National and International Systems of Broadcasting:

THEIR HISTORY, OPERATION AND CONTROL

National and International Systems of Broadcasting

THEIR HISTORY, OPERATION AND CONTROL

BY

WALTER·B·EMERY

EAST LANSING

Michigan State University Press

1969

To Jack Bain

IN APPRECIATION AND FRIENDSHIP

CONTENTS

F. *The Middle European Countries*

PART II. INTERNATIONAL BROADCASTING

ACKNOWLEDGMENTS

THIS BOOK is an outgrowth of many years of interest and study in the field of international broadcasting. Following graduation from law school in 1935, I went to Washington where I worked for a short period in the newly created Federal Communications Commission. The Communications Act of 1934 authorized the Commission to regulate not only interstate but all foreign communication by wire and radio (whether originating or being received within the United States). As a legal assistant to one of the Commissioners, I had the opportunity to acquaint myself with some of the regulatory problems concerned with domestic and foreign communications.

While yet too young and inexperienced to participate, I was in a position to listen to many high level discussions between officials of the FCC, the State Department and the White House regarding America's future role in international broadcasting. I read official reports of FCC negotiations with other countries concerning cooperative uses of the radio spectrum and I was at the Commission when plans were being drawn which resulted in the adoption, in 1937, of the North American Regional Broadcasting Agreement.

After an absence of several years, I returned to the FCC in 1943 and was given a war-time assignment which included some work with the Foreign Broadcasting Intelligence Service. The function of the FBIS was to monitor foreign broadcasts, particularly those of the enemy powers, and inform departments of the Federal Government concerning the content of these broadcasts. The volume of material was running to well over two and a half million words every twenty-four hours, and it was estimated that monitors of the FBIS heard, recorded and distributed more than one hundred and fifty thousand words daily.

Part of my job was to help analyze and interpret many of the Axis broadcasts. I came to realize the importance of international broadcasting and its tremendous influence on world opinion. I am glad, therefore, to express my gratitude to the FCC and its officials who assigned me duties which gave me first-hand knowledge about many aspects of foreign and international broadcasting and stimulated my later studies.

When I completed the preliminary manuscript of this work, I submitted portions of it to members of the FCC staff particularly concerned with international communications. Their helpful comments are greatly appreciated. I, however, take full responsibility for the book, and neither they nor others are to be held accountable for any errors of fact or interpretation which may appear.

I owe a special debt of gratitude to the Ford Foundation and the Institute for International Communications of Michigan State University for a grant of funds to spend some time in Mexico and a year in Europe doing research. I visited Mexico the summers of 1962 and 1963 and visited countries in Western and Eastern Europe in 1964–65. I interviewed more than two hundred broadcasting and government officials in Mexico and Europe and collected data concerning the history, operation and control of their radio and television systems. I am especially grateful to Dr. Jack Bain, former Director of the Institute and now Dean of the College of Communication Arts at Michigan State University who suggested these studies and whose genuine interest in and support of the project have been invaluable.

I am grateful to the Michigan State University administration for granting me a leave of absence for the field studies upon which a major portion of this work is based. Appreciation must also be expressed to my colleagues who, by adjusting curriculum and teaching schedules, made my leave possible.

I acknowledge the valuable aid given by the United States Information Agency. While in no way a sponsor of my research and travels, the Agency did assist me in preparing my itineraries. The USIA offices in the various countries helped me arrange conferences and suggested important sources of information.

I wish I might express personal thanks to each of the many officials connected with broadcasting systems in Mexico and Europe who made numerous helpful suggestions and generously provided me with documentary data, but this is not possible. The best I can do is make a general acknowledgment here, and express the hope that what I have written about them and their broadcasting systems is reasonably accurate and will promote greater understanding and appreciation of their activities and accomplishments.

The basic research and preliminary manuscripts for the chapters dealing with Chinese and Indian broadcasting were prepared by Dr. Dharam P. Yadav, a student of Asian affairs from New Delhi, while pursuing graduate studies in communications at Michigan State University. Dr. Hideya Kumata, Distinguished Professor in communications at Michigan State University and recently appointed Director of the Institute for International Communications, has contributed the chapter on Japanese broadcasting, the outgrowth of a year in Japan as the recipient of a Fulbright scholarship. He also received supplemental aid from the Institute for International Communications at Michigan State University.

I was fortunate in securing the services of Professor Donald R. Browne of the University of Minnesota who provided the chapter on African broadcasting. Professor Browne, a recognized scholar in African affairs, spent two years in Africa as an official of USIA.

I appreciate more than I can say the helpfulness of the Library staff at Michigan State University. Also, I express thanks to the staffs at the Library of Congress and the numerous national libraries in Europe who gave me access to valuable source materials.

My thanks go to the Association of Education in Journalism for permission to reproduce, with some revisions, my studies of broadcasting in Belgium, the Netherlands, Portugal, Hungary and Yugoslavia which appeared in the August 1966 issue of *Journalism Monographs*. Most of Chapter I, on the American system, is a reproduction of a paper I wrote for the Summer 1964 issue of *Centennial Review*. Chapters II, III and IX are reprints of my studies on Mexican broadcasting and Radio Luxembourg which appeared in the *Journal of Broadcasting*. Also, I acknowledge with thanks permission to reprint in the Appendix John Johnson's address which appeared in the *FCC Bar Journal*.

I express special thanks to *EBU Review* for consent to reproduce in full three articles dealing with "pirate" broadcasting, a subject which has presented some thorny problems and attracted world-wide concern. The first of these articles was written by the distinguished scholar, Albert Namurois, the legal adviser to *Radio–Télévision Belge*. A second was prepared by Karel Remes, legal adviser to the Dutch Broadcasting Organization, VARA, and a third by E. C. Robbins, legal adviser to the BBC. I am also grateful to the magazine for permission to use the succinct and informative reports of Ali Ihsan Göğüs, Turkish Minister of Tourism and Information, and his Under-Secretary, Sedat Tolga, regarding Turkish broadcasting.

The *Journal of Broadcasting* and Lee Loevinger, a former member of the Federal Communications Commission, graciously consented to a reproduction of his world survey of telecommunications systems, "The Lexonomics of Telecommunications," which was published in the Fall 1967 issue of the *Journal*. It appears as Appendix VIII.

My appreciation goes to Major Ovid L. Bayless and the *Journal of Broadcasting* for permission to reprint his discussion of the American Forces Network in Europe. Major Bayless' article appeared in the Spring, 1968 issue of the *Journal*.

The Foreword includes statements by Rosel H. Hyde, Chairman of the Federal Communications Commission, and William G. Harley, President of the National Association of Educational Broadcasters, both widely recognized for their interest and leadership in international broadcasting. I am honored by their contributions.

Joan Rae did an excellent job of typing the whole manuscript, and Lark Cowling of the Michigan State University Press contributed valuable editorial assistance.

Finally, my wife, Olive Helen Emery, and other members of my family deserve much credit for their understanding and patience, without which the task would have been much more difficult.

WALTER B. EMERY

FOREWORD

THIS BOOK represents the first attempt by an author to analyze in some depth the important broadcasting systems in all parts of the world, and to explain their origin, development, and present operation. A global study with emphasis on the managerial and regulatory aspects of radio and television, both national and international, it also covers the quantitative dimensions of the media and describes in detail their programming patterns.

This work responds to a widespread need for information regarding the control and operation of broadcast media in different parts of the world. For example, few persons in this country seem to realize that most of the broadcasting systems of Europe began as private commercial ventures and that it was not until the Second World War that there was a decided shift from private to government ownership and control. Furthermore, it is widely believed that this strict pattern of government operation still persists in most parts of the world; in fact, the pendulum generally is swinging back to commercial operation with greater autonomy for broadcasting enterprises and less control by governments. This and other significant changes in the pattern of national broadcast operations (with which all too few people are familiar) are reported in this well-documented work.

With the development of new technologies, particularly satellite transmission, the world faces a new and exciting era in broadcasting. However, along with the promise that glitters on the international horizon, there loom serious and critical problems: shortage of spectrum space, political barriers, economic scarcity, etc., which must be overcome if the maximum benefits of global communications are to be achieved. While the author does not argue the merits or demerits of existing national and international systems of broadcasting and avoids, for the most part, polemic discussion, he does describe in great detail their legal, organizational, and administrative structure, and discusses them in a meaningful historical and social context. This is the kind of knowledge which students and leaders of the broadcast media in this country and abroad need if they are to be able to solve cooperatively and effectively the pressing problems of global communications.

The author, Walter Emery, has long been a student of international broadcasting. He had opportunities to make special studies of the subject as an employee of the Federal Communications Commission in its early days. During World War II, he was assistant to a Commissioner and worked with the staff of the Foreign Broadcasting Intelligence Service then attached to the Commission. He spent a year in Europe, and has traveled widely in other parts of the world, making special studies of national and international broadcasting systems. He has taught courses in international broadcasting for more than a decade in several universities. This book, therefore, the result of more than four years of research and writing by a recognized scholar, contains much information that should be of value to broadcasters and students of broadcasting throughout the world.

Rosel H. Hyde, Chairman
Federal Communications Commission

The rapid development of new technologies and means of communication have made possible a wide range of radio and television programs for people in every part of the world. A significant aspect of this remarkable growth has been the expanded use of mass media for public enlightenment and education. What was once a multiplicity of widely separated provincial habitations has now become an informed and communicative world with its various parts linked by electromagnetic waves.

The United States can be proud of its accomplishments in educational broadcasting. More than three hundred and forty noncommercial stations (AM and FM) are operated by educational institutions in addition to over one hundred and sixty educational television stations. Thousands of American schools are now using television as an effective instructional tool. Commercial broadcasters are becoming increasingly sensitive to the educational needs of our people. With the passage of the Public Broadcasting Act in 1967, authorizing the use of federal funds for the construction or improvement of radio and television facilities and for the production of programs, further expansion of educational broadcasting can be expected.

Dr. Emery's book is of special value to those who misunderstand or do not know very much about broadcasting systems in the United States as well as to those readers who have limited knowledge of the varied systems and purposes of the media in other countries. Moreover, this book corrects simplified views of what broadcasting is or should be by demonstrating how complex and diverse an instrument it really is.

As this book reveals, for years many countries have had notable successes with educational radio and television. In fact, several European countries have used radio much more fully and effectively in the classroom than it has ever been used in the United States. European experience has demonstrated that in some areas of instruction, radio can do just as good a job, or better, than television.

In England, the BBC's Home Service has been broadcasting educational programs for many years, covering a wide range of subjects; recent reports indicate that more than thirty thousand schools make regular use of these broadcasts.

As early as 1930, Belgium was using radio in the classroom. By the end of the Second World War, French and Flemish broadcasters had established separate instructional services, and more than sixteen hundred Belgian schools were using these services. The number is much larger today.

The Scandinavian countries have had considerable success with the use of radio in the schools. They, like England and Belgium, are also making significant strides in educational TV, and their joint efforts in the production and exchange of programs would be well worth the study of all American educators.

Japan, Germany, Italy, to mention only a few other countries covered in this book, have made marked progress in media utilization in the schools and in general adult education.

Much experimental work in the development of radio and television is going on in underdeveloped countries and emerging nations. The chapters on African and Indian broadcasting should have special appeal to educators, media specialists, governmental officials and business interests concerned with the impact of radio and TV on the educational, cultural and economic growth of new nations.

Comparatively few reports of broadcasting developments in China, Russia and the countries of Eastern Europe reach this part of the world. This work provides much information about the history and present patterns of broadcast operation in these Communist countries. For example, the discussions of the "Television Peking University," and "The People's University" in Moscow, with their heavy emphasis on indoctrination, make revealing reading.

As this global study shows, national and international systems of broadcasting are feverishly presenting the messages of competing social and educational ideologies. *National and International Systems of Broadcasting* documents this world-wide struggle for men's minds.

Walter Emery, the author, and his associate contributors have long been students and practitioners of broadcasting in this country, and have had special opportunities to study, first-hand, radio and television in other parts of the world. What they have to say and the information they have assembled in this volume deserve serious study by broadcasters and students of broadcasting in this country and abroad.

William G. Harley, President
National Association of
Educational Broadcasters

INTRODUCTION

M Y FIRST INTENTION was to limit this volume to a study of European systems of broadcasting. I traveled in twenty-two countries of Western and Eastern Europe, interviewed many radio and television officials, and visited broadcasting studios and installations in all these countries. My research took me into national libraries in London, Paris, Madrid, Lisbon, Rome and other European capitals where I was able to draw upon source materials, much of which is not available in the United States. With this first-hand knowledge, I was able to complete a manuscript covering European broadcasting.

After discussing the limited scope of the study with some of my professional colleagues and other leaders in the field of educational broadcasting, I concluded that the book would be more useful if it included other selected systems. While a few global surveys of radio and television and some excellent analyses of the media in particular countries do exist, there is no single publication which includes studies, in depth, of major broadcasting systems in all parts of the world.

And so, while a large portion of this book deals with European systems, their origin, development and current patterns of operation, it also includes studies of American, Mexican, Canadian, Indian, Japanese, Chinese, African, Turkish and Australian broadcasting.

Space and time did not permit thorough coverage of all domestic broadcasting systems. Other scholars no doubt will meet this need. However, former FCC Commissioner Lee Loevinger's world survey in Appendix VIII provides essential information about most of them.

Classifying the various national systems is a problem. My original thought was to cluster them in terms of similar organization and control and patterns of operation. For example, the BBC structure shares some features with ORTF. But while there are similarities, each system is distinctive, and as Roger Skolnik has pointed out in his excellent bibliography on foreign and international broadcasting, it is misleading to "force" national broadcasting systems into neat categories which do not and cannot represent their precise character and mode of operation.* I have, therefore, grouped the systems geographically and have attempted to view each in a historical and social context, as part of and indigenous to a particular national culture. I believe this approach is essential to an understanding and appreciation of the development and present operation of each system. And

*See Roger Skolnik, *A Bibliography of Selected Publications on Foreign and International Broadcasting* (East Lansing: Michigan State University, August 1966).

I think it is an approach which deserves more stress in academic courses and in research.

I have tried to avoid arguing the merits or demerits of foreign systems of broadcasting. In Chapter I, I have attempted a rationale for the American system to which I have been exposed for almost half a century and which I have studied carefully for more than three decades. American broadcasting can be improved; however, I think, in terms of American history and culture, the U.S. system serves the country's interests and needs well. On these grounds, I am prepared to defend it. I am reluctant, however, to argue the merits or demerits of other systems. While I spent considerable time abroad, I do not believe I was there long enough to make mature, critical evaluations of the media and their operations in all the countries I visited. What I have attempted, therefore, is to explain as accurately as possible how different systems of broadcasting have developed, and how they, as mechanisms of different social orders, operate and are controlled, and to do so without condemnation or praise.

Part I deals with the origin, development and operation of national systems of broadcasting. Before analyzing each system separately, some general trends in operation may be noted. National regulatory policies in many countries have been and are being modified to permit greater autonomy, with less direct control by the government. This is certainly true in Western Europe, and to a lesser degree, in some other countries. To be sure there are counter-trends in some emerging countries and in those nations afflicted by violent social upheavals, but these appear to be in the minority.

Furthermore, there seems to be a trend in many areas toward more balanced programming. FM, television and satellites have permitted a wider range of programs for the varied interests and needs of listeners.

It should also be noted that a majority of the countries now permit some advertising. More than two-thirds of the systems of Europe and a large number in other parts of the world allow commercials, at least to a limited extent, on both radio and television. No doubt the heavy expense of television and the need for additional finances have been important factors in this development. Despite this commercial trend, the principal source of revenue in most countries continues to be the annual assessment of license fees on radio and TV receivers.

Along with more high-quality entertainment, there has been a general increase in the use of the broadcast media for adult education and classroom instruction. This has been particularly true in Great Britain, France, Japan, Hungary, Italy, the United States and some of the developing countries.

Censorship of news and political discussion still exists in many parts of the world, especially in countries governed by authoritarian regimes. There is evidence, however, that this is changing in areas where larger groups of citizens are pressing for more freedom of expression and the right to hear different points of view on controversial subjects of public importance.

Finally, Part II deals with important organizations concerned mainly with broadcasting across national boundaries—their constitution, the mechanisms used for international transmission and their functions. In a relatively short time, long-distance communication has advanced from semaphore to satellite. Through the use of satellite technology, such television systems as Eurovision in Western Europe and Intervision in Eastern Europe and the Soviet Union are providing, with some degree of regularity, direct, efficient broadcasting to peoples throughout the world.

Much international radio remains belligerent and propagandistic. However, although there still is a considerable amount of specious, vitriolic and even libelous rhetoric, the programs and messages of many short-wave stations seem to be softer and less militant than they were a decade ago.

PART I

National Systems of Broadcasting

· A ·

NORTH AND
CENTRAL AMERICA

I

The American System of Broadcasting: A Rationale

I N A DEMOCRATIC SOCIETY the supreme power of government resides in the people and is exercised, either directly or indirectly, through a system of representation and delegated authority, periodically reviewed. The laws guarantee equality of human rights, without regard to race, creed, color, or social or economic status, and require the citizens to exercise some restraints and assume some responsibilities in the interest of the common good. This, of course, is an ideal which by no means has been fully realized. But it is a basic concept upon which the U.S. Constitution was founded, and an ideal which is believed to have rational validity.

In this kind of society, the individual is important. And the affirmation and protection of his dignity and sanctity as an individual, his mature growth and ultimate destiny, are the major concerns of this society. As a corollary, he is a free person with rights protected by law. He is free to think, to inquire, to express openly his feelings and ideas and, within limits, to pursue happiness in his own way.

The rationale for this kind of individual recognition and guaranty of freedom states that in a social milieu which allows free exercise of personal powers and free expression of opinion, individuals can attain a higher level of growth, that truth pitted against error in the competition of the open market will prevail, and that the good society can be more readily attained.

An essential part of this rationale was expressed by Justice Holmes in one of his memorable dissenting opinions:

> . . . when men have realized that time has upset many fighting faiths, they may come to believe even more than they believe the very foundations of their own conduct that the ultimate good desired is better reached by free trade in ideas . . . that the best test of truth is the power of the thought to get itself accepted in the competition of the open market, and that truth is the only ground upon which their wishes can be carried out. . . .[1]

But this freedom is not absolute. As Holmes himself readily admitted, there must be limitations, for, as he explained in *Schenck* v. *United States:* "The most stringent protection of free speech would not protect a man in falsely shouting fire in a theatre and causing a panic."[2] As Holmes further noted, the increasing complexities of the modern world have made it necessary to interfere with the liberties of men in ways not contemplated by Herbert Spencer in his *Social Statics*, written more than a hundred years ago, and citizens have had to accept new responsibilities as the needs of a more complicated world have required.[3]

Sad as this may be to some, the enforcement of these obligations means more government: more exercise of police powers at local, state and federal levels; a larger Bureau of Internal Revenue; more government agencies to regulate industry; more protection of civil rights; and larger civilian and military establishments to protect our interests here and abroad.

The notion of many politicians and voters, that the sole concern of a free society is to limit government, and that the government is best which governs least, does not square with this concept of a workable and effective democracy in 1967. Government is only one form of concentrated power. Vast corporate wealth, immense labor combines, educational bureaucracies and a multiplicity of institutions, pressure groups and lobbies feverishly pursue their special interests and often exercise a coercive and restrictive influence over large segments of the American public. Robert Hutchins has stated: "Our object today is not to weaken government in competition with other centers of power but rather to strengthen it as an agency charged with the responsibility of the common good. The government is best which governs best. The Constitution must protect the citizen against the government. The government must protect him against society and the rapacity of organizations in it by seeing to it that these organizations pursue purposes and programs consonant with the common good."[4]

The primary role of government in the ideal democratic society is to promote freedom and, when necessary, under reasonable regulations, to restrain any despotic power which threatens individual liberty. An able and responsible government is essential for this purpose. However, when government assumes powers contrary to this purpose, for example, as Henry Commager has said, when it ". . . attempts to make science, education, art and letters handmaidens of the state," then the Constitution and the ballot box provide methods for the protection of personal rights.[5]

This concept of a democratic society is important to the broadcast media. In fact, the establishment and development of a national policy regulating broadcasting in the United States have been based largely upon these social ideals and the rationale discussed.

Early History of Radio

AFTER the First World War, American radio grew rapidly. With practically no regulation, broadcasters vied for the listener's attention and interest. Stations stepped up their power without restraint, jumped fre- quencies, changed hours of operation to suit their convenience, and broad- cast whatever programs they liked.

The public, including many leaders in the industry, were soon fed up with this unrestrained system. The listeners not only complained about the technical chaos, but they objected to much of the shoddy program- ming. They did not like the hard-sell commercials which flooded the air- ways. They deplored the irresponsible hucksters—the astrologers, the fortune tellers and the mercenary medicine men.

Robert J. Landry in his book, *The Fascinating Radio Business,* has given an interesting account of the activities of the radio hucksters during those early days:

> . . . There were hysterical clergymen, enemies of Wall Street, enemies of chain stores, enemies of Catholics, Jews and Negroes, promoters of patented heavens. . . . The meaning of the stars, the stock market, the future life could all be learned by enclosing cash. Falling hair or teeth could be arrested—just write. Fortunes in real estate could be made over-night—just write. Home cures for this, or the other thing were available.[6]

There were general grumblings about propagandists, religious zealots, and demagogues seeking to influence listeners with their peculiar brands of publicity. Norman Thomas spoke out against attempts by station managers to censor his speeches. There were bitter attacks against monopoly and the growing concentration of control in a few large companies. Some good programs were broadcast, of course, such as the University of Chicago Roundtable. Great musicians, opera, debate and drama were featured by some stations. But good as these programs were, they were often over- shadowed by cheap entertainment and commercialism.

Some broadcasters tried to improve the situation by voluntary restraint, agreements and self-regulation, but many others seemed unconcerned. The public, therefore, did what any enlightened public will do when an industry so essential to the national interest is floundering—it sought relief from the Government.

In *Broadcasting and Government,* I discussed the inadequacy of govern- ment power at that time to cope with the situation and will not take space to review that history here.[7] Suffice to say, Herbert Hoover, the Secretary of Commerce and Labor, tried to help but the Attorney General and the courts told him he was powerless to act. He, therefore, assumed the initia- tive in getting Congress to pass the Radio Act of 1927, which established the Federal Radio Commission, and gave it limited authority to regulate the broadcasting industry.[8]

While he wanted freedom for the broadcasters, Mr. Hoover realized that they would have to give up some of their rights, accept some restric- tions from the Government, and take on some new responsibilities, if radio was to have an orderly growth and achieve its maximum social utility.

"Radio," said he, "is not to be considered merely as a business carried on for private gain, for private advertisement, or for the entertainment of the curious. It is to be considered as a *public* concern, impressed with a *public* trust, and to be considered primarily from the standpoint of *public* interest."[9]* Mr. Hoover and many other leaders of industry, education, religion and other fields, stressed the *public* aspect of broadcasting. Since broadcasting linked *private* enterprise with the *public* interest, these leaders saw the need for some positive government regulation.

Rules established by the Federal Radio Commission helped alleviate the chaos which had afflicted radio in its formative years and the broadcasting industry grew rapidly. Simultaneously, the telephone and telegraph systems were expanding. More and more, these industries were using radio for point-to-point communication in both their domestic and foreign business. Also, broadcasting was increasingly dependent upon telecommunication, particularly in the development of network operations. The public grew increasingly aware of this interdependency of radio, telephone and telegraph communication. It became apparent that the efficiency, economy and growth of these media depended greatly upon how well their operations were coordinated. Experts in communications felt that a comprehensive national policy covering all of these media should be established and that a new government agency should be created to administer the policy. Responding to the recognized need, Congress passed the Communications Act in 1934 which abolished the old Radio Commission and replaced it with the FCC, which had the authority to regulate all radio communication and all interstate and foreign telegraph and telephone service.[10]

The Communications Act has now been in effect thirty-four years. Despite occasional amendments, its basic features remain very much the same as they were in 1934. The national policy embodied in the Act was conceived in terms of the democratic concepts and values which have already been discussed.

The importance of the individual and his freedom in the good society are important aspects of the national policy regarding radio communication. In fact, in no other country does the broadcaster have more freedom than he does in the United States. He is free to carry the kind of programming which will give him a reasonable return on his investment and serve the interests of the community. He is encouraged to use his imagination and to experiment with new types of programs, in the interest of providing a better service to the community.

No government official can restrain him in the exercise of this freedom. Those who framed the Magna Charta for broadcasting in the United States specifically prohibited censorship. Section 326 of the Communications Act reads:

*Author's italics.

Nothing in this Act shall be understood or construed to give the Commission the power of censorship over the radio communications or signals transmitted by any radio station and no regulation or condition shall be promulgated or fixed by the Commission which shall interfere with the right of free speech by means of radio communication.[11]

The rationale for this prohibition was that a multiplicity of individual broadcasters free from government restraint would provide a variety of programs offering a wide range of information, opinion and discussion.

Freedom Not Absolute

WHILE freedom was one of the keystones in the national broadcasting policy, it was not intended that this freedom should be absolute. Neither the framers of the original law in 1927 nor the public were happy with the effects of a completely free and unrestrained broadcast system. The behavior of some evil and irresponsible men in the business convinced Hoover and others that some legal restraints and responsibilities would have to be imposed.

Accordingly, as stated in the original law and in various amendments, some specific restrictions are provided. For example, stations are prohibited from broadcasting lotteries. Nor may they carry vulgar and indecent programs. They are barred from broadcasting false distress messages, deceptive advertisements or rigged quiz shows. They may not conceal the identity of sponsors, nor discriminate against candidates for public office who use radio facilities in their campaigns.

These are the statutory negatives, but there is an important statutory positive. Stations are licensed for limited periods and are under a mandate to operate in the public interest. In fact, the law says that the FCC may not grant a license or renew one unless it can find that the public interest will be served.[12] The law, however, does not spell out what this means and the FCC has had the task of developing some guidelines. The FCC has never established any hard and fast rule applicable to every station and community. It has stressed the importance of providing a program service which is designed to meet the varied interests and needs of the particular community, and to afford reasonable access to the microphone and camera for the expression of different points of view on important public issues.[13]

Some lawyers, some critics and many broadcasters object vigorously, especially those broadcasters who feature prolonged sieges of rock and roll music, interrupted with a barrage of high-pressure, hard-sell commercials, or those who provide heavy doses of old, third-rate films interspersed every thirteen minutes with two, three and sometimes four commercial spots, and do so even in communities where there may be no competing radio or television facilities. Some legal scholars and broadcasters seriously argue that such declarations of the FCC constitute governmental fiat; that they violate the First Amendment to the Constitution which guarantees free speech; and that they are contrary to Section 326 of the Communications Act which prohibits censorship.[14]

The Commission, in effect, has replied that this is not so; that it never reviews or passes judgment on programs in advance, and is only concerned with the overall program service when a station comes up for renewal of its license every three years. Newton Minow, former FCC Chairman, stated:

> I believe that the Commission clearly does *not* censor anything. We don't censor "rock and roll," or Westerns, or quiz shows, or even overdoses of brutality. Nor do we say: "Put on this program or do not broadcast that program. . . ." We never view a program in advance of broadcast and prevent its being seen by the public.
>
> . . . the Commission looks to the applicant's over-all—and I stress the word, over-all—programming proposal to determine whether granting him a license would serve the public interest. At first we look at his proposals. Later, when the station comes for renewal we also examine over-all performance during the license period; and when more than one applicant wants the same facility, we compare their programming proposals to determine which one would best serve the public interest. It is this that they call "censorship." It is this, they tell us, that violates the First Amendment and the Communication Act.[15]

Legally, censorship involves prior restraint. As early as 1644, John Milton attacked censorship in the "Appeal for the Liberty of Unlicensed Printing," on the grounds that it involved *previous* restraint; not review *after* the fact.[16]

The case of the famous Dr. John Brinkley illustrates this point. He was licensed to operate Station KFKB in Milford, Kansas. He not only advertised his hospital and his surgical skill, but he prescribed for his patients—sight unseen—over the air. One of his scripts, as reported by the FCC, ran as follows: "Probably he has gall stones. No, I don't mean that. I mean kidney stones. My advice to you is to get prescription No. 80 and 50 for men, also 64. I think he will be a whole lot better. Also, drink a lot of water."[17] When Dr. Brinkley applied for a renewal of his license, the Federal Radio Commission emphatically said "no," one of the few times when the Government has shaken its head so vigorously because of bad programming. But Dr. Brinkley was a persistent man and took the case to the Federal Court. On review of the case, the Court said:

> It is apparent, we think, that the business is impressed with a public interest and that, because the number of available broadcasting frequencies is limited, the Commission is necessarily called upon to consider the character and quality of the service to be rendered. In considering an application for a renewal of the license, an important consideration is the past conduct of the applicant, for "by their fruits ye shall know them." Matt. VII:20.[18]

Dr. Brinkley claimed: "Censorship!" The Court replied:

> There has been no attempt on the part of the Commission to subject any part of appellant's broadcasting matter to scrutiny *prior* to its release. In considering the question whether the public interest, convenience, or necessity will be served by a renewal of appellant's license, the Commission has merely exercised its undoubted right to take note of appellant's past conduct, which is not censorship.[19]

Other cases have sustained this view. Although some experts disagree, it appears that the FCC does have the authority and responsibility to establish minimum program criteria, and in so doing does not commit legal censorship.[20]

Social concern for the broadcaster as an individual and a citizen is fully recognized within the legal framework of the American system of broadcasting. The broadcaster is encouraged to be creative and is protected from arbitrary government restraints. But because he is engaged in a business that is clothed with the public interest, he has the duty to be informed of the needs and interests of the community for which he is a trustee, and to ensure that his station serves such interests. Since history has shown that some broadcasters will not measure up to this responsibility under a *laissez faire* policy, Congress created the FCC and vested it with the authority to require that they do so, if they are to maintain their licenses.

Government's Role Limited

GOVERNMENT regulation can be helpful, but its role is a limited one. How well the broadcaster meets his obligation to serve the needs of his listeners and viewers depends more on what Walter Lippmann speaks of as the "inner imperatives":[21] the broadcaster's basic values, his attitudes toward humanity in general, and his relationships to his fellow human beings. The types of programs a broadcaster presents over his station will depend much on whether he thinks of the public simply as response mechanisms to be stimulated, manipulated and exploited, or whether he thinks of them as human beings possessed of intellectual, aesthetic and spiritual powers to be cultivated. John Bachman's book, *The Church in the World of Radio-Television,* in referring to the broadcaster, raises the question:

> Does he treat the listener as man or less than man? As a man, or a machine to be operated? As a vegetable to be cultivated? As a man capable of growing and learning, or simply a creature able to react? If he is regarded as man, he should be aroused and stimulated rather than stupefied; his horizons should be enlarged rather than shrunk; he should be exalted rather than degraded.[22]

If the broadcaster has understanding of and concern for the worth, the dignity and the well-being of his listeners as individuals, and their important relationship to the growth of democratic institutions, he will give them more than programs that simply amuse and entertain, desirable as these may be at times. He will also provide programs that challenge the higher faculties.

In his provocative book, *The Public Philosophy,* Walter Lippmann speaks of the individual as acquiring a second nature when he becomes civilized, a nature made in the image of what he *is* and is living for and should become. He has seen the image in the mirror of history. Full allegiance to the community, says Lippmann, can be given only by a man's second nature, ruling over his first and primitive nature, and treating it as not finally himself. Then the disciplines and the necessities and the constraints of a civilized life have ceased to be alien to him, and are not imposed from without. They have become his own "inner imperatives."[23]

Mr. Lippmann also speaks of the principles of rational order which consist of the terms which must be met to fulfill man's capacity for the good life in this world. They are the terms of the widest consensus of rational men in a pluralistic society, not only contemporary men but those in centuries past whose ideas have been transmitted to us and constitute an important part of our cultural heritage. They are the concepts and the propositions to which all men, if they are sincerely and lucidly rational, can be expected to converge. In this regard, he is critical of popular culture, and speaks of a lack of ". . . public criterion of the true and the false, of the right and wrong, beyond that which the preponderant mass of voters, consumers, readers, and listeners happen at the moment to be supposed to want." It is possible to conduct society this way, but not the *good* society with maximum freedom.[24]

While Mr. Lippmann was speaking largely in another context, his words are applicable to broadcasting. The most enlightened and responsible broadcaster has some social philosophy with a rational base that influences his programming. This means that he does not always succumb to the whims and pressures of the moment. He will not always submit to the coercion of the advertiser seeking the mass audience who may insist on heavy doses of horse opera, vaudeville and quiz shows, and to other types of programs that John Fischer of *Harper's* magazine has referred to as dramatic "garbage"[25] and which Bob Hope recently characterized, in a satirical way, as "the outhouse in the vast wasteland" of broadcasting.[26]

Nor will program surveys, Hooper ratings and sales charts always be the broadcaster's guide. While he may not ignore them (at least not the honest ones), because they have persuasive effect on the advertiser, and are related to the station's financial security, he will not make them the sole measure of what he presents over the air. Because he understands the importance of his listeners' "second natures," he will schedule (and during good listening hours) some informational programs, news analysis in depth, and enlightened discussion on important public issues. He will broadcast some first quality programs in music and theatre, documentaries dealing with science, the arts and public affairs, and some experimental features that have intellectual and aesthetic appeal.

The architects of the American system of broadcasting gave first priority to one of these areas of programming—namely, discussion of important public issues. As Herbert Hoover envisioned the system, the development of multiple facilities and diversified ownership would lead to the expression of many points of view on social, economic and political questions.[27] The FCC has consistently stressed this in its policy statements; and has said:

> It is axiomatic that one of the most vital questions of mass communication in a democracy is the development of an informed public opinion through the public dissemination of news and ideas concerning the vital public issues of the day. Basically, it is in recognition of the great contribution which radio can make in the advancement of this purpose that portions of the radio spectrum are allocated to that form of radio communications known as radio-broadcasting. Unquestionably, then, the standard of public interest, convenience and necessity as applied to radio-broadcasting must be interpreted in the light of this basic purpose. The Commission has consequently recognized the necessity for licensees to devote a reasonable percentage of their broadcast time to the presentation of news and programs devoted to the consideration of discussion of public issues of interest in the community served by the particular station. And we have recognized, with respect to such programs, the paramount right of the public in the free society to be informed and to have presented to it for acceptance or rejection the different attitudes and viewpoints concerning these vital and often controversial issues which are held by the various groups which make up the community. It is this right of the public to be informed, rather than any right on the part of the government, any broadcast licensee or any individual member of the public to broadcast his own particular views of any matter, which is the foundation stone of the American system of broadcasting.[28]

Responsibilities of the Public

MANY people seem unaware that the radio spectrum belongs to the public and no broadcaster, whether commercial or educational, acquires any ownership rights in the frequency which is assigned him. He receives a license for only three years to use this publicly owned resource. This license is subject to renewal if he can show that his station has operated in the public interest and not simply in terms of his private and personal interests. Too many people think of radio and television stations as being owned in the same way as farm land, grocery or hardware stores. Even some well-known program producers and performers, who ought to know better, seem to think this way. For example, Mike Wallace, when considering proposed ideas for one of his network shows, was reported to have said: "Well, I'll take it up with the network, but remember, it's the network's air."[29] But as former FCC Commissioner Clifford Durr has said, it is not the network's or the broadcaster's air:

> There is need to reiterate over and over again the idea that broadcasting frequencies are *public* property, even if it has been said 99 times before. The people don't know it; they don't understand that this is *not* the property of the broadcasters. We need to create in the public mind an awareness of the fact that the people *do* have an interest.[30]

Effective communication between the broadcasters, the networks and the general public is essential. Important facts and thoughtful judgments about programs are needed to help meet the pressing, immediate problems of the community, as well as the long-range problems.

In the forties, a movement for the development of listener councils began, but was not very successful. Only a small number of such councils are still active and effective. Every community ought to have such a council, composed of people with varied interests, conducting studies and evaluating programs. Frequent conferences between management and representatives of the council would be mutually helpful. Community needs and interests would be more clearly perceived by the broadcasters, and at the same time, their problems of station operation and financial survival might be better understood by listeners who are not faced with meeting payrolls, securing advertising revenue and meeting other practical needs.

More than fourteen years ago, Senator William Benton proposed the establishment of a national Citizens' Advisory Board for Radio and Television. The Board, as he proposed it, would have issued an annual advisory report to Congress, to the FCC, to the broadcast industry and the general public. The report would have grown out of careful study, and would have contained an evaluation of the year's broadcasting service, with suggestions for improvement.[31] Such a national body, with a membership made up of distinguished citizens appointed by the President on a nonpolitical basis, and assisted by a competent research staff, could perform a real service to the broadcasting industry as well as the public.*

John Fischer made a similar proposal in the July 1959 issue of *Harper's*.[32] He felt that it was time for the enlightened leadership of the country to take positive steps toward the establishment of such an organization. The studies and reports of an advisory group, working in cooperation with state and local councils, could have an important salutary effect on radio and television programs.

Under the American system of broadcasting, radio and television li-

---

*President Johnson's recent proposal for the establishment of a public corporation to provide expanded facilities for educational broadcasting might very well include this as one of its functions.

censes have great but not unbridled freedom, for as Judge Learned Hand has said, the ways of democracy require some individual restraint:

> It is not the ruthless, unbridled will; it is not freedom to do as one likes. That is the denial of liberty, and leads straight to its overthrow. A society in which men recognize no check upon their freedom soon becomes a society where freedom is the possession of only a savage few; as we have learned to our sorrow.[33]

But along with freedom, protected by law, the broadcaster has responsibilities. He has the obligation to respect the rights of other broadcasters, and, since he makes use of public property, he has a duty to serve the public interest. In a society which recognizes the validity of free enterprise, he is permitted to use broadcasting facilities to make financial profit, but in so doing he has the responsibility, as Father John M. Culkin has pointed out, to see that ". . . these media fulfill their promises as instruments of the mind and the spirit."[34]

In a democratic society, broadcasters and the government which regulates them have responsibilities prescribed by law. The people also have responsibilities. They own the airways. They have the right to listen, to learn, to know. But citizens in a free society have the social obligation to be articulate—to communicate their best judgments, through individual, institutional and collective efforts. As Justice Douglas has suggested, the real strength of the American system of broadcasting lies "in the dignity, resourcefulness and intelligence of the people."[35]

NOTES

1. *Abrams* v. *United States.* 250 U.S. 676, 630; 40 Sup. Ct. 17; 63 L. ed. 1180 (1919).
2. *Schenck* v. *United States.* 249 U.S. 47, 52; 39 Sup. Ct. 247; 63 L. ed. 473 (1919).
3. *Lochner* v. *New York.* 198 U.S. 45; 25 Sup. Ct. 539; 49 L. ed. 937 (1921).
4. Robert M. Hutchins, "Is Democracy Possible?" *Education for Public Responsibility,* ed. C. Scott Fletcher (New York: W. W. Norton & Company, 1961), pp. 18, 19.
5. Henry Steele Commager, "Urgent Query: Why Do We Lack Statesmen?" *ibid.,* p. 39.
6. Robert John Landry, *This Fascinating Radio Business* (New York: The Bobbs-Merrill Co., 1946), p. 48.
7. Walter B. Emery, *Broadcasting and Government: Responsibilities and Regulations* (East Lansing: Michigan State University Press, 1961), pp. 10–26.
8. 44 *Stat. at Large* 1162–1174, February 23, 1927.
9. Fourth National Radio Conference, *Proceedings and Recommendations for Regulation of Radio* (Washington, D.C., November 9–11, 1925), p. 6.
10. 48 *Stat. at Large* 1064, June 19, 1934.

11. *Ibid.*, 1082–1083.
12. *Ibid.*, 1086.
13. See *Report and Statement of Policy Re: Commission en banc Programming Inquiry*, 25 F. R. 7291, August 3, 1960. Also, see *Public Service Responsibility of Broadcast Licensees*, Report by Federal Communications Commission, March 7, 1946.
14. See Theodore W. Pierson, "The Active Eyebrow—A Changing Style for Censorship," *Television Quarterly*, I, No. 1 (February 1962), 14–21.
15. Address by Newton N. Minow, former Chairman, Federal Communications Commission, to the Conference on Freedom and Responsibility in Broadcasting, Northwestern University School of Law, Chicago, Illinois, August 3, 1961, p. 5.
16. See John Milton, *Areopagitica for the Liberty of Unlicensed Printing* (London: Oxford at the Clarendon Press, John W. Hales, 1886).
17. Minow, Address to the Conference on Freedom and Responsibility in Broadcasting, p. 9; quoted by Mr. Minow from official FCC records.
18. *KFKB Broadcasting Association, Inc.* v. *Federal Radio Commission*. 60 App. D. C. 79, 47 F. (2d) 670 (1931).
19. *Ibid.*
20. For an excellent analysis of the opposing view, see Pierson, "The Active Eyebrow—A Changing Style for Censorship." Mr. Pierson, a distinguished attorney in Washington, D.C., treats the legal and cultural aspects of the problem.
21. Walter Lippmann, *Essays in Public Philosophy* (Boston: Little, Brown and Company, 1955), p. 137.
22. John W. Bachman, *The Church in the World of Radio-Television* (New York: Association Press, 1960), pp. 55–56.
23. Lippmann, p. 123.
24. *Ibid.*, p. 114.
25. John Fischer, "The Easy Chair," *Harper's*, July 1959, p. 11.
26. Speech by Bob Hope to the convention of the National Association of Broadcasters, Chicago, Illinois, April 1, 1963.
27. Fourth National Radio Conference, *Proceedings and Recommendations for Regulation of Radio*, p. 7.
28. Federal Communications Commission, *In the Matter of Editorializing by Broadcast Licensees*, Docket No. 8586, 13 FCC 1946, 14 F. R. 3055, 1 RR, Section 91:21 (1949).
29. *Broadcasting and Government Regulation in a Free Society: An Occasional Paper on the Role of the Mass Media in a Free Society*, published by the Center for the Study of Democratic Institutions, 1959, pp. 9–10.
30. *Ibid.*, p. 24.
31. *Congressional Record*, p. 5972. May 31, 1952.
32. Fischer.
33. Learned Hand, *The Spirit of Liberty: Papers and Addresses of Learned Hand* (New York: Alfred A. Knopf, 1952), p. 190.
34. Quoted by Newton Minow in a paper delivered before the Tenth Anniversary Convocation of the Center for the Study of Democratic Institutions, New York, January 22, 1963. Reverend Culkin is a consultant on Films and Television, National Catholic Educational Association.
35. *Public Utilities Commission* v. *Pollak*. 343 U.S. 451, 468; Dissenting Opinion.

II

Mexico and The United States:

Broadcasting Systems Compared

FOREIGN BROADCASTING and the international exchange of radio and television programs must, of course, be accomplished in accordance with differing national laws and systems of government regulation. For example, in many parts of Europe, Asia and Africa the laws provide for state ownership of all broadcast media, and programs are determined strictly by government authority. On the other hand, in some countries (parts of Latin America, for example) the prevailing legal pattern is private ownership with limited government regulation and control of programming. In some nations (e.g., Canada) dual systems of government and private stations operate side by side.

If foreign markets are to be developed and international broadcasting is to come to full fruition, scholars and leaders in the mass media field should become better informed about these various systems and the unique cultures which they represent and reflect. A greater understanding of these differences should lead to more willingness to cooperate in the establishment of uniform regulations and, eventually, to abrogate some of the national restrictions which now work against the free flow of information and images across national boundaries.

The 1940 Law of General Ways of Communication

BEGINNING with a 1926 statute relating to "electrical communications," supplemented by several legislative enactments in the thirties, the Mexican Congress adopted the *Law of General Ways of Communication* in 1940.[1] In accordance with previous legislation, this Law gave the Federal Government exclusive regulatory jurisdiction over broadcasting. Section 3 authorized the Secretary of Communications and Public Works to grant permits and concessions;[2] classify stations, prescribe their general functions and determine their location; establish regulations pertaining to technical operation; and modify or revoke concessions if, in the Secretary's judgment, public interest should require.

The 1940 statute made the Secretary responsible for the regulation of advertising rates charged by commercial stations. He was given broad powers to issue orders to correct and improve the services of radio stations, to suspend any services not deemed efficient, and to levy fines and inflict other penalties for violation of regulations, as defined by law.

Ownership of Stations and Program Restrictions

UNDER the 1940 Law, foreigners were not permitted to own or control broadcast stations. Nor could the ownership or control of these facilities be transferred without the prior approval of the Secretary of Communications and Public Works.

There were numerous restrictions and requirements. For example, there were specific injunctions against broadcasts which might disturb the public peace; offend existing laws or well-established customs and mores; invade rights of privacy; or lead to the commission of crime or interfere with the administration of justice. Advertising was permitted but was subject to regulatory limitations as imposed by the Secretary. Stations were required to carry, without charge, messages concerning ships and aircraft in distress, national defense or the conservation of public order. Other programs prepared by the Federal Government and considered official were to be carried at a fifty percent discount.

Inadequacy of the 1940 Law

WITH the rapid growth of broadcasting during the forties and early fifties, many legal and government experts and leaders in the industry came to feel that the 1940 Law was outdated and inadequate. Justino Jimenez de Arechega, an outstanding Latin American legal authority, observed that because the common carrier concept of radio telegraphic regulation had been extended to broadcasting, administrative practices had been adopted that seriously jeopardized the development of broadcasting, subjecting it to restrictions and sanctions not in keeping with its true nature and social function.[3]

It was this attitude that motivated the Mexican Congress to consider legislative reform. In 1959, the House of Representatives completed a study which demonstrated the need for new legislation. In its report, the House pointed out that during the preceding thirty years, Mexican broadcasting had developed greatly: the number of broadcasting stations in the Republic had reached three hundred and thirty-four in 1958, and, according to 1955 statistics, 43,210 persons were employed by the broadcast industry.

The report stated that there were 4,291,594 radio and TV receivers in 1959 with a national audience of approximately sixteen million. This remarkable growth required an adequate statute to cover the means of transmission and reception, and to encourage further development compatible with the paramount interests of the country.[4]

1960 Federal Law of Radio and Television

FOLLOWING these studies, the Mexican Congress passed the Federal Law of Radio and Television, which became effective on January 16, 1960.[5] With the exception of one provision in the 1940 Law which related to the installations of radio amateurs, all parts of the earlier statute were repealed and superseded by the new legislation.[6]

Most of the 1940 Law pertaining to broadcasting was simply absorbed by the 1960 act. There were, however, some important changes and additions. A major criticism of the 1940 legislation had been that it treated broadcasting, along with telecommunications and transports, as a public utility and failed to emphasize sufficiently its social significance. Title I of the 1960 Law supplied this emphasis with a recitation of fundamental principles.

The new statute states that the electromagnetic waves are a part of the public domain, inalienable, and may be used only under concessions or permits granted by Federal authority; that radio and television are clothed with the public interest and that the State should see that they fulfill their social function. If the broadcast media are to perform this function, the Law declares that they should: (1) provide programs that enhance respect for moral principles, human dignity and family ties; (2) avoid programs that interfere with the healthy growth of children; (3) seek to raise the cultural level of the people, preserve their customs, traditions and characteristics, and enrich the values of Mexican nationality; and (4) strengthen democratic beliefs, national unity, and international friendship and cooperation.

Moreover, the Law says that the State has an important role to play in the achievement of these moral and social objectives; that the Chief Executive, through the Federal, state and local government agencies, is obliged to promote broadcasts which contribute to the national, social, cultural and civic welfare. The State is further required to provide effective facilities for foreign broadcasting to inform other countries about Mexican life and culture, and to encourage tourist travel and commercial trade.

No specific preambular language appears in the U.S. Communications Act. While the American law indicates that its broad purpose is to provide a regulatory system serving the communication needs of all, and declares that radio waves belong to the people, it contains no list of social objectives or specific guidelines for radio and television programs. The determination of these has been left to the administrative discretion of the Federal Communications Commission, although legal scholars disagree as to how much actual authority Congress intended to give the Commission in this area. And, except for Section 303 (g) which states, in part, that the Federal Communications Commission shall "generally encourage the larger and more effective use of radio in the public interest," no responsibility is placed on the Commission or any other government agency to provide or promote actual programs for broadcasting.

José Luis Fernández in his excellent book, *Derecho de la Radiodifusion,* has praised the Mexican Congress for reciting such lofty ideals and principles of conduct in the 1960 Law. He views them, however, as desirable ethical standards rather than ironclad legal mandates. In his opinion, it was not intended that they should restrict freedom of speech as guaranteed by the Mexican Constitution. Their observance, he says, must depend primarily upon the concern and sense of responsibility of the broadcaster himself.[7]

Division of Regulatory Responsibilities

THE 1940 legislation gave the Chief Executive and the Secretary of Communications and Public Works wide regulatory authority over broadcasting. The 1960 Law reaffirmed the exclusive jurisdiction of the Federal Government, but divided responsibilities among several ministries. The Secretary of Communications and Transport now allocates and assigns frequencies for station operation; grants, modifies or revokes concessions and permits; intervenes in the rental, sale or other transactions that affect the ownership of stations; and is concerned generally with the regulation of technical operations.

The 1960 act specifies that there shall be certain classifications of broadcast stations: commercial, cultural, including governmental, experimental, and radio schools *(las escuelas radiofónics),* but the Secretary of Communications and Transport has the authority to establish additional classes of stations and determine the nature and purposes of their operations.

Under the older legislation, the Government determined the advertising rates of all broadcast stations and no changes could be made without the approval of the Communications Secretariat. This requirement was relaxed by the present Law. The Secretary of Communications and Transport sets the minimum advertising rates for all broadcast stations, but broadcasters are free to sell time at higher figures.[8]

The Powers of the Secretary of the Government

THE Secretary of the Government, as he is called in Mexico,[9] is vested with important powers relating to radio and television programs. The present statute states that his office shall see that broadcasts do not violate rights of privacy, or offend personal and moral dignity, *"se mantengen dentro de los limites del respeto a la vida privada, a la dignidad personal y a la moral,"*[10] and that they do not attack the rights of third parties, provoke crime or disturb the peace or public order.

Moreover, this office was given the responsibility of administering Article LIX of the Law which provides that all radio and television stations must carry at least thirty minutes of programming each day (continuous or interrupted) dealing with educational, cultural or social themes. These programs are prepared by the staff of the Secretary of the Government and made available to stations for regular transmission, and must be carried by them without charge. The rationale is that since the stations have the use of publicly owned frequencies for profit-making purposes, they have an obligation to provide some free broadcast time to the Government in payment for this privilege.[11]

Attached to the office of the Secretary of the Government is a coordinating agency known as the National Council of Radio and Television. Its membership, as prescribed by law, is composed of a representative of the Secretary of Government *(Secretaría de Gobernación)* who serves as Chairman, one each from the Ministries of Communications and Transport *(Secretaría de Comunicaciones y Transportes)*, Public Education *(Secretaría de Educación Pública)*, and Public Health and Welfare *(Secretaría de Salubridad y Asistencia)*, plus two from the broadcast industry and two from the workers in that industry.

The Council's duties as specified in Article XCI are: (1) to promote and organize broadcasts ordered by the Federal Executive; (2) to serve as a consultative body to him; (3) to improve the moral, cultural, artistic and social level of broadcasts; (4) to have knowledge of and make decisions regarding matters submitted to the Council for study and opinion by the Ministries and Departments of the Government and by institutions, agencies or persons concerned with radio and television; and (5) to perform other duties as prescribed by law.

In 1962 the Chairman of the Council, Señor Lic. Louis Farías, a lawyer, explained in an interview that the primary function of his office was to "see that all stations carry the official programming, and when we have programming they must use it. And of course, we put fines when there are grave violations of the law."[12]

The fines are prescribed in the statute for violations of regulations pertaining to programming. These fines may range from five hundred to five thousand pesos for an offense such as changing the text of official bulletins issued by the Government for broadcasting, to five thousand to fifty thousand pesos for offenses such as broadcasting which jeopardizes national security or for refusal to broadcast programs in the national interest.[13]

The regulatory power of the Mexican Government over programming is much greater than that possessed by the Government of the United States. While the Federal Communications Commission now has legislative authority to impose fines for infractions of the law and regulations, the Federal Radio and Television Law of Mexico is much more specific as to the types of programs which may and may not be carried by stations, and prescribes a far more detailed system of penalties for failure to observe these statutory mandates. And the Secretary of the Government is empowered to assess fines at any time if, in his judgment, violations of program requirements have occurred.

If any broadcaster takes exception to a decision of the Government which would impose fines or other penalties, he is given the right of judicial appeal in both Mexico and the United States. The Mexican broadcaster may appeal directly to the Supreme Court of Mexico. In the United States, he may ask the U.S. Court of Appeals in the District of Columbia to review the case. If that court sustains the decision of the FCC, the broadcaster may ask the U.S. Supreme Court to make a final review.

The Powers of the Secretary of Education

IN RECENT years, the Government and the citizens of Mexico have been increasingly concerned about the need for improved education. This is clearly reflected in certain provisions of the 1960 broadcasting Law. The Secretary of Public Education is under a statutory mandate to promote wider and more effective use of the radio and TV media for educational purposes. Article XI provides that this particular Ministry shall: (1) promote and organize teaching through radio and television; (2) promote and broadcast programs of a cultural and civic interest; (3) protect the rights of authors; (4) issue authorizations (certificados de aptitud) to speaking personnel employed by stations; and (5) except for copyright infringements, inform the Secretary of the Government of violations of any requirements in this Article so that the appropriate sanctions may be applied.

As previously mentioned, Article LXXXI provides for the creation of a special system of transmitting and receiving stations, or radiophonic schools, for public education. These radio schools are under the jurisdiction of the Secretary of Public Education. He and his office are responsible for the selection of personnel—teachers, announcers, technicians—who prepare and present these educational broadcasts. Municipalities, schools, labor unions, agrarian groups or other local organizations are required to finance the installation of adequate receiving equipment, if they are to participate in the program.

The Secretary of Public Education has the statutory responsibility of approving all announcers employed by stations on a regular basis. Article LXXXIX specifically provides that newscasters and news commentators shall be of Mexican nationality and shall show "certificates of accreditation" from the Secretary of Public Education. Article LXXXV states that, in special cases, the Secretary of the Government may authorize foreigners to broadcast "provisionally." It is under the latter provision of the law that Station XETRA, located in Tijuana and providing a news service for Southern California, may use U.S. citizens for news reporting and analysis.

The U.S. Government exercises no authority in the selection of any personnel employed by privately owned stations. The Mexican Law provides for two classes of announcers: the *A* group must have the equivalent of a college degree (B.A.) and the *B* group at least a high school education. Stations operating with more than ten thousand watts of power must use only announcers in the *A* classification.

The Powers of the Secretary of Health and Public Welfare

IN ADDITION to educational improvement, the Federal Government of Mexico has been increasingly concerned about the health of the nation. Article XII of the Federal Radio and Television Law provides that the Secretary of Health and Public Welfare shall promote programs for the education and health of the people, *"la orientación social en favor de la salud del pueblo."* He is authorized to prohibit the broadcasting of commercials involving the practice of medicine or related activities if, in his opinion, they may be injurious to public health. Nor does the Law permit the broadcast of any messages which advertise food, drinks, medicines, insecticides, therapeutic devices or remedies for the treatment and cure of diseases, which may be deemed harmful by this Secretary.

The functions of the Secretary of Health and Public Welfare are similar to those of the Federal Trade Commission and the Food and Drug Administration in the United States. Any kind of false advertising of products and services is prohibited by Federal law, and severe penalties are imposed for willful and false advertising that is injurious to the health of listeners.

Programming: Statutory Positives

LIKE Section 326 of the Communications Act, Article LVIII of the Federal Radio and Television Law in Mexico guarantees the broadcaster and listener freedom from government censorship. It provides that the right of expression and reception shall not be subject to judicial or administrative inquiry. But this does not mean unbridled freedom. There are statutory positives and negatives which must be observed—many more, in fact, than in the American law.

While stations in the United States are required to operate "in the public interest," and are legally prohibited from transmitting a few types of programs (lotteries, deceptive quiz shows, broadcasts containing indecent utterance, for example), the Mexican statute contains a large number of such injunctions. Statutory requirements include the daily broadcast of thirty minutes of programming prepared by the Government; the giving of priority to government bulletins related to the security or defense of the nation or the conservation of public order; making available facilities for network broadcasting of informational programs of transcendent importance to the nation, as required by the Secretary of Government or the Chief Executive; and maintenance of a prudent balance between advertising and other programs, *"Deberá mantener un prudente equilibrio entre el anuncio comercial y el conjunto de la programación."*[14] If a program might have a deleterious effect upon children, an announcement of its unsuitability must be made at the beginning.

The Law further states that stations are to carry local live programs giving expression to and stimulating artistic values, in accordance with advice given by the Secretary of the Government and members of the Radio and Television Council; that stations shall use only the Mexican language on broadcasts, unless exception is made by the office of the Secretary of the Government, and even then a transmission of the Spanish version in full or in summary form must be provided in accordance with the judgment of this office. Daily programming must include information about sports, and political, social and cultural matters of public importance.

Programming: Statutory Negatives

BESIDES the positive program requirements, there are the following negative injunctions, none of which is to be found in the U.S. Communications

Act. The Mexican Law prohibits broadcasts which may corrupt the language, violate the mores of the community, encourage antisocial behavior, belittle national heroes, offend religious beliefs or discriminate against races. There is a special prohibition against cheap comedy and offensive sounds, *"prohibido el empleo de recursos de baja comicidad y sonidos ofensivos."*[15]

Furthermore, it is unlawful to broadcast news, messages or propaganda contrary to the security of the State and public order. Rebroadcasting of programs from a foreign country or international organization without prior authorization from the Secretary of the Government is prohibited. Any publicity of centers of vice or any misleading propaganda or advertising concerning commercial products or services, the use of which might cause personal or public injury, is forbidden.

The advertising of alcoholic beverages is permitted, but if the alcoholic content exceeds twenty percent, the law says that all exaggeration (hardsell persuasion) must be avoided. With such a commercial there must also be a message concerning improvement of diet and health. Drinking of such beverages, actual or simulated, in connection with advertising, is not permitted.

While the broadcasting of lotteries is prohibited by the Criminal Code in the United States, it has legislative sanction in Mexico. Article LXX of the Mexican statute states, however, that any games of chance, if broadcast, must be approved and supervised by the Secretary of Government.

Renewal and Revocation of Licenses

THE Mexican Law provides that the term of a license for a broadcast station in Mexico may run as long as thirty years. It may be renewed to the same licensee or concessionaire who, as the Law recites, is given preference over third parties. This of course is quite different from the American law which limits licenses to three years. Furthermore, there is nothing in the Communications Act which says that licensees must be given preference over third parties at renewal time. In theory at least, the Federal Communications Commission is under a legal obligation to prefer the applicant (whether he be the existing licensee or a competing newcomer) who shows that he can more effectively serve the needs and interests of the community. Practically speaking, however, newcomers have always been at a disadvantage in the United States when competing for broadcast facilities at renewal time, and the odds are great against their being able to dispossess incumbents.

While concessions are granted for long periods of time in Mexico, the Federal Government there, as in the United States, is authorized to revoke these concessions and permits at any time for specified causes. For example, the Secretary of Communications and Transport may revoke permits and concessions for changing the location of transmitting equipment without his prior authorization, changing the frequency on which the station operates without his consent, or failure to comply with the conditions of broadcast authorization. In both Mexico and the United States, an unapproved transfer of station control constitutes statutory grounds for cancellation of a license. Also, permits of "cultural" stations may be revoked, after having been given notice, if these stations broadcast commercials or other program materials which are foreign to the purposes for which the permits were granted or if they fail to provide the specialization service for which they are licensed.

Summary and Conclusions

THE broadcasting laws in Mexico and the United States are similar in many ways. Both state that the radio spectrum belongs to the people and that its use is subject to the exclusive regulatory jurisdiction of the Federal Government. Accordingly, each statute declares that licensees (concessionaires or permittees as they are called in Mexico) have an obligation to operate in the "public interest." They must apply to the Government periodically for renewal of their licenses, giving an account of their stewardship and justifying their continued use of the frequencies which have been assigned to them.

In neither country are broadcast stations considered "common carriers" in the sense that the precise rates which they may charge are determined by the Government, as is the case with telecommunications and transportation facilities. Both legal systems recognize the validity of private enterprise and the profit motive, and sanction competition.

In addition to commercial broadcasting, the Mexican Law provides for the establishment of noncommercial, cultural, instructional (radio schools) and experimental stations. While the Communications Act does not specify these particular classes, it does give the Federal Communications Commission broad authority to make such classifications. And, in accordance with this authority, the agency has reserved channels for noncommercial, educational FM and TV stations which are similar to the cultural and instructional operations in Mexico.

In another important respect the laws are similar. The Constitutions of Mexico and the United States contain guarantees of free speech, which are implemented in the broadcasting laws of both countries. However, these assurances of free communication and reception, and prohibitions against government censorship, are offset by legislative requirements that forbid the broadcasting of certain types of programs and make mandatory an overall broadcast operation that serves public interests and needs.

Both laws prohibit the transfer of station ownership and control without the prior approval of the Federal Government. Moreover, while aliens may hold minority interests, they are not permitted to acquire majority control of broadcast operations.

The laws of both countries vest a great deal of responsibility for program service in the licensees themselves, but the Federal Governments are authorized to revoke licenses when stations do not meet their statutory and public obligations. Both Mexican and U.S. regulatory agencies are given the power to impose fines and forfeitures for failure to operate stations in accordance with legal requirements.

Differences in Laws Summarized

THE Mexican Law is much more detailed and definitive as to the standards that broadcasters should follow if they are to provide maximum program service. For example, the legislative requirement that all stations shall carry at least thirty minutes of programming per day prepared by the Government and that they should make their facilities available for special broadcasts of national interest is completely foreign to American policy. Such statutory mandates require the Federal Government of Mexico to be more actively and directly concerned with the day-to-day program operations of stations than is the case in the United States.

While the Voice of America and the U.S. Armed Forces Radio and Television Service do produce programs and broadcast to the general public (by short-wave and with programs designed for foreign reception), and other agencies of the U.S. Government do make use of frequencies for transmissions related to government business, the Federal Government normally does not produce programs for domestic broadcasting. On the other hand, the Federal Government of Mexico does produce regular programming and, pursuant to legislative authority, requires all broadcast stations in the country to carry daily thirty minutes of government programming if it is made available,[16] and to join a national network each Sunday night and broadcast a full hour of programming produced by the Government in Mexico City.

Moreover, unlike the situation in the United States, regulatory responsibilities are divided among several agencies of the Federal Government in Mexico, although there is a coordinating Council which serves in an advisory capacity and provides some cohesion in broadcasting policies. Also, broadcasters in Mexico may not, except by special permission of the Secretary of the Government, hire announcers or newscasters unless they have been approved by the Secretary of Public Education and hold Mexican citizenship.

Finally, Article LXV of the Mexican Law gives the Secretary of the

Government the power to censor the broadcasting or rebroadcasting of programs produced in other countries. No such power is given the Federal Communications Commission, and any attempt to exercise such power would be construed as a violation of Section 326 of the Communications Act which contains a blanket prohibition of censorship. The Mexican statute states that the rebroadcasting of foreign programs, whether they are produced and sponsored by private interests, governments or international organizations outside the country, and no matter how they may be received by Mexican radio or TV stations, is prohibited unless prior authorization is granted by the Secretary of the Government.

José Luis Fernández, the Mexican legal scholar, while praising the Federal Law of Radio and Television in Mexico, is critical of this particular provision. Contrary to its mandate, he favors a free flow of information and messages across national boundaries, and does not believe that before presenting programs of such organizations as UNESCO, broadcasters should be required to get prior government approval.[17]

NOTES

1. *Ley de Vías Generales de Comunicación,* publicada en al "Diario Oficial" de 19 de febrero de 1940. Señor Huberto Stein and Señor Guido Gomez de Silva aided in the translation of this law as well as the Federal Law of Radio and Television (1960) which is analyzed later. Both have interpreted for the United Nations and are of Mexican nationality, but received their university education in the United States.

2. *Concessions* are granted to commercial stations for thirty years and are renewable to the same concessionaires. *Permits* are granted to cultural stations which operate on a noncommercial basis.

3. *"De ahí que, por una indebida extensión a la radiodifusión de nociones jurídicas aplicadas de antiguo a la radiotelegrafía, se incurriera en errores tan preñados de graves consecuencias como el de sostener que el 'broadcasting' es servicio público. En ese concepto, recogido por la ley en muchos de nuestros países, se han fundado prácticas administrativas que durante muchos años han comprometido seriamente el desarrollo de la radiodifusión, sometiéndola a un régimen de policía, de restricciones y sanciones, inconciliable con su íntima naturaleza y con la función social que ella está llamada a desempeñar."*

   Justino Jiménez de Aréchega wrote the prologue to the book, *Derecho de la Radiodifusión* by José Luis Fernández, from which this quotation is taken. The book was published in 1960 in Mexico City. (*Impreso en los telleres linotipográficos de la "Editorial Olimpo," Imprenta 205.*)

4. José Luis Fernández, *Derecho de la Radiodifusión* (Mexico City: 1960), p. 146.

5. *Ley Federal de Radio y Televisión,* publicado en le "Diario Oficial," de 19 de enero de 1960.

6. *Ibid.,* Transitory Article II.

7. Fernández, p. 164. ". . . *pero obligados a enjuiciar la ley con criterio fríamente jurídico, encontramos que se trata de normas sin sanción, o más bien, cuyo cumplimiento y observancia se dejan al cuidado y sentido de responsabilidad del propio radiodifusor."*

8. To a limited extent, the Government's authority to establish minimum rate schedules in Mexico keeps broadcasting in the common carrier category. The Communications Act specifically precludes broadcasting from the common carrier classification and any attempt to establish minimum rates for stations in the United States would be viewed as a violation of the Act.

9. In Spanish the office is called *Secretaría de Gobernación.* One interpreter referred to the office in English as the Minister of the Interior.

10. *Ley Federal de Radio y Televisión,* Article X, paragraph 1.

11. See Fernández, pp. 167–168.

12. Interview with Señor Farías in Mexico City on July 18, 1962.

13. As of January 1968, one peso was equivalent to eight cents.

14. *Ley Federal de Radio y Televisión,* Article LXVII.

15. *Ibid.,* Article LXIII.

16. Because of the great expense involved, the Government does not produce enough programming to make it possible for stations to meet this daily requirement. What it amounts to is, the stations are obliged to carry the official programming if and when it is made available by the Government.

17. Fernández, p. 168. *"Pero lo que nos preocupa es que tales disposiciones contrarían los principios fundamentales de la ley y el espiritu y texto de los instrumentos internacionales que unánimemente consignan la libertad para la transmisión y recepción dentro y fuera de las fronteras. Existen organismos internacionales tan respetables como Naciones Unidas, UNESCO, la OEA, la CEPAL, etc., de las que nuestro páis forma parte, y parece inaudito que para retrasmitir programas de tales instituciones se requiera una previa autorization."*

III

Mexican Broadcasting:
Quantitative Dimensions[*]

ACCORDING TO THE OFFICE of the Secretary of Communications and Transport, as of July 8, 1964, there were three hundred and ninety-five commercial AM broadcasting stations operating on the standard band of frequencies between five hundred and forty and sixteen hundred kilocycles. Twenty-eight of these were licensed in the Federal District (Mexico City and vicinity) and the remainder were distributed throughout the country, with one or more operating in each of the twenty-nine states of the country. Their authorized power ranged from a maximum of two hundred and fifty thousand watts (such as XEW in Mexico City), to a minimum of two hundred and fifty watts, daytime only (such as XEEM, Rio Verde, San Luis Potosí).[1] XEW, licensed to *Cadena Radiodifusora Mexicana, S. A.,* has repeater stations in Guadalajara, Monterrey, and San Luis Potosí. XEX, operated by *Radiodifusora México, S. A.,* in Mexico City, has repeaters in these same cities plus Saltillo and Torreón.

According to FCC reports, there were 3,972 commercial AM stations in the United States on May 31, 1964.[2] Considering the Mexican economy and that its population is only one-sixth that of the United States, the number of standard broadcast operations there compares favorably.

There are fifteen commercial short-wave stations, eight of which are in Mexico City.[3] The remaining seven are in Hermosillo near the Gulf of California; Ciudad Mante in North Central Mexico; two in Veracruz on the Gulf of Mexico, one in Mérida, on the Yucatán Peninsula; one in León in Central Mexico and one in Tapachula on the Guatemalan border.[4]

Fifteen commercial FM stations are on the air in Mexico; eight of these are in Mexico City. The others are located in the cities of Matamoros, Guadalajara, Hermosillo and Monterrey. This number is meager compared with the 1,172 operating in the United States as of May 31, 1964.[5]

---

*Since the data for this study was accumulated, there have been some new broadcasting developments and to some extent the quantitative dimensions of Mexican broadcasting may be different as this book goes to press, but these are not significant enough to change substantially the general picture.

Estaciones Culturales

IN ADDITION to commercial stations, Mexican law provides for the establishment of noncommercial AM stations whose prescribed purpose is to broadcast educational and cultural programs. *Radio Gobernación,* an operation of the Federal Government, has an assigned radio frequency reserved for government use, but it has not been activated. *Radio Gobernación,* however, has its own staff which produces (in the studios of Station XEW) the official government programming which all stations in the country are legally required to carry. The taped programs are distributed by wire from the Government Building to a number of high-powered stations for broadcasting and are picked up and rebroadcast by all other stations in the country (providing reception is of satisfactory quality for rebroadcast).

The National University of Mexico also has one of these *estaciones culturales,* XEUN, with transmitting facilities and studios located on the University campus. Its assigned frequency is eight hundred and sixty kilocycles. In 1964 its authorized power was five thousand watts, but officials in Mexico City reported in July 1964, that its power was scheduled to be increased to fifty thousand watts in the near future.

A third educational station, XEJB (630 kc, 500 watts), Guadalajara, is licensed to the State Government of Jalisco. The remaining four are owned by universities in the state capitals of Chihuahua (XERU, 1310 kc, 1,000 watts day and 250 watts night), Jalapa (XEXB, 1400 kc, 500 watts day and 250 watts night),[6] San Luis Potosí (XEXQ, 1460 kc, 250 watts), Guanajuato (XEUG, 970 kc, 500 watts day only).

As of July 1964, ten cultural short-wave stations and two cultural FM stations were broadcasting in Mexico: XEJG (4820 kc, 250 watts) and XEJB-FM (96.4 mc, 300 watts), operated by *Gobierno del Estado de Jalisco* in Guadalajara; XERUU (6140 kc, 250 watts) by *Universidad de Chihuahua;* XESE (2380 kc, 350 watts) by the *Secretaría de Educación Pública;* XEXA (6175 kc, 100 watts) *by Radio Gobernación;* XEYU (9600 kc, 250 watts) by the *Universidad Nacional de México* in Mexico City; XEIDM (6185 kc, 1,000 watts) by *Instituto Federal de México;* XEUDS (6140 kc, 100 watts) by *Universidad de Sonora;* XEUMT (5960 kc, 250 watts) by *Universidad Iberoamericana;* and XEXQ (6045 kc, 250 watts) by *Radio Universidad Nacional Potosina.* XHD-FM (96.5 mc, 1,000 watts) was licensed to PIVM in Ixmiquilpan.[7]

Estaciones de Televisión

MEXICAN television is now in its thirteenth year. As of July 8, 1964, there were twenty-five television stations; most of them were either owned, partly owned, or affiliated with one corporation, *Telesistema Mexicano, S. A.*[8] This corporation operates three TV stations on channels 2, 4 and 5 in Mexico City, and with the use of microwave links in the mountainous areas is able to achieve coverage over a twelve state region. Channels 3, 6, 7 and 9 are used by the network to distribute the programs to the various communities served. Ten stations are operated in the larger cities of northern Mexico. According to a report dated July 31, 1963, new stations are now on the air in Acapulco and Mérida, using selected network programs.[9] However, the July 1964 official report (see footnote 4) does not list these two stations.

It has been estimated that there are over a million TV receivers in use, more than half of which are in Mexico City and its environs. Local stations in Juárez, Tijuana, Mexicali, Nogales and Nuevo Laredo near the Mexico–United States border serve a large audience in both countries.[10]

In 1962, the Federal Communications Commission granted a license to the Spanish International Broadcasting Company in Los Angeles to operate UHF Station KMEX, with authority to carry programs produced by Mexican stations. The programs of this American station are presented entirely in Spanish. A majority of KMEX's programs are purchased from the *Telesistema* network. KMEX has supplied this network with special programming, such as coverage of the 1964 visit of U.S. President Johnson and former Mexican President Mateos to Los Angeles. A similarly owned and operated station, KWEX, operates in San Antonio, Texas, and the same group of owners (which includes Sr. Azcárraga of *Telesistema* as a minority stockholder) have applied for Channel 37 in Paterson, New Jersey.

There are several independent TV stations on the air, but a large part of the nation-wide programming is produced in Mexico City by *Telesistema Mexicano, S. A.* at the *Televicentro,* a building which supports the towers, and houses all the studios, transmitters, master controls, video-tape equipment and film projectors for the network. Rates for advertising are much lower than those in the United States and broadcasting income is comparatively small. Housing all the facilities in one building lowers operating costs, provides good programs and assures financial profit.[11]

The television industry is largely a monopoly in Mexico, as compared to diversified control in the United States which has three networks and many independent stations vying for the audience and advertising dollar. Two men, Don Emilio Azcárraga of Station XEW-TV and Don Rómulo O'Farrill of Station XHTV, largely own and control Mexican television. While the initiative and helpfulness of these original entrepreneurs is appreciated, officials are disposed to make available additional TV channels and to encourage new competitive enterprise in the industry. More diversified ownership might provide greater variety in programming and more effectively serve the public interest.[12] Recent reports support this thought, but there has been no official confirmation.[13]

While commercial television has made considerable progress, educational TV has lagged behind. There is only one noncommercial TV station on the air in Mexico—XEIP, operating on Channel 11. It is licensed to the *Instituto Politécnico Nacional* in Mexico City and broadcasts a limited schedule of programs. Other educational stations are anticipated, but financing is a serious problem. The National University, for example, has been granted a permit to build but, according to University authorities, sufficient funds are not now available to build and operate a station.[14] In July 1964, government officials stated that cooperative plans were being made by the Ministries of Communications and Education, the National University of Mexico and the Polytechnic Institute to provide direct televised instruction over Channel 11. Subjects to be taught at the lower educational levels will include physics, mathematics, Spanish, history and geography.

Programs of Commercial Radio Stations in Mexico

THE pattern of programming on Mexican commercial stations is similar in many ways to that in the United States. There are occasional local live programs, and some dramatic and educational programs are produced at the local level.[15] But the bulk of the broadcasts monitored in different parts of the country during a four week period consisted mainly of brief news reports and recorded music of the popular Spanish variety, interspersed with frequent commercials.[16]

Extensive listening, and the analysis of more than fifty hours of programs taped in the northern, central and southern parts of the country indicates that broadcasting in Mexico is much more heavily commercial than in the United States. Two factors seem to account for this. One is that radio is highly competitive in most markets. For example, Mexico City had thirty AM, nine FM, eight short-wave and five TV stations in 1964. Tijuana had nine AM stations plus TV facilities. Just sixty miles south, in the small city of Enseñada, with a population of less than eighteen thousand, there were four radio stations. In the state of Sonora, one FM, one short-wave, and thirty-two AM stations operated commercially. Eight of these stations were located in Hermosillo, capital city of that state, with a population of more than ninety-seven thousand. Nogales, with a population of 37,657, had four. Ciudad Obregón, with 67,956, had seven. There were three stations in Navojoa, and the same number in Guaymas, each town having about thirty-five thousand people. Six smaller communities each had one station. The total number of people in all the towns and cities in Sonora where these stations were located was less than three hundred thousand.[17]

Economic conditions are improving, but the purchasing power of the people is not high. Business enterprises, therefore, are limited in the amounts they can spend for broadcast advertising. Accordingly, the rates are low. For example, XEQ, one of the oldest stations in Mexico City, operating on nine hundred and forty kilocycles with fifty thousand watts of power, in 1964 was selling a forty second commercial spot for the equivalent of $3.68. In Agua Prieta, Sonora, with a population of only 10,508, the published rate for a ten second spot on Station XEAQ (two hundred and fifty watts) was six cents. A competing station in the same city, XEFH (five hundred watts) charged only sixteen cents.[18]

With a high degree of saturation, keen competition in limited markets and comparatively low advertising rates, it is no wonder that radio program schedules are heavily laden with commercials, at least four or five each quarter hour. In line with the quick tempo, characteristic of most Mexican radio programs, the commercials are short and snappy. They often are the jingle and musical type, or consist of peppy dramatic dialogue and are skillfully woven into the program continuity.[19]

Radio Gobernación

ALL radio stations in the country are required to carry up to thirty minutes each weekday and a full hour each Sunday of programming prepared in XEW studios in Mexico City by the Federal Government (providing it is made available). In 1964, the man in charge of preparing these programs was Lic. Luis Farías, who was responsible to the Secretary of Government. Lic. Farías was serving as Chairman of the National Radio and Television Council, an advisory group composed of representatives of the various government agencies concerned with the regulatory aspects of broadcasting, and representatives of the industry itself and the workers in the industry. When asked to describe the nature of the programs which the Government prepares and requires stations to carry, he stated that his office cooperated with the Secretary of Agriculture and the Secretary of Public Education in preparing programs helpful to the farmers and schools in different parts of the country. He also mentioned that his office cooperated with the Secretary of Health in the promotion and distribution of health and sanitation programs. He pointed out that, as required by law, all Mexican stations are required to carry special broadcasts of national importance, if ordered by the Chief Executive or the Secretary of Government. Señor Farías explained the procedure:

> When a decision is made by the Secretary of Government (my office belongs to the Secretary), then we send out messages to all stations telling them to carry a certain program. A very interesting message by the President of Mexico, and for instance, since you are an American, the recent visit of

President Kennedy and the speeches made by him and our President were carried by all stations. And, for example, the State of the Union message that the President of Mexico presents every year on the first of September is carried by every station, and there is no time limit on that. It all depends on the President. It may take two, three or sometimes as much as four hours.[20]

He explained that the one hour show which he and his staff prepared and which all stations were required to carry on Sunday night consisted of popular music, news commentary, the reading of selected poetry and a significant newspaper editorial of the week, and information messages of interest to the Government.

A tape of one Sunday evening program showed that its content was very much in line with Lic. Farías' description. It was a well directed, first-class production featuring outstanding Mexican talent. The commentaries reflected an attempt to inform citizens about some important and interesting aspects of Mexican life and to inspire national pride and loyalty. The following are excerpts from the commentaries, as translated by Señor Huberto Sein.

To know Mexico is to love Mexico! We shall now speak of the mineral springs in Monterrey, Nuevo León. The state of Nuevo León is very rich in mineral springs. . . . There are other thermal springs with places for baths along the Inter-American Highway, Highway No. 85, between Monterrey and Laredo, Texas. . . . In no other part of the world is there such a profusion of thermal springs as we have in this part of Mexico. These springs are famous for helping keep youthful qualities in people as well as for enhancing human beauty.

After these short comments, there was an interlude of popular music, followed by a brief discourse on the attractiveness and uniqueness of some Mexican cities and a rebuke of persons who are unduly critical of Mexico.[21]

Broadcasting at the University of Mexico

THE operation of the educational station at the National University of Mexico is completely noncommercial. The schedules include a variety of programs—classical music, conferences, lectures and round tables dealing with the various arts, the theatre, painting, plastics, architecture, poetry, and with philosophical, literary, economic and sociological subjects. Except for the teaching of some foreign languages such as English and French (German and Italian were also to be taught beginning in September 1964), no instruction courses are broadcast by the station. Critical commentaries on publications, news analysis in depth, reports on significant current affairs, and student dramatic productions are also featured.

Reaching the Rural Areas with Radio

MEXICANS live in the mountains, on the deserts and in other rural areas. The inhabitants of the numerous small villages enjoy few, if any, of the modern conveniences to be found in the large cities such as Mexico City and Monterrey. The literacy rate, although improving, is still low compared to that of the large cities. Many natives living in the remote areas do not have radio receivers, though with the increasing availability of inexpensive transistor sets, the problem is being somewhat alleviated. Government officials, educators and other leaders have revealed a great interest in reaching a larger portion of the village and rural population with broadcasts designed to raise the cultural level and improve the living standards.

Señor Sein, who has lived in Mexico most of his life and has worked with the villagers on community projects, has expressed a special interest in this problem. The following is a verbatim report of an interview with him regarding the current status of radio in rural Mexico:

Emery: Would you talk about the problem of communication in the small villages and rural communities? What are their sources of information? Do they rely upon radio? What do you think the possibilities are for improving the community life of these villagers by means of broadcasting?

Sein: Before the coming of radio to rural Mexico, people relied very much on exchanges and friendly gossip at the weekly market. With the coming of radio, they have been relying a good deal for news and also for music. Sometimes, their first experience in hearing radio comes when they may be riding a bus. The passengers will listen to the radio turned on by the driver, sometimes with quite a generous volume. In villages where persons have few radio receivers, it may be two or three village storekeepers who will have a receiver operated with an automobile battery. Villagers gather in the afternoon and in the evening at these stores to hear the music and the news, and of course, the commercials as you call them in the United States. So radio has become important in Mexican village life.

With the gradual improvement in income, families have been purchasing radios. As Mexico develops its rural electrification program throughout the nation, electric radios are becoming more available. People will save in order to have a radio. The radio is sometimes covered with a neatly embroidered curtain, and is placed on a shelf in a place of prominence in the villager's simple hut. The Department of Agriculture is now broadcasting comments and advice to the farmers about soil erosion, water, plagues, marketing of crops, and also about forest fires. These programs are welcomed by the Mexican villagers. I believe that it is along these lines that improvement can be made.

Emery: I have been talking to some of the governmental officials in the Ministry of Education, Señor Sein, and they tell me about some school programs that are being presented by radio stations, and I understand many of the schools have radio receivers and the teachers use these radio programs to supplement their classroom instruction. This kind of programming would seem to have possibilities for extension, don't you think so?

Sein: Yes, I think so. The Ministry of Education has been broadening its program with the use of radio. There are places in the mountainous areas of Mexico and also places near our large deserts which are quite isolated. It is through radio that the rural school teacher feels a living contact with the Ministry of Education of the nation. These programs are supplementing the very fine work these school teachers are doing in very isolated places.[22]

Programs of Television Stations in Mexico

MOST commercial television originates in Mexico City. Señor Aurelio Pérez, the Program Manager of Television Station XHTV, one of the key stations in the *Telesistema* network, has described the station's program schedule:

We begin operation each day at 2:45 P.M., broadcasting news, and then some information about the movies that are being shown at the theatres. Then we broadcast one long feature film which may be one from the United States, or one from Mexico, Argentina or Europe. Generally, we see that Spanish is spoken by the characters in these feature films.

Following this, until 7:00 in the evening, we have programs that are of special interest to women. Then we present from 7:00 to 8:00 P.M., on weekdays, stage adaptations of movies. From 8:00 to 10:00 in the evening, we have musical programs and also have lectures. And at ten o'clock we have some "violence" programs, some stronger violence than usual, or we may have some information programs, some round table discussions of historical or political matters. At eleven o'clock, we have news, and at present, we are studying the possibility of adding from 11:15 to 11:30, or even 12:30, a musical program.

On Saturdays and Sundays, we have different programming, because the station broadcasts in the morning on these days. On Saturday morning, we have programs for children, or young people. We have documentaries or contests. On Saturday afternoon, at present, we are broadcasting the football games, and on Sunday morning there is music, generally military music or Mexican music. Then we broadcast a baseball game. This is followed on Sunday afternoon with a long high-quality feature film.

We are, at present, trying to promote the use of informational and educational programs. I think this is a general trend of Mexican television. We are also trying to promote remote control programs. For instance, when President Kennedy was in Mexico recently, Mexican television made an extraordinary effort, and broadcast twenty of the twenty-six hours he was here, during official functions.

Finally, also recently, we have another program on video-tape made in Chile, where world championship football games were played.

I also would like to add that we have an excellent relationship with the services of the United States agencies, the American Embassy, the cultural attache. We often show documentary films of our Western civilization. We showed recently a film called, "Our Planet Earth," and another film dealing with the Newport Jazz Festival.[23]

According to Señor Pérez, a current weekly series of programs, *"La Novela Semanal,"* consisting of stage adaptations and narration of novels, has received good ratings. Station XHTV recently established a department of special events with the facilities for originating remote broadcasts. This department has already covered a number of important events, such as the visit of French President De Gaulle to Mexico.

A program schedule of Station XEW-TV, another *Telesistema* outlet in Mexico City, for the week from July 16 through July 22, 1962 showed that many types of programs were similar to those appearing on Station XHTV. There were news reports, sports reviews, musicals, local live programs of special interest to women, documentaries, feature films, variety shows, comedy, educational seminars dealing with science, art and university affairs, and remote telecasts of a football game and a bull fight.[24] According to recent reports, some of the programs which are receiving high ratings in Mexico include American productions such as "Bonanza," "Untouchables," and a number of local live programs (musical, comedy, "soapers," variety) produced by the *Telesistema* network at the Television Center studios in Mexico City.[25]

The only noncommercial, educational TV station in 1963 was being operated by the National Polytechnical Institute (*Instituto Politécnico Nacional*) in Mexico City. Its hours of broadcasting and its resources are very limited. The National University of Mexico does broadcast some TV programs over commercial stations, but as Jaime García Terrés, the *Director-General de Difusión Cultural* at the University, has said, there are limitations imposed by the commercial broadcasters. "We have a few programs. We have a program dealing with the cinema, for instance, with explanations and analysis of important films, in the history of the cinema. And we have news programs, short lectures and interviews, with speeches by professors and students, etc."[26]

Outside of the major cities, TV receivers are scarce in Mexico, but there is a growing interest in television in the villages and rural areas. Señor Sein has spoken of a merchant in a small village who had a light plant providing electricity for two bulbs and his television set:

> He has placed the set in a large room and has placed benches in front of the set. When the entertainment programs come through the channels selected, the people, especially the children, of the village come and sit on these benches, after paying a few centavos admission, and they enjoy the television

programs. In this way, they are broadening their feeling of community with the rest of Mexico, and with the cities and the capital, Mexico City. They are also learning a little more about their own geography and history. For some of these are excellent cultural programs. I am happy to say that enterprises in Mexico have recognized the Mexican's interest in improving his culture and have sponsored programs of quality, and presented them in a manner intelligible to the minds of the villagers.

Señor Sein has stated what he considered to be some of the better aspects of Mexican television programming:

> The documentary films that have been shown on television are, in my opinion, the type of programs that help improve the knowledge of simple people about the world in which they live. The documentary films are being enjoyed in villages where there may be only one television set, and people will come several kilometers to see these television programs. The type of film that is carelessly selected, that is, the kind with gangsters . . . has lost its attractiveness for many people. Almost all of them are a repetition of the same plot, the same pattern, and fortunately, in my opinion, they are not liked as much as the documentary films. Also, the films that show dances of other peoples, the songs of others, trips and voyages in Africa, Asia, the United States and South America. These are the programs that have zest. They bring life from other parts of the world very close to the people and help to strengthen a sense of human solidarity. This, I think is a real mission that television can accomplish.

Visions for Future Broadcast Programming in Mexico

SEÑOR Sein has discussed the possibilities of using television to promote educational and social progress in the rural areas:

> I believe it would be very good for an enterprising television group to make some of its programs out in rural Mexico, and show how people are struggling to improve their living conditions, how they seek to grow their corn in better ways, how they are building rural schools, how they are improving elementary sanitation, how they are working on neighborhood roads, how their hope is in rural Mexico, for hope is so vital to the people. When the people have hope, and have hope for a better day for their children, there will be less a trend toward the use of violence to bring about social change. And there will be more emphasis on the persevering pursuit of the ways of peace in bringing about social change, social justice, and improved living standards and in the use of the talents and gifts that these fine people have.[27]

Dr. Ignacio Chávez, former Rector of the National University of Mexico, was enthusiastic about the possibilities of making fuller and more effective use of the broadcast media in education. He has spoken favorably of the use of television for instructional purposes: "I consider that this is a method that calls for increased development. There are some matters of a technical nature which do not lend themselves to teaching via television. There are some subjects, however, which because of the large number of students, can be handled through the use of radio and TV and both media are going to modify the classical, conventional teaching methods."[28]

Señor Farías, one of the most knowledgeable and influential persons in Mexican broadcasting, has discussed both the problems and possibilities of making a more effective use of the media:

> Everybody interested in culture and higher degrees of knowledge for the people of Mexico thinks radio and TV can do a lot in this field. But the government has a problem of budget. It costs a large amount of money to produce good programs of real interest to the public, that is, if you put them on TV. On radio, I believe it is easier and cheaper, and it also reaches a larger number of people. So, on radio we are doing something. On television, however, there are only a few programs that may be considered cultural. But if we could get the help of all the radio and TV stations who would produce their own programs; if advertising agencies and civic-minded organizations that sponsor programs would take a real interest, there is an unlimited possibility of using these mass media to carry messages to the people and to lift the cultural standard of the nation.[29]

Conclusions

MANY government, education and business leaders in Mexico are genuinely interested in making a wider and more effective use of broadcasting to serve the needs and raise the cultural standards of the people. Despite limited resources, the nation has made much progress. Under the law, the Mexican Government plays a much more active and important role in broadcasting than is the case in the United States. Señor Farias and other government officials in Mexico City, however, have expressed the hope that broadcasters, advertisers and other interested groups in the country would take more initiative and assume greater responsibilities for the production of high-quality public service programming.

Many public officials, educators, journalists, broadcasters and other leaders have expressed friendly feelings for the United States and have shown an interest in a greater cultural exchange between the two countries via radio and television. With the generous approval of government officials (a legal requirement), Mexican television and radio are using much program material produced in the United States and the Mexican people are forming images of our character and behavior by what they see and hear on these programs.

On the other hand, there is a great programming potential for American radio and television in the rich, colorful life and character of Mexico. As Señor Luis de Guevara, the Editor of the English section of the Mexican newspaper, *El Universal,* has said, "the Mexican people, and probably the same thing is true in all the Latin American countries, know more about Americans and the United States than Americans know about us." He has spoken of the tendency of the mass media to emphasize sensational events and to neglect other aspects of Latin American life which would be of as much or more interest to people in the United States. With an increased use of the media for a freer flow of information and images across our national boundaries, and with the cooperation of the two Governments and private institutions in both countries, closer understanding could be achieved.[30]

Much more research needs to be done, particularly of a quantitative character, before the full picture of Mexican broadcasting can be drawn. A few comprehensive studies are already being conducted, but others should be undertaken both in Mexico and in countries to the south.

NOTES

1. The author visited the offices of the *Secretaría de Comunicaciones y Transportes, Departamento de Radiodifusión,* in Mexico City on July 8, 1964, and received this official information. Secretary of Communications and Transport Eng. Walter C. Buchanan was very cooperative in making available these and other data. (With the subsequent change in administration, Secretary Buchanan was replaced by a new appointee.)
2. *Broadcasting,* July 6, 1964, p. 88. This figure is from the "commercial station boxscore" compiled by the FCC as of May 31, 1964. *Broadcasting*'s own compilation as of June 30, is 3,987 commercial AM stations. In both cases, the figures include both fully licensed stations and those new stations operating under authority of their construction permits.
3. The short-wave stations in Mexico City, their authorized power and assigned frequencies are: XEQK, 1000 watts, 9555 kc; XEVOZ, 5000 watts, 15200 kc; WEHH, 5000 watts, 11880 kc; XEOI, 2500 watts, 6010 kc; XEQQ, 1000 watts, 9680 kc; WERCM, 100 watts, 6130 kc; XERR, 5000 watts, 15110 kc; and XEXG, 1000 watts, 6065 kc. XEWW operates on three frequencies: 6115 kc, 9515 kc and 15160 kc, each with 10,000 watts. This information was provided by the *Departamento de Radiodifusión, Secretaría de Comunicaciones y Transportes,* July 8, 1964.
4. These stations are XEBR, 150 watts, 11820 kc, Hermosillo; XECMT, 1000 watts, 6090 kc, Ciudad Mante; XEFT, 250 watts, 9545 kc, Veracruz; XEUW, 250 watts, 6020 kc, Veracruz; XEQM, 250 watts, 6105 kc, Mérida; XEXG, 1000 watts, 6065 kc, León; and XETS, 500 watts, 6120 kc, Tapachula. This information was provided by the *Departamento*

de Radiodifusión, Secretaría de Comunicaciones y Transportes, July 8, 1964.

5. *Ibid.* Also, see *Broadcasting,* July 6, 1964, p. 88. Includes operating Construction Permits.

6. Operation of XEXB has been temporarily suspended.

7. Official records of the *Secretaría de Comunicaciones y Transportes.*

8. See *Mexican Television—1962 Report, Telesistema Mexicano, S. A.* *(Edificio Televicentro, Avenida Chapultepec No. 18, Mexico 1, D.F.).*

9. See *Variety,* July 31, 1963, p. 30. The article, "Musical Shows, Soapers Still Mainstays for Mexico's TV," is an interesting and informative discussion of recent developments in Mexican television.

10. *Variety,* January 9, 1963, p. 135.

11. *Ibid.*

12. Interviews of Mexican government officials conducted by the author in July 1962 and July 1964. These were informal discussions but no official expressed any fixed opinion on this matter.

13. *Variety,* July 31, 1963, p. 30.

14. Interviews by the author with the then Rector of the National University of Mexico and other officials of the institution, July 1962, and confirmed by Federal officials in July 1964.

15. The schedules of a few stations consist of as many as fifty percent local live programs but these are the exceptions rather than the rule.

16. With the use of a car radio, converter, and recorder, the author was able to tape for content analysis many programs in both urban and rural areas in different sections of Mexico.

17. Population figures are based upon the Mexican 1960 Federal Census. There have been increases in population since the Census was taken. The population of the State of Sonora, including rural areas, is now much larger than three hundred thousand.

18. *Medios Publicitarios Mexicanos, Tarifas E Información,* Subsidiary of Standard Rate and Data Service, Inc., May 15 to August 15, 1962, Skokie, Illinois.

19. Based on monitoring of programs of commercial AM stations in Nuevo Laredo, Monterrey, San Luis Potosí, Tamazunchale, Mexico City, Taxco, Cuernavaca, Acapulco, Tijuana, and Ensenada, and villages and rural areas near these cities. With a short-wave receiver, the author was able to monitor most of the commercial short-wave stations in Mexico. The programs of these stations consist mostly of music, news and commercials. The following short commercials are a few of a large number which were taped in different parts of Mexico. These appeared to be fairly typical of those broadcast over standard stations on the basis of extensive monitoring. They were of course broadcast in Spanish. The English interpretations are by Señor Huberto Sein.

You are a distinguished lawyer. Why don't you take this case in your hands. Excuse me, but I take . . . . Beer.

Any moment you can have a headache. Therefore, always keep close at hand . . . .!

The head thinks and the feet walk. A mixer or blender for 185 pesos? They're crazy! Well, to convince yourself that they really are crazy, come to our store at . . . . and see the attractive prices we have on many of our goods.

Buy today one peso's worth of . . . . to get rid of that toothache, that headache, that backache, or whatever ache you have. . . . for you!

American products are advertised a great deal on Mexican stations.

20. Interviews with Señor Luis Farías in Mexico City July 20, 1962 and July 8, 1964. Lic. Farías broadcast from his office via *Radio Gobernación* periodic reports on the conduct of the recent Presidential election in Mexico. These reports were carried by all stations in the country.
21. Excerpts from official government broadcast presented over national network, July 15, 1962, from 10 to 11 P.M.; translations by Señor Huberto Sein.
22. Taped interview with Señor Huberto Sein, Mexico City, July 22, 1962.
23. Interview by the author with Señor Pérez, July 20, 1962, and updated in an interview on July 7, 1964. As of August 1964, soccer games are broadcast on Sundays; translations by Señor Sein.
24. Based upon official program schedule, *"Programacion Seminal Del Canal 2 (Semana Del 16 Al 22 De Julio 1962)."*
25. *Variety,* July 31, 1963, p. 88.
26. Interview by author with Señor Jaime García Terrés, July 13, 1963.
27. Interview by author with Señor Sein.
28. Interview by author with Dr. Ignacio Chavez, then Rector of the National University of Mexico, Mexico City, July 13, 1962.
29. Interview with Señor Farías.
30. Interview with Señor Luis de Guevara, Editor, English Section, *El Universal,* Mexico City, July 21, 1962.

IV

Canadian Broadcasting:
Unity and Diversity

C ANADIAN BROADCASTING has made marked progress in recent years, despite certain geographical, economic, linguistic and cultural problems with which the country has had to contend. In such a vast area (in home territory Canada is the second largest country in the world), with much rugged and varied terrain, with comparatively limited resources, and with a total population of about twenty million (not much greater than the state of New York) located mainly in a few Eastern cities, it is understandable that the development of a national system of broadcasting has, at times, been slow and difficult.

Cultural Differences

BUT these factors explain only part of the problem. There are deep-seated and long-standing communal and cultural differences and a high degree of provincialism that have worked against the growth of strong national institutions. One-third of the present population is of French descent and carries on business in its native language.

In 1961, at a conference sponsored by the Canadian Institute on Public Affairs in cooperation with the Canadian Broadcasting Corporation, Frank H. Underhill, a Canadian historian, described the situation:

> Up to the present, this feature of a small population spread thinly over a continental area has imposed a great variety of other costs upon us. Inevitably it weakens our sense of genuine national unity. Men find it easier to feel a spontaneous loyalty to their local, geographical, sectional, or provincial community than to the wider national whole. . . .
>
> Our intellectual life suffers as well as our political life. It is hard for publishers of books and periodicals to keep going. We can have no national press. We are weak in the instruments for building up a national public opinion. . . .[1]

He went on:

> One of the chief costs of being Canadian is that of belonging to a community that has never overcome the deep divisions between its two main communal groups, French-speaking and English-speaking Canadians. Whatever else we may accomplish towards overcoming other forces that divide us, we still cannot enjoy one Canadian public opinion. We have at least two public opinions, one French and one English, which are apt to be concentrated on different subjects of interest at any given moment, and each of which remains largely oblivious of the other. . . .[2]

At this same conference, Hugh MacLennan, the Canadian novelist, spoke of the struggle to achieve a national identity and the need to develop a distinctive culture reflecting and growing out of the "Canadian Experience." He commented that "we can contribute a very great deal to the world *if Canada remains Canadian.* Culturally we can contribute, and politically we can contribute. If two centuries have produced such a nation as ours, now is not the time to give it up. . . ."[3]

While not interpreted as anti-American and unfriendly, the implication is strong that Canadians would do well to rely more upon their own genius and resources and less upon others. This attitude is pertinent to broadcasting as well as to other important activities and enterprises in the country. And, together with geographical and economic factors, it helps explain how and why the broadcasting system in Canada has developed as it has, and operates as it does.

The Early Years of Radio

CANADA adopted the first legislation relating to radio communication in 1905. The Wireless Telegraph Act provided that no person could establish any wireless telegraph station or use any apparatus for wireless telegraphy without a license granted by the Minister of Marine and Fisheries and under conditions prescribed by him.[4] This 1905 law later became Part IV of the Telegraphs Act of 1906.[5]

In 1913, the 1906 Act was replaced by the Radio Telegraph Act in which Parliament asserted the jurisdiction of the Government over all radio communication and made the licensing requirements of the earlier statutes applicable to broadcasting.[6]

The first license specifically for radio broadcasting was granted in 1919 to the Marconi Wireless Telegraph Company for experimental operations in Montreal. Three years later the Minister of Marine and Fisheries authorized regular, commercial broadcasting, and by 1923 there were thirty-four such stations in operation, most of which were located in the metropolitan centers.[7]

Eighty private commercial stations existed by 1930, but the pattern of concentration in the large cities continued, with Montreal and Toronto possessing about half of all transmitting facilities.[8]

Under regulations adopted by the Minister in 1922, all owners of radio sets were required to pay the Government an annual license fee of one dollar (this was subsequently raised to two and one-half dollars). By 1930, the Government had issued about five hundred and thirty thousand such licenses.[9]

But during these early years, as later reported by a special study commission, Canadian radio was plagued with many problems:

> Although the development of sound broadcasting in the 1920's proceeded at a fairly rapid pace, many problems arose, such as interference from stations in the United States and Mexico, poor programmes content with much material imported from the United States, and the lack of adequate extension of facilities to less populated areas.
>
> As early as 1923, Canada was experiencing interference from stations in the United States where every wave-length in the broadcast band was in use, including those used by Canadian stations.
>
> Negotiations between Canada and the United States were undertaken in 1924 to obtain some mutually satisfactory arrangement regarding the use of certain frequencies. A tentative agreement was reached allotting to Canada exclusive use of six clear channels and arranging for other channels to be shared by stations located in both countries in accordance with zoned areas. The Department of Commerce in the United States, which was responsible for conducting the negotiations, found difficulty in implementing the agreement between the two countries. As a result of litigation in the United States in 1926, it was ruled that the Department could not require licensees to adhere to any particular frequency and further, the Department was obliged to issue licenses to all applicants. Consequently, Canada was still faced with the problem of interference. Further negotiations in 1927 with the newly created Federal Radio Commission brought disappointing results, although the authorities in the United States did undertake to clear the six channels which had been allocated for Canada's exclusive use. Again in 1932, through an exchange of notes with the United States, an agreement was reached whereby Canada would have the use of fifteen channels, seven of which were to be exclusive. Even these deliberations, however, did not result in any permanent settlement of the problem.
>
> Then there was the question of programme content. Complaints were raised regarding the amount of advertising carried by licensees. The lack of live originations from local stations, the constant use of recorded material, and the failure of station operators to make good use of Canadian talent, were some of the criticisms directed against broadcasting during the 1920's. There was also the fear that the lack of east to west communication via radio, and the increasing use of programmes from the United States would have an injurious effect on Canadian unity. It was the concern of many that the possibility of cultural annexation by the United States had reached the proportions of a "new national crisis."

Yet another matter of concern was the apparent reluctance of broadcasters to enter areas of Canada which were sparsely populated. As station operators depended upon the sale of advertising time as their means of earning revenue, the natural tendency was for stations to concentrate in the larger urban areas. Coverage was not being extended adequately over the vast geographical expanse of Canada and there was multiplication of service in those areas where broadcasting was most profitable.

Such, then was broadcasting in the early years. A vigorous and growing industry, but one having to face problems which were in many respects peculiar to Canada, problems which arose because of the great size of the country, because of the sparseness of population, and because of the position of Canada as the northerly neighbour of a rich, industrious and thickly populated United States.[10]

Appointment of the Aird Commission

THE Government appointed a Commission on Radio Broadcasting headed by Sir John Aird, then president of the Canadian Bank of Commerce, to study these problems. This group was given a mandate "to examine into the broadcasting situation in the Dominion of Canada and to make recommendations to the Government as to the future administration, management, control and financing thereof."[11]

The Commission visited the United States, Britain, Germany, France, Belgium, Holland and the Irish Free State, and studied their broadcasting systems. It also held public sessions in twenty-five Canadian cities, including the capitals of the provinces, and received written and oral statements from one hundred and eighty-eight persons.

The Commission's Report was submitted to the House of Commons in September, 1929, but shortly thereafter the Stock Market Crash led to a dissolution of Parliament, and the document was not given official consideration until three years later.

This was the first comprehensive study of radio in Canada, and "was destined to become the first landmark" in the development of a national broadcasting system.[12] The Report expressed concern that many of the radio programs were of foreign origin:

> In our survey of conditions in Canada, we have heard the present radio situation discussed from many angles with considerable diversity of opinion. There has, however, been unanimity on one fundamental question—Canadian radio listeners want Canadian broadcasting. . . .
>
> At present, the majority of programs heard are from sources outside of Canada. It has been emphasized to us that the continued reception of these has a tendency to mould the minds of the young people in the home to ideals and opinions that are not Canadian. In a country of the vast geographical

dimensions of Canada, broadcasting will undoubtedly become a great force in fostering a national spirit and interpreting national citizenship.[13]

Other concerns were expressed about the existing broadcasting situation. All Canadian stations, except two provincial ones in Manitoba, were licensed to commercial interests, operating "for purposes of gain or for publicity."[14] While commending the private stations for their efforts to provide entertainment, the Report stated that the lack of revenue had "tended more and more to force too much advertising upon the listener," and that there was crowding of stations in urban centers with duplication of broadcast services, leaving other large populated areas inadequately served.

To meet the public interests and needs of Canada, the Commission stated as a fundamental principle that "public service" should be the basis of all broadcasting, and that it should be provided by one national system. The Report suggested that the financing of such a system, which would include a number of high-powered transmitters throughout the country, should come from three sources: (1) license fees on receiving sets; (2) rental of time on broadcasting stations for a limited amount of "indirect" advertising (defined as simple mention of a firm name without any promotion of products or services); and (3) an annual subsidy from the Dominion Government amounting to one million dollars to be granted for a period of five years and, after review, for an additional five years.

The Commission summarized its principal recommendations as follows:

(a) That broadcasting should be placed on a basis of public service and that the stations providing a service of this kind should be owned and operated by one national company; that provincial authorities should have full control over the programs of the station or stations in their respective areas;

(b) That the company should be known as the Canadian Radio Broadcasting Company; that is should be vested with all the powers of private enterprise and that its status and duties should correspond to those of a public utility.

(c) That a Provincial Radio Broadcasting Director should be appointed for each province to have full control of the programs broadcast by the station or stations located within the boundaries of the province for which he is responsible;

(d) That a Provincial Advisory Council on radio broadcasting should be appointed for each province, to act in an advisory capacity through the provincial authority;

(e) That the Board of the company should be composed of twelve members, three more particularly representing the Dominion and one representing each of the provinces;

(f) That high-power stations should be erected across Canada to give good reception over the entire settled area of the country during daylight; that the nucleus of the system should possibly be seven 50,000 watt stations; that supplementary stations of lower power should be erected in local areas, not effectively covered by the main stations, if found necessary and as experience indicates;

(g) That pending the inauguration and completion of the proposed system, a provisional service should be provided through certain of the existing stations which should be continued in operation by the Canadian Radio Broadcasting Company; that the stations chosen for this provisional service should be those which will give the maximum coverage without duplication; that all remaining stations not so needed should be closed down;

(h) That compensation should be allowed owners of existing stations for apparatus in use as may be decided by the Minister of Marine and Fisheries; that such apparatus should become the property of the Canadian Radio Broadcasting Company; that the more modern and efficient of these sets of apparatus should be held available for re-erection in local areas not effectively served by the high-power stations; that the cost of compensation should be met out of an appropriation made by Parliament;

(i) That expenditure necessary for the operation and maintenance of the proposed broadcasting service should be met out of revenue produced by license fees, rental of time on stations for programs employing indirect advertising, and a subsidy from the Dominion Government;

(j) That all facilities should be made to permit of chain broadcasting by all the stations or in groups; that while the primary purpose should be to produce programs of high standard from Canadian sources, programs of similar order should also be sought from other sources;

(k) That time should be made available for firms or others desiring to put on programs employing indirect advertising; that no direct advertising should be allowed; that specified time should be made available for educational work; that where religious broadcasting is allowed, there should be regulations prohibiting statements of a controversial nature or one religion making an attack upon the leaders or doctrine of another; that the broadcasting of political matters should be carefully restricted under arrangements mutually agreed upon by all political parties concerned; that competent and cultured announcers only should be employed;

(l) That consideration should be given to the question of introducing legislation which would compel users of electrical apparatus causing interference with broadcast reception to suppress or eliminate the same at their own expense;

(m) That the licensing of stations and such other matters prescribed in the Radiotelegraph Act and Regulations issued thereunder for the control of radio stations in general should remain within the jurisdiction of the Minister of Marine and Fisheries; that the authority should continue to be responsible for the collection of license fees and the suppression of inductive interference causing difficulties with radio reception.[15]

The holding of elections in 1930, some doubts as to the advisability of withdrawing licenses from private owners who had pioneered in the development of broadcasting, depression and scarcity of public money needed to finance the national system, all combined to prevent Parliament from taking immediate action on these proposals.

There was also a legal problem. Following release of the Report, the province of Quebec contested, in the Supreme Court, the validity of the 1923 Radio-Telegraph Act, under which the Federal Government exercised regulatory jurisdiction over radio. The Court upheld the validity of the Act. The matter was then carried to the Judicial Committee of the Imperial Privy Council which, in 1932, sustained the Court, holding that the Federal Government had exclusive jurisdiction in the radio field.[16]

Despite parliamentary delay, public agitation for a national system of broadcasting continued. Dissatisfaction with private operation and the growing feeling of need for change were voiced by Prime Minister Bennett in the House of Commons on February 16, 1932:

> It must be agreed that the present system of radio broadcasting is unsatisfactory. Canadians have the right to a system of broadcasting from Canadian sources equal in all respects to that of any other country. . . . The enormous benefits of an adequate scheme of radio broadcasting controlled and operated by Canadians is absolutely plain.[17]

About two weeks later, a Parliamentary Committee was appointed to consider the two year old Aird Report. In the Committee hearing which followed, there was a great deal of testimony on the issue of public versus private ownership.[18] Evidence was adduced that outside Toronto and Montreal only about two-fifths of the population could regularly pick up Canadian programs, and these consisted largely of imported recordings.[19] The Canadian Radio League argued vigorously in favor of public ownership, contending that the radio spectrum was limited and should be a part of the public domain.[20]

The commercial broadcasters countered that national service could be provided if direct advertising of commercial products and services were allowed and if license fees could be used to increase the transmitting power of stations.[21]

The proponents of public ownership won, and, on May 9, 1932, the Committee submitted the following recommendations:

> (1) The establishment of a chain of high power national stations operating on clear channels and a number of auxiliary stations of low power suitably located to provide coverage to the largest possible number of listeners;
> (2) That the cost of radio in Canada be self-sustaining and that only the money available from transmitting and receiving license fees, and advertising income be expended, and that the question of the amount of the receiving license fee be left entirely in the hands of the Governor-in-Council;
> (3) That a Commission of three be appointed and vested with the necessary powers to carry on the business of broadcasting in Canada, such powers to include
>> (a) Regulation and control of all broadcasting, including programs and advertising;
>> (b) Construction, operation and acquisition of broadcasting stations;

(c) The control of the licensing and allocation of channels to broadcasting stations.[22]

Canadian Radio Broadcasting Commission Established

PURSUANT to these proposals, the Prime Minister introduced a bill on May 16, 1932, to establish the Canadian Radio Broadcasting Commission (CRBC).[23] Upon second reading of the bill, the Prime Minister spoke in its behalf:

> *First of all,* this country must be assured of complete Canadian control of broadcasting from Canadian sources, free from foreign interference or influence. Without such control radio broadcasting can never become a great agency for the communication of matters of national concern and for the diffusion of national thought and ideals. . . . Other and alternative systems may meet the requirements of other countries. . . . But it seems to me clear that in Canada the system we can most profitably employ is one which, in operation and control, responds most directly to the popular will and the national need.
>
> *Secondly,* no other scheme than that of public ownership can assure to the people of this country . . . equal enjoyment of the benefits and pleasures of radio broadcasting. Private ownership must necessarily discriminate between densely and sparsely populated areas. This is not a correctible fault in private ownership. . . . It does not seem right that in Canada the towns should be preferred to the countryside or the prosperous communities to those less fortunate. . . . Happily, however, under this system, there is no need for discrimination; all may be served alike. . . .[24]

Speakers of other political groups in Parliament endorsed these views,[25] and on May 26, 1932, Parliament, by unanimous vote, passed the Canadian Radio Broadcasting Act (1932), providing for the creation of the Commission.

During its first year, the CRBC established stations in Vancouver, Montreal, Toronto, Ottawa and Chicoutimi. Using these new stations and the private ones already on the air, the CRBC, in May 1933, instituted a regular schedule of network programs.

By 1935, the network had been further expanded and included the CRBC facilities plus forty-three private stations. While this represented considerable progress, the Commission encountered serious problems. The Office of CBC Information Services, in a historical review of Canadian broadcasting, has described the situation:

> The two main functions of the CRBC were to regulate and control all broadcasting in Canada. . . . On the shoulders of the three commissioners was placed the responsibility of arranging networks, buying or leasing stations,

bargaining with private companies for wire line connections, and endeavouring to place on the air a representative group of the best musical and artistic talent that Canada could furnish.

Superimposed on these complexities were a number of problems attributable to the newness of the venture. The lack of revenue ($400,000 in license fees in its first year) prevented extensive operations. The geographic conditions which, by and large, have determined the development of Canada, were inexorable in their relation to national broadcasting in this country. The cost of wire lines to enable a national network to function was high. Revenues during the four years of the Commission's life proved insufficient to permit the building of the high-powered stations recommended by the Aird Commission and the Parliamentary Committee in 1932.

Two other problems faced the Commission. Both related to lack of independence from the Government. It was dependent for its finances on a Parliamentary appropriation which had to form a part of the Government estimates. The Commission's personnel were subject to the Civil Service Act. This prevented elasticity in salary schedules to attract certain personnel which the Commission required in order to carry out its activities. . . .

The Commission remained dependent on a Parliamentary appropriation for its yearly budget. The appropriation was determined by an estimate of the license revenues, payable by listeners, to the Department of Marine and Fisheries under provisions of the Radio-Telegraph Act.

By 1936, the Commission had started network broadcasting on a regular basis, with six hours of programs a day. . . . But these were confined to the evening hours. With only ten minutes of news heard on Commission stations each day, many private stations were picking up news from American stations. With the facilities at their disposal, CRBC attempted to program in both English and French but this proved unsatisfactory to both language groups. Although empowered to take over any private station required for the national system, Commission funds never permitted the operation of more than seven of its own stations and allowed very little in the way of power increases. Private stations were granted power increases to improve coverage. Even at that, coverage was lagging far behind what had been envisioned. . . .[26]

Canadian Broadcasting Corporation Replaces CRBC

A SPECIAL Committee was appointed by Parliament to study the situation and recommend remedial action. Following public hearings, the Committee, while upholding the principles of public ownership and control, unanimously proposed the complete recasting of the national broadcasting organization along more flexible lines. They recommended:

(1) That a public corporation modeled more closely on the lines of a private corporation, but with adequate powers to control, for the purpose of co-

ordination, all broadcasting, both public and private, be set up to replace the CRBC;

(2) That this corporation be managed by a general manager as chief executive and an assistant general manager, and directed as a policy by a non-partisan board of nine directors or governors, chosen to give representation to all parts of Canada;

(3) That the Corporation immediately consider ways and means of extending national coverage.

Following closely the proposals of the Committee, Parliament passed a law on November 2, 1936, establishing the Canadian Broadcasting Corporation.[27]

One of the Corporation's first tasks was to rectify coverage and interference problems. A large part of the rural population was not receiving adequate network service and numerous stations were subject to serious technical interference, both domestic and foreign. To alleviate this situation, in 1937, Canada joined with other North American countries in an international conference in Havana. The outcome was the North American Regional Agreement providing for a systematic allocation of frequencies and the suppression of interference.

By the Agreement, Canada obtained six clear channels for Class IA stations with fifty kilowatts of power or more and four clear channels for Class II stations with power range of from two hundred and fifty watts to fifty kilowatts. In addition, it was permitted to share the use of forty-one regional channels with limited power range from one hundred to two hundred and fifty watts. This helped to cut down objectionable interference and provided a basis for the orderly development of national broadcasting facilities.[28]

By 1941, there were nine CBC transmitters, four of which were operating with fifty kilowatts of power, serving large rural areas. The Board had authorized the decentralization of administration and program production into five principal divisions (a sixth was added in 1949), with the thought of serving regional interests more effectively. A French-language network had been established, and the CBC was broadcasting a total of one hundred and thirteen hours per week.[29]

War-Time Broadcasting

THE CBC has reported war-time developments as follows:

Shortly after the outbreak of war CBC sent a commentator and technician overseas with the First Canadian Division as the nucleus of a CBC overseas unit which brought first-hand accounts of Canada's fighting effort to Canadians back home throughout the war.

By 1941 CBC had established a National News Service, National Farm Radio Forum, regional farm broadcasts, started school broadcasts in the Maritimes and Radio-College in the Province of Quebec, and begun short-wave broadcasting of French Network programs from Vercheres to French-speaking listeners in the Prairies and Maritimes. The following year National School broadcasts became a reality. . . .

Perhaps the most significant change in network service during the war years came in 1944 when the CBC National Network was recast with the formation of a second English-language service. The Dominion Network immediately linked 34 private stations from coast to coast with a key CBC station in Toronto to provide a second national network service of programs produced in Canada and other countries. The National Network was re-named the Trans-Canada Network. This gave the Trans-Canada 34 stations (six CBC and 28 private affiliates), the Dominion Network 35 (one CBC and 34 private affiliates) and the French network 13 stations (three CBC and ten private affiliates).[30]

Postwar Developments

FOLLOWING cessation of hostilities, CBC expanded its facilities by adding two stations in Alberta and Manitoba and increasing the power of several existing ones. In the early fifties, the French network was extended west-ward to serve listeners in the prairie provinces. By 1956, of its twenty-two installations, the CBC had eight fifty kilowatt stations on the air and had established lower power outlets in Sydney, Cape Breton and Windsor, Ontario.

There was marked improvement in program services following the war. Educational broadcasting received a big boost, and school radio was being heard in every province. The National Farm Radio Forum had attracted one of the largest audiences in the world for a program of this kind. Important events, such as the tour of Her Royal Highness Princess Elizabeth and the Duke of Edinburgh, were being dramatically and effectively covered, and the CBC was winning many international awards for high quality programming.[31]

The Massey Commission had been established in 1949 and, among other things, had been directed to study both radio and television and recommend future policies. Its report to the House of Commons in June 1951 stressed that the grant of the privilege of radio broadcasting should continue to be made under the control of Parliament, and recommended that this control continue to be exercised by the Canadian Broadcasting Corporation.[32] The Commission stated that, because of limited channels, it was even more important that television be a part of the national system and be subject to the centralized, coordinated control of the Corporation.[33]

With the full support of a Special Parliamentary Committee on Radio Broadcasting which had been appointed the year before,[34] the CBC proceeded to implement the general plans of the Commission. New relay stations were constructed to bring better radio services to remote areas; the power of a number of transmitters was increased; and new programs were introduced.

In 1958, the CBC expanded its radio facilities to include the extreme northern section of the country. Stations were established at various locations in British Columbia, Yukon and in the Northwest Territories. Station CHAK in Inurik, N. W. T., the first CBC station established inside the Arctic Circle, and the first one in Canada to broadcast regularly in the Eskimo language, went on the air in 1960.

The CBC issued a statement in 1960 setting forth the basic principles which had motivated the expansion and improvement of its radio service and indicating some of the main features of its programs.

> The general aim in making up CBC domestic program schedules is to arrive at a satisfactory balance of entertainment on the one hand, and information and education on the other. Wherever possible these factors are combined, and presented at suitable hours. All listeners do not like the same things, and there are minority groups whose tastes must be taken into account. But whether a listener likes jazz or classical music, light opera or chamber music, discussion programs, daytime serials or book reviews, CBC feels he should have programs to meet his particular taste somewhere in its schedules. . . .
>
> In addition to presenting established Canadian orchestras and artists, CBC attempts to encourage new talent of all kinds. Throughout the week, various recital periods are scheduled on national or regional networks to give younger artists a chance to be heard and to make themselves known. The works of Canadian composers are heard frequently on CBC networks, often featured in special programs. . . .
>
> The encouragement of Canadian talent has been especially noticeable in the case of writers. During the 1959–60 season, for example, the Drama Department was responsible for the production of more than 400 radio plays, of which better than half were originals. More than 90 percent of the scripts for these plays were written or adapted by Canadians.[35]

In further justification of the Canadian system of broadcasting and its pattern of operation, CBC officials stated:

> The public system of broadcasting in Canada resulted from the natural desire and the need for a high standard of broadcasting that would express the varied facets of Canadian life and would interpret the different regions of Canada each to the other. In this way it was felt that broadcasting would be a powerful instrument for the encouragement of Canadian unity. The CBC was created out of the conviction that these aims would best be served by placing the control of broadcasting in the hands of an independent public corporation acting as a trustee for Canadian listeners. Each year the Corpora-

tion must render to Parliament an account of stewardship, and must be prepared to justify its broadcasting policies to the peoples' elected representatives. These policies are, in the final analysis, confirmed or denied by Parliament itself. It is an interesting fact that these policies have been endorsed by each of the 13 Parliamentary Committees, as well as the Massey Commission, in the past two decades.[36]

Television

CANADIANS began experimenting with television during the early thirties, but it was not until after the Second World War that the Government began a serious study of the medium. In 1951, the Royal Commission on National Development in the Arts, Letters and Sciences proposed the development of a national system. It recommended that the CBC proceed with plans for the production of television programs in French and English, and that private stations be licensed as outlets for national programs produced by the CBC network.[37]

In May 1952, the Corporation proposed the establishment of a nationwide television system, consisting of CBC stations and production centers at key locations, and private stations in other areas. It further recommended that capital costs be provided by parliamentary grants and that operating costs be derived from an annual license fee on receivers of fifteen dollars.[38]

In general, the plan was approved, although early in 1953, the license fee was dropped and an excise tax imposed on the purchase of receivers. It was provided that the proceeds from this tax were to be paid to the CBC. At the same time, the annual license fee paid by owners of radio sets was abolished.

Canadian television was initiated in September 1952, when the CBC stations, CBFT and CBLT, started operating in Montreal and Toronto. By November 1955, CBC stations were on the air in Vancouver, Winnipeg, Toronto and Halifax. There were both English and French outlets in Ottawa and Montreal. Moreover, a number of private stations had been joined by microwave, and plans were under way to establish a network from coast to coast.[39]

The Board of Broadcast Governors Established

WITH increasing interest in and the rapid expansion of television, the Government faced new financial and regulatory problems in broadcasting. The growth of both public and private stations resulted in a competitive situation which concerned the CBC as well as Parliament. To study these problems as well as others related to both radio and television, the Government appointed a third Royal Commission. Robert M. Fowler, the President of the Canadian Pulp and Paper Association, was designated Chairman.

After prolonged hearings, the Commission submitted its Report to Parliament in March 1957.[40] It recommended the establishment of a new government board, to be composed of fifteen members responsible for the regulation of both public and private broadcasting.[41]

Parliament, the next year, passed a new broadcasting law, the main feature of which was the creation of a new Board of Broadcast Governors (BBG). While this law vested responsibility for public broadcasting in a newly created CBC Board of Directors, the regulatory and operating functions, both previously carried on by CBC, were now divided between the new CBC Board and the BBG, but were not all centered in the BBG as had been proposed.[42]

The BBG was empowered to regulate both CBC and private broadcasting stations and all network operations in the country. Furthermore, the law gave the BBG authority to regulate the program content of all stations, and the type and amount of advertising.

Other provisions of the law should be noted. For example, every application for a new station, or an increase in power, a change in channel assignment or location of a station, or change in ownership, must be filed with the Minister of Transport who, before considering it, must refer it to the Board of Broadcast Governors for study and recommendation. Before recommending action, the Board is required to hold a public hearing on each application at which the applicant, the CBC, and other interested parties may make appearances and be heard. No license may be issued by the Minister without the approval of the Governor-in-Council.

The Board may recommend, as a condition to the license, that the licensee operate as part of a CBC network. Upon application from the station or the Corporation, and after both parties have had the opportunity to be heard, the Board may grant the licensee permission to affiliate with some other network. Also, the Board may, after public hearing, grant permission to any person to operate a network of broadcasting stations or revoke any permission so granted.

No alien may operate a station or network in Canada. If the licensee is a corporation, the chairman or other presiding officer and at least two-thirds of the directors must be Canadian citizens and at least three-fourths of the stock must be owned by such citizens.

In 1963, in line with the statutory mandate that broadcasting service should be basically Canadian, the BBG prescribed that no more than forty-five percent of radio and television programs may be imported from foreign countries. This, however, is actually less restrictive on outside programs than was the rule followed by the CBC prior to the passage of the 1958 law.

Other regulations concerning private commercial stations became effective in August 1963. It was provided that licenses for such stations should not exceed five years, but may be renewed for the same periods, subject to the Minister of Transport.

Each private commercial station must pay an annual license fee to the Government in the amount of one percent of its gross revenue (total income less agency commissions), if that revenue is two hundred thousand dollars or less. If it exceeds this amount, the fee is two thousand dollars plus one and one-half percent of the revenue in excess of two hundred thousand dollars. Regardless of station income, the minimum annual assessment for a private commercial station is one hundred dollars.

Applicants for new broadcast facilities are required to deposit one hundred dollars with the Minister of Transport, if the power requested is less than one thousand watts, and five hundred dollars if it is one thousand watts or more. If the application is granted, the sum deposited is applied to the payment of the first license fee. Should any amount of the deposit remain after the first license fee has been paid, it is applied to the payment of the fees for subsequent years.*

Current Radio Facilities

RADIO is now reaching almost all the homes in Canada. According to the CBC's *1965–66 Annual Report,* the Corporation is operating two AM networks. The first, Trans-Canada, broadcasts in English and spans the nation with thirty main CBC stations, one hundred and seventeen low-power relay transmitters and fifty-five private affiliates and two relays. The second, the French network, broadcasting to the French-speaking population in Quebec, Ontario, New Brunswick, and the Prairie Provinces, is composed of seven main CBC stations, twenty-four low-power transmitters and twenty-five private stations plus two relays.[43] The headquarters and principal production facilities for Trans-Canada are located in Toronto, while those for the French network are in Montreal.[44]

Prior to 1963, the CBC had been operating two English-language networks, Trans-Atlantic and Dominion. These were consolidated in 1964. This merger changed the role of radio station CJBC in Toronto. No longer an anchor operation of the former Dominion network, CJBC was converted into a partial French-language station to serve a substantial minority of listeners in the area.[45]

In April 1960, the CBC inaugurated a bilingual FM network with key stations in Toronto, Montreal and Ottawa. There were, at the time, two

*For further study of important BBG program regulations governing all Canadian stations, see Appendix I.

additional FM stations operating independently in Montreal and Vancouver. Economic conditions made it necessary for the CBC to suspend its FM network broadcasting for a time, but during the summer of 1964 the Corporation made plans to reactivate the network. As pointed out by the Government in 1965, "the initial goal of the reactivation was to provide, by late 1964, CBC FM stations in Montreal, Ottawa, Toronto and Vancouver, with a program service completely separate from the AM service, and to be distributed, in the initial stages at least, largely on tape."[46] Not only have these goals been accomplished, but an additional FM station has recently been built in Winnipeg.

Radio Programming

THE CBC English AM network broadcast one hundred and nineteen hours per week during 1965–66. A substantial part of its programs came from regional networks which connect with it. The total program output of this national chain, not including that of commercial affiliates, was divided as follows:[47]

Program Type	Percent
Music	40
News and Special Events	12
Discussion and Documentaries	25
Educational (formal and informal)	12
Drama, Story, Poem	6
Sports	4
Religious, Variety, Quiz, Game, Etc.	2

The French AM network operated about one hundred and twenty-four hours per week in 1965–66. As reported by the CBC, the approximate percentages of time devoted each week to French programs that year were:[48]

Program Type	Percent
Music	44
News and Special Events	10
Discussion and Documentary	15
Religious	1
Education (formal and informal)	10
Drama, Poem and Story	9
Miscellaneous (science, variety, quiz, game, sports)	12

As of June 30, 1966, the English FM network was on the air one hundred and two hours per week. At that time there was no French FM network, but there was one FM station broadcasting eighty-four hours per week in Montreal. More than eighty percent of the time of these FM stations was devoted to recorded music, with the remainder divided among news, discussion and documentaries.[49]

In recent years, the CBC has been experimenting with what it calls magazine formats.[50] In 1965 the French radio network introduced *"Présent,"* a program running ninety minutes a day, five days a week. The CBC states that "With national and local editions using CBC reporters throughout Canada, and in Paris and in New York, with fast moving items on current events, science, the arts and anything else that is interesting, all interspersed with music—*Présent* is a step towards enabling the listener to turn on his radio at any time to find something of interest."[51]

English radio has followed a similar pattern in the morning and late afternoon hours. In addition, it has developed a program, "Country Check-up," for Sunday evenings which has attracted a wide audience. Listeners anywhere in Canada may telephone collect to the Montreal studios and talk on the air with experts regarding the subject being discussed in the broadcast.[52]

In its *Annual Report 1965–66,* the CBC stated:

> The differences in techniques of radio and television caused changes in corporate organization last year when program planners for the two media were separated into distinct departments. Programming emphasis this year in radio was on speed of delivery and omnipresence (for instance, coverage on the FM network of the international "teach-in" on Viet Nam from the University of Toronto), on network flexibility leading to live regional participation, and on greater audience participation; and on a generally more relaxed style of broadcasting.
>
> The year, therefore, brought more steps in fitting radio programs to listening needs. The problem is to do this and still maintain the distinctively high quality and diversity traditionally offered on CBC radio. Such programs as the two-hour dramas, *The Play of Jesus* on *CBC Tuesday Night,* or the weekly 90 minute *Concert du mercredi* on the French network, or all the others listed under "Representative Programs" suggest that CBC standards and diversity have indeed been maintained.[53]

International Broadcasting

THE CBC started foreign, short-wave broadcasting during the Second World War, with studios located in Ottawa. The service is now being provided by two fifty kilowatt transmitters in eleven languages for listeners in

Europe, Africa, Latin America, the Caribbean, North America, Australia, New Zealand and the South Pacific.

A heavy component of the short-wave service consists of news reports and commentaries. Programs such as that identified with the Radio-Canada Shortwave Club and special ones such as those designed for philatelists have resulted in a marked increase in mail response from foreign listeners. In 1965–66, the CBC received sixty-one thousand letters and cards from all parts of the world (a sixty-five percent increase over the preceding year). Four times a year the CBC supplies one hundred and fifty thousand listeners in many countries with Program Schedules.[54]

A variety of programs are transcribed and made available to foreign broadcasting organizations. At the same time, Canada participates in an exchange service and receives programs from all parts of the world, including communist countries. Many of these foreign programs are broadcast domestically on the AM and FM networks.

Private Radio

THERE has been a tremendous development in private broadcasting during the past decade. It has been reported that as of January 1966, there were three hundred and forty-nine privately owned broadcasting stations in Canada.[55] The Canadian Association of Broadcasters represents a substantial number of these (two hundred and twenty-eight radio stations and fifty-five television stations), and has been active in promoting their operation and interests.

The 1965 Report of the Canadian Committee on Broadcasting points out that the private radio stations "concentrate on events of local interest. Many of them have developed speedy information. They often develop a dynamic pace which may at times seem over-excited and excessive. They are in close contact with their public, using telephone communications extensively, and this too occasionally becomes excessive and goes beyond the limits of common sense and good taste. . . ."[56]

The Report commends some of the private stations, particularly those broadcasting in French, for increased use of Canadian artists in their programs, and also makes special mention of a program exchange system initiated by the Canadian Association of Broadcasters "in which more than 140 stations participate. These stations pool programs which are available to members at practically no cost other than that of supplying recording tapes. The system was inaugurated in 1962, and by 1964 more than 2,100 program hours were exchanged."[57]

Generally, the program format of private broadcast stations in Canada is similar to that in the United States—related to local happenings, with a heavy component of recorded popular music and a large number of commercials.

The Canadian Association of Broadcasters has provided the following information regarding the number and income of private stations:

1956	PRIVATE RADIO (160)	PRIVATE TV (27)
Network and National Advertising	$16,366,921	$ 8,338,520
Local Advertising	21,252,056	4,013,799
Other Operating Revenue	796,409	289,302
Total	$38,415,386	$12,641,621

1965	PRIVATE RADIO (194)	PRIVATE TV (55)
Network and National Advertising	$27,668,396	$50,745,024
Local Advertising	40,987,703	17,769,736
Other Operating Revenue	1,876,429	6,747,504
Total	$70,532,528	$75,262,264

In less than ten years, revenue from private radio has almost doubled and increased almost six times in private television.[58]

Present Television Facilities

As IN radio, the CBC is operating two television networks, both English and French, with five hundred and twenty-nine line definition. There are eleven basic stations with twenty-four relay and rebroadcasting units in the English network, all owned and operated by the CBC. Thirty-seven privately owned affiliated stations plus their sixty-seven relays are linked to the English system. In addition, twenty-six independent stations, not affiliated with the network, carry its programs.

In the French chain there are five basic stations and nine relays owned and operated by the CBC, plus eight privately owned affiliated stations with their twenty-three relays. Moreover, four independent rebroadcasting stations, not owned by affiliated stations, carry the CBC TV service.[59] The French TV network is largely located in the Quebec area but has outlets in Ontario, New Brunswick, Nova Scotia and as far west as Manitoba.[60]

In 1960, the Board of Broadcast Governors authorized the establishment of a privately owned network—Canadian Television (CTV). It began operating in October of that year, is wholly Canadian owned, broadcasts in English, and, through coast-to-coast reversible microwave channel, now provides a national network service.[61] Also, as in the United States, there has been a large growth in the number of community antenna television systems in Canada. These systems, which relay television programs via wire to subscribers who pay a fee for the service, have been a matter of concern to the Government, the CBC and private broadcasters, and have been the subject of a special study by the Board of Broadcast Governors.[62]

CBC Television Programs

IN 1965–66, the CBC English TV network was on the air about seventy-three hours per week. Since that time, morning telecasts have been added to the schedules and, for the period April 22–28, 1967, the network was operating about sixteen hours daily with a total of one hundred and ten hours for that week. As reported by the CBC in 1966, the percentage breakdown for programs was about as follows:[63]

Program Type	Percent
News and Special Events	5.7
Documentaries and Discussion	16
Religious	.7
Education (formal and informal)	19
Music and Dance	7
Drama, Poetry, Story	30
Variety, Quiz, Game	12
Sports	8
Criticism and Science	1

In 1965–66, the French TV network was averaging approximately one hundred hours of broadcasting per week. A review of the program schedules for seven days in April 1967, showed an increase of about eight hours.[64] Again using the program categories as stated by the CBC, in 1965–66, the division of time was approximately as follows:[65]

Program Type	Percent
News and Special Events	5.5
Documentaries and Discussion	11
Religious	2
Education (formal and informal)	16
Music and Dance	3
Drama, Story, Poem	47
Criticism and Science	1
Variety, Quiz, Game	5
Sports	8

The CBC has pointed out that in the afternoon and late evening the French television network carries feature films, which the individual English stations in the other network schedule on a local basis. This accounts, in the main, for the larger number of French hours shown for "Drama and Story."

In 1966, about sixty percent of the programs carried by the English and French TV networks were Canadian. About forty percent of those imported by the English chain were produced in the United States and one percent in the Commonwealth. On the French network, thirteen percent of the foreign programs came from the United States, fifteen percent from French-speaking countries, twelve percent from other foreign countries, and less than one percent from the Commonwealth.[66]

A perusal of recent schedules shows that the English network carries regularly a number of U.S. shows, such as "Tarzan," "Beverly Hillbillies," "Bonanza," the "Ed Sullivan Show," "Bob Hope Theatre," and occasionally features special films made in Hollywood. In one week, April 22 through April 28, 1967, on the French network, eighteen foreign feature films were shown: five French, four German, three Italian, one American, one Hungarian, one Spanish, one Japanese, one British and one Russian, not to mention a number of shorter films produced abroad.[67]

CTV Television Programs

CTV, the independent, commercially operated TV network, began operating in October 1961, with eight charter affiliates, all broadcasting in English. Later, three former CBC affiliates were added.[68] CTV is entirely dependent upon advertising for revenue, and its programs tend to be of the light entertainment variety, with a sizeable number imported from the United States. It has developed what the Committee on Broadcasting describes as an "adequate" news service and has carried on a "relatively inexpensive weekly Sunday afternoon program called 'Telepoll,' reporting the opinions of Canadians."[69] Sports received considerable coverage in 1967, for the network had the exclusive rights to cover all sports events connected with EXPO 67. Also, in March of that year, CTV telecast the Centennial Year edition of the world hockey championships from Vienna. All games involving Canada and the Russia-Czechoslovakia one were videotaped in Austria and the films flown by jet to Canada for CTV showing.[70]

A series of programs, "This Land is People," featuring interviews with Canadians who have achieved recognition in special fields, was carried in the early part of 1967. This series was not renewed but did enjoy some degree of popularity while it was on the air. In April 1967, the CTV network presented two special Centennial shows which featured interviews with both well-known and "ordinary" citizens revealing their opinions about a variety of timely subjects.[71]

Color Television

THE Government announced in 1965 that Canadian television stations could apply to the Board of Governors for licenses to broadcast in color, and authorized the CBC to convert certain network facilities at a maximum capital cost of fifteen million dollars.[72] Both English and French networks now broadcast from three to as many as ten color programs daily, and, with the promotional efforts being made by both the Government and industry, the quantity of color TV in Canada is expected to increase rapidly.

CBC Financing

THERE are now no license fees on radio or TV sets. There is the sales tax on sets and spare parts. Privately owned commercial stations, as previously mentioned, pay annual license fees. The CBC is financed by advertising revenue and parliamentary grants.

The CBC's total expense for 1965–66 was $133,447,000,[73] a seven and four-tenths percent increase over the preceding year. Of this amount, $21,893,000 was spent for radio, including the production and transmission of programs and the acquisition and building of some new facilities; $80,810,000 was spent for television, including programming and the introduction of five new auxiliary stations and the extension of service to twenty-one additional communities.[74]

The CBC received a parliamentary grant for the year of $97,044,000 and derived gross revenues of $33,562,816 from commercial advertising. Of this amount, $4,590,870 went to privately owned affiliates and $3,944,840 to advertising agencies.[75]

The Corporation operates the International Service on behalf of the Government of Canada. All operational costs are borne by the Government. The CBC shows on its books, as a separate item, the total cost of the Crown's property together with a like sum as a liability to the Government. Gross expenditures of the International Service during 1965–66 totaled $2,821,000, an increase of thirteen percent over the preceding year.[76]

A Special Committee on Broadcasting Appointed

A SPECIAL Committee on Broadcasting was appointed by the Government on May 25, 1964 to study the broadcasting law and recommend what changes, if any, should be made to meet new conditions. Robert M. Fowler, a Montreal industrialist, who headed the Royal Commission on Broadcasting in 1956–57, was made Chairman. After exhaustive study, the Committee made its report to the Secretary of State in September 1965.

With respect to programming, the Committee reiterated the lofty objectives of previous committees and commissions: a wide choice of high-quality programs, responsible broadcasting, and that which awakens the listener to "Canadian reality." While the Committee did not favor any kind of "broadcasting ghetto," it deplored what it called the "escapist and insubstantial" variety of programming secured from the United States. It strongly urged more exchange of programs between different regions of the country and was critical of the CBC for "failing to discharge adequately its duties to foster understanding between the two main cultural groups" in the country.[77]

The Committee further recommended that the administration and control of the broadcasting system be vested in one independent authority with a single board, which would replace the Board of Broadcast Governors and the present CBC Board of Directors. This authority would develop general program policies for both public and private stations and networks but would not be concerned with the production of particular programs. In addition to its licensing responsibilities, it would carry on research, perform public relations functions (encourage dialogue between broadcasters, the public and Parliament), and report annually to Parliament on important aspects of the media, including the financial status of private broadcasters and the programming performance of both public and private stations and networks.

The Committee further recommended that the International, Northern and Armed Forces Services all be expanded. Educational broadcasting, including classroom uses, was given a strong boost, and it was proposed that licenses be granted to qualified educational institutions or corporations.

It was proposed that the CBC continue to seek commercial revenue from both radio and television, with minimum targets set at twenty-five percent of the television market and four percent for radio. In view of mounting program costs, the Committee urged that production procedures be standardized and that other savings and economies be effected.[78]

CBC Replies

IN THE March 1966 issue of the *EBU Review,* the CBC summarized its reactions to the Committee's Report.[79] There was virtual agreement on matters pertaining to broad principles and basic objectives and the need for some improvements in CBC operations, but marked differences of opinion as to how best these might be achieved, and disagreement as to the amount of money needed and the source from which it should come.

First, the CBC objected to the proposed concentration of control, with powers over broadcasting vested in one man, the *chairman* of a board— "an unprecedented departure from normal practice."[80]

Second, the Corporation agreed with the Committee that there should be more Canadian and better programs, more variety, greater understanding between French and English cultures, more public service programs in prime time periods, more exchange between regions, more attention to radio and more long-range planning. But, to achieve these ends, the Corporation contended that commercial operations would have to be reduced rather than expanded as proposed by the Committee, and that more public funds should be made available to replace some imported programs (Hollywood syndicated film, for example) with Canadian-produced shows. Only limited improvement in this and other areas of programming could be made, said the Corporation, "within present resources."[81]

Furthermore, the Corporation had reservations about devoting morning television solely to educational programs. It also objected to a proposed five year "freeze" on CBC construction of new stations and restrictions on the development of color TV:

> The Corporation believes that such a "freeze" on CBC development over a five-year period would be detrimental to the national service. This would leave CBC Canadian productions largely in black and white while most U. S. television imports would be in colour and Canadian private stations could develop color at will. This would increase the imbalance in U. S. versus Canadian programme viewing; it would work against the Committee's recommendations that more CBC network programmes should originate in the regions (regions would have no color studios); it would negate the Committee's view that the national service be paramount; it would affect the Corporation's commercial revenue position; and it could place all CBC stations in a secondary position to other stations for color viewing.[82]

The Corporation welcomed the Committee's recommendation that CBC's financing be placed on a five year basis, and that it be authorized to borrow up to two hundred million dollars for "general and working capital requirements."

While recognizing that great efficiency and economy might be achieved, the Corporation replied that limits should be recognized:

> . . . Present indications are that the Committee prediction of $8,000,000 in savings by 1970 is optimistic and that a target of $3,000,000 to $3,500,000 is more realistic. All savings achieved through improved efficiency in operations and administration will be devoted to improvements in the Corporation's programme services.
>
> While the Corporation intends actively to seek further savings, it is essential to remember that CBC already has one of the most efficient network

production operations in the world. This does not mean that still greater efficiency cannot be achieved but rather that the limits of efficiency must be recognized. The quality of program service must not suffer through an unrealistic approach to efficiency. An example of CBC's continuing efficiency programme is that between 31st March 1961 and 31st March 1965, the Corporation's television production hours, live and on film, increased by 38 percent. The increase was accompanied by a sizeable drop in the average cost per programme hour of 7 percent on live programmes and 12 percent on film.[83]

The Canadian Association of Broadcasters Replies

THE Canadian Association of Broadcasters also responded to the Fowler Report. It objected to the proposed establishment of a "Canadian Broadcasting Authority." The Association declared that under the Fowler proposal the Authority would have too much power:

> It would be assigned enormous powers of a nature which we are confident have seldom, if ever, been assigned to the administrative procedure in any democratic country. We agree with the Fowler of 1957, rather than the Fowler of 1965, that the licensing function is too important to be removed from the hands of the elected representatives of Canadians and placed in those of an administrative tribunal.
>
> We believe the powers of the impartial agency of regulation in regard to licensing should be those of recommendation to the Cabinet through one of its Ministers and that final decision concerning new or changed broadcasting facilities must rest with Governor in Council.
>
> The Fowler-proposed "Canadian Broadcasting Authority" would have a full-time Chairman and fourteen part-time members. We have had sufficient experience with administrative tribunals, especially those operating in a field as complex and swiftly developing as broadcasting, to realize that in fact this creates a one-man Board.
>
> Such an unusual situation offers no discernible benefit to the public of Canada, let alone to the encouragement of broadcasting development in either the public or private sectors. On the contrary, we think such a situation would create serious difficulties for all concerned including the government.[84]

The Association further contended that the affairs of the CBC were sufficiently important to warrant "sole attention by its own Board of Directors" and that the affairs of private stations were "equally complex" and warranted a separate regulatory board. It proposed, therefore, the continued existence of an "impartial agency" of regulation not in any way involved in the actual operation of stations or networks. While this agency would be mainly concerned with private broadcasting, it would have limited jurisdiction over the CBC in such matters as commercial content of programming, or in conflicts between the CBC and private stations having to do with allocation of facilities or network affiliations.[85]

White Paper Issued

RESPONDING to the Report of the Fowler Committee and public and private comments regarding it, the Government issued a *White Paper on Broadcasting* in 1966. The Government stated that it thought the Committee's Report in many respects was valid, and that many of its recommendations should be implemented as soon as possible, but not necessarily in every detail. Accordingly, the Government proposed to introduce new legislation along the general lines suggested.

With respect to control of the broadcasting system the Government stated:

> The Canadian broadcasting system, comprising public and private sectors, must be regarded as a single system which should be regulated and controlled by a single independent authority. It is therefore proposed that the powers and authority of the Board of Broadcast Governors, which require extension and clarification, shall be applicable to all broadcasters alike, and that the Board itself shall be reconstituted. The Government does not concur in the recommendation of the Advisory Committee that the regulatory authority should be responsible for the management of the Canadian Broadcasting Corporation. However, the legislation will make it clear that the Corporation will be subject to the regulatory powers of the Board of Broadcast Governors in all matters affecting general broadcasting policy in Canada.[86]

Regarding programming, the Government stated that the new legislation would provide for minimum standards of public service broadcasting and that Canadian content would be "determined by the Board of Broadcast Governors on an individual basis, taking account of the circumstances of the licensee or of groups of licensees, including the Canadian Broadcasting Corporation." It was further stated that these minimum standards would be incorporated into the conditions of the license so as to be legally enforceable.

The *Paper* declared that Parliament would be asked to authorize the Government to "give guidance to the Board of Broadcast Governors aimed at preventing foreign control of broadcasting facilities, the domination of a local situation through multiple ownership, or the extension of ownership geographically in a manner that is not in the public interest."[87]

The Government acknowledged the growth and importance of educational broadcasting and stated that it was prepared "to give immediate consideration to the creation of a new federal organization licensed to operate public service broadcasting facilities." "This organization," it was said, "would be empowered to enter into an agreement with any province to make such facilities available for the broadcasting within the province, during appropriate periods of the day, of programs designed to meet the needs of the provincial educational system as determined by the responsible provincial authorities. As a component of the Canadian broadcasting system, the new organization would be subject to the authority of the Board of Broadcast Governors in respect of the licensing of stations, the hours of broadcasting, the interpretation of its purposes, and generally the regulatory power of the Board in all matters affecting general broadcasting policy in Canada. . . ."[88]

It was also proposed that community antenna television systems should be treated as components of the national broadcasting system and that the new legislation should provide for their licensing, regulation and control by the Board of Broadcast Governors.[89]

Finally, the Board of Broadcast Governors would be empowered to inflict monetary penalties for breaches of regulations or failure to comply with the conditions of a license and, in the latter case, have the authority to suspend or revoke the license. There would be opportunity for appeal to the courts on questions of law but not of fact.[90]

CBC Responds to the White Paper

The Canadian Broadcasting Corporation made a lengthy response to the White Paper, recommending a retention and strengthening of the "two-system" concept within the total structure as the new basis for the country's broadcasting policy.

The CBC stated that it did not believe responsibility for the national broadcasting service could be divided between two public boards. "CBC program policies and operations are indivisible," said the Corporation, and "to divide responsibility for them is to divide the Corporation—to weaken CBC—and to weaken CBC is to weaken the service it provides."[91]

Accordingly, the CBC recommended:

(a) that the Board of Broadcast Governors be given full authority and responsibility for (1) the planning and administration of Canadian broadcasting's physical structure; (2) general broadcasting regulations; and (3) the broad performance of private broadcasting.

(b) that the Board of Directors of CBC be given full authority and responsibility for the policies, programs and operations of the national broadcast service.

(c) that BBG and CBC should each answer directly to Parliament through a designated Minister for their respective responsibilities.[92]

Furthermore, the CBC urged that the proposal to prescribe individual conditions of license for each CBC-owned station be dropped, since they operate under legislative mandate and a common policy of direction and control, whereas private stations do not, and, having varying responsibilities, their licenses should be subject to individual conditions.[93]

As in previous comments, the CBC took exception to the proposed requirement that the Corporation achieve commercial revenues totaling twenty-five percent of *all* television advertising expenditures in Canada and four percent of *all* for radio. Moreover, it disagreed that there was need for a new federal agency to carry on public service broadcasting, thought it would be wasteful, lead to conflicts, and be ineffective.[94]

New Legislation Imminent

AS OF October 30, 1967, new legislation seems imminent. In a speech to the Canadian Association of Broadcasters in Toronto the week of April 17–26, 1967, Dr. Andrew Steward, the Chairman of the Board of Broadcast Governors, stated that new legislation would give the Board new powers and that the BBG was preparing itself for new responsibilities.[95] However, not all broadcasters at the Association meeting were agreeable to further government controls and some contended that the industry should resist moves in that direction.[96]

What the provisions of the new law will be cannot now be stated with certainty.* However, the recommendations of the Standing Committee on Broadcasting, Films and Assistance to the Arts in the House of Commons may be noted. This Committee held long and exhaustive hearings on the *White Paper on Broadcasting* beginning December 1, 1966. Testimony was presented by the Board of Broadcast Governors, the Canadian Broadcasting Corporation, the Canadian Association of Broadcasters, the National Community Antenna Television Association of Canada, the Association of Canadian Television and Radio Artists, the British Broadcasting Corporation and the Independent Television Authority, Canadian Broadcasting League, Canadian Association for Adult Education and the Secretary of State.[97] Upon the basis of the testimony, the Committee issued a report expressing substantial agreement with the *White Paper*. It approved the basic principles of the *Paper* and a reconstitution of the BBG with legis-

---

*Since this was written, Parliament has passed new legislation which became effective in April 1968. See Appendix IX for selected provisions of the new law.

lative clarification of the areas of responsibility of the BBG and CBC. The Report stressed the need for one "common regulatory authority" to oversee the whole broad cost structure (both public and private) and advise Parliament periodically.[98] The following excerpts from the Report suggest the important provisions which are expected to constitute the legislation which will soon be passed and will govern Canadian broadcasting in the years ahead.

. . . .

The Committee concurs with the White Paper's statement of objectives. We are convinced that Canadians want radio and television programs of Canadian origin and character, although programs produced in the United States are available to a majority of Canadians who obviously enjoy them. A Canadian identity demands public affairs and news programs about Canada and about the world through Canadian eyes. Canadian broadcasters have a special responsibility to provide such programs because they will not come from any other source. Although the United States will continue to be the source of many dramatic and variety programs on Canadian stations, Canadian broadcasters must develop such programs in Canada to the fullest extent which availability of talents and resources permits.

. . . .

The Committee concurs with the general principles stated in the White Paper. We urge, however, a clear legislative declaration of the pre-eminence of the public sector. We agree that, although the CBC's responsibility is paramount, all broadcasters share a duty to serve the public interest and must share it more equitably and effectively. We earnestly hope that the proposed "total delegation of authority over programming" will end Parliament's frequent involvement with broadcasting matters.

. . . .

If public and private components are part of a single structure, as the Fowler Committee Report and the White Paper see them to be, a common regulatory authority is needed to oversee this structure and, as an "auditor general" of broadcasting, to advise Parliament periodically as to the performance of Canadian broadcasting.

Although the ultimate authority and responsibility of Parliament is clear, it is equally clear that Parliament cannot administer or supervise broadcasting. Nor do we believe a Minister of the Crown should have such power. A reconstituted BBG should provide an assessment of our broadcasting system. In order to do so, it must have clear-cut directives from Parliament as to how it will be expected to act on Parliament's behalf.

The CBC, as the prime instrument of public policy in broadcasting and one of the world's largest broadcasting organizations, needs a strong Board of Directors. Its directors would continue to be challenged with the management of one of our country's most important corporations. Legally, they are the Corporation. Although they hold this public asset as trustees for the Canadian people, it is natural that they should develop loyalties to its personnel, its programs and its welfare. It is in the public interest, as well as in the interest of the CBC, that they do so, within the context of their responsibility to Parliament on behalf of the people. At the same time, the CBC (and the public) should benefit from continuous and co-operative liaison with a BBG bearing responsibility for overseeing performance of the entire broadcasting system. The BBG, however, should not be involved in the Corporation's day-to-day decision-making or in policy-making concerned with the internal workings of the Corporation. These must be the responsibility of the CBC Board of Directors.

The responsibility of the BBG, in the first instance, would be to amplify the broad principles for Canadian broadcasting laid down by Parliament and to set general standards following public hearings. The legislation must say, with a good deal of precision, what these principles are, as they apply to the various components of the system, both public and private. Obviously, the most important of them will concern programming. In the case of the CBC, responsibility for programming must rest with its Board and management. We welcome the assurance that the BBG "will not, however, be empowered to give directions, other than by generally applicable regulations or in the conditions of a license, to any broadcaster in respect of specific programs."

In case of conflict between components, the BBG should have the power to arbitrate any dispute. It should seek to resolve complaints which fall within its purview by consultation with the component or components concerned before resorting to penalties or public censure, either of which should be a final resort but firmly used if necessary.

· · · ·

The Committee approves of the licensing procedure, regulation of affiliation agreements, and composition of the BBG as outlined in the White Paper. The Committee believes, however, that the authority of the Board should not reside only in the full-time members but that part-time members should have the right to vote. We also recommend that the total number of members be eleven; five full-time and six part-time. We suggest that the full-time members constitute an Executive Committee empowered to deal with matters delegated to it by legislation or by the full Board.

· · · ·

The Committee concurs with the statement on structure appearing in the White Paper, particularly with reference to extending coverage to all Canadians, and to full network services in both official languages. We recommend further that, wherever practical, in areas now receiving only one Canadian service, if the service is through a private outlet, the alternative should be provided by CBC. If CBC is now the sole service, the second service should be private. Where there are serious obstacles to such parallel development, however, these should not prohibit the extension of alternate service by other means, at least on a temporary basis. We urge that the introduction of dual service proceed as rapidly as CBC finances and local market conditions permit.

· · · ·

The Committee agrees with the comments of the White Paper on programming. We approve of a flexible formula of expectations for performance by individual stations or groups of stations but with strict enforcement of standards imposed as a condition of licence. We believe it is essential to avoid monopolization of prime time by foreign programs, and to increase true Canadian content in radio as well as television. We also believe that public affairs programs should be included among those shown during prime time.

The Committee supports the White Paper's proposal that the BBG be required to investigate and report on public complaints or representations about situations where control of broadcasting and another communications medium may tend to create a monopoly of information. We suggest that similar action would be justified where there appears to be danger of an undue concentration of control within broadcasting media. We also recommend that the BBG be authorized to initiate such investigations in the absence of public complaints when it deems advisable. We believe, too, that careful attention should be paid to these considerations in the granting of licences and in formulating conditions of licences, particularly in any area where there is unlikely to be more than one station, either radio or television. The Committee has noted that in the United States there is a limitation on the number of stations which can be licenced to any one owner, and feels the merits of such a restriction should be considered.

The Committee concurs with the proposals of the White Paper with respect to community antenna systems. We recognize the value of these systems but we agree that they should be treated as part of the broadcasting system. While they do not at present use the airwaves, they nevertheless distribute broadcast programs which may compete with those of other broadcasting outlets and therefore, should be under the jurisdiction of the BBG.

The Committee concurs with the proposal in the White Paper that the CBC will be subject to regulation and control by the BBG on the understanding that this does not imply any power to give directions in respect of specific programming except by general regulation or conditions of licences.

The Committee concurs with the proposal in the White Paper for financing of the CBC, and considers this basic to accomplishment of the goals which justify the Corporation's existence.

The Committee recommends reconsideration of the commercial target on which the grant is to be based. If the Corporation is to carry out its mandate, improving quality and expanding Canadian content of its programming, its first concern must not be competition for commercial sales. A revenue target based on a share of the advertising market could require the Corporation to place an excessive emphasis on this aspect of its activities.

An alternative is suggested that would relate CBC commercial revenues to the proposed statutory grants. Having determined the over-all revenue needs of the Corporation for operational purposes, and the desired level of commercial activity, the number of dollars to be derived from advertising sources would not be specified. This must be a realizable target and the Corporation should be expected to use aggressive advertising and program sales policies to the degree necessary to achieve it.[99]

NOTES

1. Canadian Institute on Public Affairs, *The Price of Being Canadian, 7th Winter Conference,* ed. D. L. B. Hamlin (Toronto: University of Toronto Press, 1961), p. 10.
2. *Ibid.,* p. 11.
3. *Ibid.,* p. 33.
4. *CBC, A Brief History and Background,* published by CBC Information Service (Ottawa: April 1966), p. 1.
5. *Canada, Report of Royal Commission on Broadcasting* (Ottawa: Queen's Printer and Controller of Stationery, March 15, 1957), p. 297.
6. *Ibid.*
7. *Ibid.*
8. *Ibid.,* p. 298.
9. *Ibid.* As of January 1968, the Canadian dollar was equivalent to ninety-two cents.
10. *Ibid.,* pp. 298–299.
11. *Report of the Royal Commission on Radio Broadcasting* (Ottawa: F. A. Aclaud, Printer to the King's Most Excellent Majesty, 1929), p. 5.
12. Canadian Broadcasting Corporation, *Broadcasting in Canada: History and Development of the National System,* November 15, 1960, p. 4.
13. *Canadian Royal Commission on Broadcasting,* 1929, p. 6.
14. *Ibid.*
15. *Ibid.,* pp. 12–13.
16. *In re Regulation and Control of Radio Communication in Canada* (1932), A.C. 304 (P.C.).
17. *Canada, House of Commons Debates,* LXVIII, No. 1, February 16, 1932, 266–267.
18. *Ibid.,* No. 20, March 2, 1932, p. 786.
19. Canadian Broadcasting Corporation, *Broadcasting in Canada,* p. 7.
20. *Ibid.*
21. *Ibid.*
22. *Canada, House of Commons Debates,* LXVIII, No. 64, May 9, 1932, 2935–2938.
23. *Ibid.,* May 16, 1932, p. 3225.
24. *Ibid.,* pp. 3290–3291.
25. Rt. Honorable Ernest Lapointe spoke for the Liberals; *ibid.,* pp. 3290–3291. J. S. Woodsworth, leader of the Co-operative Commonwealth Federation, also voiced approval, *ibid.,* p. 3291.
26. Canadian Broadcasting Corporation, *Broadcasting in Canada,* pp. 10–11.
27. *Canada, House of Commons Debates,* LXXII, No. 84, June 15, 1936, 4025. Also, see Canadian Broadcasting Corporation, *Broadcasting in Canada,* p. 13.

28. *Ibid.*, p. 14.
29. *Ibid.*, pp. 14–15.
30. *Ibid.*, p. 17.
31. *Canada, Royal Commission on National Development in the Arts, Letters and Sciences*, 1949–51 (Ottawa: Edmond Cloutier, Printer to the King's Most Excellent Majesty, 1951), pp. 286–287.
32. *Canada, House of Commons Debates*, LII, No. 82, June 1, 1951, 3613.
33. *Ibid.*
34. Canadian Broadcasting Corporation, *Broadcasting in Canada*, p. 19.
35. *Ibid.*, p. 20.
36. *Ibid.*, p. 21.
37. *Canada, Royal Commission on National Development in the Arts, Letters and Sciences*, 1949–51, pp. 302–303.
38. Canadian Broadcasting Corporation, *Broadcasting in Canada*, p. 25.
39. *Ibid.*, p. 29.
40. *Canada, Report of Royal Commission on Broadcasting* (Ottawa: Edmond Cloutier, Queen's Printer and Controller of Stationery, March 15, 1957).
41. *Ibid.*, p. 94.
42. Canadian Broadcasting Corporation, *Broadcasting in Canada*, p. 31.
43. Canadian Broadcasting Corporation, *Annual Report 1965–66*, Appendix, Ottawa, June 30, 1966.
44. UNESCO, *World Communications: Press, Radio, Television, Film* (New York: UNESCO Publications Center, 1964), p. 139.
45. *Canada Year Book 1965* (Ottawa: Queen's Printer, 1965), p. 841.
46. *Ibid.*, p. 842.
47. Canadian Broadcasting Corporation, *Annual Report 1965–66*, p. 40.
48. *Ibid.*
49. *Ibid.*
50. *Ibid.*, p. 37.
51. *Ibid.*
52. *Ibid.*
53. *Ibid.*, p. 39.
54. *Ibid.*, p. 41.
55. Canadian Association of Broadcasters, *Comments by the Canadian Association of Broadcasters on the Legislative and Structural Framework of Broadcasting in Canada*, January 16, 1966, p. 3. These comments were in response to the *Report of the Committee on Broadcasting*, 1965, popularly known as the Fowler Report.
56. *Ibid.*, p. 51.
57. *Ibid.*, pp. 51, 52.
58. Correspondence with Canadian Association of Broadcasters, October 18, 1967.
59. Canadian Broadcasting Corporation, *Annual Report 1965–66*, Appendix.
60. *Ibid.*
61. *Canada Year Book 1965*, p. 841.
62. *Ibid.*
63. Canadian Broadcasting Corporation, *Annual Report 1965–66*, p. 40.
64. *CBC Times*, XIX, No. 43 (April 22–28, 1967), 8II–8XV.
65. Canadian Broadcasting Corporation, *Annual Report 1965–66*.
66. *Ibid.*, p. 40.
67. *CBC Times*, April 22–28, 1967.
68. *Report of Committee on Broadcasting, September 1, 1965* (Ottawa: Queen's Printer), p. 235.

69. *Ibid.,* p. 236.
70. Centennial Commission, *Bulletin,* No. 28, March 10, 1967 (P.O. Box 1967, Ottawa), p. 2.
71. *Ibid.*
72. Canadian Broadcasting Corporation, *Annual Report 1965–66,* p. 56.
73. *Ibid.,* p. 18.
74. *Ibid.*
75. *Ibid.,* pp. 18, 60.
76. *Ibid.,* p. 19.
77. *EBU Review,* 95B, January 1966, pp. 18–20.
78. *Ibid.,* pp. 20–22.
79. *EBU Review,* 96B, March 1966, pp. 19–23.
80. *Ibid.,* p. 19.
81. *Ibid.,* p. 20.
82. *Ibid.,* p. 22.
83. *Ibid.*
84. *Comments by the Canadian Association of Broadcasters on the Legislative and Structural Framework of Broadcasting in Canada,* January 13, 1966, p. 2.
85. *Ibid.,* p. 3.
86. Honorable Judy LaMarsh, Secretary of State, *White Paper on Broadcasting* (Ottawa: 1966), p. 8.
87. *Ibid.,* pp. 11–12.
88. *Ibid.,* pp. 12–13.
89. *Ibid.,* p. 13.
90. *Ibid.,* p. 14.
91. *White Paper on Broadcasting 1966, Comments by the Canadian Broadcasting Corporation,* November 1, 1966, pp. 2–4.
92. *Ibid.,* p. 5.
93. *Ibid.,* p. 6.
94. *Ibid.*
95. *Broadcasting Magazine,* April 24, 1967, p. 74.
96. *Ibid.,* p. 75.
97. See *Minutes of Proceedings and Evidence,* Standing Committee on Broadcasting, Films and Assistance to the Arts. Nos. 29–42, December 1, 5, 6, 12, 15, 20, 1966; January 9, 10, 17, 19, 31, 1967; February 2, 3, 7, 9, 14, 1967; March 9, 10, 13, 14, 15, 16, 1967. These hearings related to the *White Paper on Broadcasting 1966.*
98. *Ibid.,* No. 42, *Eleventh Report to the House* (Respecting *White Paper on Broadcasting*).
99. *Ibid.*

· B ·

THE UNITED KINGDOM
AND IRELAND

V

The United Kingdom:

From Monopoly to Diversity

THE BRITISH were among the first to realize the importance of and to make use of electromagnetic communication. The first English patent for a telegraph was issued to Cooke and Wheatstone in 1837, only two years after Morse had conducted his successful experiments.[1]

The Napoleonic Wars and the Industrial Revolution combined to make Great Britain a major political and military power. During the eighteenth and nineteenth centuries, she became queen of the seas, and through effective diplomacy, aided by the use of land and oceanic cables as well as wireless communication, she maintained and extended her Empire.

Early Radio Developments

FROM the beginning, the British Post Office exercised regulatory jurisdiction over wire and wireless communication. This authority was derived from two statutes. The first, enacted in 1869, gave the Postmaster General the exclusive privilege of transmitting telegrams within the United Kingdom.[2] The second, passed in 1904, extended his powers to wireless telegraphy, and laid down the principle that no person should establish a wireless telegraph station without first securing a license from the Postmaster General, or transmit messages except under conditions as prescribed by him.[3]

Some of Marconi's earliest experiments in radio attracted the favorable attention of the postal authorities,[4] and the political leadership in England talked enthusiastically of strengthening the ties between the mother country and her colonies through the use of this marvelous new medium.

Asa Briggs, in his monumental work, *The History of Broadcasting in the United Kingdom,* has told the fascinating story of the development of radio during the early part of the twentieth century.[5] At first, little thought was given to using radio for broadcasting. The main concern was to develop it as an effective device for communication with and among ships at sea, and with outlying islands. The interest was in point-to-point communication rather than in broadcasting to the general public.

Briggs has attempted to see the development of broadcasting in a historical and social perspective. He has pointed out that between 1890 and the end of the First World War, a new pattern of national life developed. "The ordinary man had begun to assert his social claims, and there was no shortage of agencies in society which were seeking to satisfy or to exploit them." Barriers between classes and groups had broken down, and "it was the war itself which had produced the final jolt, and inevitably it left many social vacuums to fill. Broadcasting was of the greatest possible importance in relation to this changing social pattern."[6]

Commercial Interests Take Initiative

AFTER the First World War, as was true in many other European countries, commercial interests in England took the initiative in developing organized broadcasting. The Marconi Company established experimental stations, first in Ireland and later at Chelmsford. Amateurs, or "ham operators," as well as sailors at sea, constituted a large part of the listening audience.

Musical programs and newscasts aroused the interest of the general public. Furthermore, the broadcasting boom in the United States had a stimulating effect on British government officials and commercial entrepreneurs.

Because of complaints of interference from listeners and the feeling of some that the broadcasting of musical programs was a wasteful and even a "frivolous" use of radio, the licenses of the Marconi Company were suspended.[7] But this by no means impeded the growth of broadcasting. Representatives of more than sixty wireless societies filed a petition with the Post Office in December 1921, voicing resentment that "permission to transmit weather reports, news and music by wireless telephony should be refused to companies competent and willing to provide the service and do so without interference with the defensive services of the country."[8]

The result of this petition was that the Postmaster General renewed the authority of the Marconi station to broadcast speech and music for a short period each week for the benefit of the wireless societies.[9] With the sanction of the Government, a small group of lively, imaginative and talented young men, in charge of the station, initiated a program service that became increasingly popular with the public and "guaranteed the future of broadcasting in Britain."[10]

A number of other commercial companies were authorized to broadcast experimentally, and it appeared that a system of private broadcasting similar to that in the United States might develop. But this was not to be. The postal authorities believed that it would be better for the various manufacturing firms to join in one broadcasting company, rather than compete. As Terence O'Brien has pointed out, this opinion "was undoubtedly influenced by the experience of the broadcasting boom in the United States, which had led to a condition bordering on chaos in that country as the result of competition for and in the air between a large number of independently-owned stations. . . ."[11]

British Broadcasting Company Established

In December 1922, after much haggling and negotiation, the radio manufacturers achieved a sufficient consensus to join in establishing the British Broadcasting Company. On January 18, 1923, the Company was authorized to construct and operate eight broadcasting stations. The license permitted the Company to transmit programs daily until January 1, 1925, with a proviso that the programs should meet with "the reasonable satisfaction of the Postmaster General."[12]

The Articles of Association provided that any manufacturer of wireless equipment was eligible for membership upon acquiring one or more shares of stock. The bulk of the stock was owned by six large companies, including Marconi. These large firms nominated six of the Company's eight directors. Under an agreement approved by the Company and the Postmaster General, all members were obliged to sell only radio apparatus of an approved type manufactured in Britain, pay royalties to the Company on all equipment sold, and refrain from selling advertising without special consent. All owners of radio receivers were required to pay an annual license fee of ten shillings on each set, half of which went to the Company and half to the Government.

The original authorization for this broadcast station was of an experimental nature, "the future of which was from all points of view highly conjectural." It had three basic features which continued to characterize the system for many years. It reaffirmed the principle that the radio spectrum is a part of the public domain and that the State should exercise regulatory control over both transmission and reception. The Postmaster General had assumed this from the very beginning. It required that all transmitters and receivers should be licensed by the Government and that it was more desirable to finance the system by license fees rather than by public taxation or by the sale of advertising.[13]

Early Problems

THE first few months were a trying time for the new Company. There were disputes with the postal authorities. The monopolistic aspect of the Company's operation disturbed Parliament and segments of the public. In some quarters, the authority of the Postmaster General to collect license fees under the Wireless Telegraphy Act of 1904 was questioned.

A matter of great concern was that some firms were importing an increasing number of cheap, ready-made parts for radio receivers. These parts could be readily assembled, and as Briggs has noted, "such firms avoided the necessity of paying royalty to the BBC on the purchase price of the apparatus."[14] Furthermore, the Postmaster General was issuing numerous experimental licenses to amateurs who were not required to pay fees on receivers. Thus, the revenue from royalties and licenses was much less than had been anticipated.[15]

Moreover, there was the growing conflict between the press and the broadcasting enterprise. The powerful newspapers and news agencies expressed, in no uncertain terms, their determination to maintain supremacy in the news field. On the other hand, there were the radio manufacturers with large investments in the Company eager to make the broadcasting service more widely appealing and arguing the need for experiment and change.[16] The clash of these vested interests had a shuddering effect on the Postmaster General and made his regulatory position increasingly difficult.

Formal Inquiry Instituted

HOPING to alleviate the situation, the Postmaster General appointed a Committee of ten members to make a formal public inquiry. The Committee was broadly representative of Parliament, the Postmaster General, the Company, the press and the Radio Society of Great Britain. Major General Sir Frederick Sykes was made Chairman.[17]

After holding thirty-four meetings and eliciting much information and many points of view, the Committee issued a Report. One of its most important recommendations was that broadcasting should be subject to a large measure of state control. The Committee stated that "broadcasting holds social and political possibilities as great as any technical attainment of our generation," and that, therefore, "the control of such a potential power over public opinion and the life of the nation ought to remain with the State," and that "operation of so important a national service ought not to be allowed to become an unrestricted commercial monopoly."[18]

The Report further said that "ultimate control" should be vested in a minister responsible to Parliament, assisted by an advisory committee or board, representing various interests. While affirming the importance of centralized control, it spoke of the desirability of establishing a number of stations in different parts of the country which would be managed by a variety of local groups.

The Committee considered various methods of financing the broadcasting system—the use of public funds, customs and excise taxes on apparatus, licensing of radio manufacturers and dealers, advertising, and license fees. The latter method—a license fee of ten shillings on each radio set—was decided upon.

The recommendations of the Committee were, for the most part, approved by the Government. The requirement that members of the Company pay royalties on the sales of radio equipment was abolished, and the ban on foreign receivers removed. The Company's license was extended for two years, until December 31, 1926.[19]

Prior to the expiration of this license, British broadcasting developed rapidly. The number of receiver licenses increased from about one million at the end of 1924 to more than a million and a half in early 1926. Nine broadcasting stations plus eleven relays were in operation. A high-powered station in Daventry began experiments in long-wave broadcasting, and with the opening of this station in July 1925, radio became available to eighty percent of the population. The variety and scope of programming was vastly improved, and the hours of broadcasting were more than doubled.

As Terence O'Brien has pointed out, "in proportion as broadcasting grew out of the embryonic stage into sturdy infancy, both the practical difficulties and the theoretical objections involved in entrusting its operation to a private company representative of the wireless trade became more apparent . . ." and "the view was becoming widespread that introduction of a more definite measure of public control and a more impartial form of operation should no longer be delayed."[20]

As a result of this growth, the Postmaster General, in August 1925, appointed another committee, with the Earl of Crawford as Chairman, to "advise as to the proper scope of the Broadcasting service and as to the management, control and finance thereof after the expiration of the existing license on December 31, 1926."[21]

The Crawford Committee endorsed most of the proposals of the Sykes group. It was the Committee's view that monopolistic control of broadcasting should be continued, but added that a public corporation should take the place of the commercial Company, and that this corporation should serve as a "trustee for the national interest in broadcasting."

On July 14, 1926, the Postmaster General announced in the House of Commons that the Government had decided to adopt, in substance, the recommendation of the Crawford Committee, and would petition the Crown for a Royal Charter of incorporation. He explained that he preferred not to have the new corporation created by statute, because he felt that the public might believe that it was a creature of Parliament and therefore subject to political influence. While it would be constituted as a public institution, he wanted to insure that it had reasonable autonomy and "the greatest possible latitude" in the conduct of its affairs.[22]

Establishment of the British Broadcasting Corporation

THE Charter creating the British Broadcasting Corporation was issued and the Postmaster General granted the Corporation a license for ten years, beginning January 1, 1927. The commercial Company was dissolved. The private shareholders were reimbursed for their stock subscriptions, and the entire capital and property of the Company was transferred to the new public Corporation. Thus the basic pattern for future broadcasting was determined, and as Burton Paulu has noted, "broadcasting became a monopoly, financed by license fees on radio receivers, and administered by an independent public corporation." And, until 1954 when the establishment of the Independent Television Authority ended the BBC monopoly, these three features remained the essential characteristics of British broadcasting.[23]

Some changes were made in the BBC operation in the years following its creation. These were a result of studies made by committees in the periods of 1937–46, 1947–51, 1952–62 and 1960–62, but the fundamental nature of the BBC operation has remained the same.[24]

Domestic and Foreign Services Expanded

DURING the early years, two BBC programs were on the air, one providing a uniform national service with broadcasts emanating from the London studios, and the other providing a regional service, with some local originations. Under the leadership of Sir John Reith, the BBC emphasized "serious," "educational" and "cultural" broadcasts. While popular tastes were not ignored, the prevailing philosophy was to provide a service that would raise the level of intellectual and aesthetic tastes, to give the public "something slightly better than it now thinks it likes."[25]

From the beginning the British have exploited the full uses of wire and wireless communication to promote the interests of the nation and the Commonwealth. Supported by numerous colonial and imperial conferences, the BBC in 1932 instituted a regular short-wave service. This Empire Service, as it was called, was primarily intended to strengthen the economic, political and cultural ties with the colonies and all important areas of the Commonwealth. Noting that other countries such as France, Germany, Italy and the United States were broadcasting via short-wave, and believing that "the British Commonwealth, both as a community and as idea, cannot but take its turn on the platform,"[26] the BBC expanded the Empire Service further in 1935.

These foreign broadcasts featured news reports and talks by high government officials. The voices of the great—H. G. Wells, George Bernard Shaw, J. B. Priestly, Aldous Huxley, Winston Churchill, to mention only a few—were carried, on a regular basis, to eager listeners throughout the world. In 1938, foreign-language broadcasts were initiated, and within a short time programs were being transmitted in most European languages. Important radio links with American networks were established, and in November 1935, the BBC set up an office in New York to facilitate the distribution of its programs and to develop an exchange service between Britain and the United States.

Broadcasting During the War

WITH the coming of the Second World War, all domestic radio was consolidated into one national network, the Home Service. The Ministry of Information assumed the general supervision of broadcasting, both domestic and foreign, but the BBC continued to select the subject matter for programs, consistent with war-time policies and objectives, and was able to carry on its newscasts with some degree of independence and objectivity.

Shortly after the war began, a second national service was introduced, the General Forces Programme, designed primarily for the entertainment of British troops. H. H. Wilson has stated that "there is little doubt that British soldiers and civilians alike thoroughly enjoyed the more relaxed, informal atmosphere of American style broadcasting and found the entertainment more sprightly than that of the pre-war BBC."[27]

As the Nazis and other belligerents stepped up their propaganda broadcasts via short-wave, the BBC became increasingly active in the war of words. Its newscasts and commentaries, however, were more factual and less vituperative than those from Berlin, Rome and other communication centers then under the control of the Nazis. With false, abusive and conflicting messages flooding the airways, the BBC endeavored to preserve the image of accuracy and reliability which it had established. Throughout the world, especially in German-occupied territory, it was regarded as the most dependable source of news about the war.

Burton Paulu has given an excellent, detailed account of British broadcasting during the war—how London became the communications center for the Allies, how the BBC tailored its broadcasts to appeal to the varying interests of foreign audiences, and cooperated with the United States and other Allies in the development of an extensive international network and exchange program service.

> Program objectives and content varied with the intended audience. There were broadcasts for the Empire, the Allies, occupied countries, the enemy, neutrals, and the Armed Forces. Broadcasts for the dominions and colonies stressed the war against the common enemy. The basic features of the Empire Service were retained, and were reinforced by many news programs, particularly about events and people centered in Britain. Broadcasts to the United States and other Allies emphasized the theme of unity. Talks and discussions by prominent people explained British policies and actions. . . .[28]

And, as Paulu has further pointed out, the effectiveness of these programs was greatly improved by extensive rebroadcasting. For example, in the United States, on D-day, seven hundred and twenty-five out of nine hundred and fourteen American radio stations then on the air rebroadcast BBC reports. American correspondents, such as Edward R. Murrow broadcasting from London during the "dark and dismal" days, helped keep the spirit of victory alive.[29]

Radio and TV After the War

THE Second World War undoubtedly had a modifying effect on the BBC. Following the Allied victory, the Home Service with regional programs was restored. The General Forces Programme which had been so popular with American and British troops was continued as a new national service, the Light Programme, emphasizing entertainment with a broad mass appeal. This was balanced, however, in September 1946, by the creation of a Third Programme, designed to appeal to minority tastes and "to broadcast, without regard to length or difficulty, the masterpieces of music, art, and letters which lend themselves to transmissions in sound."[30] H. H. Wilson has remarked that "whatever their views on the Third Programme, most listeners were likely to agree that the post-war BBC was offering far more attractive fare than ever before. It had come a long way in meeting the needs of the British public, without deviating from its public service mission."[31]

British television, which had been initiated experimentally in 1936 and was interrupted by hostilities, was restored in June 1946. The BBC concentrated on the development of a national TV network and began plans for a second program.

The BBC Charter and License, due to expire in 1946, were renewed to December 31, 1951. There was some agitation for a formal inquiry and re-evaluation of the BBC's performance, but this was postponed pending the nation's recovery from the disruption of the war.

For the next three years there was much heated discussion in Parliament, in the press, and among commercial and cultural groups regarding the BBC's future. There was an intensification of debate on important issues which had been raised prior to the renewal of the BBC's Charter and License. Should British broadcasting continue to be a monopoly? Should competitive, commercial service be introduced? And, if so, would this provide better and more balanced programming in keeping with the changing character of British society?

Appointment of the Beveridge Committee

THE pressures for a formal investigation led to the appointment of the Beveridge Committee on June 21, 1949. This Committee made the most comprehensive study of the BBC yet undertaken. Its report to Parliament, dated January 18, 1951, included a detailed analysis of the issues pertaining to monopoly and the introduction of commercial broadcasting. The many recommendations included support for a continuation of the BBC monopoly for an unlimited period and a prohibition against advertising without the written consent of the Postmaster General.[32]

The Labor Government which came into power after the war withheld action on renewal of the BBC Charter and License while it considered the Beveridge Report. In July 1951, the Government submitted its White Paper to Parliament for legislative action.[33] It supported the Beveridge recommendations for continuation of the broadcasting monopoly and the prohibition of advertising. It proposed a fifteen year license, the establishment of broadcasting commissions made up of local authorities in large urban communities and of members of county councils, and the withholding by the Treasury for three years fifteen percent of the net license revenue pending more careful consideration of future broadcasting needs.

Parliamentary Debate

THESE proposals evoked great controversy in many quarters, including the BBC itself, and led to vehement debate in Parliament. Before the issues could be resolved, the Labor Government lost the election of October 1951, and was succeeded by the Conservatives. Since the BBC Charter and License were due to expire in December of that year, the new Government granted a six month extension.

The parliamentary debate continued. The Conservative victory increased the support for those urging the introduction of commercial broadcasting. Radio Luxembourg and other foreign systems of commercial radio had attracted large British audiences. Their patterns of operation had won the support of many listeners and particularly certain advertising firms and business interests. A small but effective group of back-bench Conservatives committed to "private enterprise" worked assiduously and succeeded in persuading the new Government to change its thinking about commercial broadcasting.[34] In May 1952, the Government announced that, while it favored a continuation of the BBC monopoly in radio, it would support the introduction of "some element of competition" in television.[35]

In the debate in the House of Lords, Lord Reith, who had been the BBC's chief executive officer for sixteen years, severely criticized the proposals and the Government which made them. He accused the Government of attempting to scuttle a system which, he said, had won the admiration of the world. He expressed in no uncertain manner his opposition to the introduction of commercial sponsorship in any form, which he believed was clearly implicit in the proposal for a competitive TV system. He declared that moral and intellectual values were at stake. Arguments pro and con continued in the House of Lords for two days.[36]

On June 11, 1952, a motion was made in the Commons to approve the Government's proposals.[37] The purposes of these proposals were summarized by the Government: ". . . to achieve three objectives—the first is to introduce an element of competition into television and enable private enterprise to play a fuller part in the development of this important and growing factor in our lives; the second is to reduce to a minimum the financial commitments of the State; and the third is to proceed with caution into this new field and to safeguard this medium of information and entertainment from the risk of abuse or lowering of standards."[38]

After a heated debate, the BBC License and Agreement were approved in the House of Commons by three hundred and two votes to two hundred and sixty-seven, and the Charter, granted under Royal prerogative, was issued, effective July 1, 1952.[39] For the first time, the BBC License was a nonexclusive one, enabling the Government to establish a competitive, commercial system.

During the next two years there was much debate regarding commercial TV in Parliament, in the press, and in private and public meetings. While some of the supporters of the Government's proposals had stated in Parliament that it would be "several years" before commercial television would be initiated, the pressures in its behalf increased rapidly. Once Parliament had acted, business interests campaigned more vigorously for its introduction.[40]

Independent Television Authority Established

H. H. WILSON, in *Pressure Group,* has given a detailed and interesting report of how commercial groups and "back benchers" in Parliament conspired to overcome resistance and pushed through legislation which established the Independent Television Authority (ITA), and authorized it to provide commercial programs.[41] Space does not permit a full account of this history here. Suffice to say, the bill to create the Authority was introduced in Parliament on March 4, 1954. After a prolonged debate and the incorporation of many amendments, it became law on July 30, 1954.[42] The Postmaster General granted the Authority a license for ten years and it began operation on August 4 of the same year.[43]

The next six years were a testing period for both the BBC and ITA television systems. Burton Paulu wrote in 1961 that "any objective comparison of British television in 1955 and 1961," clearly showed that things were better because of ITA. He stated that "public acceptance of the new service" had been so overwhelming that "even the Labour Party had to change its position from one of outright opposition to qualified acceptance."[44]

Despite Mr. Paulu's favorable appraisal, there was considerable criticism of the ITA and its programs. Some Members of Parliament decried the enormous profits being made by the commercial contractors who provided the television service for the ITA. The press, in general, was not happy with the competition for the advertising pound, and many civic and cultural leaders were complaining that ITA program standards were too low.[45]

The BBC Charter and License were due to expire on June 30, 1962, and that of the ITA two years later. The Government extended the authority of the BBC to operate until July 29, 1964, making the Charter and License for both organizations terminate at the same time.[46]

Appointment of the Pilkington Committee

IN the meantime, the Postmaster General, in line with previous practice, appointed a committee of inquiry headed by Sir Henry Pilkington to study the performances of both the BBC and ITA and make recommendations for the future of both operations.[47]

This Committee made its report in June 1962, after holding public hearings for seventy-eight days, and receiving more than eight hundred written statements from interested parties.[48]

In general, the Report commended the BBC and its programming but was highly critical of the ITA. It concluded that the BBC's television service was a "successful realization of the purposes of broadcasting as defined in its charter, but that the service of the ITA did not successfully realize the purpose of broadcasting as defined in the Television Act."[49]

Furthermore, the Committee believed that the contracting companies, commercially motivated, were largely responsible for the planning and production of television programs, and that the Authority itself, as a trustee for the public interest, should have the controlling influence.

> The authority's formal powers are to regulate programming in the public interest. Because the regulatory function is separated from the creative function of program planning and production, it is negative and prohibitive. The initiative is held by the program contractors and, for most practical purposes by the four major companies.
>
> The positive and creative activity essential for a good service of broadcasting is theirs. This essential activity cannot be generally compelled by the exercise of regulatory powers. Nor do we believe that a regulatory body, not organically involved in planning and production, can develop a sufficiently perceptive comprehension of the creative aspect. . . .[50]

The Committee recommended that the Authority be empowered to plan the programming and to sell the advertising time. As proposed, the commercial companies would produce and sell to the Authority particular programs for inclusion in the schedules made up by the Authority, and that any surplus income, after making provision for reserves, would be paid to the Exchequer. Responsibility for programming, said the Report, would move from the companies' administrators to those of the Authority, which would be expected to produce some programs itself.[51] As *The Times* put it, "the companies' producers would be free from any need, implicit or explicit, to consider the market for advertising time and because their commercial success would depend entirely on the worth of their programmes, the producers would be encouraged to employ their talents as creatively and widely as possible."[52]

Other important recommendations in the Report were: (1) a change in the definition standard for television from four hundred and five to six hundred and twenty-five lines; (2) the introduction of UHF color television on six hundred and twenty-five lines as soon as possible; and (3) the grant of rights and responsibilities to the National Broadcasting Council for Scotland regarding the BBC's TV service in that area, comparable with those it had exercised in connection with the Home Service in radio, and an extension of similar rights and duties to the National Council of Wales.

The Committee's chief criticism of the ITA was that the private objective to sell advertising time did not coincide with what it considered the primary and essential public objective, the best possible service to the public. In the Authority, as it was then constituted and organized, the dynamic of profitability was applied to the realization of the objective which the Committee considered incidental, that is, the production of programs to sell advertising; and the regulatory function of the ITA could not ensure the realization of the purposes of broadcasting. The Committee recommended, therefore, organic changes that would (1) vest real power in the Authority; (2) remove from program planning and production the commercial incentive always to aim at maximum audiences and at maximum advertising revenue; (3) apply the incentive of profitability to the production of the best programs; and (4) promote real competition in program production among program contractors, and competition in high-quality programming between the BBC and the ITA.[53]

Television Act of 1964 Adopted

THE criticisms and recommendations of the Pilkington Committee were widely reported in the British press,[54] and provoked much discussion throughout the United Kingdom.[55] It was the object of intense study and debate by Members of Parliament and the Government, and had an important influence on the legislation which followed.

Parliament passed the Television Act of 1964 which consolidated provisions of the 1954 law and those of an Amending Act of 1963. On June 10, 1964, the Postmaster General, exercising his powers under the Telegraphy Act of 1869 and the Wireless Telegraphy Act of 1949, and pursuant to the 1964 law, renewed the License of the Independent Television Authority for the period ending July 31, 1976.

Present Organizational Structure of ITA

THE ITA's basic organization was preserved. As presently constituted, it consists of a board of thirteen members representing different walks of life, appointed by the Postmaster General, one of whom he designates as Chairman and another as Deputy-Chairman. All serve in a part-time capacity, although the Chairman is expected to give his major attention to the work of the Authority. Three members are required to give special attention to the interests and needs of Scotland, Wales and Northern Ireland.

The Authority has a staff of about six hundred, more than two hundred of which are administrative and technical personnel at the London headquarters. Almost four hundred engineers operate more than twenty transmitters with studio centers located in London, Birmingham, Manchester, Glasgow, Cardiff, Bristol, Southampton, Dover, Newcastle-upon-Tyne,

Norwich, Belfast, Plymouth, Carlisle, Aberdeen and St. Helier. In addition, UHF facilities are being constructed at various sites for joint use by the ITA and the BBC. Ninety-eight percent of the people in the United Kingdom are now within range of one or more of the Authority's twenty-two transmitting stations.

The 1964 law provided for the establishment of numerous advisory councils. The General Advisory Council, concerned with overall TV programming, consists of more than twenty distinguished members. Its function is to review ITA programs, to advise the Authority on the general pattern and content of programs and to consider such other matters affecting the Independent Television service as may from time to time be referred to it by the Authority.[56]

Special committees have been established to consult with the Authority about programs relating to religion, education and advertising. There is also a Central Appeals Advisory Committee to advise on the choice of subjects for charitable appeals broadcast over the ITA network on Sunday evenings.

ITA Responsibilities Increased

IN response to the Pilkington Report, Parliament, in the 1964 Act, granted the Authority considerably more power.[57] While Section 1(5) of the 1964 law states that the programs broadcast are to be provided by program contractors and not the Authority, Section 2(2) qualifies this to the extent that the Authority may arrange for the inclusion of particular material which, in its opinion, is "necessary for securing a proper balance in the subject matter of the programmes and cannot, or cannot as suitably, be provided by programme contractors."

The new law requires the Authority to insure "that the programs in each area maintain a high general standard in all respects, and in particular in respect of their content and quality, and a proper balance and wide range in their subject matter, having regard both to the programmes as a whole and also to the days of the week on which, and the times of the day at which, the programmes are broadcast."[58]

The Act also provides that all program schedules must be drawn up in consultation with the Authority and approved by the Authority in advance. To implement this requirement, a Program Policy Committee was established in 1964 to serve as the principal channel for making known to the companies the Authority's views on program policy. It works closely with the Network Planning Committee of the program companies in determining network schedules. Arrangements are also made for regular consultation between officials of the Authority (national and regional) and the individual companies.[59]

Section 3(1) of the Act requires the Authority to insure that "nothing is included in the programs which offends against good taste or decency or is likely to encourage or incite to crime or to lead to disorder or to be offensive to public feelings"; to see that sufficient time is given to news and that it is presented with "due accuracy and impartiality"; that "proper proportions" of the programs are of British origin and performance; that stations carry "suitable" proportions of material with appeal to the viewers in local and regional areas; and to insure that "due impartiality" is preserved as regards matters of political or industrial controversy or those relating to "current public policy."[60]

Subliminal persuasion is specifically prohibited. The granting of prizes or "gifts of significant value" on programs is forbidden and, except with the previous approval of the Authority, no program may be broadcast which contains a religious message or which promotes any charitable enterprise.[61]

As pointed out by the Authority, it exercises a continuing surveillance function, and, as occasion may require, it reviews program scripts to make sure they do not infringe the law. However, the Authority has stated that "such interventions are rare in relation to the totality of the output and they have never been on such a scale or of such severity as could be said to hamstring creative artists."[62]

The Authority has further commented that "wrong impressions are apt to be formed of this part of the Authority's work depending on people's own attitude towards the control of television standards. The Authority does not expect to satisfy everyone all of the time. It is sometimes criticized for being too liberal or even lax in its interpretation of its duties and occasionally also for being too restrictive. In a free society, it could hardly be otherwise."[63]

As required by Section 4, the Authority has drawn up a code giving guidelines to be observed in regard to the showing of violence, particularly when children may be expected to be viewing programs. Before sanctioning such programming, the questions to be answered are: (1) Is it socially defensible when viewed as a part of the dramatic context in which it occurs? (2) Does the violence, whether mental or physical, appear simply to attract attention and exceed quantitatively what is needed to accomplish dramatic purpose? And (3) is the intensity of the material such that it produces an unhealthful and horrifying effect on children?[64]

ITA Financing and Advertising

INDEPENDENT Television is financed entirely from advertising revenue. Fourteen program companies, as approved by the Authority, sell advertising time and from this income provide the programs, pay a rental to the

Independent Television Authority and a levy, based upon net advertising receipts, to the Exchequer.

The amount and content of television commercials (limited to an average of not more than six minutes per hour) are controlled by the Authority. Rules controlling the content are set out in a code of Television Advertising Standards and Practice, as required by the 1964 Act. To administer this code, the Authority has the aid of an Advisory Advertising Committee and a group of independent medical experts. The preamble to this code reads:

> The general principle which will govern all television advertising is that it should be legal, clean, honest and truthful. It is recognized that this principle is not peculiar to the television medium, but is one which applies to all reputable advertising in other media in this country. Nevertheless, television, because of its greater intimacy within the home, gives rise to problems which do not necessarily occur in other media and it is essential to maintain a consistently high quality of television advertising.[65] (The complete code is reproduced in Appendix II.)

Current ITA Programming

ACCORDING to the ITV 1965 Report, from sixty to sixty-five hours of programming per week are available in each Independent Television Service area. The kinds of programs provided by the contracting companies vary somewhat to suit the particular interests and needs of the different areas served. However, under the general guidance of the Authority, the division of output among the different program categories is essentially the same.

What ITA calls "serious programming" was running about thirty-six percent on Independent Television during the last quarter of 1966 compared to only nineteen percent in October 1956. The following table reflects the estimated percentages of time per week devoted to different program categories in the London area from October to December, 1966. This is fairly typical of other areas served by the ITA.[66]

Programs	Percentage
News and news magazines	7
Documentaries and news features	9
Adult education (including repeats)	4
Religion	5
School programs (including repeats)	9
Children's programs	
informative	2
entertainment	6
Plays	5
Drama series and serials	19

Feature films	9
Entertainment and music	12
Sports	13

The contracting companies produce about seventy percent of the programs. The remainder consists of recorded programs made in the United States and films produced in Britain and Commonwealth countries.

The Authority emphasizes the regional pattern of ITA broadcasting. "During a period," says the Authority, "when more and more institutions have tended to be concentrated in the Capitol, the development of Independent Television on the basis of fourteen separate programme companies each serving a particular part of the country has brought a new emphasis to local life and customs and provided creative centers in the provinces stemming from local initiative."[67] Studio centers and transmitters are located in London, the Midlands, Lancashire and Yorkshire (North), Scotland, Wales and the West of England, Northern Ireland, Southern England, Eastern England, Southwest England and the Channel Islands. Within these areas, ITV serves a total population of about fifty-five million.

Organizational Structure of the BBC

As previously pointed out, the basic constitutional position of the BBC has remained largely unchanged since the first Charter was granted in 1927. It is a nonprofit, corporate body set up by Royal Charter, with a Board of Governors (nine members at present) appointed by the Queen in Council. (The complete text of the BBC Charter appears in Appendix III.) The Governors serve for terms of five years, and determine the basic policies of BBC operation. These policies are carried out by a permanent executive staff, headed by a Director-General, who is the chief executive officer of the Corporation.

Under Article X of the Charter, broadcasting councils have been established in Scotland and Wales, whose functions are to "control the policy and content of the BBC's Scottish Home Service and Welsh Home Service" and to "control the policy and content of those programs in the television services of the BBC which are provided primarily for reception in Scotland and Wales."[68] The Charter also provides for the setting up of a similar council for Northern Ireland, should the Government there at any time formally request it.

Except for network links which are provided by the Post Office, the BBC's responsibilities extend over the whole field of broadcasting, "from the organization of performance in front of the microphone, or microphone and camera in the case of a television program, to the radiation of signals from the transmitting aerial."[69]

The BBC is licensed to operate by the Postmaster General, who exercises regulatory powers as provided under the Wireless Telegraphy Acts which were consolidated in 1949. The BBC License and Agreement (reproduced in full in Appendix IV), which runs to July 31, 1976, and is coextensive with that of the ITA, states the terms and conditions under which the BBC may use its technical facilities.

BBC Financing

MOST of the money for financing the BBC's domestic services is derived from annual license fees on radio and television receivers (£1 for radio only and £5 for both radio and TV).[70] These fees are collected by the Postmaster General, who retains an amount necessary to carry on his broadcast function, and gives the balance to the BBC. The gross license revenue in 1963–64 was £50,039,514. The Postmaster General deducted £3,281,213 for his own broadcast expenses, and paid the remainder, £46,758,301, to the Corporation. Of this amount, radio received £14,833,729 and television £31,924,572.[71]

The External Services, directed to overseas listeners and an important part of BBC operations since the early days, are financed by grants-in-aid from the Treasury. In 1963–64, £8,063,000 were allocated for these broadcasts.[72]

Government Program Controls

UNDER the BBC License and Agreement, the Postmaster General reserves for the Government some important powers over programming. For example, Section 14(4) states he "may from time to time by notice in writing require the Corporation to refrain at any specified time or at all times from sending any matter or matter of any class specified in such notice. . . ."

While this provision does give the Government of the day and Parliament formal veto power over programs, from the beginning, the BBC has enjoyed a large measure of independence. The Postmaster General, who led in the establishment of the Corporation in 1926, stated in November of that year that while he assumed responsibility for broad issues of policy, "on minor issues and measures of domestic policy and matters of day-to-day control" he wanted the BBC to be free to exercise its own judgment.[73]

This, to a large extent, has continued to be the policy of succeeding

Governments and has carried the sanction of Parliament. But as the BBC has pointed out, Section 14(4) of the License does provide a means which enables Parliament "to secure the compliance of the Governors on matters to which Parliament attaches basic importance and to have the last word on any issue in which the views of the Governors may be in conflict with those of the Government or of Parliament."

The Government has imposed some specific restrictions on programming. In the interest of maintaining a policy of impartiality, there is a rule, originally adopted in 1927, which forbids the BBC from broadcasting its own opinions on controversial subjects of public importance. In 1955, after much discussion between BBC officials and political leaders, the Postmaster General issued a formal order which stated: "(a) that the Corporation shall not, on any issue, arrange discussion or exparte statements which are to be broadcast during a period of a fortnight before the issue is being debated; (b) that when legislation is introduced in Parliament on any subject, the Corporation shall not, on such subject, arrange broadcasts by any member of Parliament which are to be made during the period between the introduction of the legislation and the time when it either received the Royal assent or is previously withdrawn or dropped."[74]

This notice was the subject of debate in Parliament and the study of a Select Committee. After assurances from the BBC that it would act "within the spirit" of the House of Commons resolution that there should be limitations on such broadcasts, the Postmaster General revoked the order in December 1956.[75]

Political party broadcasts other than those intended for reception throughout the United Kingdom are prohibited, and, unless there is agreement with the main political parties, no such broadcasts designed exclusively for the home services of Scotland and Wales are permitted. In 1961, however, the Postmaster General did allow the BBC to arrange for election broadcasts on behalf of the leading parties in Northern Ireland during a general election of the Northern Ireland Parliament.[76]

In addition to the powers of restraint which may be exercised by the Government, under the terms of the License, the Government may impose some positive obligations on the Corporation. Under Section 14(3), the Government may require the broadcasting of any announcements such as police messages or "emergency" messages concerning public health, welfare and security. Also, the Government requires the BBC to broadcast, on an impartial basis, daily accounts of the proceedings in both Houses of Parliament.

The BBC is not permitted to sell broadcast time and may not carry commercial advertising of any kind. In this connection, the Corporation has stated that it seeks to reconcile a policy of "no advertising" with "the abiding need to provide a full service of news, comments, and information generally," and it avoids giving publicity to any individual person, firm or organized interest "except in so far as this is necessary" to provide informative and effective programs under its Charter.[77]

Current BBC Programming

SINCE the Second World War, the BBC has been providing three programs —the Home Service, the Light Programme and the Third Programme.* Each has a distinct character, and an effort is made to avoid duplication. The general plan is to serve a variety of interests and to cater to minority as well as majority audiences. Programs range from those with an entertainment format attracting a weekly audience of as many as twenty million to others of an informational or didactic nature which may attract only a few thousand.[78]

The Home Service is designed to appeal to the "broad middle section" of the community. While there is some degree of overlapping with the other two programs, it does have its own distinctive characteristics. A heavy component of its daily broadcasts consists of news and reports of parliamentary proceedings. Special attention is given to reporting and analysis of world affairs.

Furthermore, the Home Service includes instructional broadcasts for the schools. These cover a wide range of subjects at the elementary grade levels, and in 1963–64 more than thirty-one thousand schools in the United Kingdom were making regular use of them. In developing these school programs, the BBC relies heavily upon School Broadcasting Councils made up of educational experts, representing all parts of the United Kingdom.

Another feature of the Home Service is its emphasis upon musical programs of great works, and dramatic shows, including stage plays, serials and radio adaptations of popular novels.

The Light Programme is designed to appeal to a large audience, primarily interested in entertainment and relaxation. The broadcasts consist mainly of popular music, comedy, light drama, and frequent, brief news and weather reports.

The Third Network carries what is called the Third Programme, intended for those "whose tastes, education, and mental habits enable them to take pleasure in close and responsible listening to broadcasts of artistic and intellectual distinction." For example, masterpieces of music and drama

---

*Reports from the BBC dated October 31, 1967 reveal that the BBC now has four national radio networks: Radio 1 (a new popular music program); Radio 2 (formerly the Light Programme); Radio 3 (classical music); and Radio 4 (the former Home Service). Also, a two year experiment with local radio has begun. The first local station, BBC Radio Leicester, started November 8, 1967 and will be followed by eight other stations in different parts of England. The regional services remain unchanged.

—Beethoven and Shakespeare—are regularly presented.[79] Special attention is given to experimental drama, news analysis in depth, and analytical discussions of important domestic and foreign affairs.[80]

The Third Network also provides another service known as the Music Programme. This is being introduced in stages and, when fully developed, will provide daily a wide range of high-quality music including orchestral concerts and operas.

Special mention should be made of the "Study Session" broadcast over the Third Network each evening, Monday through Friday, serving groups wishing to increase their knowledge in specialized fields (for example, foreign languages, history, art), and "Sports Service" on Saturday afternoons, with play-by-play broadcasts of games and commentaries on the important sporting events.

The BBC has broadcasting studios in more than a dozen cities in Britain and considerable emphasis is placed upon regional broadcasting. There are three English areas: The Midlands, the West and the North. In addition, Scotland, Wales and Northern Ireland are classified as "National Regions."[81]

The charts on the following pages from the *BBC 1965 Handbook* reflect the content of radio programs in the national and regional services for the year ending March 27, 1964.[82]

BBC Television

THE BBC now provides two television services: BBC-1 and BBC-2. BBC-1, operating on the four hundred and five line standard, began in 1936, was interrupted by the war, but has since been expanded to provide nation-wide coverage. BBC-2, operating with six hundred and twenty-five lines on UHF channels, was initiated in 1964 in London and Southeast England and was extended to the Birmingham area in the autumn of 1964. Present plans envision its expansion to provide nation-wide service.

Headquarters for television production are located at Television Center in West London, where six production and two presentation studios are in use. Plans include the construction of additional facilities for color television which is being introduced in three stages. Initiated in July 1967, full color service was scheduled to begin December 2, 1967. Later, the present four hundred and five line VHF service (BBC-1) will be duplicated with color on six hundred and twenty-five lines UHF.

Besides the Television Center, there are six other production locations in the London area, as well as eight production units and eleven news studios in other regions.

More than eighty-five percent of the television programs are produced

Content of Radio Programmes

Combined Output—London (Analysis by Services)

For the 52 weeks ended 27 March 1964	HOME SERVICE		LIGHT PROGRAMME		THIRD PROGRAMME		THIRD NETWORK		TOTAL	
	Hours	%	Hours	%	Hours	%	Hours	%	Hours	%
Serious Music	1,365	22	176	3	760	52	181	21	2,482	17
Entertainment Music	604	10	3,674	57	8	1	36	1	4,322	29
Light Entertainment	209	3	384	6	—	—	—	—	593	4
Outside Broadcasts	96	2	134	2	—	—	217*	25	447	3
Features	283	5	77	1	146	10	1	—	507	3
Drama	385	6	407	6	207	14	—	—	999	7
News	841	14	648	10	59	4	34	4	1,582	11
Talks	1,026	17	293	5	233	16	36	4	1,588	11
Religious	304	5	105	2	8	1	38	4	455	3
Schools	398	6	—	—	—	—	18	2	416	3
Other Educational	20	—	—	—	—	—	167	19	187	1
Special Minorities	507	8	460	7	—	—	133	16	1,100	7
Miscellaneous	147	2	42	1	30	2	7	1	226	1
	6,185	100	6,400	100	1,451	100	868	100	14,904	100
Presented by London	4,923	79	5,398	84	1,356	93	622	72	12,299	82
Regions	1,262	21	1,002	16	95	7	246	28	2,605	18

*This figure includes 115½ hours of "ball-by-ball" commentaries on Test Matches against West Indies and 71 hours of Saturday sports, which were broadcast in the Third Network wavelength.

Regional Home Services

	MIDLAND	NORTH	WEST	SCOTLAND	WALES	NORTHERN IRELAND	TOTAL
	Hours	*Hours*	*Hours*	*Hours*	*Hours*	*Hours*	*Hours*
Serious Music	157	177	50	363	170	56	973
Entertainment Music	80	91	147	114	74	95	601
Light Entertainment	28	17	—	27	12	—	84
Outside Broadcasts	17	30	25	45	68	20	205
Features	15	13	3	64	31	12	138
Drama	14	19	21	30	20	21	125
News	324	243	456	271	332	125	1,751
Talks	187	191	161	153	180	69	941
Religious	48	48	45	156	183	41	521
Schools	—	3	—	90	83	11	187
Other Educational	—	—	—	—	13	—	13
Special Minorities	142	120	93	146	135	80	716
Miscellaneous	34	18	19	54	55	89	269
	1,046	970	1,020	1,513	1,356	619	6,524

The Welsh-language broadcasts, excluding sports commentaries, for the 52 weeks ended 27 March 1964 amounted to 174 hours.

by the BBC itself, of which about thirteen thousand prints are exported for use in other countries. Since the establishment of Eurovision in 1954, the BBC has been one of the largest suppliers and users of the programs of the Western European TV network.

As reported by the BBC in 1965, the Postmaster General prescribed a limit of fifty hours per week for BBC-1 and thirty for BBC-2. Additional time, however, may be used for special religious and educational broadcasts and for programs in the Welsh language.

The following excerpts from the *BBC 1965 Handbook* provide information regarding the general nature of television programming on both networks:

> . . . While a high proportion of television programmes come under the headings of information and entertainment, over the past year there was a significant increase in educational programmes, as distinct from the schools service.
>
> Among the adult educational series on BBC-1 were "An Introduction to Relativity," "The Science of Man," "Parliamo Italiano," "Money Matters," "The Painter and his World," and practical advice on maintaining a motor car. In "Tuesday Term" on BBC-2 were "Power and British Politics," "100 Years of Marxism," and "Studying the Social Sciences." . . .
>
> Drama on BBC Television presents some hundred different plays a year, many of them specially commissioned, as well as series and serials. . . .
>
> Light Entertainment pursues the policy of finding new talent and producing wider scope for established artists. . . .
>
> Television News is served by staff correspondents in many parts of the world, who are supplemented by reporters and camera teams on special assignments. Every opportunity is taken to speed up reception of news and pictures by the use, when possible, of the transatlantic telephone cable and of communication satellites.
>
> Since the advent of BBC-2 it has been possible to introduce a weekly news magazine for the deaf and hard of hearing, using new methods of presentation, such as simplified captions, and sign language. . . .
>
> But BBC Television as a whole aims to cover the full range of public tastes and interests, to expand the viewer's awareness of the world in which he lives, and to set and maintain high professional standards. . . .[83]

The following charts from the *1965 Handbook* show the percentages of time devoted to national and regional programs:[84]

Regional Programmes: Hours of Television

For the 52 weeks ended 27 March 1964	MID-LAND	NORTH	WEST	SCOT-LAND	WALES	NORTH-ERN IRELAND	TOTAL
	Hours	Hours	Hours	Hours	Hours	Hours	Hours
1. Programmes produced by Regions for their own Service and not taken by the National Network	204	194	262	277	332	131	1,400
2. Programmes produced by Regions for the National Network	136	160	92	62	67	11	528
3. Total Programmes produced by Regions (1) and (2)	340	354	354	339	399	142	1,928
4. Programmes taken by Regions from the National Network and other Regions	3,569	3,555	3,675	3,336	3,423	3,508	21,066
5. Total Regional Programme Hours (1, 2 and 4)	3,909	3,909	4,029	3,675	3,822	3,650	22,994

In addition to the above, 90 hours of News programmes were broadcast on the transmitters covering the London area and South-east England only.

Content of Television Network Programmes

For the 52 weeks ended 27 March 1964	Hours	Per cent
Outside Broadcasts	593	16.8
Talks, Documentaries and other Information Programmes	531	15.0
British and Foreign Feature Films and Series	469	13.3
Drama	380	10.8
Schools Broadcasts	313	8.9
Children's Programmes	290	8.2
Light Entertainment	258	7.3
News, Weather and other News Programmes	217	6.1
Presentation Material	172	4.9
Religious Programmes	141	4.0
Adult Education Programmes	71	2.0
Music	52	1.5
Sport News and Reports	43	1.2
	3,530	100.0

Programmes in Welsh Language carried by all
   Network Transmitters   25

Presented by: London 3,027   Regions 528   3,555

NOTES

1. Charles F. Briggs and Augustus Maverick, *The Story of the Telegraph and History of the Great Atlantic Cable* (New York: Rudd and Carlton, 1958), p. 25.
2. Asa Briggs, *The Birth of Broadcasting: The History of Broadcasting in the United Kingdom* (New York: Oxford University Press, 1961), I, 95.
3. *Wireless Telegraphy Act,* adopted August 15, 1904, 4 *Edward* VII, Chap. 24, *Chiffy's Statutes,* 6th ed.
4. Degna Marconi, *My Father Marconi* (New York: McGraw Hill Book Company, Inc., 1962), pp. 39–43.
5. See Briggs.
6. *Ibid.,* p. 43.
7. *Hansard,* CXXXV, Col. 204, November 23, 1920.
8. *Wireless World,* January 21, 1922.
9. Marconi Company Archives.
10. Briggs, I, 58.
11. Terence H. O'Brien, *British Experiments in Public Ownership and Control* (London: George Allen and Unwin, Ltd., 1937), p. 98.
12. *Cmnd.* 1822/1923.
13. O'Brien, pp. 99–100.

14. Briggs, I, 146–147.
15. *Ibid.*
16. *Ibid.*, I, 145–183. Also, see Burton Paulu, *British Broadcasting: Radio and Television in the United Kingdom* (Minneapolis: University of Minnesota Press, 1956), pp. 9–11.
17. See §§ 14–20, *Sykes Report*, for discussion of factors leading to the appointment of the Committee.
18. *Ibid.*, §§ 4, 6.
19. *Supplementary Agreement: Wireless Broadcasting License, Cmnd.* 1976.
20. O'Brien, p. 105.
21. *Report of Crawford Committee 1925*, p. 2, *Cmnd.* 2599/1926.
22. See O'Brien, pp. 107–110, for discussion of this point. Also, see 199 *H. C. Deb.*, 5 s. pp. 1563–1650, for debate in Parliament on establishment of the Corporation.
23. Paulu, *British Broadcasting: Radio and Television in the United Kingdom*, p. 12.
24. *Ibid.*, p. 12. Also, see *BBC 1965 Handbook*, British Broadcasting Corporation (Broadcasting House, London W. 1).
25. See H. H. Wilson, *Pressure Group: The Campaign for Commercial Television in England* (New Brunswick: Rutgers University Press, 1961), p. 22.
26. *Annual 1935*, p. 131.
27. Wilson, pp. 22–23.
28. Paulu, *British Broadcasting: Radio and Television in the United Kingdom*, p. 391.
29. *Ibid.*, p. 392.
30. *Beveridge Report II*, p. 25.
31. *Wilson*, p. 24.
32. *Report of the Broadcasting Committee 1949, Cmnd.* 8116; *Appendix H; Memoranda Submitted to the Committee, Cmnd.* 8117.
33. *Cmnd.* 8291.
34. See Wilson for a detailed account of this back-bench triumph.
35. *1952 White Paper*, §§ 4–11.
36. *H. L. Debs.*, May 22–26, 1952, 176: 1293–1451.
37. *Ibid.*, pp. 502, 213–342.
38. *Ibid.*, June 23, 1952, 502, 1936.
39. See Wilson, pp. 127–128.
40. *Ibid.*, pp. 128–150.
41. Wilson's informative and well-written history appears in Chaps. VI–VIII.
42. *ITV 1965, A Guide to Independent Television*, Independent Television Authority (10 Brompton Road, London, S. W. 3), January 1965, p. 24.
43. *Ibid.*
44. Burton Paulu, *British Broadcasting in Transition* (Minneapolis: University of Minnesota Press, 1961), pp. 207–208.
45. For example, see sermon of Reverend H. W. Montetoire, "The Pilkington Report," delivered on July 29, 1962, in the University Church, Cambridge, England.
46. *Cmnd.* 1724, July 29, 1964.
47. See *H. C. Deb.*, 145: 1402–1406, July 13, 1960; also, see *The Times* (London), July 14, 1960, p. 3.
48. *Report of Committee on Broadcasting 1960, Cmnd.* 1753, June 1962.
49. *Ibid.*
50. *Ibid.*
51. *Ibid.*

52. *The Times,* June 28, 1962, p. 8.
53. *Report of Committee on Broadcasting 1960.*
54. See *The Times,* June 28, 1962; *Manchester Guardian,* July 5, 1962; *Evening Standard,* June 27 and July 18, 1962; and *The Evening News,* June 27, 1962.
55. For example, see sermon of H. W. Montetoire.
56. *ITV 1965, A Guide to Independent Television,* pp. 13–14.
57. *Ibid.,* p. 17.
58. *Ibid.*
59. *Ibid.*
60. *Ibid.,* p. 18.
61. *Ibid.,* p. 59.
62. *Ibid.,* p. 18.
63. *Ibid.*
64. *Ibid.,* pp. 19–20.
65. *The Independent Television Code of Advertising Standards and Practice,* 1st ed., July 1964, § 1.
66. *ITV 1965, A Guide to Independent Television,* p. 21.
67. *Ibid.,* p. 22.
68. *BBC 1965 Handbook,* p. 131.
69. *Ibid.,* p. 123.
70. These figures are for 1963–64; at that time, the pound was valued at $2.80.
71. *BBC 1965 Handbook,* p. 160.
72. *Ibid.*
73. *Ibid.,* p. 126.
74. *Ibid.*
75. *Ibid.*
76. *Ibid.,* pp. 128–129.
77. *Ibid.,* p. 130.
78. *Ibid.,* p. 49.
79. *Ibid.,* pp. 51–52.
80. *Ibid.,* p. 64.
81. Cohn Shaw, "The Regional Structure of the BBC," an excellent article in the *EBU Review,* 90B, March 1965, pp. 13–17.
82. *BBC 1965 Handbook,* pp. 52–53.
83. *Ibid.,* p. 38.
84. *Ibid.,* pp. 42–43.

VI

Ireland: Independence
and Nationalism

THE IRISH FREE STATE, consisting of twenty-six southern counties, was established as a Dominion in 1922, with the six northern counties remaining part of the United Kingdom, a separation which Ireland has never officially recognized. A new constitution, adopted by a plebiscite, became effective in 1937. It declared Ireland to be a sovereign democratic state and gave it the name of *Eire*.[1]

Article XL(i) of the Constitution guarantees citizens the right to express freely their convictions, but "the education of public opinion being, however, a matter of such grave import to the common good, the State shall endeavor to ensure that organs of public opinion, such as the radio, the press, the cinema, while preserving their rightful liberty of expression, including criticism of Government policy, shall not be used to undermine public order or morality or the authority of the State." The Article further declares that "the publication or utterance of blasphemous, seditious, or indecent matter is an offence which shall be punishable in accordance with law."

Early Regulation of Wireless Communication

THE British Wireless Telegraphy Acts of 1904 and 1906 gave the U.K. Minister of Posts and Telegraphs regulatory authority over wireless communication throughout the British Isles. With the coming of independence it was necessary to pass a new law repealing these earlier statutes and extending the new Government's authority to broadcasting. This was passed in 1926.[2] Part II of the 1926 law provided that the Minister of Posts and Telegraphs, with the approval of the Minister of Finance, might acquire or establish broadcasting stations and operate them as he saw fit. He was also empowered to charge fees for the distribution of programs, the fees to be determined by him with the sanction of the Minister of Finance.

Furthermore, the law required that the Minister establish by order an advisory committee to assist him in the operation of the stations, including "the selection and control of broadcast matter distributed."[3] It was prescribed that this committee should consist of at least five members, appointed for two year terms, one of whom was to be nominated by the Minister of Education, one by the Minister for Lands and Agriculture and the remaining three by the Minister of Posts and Telegraphs.

Early History of Broadcasting

THE first broadcasting station in Ireland was established in Dublin in 1926 with the call letters 2RN and a power of one kilowatt. This station came to be known as *Radio Éireann*. A second station with one kilowatt transmitting power was established in Cork in 1927. This was followed by the installation in 1932 of the main transmitter (one hundred kilowatts) for the national program in Athlone. Following the Second World War, the power of these transmitters was increased to provide an efficient, nationwide network service.

Radio Éireann was reorganized in 1953. A radio council (*Comhairle Radio Éireann*) was established to advise and assist the Minister of Posts and Telegraphs in the conduct of the broadcasting service. This council had no legal status but was a creation of the Minister under the broad, discretionary authority granted him by the 1926 law. It functioned in a supervisory fashion under his direction, was permitted to recruit a staff without going to the Civil Service Commission as was previously required and, with some reservations, could spend money without authorization from the Ministry of Finance.

This move toward greater autonomy resulted in improved efficiency and more effective programming. In early 1955, the officials of *Radio Éireann* reported on its organization and programming. They pointed out that the organization comprised "the usual divisions of Programme, Engineering and Administration," and that within the Programme Division there were "sections of music, talks and features, drama and variety productions, children's programmes, news and some smaller sections."[4]

Reference was made to the *Radio Éireann* Symphony Orchestra of seventy musicians which gave public concerts twice a week in Dublin and occasionally in other parts of the country. Other sources of programming included a light orchestra of twenty-seven members and a repertory company of twenty-four actors which presented plays in both Irish and English.

Other types of programming which were emphasized included local, national and international news prepared by a large staff of reporters, feature writers and others.

A Study Commission Appointed

As the years passed it became increasingly evident that the radio organization needed to be stabilized and improved. Administrative functions were
not clearly defined and job security for a majority of the employees was
tenuous. Added to this was the need to provide for expanded facilities
with authority to develop and operate a television system.

Recognizing these needs, the Minister of Posts and Telegraphs, on March
26, 1958, appointed a study commission, with a mandate to review the
whole broadcasting situation and come up with recommendations regarding
the following questions:

(1) the practicability of establishing a television service,

(2) the arrangements that can be made to ensure that the television system
will be owned by the State, either from the outset or after an interval,

(3) the proposals that have been made to the Department of Posts and Telegraphs and any further proposals that may be received,

(4) the powers and duties of the television authority and the manner of its
constitution,

(5) the special arrangements that should be made

(a) to provide for the use of the Irish language and for the adequate
reflection of the national outlook and culture and

(b) to govern the presentation of information and news in the television
service,

(6) any other relevant matters to which the Commission deems it advisable
to draw attention.[5]

The Commission Reports

THE Commission made its report in 1959. At the outset, television's importance as an educational medium was recognized. "Properly managed,"
said the Commission, "television can bring into the home entertainment
of a kind that is ordinarily beyond the reach of most, and more important,
can impart a breadth of knowledge of history, world affairs, art, science
and crafts hitherto unknown and completely unattainable by the public
generally before the advent of television."[6]

The Commission reported on the personnel and financial situation of
Radio Éireann.

The staff of Radio Éireann is now 377 persons, including 28 actors, 97
members of the orchestra and 10 singers. The members of the staff are civil

servants. The majority are unestablished, and under present circumstances are incapable of being established, and consequently are not pensionable. Though unestablished, there are certain members of the staff with at least 15 years service who are entitled to get gratuity on retirement based on the number of years service. The Commission was informed that one of the disquieting things about Radio Éireann was that at present the majority of the staff are very dissatisfied due to the fact that they cannot become established. This position is aggravated by the fact that this majority are employed side by side with a minority who were recruited from other branches of the Civil Service and having retained their established Civil Service status are eligible for pension.

The Radio Éireann Staff Panel is apprehensive as to what may happen to people at present employed by Radio Éireann if it should be decided that the control of Radio Éireann should be taken over by some form of public authority outside the Civil Service. The Commission would assume that in any reorganization of the structure of the radio organization no person at present employed by Radio Éireann would suffer in the conditions of his employment, and that the rights of unestablished civil servants entitled to a gratuity on retirement would be protected, but the Commission does not feel called upon to deal with the conditions of employment under such public authority.

The present broad financial structure of Radio Éireann is that the total of license fees and sponsored programme fees amounts to approximately 529,000 pounds. The sum just about meets requirements for normal operation but allows no provision to be made for capital or interest. Radio Éireann is not in fact charged the amount which it costs the Post Office to collect the license revenue, which the Commission was informed was the very large sum of 105,000 pounds per annum. Radio Éireann in addition gets services from other Government Departments valued at approximately 26,000 pounds without actual cost to Radio Éireann. The revenue from sponsored programmes is about 90,000 pounds per annum. The general opinion is that all or some of this advertising revenue would be lost on the advent of a commercial television service.

Radio Éireann considers the premises at present available to it unsuitable. It was strongly represented on behalf of Radio Éireann that television and radio should be controlled by a joint authority. It was submitted that it would be a desirable thing to get integration, in order to share resources instead of competing for them and to make the most economical use of the limited resources available in Ireland. Radio Éireann has found it difficult to build up and keep together the qualified staff it has, as, for instance, the hundred professional musicians, some of whom have had to be recruited outside Ireland.[7]

Commission Recommendations

THE Commission recommended that the Government provide for the establishment of television; that two separate, independent public bodies be created, and that, for "some years to come," one control radio and the other television. The Commission thought, however, that eventually the control of both media should be centralized in one public authority.

The Commission further proposed that television be financed largely from commercial advertising, but expressed these reservations and conditions:

> . . . Experience tends to suggest that commercial forces have an undesirable influence on programme performance. This influence is not necessarily direct, but often stems indirectly from the demands of advertisers. A private organization, however anxious its individual members may be to provide worthwhile programmes, will, on account of these forces, be primarily interested in reaching the largest possible audience most of the time, and with programmes intended primarily for mass entertainment. It will therefore be faced with a conflict of interests and motives, namely, whether to try and serve the public interest by treating television as much more than just another medium of mass entertainment, or to endeavor to please its advertisers by attracting maximum audiences and at the same time make greater profits for itself. It is, therefore, imperative that if television provided by a private organization is to serve the public interest, there must be externally enforced standards in order to counter the influence of commercial pressures. If the control is not effective, commercial pressure will probably prevail to the detriment of the programme material.[8]

A Broadcasting Authority Established

FOLLOWING submission of the Commission's report, Parliament passed a law in 1960, enabling the establishment of an authority to provide a national television and sound broadcasting service.[9] The same name, *Radio Éireann,* used to identify the previous radio organization, was given to the new authority, which, since the introduction of television, has been known as *Radio Telefis Éireann.*

The law provided that the Authority should be a corporate body, composed of not less than seven and not more than nine members appointed by the Government, with terms of office not exceeding five years.

Section 16(2) vests the Authority with the following powers:

(a) to establish, maintain and operate broadcasting stations and to acquire, install and operate apparatus for wireless telegraphy;

(b) to provide, by arrangements made for the purpose with the Minister and any other person, for the distribution, by means of relaying, of programmes broadcast by the Authority;

(c) to originate programmes and procure programmes from any source;

(d) to make contracts, agreements and arrangements incidental or conducive to the objects of the Authority;

(e) to acquire and make use of copyrights, patents, licenses, privileges and concessions;

(f) to collect news and information and to subscribe to news services and such other services as may be conducive to the objects of the Authority;

(g) to subscribe to such international associations, and to such educational, musical and dramatic bodies and such other bodies promoting entertainment of culture, as may be conducive to the objects of the Authority;

(h) to arrange, with other broadcasting authorities for the receipt, exchange and relay of programmes;

(i) to organise, provide and subsidize concerts and other entertainments in connection with the broadcasting service or for any purpose incidental thereto and, in relation to any such concert or entertainment, to provide or procure accommodation and, if desired, to make charges for admission;

(j) subject to the consent of the Minister, to prepare, publish and distribute, with or without charge, such magazines, books, papers and other printed matter as may seem to the Authority to be conducive or incidental to its objects;

(k) subject to the consent of the Minister, to compile, publish, distribute, sell and exchange recorded aural and visual material.[10]

The Authority may appoint a Director General and other personnel needed, but none may be employed except by public competition. A retirement system, subject to the approval of the Minister of Posts and Telegraphs, was made mandatory in Section 15 of the Act.

Programming Requirements

THE law imposed a number of restrictions and conditions on programming. For example, it was prescribed that "in performing its function, the Authority shall bear constantly in mind the national aims of restoring the Irish language and preserving and developing the national culture and shall endeavor to promote the attainment of those aims."[11]

Section 18 states that "any information, news or feature which relates to matters of public controversy or is subject to current public debate," must be presented "objectively and impartially and without any expression of the Authority's own views."

Furthermore, the Authority is prohibited from accepting any advertisement which is "directed towards any religious or political end or has any relation to any industrial dispute." Priority for Irish advertising is emphasized and the Authority is empowered to fix reduced charges and preferential conditions for such advertising.

Ministerial Powers

THE law provides that the Authority may not operate without a license granted by the Minister of Posts and Telegraphs and in accordance with conditions prescribed by him. In the event of a "national emergency," the Minister is empowered to suspend the license and, while the suspension continues, to assume active control of the broadcast operations.[12]

He is vested with general, regulatory power, and the operations of *Radio Telefís Éireann* (RTE) are subject to rules which he promulgates. The Minister recommends to Parliament the terms of employment and the remuneration of members of the Authority, approves periods of time for broadcasting as proposed; and on recommendation from the Authority, determines the amount of time to be devoted to commercials and their distribution throughout the program schedules.

Section 21 of the statute states that the Minister may direct the Authority in writing to refrain from broadcasting any particular matter or material of any particular class, and may require the allocation of broadcasting time for any announcements by or on behalf of any Minister of State in connection with the functions of his office.

To insure that the Authority has expert advice in the performance of its functions, the Minister, after consultation with the Authority, may from time to time appoint advisory committees. These committees, each consisting of at least three members, meet whenever called together by the Minister or by the Authority. While the Authority and the Director General are required to consider the advice of these committees, they are not bound to follow it.

The Minister of Finance also plays an important role in the Authority's operations. Any plans for pensions, gratuities or allowances must have his approval. The law specifies that the Minister of Posts and Telegraphs may pay each year to the Authority, out of monies provided by the Parliament, an amount equal to the total receipts derived that year from broadcasting license fees and any other expenses incurred in connection with the functions of his office. All these disbursements, however, must first be approved by the Minister of Finance.

Furthermore, upon recommendation of the Minister of Posts and Telegraphs, the Minister of Finance is empowered to make advances to the Authority for capital purposes, not to exceed two (now three) million pounds in the aggregate, and may specify the terms and conditions for repayment.[13] He must be consulted about the establishment of any system by which the Authority keeps its accounts, and the method by which they are audited.

Section 27 of the law empowers the Authority to borrow money by "the creation of stock or other forms of security," but any such transaction must have the consent of both the Minister of Posts and Telegraphs and the Minister of Finance.

Current Facilities

SINCE the establishment of the Authority, Irish broadcasting has made considerable progress. The radio studios and the technical staff are housed in the General Post Office Building in Dublin. Work on new buildings and transmitters to replace the old in Dublin and Cork was begun in 1966. In addition to the nation-wide service provided by the medium-wave transmitters at Athlone, Dublin and Cork, a VHF radio network is presently under construction.[14] In 1965, there were 555,409 licensed receivers. Of these, 258,837 were sound receivers only. The remaining 296,572 were of the combination type, with both radio and TV.[15]

The construction of television studios was started on twenty-two acres at Donnybrook in 1960; on December 31, 1961, regular television was initiated.[16] Since then, TV facilities have been expanded and a nation-wide network is now in operation, with five main high-power transmitters and thirteen satellite transposers. National coverage is estimated to be ninety-eight percent of the population.[17] The national technical standard (six hundred and twenty-five lines) conforms to that used by most of the Western European countries, but programs are also broadcast on the four hundred and five line standard from the Kippure and Truskmore transmitters to serve listeners in the eastern, northern and northwestern areas.

Except for outside programs (Eurovision, for example), all television transmissions originate at the central RTE location in Donnybrook, Dublin. There are two spacious and fully equipped studios used for drama, light entertainment and elaborate productions. A third, more modest in size, is used mainly for interviews and other unpretentious shows.

As of September 1966, *Radio Telefís Éireann* had a staff of more than eleven hundred, made up of writers, journalists, musicians, actors, singers, artists, program planners and producers, the technical staff, and a large number concerned with administration, sales and publications.[18]

Programming Philosophy

IN the Third Annual Report (1963), the Authority stated its general program philosophy:

> Radio Éireann . . . believes that broadcasting has a positive role in public life which transcends, but includes, the provision of entertainment. The serv-

ice must maintain contact at all times with a mass audience, and its need for commercial revenue will ensure that it does so.

It does not follow that its duty is to please most of the people all of the time. It must have regard to the needs and rights of the smaller sections of the community. It must not, however, allow the interests of organised minorities to override the wishes of the unorganised majority. . . .

In particular, Radio Éireann continues to keep in mind its special responsibility toward the Irish language and the preservation and development of the national culture. . . .

The Broadcasting Authority Act, 1960, requires the Authority to be impartial in matters of public controversy. Such impartiality is fundamental to the concept of a national service; a complimentary duty, which must equally be recognized is to bring issues of controversy and debate before the public. Freedom of the press is secured, very largely, by the existence of different journals of varying opinions, which act as a check and balance one upon the other. In a single national broadcasting service, where no such checks exist, it is of the greatest importance that all necessary steps be taken to ensure that conflicting interests and viewpoints shall be fairly represented.

Broadcasting is one of the miracles of the twentieth century, but it is a miracle of technology only. The influence it may have, for good or ill, depends on the use that is made of it. The *Oireachtas* has set up Radio Éireann as a national service, it is the Authority's intention to fulfil this.[19]

Radio Service

A RECENT report of *Radio Telefís Éireann* indicated that radio programs are broadcast from medium-wave transmitters at Athlone, Dublin and Cork. Normally, one program is broadcast on all three stations, but the intention is to carry it also on the VHF service which is being developed.[20]

RTE now has a repertory company of twenty-eight actors. It also maintains a symphony orchestra of seventy-one musicians, a light orchestra of thirty-two players, a choir of ten singers and a string quartet. Broadcasts are presented both in Irish and English. Drama constitutes a substantial portion of the radio output, and in 1961 and 1965, the repertory company won the *Prix Italia,* the outstanding European award for radio drama.

The two orchestras broadcast regularly. The symphony is the only full-time one in Ireland, gives many concerts throughout the year, takes part in two opera seasons each year under the auspices of the Dublin Grand Opera Society, and gives regular public concerts for school children. Actually, the RTE Symphony is the national orchestra and contributes greatly to the cultural life of Ireland.[21]

As reported and classified by RTE, its program output for the year 1964–65 showed the following pattern:[22]

	Hours	Percent
Music	892	21
Talks and Features	443	10
Plays	185	4
Variety	194	5
News (Irish)	197	5
News (English)	648	15
Sponsored	1031	25
Religious Services	82	2
Children's	329	8
Sport	153	4
Women's	40	1

Television Service

Television programs are broadcast approximately forty-four hours per week. Two and a half hours of this are used to transmit special programs to the schools. As of September 1966, half of the RTE programming was "home-produced," covering news and current affairs, light entertainment, drama and documentaries, children's programs and sports.[23]

An analysis of the TV program schedules for the year 1964–65 showed the following percentages of time devoted to different program types as classified by RTE:[24]

Home Originated	Hours	Percent
News	182	8
Public Affairs and Religious	391	17
Sports	133	6
Light Entertainment	280	12
Children's	110	5
Women's	33	1
Drama	56	2
Schools Broadcasts	68	3
Total	1253	54

Imported	Hours	Percent
Detective/Adventure	105	4
Comedy	202	9
General Drama	373	16
Light Entertainment	59	2
Westerns	96	4
Children's	79	3
Documentaries and Public Affairs	115	5
Sports	64	3
Total	1093	46

Radio Telefís Éireann is affiliated with the European Broadcasting Union and receives programs from abroad via Eurovision. It also produces programs which are carried by the network. The first live sports event broadcast from Europe to the United States by means of space satellite was that of the 1965 Hospitals Sweep Derby at Curragh, County Kildare.[25]

Financing

THE 1960 Broadcasting Authority Act requires that the RTE be self-supporting; that it conduct its affairs so that its revenue is sufficient to pay for all operations and provide for capital expenditures. The Authority has two main sources of income—license fees and advertising. The fees are determined by the Minister of Posts and Telegraphs and collected by the Post Office. The annual license fee for a combination radio and TV receiver is five pounds. These fees constitute less than half of the Authority's income, the remainder coming from advertising which has doubled since 1963.[26]

Earned surpluses have been used to expand technical facilities and help provide a new FM service. The Exchequer, however, has provided most of the funds for capital expenditures. Interest bearing loans are made to the Authority. As previously indicated, the statutory limit of these advances is three million pounds. As of March 31, 1966, the Authority had drawn £1,816,000, although at that time capital investment by the Authority was almost twice that amount.[27]

NOTES

1. *Constitution of Ireland,* Article IV (Government Publications Sale Office, G. P. O. Arcade, Dublin), p. 4. Also, Brian Inglis, *The Story of Ireland* (London: Faber and Faber, 1956), p. 215.
2. Wireless Telegraph Act, 1926; approved December 24, 1926. *Irish Free State, Public General Acts;* passed by *Oireachtas of Saorstát Éireann,* 1926, Dublin, No. 45, pp. 565–589.
3. *Ibid.,* Part II, Section 19.
4. *EBU Bulletin,* March-April 1955, p. 103.
5. *Report of the Television Commission,* 1959 (Dublin: Stationery Office), pp. 5–6.
6. *Ibid.,* pp. 11–12.
7. *Ibid.,* p. 31.
8. *Ibid.,* p. 22.
9. *Broadcasting Authority Act,* 1960, No. 10 (Dublin: Stationery Office).
10. *Ibid.,* pp. 21–22.

11. *Ibid.*, Section 17, p. 23.
12. *Ibid.*, Section 16(3) (a) and (b), p. 23.
13. As of January 1968, the Irish pound was equivalent to $2.80.
14. *Radio Telefís Éireann,* "The Irish Broadcasting Service," *EBU Review,* 99B, September 1966, pp. 14, 17.
15. *EBU Review,* 96B, March 1966, p. 37.
16. *Ibid.,* 99B, September 1966, p. 14.
17. *Ibid.,* p. 15.
18. *Ibid.*
19. *Radio Éireann, Third Annual Report,* 1963, p. 9.
20. *EBU Review,* 99B, September 1966, p. 15.
21. *Ibid.*
22. *Ibid.* As of November 1967, the program output was about the same (letter from *Radio Telefís Éireann,* November 2, 1967).
23. *Ibid.,* p. 16.
24. *Ibid.*
25. *Ibid.*
26. *Ibid.,* p. 17.
27. *Ibid.*

· C ·

THE BENELUX COUNTRIES

VII

Belgium: Cultural Duality

FLEMINGS AND WALLOONS MAKE UP the bulk of the Belgian population.
Their racial backgrounds and mother tongues are vastly different, and
they have vigorously resisted all efforts toward cultural amalgamation.
This, however, has not prevented them from developing a community and
national life. For economic reasons, as well as national stability, both
groups have found it necessary to cooperate.[1]

The problem of language, however, has provoked some tempestuous
controversy. For example, representatives of the Flemish-speaking people
in Parliament have insisted that their mother tongue have equal status
with French. The achievement of this equality is the result of a long and
arduous struggle and has been accompanied by a persisting bitterness. In
all other important areas of Belgian life the same equality has been demanded, and granted.

A Belgian writer has described it in this way:

> Can you imagine a Parliament where every word—except the insults (those
> words everybody understands instinctively)—has to be translated? Or a
> religion in which, 20 miles from his home, a parishioner cannot follow the
> sermon and may be absolved without being sure that his confession has been
> understood? Or courts of justice where the accused, if arrested in a place but
> two hours' walk from his dwelling, may well be unable to prove his innocence
> because he does not speak his judge's language? Or an army where regiments
> march side by side to songs whose words are unintelligible to half of the men?
> Or factories where foremen must give their directions in two different
> languages? Governing such a state has its problems. Most of them costly.[2]

To meet the unyielding demands of these two groups, there must be a
double set of schools (elementary, secondary and university), each promoting its own culture and language with little concern for those of the
other. Newspapers, magazines and books necessarily have limited circulation.[3] Those who read Flemish publications are not exposed to (and
generally have little interest in) what is written in French, and vice versa.
This situation, of course, has not been conducive to intercultural relations.

It is therefore understandable that the Belgian system of broadcasting
is what it is—a system which recognizes the cultural and linguistic autonomy of both Flemish and French groups and which provides separate
channels of communication.

Early Years of Radio

THE first law concerning radio communication in Belgium was passed in July 1908, after the Berlin Conference which established the first general convention on wireless telegraphy.[4] Experimental broadcasts were conducted by amateurs prior to 1914, but these operations were suspended by the Government during the First World War.

Following cessation of hostilities, private enterprise was allowed to enter the radio field. In 1923, *Radio Belgique,* a corporation with capital subscribed by industry and banking establishments, was authorized by the Government to provide the first regular commercial broadcast service. Several years later, a second company, *N. V. Radio,* was licensed. These two stations, broadcasting in French and Dutch respectively, were supported by revenue from advertising and voluntary contributions from listeners.[5]

As was true in some other parts of Europe, radio developed rapidly in Belgium during the twenties. Government officials and other leaders increasingly realized its potential for public service. The international radio conference held in Prague in 1929 allocated two wave lengths for exclusive use in Belgium and a third one to be shared with other countries.[6] To justify retention of these frequencies, Belgian officials were eager to activate them as soon as possible.

Institut National Belge de Radiodiffusion

IN accordance with this purpose, Parliament established a new public corporation, the *Institut National Belge de Radiodiffusion* (INR/NIR),* and assigned to it the three available wave lengths. On June 18, 1930, Parliament passed a new law, setting forth the general principles by which the *Institut* was to be governed.[7] Ten days later, these principles were implemented by Royal Decree.[8]

This new legislation gave the *Institut* a monopoly. The installation and operation of transmitting and receiving equipment was subject to authorization by the *Ministre des Postes, Télégraphes et Téléphones,* with a new set of regulations administered by this Ministry. The commercial stations were permitted to operate until 1931, at which time their installations were taken over by the *Institut* as authorized by the 1930 law.[9]

Albert Namurois, legal adviser to *Radiodiffusion–Télévision Belge,* the

---

*INR represents *Institut National Belge de Radiodiffusion* and NIR represents *National Institut Voor Radio-Omroep.*

successor to INR/NIR, has written that the reasons for the change from a private, commercial system to a public one were twofold. First was the need to "occupy the wave lengths as soon as possible with sufficient power to discourage any other countries that might take a fancy to them." Furthermore, "in consideration of the fact that broadcasting has a public mission to perform that is incompatible with a private business operation," public authorities ought to "take a hand in this powerful medium of communication."[10] Parliament also wanted to guarantee that segments of society other than the Government had the opportunity to broadcast, and specified in the law that the *Institut* was required to allocate air time to organizations, groups and individuals having messages of interest to the public.

Administration and Financial Support of INR/NIR

THE law provided that INR/NIR should be administered by a Board of Governors, presided over by the Minister of Posts, Telegraphs and Telephones. There were nine members (subsequently the number was increased to sixteen): three appointed by the Government, three by the Senate, and three by the House of Representatives, each for a six year term. As the *Institut* was then constituted, the Minister played an important role in determining policies and conducting the *Institut's* affairs. This pattern of control was typical in Europe during radio's early period.[11]

The statute authorized the *Institut* to operate for twelve years. It was to be financed largely from two sources: a state grant equal to ninety percent of the estimated proceeds from an annual license tax levied on all receivers, and a grant equal to the estimated tax revenue on the sale of radio tubes and other parts. The *Institut* was also permitted to accept gifts and legacies, and could negotiate loans if necessary.

The 1930 Act contained some specific provisions relating to programs. The *Institut* was forbidden to broadcast commercials. Programs were prohibited which were contrary to law and order or the mores of the community, or which would "outrage" the widely held beliefs of listeners or offend foreign states.

The Royal Decree, which implemented the Act, specified that the *Institut* had a responsibility to provide educational programs and a strictly objective service. The Decree further prescribed that twelve hours of broadcast time per month were to be made available to the Government for official communications. And, in line with parliamentary concern for linguistic and cultural duality, broadcasts must "respect each of the national languages equally."[12]

The law stated that in planning its program service, the *Institut* should utilize the resources of organizations whose messages might be of special interest. Pursuant to this mandate, the *Institut* arranged broadcast time for a number of French-speaking political groups, namely *Radio Catholique Belge, Solidra (Société Liberalede Radiodiffusion), Resef (Radio Socialiste D'Expression Française)*; and similar Flemish organizations, *Katholieke Vlaamse Radio Omroep, Librado* and *Sarov*. Two other nonpolitical groups, *Radio Wallonie* and VLANARA (*Vlaamse Nationale Omroep*), were also assigned time. While these organizations were subject to the law and regulations, they did have a reasonable amount of autonomy. This minimized the effect of the monopoly and assured a broad participation. Both Flemish and French groups would have equal access to the microphone, each presenting programs in its own language and promoting its own culture.

The War Years

FOR ten years, INR/NIR functioned under the 1930 statute and the regulations based upon it. Broadcasting hours were increased, program quality improved, and the physical facilities enlarged. The completion of its Broadcasting House (*La Maison de la Radio Belge*) in 1937 gave the *Institut* attractive studios and office space for its program and administrative personnel, and one of the best transmitting installations in Europe. This structure is still the center for broadcasting service in Belgium; additional facilities have met the needs of a vastly expanded operation.

The German invasion in 1940 disrupted broadcasting. On July 31, 1940, the *Institut* and all its functions were taken over by an administrative commission under the direction of the German Military Government. Some of its staff withdrew to France with the Brussels Government and continued broadcasting for a short time with makeshift equipment.[13] The exiled Belgian Council of Ministers, in a legislative decree of October 13, 1942, established an official wartime agency, the *Office de Radiodiffusion Nationale Belge* (RNB/BNRO),* with headquarters in London.[14] It was administered by a board of directors appointed by the Belgian Government and broadcast programs over a fifty kilowatt transmitter in Leopoldville (Belgian Congo), as well as on wave lengths from London.

Postwar Developments in Radio Control

FOR a brief period following the war, INR/NIR and RNB/BNRO maintained a joint operation, with INR/NIR responsible for technical trans-

---

*RNB represents *Office de Radiodiffusion Nationale Belge* and BNRO represents *Belgische Nationale Radio-Omroep*.

mission and RNB/BNRO in charge of programming. On September 14, 1945, legislation terminated the RNB/BNRO operation and authorized the INR/NIR to conduct the total broadcasting service as it had done prior to the war.[15] The basic provisions of the 1930 statute were reconfirmed, although some modifications of the organization and administration of the *Institut* were made.

The number of the Board of Directors was increased from nine to sixteen with ten appointed by the Government, three by the Senate and three by the House of Representatives. The organization was structured with three main departments, two concerned with the production of Flemish and French programs respectively, and a third responsible for the technical operations of both. Under the combined leadership of the directors, there was a unit for foreign broadcasts and for the organization and maintenance of services such as the symphony orchestra and recording library in which the Flemish and French personnel had a common interest.

Radio Programs

WITH this organization and with increased revenue from the fees on receivers, Belgian radio made much progress in the next fifteen years. Transmission facilities were greatly extended and improved to provide more efficient reception by listeners throughout the country. New and outstanding talent was brought before the microphones, providing a wide variety of quality programs—symphonic and light music, domestic and foreign news and commentaries, classical and contemporary drama, literary and religious features, and sports.

Educational radio received a special boost from the new INR leadership. School broadcasting had been initiated on an experimental basis prior to the war. As early as 1928, a commercial firm was attempting to interest educators in the possibilities of using radio in the classroom. Some instructional broadcasts were carried by *Radio Belgique* in 1930, and in 1931 the Minister of Arts and Sciences set up a commission to study the educational uses of radio. On the basis of the commission's report, INR/NIR, in collaboration with the Ministry of Education, conducted a series of educational programs from 1932 to 1935. Thereafter, the *Institut* established a School Broadcasting Secretariat which worked closely with the Ministry of Education to provide instructional radio until 1940. At the time of the German invasion, there were four hundred and fifty schools using the radio lessons broadcast from Brussels.[16] After the war, new emphasis was put on educational radio, and separate services were created to provide instruction in Flemish and French.

A special effort was made to enlist the support and advice of the school administrators and teachers. An advisory committee representing both private and public education was established to determine program objectives and standards. French educational leaders were careful to stress that radio was a tool and not a substitute for the instructor:

> School broadcasting is a new tool which we must learn to use. . . . While the choice of programs is obviously of paramount importance, we in the studios shall always have need of the sympathetic atmosphere which the teacher must create in his class. There can be no school broadcasts without the cooperation of the schools.[17]

Similarly, Flemish leadership stated:

> It must first be realized that school broadcasts cannot and must not in any circumstances compete with school teaching. We make no claim to take the place of ordinary teaching. . . . What we want to do is not to take the teacher's place but to supply him with teaching material that he can use to illustrate his lessons.[18]

By 1948, more than sixteeen hundred schools were using the instructional broadcasts. Foreign languages, the sciences, history and music were a few of the subjects taught. The broadcasts were being used not only by Flemish and Walloon schools, but also by schools in France, the Netherlands, Germany and even Wales.[19]

Beginnings of Television

THE 1930 Act had authorized INR/NIR to provide television as well as radio programs, but a regular television service was not initiated until 1953. Following the Second World War, Belgian authorities gave serious attention to the problems of developing the new medium. One of the big issues was whether to adopt the eight hundred and nineteen or the six hundred and twenty-five line system for TV transmission. After much discussion, a compromise was reached. Both standards would be used: French programs would be telecast with eight hundred and nineteen line definition, and Flemish programs with six hundred and twenty-five lines.[20]

In June 1952, the Stockholm Conference allocated channels accordingly, and in September it was announced that the *Institut* had been instructed to begin the preparation of programs. The first telecasts were presented on October 31, 1953, with much fanfare in the Belgian press.[21] The program schedules were limited to about twelve hours per week for each of the linguistic groups, but by 1960 these hours had been almost tripled, and the number of television receivers had grown to almost four hundred thousand, a remarkable figure for a country with less than nine million people.

Although some writers had urged that the Government consider authorizing commercial television,[22] Parliament refused to sanction any type of advertising. The *Institut,* therefore, was largely dependent upon annual fees levied against the owners of television receivers. The original assessment on radios was sixty Belgian francs.[23] In 1947, this was increased to one hundred and forty-four francs.[24] The act of December 24, 1957, maintained this same fee for radio but established an annual fee of eight hundred and forty francs for television.[25] Latest reports indicate that present fees are two hundred and four francs for a radio receiver and eight hundred and sixty for a TV set, with a fee of nine hundred and sixty francs for both.

Early Television Programming

WITH these financial resources, the *Institut* not only increased its hours of telecasting but was able to offer a wide variety of programs. In 1955, on the twenty-fifth anniversary of the *Institut National Belge de Radiodiffusion,* it was recalled that the Belgian television system was the first and only one in Europe to have, from its inception, a double service, one intended for French-speaking viewers and the other for Flemish.[26] The French and Flemish programs were broadcast from Brussels and relayed by regional transmitters in Liège and Antwerp.

In addition, viewers in southwest Belgium from the French frontier to Brussels could, with suitable antennas, receive programs from Paris, relayed by the *Radio Télévision Française* station in Lille on the eight hundred and nineteen line system. Thus viewers in the Belgian capital and its environs and in several of the provinces (West Flanders, East Flanders, Hainaut and Brabant) had the choice of three transmissions, i.e., two in French from Paris and Brussels, and one in Flemish from the latter city. Some limited television service was also provided by stations in the Netherlands (Lopik and Eindhoven) and in Germany (Langenberg). Since nearly all the television receivers on the Belgian market were the multistandard and multi-channel type, a wide variety of programs was available to much of the population. "These circumstances," said one writer, "make it possible to assess the possibilities offered by television for the projection of culture from one country to another."[27]

Each section of the INR/NIR presented its own television programs. In 1956 the French section carried more than forty full-length dramatic shows, a number of transmissions from theaters in Brussels, and eighteen relay programs from *Radio Télévision Française* (RTF) in Paris. Emphasis was placed on musical programs, including classical concerts, operettas, and dance and cabaret music. Ten programs were devoted to the direct transmission of spectacles such as the Moscow and Peking circuses. Seventy-six feature films and more than five hundred short films were shown. For the daily news, 2,884 filmed sequences were used, half of which related to international subjects. Numerous programs were devoted to literature, the arts and science, and a special series of twenty programs about the life and culture of the Walloon province was presented. Sports and special programs for children occupied important places in the schedules. As reported by the French section of the *Institut,* Belgian televiewers in 1956 saw the work of approximately ten thousand performers, reporters, commentators and collaborators.[28]

The Flemish division of the *Institut* was equally effective. A 1958 report on the first five years of its operation showed that in 1957 its total transmission time was more than fifteen hundred hours, with about seventeen percent of that time devoted to news and commentaries, five percent to drama and literature (including nine original Flemish works), seven percent to light entertainment shows, four percent to documentaries, five percent to children's programs, eight percent to "cultural and educational" broadcasts, and twenty percent to films, excluding news features. The remainder of the time was used for Eurovision shows, relays from other stations and pickups from the Netherlands television service.[29]

School Television. As early as February 1956, INR/NIR produced some experimental educational telecasts. Films about animal life, geography and mine operations were televised to forty schools in the Brussels and Liège districts. Those working on the project concluded that there was a need for the development of programs, particularly at the elementary level, and that further studies should be made about the problems and possibilities of utilizing television in the classroom.[30]

Establishment of RTB–BRT

THE rapid growth of radio and television during the fifties required a new and improved charter for broadcasting. The 1930 law was inadequate to meet Belgium's communication needs in the postwar period, and Parliament attempted to enact new legislation. A number of bills were introduced and debated, but all were tabled. It was not until 1958 that the Government took steps which resulted in a new law. The Minister of Cultural Affairs, a newly created office, was directed to make a study and propose a new organization for radio and television. The following year, Parliament passed legislation providing that thereafter the Government would designate the Minister to hold the chairmanship of the INR/NIR Board of Directors and exercise regulatory powers over the *Institut.*[31] Accordingly, the Minister of Cultural Affairs was designated as a replacement for the PTT Minister, who had occupied the office since the creation of INR/NIR.[32]

One factor delaying the passage of legislation was Parliament's insistence that cultural duality be respected, that the two linguistic groups have organizational autonomy and be independent in their program operations. Parliament debated whether there should be one centralized agency in charge of all radio and television or three institutes operating as separate entities.[33] The latter concept was embodied in law on May 18, 1960.[34]

This new legislation abolished INR/NIR and replaced it with a new organization. As M. Namurois has pointed out, "The essential principle underlying the act was to ensure the fullest possible cultural autonomy in the field of broadcasting. Separate boards were created and separate powers vested in two independent bodies, one for the French-language and the other for the Dutch-language broadcasting service." And, as he indicated, considering the deep-seated aversion of the Flemings and Walloons to any kind of cultural amalgamation:

> It was hardly possible to imagine these boards operating and these powers being exercised otherwise than in the context of two different corporations, each possessing legal personality, and each having its own budget and its own staff. A number of services, however, had to be administered in common, and so a third body of a mainly technical and administrative character was set up and likewise established as a corporate entity.[35]

Organization. Three separate sections make up the new organization: the Institute for Belgian Radio and Television, French Broadcasts (RTB); the Institute for Belgian Radio and Television, Dutch Broadcasts (BRT); and the Institute of Common Services. Each is vested with independent legal status and each of the first two is charged with providing programs in its own language, has its own budget and manages its own affairs. The Common Services Institute is responsible for administration, technical and financial matters, cultural services common to French, Dutch, German and world-wide transmissions. Furthermore, this Institute is vested with ownership of the real estate and transmission facilities of the total organization, with an obligation to provide the necessary technical personnel and equipment for both French and Flemish broadcasts.

Each organizational unit has a ten member board, eight of whom must be appointed alternately by the House of Representatives and the Senate and the remaining two chosen by the parliamentary appointees. Terms are for six years. Members may succeed themselves but, following one successive term, six years must elapse before re-appointment.

The law requires that board members be appointed from a list of candidates submitted to Parliament by provincial councils. These lists must be compiled and selections made under a formula which attempts to equalize representation among different geographical, cultural and linguistic groups, including the Royal Academies of Science, Art, Language, Literature and Medicine together with the universities. Precluded from appointment are aliens, members of Parliament, permanent employees of the Institutes, and persons over the age of sixty-five.

Each Institute has a general director and two program directors in charge of radio and television respectively, all of whom are chosen by the Government upon the advice and counsel of the Institute's board of directors. The Common Services unit is directed by a General Council composed of board members of both French and Flemish Institutes, with the presidency and vice-presidency of this Council held alternately for one year by the presidents of the two boards. Two general directors, selected by the Government upon recommendation of the General Council, oversee the technical, administrative and financial functions of the whole organization.

The general directors of the three Institutes participate in an advisory capacity in the meetings of the General Council and its standing committee made up of the presidents and vice-presidents of the French and Dutch boards. These same general directors, working with the president of the Council, are in charge of the cultural services common to both Institutes (for example, the symphony orchestra and recording libraries), all broadcasts in German and all foreign transmissions.

Government Supervision

WHILE the Institutes have considerably more autonomy than did their predecessor, they are subject to some government controls. The Government, with the Minister of Cultural Affairs in a key role, exercises general regulatory authority. The Institutes establish their own policies and procedures, but these are subject to the approval of the executive branch of the Government. Likewise, the Government allocates the financial allowances for the boards and the General Council, regulates the salaries and determines the pensions of the general directors, program directors and other important personnel. In case of need, it may authorize the Institutes to accept donations and inheritances and negotiate loans.

The Government is empowered to authorize Common Services to acquire or dispose of real estate or to mortgage such property. Moreover, it may establish advisory commissions to study the Institutes, their policies and practices, and to investigate any general questions relating to broadcasting. These commissions are chosen by the Minister of Cultural Affairs, to whom the Institutes are responsible, from a double list submitted to him by the boards and the General Council.

The three Institutes are required to prepare annual reports of their activities, which must be approved and submitted by the Ministers to Parliament. These combined reports must include up-to-date financial statements and proposed budgets for the ensuing year. A specific appropriation for each Institute is granted by Parliament and is included in the

State's general budget. For example, for the fiscal year 1965, Parliament appropriated 1,562,000,000 Belgian francs for radio and television. A little less than one-third of this amount was designated for French broadcasting, the same amount for Dutch, and the rest for Common Services, including broadcasts designed for Germans residing in the eastern region of Belgium, and for an extensive world-wide service.[36]

As was true before the 1960 legislation, appropriations for radio and TV are made from the Government's general fund. Annual fees assessed against the owners of receivers and taxes on the sale of tubes are deposited in this fund. Parliament annually allocates for radio and TV operation an amount roughly equal to the total income from these sources, after allowing some deduction for collection expenses. In 1964, the revenue from these fees and taxes totaled 1,590,000,000 Belgian francs.[37]

Statutory Provisions Concerning Programming

THE 1960 statute prescribed that news broadcasts of each Institute must be made in "strict objectivity" and without any prior censorship by the Government. The general directors of the Institutes and the collegiate body in charge of overseas and German-language broadcasting are responsible for seeing that this mandate is complied with. This means that the Minister of Cultural Affairs cannot exercise any prior restraint. However, under the law, this does not preclude the Minister's influence on the overall news policies and practices of the Institutes. His office is empowered to take disciplinary action against those responsible for newscasts which it believes have been slanted, distorted, false, or which lack objectivity.

A general provision forbids broadcasts "contrary to the laws or the public interest," those which disturb the public peace, or which offend foreign states. Likewise, programs which affront public morality or "do violence to the opinions and convictions of others" are prohibited. These taboos were carried over from the previous legislation.

If the property of any program or programs is seriously questioned, the law authorizes the RTB–BRT to seek outside counsel. The General Council may set up a consulting committee composed of eight members; four must be chosen to give special aid to the general director of the French Institute and four to assist the general director of the Dutch.

The new legislation continued the prohibition against commercial broadcasting. When the 1960 bill was pending, some argued vigorously for advertising, particularly on television. Others urged that the intervals between programs could, with propriety, be used for spot announcements, and that the additional income would make it possible to improve the quality of programs. The Government took the position that there were unresolved questions about commercial broadcasting which deserved further study.[38] Parliament agreed and continued, for the time being at least, the prohibition against commercial broadcasts. It also continued the injunction against the publication of any materials except those relating to programs.

Since they possess a broadcasting monopoly, the law specifies that the Institutes should release radio and television time to private organizations and foundations as their predecessor had been required to do. The purpose is to maintain cultural and linguistic duality, and to protect the public interest against a possible program imbalance.

And so, in accordance with the spirit of the present statute, the Institutes make broadcast time available to a variety of individuals and organizations. Religious bodies, both orthodox and unorthodox, groups representing different shades of political opinion, trade unions, educational institutions, writers and other professional organizations—all have the opportunity to provide information and express their points of view.

Present Facilities and Operations

THE main quarters for Belgian broadcasting, both Dutch and French, are located in *La Maison de la Radiodiffusion–Télévision Belge* at Place Flagey in Brussels. This facility has twenty-nine studios, two of which have been converted to television use. To meet the needs of the expanding broadcasting services, additional building space is being rented in Brussels. A new site has been secured and construction of an elaborate, up-to-date broadcasting center is under way. The completion of the project is expected to require from ten to fifteen years and cost two and one-half billion francs.

The national and regional radio operations are carried on by eight medium-wave transmitters with a combined power of three hundred and fifty kilowatts, and sixteen FM transmitters with a combined power of three hundred and ninety kilowatts. To maintain these facilities and carry on the work in 1964 required 2,790 employees, 566 of which were concerned with French operations, 504 with Dutch and the remainder with the work of the Common Services Institute.

With their present facilities, the French and Dutch Institutes each broadcast three separate program schedules, totaling more than five hundred and twenty hours per week. As of January 1965, the Common Services unit was transmitting fifteen additional hours per week in programs designed for the German-speaking population in Belgium.

Domestic Programs. Three radio networks operate in Belgium, providing what are called the First, Second and Third Programs. The First Program of both the French and Dutch Institutes is designed to have wide appeal. A sampling of late 1964 logs revealed that from six to seven percent of the total time was devoted to news reporting and analysis. Music is a heavy component of the broadcasts. The French schedule for one day in October 1964, showed approximately thirty percent of the total broadcast time given to light and classical music, with about one hour of the classics presented during the afternoon. Dutch offerings in November of the same year were much the same.

Other entertainment programs included travelogues, quiz shows, live and remote broadcasts, national and international sports and a variety of dramatic offerings.

Since the beginning of Belgium radio, the authorities have emphasized educational and religious programming. Time is allocated to representatives of political parties and other organizations for the discussion of important issues; for talks on cooking, farming and other practical pursuits; for literary forums and language instruction. Special informational broadcasts are designed for both children and adults and numerous taped programs from other countries are aired. Time is made available for both Catholic and Protestant services and for other religious programs.

The Second Program, while varied, tends to emphasize light subject matter with more appeal to regional interests. Short news bulletins are frequently presented, with reports on weather and traffic conditions. As announced by the Belgium Radio and Television Service, the 1964–65 schedules emphasized "recreation with various light programs intermingled with news bulletins."[39]

While some light music is presented, the Third Program consists mostly of musical works of the great composers, interspersed with news reports and lectures by distinguished professors and other experts.

School Radio. Belgian authorities traditionally have been interested in the classroom uses of radio. In November 1964, the program schedules included two instructional periods per week for the French schools and daily instruction for the Dutch schools. Subjects being taught by one or both of the Institutes include history, biology, languages, literature, geography, music, philosophy and economics. While use of these broadcasts was not compulsory, in 1964 more than forty-seven percent of the lower grade schools in the Flemish regions tuned them in. Reports were equally good in the French area.

Foreign Broadcasting. RTB–BRT has participated in and encouraged program exchanges with other countries since the last war. Three shortwave transmitters, with a combined power of two hundred and twenty kilowatts, broadcast twelve hours daily in French, Dutch and several African dialects. These transmissions reach various parts of Europe, Africa, North and South America, and the Far East, with programs designed to appeal to listeners in each reception area.

The Overseas Service supplies transcriptions of Belgian music to foreign broadcasting organizations free of charge. The recordings are sent either as complete programs combining music and commentary, or are provided with a printed commentary. The catalog issued by the Director of *Emissions Mondiales* in the fall of 1964 listed the types of Belgian music available for foreign use: chamber, contemporary piano, ballet, bel canto and melodies, folksongs, military bands, chimes and choirs. It also mentioned important features of the overseas broadcast service, such as weekly press reviews in numerous languages.

Current Television Programming. As with radio, the Dutch and French Institutes are responsible for their respective television shows. French programs are presented forty hours per week and distributed via three main transmitters and three relays; the Dutch programs are broadcast the same number of hours over two main and two auxiliary transmitters.

Considerable time is devoted to regular news reports and analysis. Within limited schedules, the following program types have recently appeared: live dramatic shows produced in Brussels, symphony concerts, film serials such as "Father Knows Best," documentaries, sports broadcasts and children's programs. As reported and classified by the Dutch Institute, the breakdown of programs for the 1963–64 season was approximately: news (newsreels, sports results), twelve percent; general informative, including documentaries and telecasts of athletic events, fifteen percent; cultural programs, eleven percent; instructional programs (language courses, etc.), nine percent; fictional presentations (feature films, live drama, serials), twenty-one percent; light programs (variety shows, popular songs, games), fourteen percent; programs for young people, fourteen percent; and miscellaneous programs (guest interviews, religious programs, etc.), four percent.

Percentages for French programs for the same period were reported to be: feature films, twenty-seven percent; cultural programs (dramatic, literary, etc.), seven percent; entertainment (light and popular music and variety shows), ten percent; instructional telecasts, including formal courses for the schools, seventeen percent; service coordination and continuity, six percent; and miscellaneous, three percent.

School Television. Instructional television is offered by both the French and Dutch Institutes. *TV Scolaire* (French), designed for different age groups, followed a set schedule of weekly transmissions during the 1964–65 school year with a wide variety of offerings including zoology, geography, languages and literature. *School Televisie* (Dutch) had a similar program. Both organizations send out printed schedules and other materials to schools to help in the planning and utilization of the telecasts. *Television Scolaire* and *School Televisie* have been in operation for several years. During this time, the interest among schools has grown. Responses from educators using the telecasts have been actively solicited. According to a published report of *Television Scolaire* in 1963–64, two hundred and sixty-seven schools in one hundred and thirty communities returned questionnaires reporting use of the French programs and offering comments on content and quality. *School Televisie* reported similar communications from twelve hundred schools in the Flemish part of the country.

Eurovision. Since 1954, Belgium has participated in Eurovision, an enterprise of the European Broadcasting Union. The legal and programming offices of EBU are located in Geneva, but the technical and engineering offices are in Brussels. The RTB–BRT stations serve as important links in the Eurovision network. Belgium has been one of the largest consumers of EBU television programs. For example, from June 6, 1954, to August 12, 1958, Dutch broadcasts carried five hundred and sixty-four of a total of eight hundred and six EBU offerings. In 1958–59, the French Institute broadcast one hundred and sixty-eight hours of Eurovision out of a total of 1,815. This constituted about six and one-half percent of all the broadcast time of the Institute that year.

The use of Eurovision has not diminished in more recent years. Programs have included many important telecasts such as President Kennedy's funeral, the pilgrimage of Pope Paul VI to the Holy Land, Telstar relays of the Olympics, and a number of Early Bird transmissions.

Because of comparatively limited resources, Belgium has not been one of the larger producers of programs for EBU. However, those which it has produced for the network—pageants, festivals, broadcasts of sports events —generally have been of high quality and have attracted favorable response from a large foreign audience.

Commercial Broadcasting

ALTHOUGH commercial stations and advertising are prohibited in Belgium, foreign stations transmit commercial programs across the Belgian boundaries. Radio Luxembourg, for example, is one of the most popular stations in the area. It has recording studios and business offices in Brussels with a large programming and sales staff. Belgians listen to Europe No. 1 and other commercial stations on ships at sea, featuring news and light music.

There have been pressures on the Government to authorize commercial broadcasting. Some Belgian writers and communications experts favor it. Some have expressed concern over the increasing public expense incurred by broadcasting operations, particularly television, and believe that advertising on a limited basis may offer some relief. Some local commercial interests feel that their products are at a disadvantage when competing against those promoted by foreign radio programs. Whether the Belgium Parliament will eventually yield to these pressures is questionable. At present, there is no great public clamor for commercial broadcasting. And, should positive moves be made in that direction, negative reactions will ensue from many Belgian listeners, and much heated debate in Parliament, in the press and in other public forums can be expected.

NOTES

1. For a history of Belgium, see Henri Pirenne, *Early Democracies in the Low Countries* (New York: Harper and Row, 1963); Therese Henrot, *Belgium* (New York: Viking Press, 1960); and Leon Van der Essen, *A Short History of Belgium* (Chicago: University of Chicago Press, 1915).
2. Henrot, p. 7.
3. Flemish publications can be and are read in Holland, while French-writing Belgians do publish works in Paris. This increases slightly the circulation of Belgian publications.
4. *Bulletin usuel des lois et arretes,* 1906–10, p. 250 (hereafter referred to as *Bulletin usuel*); *Moniteur belge,* August 3–4, 1908 (hereafter referred to as *Moniteur*). Both official publications are issued in Brussels.
5. Albert Namurois, "The New Charter for Broadcasting in Belgium," *EBU Review,* 63B, September 1960, p. 2. Mr. Namurois includes in his excellent article a short history of Belgian radio.
6. *Ibid.*
7. *Bulletin usuel,* 1930, pp. 1041–1043; *Moniteur,* June 23–24, 1930.
8. Royal Decree of June 28, 1930, *Bulletin usuel,* 1930, pp. 1079–1081; *Moniteur,* July 3, 1930.
9. See Namurois for discussion.
10. *Ibid.,* pp. 2–3.
11. Royal Decree, June 28, 1930.
12. *EBU Bulletin,* May 15, 1950, pp. 41–45.
13. Namurois, p. 3.
14. *Bulletin usuel,* May 1940–December 1943, pp. 106–107; *Moniteur,* November 13, 1942.
15. *Bulletin usuel,* 1945, p. 591; *Moniteur,* September 24–25, 1945.
16. J. Gorus, "Flemish-Language Sound Broadcasts to Schools," *EBU Review,* 70B, November 1961, pp. 6–9. M. Gorus, the Head of School Broadcasts, *Belgische Radio en Televisie,* reviews the early history of educational radio in Belgium in the last part of his article.
17. Jules Ghaye, "French-Language Sound Broadcasts to Schools," *ibid.,* p. 5.
18. Gorus, p. 8.
19. *EBU Review,* 52B, December 1958, p. 16.
20. Royal Decree of January 3, 1952, *Bulletin usuel,* 1952, pp. 36–37; *Moniteur,* June 21–22, 1952; also, Royal Decree of June 11, 1952, *Bulletin usuel,* 1952, pp. 360–361; *Moniteur,* July 14–15, 1952.
21. *La libre Belgique* (Brussels), October 31, 1953, p. 2, reports on the inaugural TV program of INR/NIR and discusses the technical, organizational and budgetary problems. See also issue of November 1, 1953, p. 4, *"La télévision-belge est en marche,"* a favorable account of the first INR/NIR telecasts.
22. For example, see Renaud Strivacy, *La Télévision Commerciale en Belgique,* a study published by the *Office de Télédiffusion,* Brussels, 1948. Mr. Strivacy

was then Secretary General of the *Société d'Expression de la Télévision* and Chairman, Administrative Council, *Office de Télédiffusion.* He presented arguments in favor of commercial television.

23. Royal Decree of June 28, 1930, *Bulletin usuel,* 1930, p. 1097; *Moniteur,* July 4, 1930. As of January 1968 the Belgian franc was equivalent to two cents.
24. *Bulletin usuel,* 1947, p. 651; *Moniteur,* September 20, 1947.
25. *Bulletin usuel,* 1957, p. 888; *Moniteur,* December 29, 1957.
26. J. Gantelae, *EBU Bulletin,* July-August 1956, p. 503.
27. *Ibid.*
28. *Ibid.*
29. *EBU Review,* 52B, December 1958, pp. 15–16.
30. Henri Dieuzeide, "The Present Position of School Television in Europe," *EBU Review,* 61B, May 1960, p. 6. Professor Dieuzeide is Head, Schools Television Service, *Institut Pédagogique National,* Paris, and Head, Audio-Visual Laboratory. His article contains an excellent discussion of the status of educational TV in Europe as of May 1960. He also includes a short history of experimental school broadcasts in Belgium, the Netherlands, Switzerland, Great Britain, Austria, France and Italy, and discusses possibilities for the expansion of educational television in Europe.
31. *Bulletin usuel,* 1959, p. 47; *Moniteur,* January 8, 1959.
32. Royal Decree of January 3, 1959, *Bulletin usuel,* 1959, p. 47; *Moniteur,* January 8, 1959.
33. See reports of debates in *La libre Belgique* (Brussels), May 5, 1960, p. 2 and May 11, 1962, p. 2.
34. Act of May 18, 1960, *Bulletin usuel,* 1960, pp. 355–361; *Moniteur,* May 27–28, 1960.
35. Namurois, p. 4.
36. Figures supplied by staff officials of RTB–BRT, Brussels.
37. *Ibid.*
38. Namurois, p. 10.
39. Press Section, Belgium Radio and Television Service, July 1964.

VIII

The Netherlands:

Pluralism with Freedom

R ELIGION HAS MAINTAINED a dominant position in the Netherlands for centuries. Long before Holland became independent, Catholicism and Calvinism were powerful social and political forces. Later, despite the strong hold of the traditional groups, constitutional liberality enabled new ideologies to develop. Bernard Pingaud has written that "The Dutchman is pious by definition, even if he has ceased to practice his religion. . . ."[1] This characteristic is revealed by the numerous denominational political parties, schools and businesses.

Nevertheless, despite the rivalry among the various interest groups—political, educational, business and labor, as well as religious—the Dutch have exhibited a genius for negotiation and the maintenance of domestic order. In times of national peril or as the public interest has required, they have been able to resolve their differences. As one writer has pointed out:

> Against the German invader Holland presented an almost unified front, and the history of this period is marked by a fine series of acts of defiance, attacks and protestations emanating from people of every category of social or religious opinion.[2]

Early Developments in Broadcasting

BROADCASTING in the Netherlands was initiated in 1920. A radio transmitter was installed in Amsterdam that year and used by the Amsterdam Stock Exchange to transmit stock quotations and financial bulletins. Subscribers to the daily service received the transmissions on special sets.[3] Two years later, the same transmitter was used by the Vaz Dias Press Agency in Amsterdam to broadcast news reports to fifty provincial newspapers.[4] In 1923, a transmitter was built by manufacturing interests in Hilversum and used to broadcast programs to the general public.[5] These programs evoked widespread interest, and in 1925 a new five hundred watt transmitter was installed to improve and increase broadcast coverage. At the same time a foundation, *Hilversumche Draadloze Omroep* (HDO), was established in the Hilversum area. Its Board of Directors was made up of representatives of equipment manufacturers and radio listeners.[6] Thus it was a joint enterprise of business and the public to promote the commercial as well as the public service aspects of broadcasting. By 1927 radio receivers were being produced in the tens of thousands. And, under the HDO's leadership, the quality of receiving equipment and program service was greatly improved.

These improvements stimulated the development of broadcasting. Under the aegis of amateurs, a new organization known as *Algemeene Vereeniging Radio Omroep* (AVRO) was formed and assumed the programming responsibilities previously exercised by the HDO.

During the same period, religious and political groups organized separate corporations for the purpose of broadcasting. The Catholics created *Katholieke Radio Omroep* (KRO). Orthodox Protestants set up *Nederlandsche Christelyke Radio Vereeniging* (NCRV). A group of liberal Protestants established their own organization, *Vrijzinnig Protestantse Radio Omroep* (VPRO).[7] In 1928, amateur operators organized another broadcasting group known as VARA.

These five groups filed applications and received broadcasting concessions from the Government. Since that time most of the broadcasting in the Netherlands has been conducted by these organizations.

Dutch broadcasting was conceived as a commercial enterprise. The religious groups and amateurs, however, motivated by other objectives, preferred not to follow the commercial line. Until 1940 they maintained their operations with voluntary subscriptions from members. As one author has commented:

> From 1924 to 1940 the members of the associations made great sacrifices of time and money to secure the necessary funds each year for their own society. The radio buildings in Hilversum, which were erected for the greater part before 1940, must surely inspire great respect in the beholder prompted by the spirit of sacrifice of the various denominations who built Dutch broadcasting.[8]

At the time these corporations were established, no special law covered broadcasting. A statute, passed in 1904, and amended from time to time, provided for state ownership and operation of the postal service and telecommunications, and gave regulatory jurisdiction to the Postal, Telegraph and Telephone Administration (PTT). Under the general provisions of this law, the PTT assumed limited regulatory authority over broadcasting, which consisted largely of allocating frequencies, granting licenses and controlling technical operations.

In Hilversum, the societies originally operated with one transmitter. A second one was built nearby in 1927. These were replaced in 1940 by improved facilities near Utrecht, a location more desirable from the standpoint of coverage. This central equipment was later augmented by several low-power transmitters placed along the eastern border.

These transmitting facilities became the property of a public corporation, NOZEMA, Ltd., which was established in 1935, with shares divided among the Government and the private corporations (the four private groups together had forty percent and the remainder was owned by the Government).[9]

Although using the same transmitting facilities, each of the associations has, from the beginning, produced its own programs. In 1930, Parliament passed a law dividing equally among them the available transmitting time, except for the smaller VPRO, which was allotted seven hours per week.[10]

War-Time Radio

DURING the Second World War, the Germans liquidated the private broadcasting organizations and used the facilities for propaganda. But this did not end the creative and independent spirit of the leaders who had established these associations. As the report of the *Nederlandse Radio Unie* (1958) has pointed out:

> In spite of the diversity of religious and political convictions, the Dutch people form a unity. This characteristic became evident during the war which put an end to the independent life of the broadcasting societies, but the former leading personalities of the broadcasting world continued to meet and plan for the future.[11]

While the guns were still firing, these enterprising men made plans for a federation of broadcasting societies which would both increase efficiency and preserve the traditional autonomy of the individual groups.

For a short period after the war, a political movement attempted to create one national system of broadcasting, as was the pattern in many other European countries. But the forces for pluralism won, the societies regained full possession of their buildings and equipment, and their authority to broadcast was fully restored.[12]

Postwar Developments

IN February 1947, the five groups worked out a plan by which each maintained the title to its own properties but, in the interest of efficiency and economy, shared them with all the others. To implement this arrangement, they joined in the establishment of a foundation, *Nederlandse Radio Unie* (NRU), with each member-corporation represented on its Board of Directors. While sharing facilities, each member-corporation maintained autonomy in the production and presentation of programs.[13]

This new broadcasting structure was recognized by the Minister of Education, Arts, and Sciences, and, by administrative orders dated January 15 and April 14, 1947, he assumed regulatory jurisdiction over the NRU and its members and set forth the principles by which they would be governed. It was specified:

> 1) That regulation of broadcasting in general—excluding the operation of transmission facilities for which the Postal Administration is responsible— would be exercised by a commissioner nominated by and responsible to the minister; 2) That the union board would consist of two representatives from each of the four large organizations and one from VPRO (with its smaller membership); 3) That associations together should provide 780 hours of programs per week.[14]

In line with the traditional concern for religious institutions, the Minister decreed that a part of the broadcasting time should be allocated to the various churches and that they might produce their own programs or delegate such responsibilities to other agencies.[15] To finance overall operation, various bodies of the NRU were to receive annual grants based upon estimated expenses. These grants were to be made by the Minister from fees on licensed radio receivers collected by the Postal Administration.[16]

In 1945, the annual tax on a single radio receiver was set at twelve guilders (since raised to eighteen).[17] In 1962, the annual income from fees on all licensed radio sets was approximately thirty-six million guilders. In 1964, the number of licensed radio sets was more than three million. This included four hundred and sixty thousand used by subscribers to a special radio service provided by state-owned relay-exchange systems which feed programs from domestic stations and selected foreign programs. Total annual receipts were distributed to the various licensed broadcasting organizations and to the NRU to defray expenses of domestic programs, to Radio Netherlands for costs of foreign broadcasting, to the commissioner and his staff for administrative expenses, and to the PTT to pay the costs of collecting the annual license fees.[18]

The programming associations receive additional income from the sale of program schedules and from members' subscriptions. It has been recently estimated that the largest group (KRO) in the NRU has about six hundred thousand subscribers and that the smallest (VPRO) has about one hundred and fifty thousand.[19]

Expansion of Radio Programs

PROBABLY no European system of broadcasting is subject to less government influence on programming than Holland's. However, because of the Government's important connection with the financial needs of the NRU and its affiliated bodies, the commissioner sits in on the NRU Board meetings and is authorized to refer policy decisions of the Board to the Minister of Education, Arts and Sciences for review and possible annulment. But the Government's role in the development of programming has been minimal. The private groups licensed to operate broadcast facilities have enjoyed autonomy, and with the resources available have established a program service of the highest quality.

The five religious, cultural and political groups which make up the *Nederlandse Radio Unie* share the broadcast time on two national network programs. These programs originate in the Hilversum studios and are sent out by two medium-wave transmitters, each having a power of one hundred and twenty kilowatts. Nation-wide coverage is achieved by three additional auxiliary relay transmitters, each with two and one-half kilowatts of power, located at Hoogezand (Greningen), Hengelo (Overijssel) and Hulsberg (Limburg).

Additional programs are provided by a nation-wide network of sixteen FM stations, located in Goes, Hoogezand, Irnsum, Markelo, Hulsberg, Roermond and Lopik. Plans are under way to enlarge the FM facilities.

A variety of programs is presented over both AM and FM networks. Considering the Dutch temperament and traditional concern for religion, it is not surprising that about eight percent of the programs consist of church services, ceremonials and religious talks. Each society sees that its broadcasts reflect its own religious views, but is careful not to criticize the doctrines espoused by the others.

Musical programs are allotted from sixty to seventy percent of the broadcast time. Classical music is given considerable emphasis. However, popular music with wide appeal is presented regularly to an increasing audience.

The NRU employs more than four hundred musicians who contribute to the programs of the various groups. The Radio Philharmonic Orchestra, made up of NRU personnel, is one of the leading orchestras and regularly provides programs. In addition, the NRU conducts international courses for orchestral conductors. Some of the world's foremost directors, including the conductor of Holland's leading orchestra, received their early instruction in these training programs.

News and discussion programs are popular in the Netherlands and are given considerable time. In preparing and presenting the news and discussion of public issues, each organization is relatively free of censorship. But, as is generally true throughout Europe, there are statutory prohibitions against broadcasts which may endanger the security of the State, offend public morale or unduly disturb the peace.

The private societies have not overlooked the value of radio as an instructional medium. Programs for the schools are broadcast five days per week and are used by an increasing number of schools throughout the country. A large percentage of these educational programs are designed for the primary grades, although some are planned for the secondary schools. A variety of subjects is taught and the instruction is supplemented with class outlines and other printed materials for which the schools pay nominal fees.

While a majority of the radio programs broadcast in Holland are produced by the societies, from thirty to forty percent are imported. Taped programs of orchestras, dramatic shows, entertainment features and educational broadcasts produced in England, France, the United States, Canada and other countries are frequently used by the Dutch networks.

Foreign Broadcasting

BEFORE and during the Second World War, Holland had engaged in international broadcasting. After the liberation, Dutch leaders in broadcasting felt that the Netherlands should continue to be heard.[20] Thus, on April 15, 1947, *Stichting Radio Nederland Wereldomroep* (Radio Netherlands World Broadcasting Foundation) was established to provide short-wave programs for foreign reception. As officially stated, it had two tasks: to maintain contact with compatriots in all parts of the world and to "protect" the Netherlands image abroad by broadcasting to non-Dutch listeners. Accordingly, daily transmissions go out in foreign areas of the world where large numbers of Dutch reside. Daily programs in other languages—English, Spanish, Arabic, Afrikaans and Indonesian—reflecting Dutch scientific thought and business and cultural matters are broadcast. Care is taken that they are prepared by persons "fully conversant with the languages used and with the habits and customs prevailing" in the foreign areas for which reception is intended.[21]

In addition to direct broadcasting, Radio Netherlands also provides transcriptions free of charge to foreign stations. In 1964, it supplied a large number of such programs in more than thirty languages to about one hundred countries. It also transmits special programs by short-wave for relay by local stations in North, Central and South America. One of these is "European Review" in which a team of correspondents in fifteen European capitals provides information on significant world events.

It should be noted that the Netherlands World Broadcasting Foundation is an independent organization and is not financed by the State. It is supported, as are the domestic broadcasting organizations, by the license fees which are paid by every Dutchman who owns a radio or television set.

The Development of Television

HOLLAND has made considerable progress in recent years in the development of television. Experimental operations had been conducted by industrial enterprises prior to the war. After the Armistice, further experimental licenses were granted by the PTT. In 1948, the Minister of Education, Arts and Sciences and the Minister of Communications jointly established a special commission to study the problems of developing the medium. After careful study, the commission recommended the adoption of a six hundred and twenty-five line system, and proposed that six channels be allocated for television use. The commission suggested a two year trial period, with the broadcasting societies bearing the programming costs.

Pending the Government's action on the commission's recommendations, the programming organizations, on May 31, 1951, joined in the creation of a new foundation, a coordinating body which they named *Nederlandse Televisie Stichting* (NTS).[22] As was the case in *Nederlandse Radio Unie,* the by-laws of the new foundation provided for the development and sharing of facilities, the division of broadcasting time among the groups and the coordination of program schedules. Each member, however, was to retain its independence and provide its own programming.

In September 1951, the Minister of Education, Arts and Sciences authorized television for the trial period of two years. It was a cooperative project in which the societies financed the programs, the firm of Philips, Ltd., furnished the transmitter and studio, and the Postal Administration supplied the tower and antenna.

The experiment having proved successful, the Government extended the license to 1955, and in 1956 an administrative order was issued authorizing television on a permanent basis. Parliament enacted legislation and established an annual license fee of thirty guilders on all television sets.[23] The fee has since been raised to thirty-six guilders.

TV Organization and Administration. One organizational difference between the NTS and the NRU should be noted. Whereas the NRU Board of Directors is made up of ten members of the programming societies (two from each), the 1956 decree specified a maximum of fourteen for the TV Board, and provided that three of them might be nominated by the Minister of Education, Arts and Sciences, with the remainder chosen by the societies. The Crown appoints an additional member to serve as Chairman of the Board.

A recent statement of the Department of Radio and Television in the Ministry set forth the ways in which the societies must cooperate and the basis on which time and funds are allocated for television broadcasting, as was provided in the original statute:

> The aim of the foundation has remained the same since the start, and Article 3 of the statutes states that the NTS must guarantee cooperation between the broadcasting societies in the field of television. This cooperation covers the administration of the technical services, the coordination of programmes, the exchange of programmes with foreign organizations, the building, acquisition and furnishing of television studios and the regulating of staff matters in cooperation with the NRU. The financial resources consist of government grants and the net revenue from television license fees in accord-

ance with estimates submitted by the NTS and the broadcasting societies. Time on the air is allocated according to a scheme set out in a circular letter from the minister dated 21st December 1956, under which the broadcasting societies, the NTS and the churches receive an appropriate share of the available broadcasting time for their programmes.

Each of the broadcasting associations has its own governing board which directs its radio and television operations. The day-to-day affairs of the NTS are conducted by a Board of Management made up of members of the various governing boards of the associations plus the Chairman of the NTS. A Program Commission, consisting of five members of the NTS Board and its Chairman, supervises and coordinates programming and determines general policies in this area.

As is true in radio, the Minister of Education, Arts and Sciences has general supervisory powers over the NTS. He is represented by a commissioner who has the authority to attend the NTS Board meetings.

Early TV Programming. Following the experimental period, TV programming expanded rapidly. In 1956, the NTS reported that during the previous year it had telecast three hundred and twenty-four programs with a total of five hundred and seventy-seven hours. A year later the number of programs had more than doubled, with a substantial increase in the hours of transmission. In 1956, broadcasting time per week averaged twelve hours and forty-six minutes.[24] Since that time the number of hours has gradually increased and in 1965, the associations and the NTS were sending out programs thirty-two hours per week on one channel. As of October 1, 1964, the NTS began operation on a second channel providing an additional seventeen and one-half hours.[25]

About forty percent of all TV time was being used by the NTS. The remainder was programmed by the broadcasting associations, by churches (five percent of the total time), and by the democratic political parties, each of which was permitted ten minutes every eight weeks. Ten parties in Holland have used television to espouse their policies. The principal ones include the Catholic People's Party *(Katholieke Volkspartij)*, the Calvinist Protestant Party *(Anti-Revolutionaire Partij)*, the Liberal Party *(Volkspartij voor Vrijheid en Democratie)*, the Labor Party *(Partij van de Arbeid)*, the Pacifist Labor Party *(Pacifistisch Socialistische Partij)* and the Protestant Party *(Christelijke Historische Unie)*. The Communist Party is also provided with broadcasting time.

The pattern of these political programs has varied. Sometimes party representatives have delivered personal messages, illustrated by photographs or films. In other broadcasts, short commentaries have discussed the duties and problems of government. Occasionally, members of the press have been invited to question the political leaders on matters of general concern.

The associations and the NTS have provided a wide variety of programs

—newscasts reporting significant local, national and international affairs; sports events; programs dealing with domestic problems of agriculture, business, religion, government and other important areas of Dutch life. Broadcasts have included regular Eurovision and Telstar news exchanges (the Netherlands has played an active role in these exchanges). Other special telecasts have been historical documentaries, informational broadcasts dealing with critical social problems such as the exploding population, the administration of the courts and the enforcement of the law. A dramatic presentation was a visit with the Royal Family, commemorating the one hundred and fiftieth anniversary of the Monarchy.

The following are some of the specific programs presented by the associations on the two networks, *Nederland 1* and *Nederland 2*, during August 1965. In the "actualities and documentaries" category, viewers toured Rome with Sophia Loren. A film about the war in the Pacific, with shots of Japanese pilots crash-diving on American cruisers, was presented. Other broadcasts in this same category were an unrehearsed program, "Off the Cuff," from a seaside resort; a documentary dealing with the problems and the future of the Jews; another special called *"Keirei,"* concerning the Japanese surrender and giving viewers an impression of life in Japanese captivity; and *"Europees Panorama"* (European Panorama) with excerpts from the *"Journal de l'Europe"* (European Newsreel), an international feature prepared by the editorial staffs of broadcasting systems in six other European countries.

Programs in the "entertainment" category included musical shows featuring outstanding orchestras and vocalists, television plays such as "Hannibal," by the Yugoslav playwright, Vantsja Kljakovitch, and "Hallo Out There" by the American playwright, William Saroyan. There were films of the popular variety plus some folk singing and opera.

Instructional TV. According to a report of the NTS dated October 10, 1963, the first TV program for the Dutch schools was scheduled to begin on October 22 of that year. After stating that during a two year trial period, there would be twenty programs for four different groups of children broadcast on Tuesdays and Fridays, and that careful evaluation of these programs was to be made by educational experts, the NTS press release continued:

> The programmes will materialize in close collaboration between the NTS and the Netherlands School Television Foundation (*Stichting Nederlandse Onderwijs Televisie,* or NOT for short). The foundation was set up in 1962 by representative bodies of the three denominational and social groupings in Dutch education. This ensures that the nature and content of the programmes will be decided by educationalists, thus guaranteeing their didactical and pedagogical quality. A two-year contract has been concluded between NTS and NOT, providing that the scripts shall be supplied by NOT and programmes produced and transmitted by NTS and the Dutch broadcasting association.

The school television programmes may be classed according to their nature in two main groups; those of a general nature, and others of a religious or social outlook, provided by the three collaborating educational bodies. The structure of Dutch education is such that special attention must be devoted to programmes which meet the varying requirements of the Protestant, Roman Catholic and non-denominational schools. The programmes for the 1964 school year were predominantly concerned with geography, society, natural sciences, foreign languages and traffic safety. At the end of the initial series of school television programmes a classical Dutch play was to be staged, to be introduced in another separate programme.[26]

Indicative of the interest in the educational use of television was the establishment of the Television Academy *(Stichting Televisie Academie)* in The Hague on December 16, 1964. The Minister of Education, Arts and Sciences took the lead in the organization of the Academy. TELEAC's purpose, as reported, is to provide instruction in various fields, to inform the public about technical and scientific progress and to help the individual to adapt "to the changing demands of the times and to changing environment."[27]

The first courses, "Modern Didactics" and "First Aid," began in early 1965. It was reported that TELEAC would draw upon the resources of and collaborate closely with the universities, the scientific institutes, trade and industry in preparing the courses. The foundation has a fully equipped television studio in Delft (the first town in the Netherlands to have a technical college), and mobile tele-recording equipment which is used to produce instructional programs in laboratories, workshops and university classrooms.

Commercial Broadcasting

UNTIL recently any type of advertising over radio or television was forbidden. However, support for commercial broadcasting has been increasing.

While there was some occasional agitation for commercial radio, it was not until the advent of television that business and other groups began to press vigorously for authority to use the media for advertising. In the middle fifties, two groups, working independently, hoped to introduce commercial television. The Independent National Television Foundation (ONTV) requested the Minister of Education, Arts and Sciences to authorize advertising, the plan being to have programs produced by a contractor with the foundation acting in a supervisory role. The Society for the Development of Television (TEM) put forward a similar request.

These organizations were made up of bankers, industrialists (including some manufacturers of radio receivers), certain newspapers and other commercial interests. ONTV proposed to abolish the existing system of broadcasting and replace it with a "national" system. TEM recommended that the status quo be maintained, but with some broadcasting time allotted for commercials.

All the programming organizations participating in the broadcasts of *Nederlandse Televisie Stichting* opposed these plans, although VPRO was willing to consider them further. A committee representing the Socialist Party issued a report for VARA in which it was pointed out that radio had developed without the use of commercial revenue, and it was predicted that TV would become self-supporting by 1961 by means of the annual license fee of thirty guilders.[28]

The Catholic group, KRO, took the same position and alleged further that noncommercial broadcasting had been able to preserve its independence and that this should be the case with television. Among other things, it was contended that commercial TV would bring little that would be new in programming, and that the existing system, operating on a limited subsidy and competing with a commercial service having more abundant resources, would be doomed. The conclusions of the VARA Report, to which the KRO agreed, were:

1) TV should be entrusted to reliable organizations with desirable moral and cultural aims.

2) Taking into account creative talent available, the influence of TV on the viewer and the general economic situation, a gradual increase in the hours of transmission was desirable (at that time Dutch telecasts were limited to twelve hours per week).

3) Funds for TV should be provided by the viewers through license fees as was the case in radio, and, if necessary, the state should assist by providing subsidies.

4) The proposals of the business groups, commercially motivated as they were, would not serve the best cultural and educational interests of Dutch society.

5) Financing by means of advertising would endanger, might even preclude, freedom in program production.

6) TV can be developed and financed with license fees and with a gradually decreased state subsidy.[29]

The Government took no action on the ONTV and TEM recommendations, but the pressure for commercial television continued. This pressure, plus the growing demand for greater variety in programming, prompted the Minister, in 1961, to propose the establishment of a second program. It was his idea that the existing broadcasting organizations should continue to program on the first channel, but that business interests should play some part in the development of the second one.

His proposal met with great opposition in Parliament and in broadcasting circles.[30] An amendment to limit commercial programming on the second channel to one-third of the time was likewise rejected by a majority in Parliament. A special commission was then set up to negotiate a solution. It was composed of representatives from the Government, the broadcasting organizations and interested business groups. This "peace-keeping commission" was given until July 1965, to study the problem and make recommendations regarding the control and nature of the second program. In the meantime, all broadcasts on the second channel were to be presented by the existing licensees, the *Nederlandse Televisie Stichting* and its affiliated societies.[31]

"Pirate" Stations

SINCE the late fifties, a number of stations operating on ships at sea have been beaming commercial programs to Holland and other European countries. These stations are of the "disc jockey" type, featuring light music and news interspersed with commercials. While many persons in Holland object to this type of programming, there are large numbers, particularly younger people, who listen to them regularly.

Until early December 1964, a commercial television station was operating in the North Sea just six miles from Rotterdam, outside Dutch territorial waters. Construction of the station was completed in April of that year by a limited company known as *Reclame Exploitatie Maatschappij* (REM), owned by Dutch citizens and foreign nationals. It was erected on an artificial island and rested on stilts standing forty feet in the water. The platform supported a three hundred and sixty foot tower, housed transmission equipment, a studio and control rooms, and provided living quarters for technical and programming personnel.

TV-Nordzee, as it was called, provided light entertainment, featuring films such as "Ben Casey" and "Wagon Train," and its programs became quite popular with many Dutch viewers. According to the REM publicity, in October 1964, seventeen percent of the owners of TV sets in Holland (at that time there were about two million licensed sets) had installed the special antennas needed in many areas to get the best reception from the station.

Transmitting from outside territorial waters, the station had not been licensed by the Dutch Government and commercial broadcasting was then prohibited by law in Holland. While the station was on the air, there was a lively debate in the press, in Parliament and among the legal experts as to its propriety. Finally, Parliament passed a law prohibiting the *Noordzee* operation, and in December 1964, the Royal Navy and police dropped down in helicopters and silenced the transmitter.[32]

The growing popularity of some of the programs transmitted by this "clandestine" station no doubt was a large factor in convincing the Government and the private broadcasting association that limited commercial broadcasting should be authorized. Pursuant to parliamentary discussion on July 6 and 7, 1965, the Government took immediate steps to bring this about and to effect other regulatory changes in broadcasting for which there was a growing public demand.[33]

New Broadcasting Law and Regulations

As pointed out by *Televisie Nieuws,* published by the NTS Press Department in Hilversum, Holland, 1965 was "an eventful year in Holland's television history, and one which brought important changes in the organization of the Dutch broadcasting system."[34] In fact, serious differences of opinion as to policies and methods of operation caused the Government to resign in 1965. A new coalition Government was able to effect some political compromises and establish the basis for a new broadcasting bill. In the meantime, the existing law and regulations were amended by government decree to bring them in line with the agreement.

Televisie Nieuws, in January 1966, explained the reasons for these regulatory changes. After describing the previous organizations and administrative set-up by which radio and television had been carried on by the various religious and political groups and the NTS, it stated:

Despite the uniqueness of the Dutch broadcasting system, which coupled artistic and creative competition with technical and material cooperation, there was still some measure of discord among certain groups of the population, mainly because they felt themselves inadequately represented in the programming. This in turn has been a source of unrest in the evolution of television in this country. Attempts to introduce advertising on television by entrusting a second network to independent commercial companies after the example of Britain misfired by being voted down in Parliament by a large majority.

The political struggle reached a peak in the spring of 1965 with the resignation of the Cabinet, which was not brought about by a parliamentary conflict but by dissension among the Cabinet members themselves with regard to the definitive pattern of the broadcasting system.

The parties which formed the new coalition reached agreement on a number of preliminaries, which on the one hand respected the rights of the existing broadcasting associations, while on the other hand facilitated the contemplated greater openness. These principles were worked out in more detail in the amendments to the Television Decree mentioned earlier.[35]

After considerable debate in both houses of Parliament, a new law was passed which "dovetailed the trends" laid down in these transitional regulations.[36] This statute sanctioned a limited amount of advertising for both radio and television. It broke up the monopoly which had been enjoyed by the five broadcasting licensees (AVRO, KRO, NCRV, VARA and VPRO) for many years. While they retain their autonomy and will continue to produce programs for network distribution, some of the time which they had garnered for themselves in the past has now been given to other organizations that meet the requirements prescribed by the new law.

Subject to the approval of the Minister of Culture, Recreation and Social Work, four types of organizations are eligible for broadcasting privileges: (1) those such as the existing licensees that have as many as one hundred thousand members; (2) applicants from broadcasting organizations with as many as fifteen thousand registered members; (3) groups with no special broadcasting mission but which desire facilities for incidental broadcasts; and (4) the new Netherlands Broadcasting Foundation *(Nederlandse Omroepstichting)*, which will be described later.[37]

The large bodies are allocated time in proportion to the size of their membership and, as of October 1967, were using thirty-three hours per week, more than half of the total broadcasting time.[38] Each new applicant with as many as fifteen thousand members is granted one hour per week for television and three for radio, but must attain a membership of one hundred thousand within two years to retain these privileges.[39] The smaller organizations may not be allocated more than ten percent of the total transmitting time.

The new law provides for a merger of the Netherlands Radio Union (NRU) and the Netherlands Television Foundation (NTS), forming the Netherlands Broadcasting Foundation (NOS) previously mentioned. The NOS has taken over all functions (both radio and television) hitherto performed by the NRU and the NTS. It has at its disposal for the network programs at least fifteen percent of the total transmitting time for radio, and twenty-five percent of the total time for television. The maximum time available to the NOS for both media is forty percent.[40]

The new regulations, implementing the statute, provide that advertising is to be prepared by an independent foundation *(Stichting Ether Reclame,* STER). This body has the exclusive authority to produce and sell commercials for television, and, as of October 1967, was using two hours and five minutes per week for advertising.[41] The Foundation, however, must follow the directives of a newly created Advertising Council whose members are appointed by the Government and who represent varied segments of Dutch society, including the press. This Council regulates commercials to see that they comply with standards set by the Minister and also determines the rates to be charged for these messages.* Advertising must be so prepared and presented as not to "interfere with the programmes."[42]

---

*An interesting note is that beginning January 1,1968, alcoholic beverages will be advertised on TV. The spots must not be such that they promote excessive drinking and must not be directed at children. Advertising tobacco on TV will be strictly prohibited in 1968. *(Televisie Nieuws,* No. 7–8, July-August 1967, p. V–I.)

The net proceeds from advertising must be used largely to defray the costs of programming, and during the first three years a part of the revenue must be put in a reserve fund to be used to compensate the press for any losses which it may suffer in advertising revenue.*

Under the new law, the NOS is assigned important tasks, including (1) the coordination of all radio and TV programs; (2) handling all technical operations, including the directing of the use of all studios; and (3) the production of network programs (within fixed percentages as mentioned above). In the performance of the last task, more responsibility is now assumed by an expert NOS staff, and there is less dependence on the program personnel of the individual broadcasting organizations.[43] Assisting the NOS is a new Programme Council, with members broadly representing existing licensees and other important national cultural organizations. This Council provides continuing advice and criticism regarding network programming.

Ministerial Control

THE present laws give the Minister of Culture, Recreation and Social Work important overall regulatory responsibilities. He is assisted by a Government Commissioner who "watches over the observance of the legal regulations and is empowered to issue instructions to facilitate his supervisory tasks, which are binding for all bodies which have acquired transmitting time."[44]

In the Minister's behalf, he is authorized to enter the buildings and to attend the board meetings of the various broadcasting organizations; may require them to furnish information which may be helpful to him in performing his duties; and he may examine any of their books, documents and other records if they relate to broadcast operations.[45]

One-fourth of the members and the Chairman of the NOS Board are appointed by the Crown, but the Minister fixes the total number of the Board and appoints three-fourths of the members. The Minister also names two-thirds of the appointees to the Programme Council and half the appointees to a program coordination committee.[46] *Televisie Nieuws,* however, has emphasized that "all these appointments concern independent people, who are in no way to be regarded as government representatives."[47] It further elaborates on the Minister's authority and responsibilities:

> . . . the Crown can suspend or annul the decisions of the Board, though in such cases the Minister is required to publish in the government statute

---

*Recent reports indicate that newspapers in Holland have already begun to suffer from broadcast competition, with a loss of as much as ten percent of their advertising during the first year of commercial broadcasting.

book which decision is involved and the reasons for its suspension or nullification, so as to exclude all suspicion of arbitrariness.

The Minister is also authorized to instruct the Foundation to supply regional programmes. He has a finger in the pie with regard to rediffusion, he gives life to the Advertising Council, nominates the Board of the Advertising Foundation and settles differences which might possibly arise there. He is also concerned with *Radio Nederland Wereldomroep* (the Dutch Overseas Service) and is, to all intents and purposes, "treasurer" to the entire broadcasting system, insofar as he is responsible for the distribution over the various broadcasting organizations of the listener/viewer license revenue and the proceeds from advertising. This part of his task entails the approving of the budgets of all the licensed broadcasting organizations, and, later, their annual accounts.

This resume would not be complete without reference to the final article in the Act, which deals with the sanctions which the Minister can apply in cases of infringement. This article (61) runs: "Our Minister can reprimand or, in consultation with the Broadcasting Council, exclude from broadcasting activity for a given period, any institution which, having acquired transmitting time, infringes any of the terms of this Act, or any regulation pertaining to the execution thereof." Further, the Minister can withhold or withdraw, partially or wholly, that part of the financing allocated to a licensed broadcasting organization, if it does not comply with the provisions of the Act.[48]

The *Nieuws* further points out that "notwithstanding all the powers vested in the government with regard to broadcasting, one thing is expressly guarded against: the authorities have no say in what shall be broadcast, other than via supervision of the observance of the general regulations. As long as the Dutch broadcasting system has been in existence the transmissions have not been allowed to contain anything that could endanger the security of the state, the public order or good morals, nor could they, except with the permission of the Minister, be used for advertising purposes."[49]

The new Act provides that films shall be subject to review by the Central Board of Film Censors, and, unless approved by this Board, may not be broadcast. There is a proviso that films, or parts thereof, which the Board finds objectionable and unsuitable for persons under eighteen may not be presented before nine o'clock in the evening. Except for these restrictions, program content is left to the judgment of the licensees and there is a minimum of interference from the Government.[50]

The Outlook for Dutch Broadcasting

THE outlook for Dutch radio and television appears most promising. With expanded program schedules on a new FM network and the second TV channel, plus the financial support from both license fees and advertising, the variety and quality of the broadcast service should be greatly improved.

Plans are under way to enlarge the television facilities. Studios now in use are located in four converted buildings near Hilversum. Programs are also originated at various locations in Amsterdam, The Hague, Laren and other places. Two new studios with a floor space of about seven hundred square yards are being built, and further expansion of facilities, including assembly halls, is contemplated. When these plans are realized, the Netherlands will have one of the finest TV establishments in Europe.

On October 2, 1967, color television was introduced in Holland. During the first year of experimental operation, programs will be presented seven hours per week. The broadcasting associations will be responsible for the production of five hours and the NOS will provide the rest. It is expected that the number of hours will be gradually increased and that by 1970 color programs will be on the air twenty-two hours per week.[51]

There has been a considerable increase in the number of radio and TV receivers in recent years. As of July 1967, there were almost three million registered radio sets and more than two and one-half million television sets in a country with a population of about thirteen million.[52]

NOTES

1. Bernard Pingaud, *Holland: A Land Afloat* (New York: Viking Press, 1962), p. 73.
2. *Ibid.*, pp. 84–85.
3. *Nederlandse Radio Unie,* "The Origin, Development and Present Organization of Sound and Television Broadcasting in the Netherlands," *EBU Review,* 48B, April 1958, p. 9.
4. *Ibid.*
5. *Ibid.*
6. *Ibid.*
7. *Ibid.*
8. *Ibid.*
9. *Stattsblad,* 10403, 1935, The Hague.
10. *Nederlandse Radio Unie, EBU Review,* April 1958, p. 9.
11. *Ibid.*
12. *Ibid.*
13. *Ibid.,* p. 10.
14. *Ibid.*
15. *Ibid.*
16. *Ibid.*
17. *Nederlandse Radio Unie,* publicity release, March 1964. As of January 1968, one guilder was equivalent to 27.6 cents.
18. *Ibid.*
19. Official correspondence from NRU.
20. *Radio Nederland,* press release (undated), Hilversum.
21. *Radio Nederland,* undated publication, Hilversum.

22. *Nederlandse Radio Unie, EBU Review,* April 1958.
23. *Ibid.*
24. NTS, *Jaarverslay,* 1956; *EBU Bulletin,* July-August 1957, p. 496.
25. Official correspondence from *Radio Nederland,* Hilversum.
26. *Televisie Nieuws uit Nederland,* October 10, 1963 (NTS Press Department, P.O. Box 10, Hilversum), p. 1.
27. *Ibid.,* No. 23, January 1963, p. 2.
28. *Ibid.; EBU Bulletin,* September-October 1957, p. 558.
29. *Ibid.,* p. 559.
30. *EBU Review,* 89B, January 1965, p. 14.
31. *Ibid.,* pp. 14–15.
32. *New York Times,* International Edition, January 12, 1965, p. 5.
33. *EBU Review,* 93B, September 1965, p. 35.
34. *Ibid.* Also, see *Televisie Nieuws uit Nederland,* No. 9, September 1966, p. 1.
35. *Televisie Nieuws uit Nederland,* No. 2, January 1966, pp. 3–4.
36. *Ibid.,* No. 4, April 1967, p. 3.
37. *Ibid.*
38. *Ibid.,* No. 7–8, July-August 1967, p. II–3.
39. *Ibid.,* p. II–1.
40. *Ibid.,* No. 4, April 1967, p. 3.
41. *Ibid.,* No. 7–8, July-August 1967, p. I–1.
42. *Ibid.*
43. *Ibid.,* No. 4, April 1967, p. 1.
44. *Ibid.,* No. 7–8, July-August 1967, p. I–2.
45. *Ibid.*
46. *Ibid.,* p. I–3.
47. *Ibid.*
48. *Ibid.,* p. I–2.
49. *Ibid.*
50. *Ibid.*
51. *Ibid.,* No. 9, September 1967, p. I–1.
52. *Ibid.,* No. 7–8, July-August 1967, p. V–2.

IX

Radio Luxembourg:
"The Station of the Stars"

COMMERCIAL AND NONCOMMERCIAL BROADCASTERS in the United States would do well to study the history of Radio Luxembourg and its far-flung commercial operations. Its sales agent in the United States and Canada, RKO General, Inc., has claimed that "Radio-Luxembourg's unique set-up, the territories it covers, its multi-language broadcasts, all contribute to make it a major international medium, a crossroad of European culture and a unifying force in the Common Market." It is a unique broadcasting system in which the Government and private enterprise share the profits and which, according to its officials, is, since 1966, the largest source of revenue for the Grand Duchy.[1]

Luxembourg has only nine hundred and ninety-nine square miles and fewer than three hundred and fifty thousand people, but the commercial messages and programs of its radio station reach a Common Market audience of more than one hundred and twenty million people in an area with an aggregate national product of more than one hundred and twenty-six billion dollars.[2] It has been estimated that the station offers, per thousand homes, one of the lowest advertising rates of all the mass media in Europe.[3] RKO General, Inc., has stated that if a typical French-language program is considered, dividing "the average price paid by the average number of homes tuned in, we arrive at an average cost of 25 cents per thousand homes reached for a 30-second commercial announcement. If we count on two to three listeners per set, the average cost varies between 8 cents and 13 cents per thousand listeners reached."[4] With such comparatively low rates and wide coverage, it is not surprising that more than one hundred businesses have used its television facilities to sell their products and services; the radio broadcasts are similarly used.[5]

Early History

THE first transmitter in the Grand Duchy was built in 1924 by a young technician, Francois Aneu. He installed it in his attic and operated it with a power of one hundred watts. His broadcasts of musical concerts and plays in the city of Luxembourg interested the entrepreneurs in the possibilities of developing a commercial enterprise profitable to the Government as well as to private investors. Accordingly, he and a number of other imaginative citizens joined a group of French industrialists and on May 11, 1929, established the Luxembourg Society for Radio Studies *(La Société Luxembourgeoise d'Etudes Radiophoniques).*[6] The object of this organization, as provided in its by-laws, was to operate a commercial broadcast station in the Grand Duchy.[7] On December 19, 1929, under pressure from the Society and other radio enthusiasts, Parliament enacted a law providing that no station could operate in Luxembourg without authority from the Government and that any operation which might be approved would be subject to the conditions set forth in a contract to be agreed to and signed by both the Government and the broadcaster.[8] This law constituted the basis on which the Government, on December 29, 1930, granted a contract of concession to the Society for the establishment and operation of a commercial station.[9] The Society was granted a monopoly and, in case of need, subject to the approval of the Government, was authorized to reorganize itself to carry out more effectively the purposes of the concession. Pursuant to this authorization, the Society reconstituted itself and established the Luxembourg Broadcasting Company *(Compagnia Luxembourgeoise de Radiodiffusion)* which became the operating company for Radio Luxembourg.[10]

For more than thirty-five years, the station has provided a commercial service to a large portion of Europe. Its studios and main offices have been, from the beginning, in the *Villa Louvigny* in the city of Luxembourg. Its three inter-connected long-wave transmitters with a total power of eleven hundred kilowatts and three eight hundred and twenty-two foot towers, plus two medium-wave transmitters with a total power of twelve hundred kilowatts are located in the cities of Junglinster and Marnach near the Luxembourg border. The first three operate on 1293 meters (232 kc), while the latter two operate on 208.4 meters (1439 kc). Five short-wave transmitters, three of which are ultra-high, are also operated by the Company.

The concession, as modified from time to time, states that Radio Luxembourg shall provide high-quality educational broadcasts, including news and informational programs. The station is also required to broadcast some programs in the native or various foreign languages authorized by the Government.[11] Free time must be given for official government communications concerned with the protection of human life, and the security and well-being of the State. The concession also contains the usual prohibitions against programs which may disturb the peace or unduly offend established mores. Likewise, anti-religious broadcasts, or those reflecting a political bias, are prohibited.[12] Regulatory authority is exercised by two commissions appointed by the Government. One is concerned with technical operations, the other with programming. Thus the interests of the State are safeguarded and programs may be prohibited which are believed contrary to law and regulations.[13] In accordance with function, the concessionaire is required to retain copies of program scripts and upon demand from the Government make them available for study and review.[14]

The contract of concession authorizes Radio Luxembourg to sell commercials and provides that the Government shall share in the profits. One important function of the Government is to see that proper accounting procedures are followed and that the income is properly distributed to the Government and the stockholders in accordance with the conditions of the concession.[15] A majority of the Board of Directors and of the Company's employees must be Luxembourg nationals and live in the country. Also, insofar as possible, equipment used by the station must be manufactured and sold in the Grand Duchy.[16] Furthermore, regarding broadcasting, the Company is under a mandate to observe all international treaties and conventions to which Luxembourg is a signatory.[17] The organizational structure of the Company consists of the General Assembly of stockholders, the Board of Directors, an Executive Committee, an Oversight Committee, the Director and his deputies. While the organization must function in accordance with the contract of concession and is subject to government regulation, it is reasonably independent, and enjoys financial and administrative autonomy.

In 1961, Radio Luxembourg celebrated its thirtieth anniversary. In a document published that year, a number of contributors paid tribute to the many achievements of the station.[18] Gust Graas, the Company's Secretary, described a part of the enterprise's dramatic history. As he has said, from the very beginning, the station conceived its function to be international and set about to attract a wide European audience. Whole evenings were given over to programs designed for particular areas. On Monday evening the entire schedule might be in English to appeal to countries in the United Kingdom, followed on successive evenings by programs for the French, Germans, Luxembourgeoise, Belgians, Dutch, and at greater intervals for Italians, Swiss, Czechs and Poles.

The formula was simple—much music with comparatively little speech. Classical music was featured and many soloists of international renown appeared before the microphones between 1933 and 1939. The broadcasting of great music with an international appeal, using distinguished artists was, for the time, a revolutionary accomplishment in European radio. The station came to be recognized as the "Station of the Stars." From the beginning, news also constituted an important aspect of the programming. World news, presented several times per day in various languages, attracted many European listeners. These news programs, accompanied by advertising, presented a threat to the print media. Newspapers and magazines at first expressed concern and even hostility. However, because the station's audience was rapidly increasing into the millions, the press could no longer afford to be antagonistic. By 1936, newspapers in seven European countries, in response to public demand, were publishing regularly the station's program schedules.

In addition to music and news, these schedules included other types of programs. For example, beginning in 1935, regular reviews of contemporary literature were presented. There were discussions of social and economic affairs. Sports events such as the *Tour de France* were dramatically covered. And regular educational broadcasts for children such as "Art and School" were finding their place in the program schedules. Time was allowed for religious broadcasts presented under the auspices of both Catholic and Protestant churches.

Desiring to reach the largest possible audience, the station began to feature more entertainment programs in 1936. More time was devoted to light music. Entertaining documentaries, dramatic shows, direct news reports via mobile transmitters—all this and more gave the station widespread appeal and made it increasingly attractive to advertisers. While entertainment was stressed, serious programs were not neglected. Religious services for shut-ins were broadcast. In the midst of the growing disorder in Europe, discussion programs such as "The Youth of the World," and "International Friendship" were presented regularly and heard by millions of people over Europe. With conflicting propaganda flooding the airways, Europeans, particularly those across the Rhine, turned to Radio Luxembourg for objective news reports and analysis.

As its programs became more popular, the station increased its hours of broadcasting. In 1933, it was broadcasting only forty hours per week. This was more than doubled in 1935. By 1937, the weekly schedule had grown to more than one hundred hours, with programming from seven until one o'clock in the morning on two days of the week. The station became increasingly popular as an advertising medium. Arrangements were made with advertising agencies in the different countries for the sale of commercials. Stockholders who had risked capital in an uncertain, pioneering venture began to realize dividends. This continued growth called for expanded facilities. In 1936, the Company purchased the land and buildings in the *Villa Louvigny* which it had previously rented. Modifications were made and new facilities added. By 1939, Radio Luxembourg was housed in a grand *Maison de la Radio*.

The War Years

ON September 21, 1939, in accordance with its then strict policy of neutrality in war-time, the Luxembourg Government ordered the station to cease operations.[19] On May 10, 1940, the Nazis invaded the small country and took control of the radio installations. Four weeks later, they put the station back in operation as a military medium and later made it an important link in the European network of the German Reich. For four years its transmitters were used to disseminate propaganda and serve the military purposes of the Wehrmacht.

On May 24, 1944, foreseeing the liberation, the Luxembourg Government (with war-time offices in Washington) agreed to make the station's facilities available to the Allies. On September 10, 1944, the German armies fled the country. Before doing so, however, they dynamited the installations at the *Villa Louvigny,* confiscated much of the studio and transmitting equipment, and destroyed important records. Although considerable damage had been done, the transmission facilities at Junglinster were still working because of the help of some technical personnel. For ten months, the station was used by SHAEF (Supreme Headquarters, Allied Expeditionary Force), and for a period after July 1945, was operated by the United States Office of War Information.[20]

Financial Problems and Postwar Expansion into TV and FM

AT the conclusion of the war, Radio Luxembourg faced a grim situation. Its equipment was in a state of disrepair. Its financial resources were almost nonexistent. England, from which the station had derived a substantial portion of its advertising support prior to the war, now prohibited the transfer of currencies. In France and other European countries ravaged by the war, there was a critical shortage of consumer goods. Since the meager supplies were stringently rationed, there was practically no market for the sale of radio advertising. With only enough in its treasury to keep the station operating for about a month, the Company officials sought desperately to secure additional financing. A group of Belgian business concerns responded with an investment of six million francs in the purchase of new stock. The International Bank provided a loan of fifteen million francs. With this additional capital, the reconstruction and improvement of the station facilities began. In December 1948, a directional antenna was constructed and long-wave transmissions were initiated which increased the station's French coverage by forty percent. New studio equipment and teletype machines were installed. Program service was expanded.

Income from the sale of advertising began to come in, but the different devaluations of the English and French currencies during the postwar period caused the Company to suffer substantial losses and to experience continuing financial problems. In 1949, the situation was so critical that the officials considered dissolving the Company. But some stockholders and government officials were willing to risk additional capital. Severe economies were effected. Personnel was reduced and, by 1952, with economic recovery on its way to Europe, revenues from the sale of advertising began to grow. The station survived the financial crisis and since that time has become an increasingly profitable enterprise, paying good dividends to the Government and the private stockholders.[21]

In addition to using long-wave facilities for French listeners, by 1951, the station was transmitting from Junglinster via medium-wave new programs in English, Flemish and Luxembourgeoise. At the *Villa Louvigny,* new studios were constructed over the six thousand square meter auditorium in which the concerts of the Radio Luxembourg Symphony Orchestra were held. This permitted the simultaneous transmission of concerts on four different frequencies designed for different European audiences, and provided new recording facilities for the musical programs. By 1956, with the increases in power and the addition of both medium- and long-wave facilities, Radio Luxembourg was achieving effective coverage throughout a large part of Europe, with excellent reception in France, Germany, England, Belgium, Holland and the Scandinavian countries, as well as satisfactory reception in Austria and Switzerland.

On July 1, 1954, the Government authorized the Company to establish a television station, with studios located in the *Villa Louvigny,* operating with eight hundred and nineteen line definition, and with transmission facilities at Dudelange at a place called "Ginzebierg."[22] Construction was completed about seven months later and the station began regular, commercial service on May 14, 1955, with an inaugural telecast which included the Grand Duchess, the Prince Consort and the President of the Luxembourg Parliament.[23] New television studios and production facilities, housed in an imposing tower constructed on the ancient bastion of the *Villa,* were added in 1957. Today, Tele-Luxembourg operates with a transmitting power of one hundred kilowatts. With a coverage radius of approximately one hundred miles, it provides service to Lorraine Province, the most densely populated and industrialized section of eastern France, the French-speaking part of Belgium, the Saar, and a section of West Germany close to the French-Belgian border. This market has a population of 5,770,000.

In October 1960, a FM station was established. With its limited range, this new facility has been dedicated especially to the service of the Luxembourg people. Whereas the program service on medium- and long-wave is largely designed for an international audience and geared to attract advertisers, the FM programs are prepared to meet the particular interests of a well-educated populace in the Grand Duchy and contain a heavier component of broadcasts with intellectual and aesthetic appeal. Radio-Tele-

Luxembourg officials have stated that two additional FM transmitters for German programs began operations in 1965 and 1967.

Current Radio and Television Programming

AFTER the war, the international service of Radio Luxembourg continued to emphasize entertainment. Those who are responsible for the programs frankly admit that, since the station's only source of revenue is advertising, the programs must have broad appeal. This, they say, means some degree of servitude to the advertiser. "Common sense," says Jean Luc, the Program Director, "forbids dedication of the station to *l'experience esthetique d'avant-garde.*"[24] The management holds that popularity is the criterion of the station's success, and to be widely popular, the programs must be intelligible to the masses, *la radiodiffusion populaire dort parler le language de tout la monde.* It is also stressed that care must be taken not to offend the feelings and conventions of the majority in the various countries served.

Approximately two-thirds of Radio Luxembourg's current programs are devoted to popular music. Musically knowledgeable disc jockeys play an important part in the programming and are chosen with great care. The station seeks to avoid the jukebox image and, while generally catering to unsophisticated musical tastes, it does not depend entirely upon the top ratings. Radio Luxembourg attempts to establish new patterns of musical taste by frequently featuring new music which it believes has merit and potential popular appeal.

The station also devotes much time to the *feuilleton* type of drama, or simple, serialized broadcasts with a familiar tone or reminiscent content. While these programs are light and entertaining, the producers consider their *literature radiophonique populaire* superior to American soap opera.[25] They believe that these short dramas meet a need for escapism and may present as many as ten in any one day. Station surveys have shown them to be popular with a large percentage of the listeners.

Although emphasizing popular music and drama, the station occasionally includes informational broadcasts in its entertainment shows. While the didactic is generally avoided, at times interesting historical, biographical and scientific facts are presented. The station's management feels that the great majority listen to radio primarily for entertainment but that they will give attention to educational messages if they are skillfully woven into the program structure, are not too heavy, and are readily intelligible.

Another important aspect of programming is the reporting and analysis of news. Radio Luxembourg prides itself on world-wide coverage and strives for accuracy and objectivity. While it does feature analyses and interpretations of world events, it seeks to avoid polemics and advocacy. The station, as often as possible, brings to its microphones responsible people with conflicting viewpoints who relate their stories and opinions directly. One of the outstanding news programs is *"Service d'Information de Radio Luxembourg."* The directors of this program speak with pride about the manner in which the news items are prepared and reported. Sources of information are critically evaluated and identified for listeners. Careful crosschecks are made. While hypotheses are analyzed and facts are interpreted, strict regard for objectivity is maintained.

Special mention should be made of the International Night Service which was first broadcast in September 1961. It now begins at midnight and is broadcast simultaneously on long-wave, medium-wave and short-wave until three o'clock in the morning. Reports indicate good reception in France, Belgium, Switzerland, Luxembourg, Germany, Austria, Holland, Great Britain, Ireland, Norway, Denmark and Sweden, as well as a considerable audience in such countries as Finland, Hungary, Poland, Yugoslavia and Czechoslovakia. The program is broadcast from the studios in Luxembourg by French, German and English disc jockeys and consists largely of "pop" European and American tunes, time checks and frequent reports on the weather and road conditions. It was estimated in 1963 that the total European audience for this program was more than eight million.[26]

Tele-Luxembourg programming is varied and includes quality American and European films as well as the TV series produced by Radio Luxembourg's subsidiary production company, Paris-Television. Live broadcasts consist of variety shows, plays, contests, sports (especially wrestling, which is popular with European viewers) and news programs. The station attempts to keep in touch with important activities in the various communities of its coverage area. Special programs are broadcast from industrial and trade fairs. Telecasts, often sponsored by local newspapers, are occasionally devoted to particular cities. Community and public affairs programming make up an important part of the Tele-Luxembourg schedules. A 1963 brochure lists more than one hundred key advertisers as having purchased time on the station.[27]

Commercial Competition

UNTIL recent years, Radio Luxembourg had little commercial competition. However, since the late fifties, a number of stations operating on ships and fortifications at sea beyond national boundaries have been beaming commercial programs to European countries within Radio Luxembourg's coverage area. These stations are of the "disc jockey" type, featuring light music and news, interspersed with commercials. Located in international waters and unlicensed to broadcast from the countries to which they direct their programs, they operate on frequencies without any authorization from the International Telecommunications Union, the agency in Geneva with which most countries are affiliated and which officially approves channel assignments for domestic and international broadcasting. The European Broadcasting Union and several European governments are increasingly concerned about these "pirate" stations and are exploring legal means to prohibit all such transmissions.[28] While many persons within the coverage areas of these stations object to their programs and mode of operation, their broadcasts attract a large number of listeners, particularly the young people. As long as they continue to reach masses of people in Europe, advertisers will continue to use their facilities, and Radio Luxembourg will not have the virtual monopoly on the sale of radio advertising which it once had.*

Radio Luxembourg must also compete with the land stations located within its service areas. The trend of European broadcasting is toward commercialization. For example, Switzerland, Germany, Holland, Great Britain, Ireland and some of the Eastern European countries (all within the range of Luxembourg transmission) now permit advertising on their television stations. West Germany and Holland also sanction a limited amount of advertising on their radio stations. It is true that France and Belgium as yet have not commercialized either their radio or TV broadcasting, but indications are that they are moving in that direction.[29]

In Belgium, where Radio Luxembourg maintains recording studios and a large sales staff and has one of its largest audiences, there are strong pressures on the Government to authorize *Radio–Television Belge* to broadcast commercials. Some Belgian authorities believe that the revenue from advertising would offset the increasing public expense incurred by broadcasting and would permit expanded facilities and improved service. Moreover, some business interests feel that their products and services are at a disadvantage when competing against those promoted by foreign stations.[30]

For a long time there has been intermittent agitation in France for the introduction of commercial broadcasting. Although there are some indications that advertising might eventually be permitted, the Government has not yet sanctioned any commercialization of radio and television.[31]

Perhaps one cause for the delay in authorizing transmitters to carry advertising is that the French Government already owns interests in Radio

---

*Recently, the British Parliament enacted legislation prohibiting "pirate" broadcasting near English shores and Radio Caroline and Radio London, operating in that vicinity, have been forced to close down. This eliminates some of Radio-Tele-Luxembourg's competition in that area.

Luxembourg and other foreign commercial stations operating near the French borders. A news item dated May 21, 1965, in the international edition of the *New York Herald Tribune* stated that the French Government holds fifteen percent of Radio Luxembourg's stock in the name of *Havas,* described as a "state-controlled advertising agency." The article stated further that "informed sources" confirmed reports that the Government was negotiating to buy an additional thirteen percent owned by the *Companie Generale de Telegraphie Sans Fil* (CSF). (The Luxembourg Government would not agree to this and the stock was sold to other parties.) It was also pointed out that the French Government's "big radio interests are held by the state group *Societe Financiere de Radiodiffusion* (Sofirad) which is said to own one half of Europe No. 1, 83 percent of Radio Monte Carlo, 35 percent of Tele-Monte Carlo and 97 percent of Andorra radio."[32]

All these are profitable commercial stations which compete with Radio Luxembourg for listeners and advertisers. Europe No. 1's transmitters, located in the Saar region, have attracted large French and German audiences. No official French documents regarding these matters were made available to the author after the *Herald Tribune* article appeared. However, conversations with informed persons in Paris and Luxembourg and recent reports from Radio Luxembourg officials leave no doubt that the French Government not only holds substantial interests in these commercial stations but also desires to secure more.

In France as well as in other European countries, where Radio Luxembourg has tended to dominate the broadcasting advertising market, there is now a marked trend toward commercial domestic stations. However, with a program format which has achieved such popularity in a major portion of Europe and with the enterprise, imagination and faith exhibited by its owners and managers through the years, Radio Luxembourg should continue to be a prosperous operation. This seems confirmed by recent financial reports and audience surveys.

In October 1965, Radio Luxembourg announced that it had begun transmission on a new one million dollar transmitter which, the station claimed, is one of the most powerful in Europe. The results of a survey conducted by the Social Surveys Gallup Poll, Ltd., were also revealed. The poll stated that Radio Luxembourg's audience in Great Britain and Ireland exceeded thirty-seven million compared with the combined audience of a little more than thirteen million claimed by the "pirate" stations, Radio London and Radio Caroline, which operated off the English coast until September 1967.[33] The survey also showed that several of Radio Luxembourg's top shows had been attracting over two million late night listeners as compared with the five hundred thousand the BBC reported it had after midnight. The managing director of Radio Luxembourg, Geoffrey Everitt, stated, "Our revenue has rocketed in the year since the pirate stations started business. Our advertising earnings this year are estimated at $1,800,000 which represents an increase of nearly 30 percent over the 12 months prior to the advent of pirate broadcasting."[34]

NOTES

1. *Radio Luxembourg, The Station of the Stars* (London: Gordon Ross Company, undated), p. 4. (The publication is available at Radio Luxembourg, Inc., 38 Hertford Street, London W. I.)
2. *Radio Luxembourg,* a presentation of RKO General, Inc., p. 5. RKO General exclusively represents Radio-Luxembourg and Tele-Luxembourg in the United States and Canada. This brochure contains information about the station's coverage areas, including maps. It also provides information regarding the types of programs presented to the various countries within the station's coverage area—France, Belgium, Holland, Germany, Switzerland—and supplies research data relating to the number and types of listeners.
3. *Ibid.*
4. *Ibid.*
5. *Radio Luxembourg, The Station of the Stars,* pp. 8–9.
6. Raymon Mehlen, *Les Cahiers, Luxembourgeois, Radio-Tele Luxembourg, Imprimeria Bourg* (Luxembourg: Bourger, 1961), p. 30. This volume contains an excellent study of Radio Luxembourg, its origin, development and control, plus a detailed discussion of the station's policies and program practices. Written in French, it was published as a tribute to the station on its thirtieth anniversary. It was prepared by officials of the Company and carries the endorsement of the Luxembourg Prime Minister who wrote the introduction. Much of this chapter is based upon translations of this book.
7. *Ibid.*
8. Law of December 19, 1929. *Pasinomie, Luxembourgeoise, Recueil des Lois, Decrets, Arrets, Reglements Generaux & Speciaux, et., Le Grand-Duche de Luxembourg,* 1929–32, pp. 218–219.
9. Mehlen.
10. *Ibid.,* p. 31.
11. Article I, Contract of Concession, dated August 20, 1930. This concession was authorized by the law of December 19, 1929, which set forth the conditions for the establishment and use of a broadcasting station in the Grand Duchy of Luxembourg.
12. *Ibid.,* Article IX.
13. *Ibid.,* Article XI.
14. *Ibid.*
15. *Ibid.*
16. Mehlen, p. 32.
17. *Ibid.*
18. *Ibid.*
19. *Ibid.,* p. 41.
20. *Ibid.,* p. 42. For details of its "black propaganda" use toward the end of World War II, see also U.S. Army, 12th Army Group, *Report of Opera-*

tions (Final After Action Report), XIV, Publicity and Psychological Warfare Section, 160–161, 190–195; and Psychological Warfare Division, Supreme Headquarters, Allied Expeditionary Force, *An Account of Its Operations in the Western European Campaign, 1944–1945,* Bad Homberg, Germany, October 1945, particularly pp. 39–42. These volumes contain the details of the liberation and use of Radio Luxembourg.

21. *Billboard,* October 16, 1965, p. 24.
22. *EBU Bulletin,* November-December 1954, p. 718. Also, see Mehlen, p. 46.
23. *Ibid.,* July-August 1955, pp. 437–438. Also, see Mehlen, p. 46.
24. Mehlen, p. 69.
25. *Ibid.,* pp. 70–72.
26. See *Radio Luxembourg, The Station of the Stars,* p. 15, for more detailed information about this international night service.
27. *Radio Luxembourg,* RKO General, Inc., pp. 26–28.
28. See report from Hamburg (WPS) in *State Journal* (Lansing, Michigan), December 20, 1964, p. D.14. Also, see recent issues of the *EBU Review.*
29. For example, regarding France, see article by John Urquhart, *New York Herald Tribune,* International Edition, April 10 and 11, 1965, p. 7.
30. For further discussion of the status of commercial broadcasting in Belgium, see Chapter VII.
31. For further discussion of the status of commercial broadcasting in France, see Chapter XIV.
32. *New York Herald Tribune,* International Edition, May 22–23, 1965, p. 7.
33. *Billboard,* October 16, 1965, p. 24.
34. *Ibid.*

· D ·

THE NORDEN COUNTRIES

X

The Danish Kingdom and Iceland: Individualism and State Control

Introduction

THE Norden countries include Denmark, Finland, Iceland, Norway and
Sweden. The Faeroe Islands now have home rule but still remain under
Danish sovereignty. The languages and ethnographic, political and cultural
development of these countries are closely related, and their patterns of
broadcasting are similar.

As Nils Andrén has indicated, there are many ways in which these countries differ and these differences have intermittently affected their mutual
relationships; however, "during the last decades the gradual progress of
Nordic cooperation and the general development of Nordic interrelations
have actively contributed towards increasing the awareness of common ties
among the five nations of the region."[1]

Private initiative, free enterprise, democracy and representative government are important aspects of the national life in all these countries. However, as one Scandinavian authority has said, "the state has become a potent
factor in controlling economic individualism to the end that the benefits of
individualism shall be more widely shared and the evils mitigated."[2] The
result has been much economic planning and control. Many industries are
state-owned and operated. For example, in Norway, the Government has
ownership interests in mines, factories and in other industries such as alu-
minum, hydro-electricity, chemicals, transportation and communications.
State monopolies over grain and alcohol were established before the Second
World War. Similar patterns of state control are to be found in the other
Nordic countries.

Traditionally, these countries have emphasized education. For example,
in Sweden, thousands of study groups provide knowledge and training in
many areas. The Government allows substantial subsidies for these and
other educational activities. Thus Swedish citizens generally are enlightened
and illiteracy is practically nonexistent.

Religion has always played an important part in the life of these peoples, most of whom are Lutherans, the official church of the Nordic countries. However, freedom of worship is recognized and a small minority of other religious groups are active.

Broadcasting in the Norden countries has been greatly influenced by these social and cultural patterns. The systems all enjoy a monopolistic privilege, are subject to a minimum of state control and are allowed maximum freedom of expression. Monopoly is balanced by the wide participation of citizens in councils of administration. While entertainment is not neglected, educational and cultural programs are emphasized and, so far, pressures for commercial broadcasting have been resisted. As might be expected, religion finds an important place in the program schedules.

The increasing cooperation (Nordisk samarbejde) between the Scandinavian countries has been compared to that between the members of the British Commonwealth of Nations. One important basis for this cooperation has been a mutual understanding of the various languages. While it is true that modern Icelandic is not well understood outside Iceland and the Faeroe Islands; and Finnish, a language of Asiatic origin, is not intelligible to Germanic Scandinavians, still Danish is taught in the Icelandic schools and Swedish is recognized as the second official language in Finland. Whenever nationals of the five countries get together, they usually can communicate simply by alternating speech in Danish, Norwegian and Swedish. And, as will be explained later, the cooperative movement among these countries has found an important expression in broadcasting. For several decades knowledge has been shared and broadcast resources pooled, and plans point to an even greater cooperative effort in the Nordic area and with other countries in Europe and other parts of the world.

Early Radio Regulation in Denmark

THE regulation of radio in Denmark dates to 1907 when a law was enacted giving the Minister of Public Works the authority to grant licenses for wireless communication.[3] In succeeding years, amateurs played an important part in early developments.

A public institution, the Statsradiofonien, was established on April 1, 1925,[4] and in accordance with the authority granted in the 1907 Act, the Minister, on February 26, 1926, issued an order transferring control of all radio from private interests to this new institution.[5]

The Statsradiofonien, as subsequently constituted by a 1930 law, consisted of a Radio Council of fifteen members representing various agencies of the Government, the press and listeners' associations (made up mainly of amateurs). It was granted an exclusive franchise for broadcasting by the

Minister of Public Works who continued to act in a regulatory capacity over all radio communication.[6]

In 1934 a technical commission worked out plans for a broadcasting center. A building committee was appointed, and in 1938 construction was started. The project was not completed until 1945 when the building was officially dedicated and named "Radio House." The introduction of a second radio network, and the development of television in the early fifties necessitated the construction, in 1958, of a new wing and an additional story on the building. This represented a forty percent expansion of the facilities, totaling 4,235,000 square feet.[7]

For more than a quarter of a century the national development of broadcasting was in the hands of the *Statsradiofonien*. A network of stations was established to provide radio service for the whole country. The system was financed by an annual assessment paid by the owners of radio receivers.

As was true in most of Western Europe, Danish broadcasting during the Second World War was subject to German control. During the Occupation, the official Danish Press, as well as the *Statsradiofonien*, were subject to strict Nazi censorship. The propaganda efforts of the Nazis, however, were thwarted by the growth of underground newspapers and radio transmissions carried on by groups active in the Resistance Movement.[8]

Postwar Radio Growth

FOLLOWING the war, broadcasting was expanded. Until 1951, however, there was only one radio network with four connecting stations. But in the spring of that year, the *Statsradiofonien* initiated a second network and enlarged its facilities to include two additional AM and two FM stations.[9] To achieve a more balanced program service one network emphasized entertainment, while the other presented the more serious programs.

According to its 1953–54 *Annual Report,* the *Statsradiofonien* had four hundred and twenty-nine permanent employees on its payroll, including the members of both the symphony and the light orchestras.[10] The 1954–55 *Report* showed that the number of radio licenses had increased to 1,329,338.[11]

Development of Television

PLANS for the development of television began in the late forties, and in early 1950 an experimental station, using the six hundred and twenty-five line system, started broadcasting four times a week.[12] The service was subsequently regularized and by 1956 it was estimated that there were thirty thousand TV receivers in use.[13]

Establishment of Radio Denmark

ON June 11, 1959, a new broadcasting law (*Radioloven*) was passed.[14] This statute provided for the establishment of an independent, self-governing public institution and granted it a monopoly in the field of both sound and visual broadcasting. It replaced the *Statsradiofonien* and was given the name Radio Denmark (*Danmarks Radio*).

As it was created then and functions today, its organization includes a Radio Council of eighteen members. Twelve of the members are nominated by the Minister for Cultural Affairs, two to represent his office and ten to represent viewers. Each political party represented on the Parliamentary Finance Committee (five parties were represented on this Committee in 1960) designates a member to the Council. The Minister of Public Works appoints one member who, under the law, must be a technical expert in communications.

The Radio Council meets monthly and formulates general policies with respect to administration, finances and programming. It appoints and has the service of two important committees—Administrative (*Forretningsudvalget*) with six members and Program (*Programudvalget*) with ten members.

The Minister of Cultural Affairs may appoint as many as ten additional members to the Program Committee with specialized knowledge about various aspects of Danish life. Its duties consist of reviewing, criticizing and approving projected programs as well as evaluating and criticizing programs already broadcast. Matters that must be submitted to the Council for approval include repertoire plans, plays, films, manuscripts of speeches, discussions of controversial subjects, and questions of principle concerning political broadcasting.[15]

The Minister also appoints, on recommendation of the Radio Council, the Director-General (*Generaldirektoren*) of Radio Denmark. Working under the Director-General are two program directors, one for radio and one for television.

There are four program departments operating jointly for radio and television: Talks and Actualities, Drama and Literature, Music, and Entertainment. The heads of these departments are responsible to the Program Committee and the Radio Council for the content of the broadcasts and to the Director-General for financial matters.

Also working under the Director-General are the Secretariat and the

Administration, Technical, Press and Foreign Relations departments. An important function of the latter department is to conduct the overseas short-wave service.[16]

Present Facilities

DOMESTIC broadcasting is presently supplied by one long-wave transmitter of one hundred and fifty kilowatts, seven medium-wave transmitters totalling 144.50 kilowatts and eight powerful FM stations.[17] Nation-wide TV coverage is achieved with eight main and three auxiliary transmitters.[18] Short-wave facilities provide regular transmissions to the Americas, the Far East, Australia and New Zealand, Southeast Asia, Africa, the Near East and Greenland. In 1964 more than seven hundred thousand radio sets and almost a million television receivers had been licensed for use in Denmark.[19]

The growth of television has necessitated the renting of premises outside the Radio House to provide studio space. A separate television center, however, is being constructed on the outskirts of Copenhagen. Three studios have already been completed and are in use. The Technical Center with elaborate video-tape and telecine facilities was approaching completion at the time of this writing. Future plans include the erection of a canteen, office building, spacious facilities for news and public affairs programming, costume workshops, rehearsal halls and residential housing units for staff members.[20]

Recent Program Patterns

ACCORDING to the 1964 official *Handbook of Denmark,* Program I and Program II broadcast more than eight thousand radio-hours that year. Two programs were presented concurrently every evening and on Sundays and holidays. Program III was on the air about five thousand hours in 1964, with half of its broadcast time devoted to original musical productions. The Danish Radio Symphony Orchestra, which has performed at the Edinburgh Festival and has taken numerous foreign tours, is featured on Program III and has achieved a central position in the musical life of the nation.

The Danes are great lovers of music and a large percentage of both radio and television programs are musical. However, in radio, "talks, outside broadcasts, parliamentary broadcasts, drama and literature, as well as entertainment, all get their fair share of broadcasting hours."[21]

In television (about twenty-eight hours per week with a six hundred and twenty-five line definition), about half of the broadcasting time is devoted to talks, news and discussions and the remaining fifty percent is allotted to sports, theatre, literature, entertainment and classical music. Denmark is affiliated with the Scandinavian television network (Nordvision) and the European network (Eurovision) and is an important contributor to these international organizations.

Special mention should be made of newscasts which occupy important positions in program schedules. The News Service (*Presseus Radioavis*) is administered by a committee consisting of five members of the Radio Council and five representatives of the Press. The committee is responsible for the finances of the news service and appoints the Editor-in-Chief (*Chefredaktoren*). The representatives of the Press decide editorial matters, but Radio Denmark bears all costs of the news service.[22]

All political parties are allowed to present programs, but such broadcasts must be approved by the Program Committee of Radio Denmark. There is a "political quarantine" one month prior to elections, except for the official election broadcasts, when each party is allowed thirty minutes to discuss its policies and promote its candidates.[23]

Educational Broadcasting

BECAUSE of the great emphasis which the Danish people have placed upon education, there is practically no illiteracy. Both the public and the private schools are of comparatively high quality and, in general, the citizens are enlightened.

As early as 1928, the *Statsradiofonien* cooperated with educators by making its facilities available for instructional programs, consisting of lectures, readings, music demonstrations and lessons for the classroom. This educational service was suspended in 1945 but was resumed on an experimental basis in September 1947. In 1949, the Danish School Broadcasting Service was established, with the Radio Council of *Statsradiofonien* and its Talks Department in charge of operations.[24]

As established then and still in effect, its pattern of operation includes a day-to-day manager responsible to the Director of Talks in Radio Denmark (successor to *Statsradiofonien*) who in turn is responsible to the Radio Council. The Working Committee of School Broadcasting is made up of two members of the Radio Council, one member of the Program Committee of Radio Denmark, the chief inspector of primary schools and training colleges, the chief inspector of secondary schools, the Chairman of the Board of School Broadcasting, and two members of the executive board of the Danish Teachers' Association. The Board of School Broadcasting consists of twenty-two persons representing all types of Danish schools.

The Working Committee and the management meet periodically for consideration of school broadcasting problems and meet once each year with the Board of School Broadcasting for a joint discussion of past performance and future plans. Any projected program for instructional broadcasting must have the final approval of the Radio Council.

The objectives of school broadcasting in Denmark have been expressed officially as follows:

> . . . educational broadcasting *must not, cannot,* and *is not* intended to replace the teacher. Teaching cannot be based on the school radio, because the school radio does not teach. On the other hand the cooperation of the teacher is indispensable, and often a "school radio lesson" must be reckoned to take up more of the teacher's time than a "normal lesson" and on the whole to make heavier demands on him. School radio is an educational aid ranking with motion pictures, slides and other audio-visual aids. A broadcast is to constitute only a supplement to daily teaching, but provided that
> (1) the teacher has prepared the children for listening in (studied the broadcast with them in advance),
> (2) the broadcast is well arranged by the school broadcasting section,
> (3) the technical equipment is in working order.
>
> School radio may become quite an excellent instructional aid and a most valuable supplement to daily teaching, as it is able to corroborate and emphasize the statement of the teacher and the words of the text-book.[25]

Language lessons have been featured in Danish radio almost from the beginning.[26] The number of subjects taught on a regular basis has been increased in recent years and now includes Danish, Swedish, English, German, French, Italian, Spanish and Russian.[27]

Adult education holds a relatively important place in broadcast schedules. The so-called "Evening High School" and the "Sunday University" involving study groups at different reception points have proved to be quite popular in some areas of the country. In 1966, a series, "How Your Body Works," was presented on the TV network. Also, a number of experimental television series in chemistry, mathematics and biology with direct appeal to the adult population have been completed.

Financial Problems

IN the November 1965 issue of the *EBU Review,* Mr. Valdemar Christensen, the Head of School Broadcasting, *Danmarks Radio,* wrote:

> The prospects of adult education are so immense that they are hard to imagine. The financial and technical requirements, though, are far more per-

spicuous, and facing them will probably leave us with sufficient food for thought for a while.[28]

As in the other European countries, the financial aspects of broadcasting, particularly in television, pose serious problems. It is this situation generally which has caused a large percentage of European countries in recent years to authorize, on a limited basis, commercial sponsorship of programs. Denmark, thus far, has resisted this trend and depends entirely upon the Broadcasting Fund (*Radiospredningsfonden*) made up of the proceeds from license fees on radio and TV receivers. The annual fee for one or more radio receivers in a household is forty Kroner.[29] Rough calculations, based on the number of receivers licensed (both radio and TV), indicate that between twenty and thirty million dollars are available annually for broadcasting operations and expansion of facilities.

Faeroe Islands

THIS group of twenty-one islands, with a population of about thirty-five thousand, is located in the North Atlantic about two hundred miles northwest of the Shetland Islands. They are a part of the Danish Kingdom but under a law enacted in 1948 the Faeroe Islands acquired home rule and two representatives in the Danish Parliament (*Folketing*).

The Islands are now equipped with a five kilowatt medium-wave transmitter which broadcasts about two hours daily, Monday through Friday, and three hours on Saturdays and Sundays. Programs, presented in Faeroese, consist of local and international news, commentaries, music and lectures. Much of the programming consists of recorded music imported from Denmark. Broadcast operations are financed by government subsidy. About eight thousand receivers are in use. There is no television.[30]

Greenland

GREENLAND, the world's largest island, located between the North Atlantic and the Polar Sea, is a part of the Danish realm, and has two representatives in the Danish Parliament. Its population is about thirty-six thousand.

Broadcasting service on the island was initiated at the beginning of the Second World War. The facilities, including a low-power transmitter, were housed in a small room of a telegraph station in the capital city of Godthaab. Because of the war, all communications with the mother country had been severed and the people welcomed the chance to hear the news which emanated from this station. The program service was gradually expanded to include educational and entertainment programs, but the growth in technical facilities, however, was not commensurate with the improvement in program service. Reception was poor in many areas and listeners pressed the Provincial Council to do something about it. In response, the Council took action to persuade the Danish Government to provide additional facilities.

The appeals were not realized until 1956 when building operations for an expanded system were begun. A new Broadcasting House was completed in 1958.[31] Today, *Grønlands Radiofoni,* government-owned, operates three AM and one FM station. Programs are broadcast in Eskimo, Danish, Norwegian and Faeroese.

More than fifty percent of the programs consist of music, much of which is recorded and supplied by Radio Denmark in Copenhagen. The remainder of the broadcasts cover a wide range of material—news, serious talks, broadcasts for schools given three times per week, church services, special entertainment and informational programs for fishermen.

Owners of radio receivers in Greenland pay no license fees. All broadcasting is controlled and subsidized by the Government in accordance with the policies established by the Danish realm and implemented by *Grønlands Radiofoni.*[32]

Iceland

THIS small republic, located midway between Europe and America, with a population of less than two hundred thousand, originally was an independent state. Later (1262–64), it was ruled by Norway. Subsequently, through the formation of the Union of Kalmar in 1483, it came under Danish control. In 1874, Iceland obtained its own constitution, and in 1918, Denmark recognized it as a separate state. For more than twenty-five years thereafter, it nominally remained a part of the Danish Kingdom. On June 17, 1944, however, the royal ties were severed when, following a popular referendum, the Parliament proclaimed the complete independence of the country.

Although the Icelanders are Scandinavians by language and origin, they have developed cultural and commercial links with many European and American countries. The Icelandic language has maintained its purity for a thousand years, but both Danish and English are taught in the schools. Much emphasis is placed upon formal education and there is no illiteracy in the country. The national religion is Evangelical Lutheran, but there is complete freedom of worship.

Iceland has had a radio service since 1930. Broadcasting is carried on by the Iceland State Broadcasting Service (*Rikisutvarpid*), and is under the authority of the Minister of Education. The *Rikisutvarpid* operates five AM transmitters, including a one hundred kilowatt long-wave and a six hundred watt FM transmitter at Reykjavik. It also operates a seven kilowatt short-wave transmitter for listeners abroad. In 1964, there were about fifty thousand radio receivers in the island.[33]

The United States Air Force at Keflavik Airport operates a two hundred and fifty watt medium-wave transmitter for its personnel in that area. It also has been operating there, since 1955, a television station, using a five hundred and twenty-five line definition.[34] As of 1964, the *Rikisutvarpid* had no television facilities of its own, but according to reports in May 1965, plans were under way to establish a station.[35]

Despite glaciers, volcanoes and the irregularity of the terrain, the broadcasting system reaches all parts of the country and the citizens enjoy good radio reception. The system receives no government subsidies but is financed from revenues derived from license fees on receivers (sixty percent) and from advertising (forty percent). The license fee is five hundred and thirty Icelandic Kroner per year, of which the *Rikisutvarpid* receives about five hundred Kroner, and the remainder goes to the Government in tax. The estimated income from these two sources for the year 1965 was forty and one-half million Kroner.[36] In addition, the *Rikisutvarpid* has a monopoly on the sale and repair of radio sets from which it derives some income.

Programs

THE program schedules include frequent weather reports, daily reports on parliamentary proceedings with occasional, direct reports of debates, and political discussions prior to elections covering a wide range of viewpoints. There are special bulletins for farmers and fishermen, since these are the main sources of livelihood for the Icelandic people.

All news, as well as other programs, is presented in the traditional Icelandic language. The Director-General of the *Rikisutvarpid* recently stated:

> . . . Icelandic is the national language and has been spoken and written in the land for the 1,000 years and more covered by the nation's history. . . . Thus the daily radio news bulletins are read in the same language as is to be found in the old sagas . . . .
>
> News, domestic and foreign, is read by special announcers, or by the news correspondents themselves, nine times throughout the day. . . . Special weather reports are broadcast 11 times a day . . . . Debates are sometimes broadcast direct from Parliament . . . . Various political discussions are also

broadcast from meetings or from the studio, before an election, for example, besides a great variety of political news. The morning programs include an account in some detail of the leading articles in the daily press. There are also special bulletins of farming and fishing news . . . . There are, besides, often special talks and features about literature, with readings from new books.

In general the radio newsroom also broadcasts special news commentaries on various subjects and current topics, both foreign and domestic, though especially the latter, with talks and interviews. These are usually given daily, and last year there were, in all, more than 400 programs of this kind. The radio sends its representatives all over the country, by road and by air, to collect such material.

To some extent linked with radio news, and transmitted in close connection with it, are advertisements and announcements, broadcast for a fee. These are for the most part, announcements about meetings, entertainments and travel, but also include personal announcements such as deaths, and trade advertisements. This material is broadcast at fixed times, twice a day, for 15–20 minutes, or sometimes longer, but is otherwise kept separate from all other program material, while program time is never sold to advertisers for sponsoring.[37]

The Director-General has further pointed out that the *Rikisutvarpid* receives frequent visits from news correspondents from abroad and maintains useful and friendly contacts with foreign radio organizations, besides being a member of the European Broadcasting Union. He has written with some pride about the recent cultural growth of Iceland and the important role radio has played in this development:

> Iceland, which has been an independent republic since 1944 (though an Icelandic state was first founded in 930), is firmly based on an ancient tradition; but in recent years it has developed for itself new occupations and up-to-date practical projects, and new cultural institutions, such as a university, national theatre and symphony orchestra, and a considerable publishing industry. But of all these institutions it is the Radio that reaches most effectively to the public as a whole, and one which, with its news service and other programs, keeps open the lines of communication between this remote land and the outside world.[38]

As of 1966, regular in-school broadcasting had not been initiated, but special emphasis has been placed upon cultural and educational programs, which have been presented during the best hours of the day. Lectures covering a wide range of subjects—philosophy, sociology, history, political science and languages, to mention only a few—are frequently broadcast. In November 1961, Andrés Björnsson, the Program Director of the system, commented on Icelandic listeners and their interest in programs which appeal to the higher tastes:

> It is a well-known fact that the Icelandic people possess an extensive and outstanding literature from medieval times. Every winter one or more of the ancient sagas is read over the radio once a week.[39]

During one year classical music covered more than eight hundred hours, an average of more than two hours daily. This included symphony concerts with explanations by specialists once a week and the concerts of the Iceland Symphony Orchestra which is partly supported by the State Broadcast Service.[40]

The Icelanders have an extensive modern educational system and are unusually keen readers. The general public therefore possesses fundamental knowledge in some respects ranging far beyond the daily tasks of the individuals. They are grateful that the radio brings them fairly serious subjects at such times of the day as are most convenient for listening. The Icelanders do not at all object to lengthy lectures. Such programs, intended for all those who wish to enrich their knowledge, are among the most popular.[41]

NOTES

1. Nils Andrén, *Government and Politics in the Norden Countries* (Stockholm: Almquist and Wiksell, 1964), p. 13.
2. Statement by Lithgow Osborne, President, American-Scandinavian Foundation.
3. *Lortidende for Kongeriget Danmark, 1907* (Copenhagen: Trukt hos J. H. Schultz A/S, 1908), No. 99, pp. 357-358.
4. *Denmark, Official Handbook*, prepared by the Press and Information Department, Royal Danish Ministry of Foreign Affairs (Copenhagen: 1964), p. 418.
5. *Lortidende for Kongeriget Danmark, 1926*, No. 30, pp. 48-49.
6. Law of Broadcasting, March 21, 1930. *Lortidende for Kongeriget Danmark, 1930*, No. 76, pp. 257-259.
7. Radio Denmark, Press Department, "Facts about Radio Denmark," Copenhagen, undated press release.
8. See *Denmark, Official Handbook*, pp. 93-95.
9. *EBU Bulletin*, November 15, 1951, p. 570.
10. *Ibid.*, May-June 1955, p. 257.
11. *Ibid.*, January-February 1956, p. 54.
12. *Le Haut-Parleur*, August 10, 1950; reprinted in *EBU Bulletin*, September 15, 1950, p. 271.
13. *Ibid.*, November-December 1956, p. 859.
14. *Denmark, Official Handbook*, p. 419. The provisions of the law are fully explained in this highly informative book.
15. *Ibid.*, p. 420.
16. *Ibid.*, p. 424.
17. UNESCO, *World Communications: Press, Radio, Television, Film* (New York: UNESCO Publications Center, 1964), p. 276.
18. *Ibid.*
19. *Ibid.*
20. *Danmarks Radio, TV-Byen I Gladsaxe*, April 1965, pp. 22-23.
21. *Denmark, Official Handbook*, p. 421.

22. *Ibid.*
23. *EBU Bulletin,* September-October 1957, p. 580.
24. *EBU Review,* 70B, November 1961, p. 10.
25. *Ibid.*
26. UNESCO, *World Communications.*
27. *EBU Review,* 94B, November 1965, p. 35; also, see UNESCO, *ibid.*
28. EBU Review, *ibid.*
29. *Denmark, Official Handbook,* p. 424. As of January 1968, one Kroner was equivalent to 13.3 cents.
30. UNESCO, *World Communications,* p. 277.
31. *EBU Review,* 51B, October 1958, pp. 4–5; also, see UNESCO, *ibid.,* p. 147.
32. *Ibid.*
33. UNESCO, *ibid.,* p. 299; also, see Vilhalmur Th. Gislason, "Vigorous Radio News Policy Helps to Combat Isolation," *EBU Review,* 91B, May 1965, p. 46.
34. UNESCO, *ibid.,* p. 299.
35. Gislason, p. 46.
36. *Ibid.,* p. 47.
37. *Ibid.*
38. *Ibid.*
39. Andrés Björnsson, "Instructional Broadcasting Programs," *EBU Review,* 70B, November 1961, p. 32.
40. *Ibid.*
41. *Ibid.*

XI

Norway: The Social Welfare State

ORWAY HAS TRADITIONALLY ALIGNED HERSELF with organizations
concerned with international cooperation and world peace. She
was a member of the League of Nations, has been active in
UNESCO, UNRRA and other agencies of the UN, and has given her full
support to NATO. In 1959, Norway took a leading part in the establishment of the European Free Trade Association, the counterpart to the
Common Market.

Of special note is the country's participation in the Norden Council
which was established in 1952 to promote the common interests of Denmark, Finland, Iceland, Norway and Sweden. This Council is concerned
with economic, social and cultural cooperation, and, as will be pointed
out, has effectively used the broadcast media in carrying out this objective.

Early History of Broadcasting

FROM the beginning, wire and wireless communication has been subject to
state control in Norway. By an Act of April 29, 1899, Parliament gave the
Government the exclusive right to control communication by telegraph
wires and similar constructions.[1] At first, on the basis of this law, private
interests were given franchises to operate radio stations. On December 13,
1924, the Government granted the first license for regular broadcasting
to a company known as the *Kringskastingselkapet, A. S.*, with authority to
broadcast in the Oslo area.[2] Shortly thereafter other companies were licensed to operate outside the Norwegian capital.

The Advent of State Control

THESE private companies provided all the broadcast services in the country for several years. In 1925, there were eight transmitters with a total
power of 4.8 kilowatts, serving about twenty-five thousand homes in the
Oslo area. By 1929, the number of stations in the country had increased

to thirteen, including one sixty kilowatt operation, which at that time was the most powerful in Europe.[3]

The Government became increasingly interested in the social and educational uses of the growing medium. Accordingly, in line with control patterns already established in Sweden and Denmark and many other European countries, on June 24, 1933, Parliament passed a law conferring a monopoly over all radio to a newly created national organization, the Norwegian Broadcasting Corporation (*Norsk Rikskringkasting*).[4] The private companies were dissolved and their facilities and operations were taken over by the new organization. Thus the State assumed a progressively important role in the development of broadcasting.

The Act of 1933, as amended from time to time (May 12, 1939, June 25, 1948, March 18, 1949, October 23, 1959 and June 21, 1963), governs the present pattern of Norwegian broadcasting. It provides that the Norwegian Broadcasting Corporation shall have the exclusive right to establish and operate all radio and television in the country, except that government agencies such as the Telecommunication Administration may, upon permission, use radio communication to conduct official business. The King is authorized to use broadcast facilities for special purposes and may define the spheres of activity of the Corporation and the Telecommunication Administration.

The law further states that the King shall appoint a Board of five governors (plus an equal number of deputies). One governor must be a "technical" expert. Each member and deputy is appointed for a period of four years.

Section 3 of the Act provides for a Broadcasting Council of twenty-three members (plus an equal number of deputies), twelve of whom are chosen by the Parliament (*Storting*), and eleven of whom are appointed by the King, including the Chairman and Vice-Chairman. Members of the Council and their deputies serve four year terms.

The Broadcasting Council is required to assemble at least once every six months. The Government appoints from the Council members two program committees, one for radio and one for television. Their functions and operations are prescribed by the King and their salaries are stipulated by the Parliament.

Section 4 states that the Telecommunication Administration is responsible for technical operations except in matters "directly related" to programming.

The King, upon information received from the Board and the Council, appoints the Director-General. Assistant directors are chosen by the Government. The Board, or whomever it authorizes, selects other staff members of the organization. General regulations for staff appointments and salary schedules are determined by the King, subject to the approval of Parliament.

The Parliament specifies license fees and sales taxes on receivers, and makes decisions regarding the construction and expansion of transmitting facilities and the negotiation of loans for such purposes.

The Board is required to make a report for the King each year. This report is addressed to the Parliament which in turn must approve the annual budget for the Corporation and appropriate funds in accordance therewith.

Section 9 declares that broadcast facilities, in accordance with directions issued by the King, shall be at the disposal of the Government for the transmission of communications "of interest to the State."

Following the adoption of the original statute in 1933, the State continued to expand transmission facilities and at the time of the German invasion in 1940, a new Broadcasting House was being constructed. Work on the building continued, but toward the end of the war, the Germans demolished the building and transmission equipment as they withdrew.

Postwar Growth

WITH peace restored, the Broadcasting House was reconstructed in Oslo, and studios and transmission facilities were built in a number of other Norwegian cities.[5] Under a cooperative arrangement, the Corporation was broadcasting on a network of twenty-two stations with a total transmitting power of over four hundred kilowatts by 1950. Plans were under way to construct twenty more stations. As of January 1, 1950, the number of licensed receivers had risen to more than seven hundred and forty thousand.[6]

A 1953 report showed a variety of programs, with some emphasis on educational and religious content. These included regular lectures by professors at Oslo and Berger universities, popular science talks, discussions of important social, economic and political problems, and educational broadcasts on history, art, the theatre, literature and world events.

A morning feature, "House and Home," and an evening one, "Parents' Hour," both providing a wide variety of information on problems of family life, were attracting large audiences.

A weekly Sunday broadcast was designed to aid agriculture and industry, to improve methods of production and marketing, and to increase the income and raise the living standards of the workers.

An important part of the schedules consisted of broadcasts for the schools. These were originally started in February 1931 and, except for the years of the German Occupation when all receivers were confiscated, had been continued on a regular basis. In fact, prior to the Nazi invasion, nearly eighteen hundred schools received the school broadcasts of the *Norsk Rikskringkasting*.[7]

Postwar restoration of this school service was delayed because of the shortage of receivers, but by 1951 there were over nineteen hundred elementary schools and about one hundred and thirty-five high schools participating in the instructional program.[8]

As reported, there were two hundred and fourteen lessons for both elementary and secondary grades broadcast during the 1951–52 academic year. These broadcasts, prepared by a standing committee assisted by advisory groups of teachers and other educational experts, covered a wide range of subjects. Supplementary reading materials, financed by subsidies from the *Norsk Rikskringkasting* and by nominal fees paid by the schools, were provided.[9]

As might be expected, religious programming constituted a sizeable segment of the weekly schedules. About six percent of the broadcast time was allocated for religious talks and worship services. Every Sunday morning from 10:55 to 12:30 a complete worship service was transmitted live from one of the Lutheran Evangelical Churches.[10]

The works of Ibsen, Bernard Shaw and various French writers were included in the schedule of radio plays. During the latter part of 1953, the *Norsk Rikskringkasting* collaborated with the Danish, Finnish and Swedish broadcasting organizations in presenting historical documentaries of common interest to the Scandinavian countries.[11]

Musical programs were of the finest quality. The 1953–54 season included a series of major symphony concerts under the direction of internationally known conductors. Some of these were relayed to other Nordic countries as a part of Scandinavian Music Week.[12]

In line with the renewed interest in politics after the war, broadcast facilities were made available to the various political parties. For example, a series of broadcasts, "Awaiting the Elections," in which candidates and parties expressed their views and solicited the support of the voters, was featured in 1953.[13]

The 1955–56 report of the *Norsk Rikskringkasting* showed the total transmission time for that year to be almost five thousand hours, or an average of about twelve hours per day. Percentages of time for various program categories were allocated approximately as follows:[14]

Program	*Percent*
Music	40
News	10
Talks and educational programs	5
Variety	4
Programs for children and young persons	4
Religious programs	4
Sports	2
Broadcasts to schools	2
Miscellaneous programs, including drama, station announcements and intervals	25

The broadcasts included one hundred and forty-eight hours of symphonic music presented by the Oslo Philharmonic Society and Marmonien group of Bergen. The *Norsk Rikskringkasting's* own orchestra of thirty musicians provided one hundred and thirty-five hours of light music. The internationally famous Bergen Festival was broadcast to the nation and was carried either by direct or delayed transmission by the systems in Canada, Denmark, Finland, France, Germany, Hungary, Poland, Rumania, South Africa, Sweden, Switzerland, the USSR, the United Kingdom and the United States. There were also sixty-eight dramatic shows, nine hundred lectures and talks, two hundred and forty-five school programs, and a number of language courses in English, French and Italian.[15]

With the increase in programming and the extension of facilities, the number of listeners grew substantially. In a brochure published by the Norwegian Broadcasting Organization in 1955, it was reported, on the basis of nation-wide research, that there were more than two million and two hundred thousand persons above sixteen years of age who listened to radio programs in their homes.[16] Revenues from license fees, plus stamp taxes on receivers and other radio equipment, which amounted to twenty-two million Kroner in 1952–53,[17] had risen to thirty-one million Kroner in 1956–57.[18]

Development of National Service

BECAUSE of the weather conditions and the rugged terrain, the building and maintenance of broadcast facilities in Norway has presented technical and financial difficulties. There are many high peaks to which access is difficult, and the heavy ice and strong winds in the mountainous regions make severe demands on buildings and transmission equipment. Such an irregular topography makes efficient broadcast coverage in every part of the country extremely difficult.

Despite all this, not long after the Second World War, Norway initiated plans for the development of nation-wide coverage. This had not been possible with the long- and medium-wave facilities then in use. The post-war plans called for the building of more than twenty-five transmitting stations with an accumulated power of almost nine hundred kilowatts to be located on mountain peaks in different parts of the country.[19] Actual construction of the first station began in 1955. By June 1965 these plans had been more than completed. There was one long-wave station in Oslo and a number of repeaters in other cities. More than thirty medium-wave stations were on the air. In addition, there were FM transmitters in more than seventy different locations. All these facilities were providing effective radio service throughout the country.[20] As reported in March 1965, there were more than six hundred and sixty thousand licensed radio receivers in use, plus more than four hundred thousand combinations sets (both radio and television).[21]

Current Radio Programming

THE enlargement of the technical facilities has been accompanied by the expansion of program service. As reported by officials in June 1965, the Home Service was on the air more than one hundred hours per week. About one-fifth of the time was devoted to news and public affairs.[22] The 1964 Annual Report of *Norsk Rikskringkasting* shows many interviews with international figures including heads of state, ambassadors such as Margaret Joy Tibbets and celebrities such as Charles Chaplin.[23]

A large component of the program schedules consisted of music, both light and classical. Recordings of some of the best Norwegian music were made available to a number of foreign broadcasting systems and were heard by listeners in other parts of the world.

As will be more fully discussed later, emphasis was placed upon programs for children and, for four hours per week, broadcasts in a variety of subjects, especially designed for the classroom, were received by about twenty-five hundred schools.[24]

Foreign Broadcasting

THE *Norsk Rikskringkasting* operates six short-wave transmitters with a total power of 127.2 kilowatts. Programs are beamed to North and South Atlantic areas, the Americas, Africa, the Middle and Far East, Europe and Oceania. These broadcasts, mostly in Norwegian, are designed "to link Norwegians all over the globe to their homeland."[25]

"Norway this Week," a one-half hour program for English-speaking listeners is presented every Sunday. This program, as of August 1965, included a news bulletin, some Norwegian music, and interviews with knowledgeable persons concerning Norway's cultural, social, political or economic life.[26]

Television

IN 1952, proposals supporting the introduction of television in Norway were submitted in Parliament. It was suggested that experimental transmissions be carried for two years, using a channel width of seven mega-cycles and six hundred and twenty-five horizontal scanning lines. It was further proposed that viewers should be required to pay an annual license fee of five Kroner during the experimental period.[27]

In January 1953, the Norwegian Parliament authorized the *Norsk Rikskringkasting* to conduct the experiments as requested. At the same time, an Executive Committee, with the Director-General of *Norsk Riks-kringkasting* in charge, was given a mandate to study television in other countries—including color TV—and in terms of technical facilities and costs to project a plan for nation-wide service.[28]

Experimental work began in January 1954. The studies were completed in 1956, and in August of that year, the Committee made its report. It recommended that regular television service be established; that construc-tion of a network (twenty-eight main connecting stations and nineteen satellites) be undertaken over a period of years; that the first transmission facilities be built in the more densely populated Oslo area; and that the construction and operation be financed by an annual license fee and a ten percent purchase tax on television receivers. Advertising as a source of revenue was considered but was rejected in the final plans.[29]

It was recommended that a new department in *Norsk Rikskringkasting* be created with responsibility for all television operations and that there be regular exchanges of technical and programming personnel between the television and radio services.[30]

In general, these plans were approved by the Parliament. Experimental programming was continued for a time, and, in October 1959, the *Norsk Rikskringkasting* became a member of Eurovision and also linked up with Nordvision transmissions. These added connections provided new pro-grams which became increasingly popular with the viewers.[31]

By June 1960, the income from license fees and the purchase tax on TV sets had reached a total of 5,821,297 Kroner, the plant and equipment had been greatly expanded, and more than a hundred people were engaged in operations.[32]

As of June 1965, Norway was ringed with a TV network, consisting of main stations in Oslo, Bergen, Stavonger and Kongsberg and a sizeable number of auxiliary transmitters, providing service to about sixty percent of the population.[33] There were more than four hundred thousand licensed TV receivers in the country.[34] Plans were under way to extend the network, and it was expected that eighty-five percent of the Norwegian population would be served by 1970.[35]

As of June 1965, TV programs, emanating from the Oslo studios, were being transmitted twenty-five hours per week, including news, discussions of public affairs, religious services, special programs for children and school telecasts. In 1964, the network carried Eurovision programs for ninety-seven hours, including a number of satellite transmissions.[36]

School Broadcasting

As previously pointed out, the *Norsk Rikskringkasting* has provided regular programs for the classroom since 1931, except during the Nazi Occupation. An independent branch within the section of Lectures and
Education, with a full-time director and staff, is in charge of school broadcasting.

Programs from fifteen to thirty minutes, designed for pupils in both
elementary and secondary schools, are broadcast four hours per week and,
according to a 1964 report, about twenty-five hundred schools were using
these broadcasts. A wide range of subjects has been covered in recent
years—humanities, music, history, geography, gymnastics, languages, including English and French, and current affairs.[37]

Programs are of a composite nature rather than lengthy lectures. Teachers present brief discussions which are supported and illuminated by
stories, plays, music and other audio aids. An attempt is made to activate
and maintain the interest of the pupils by asking questions that call for
responses and suggest follow-up activities.[38]

The *Norsk Rikskringkasting* produces color filmstrips which are available to the schools at nominal costs. These relate to such subjects as geography, science, art, literature, industry, health and safety. A manual of instruction is supplied with the filmstrips, and experts give appropriate
commentaries directly to the schools as the teacher shows the filmstrips in
the classroom. Sound effects are inserted in the broadcasts to make the
strips more meaningful and effective. This combination of audio-visual
material, including direct radio commentary, has been well received and
widely used by Norwegian schools.[39]

For a nominal fee, the schools may obtain numerous publications pertaining to the broadcasts—a year's time table and schedules of broadcasts
and booklets containing explanatory materials. Standing committees made
up of outstanding teachers in the different subject matter fields provide
continuing advice and help in the preparation of these printed materials
and in the planning of the school broadcasts.[40]

School Television

THE first experiments in school television began in the spring of 1962.
Nine programs were broadcast during a two week period for one hundred
and seventy-six elementary schools.[41] A second period with seventeen

school telecasts was completed in early 1964 and forty additional ones were transmitted during the school year, 1964–65.[42]

As of March 1965, programs were being presented only to the elementary schools, but it was expected that ultimately the secondary schools would be also included. Hans J. Birkrem, the Head of School Television in *Norsk Rikskringkasting,* writing in the *EBU Review* for March 1965, pointed to the difficulties of developing instructional TV in Norway:

> It is not easy to ensure good television reception throughout Norway, with its high mountains, deep valleys, elongated shape and small, scattered communities; but by now, only four and a half years after the introduction of television, it has reached Bodø, north of the Polar Circle, two years ahead of the plans. . . .
>
> The good progress made in the fifties and sixties might be thought to be a good moment for the establishment of school television: this may be the case in many countries, but not in Norway. Unfortunately, the experiments in school television clash with the introduction of compulsory nine-year schooling which is to replace the seven-year *folke* schools and the three-year *realskole.* This entails a complete reorganization of our school system and enormous expense for new school buildings, equipment, etc. In short, school authorities have to decide whether or not to introduce school television at a time when their resources are already overstrained. No explosive development of our school television can be expected, then, but as the reaction of the teachers is very positive the parents' associations will certainly lend a helping hand if the school authorities have to backpedal for financial reasons.[43]

Mr. Birkrem then explained that the present TV school offerings are arranged in short series of three or four programs. Some subjects covered so far have been religion, history, music, science, biology, language teaching and geography.[44]

Norway cooperates closely with other Scandinavian countries in school telecasting. There is a regular exchange as well as joint production of courses. In February 1965, representatives of the Nordic countries met in Oslo and agreed upon cooperative efforts along this line.

Commenting on the future pattern of school television in Norway, Mr. Birkrem recently stated:

> Norwegian school television is part of the educational television department with a budget of its own, a parallel to the situation of school sound broadcasting. We do not yet know if school television will in future be completely independent or will be run in cooperation with school radio. If we follow the example of Denmark and Sweden, we shall perhaps at some not very distant date have one large school program department, with a school program director and two assistant directors, one for school radio and one for school television. But other solutions are also possible.[45]

Adult Education

As is the case with other Scandinavian countries, Norway is concerned that broadcasting do more in adult education. Because of financial and technical problems it has not been possible to expand this area of programming as rapidly as desired. Norwegian television, as of the latter part of 1965, was presenting thirty-five hours of adult education per week, including special series of programs such as "The Great World Religions" and "A Brief History of Philosophy." It was planned to expand this type of adult instruction during 1966.[46]

NOTES

1. Act of April 29, 1899, *Norges Love II, 1891–1908*, H. Aschehoug and Co., Oslo, No. 1899, pp. 557–559.
2. *EBU Bulletin*, May 15, 1950, pp. 73–74.
3. *Ibid.*
4. Act of June 24, 1933, *Norsk Lovtidende, lste Avdeling*, 1933, Grondahl and Sons, Boktrykkeri, Oslo, No. 13, pp. 434–437.
5. *EBU Bulletin*, May 15, 1950, p. 74.
6. *Ibid.*, p. 73.
7. *Ibid.*, March 15, 1953, pp. 182–183.
8. *Ibid.*, p. 183.
9. *Ibid.*
10. *Ibid.*
11. *Ibid.*, November 15, 1953, p. 688.
12. *Ibid.*, pp. 688–689.
13. *Ibid.*
14. *Ibid.*, March-April 1957, p. 151.
15. *Ibid.*
16. *Ibid.*, September-October 1956, p. 701.
17. *Ibid.*, March-April 1954, p. 161. As of January 1968, the Norwegian kroner was equivalent to fourteen cents.
18. *EBU Bulletin*, November-December 1957, p. 690.
19. *Ibid.*, January-February 1957, p. 56.
20. Reports of officials of the *Norsk Rikskringkasting* to the author in Oslo in June 1965. Also, see 1964 Annual Report of *Norsk Rikskringkasting*, Oslo, pp. 41–42.
21. *EBU Review*, 90B, March 1965, p. 29.
22. Reports of officials of the *Norsk Rikskringkasting* to the author in June 1965.
23. 1964 Annual Report of *Norsk Rikskringkasting*.
24. UNESCO, *World Communications: Press, Radio, Television, Film* (New York: UNESCO Publications Center, 1964), p. 313.

25. *Radio Norway Overseas Service, Short Wave Schedule*, May-August 1965.
26. *Ibid.*
27. *EBU Bulletin*, November 15, 1952, p. 685.
28. *Ibid.*, May-June 1957, pp. 352–353.
29. *Ibid.*, p. 354.
30. *Ibid.*
31. *EBU Review*, 66B, March 1961, p. 29.
32. *Ibid.*
33. Based upon conversations of the author with officials of *Norsk Rikskring-kasting* in Oslo in June 1965. Also, see UNESCO, *World Communications*, p. 314, and 1964 Annual Report of *Norsk Rikskringkasting*, pp. 77–79.
34. *EBU Review*, 90B, March 1965, p. 32.
35. *Ibid.*
36. The take-off of American astronauts from Cape Kennedy in early June 1965 was transmitted via Early Bird, picked up by Eurovision, and carried to the Norwegian area by the *Norsk Rikskringkasting*. The reception in Oslo was excellent.
37. *EBU Review*, 90B, March 1965, pp. 32–33. Also, see Hans J. Birkrem, Editor of School Broadcasts, "Broadcast Programmes for Schools," *EBU Review*, 70B, November 1961, pp. 36–37.
38. *Ibid.*, p. 37.
39. *Ibid.*
40. *Ibid.*
41. *Ibid.*, 90B, March 1965, p. 32.
42. *Ibid.*
43. *Ibid.*
44. *Ibid.*, pp. 32–33.
45. *Ibid.*, p. 33.
46. *Ibid.*, 94B, November 1965, pp. 34–35.

XII

Sweden: Welfare State
with Private Enterprise

Radio Controls

THE MINISTER OF COMMUNICATIONS has general regulatory authority over broadcasting in Sweden. The first law governing radio communication was passed by the Parliament on August 31, 1907. This Act provided for the licensing of wireless stations operating on ships at sea, and recognized the 1906 international convention in Berlin which established regulations for the operation of such stations.[1]

As was true in many other countries, Swedish broadcasting owes its early development largely to amateur operators who banded together to form local clubs and who built and operated their own transmitters. The first official pilot transmissions were conducted by what was called the Royal Telegraph Board.[2] Beginning in 1924, the Government extended its regulatory jurisdiction over all broadcasting, both private and public, and required the payment of fees for the use of receivers.[3] Since January 1925, sole broadcasting rights have been vested in a single company (originally called *Radiotjänst* but now called *Sveriges Radio*), while the State has continued to own and operate the transmission facilities, including the connecting circuits.

Prior to the Second World War, the *Radiotjänst* developed both national and regional program services. Unlike most other countries in Europe subject to the Nazi yoke, Swedish broadcasting was able to maintain control of its operations during the hostilities, although program content was necessarily limited, especially in the area of news and controversial discussion, because of the Swedish Government's policy of neutrality.

Postwar Programming

THE decade after the war was one of rapid growth for Swedish broadcasting. According to reports issued by the *Radiotjänst* in 1953 and 1954, the density of radio listening was greater in Sweden than in any other country where license fees on receivers were charged. In 1954, the total number of receivers had reached 2,353,542, or approximately one receiver for every three inhabitants.[4]

This increasing public interest in the medium was due largely to the enlightened leadership of the *Radiotjänst* which stressed quality and variety in programming and whose objectives had the enthusiastic support of the postwar Government. Many of the programs emanating from the Stockholm studios consisted of classical music. For example, during the autumn and winter seasons of 1953–54, numerous programs featuring the works of Franz Schubert were broadcast. On Sunday afternoons symphony and chamber music, including the first performances of modern Swedish compositions, were presented with historical commentaries.

Various types of drama and literature were emphasized in the schedules. Original plays concerning the everyday life of the Swedes, literary readings, including popular lyrical poetry, novels of special interest to young people, and other types of literary material made up much of the program offerings.[5]

During the early fifties, the intellectual interests of a highly literate people were served by uncensored and unscripted discussions on a wide range of subjects. For example, the *Radiotjänst,* during the 1952–53 season, carried a series of broadcasts, varied in format, dealing with vital issues of the day, "the aim being to cast light . . . from as many angles as possible."[6] Among the topics treated in these programs were: espionage and sabotage, abolition of passports for travel by Scandinavians in Nordic countries, the housing problem, wage differences, alcoholism, social legislation, the mania for medicines, and legal abortion and its problems.

Weekly programs called "Housewives' Half Hour," dealing with practical problems in the home, and "Outlook," concerned with political, economic, social and cultural matters, were other types of programs presented.

A variety of professional people and experts participated in these educational broadcasts—clergymen, physicians, educators, psychologists, authors and literary critics, sociologists, political leaders and others. Many of the programs were designed for national reception and were carried by the networks. Some, however, were prepared and broadcast for regional and local appeal.[7]

In line with the progress in Nordic cooperation, the *Radiotjänst* joined the broadcasting systems of Denmark, Norway and Finland in an exchange of programs with wide Scandinavian interest.[8]

Courses in a variety of languages—Danish, Finnish, Italian, German, French, English, Russian and Spanish—were presented both at the national and regional levels. Textbooks related to the language courses, with attractive, illustrative material, were available to the listeners at minimum cost.[9]

Special mention should be made of the *Radiotjänst's* policy regarding political broadcasting. Because of Sweden's multiple party system, the Company has always viewed broadcasting as an important medium for political education, and has followed the practice of allocating equal air time to the various parties, their leaders and candidates. For example, in 1951, M. Henrik Hahr, who was then the head of *Radiotjänst's* news section, stated:

> In election years the Swedish broadcasting organization makes a habit of allowing the leaders of the political parties represented in Parliament to meet before the microphone and carry on a debate intended for the ears of the entire nation. . . . The public has the right to require that such debates on questions of national importance take place although there is a risk of violent clashes between the most widely differing points of view.[10]

Mr. Hahr further stated that with propaganda so rife, in the interest of preserving freedom, such radio discussion seemed imperative.[11]

Expansion of Facilities

A SECOND national network service using FM facilities was initiated in 1955. At the same time, the service on Programme I was expanded. During the next four years, the amount of broadcasting time was increased more than fifty percent. By 1960, the facilities had been expanded to provide nation-wide coverage on the First Programme and from sixty to seventy percent coverage on the Second.[12]

Foreign as well as domestic broadcasting was expanded. A new international short-wave service was instituted in January 1952. Programs were beamed in Swedish and English to listeners in the Americas, the Middle and Far East, South Asia and Africa. Programs in Swedish, German, English and French were transmitted throughout Europe.[13]

During the fifties, there was a substantial growth in the broadcasting staff. In 1948–49, there were fewer than three hundred employees; by 1958–59, this number had almost tripled.[14] This increase was in part a result of the development of television which, by 1956, had been established on a regular basis.

Television

AFTER much planning in the late forties, the Company officially asked the Government for the authority to operate a television service.[15] In line with this, the Posts, Telegraphs and Telephones Administration, which operated the transmission facilities for radio, requested the Government to provide two million and two hundred thousand Kronor to finance television tests.[16] These requests were rejected. Instead, the Minister of Communications set up a Commission of six members, representing the Parliament, the communications industry, the PTT and the *Radiotjänst,* to study the technical and financial problems.[17]

On October 29, 1952, the Commission made its first report which recommended that the State provide the funds for experimental television. As reported by the *EBU Bulletin* in July 1953, the status of television and the Commissioner's concern at the time were as follows:

> Members of the Commission have arranged for discussions with representatives of various organizations and institutions interested in the development of television in Sweden, especially with representatives of the Ministry of Education. Furthermore, various questions are under survey such as commercial broadcasting, cooperation with the Swedish association of newspaper editors, the Swedish advertising agencies and other organizations concerned. Meetings with representatives of the film industry are likewise envisaged, whereas discussions with representatives of sporting circles have already taken place.
>
> The Government has not as yet acted upon the Commission's recommendation contained in the above-mentioned report that financial support from the State should be made available. In accordance with directives received, the Commission will concern itself primarily with financial and organizational problems, and will likewise review alternative methods for the development of television. As to future programme production, the Commission, bearing in mind experience gained in this field in other countries, will endeavor to estimate expenditure likely to arise in connection with the various types of transmissions envisaged, as well as their length and general structure.[18]

The Commission completed its studies in late 1954 and issued a final report recommending that television service be started in the late summer of 1956; that main transmitters be installed first in Stockholm and Uppsala, and auxiliary ones in Gothenburg and Malmö. A nine year plan was envisioned, with an ultimate network linked by about fifty transmitting stations operating with six hundred and twenty-five line definition and requiring investments of over seventy-eight million Kronor.

It was recommended that the *Radiotjänst,* along with its monopoly in radio, be granted exclusive rights in the field of television, and that the number of members on the Company's Board be increased and the representation of various share-holding interests and organizations be broadened.

The Commission further recommended that the Telephone and Telegraph Administration be responsible for technical TV transmission, and the collection of license fees, as was the case in sound broadcasting.[19]

Prior to this report, some private groups had expressed interest in the establishment of commercial television as a profit venture.[20] In fact, some experimental television, partially financed by advertisers, was presented in May 1954. The programs were produced in private studios and transmitted by an experimental transmitter at the Technical University of Stockholm.[21]

While a minority of the Commission were against granting a monopoly for television broadcasting and favored the introduction of some commercials, the majority recommended that the *Radiotjänst* be given exclusive rights and that all broadcast financing (both radio and TV) come from state subsidies and license fees on receivers.[22] The majority report stressed the public service aspect of television and the need for regular educational and cultural programs, including those designed to improve and strengthen home life.[23]

After studying the report and the Government's subsequent proposals, the Parliament, on May 24, 1956, authorized the establishment of television on a regular basis. It was decided that the programming should be entrusted exclusively to the *Radiotjänst*, that it should be noncommercial, and that the PTT should be responsible for the construction and operation of the transmission facilities and the collection of the license fees.[24]

On September 15, 1956, regular programming began in the Stockholm area, with daily schedules running from seven to eight hours. With the help of government subsidies and loans, plus the income from license fees, facilities were expanded, and the hours of telecasting were increased.

Establishment of Sveriges Radio

IN view of the expanded activities in both radio and TV, it was decided that the *Radiotjänst* should be reorganized. Shares in the Company, which until then had been owned exclusively by newspapers and radio manufacturers, were offered to other interests. Capital was increased from five hundred and forty thousand to one million and eighty thousand Kronor. New shareholders included organizations concerned with the cooperative movement, trade unions, religious organizations and temperance societies. The membership on the Board was increased from seven to eleven, six of whom (including the Chairman) were appointed by the Government and the remaining five by the shareholders.

The full name of the old company, *Aktiebolaget Radiotjänst,* was changed to *Sveriges Radio Aktiebolag.* The last word in the name (meaning joint stock company) is omitted except in business transactions when full legal identification is necessary.[25] Government regulations, adopted September 25, 1953 and providing for a division of labor between the Company and the Board of Telecommunications, remained in effect. The Company was responsible for the programming and the Board of Telecommunications operated the transmission facilities (both radio and TV).

Requirements concerning the coordination of broadcast engineering between the two organizations continued in force.

After much deliberation by the Government and the Company, an Agreement with new regulations was approved on May 15, 1959.[26] Article XVII of the Agreement provided that it would become effective June 1, 1959, and remain in force until June 1964. It was further provided that it would be extended for five year periods unless notice of termination was given one year prior to the expiration of any such period.

As was the case with the *Radiotjänst, Sveriges Radio* has a monopoly in broadcasting and is responsible for all program production in radio and television, whereas, the Telecommunications Administration is in charge of all transmissions, the suppression of technical interference, and the collection of license fees.

Programming Requirements

PROVISIONS in the Agreement regarding programming are quite specific. Article IV reads:

> *Cl. 1.* The broadcasting services shall be conducted with regard for the central position of sound radio and television in the country's cultural and social life.
>
> Programmes shall be diversified in nature and content, and shall be calculated to uphold and to strengthen the interest of the general public in broadcasting.
>
> In the presentation of programmes the Corporation is required, inter alia,
>
> to disseminate, in objective, impartial and suitable form, information on current events and to orient the general public towards more important cultural and social issues, as well as to encourage debate on such issues;
>
> to satisfy, on a reasonable scale, different schools of thought within religion, music, art, literature and science;
>
> and to provide good diversion and entertainment.
>
> When two or more programmes in sound radio or television are being broadcast at the same time, the Corporation should aim to vary these so as to satisfy the preferences of different audiences. In this matter the more specialized interests of minority audiences should also be catered for wherever possible.
>
> *Cl. 2.* The Corporation shall give principal emphasis in its broadcasting services to national programmes. However, the needs of local and regional areas with their own special interests should also be considered. The Corporation shall maintain good contacts with various parts of the country to meet this aim to the greatest possible extent.
>
> *Cl. 3.* In addition to providing programmes which are chiefly intended for Swedish listeners, the Corporation is required to produce special programmes

for transmission to other countries, either by short wave or by other means, with the objective of enabling foreign audiences to obtain information about Sweden and Swedes living abroad to maintain their ties with the homeland.

Article V requires that the Corporation, in planning its programs, co-operate "on the best possible terms" with community and cultural organizations, particularly those in religion, music, theatre, art, science and education, with government officials at the national and local levels, and with Swedish commercial and industrial interests.

Cooperation with government officials is required, and upon the request of a government department for time to broadcast an important announcement to the public, it is the Corporation's duty to grant the request. However, *Sveriges Radio* has the right to word the message so that it does not "prejudice the broadcasting services."[27]

Under the Agreement, the Corporation is entitled to receive every year that share of the revenue from receiver licenses which the Government decides is necessary to finance the broadcasting services. Accordingly, the Corporation is required to submit, not later than September, its program proposals and an estimate of its financial needs for the coming fiscal year. The preparation of this estimate is to be preceded by consultations with the Telecommunications Administration, and, when necessary, with the Board of Building and Town Planning.

Article XII provides that the Government shall appoint a special Radio Council *(Radionämuder)* of twenty-four members to see that programs comply with the provisions of the Agreement. The Council is authorized to act upon the complaints of organizations and individuals. Its function, however, is to review programs *after* the fact and it does not exercise any powers of censorship in terms of prior restraint.

Article XIII states that "if there are grounds for assuming that the Corporation has fallen short of its responsibilities as defined by the Agreement," the Government may assign three investigators to conduct an inquiry and should the findings of the inquiry warrant, the Government may divest the Corporation of its broadcasting authority.

Broadcasting Code

FOLLOWING the adoption of the Agreement, the Parliament instituted an official inquiry into the whole field of broadcasting with instructions to make long-range plans and recommendations for its future development which might become the basis for further legislation. Pending the completion of this study (the final report was not issued until 1965), *Sveriges Radio* appointed a special committee to prepare a *Code of Broadcasting Practice* to implement the provisions of the 1959 Agreement. In two articles in the *EBU Review,* Henrik Hahr, the Director and Chief Assistant to the Director-General, discussed the contents of the *Code.* In November 1962, he wrote that it consisted of three parts: (1) general rules meant to guide all broadcasting; (2) special rules applicable to certain programming areas; and (3) a collection of documents containing, among other things, guiding statements made by the Board of Governors and the Broadcasting Council.

Mr. Hahr mentioned Article IV of the Agreement which calls for objectivity in news reporting and the broadcasting of programs on issues of public importance. He discussed the section of the *Code* which implements the provisions of this Article and explains the philosophy of *Sveriges Radio* regarding this area of programming:

> . . . The first clause of this article emphasises the central position of sound radio and television in Swedish cultural life, and states that programmes shall uphold and strengthen the interest of the general public in broadcasting. The structure and general tendency of programmes is clarified in principle when this clause goes on to say that Sveriges Radio is required "to disseminate, in objective, impartial and suitable form, information on current events and to orient the general public towards more important cultural and social issues, as well as to encourage debate on such issues."
>
> Unlike the press, wherein a balance of divergent views evolves out of discussion and competition between organs, broadcasting must achieve this balance by means of special measures. Put succinctly, this means that the exclusive technical rights which Sveriges Radio now has for its broadcasts shall be used to create a platform on which conflicting opinions can make themselves heard, in accordance with established and guaranteed democratic principles. Accordingly, the requirement of impartiality assumes fundamental importance. This is a cardinal rule for all programming and a prerequisite for the retention of public confidence in Sveriges Radio. By virtue of the operational form which was laid down for them a long time ago by the Riksdag, our radio and television services are required to cater not only for the interests of powerful opinion-moulding groups but also—as specified in the agreement —for the specialised interests of minority audiences. Such a balance of programme presentation is held to be in the best interests of both the individual and the community at large.
>
> To begin with, the impartiality requirement means that Sveriges Radio may not take sides in controversial matters; to this there is one natural exception, and that is to uphold democratic and equivalent values. Secondly, the requirement means that conflicting opinions shall be allotted programme time and be balanced in a fair manner. This is not to say that all such opinions must be represented on one and the same programme. The observation was made back in 1948 by the then programme directors that impartiality cannot always be adhered to in individual programmes but must be applied to programming as a whole. Thus, controversial issues may be discussed either in a single debate or divided into separate programmes, with one view argued on each occasion. The Committee, however, has seen fit to introduce a modification: the more controversial a programme is expected

to be, the more necessary it is to make provision for balanced representation of opinions either concurrently or within a relatively short time. This point must accordingly be considered in programme planning.

The impartiality requirement is not to be viewed in isolation. It may interact in some way with the requirements of objectivity and suitable form. For instance, Sveriges Radio feels that the interests of truth are better served by aligning itself with scientific objectivity as against the distinctly unscientific approaches inherent in superstition, magic, astrology, religious hallucinations and the like.

With regard to orientation of the public towards cultural and social issues, it is essential that this be as comprehensive as possible. It follows from this requirement that Sveriges Radio cannot avoid programmes of controversial content on the grounds that they might make it a target of adverse criticism. In emphasising the importance of being scrupulously careful in such matters, the Committee has cited a guiding pronouncement of the Broadcasting Council, which it made in 1960 with reference to "public affairs" programmes that may entail the critical examination and appraisal or description of obvious social evils. The Council initially observes that such programmes have a definite place in our programming. It goes on to say that radio and television programmes dealing with an instance of some act or omission by an authority, institution or company, which has caused annoyance or dissatisfaction to the public, should be designed so as to give the criticized party a fair chance and reasonable transmission time to present its case. Moreover, such party should be informed in advance of the criticism that is going to be broadcast.

Another statement of guiding importance made by the Council on this occasion is directly related to controversial programmes. For instance, a special interest may seek to prevent such a programme by refusing to take part. In so doing, the special interest assumes that the programme would become biased, thus violating the rule of impartiality. The projected program might then be cancelled or, if broadcast, would perhaps be meaningless.

In reviewing this matter, the Council observes that it had earlier been given cause to determine whether refusal to take part in a controversial programme should be permitted to prevent its broadcast. Of course, there is no question of denying anyone's right to refuse to participate. But in its earlier statements the Council has maintained that such refusal must not be allowed to stand in the way of carrying out a programme. Any decision on the measures to be taken in consequence of a refusal rests with Sveriges Radio, and not with the special interest whose participation has been invited.[28]

In January 1963, Mr. Hahr summarized sections of the *Code* concerning news as stated by a special committee set up by *Sveriges Radio* to deal with the legal responsibility of broadcasting:

On the subject of broadcast news, the Committee makes it clear that an objective, impartial, independent and prompt news service is in the interests of a democratic society. It should be conducted in principle to conform with regular journalistic practice, though paying careful attention to the difference in status between Sveriges Radio and the press. Since the general public is supposed to be able to rely on the news broadcast by Sveriges Radio, staff members are required to make sure that their news sources are trustworthy. The editorial staff or department which produces the programme is to be responsible for the evaluation of news. Attempts by outsiders to influence the evaluation of news or the wording of a news communication on irrelevant grounds shall be disregarded. An item of news shall be made public as soon as possible. Of particular relevance to Sveriges Radio, however, is that speed must not be obtained at the cost of accuracy.

When dealing with the task of treating certain rules of news broadcasting in greater detail, the Committee has found it most suitable to draw on the rules of the Publicists' Club (PK) dating from January 1st, 1953. Although admittedly formulated with reference to the Freedom of the Press Act, these rules constitute a well worked out and valuable body of material which offers a good foundation in the present context. The rules have been accommodated to the unique position of Sveriges Radio and the special nature of radio and television media.

Under the heading "Correct Information," our Code states (following a number of practical directives to the editorial staffs):

"Before any item of news is passed on to the public, its *veracity* should be checked, careful thought given to *precision* of vocabulary—not least with regard to the classification of crime and other legal terms—and *restraint* observed in its wording, not least if the item is of doubtful nature or pressing urgency. Especially in perplexing situations, each and everyone must act so that the public can put its reliance on Sveriges Radio as a communicator of news."

An essential point is taken up by the PK rules under the heading, "Make provision for justifiable replies." We quote: "The individual's right to protection of his reputation and integrity shall be respected. Publicity which violates the sanctity of private life must be avoided, unless it is imperative in the public interest to demand disclosure. Allow time for the right to reply, preferably equal in length to that already given to the statements concerned."

The Committee has annotated PK's discreetly presented considerations thus: Given its special status, Sveriges Radio must approach the difficult task of weighing private against public interest with scrupulous care. In the matter of replies, controversial programmes are usually devised (as was mentioned earlier) to permit different interests to present their views either in one programme or in a series of consecutive programmes. If a reply from an interest is warranted, the form this should take is to be discussed with the management of Sveriges Radio in each instance. In the event of a wrong item of information being mistakenly broadcast in a news bulletin or other programme, it shall be retracted as soon as possible in a similar type of programme. The restraint which the PK rules call for in the reporting of crimes is of course echoed in the Committee's annotations. A related point made by the Committee is that Sveriges Radio should, as a rule, refrain from tracking down and publishing material on criminal investigations which have not been released to the general public. Any such attempts, besides the undeserved suffering they can cause, might constitute grounds for defamation suits. The rules under this head further stress that persons who supply Sveriges Radio with information do not enjoy the protection of anonymity that is theirs when they turn to the press, the Swedish and other news agencies.

A rule which applies with particular force to Sveriges Radio is that individual complaints lodged with public officials against such occupational groups as doctors, teachers and lawyers must first be carefully examined; the same is true of complaints against different acts by public officials. In dealing with such cases, however, staff members must not be misled into the kind of cautious behavior which might be interpreted as submissiveness towards public officials and other persons in public life.

An area as delicate as it is important has to do with publishing the name of a person who is suspected of a crime, or who is apprehended, arrested, indicted or convicted. The building principles contained in the rules are: no names are published in respect of *apprehension,* unless it concerns a gross crime to which the offender has confessed; in respect of *arrest* or *request for arrest,* unless the investigation in hand supports the assumption that several years of imprisonment will follow; in respect of *indictment,* unless a confession is obtained or full substantiation produced, and if the crime is so gross as to rule out a suspended sentence; in respect of *criminal verdicts,* unless punishment exceeds one year of imprisonment and the offender is more than 21 years of age; and in *civil verdicts,* unless publication of name cannot harm the person concerned. The names of juvenile delinquents or mental defectives are never published.

In view of the risks involved, however, staff members are required to keep in close touch with the management of Sveriges Radio with regard to doubtful cases of name publication.

A last point to be made under this head is related to the requirement of objectivity in court reporting. The rules prescribe that judicial proceedings and crimes be dealt with as far as possible by permanently employed staff of Sveriges Radio. Staff members who receive such assignments are required to observe the strictest objectivity especially when they have dealings with parties to a case or their representatives. A Sveriges Radio man must not allow even the mere suspicion that his reporting of the facts may be coloured by the acceptance of hospitality or the like.

A general comment concerning all rules in the Code might be in order: they apply with equal force to radio and television. However, the Code has made a special reference to the latter by observing that detailed pictures of violence in a filmed news sequence can become very upsetting and obtrusive when shown on television. Neither may the pictures suggest what the commentary does not say, and editors are urged when cutting films prior to broadcast to be careful that innocent parties are not negatively implicated.[29]

In the same issue of the *EBU Review,* Mr. Hahr referred to that section of the *Code* which prohibits advertising. In making contracts for the broadcast of programs (e.g., sports events), *Sveriges Radio* requires that "the other contracting party pledge itself not to involve a third party in this agreement or to enter into a contract with a third party that permits it to display advertising during broadcasts." In connection with the broadcast of consumer information and research, the names of some products, prices, and quality may be mentioned, but "with the understanding that considerations of impartiality must be scrupulously observed."

The *Code* permits *Sveriges Radio* to promote its own programs so long as such promotion helps the public "to better assimilate the contents" of the programs. Extraneous advertising which exploits the goodwill of a program for private ends (except in such cases as the advertising of books) is discouraged by *Sveriges Radio*.[30]

Current Status of Sveriges Radio

Sveriges Radio continues to operate as a private company with the press owning about two-fifths of the shares, large national organizations and popular movements two-fifths, and commercial interests, primarily the wireless industry, one-fifth. The Government has no financial interest in the Company, although it can exercise majority control by appointing the Chairman and five additional members of the Board, whereas, the shareholders elect only five. The Board constitutes the highest administrative authority and is responsible for the establishment and interpretation of general policies and regulations, but does not concern itself with the day-to-day operations. As of June 30, 1964, the outstanding stock amounted to one million and eighty thousand Swedish Kronor with the dividends fixed at five percent.[31]

The Radio Council, consisting of twenty-four members appointed by the Government, still functions as an agency for program review, handles complaints from the public, and submits an annual report which evaluates the past program performance and recommends improvements.

Ultimate administrative responsibility is vested in a Director-General, who is appointed by the Board. There are separate organizations for radio and television, each headed by a program director. These two organizations are jointly served by a single technical unit as well as by other departments concerned with supplies, personnel administration and training, external relations and educational activities.

The program departments report directly to the Director-General who also exercises overall administrative control over programming operations at the regional level. He is in charge of the library and records section, the information department and the central newsroom, and his office conducts audience surveys.

There was only one national radio service until the Second Programme (P2) was initiated in November 1955. Shortly thereafter, a third network of FM stations was established on a trial basis. As of June 1964, only about one-half of the population could receive this latter service. With the Parliament's approval, plans called for the establishment of a nation-wide FM service by 1967.[32]

Current Radio Programming

Sveriges Radio recently has provided information about its various radio services. On Programme 1, the original network, the programs consist mainly of light entertainment and informational materials with a broad appeal. Some "serious" broadcasts dealing with the sciences, literature and art are carried during the day "on the principle that listeners shall be offered a varied choice of programs," but the stress is on "simple" subject matter.[33] Programme 2, operating in the evenings, concentrates on materials that appeal to a limited and sophisticated audience. Programme 3 presents light music during the best listening hours, but is limited largely to FM transmission in metropolitan areas.

Sveriges Radio has described its operation as of October 1964:[34] four radio services (three national and one overseas); Programme 1 transmitted from six in the morning until midnight by thirty-six AM stations on long- and medium-wave and forty-seven FM stations on ultra-short-wave; Programme 2 with its *melodiradio* (light music) carried from quarter past six to eleven in the evening by twenty-six medium-wave stations of limited range and forty-seven FM stations; Programme 3 transmitted by six FM stations in the larger cities. In addition, both P1 and P2 are relayed over wired facilities which are particularly extensive in northern and southeastern Sweden.[35]

The fourth service, Radio Sweden, designed for foreign listeners, is carried by two short-wave transmitters. It is transmitted twenty-four hours per day to different parts of the world in Swedish, English, German, French, Spanish and Portuguese. Transcriptions of selected programs are made available for rebroadcasting in many other countries.[36]

Current Financial Status

As of April 1966, there were about three million radio licenses in Sweden, or almost one set for every three persons. As of the same date, only ten years after the introduction of television, there were almost two million TV licenses. According to *Sveriges Radio,* this represents the highest per capita license ratio in Europe for radio and the second highest for television.[37]

In 1965 the annual license fees were thirty-five Kronor per home for radio and one hundred Kronor per home for television.[38] Total revenue for the fiscal year 1964–65 from radio licenses were estimated at one hundred and two million Kronor. Of these amounts, *Sveriges Radio* received 66.3 million Kronor to carry on its domestic radio service and 101.4 million Kronor to finance its television.[39]

In addition, *Sveriges Radio* received in 1964–65 a special grant from public funds of 9.8 million Kronor, a little more than half of which was used to carry on school programs and the remainder to provide the overseas service.[40]

Present Television Facilities

THERE is at present only one television network. As of June 1964, the service was carried by ninety-five transmitters, forty-eight of which were relays. It was reported that the telecasts were usually presented in the evening from six to half past ten, with a weekly total of about forty-four hours per week, including school programs. Eurovision and Nordvision programs and a limited number of repeat broadcasts are carried during the afternoons.[41]

Educational Broadcasting

As previously indicated, education has always been given high priority in Swedish broadcasting. School television, which was inaugurated in 1961, may be considered as an extension of school radio which has been operating in Sweden since 1929. In 1958, the Swedish Broadcasting Corporation began a study of the possible uses of television in education. On the basis of this study, in May 1959, it was recommended that an experimental project be undertaken.

Accordingly, the first classroom instruction for an academic term was started. It consisted of thirty programs designed for fourteen to sixteen year olds, presented in four different series: current events, vocational guidance, elementary physics and quiz programs in the Danish language.[42] This experiment proved successful and regular classroom instruction for all age groups, involving a variety of disciplines, was initiated, with the costs defrayed by a special grant from the Government.[43] The Swedish Board of Education has taken the lead and cooperated with the Corporation in the preparation of these broadcasts.

Recent reports from the officials in charge of the Swedish school broadcasts indicate that great progress has been made, and that the patterns of operation have changed considerably during the past decade. A 1967 report of the School Programmes Department of the Corporation explains the shift in educational policy:

School broadcasts have undergone considerable metamorphosis—largely as a result of a gradual shift in educational policy, which now conceives of them as essential parts of an integrated whole. Earlier, they were designed merely to supplement instruction; at times, the broadcasts were not even centrally related to the curricula at all but were offered instead as "extras," standing, as it were, outside the main work of the the students concerned. Today, however, schools are offered complete study "packages" or what might aptly be called teaching systems. Among other advantages of these broadcasts "packages" is the fact that they will assist long-term educational planning by forming the bases of continuity in curricula.

Educational authorities are generally agreed that this has been a good development. Now, program production is spread over considerable time and represents the professional contributions of numerous people. Broadly speaking, the School Programme Department provides two kinds of services to schools:

1. Study material in the form of radio and television *programmes*.

2. *Courses* that form the foundation (for the whole or part) of the teaching.

This procedure, supplying broadcast and printed material as integral elements of school curricula, is the traditional policy of school broadcasting in Europe. The programmes may be complete in themselves or they may be parts of series; either way, they need not materially alter a teacher's plans for the year.

It is a relatively recent development, however, that school broadcasts are providing courses that are designed as the very foundations of the teaching itself. In such cases, the broadcasts are designed as lessons (as distinct from programmes) and are built around a course textbook. These broadcast courses can range in scope covering an entire year's syllabus to detailing some concentrated aspect of a syllabus.

Planning for a school year (1967–68, for example) is begun in February of the previous year (1966). Programme quotas are worked out on the basis of the budget applied for. The Swedish Broadcasting Corporation's proposals and general questions are then presented to the Swedish Board of Education.

In March, the Board replies, comprehensively outlining the requirements of different kinds of schools and stating its wishes regarding priorities.

The Swedish Broadcasting Corporation and the Board of Education both continue the refining and coordination of the programme plan until the autumn. In November, the plan is completed, tasks are allocated, and production begins.

It is estimated that in school year 1967–68, the schools will be offered about 1,650 broadcasts: 250 on television and 1,400 on radio.

The Department uses various methods to maintain contact with teachers and keep them informed. Important information regarding curricular content and suggestions for use of broadcast materials are disseminated through a periodical called AVIN. Different editions of AVIN are published for teachers at various levels of instruction. Between six and eight issues (100,000 copies of each issue) are published each school term.

The Department places great emphasis on pupil participation in its broadcasts. This and other matters relating to program production are discussed in a 1967 brochure published by the Department:

In the view of the School Programmes Department, it is important that productions actively engage the pupils. This emphasis on engagement must be integrated into both programmes and printed materials. Active engagement has proved far more motivating than mere passive reception of information. The results: interest, stimulation, self-activity.

Another essential of school-broadcast production is that programmes and printed matter must function as integrated wholes, and broadcasts must always be compatible with the most modern accepted teaching methods and concepts. Earlier, printed matter merely supplemented the broadcasts. Today, however, both these elements are thoroughly integrated: each determines the efficacy of the other in the classroom.

Before a programme (or a booklet, still-film series, or textbook) can be evaluated, the full "package" (programme and printed matter) must be taken into account. The judged "package" should also include AVIN. And finally, the role of each of these elements in the general school-year plan must be known. THEN, a valid opinion is possible.

The members of the staff primarily involved in productions are the broadcast producer and the printed-matter editor. Often, a planner is involved as well, and each section (radio, television, editorial) works in its own area of responsibility. This separation of professional functions does not, however, detract from the integral unity of the final product: coordination is maintained between sections, with the broadcast producer having ultimate responsibility and authority for the project.

In their final form, the broadcast and the printed matter will bear the stamp of this producer: his ability, his experience, his imagination. This is a great deal of responsibility to be placed on a producer, but there are very few people who are completely competent in both programme-production and education. Still fewer of these are, at the same time, experts in some field of instruction and good, clear writers besides. Therefore, to create a sound basis for production, various outside experts are called in whenever need arises.

Municipal audio-visual centres, about 75 of them, constitute an external system of broadcast distribution. Their functions include the tape recording and post-broadcast distribution of radio programmes.

Research Activities

Sveriges Radio has shown much interest in research. A special department in the Corporation makes continuing studies of audience composition and response. For example, a 1965 report of this department states that research regarding adult education programs in radio and television had been conducted with the following objectives:

(1) Description of audience, size and social composition
(2) Discovery of why persons listen or watch certain programs
(3) Ascertainment of effects on behavior
(4) Registration of *desiderata* of the audience with respect to future programming.

In the long range planning of the research, the emphasis had been on developing a conceptual framework and determining the main functional aspects of the programs. Most of the investigation thus far has consisted of statistical field studies, but certain hypotheses (i.e., some concerning interaction processes of listeners in study groups) have been experimentally tested.[44]

Sveriges Radio devotes considerable time to research relating to school broadcasting. For example, one 1965 survey was designed to determine the use which fifth and sixth grade schools made of a series of five broadcasts on sexual education, and to ascertain how the pupils, teachers and parents reacted. The findings were:[45]

84% of all the 725 teachers sampled had given classroom instruction in sexual education during the 1964/1965 academic year.
Of these 84% (612 teachers), the greater number (462 or 76%) had devoted 2–5 lessons in the subject, but sometimes as many as 10 lessons were used.
339 teachers, comprising 47% of the total sample (54% of those who had taught sexual education) drew on one or more of the broadcast programmes. Most of the teachers who made use of the series listened to all 5 programmes. Tape recording of the programmes occurred to a greater extent than direct listening. 30% of all the teachers sampled listened on tape, 19% listened directly. 2% of the total sample listened to the same programme both directly and on tape.
The first programme was heard by 44% of all the teachers sampled, the second by 43%, the third by 42%, the fourth by 41%, and the fifth (question-and-answer programme) by 26%.
58% of the teachers who drew on the series prepared their class in some way beforehand. 43% of the teachers who reported making such preparation did so with reference to the section of the text dealing with the human body. 18% had studied the booklet issued by Sveriges Radio in conjunction with the series. . . .
8% of the parents having children who heard one or more of the programmes gave their opinions of the series. Most of the opinions were favourable.
Most of the teachers, or 65%, drew on the programme series to the extent where it formed the basis for their instruction in the subject. 9% drew on only single programmes or segments thereof and formulated the rest of the instruction themselves. For 9% the programmes comprised the sole form of

instruction, and for 4% the series did no more than amplify their own instruction.

70% of those who listened to the series drew on Sveriges Radio's booklet.

In 82% of the classes using the booklet, the pupils studied it while the programmes were in progress; 63% of the classes before the programmes were broadcast, and 52% afterwards.

The booklet contained examples of discussion for the teacher. 70% of the teachers in classes using the booklet felt they were helped by the discussion examples.

16% of all the teachers sampled expressed a need for more information on the content of the series and for different ways in which the series can be utilized in instruction.

3% of the teachers who drew on the series felt that the subject matter was treated too extensively. 81% held that the treatment was adequate, 3% inadequate, and 13% did not answer the question.

Another study was made in 1965 to determine the extent of listening to school broadcasting in the junior grades. The findings were:[46]

Schools Radio

All 467 classes in the sample were in a position to listen to the radio broadcasts, either directly or on tapes. 95% of the classes availed themselves of this facility during the 1964 autumn term.

49% of the classes had their own radio set in the classroom, 14% fetched a set from another part of the school premises, and 34% listened to a central radio. About 80% of the junior classes have a tape recorder in school. 15% of the classes in our sample said they had a tape recorder in the classroom, and 40% that they obtained a recorder from another part of the premises. Thus about 25% of the classes did not use a tape recorder for various reasons, even though their school has one.

95% of the entire sample listened to some School Radio programme during the term. Of these 95% (443 classes), 23% listened to 11–15 programmes, which is the number most frequently listened to per class. 20% listened to 16–20 programmes, and 18% to 6–10 programmes. The largest number of programmes listened to by any one class is 41–44 (1%).

60% of the listeners heard only live broadcasts, 10% only tape recordings, and 29% both live and tape.

On an average, musical programmes were heard by 46% of the total sample, religious programmes by 37%, Swedish by 27%, local culture by 25%, mathematics by 22%, and gymnastics by 14%.

Sveriges Radio airs its radio programmes over three channels. Up to now Schools Radio has been broadcasting over Channel 1, but will switch to Channel 2 beginning in the spring of 1967. . . .

Schools TV

Out of the total sample 302 classes, or 65%, had access to a TV set. The sets were variously located as follows:

In the classroom	4%
Elsewhere in the same building	40%
In another building of the school	21%
No access to TV	35%
	100%

41% of the classes having access to TV shared the set, intended for junior, intermediate and upper grades, with nine or more classes.

Out of the 65% (302 classes) in the sample having access to TV, 68% (205 classes) watched some programme during the term. If the number of viewing classes is related to the total sample, the viewing proportion comes to 44%. Out of the TV viewers, 53% had seen 1–5 programmes, 34% 6–10 programmes and 13% 11–14 programmes.

65% of the 205 classes who watched TV during the term did not see any programme with only their own class in the receiving room, but always together with some other class. 24% of the TV viewers saw 1–5 programmes with only their own class, 8% saw 6–10 programmes and 4% saw 11–14 programmes.

The Future of Swedish Broadcasting

THE future for Swedish broadcasting appears extremely promising. Construction of an elaborate radio and TV center is under way in Stockholm. The office and library sections for radio were occupied in 1961. Mr. Olof Rydbeck, the Director-General of *Sveriges Radio,* reported that the completion of a modern studio block was expected by January 1965 and that the first stage of television construction would be completed by 1966 or 1967. He further stated that a large concert hall to serve both radio and television, plus additional TV studios and office buildings, were already on the planning boards. A large scale radio and television center is to be built in Gothenburg. A similar center was opened in Malino in southern Sweden in 1958. Well-equipped facilities for radio and TV are already in use in numerous other cities and construction is contemplated in several other places.[47]

On April 7, 1965, the Swedish Committee on Broadcasting, which was created in 1960, presented a seven hundred and fifty page report, *The Future of Radio and Television in Sweden.*[48] This report pointed out that in 1965 Sweden's single TV channel carried forty-five hours per week of programming (including three hours of school programs and six hours of afternoon repeats). The Committee's study lists as a primary objective the introduction of a second channel with the completion of TV studios in the new Broadcasting House in 1968. It is anticipated that the total hours of TV programming will then approach sixty-five hours. Also, it is expected that some color television may be introduced by that time. The hope is that by 1975 the two schedules will be running one hundred hours weekly with a program breakdown as follows:

Production by *Sveriges Radio*	45 hours
Production by independent agencies in Sweden	3 hours
Films	27 hours
Afternoon repeats	8 hours
TV college	17 hours

The second network will operate on UHF channels, using, at the start, thirty transmitters, and furnishing service to sixty-five percent of the population. The facilities are to be expanded later and, by 1975, it is anticipated that nation-wide coverage will be achieved, provided by a total of one hundred and twenty-three major transmitters and about one hundred and fifty repeaters.

Presently, as previously indicated, *Sveriges Radio* presents three radio services, using only two networks. Plans call for the completion of the third FM network and to transfer to it light music from Programme 2 and some "talk" entertainment from Programme 1.

As projected by the Committee, programs on the three radio networks will follow somewhat the British Broadcasting Corporation and the *Radio Telefís Éireann* patterns. Total broadcasting time will run about three hundred and sixty-five hours per week, with P1 on the air from six in the morning until eleven in the evening daily, P2 from nine in the morning until half past eleven in the evening (with the morning and early afternoon hours devoted to school programs), and P3 twenty-four hours per day.

The Committee's plans for the future call for the elimination of "wired radio systems," a reduction of the AM transmission, and an expansion of the FM transmissions. Regional broadcasting, which now averages only about three and one-half hours per week in ten areas, will be substantially increased. Greater emphasis will be placed upon the use of local live talent and the development of diversified and indigenous programming, reflecting the varied interests and needs of the country.

Special Programming Planned

ONE of the most important changes contemplated by the Committee is the development of what it calls "special programming." While it believes that a public monopoly for "general programming" is desirable and that *Sveriges Radio* should continue to serve this function, the Committee maintains that some facilities should be available for private nonprofit groups. For example, it is felt that school authorities should be mainly responsible for institutional broadcasting. Moreover, some of the so-called "popular movements" in Sweden are pressing for more broadcasting time to serve their special interests and needs. Accordingly, it is envisioned that the Board of Telecommunications (which also serves *Sveriges Radio*) will establish and operate two radio networks, and a large number of widely distributed, low-power stations. Organizations, including educational institutions, meeting the eligibility requirements, upon application to the Government, will be granted permits to rent time on these projected networks and stations. Broadcasting time will be allocated by a small government bureau made up of national and local officials "whose most exacting task will be to divide the desirable time slots impartially."[49]

Educational programs, designed for general reception, for the most part will continue to be the responsibility of *Sveriges Radio* and will be financed out of funds derived from the license fees. Instructional broadcasting, such as that designed to supplement classroom teaching, courses leading to diplomas and other formalized uses of radio and television for student instruction, will be carried on by other groups who will be expected to bear all production and rental costs.

Since no national TV network will be established for this "special programming," *Sveriges Radio* will be expected to continue the televising of adult education with a wide appeal (language instruction, for example). In some cases, if suitable arrangements can be made and time is available, a college or university may sponsor an instructional program on the TV network and share in the costs.

One of the most important proposals of the Committee is the establishment of a "TV College" which would occupy the time slot on the second network from six to eight in the evening, five days per week, with repeats on weekend afternoons.

Proposed Reorganization of Sveriges Radio

ANOTHER major proposal concerns the reorganization of *Sveriges Radio*. It is now a limited liability company but will be transformed into a foundation, and the Board of Control will be cut from twenty-one to seven, with the Government appointing three of the members and the Chairman, and the shareholders (press, popular movements and business interests) choosing the other three. The Broadcasting Council will be reduced from twenty-four to seven members and will continue its principal task of considering "after the event, complaints against individual programs" and any infractions of the rules governing broadcasting.

This far-reaching plan calls for large expenditures. The total annual costs of operation now (including both radio and TV) are about two hundred and fifty million Kronor; the projected plan is estimated to cost about three times that amount in 1974–75. Since no commercials are to be allowed, the license fee system will be continued. A "combined" annual fee (covering both radio and TV) will be charged and will be progressively increased as follows to meet additional costs:[50]

1967	170 Kronor
1969	210 Kronor
1971	240 Kronor
1973	1,973 Kronor

On April 18, 1966, Mr. Olof Palme, the Swedish Minister of Communications, in a speech before the Conference on Culture at Stockholm, made some predictions about the future of broadcasting in the country. He said that the School Radio programs would soon be moved to Programme 2, and the transmission network for Melody Radio on Programme 3 would become fully operational. He further stated that there was a great interest in the introduction of a second TV program, but it would probably be January 1, 1969, before it could be accomplished. Because of the financial and technical problems, he was not prepared to fix an exact date for the introduction of color television.

Despite some pressures from business interests for commercial television, Mr. Palme declared that such an idea would be rejected by the Government. Quoting from Olof Lagercrantz in the *Dagens Nyheter,* he was highly critical of commercial broadcasting in the United States:

> Once the morning newscasts are done with, and their content is often of excellent quality and not marred by too many commercials, every home is turned into a lunatic asylum at about nine o'clock. Or perhaps it would be more adequate to call the offerings of American TV between nine in the morning and ten at night—with certain breaks for news—a nightmare of insipid sweetness, a hell where the instruments of torture have been fetched from some earthly amusement park. Soapy-voiced tenors sing of sweethearts and mothers, and quiz-contest M.C.'s put on machine-made smiles when they hand over absurd prizes to winners who know the answer to two times two. Cowboy heroes lash out one uppercut for every yard of footage, shouting their homily for one and all to hear: "I'll teach you that rough stuff doesn't pay."

Despite Mr. Lagercrantz' description, Mr. Palme thought the picture of TV might be "more finely shaded." "For example," said he, "the debates and news-in-depth programs contain a frankness and freedom which are fine expressions of American democracy. Some of the steadily grinding serial programmes are of good quality. Excellent programmes of serious content are also broadcast, though usually late at night or early in the morning. Brilliant heights may be reached on occasion, as witnessed by the coverage of President Kennedy's funeral and the Senate hearings on Vietnam.

Unfortunately, however, these are exceptions, and in their way sadly confirm the fantastic potentialities of the TV medium—for the one who has both the will and the resources."

Mr. Palme concluded that the Swedish broadcasting system should and *would* continue to be a noncommercial one. He anticipated that further legislation would make clear that broadcasting is a "public service" and that it should be detached from both commercial and government controls. He opposed setting up a system of competitive broadcasting since he believed that "the experience of other countries convincingly demonstrates that competition between different enterprises means having to choose between very similar alternatives," and "the remorseless tendency for competing broadcasters to schedule so-called minority programs at inconvenient hours." On the other hand, he favored a single, cohesive system but with maximum autonomy at the national and regional levels. He envisioned a flexible system in which regions would be allocated their own budgets to produce programs and to enjoy independence in their operations.

The legislation which Mr. Palme proposed to submit would provide for an integrated organization with a Board of Directors, a Director-General and a Central Office. There would be four independent program departments: one for radio, one for TV-1, one for TV-2, one for educational programs, and a department for engineering. It was expected that the Parliament would enact new legislation soon to put into effect the Minister's proposals.

NOTES

1. Act of August 31, 1907, *Svensk Författnings-Samling Med Bihang*, 1907, Sweden; Laws, Statutes, Etc.; Stockholm, *Kungl Boktryck Eriet, F. A. Norstret and Sóner*, 1908, No. 94, pp. 2–3.
2. See Olof Rydbeck, "Broadcasting in Sweden," *EBU Review*, 80B, July 1963, p. 6.
3. See Act of May 16, 1924, *Svensk Författnings-Samling Med Bihang*, 1924, No. 121, pp. 171–172.
4. *EBU Bulletin*, March–April 1955, p. 143.
5. *Ibid.*, September 5, 1953, pp. 269–270.
6. *Ibid.*, May 15, 1953, p. 319.
7. *Ibid.*, pp. 320–321.
8. *EBU Bulletin*, March–April 1955, p. 569.
9. *Ibid.*, September 15, 1953, p. 574.
10. *Ibid.*, November 15, 1951, pp. 591–592.
11. *Ibid.*
12. *EBU Review*, 57B, September 1959, p. 2.
13. *EBU Bulletin*, March 15, 1953, pp. 177–178.
14. *EBU Review*, 57B, September 1959, p. 3.
15. *EBU Bulletin*, September 1950, p. 295.

16. As of January 1968, the Swedish Kronor was equivalent to nineteen and one-half cents.
17. *EBU Bulletin*, May 15, 1951, p. 295.
18. *Ibid.*, July 15, 1953, p. 475.
19. *Ibid.*, January–February 1955, p. 67.
20. The Swedish Philips Company, Ltd., formally requested the Government to grant it a concession for fifteen years to broadcast commercial programs on FM. (See *EBU Bulletin*, May–June 1954, p. 306; also, see July 15, 1953, p. 475.)
21. *Ibid.*, July–August 1954, p. 515.
22. *Ibid.*, January–February 1955, p. 67; also July–August 1955, p. 444.
23. *Ibid.*, January–February 1955, p. 67.
24. *Ibid.*, September–October 1956, p. 735.
25. *Ibid.*, November–December 1957, pp. 690–691.
26. Agreement between Swedish State and the Swedish Broadcasting Corporation with reference to broadcasting services and regulations governing the division and coordination of broadcasting engineering between the Telecommunications Administration and the Swedish Broadcasting Corporation, Stockholm, May 15, 1959. See report on this Agreement and these regulations in *EBU Review*, 60B, March 1960, pp. 23–24.
27. *Ibid.*, Article VI of Agreement.
28. *EBU Review*, 76B, November 1962, p. 43.
29. *Ibid.*, 77B, January 1963, pp. 25–27.
30. *Ibid.*, pp. 26–27.
31. The Swedish Broadcasting Corporation, Stockholm; an informational document published in English by *Sveriges Radio*, dated October 1964.
32. *Ibid.*, p. 4.
33. *Ibid.*, pp. 4–5.
34. *Ibid.*, p. 5. Also, see "Broadcasting in Sweden: Material Resources," *Sveriges Radio*, Stockholm, June 1963. This is an informational bulletin which was prepared by the Engineering Division, *Sveriges Radio*, for the delegates of the EBU General Assembly which convened in Stockholm on June 28, 1963.
35. *Ibid.*
36. *Ibid.*
37. The Swedish Broadcasting Corporation, informational document, October 1964, p. 3; also, see speech by Olof Palme, Swedish Minister of Communications, Stockholm, April 18, 1966.
38. *EBU Review*, 98B, July 1966, p. 32.
39. Swedish Broadcasting Corporation, informational document, October 1964, p. 3.
40. *Ibid.*
41. *Ibid.*
42. "School Television," report of *Sveriges Radio*, Stockholm, May 1961.
43. UNESCO, *World Communications: Press, Radio, Television, Film* (New York: UNESCO Publications Center, 1964), p. 327.
44. See report of Bengt Högland, "Research Perspectives on Adult Education in Radio and Television," *Sveriges Radio*, Stockholm, 1965.
45. See report on survey dealing with "Series of Programs on Sexual Education for Schools Radio," Margarete Lihr, Research Department, *Sveriges Radio*, Stockholm, 1965.
46. See "Report on a Poll on the Use of Schools Broadcasting in the Junior Grades During the 1964 Autumn Term," Margareta Lihr, Research Department, *Sveriges Radio*, Stockholm, 1964.

47. See Olof Rydbeck, "Broadcasting in Sweden," *EBU Review*, 80B, July 1963, p. 6.
48. Statement of Dr. Ingemar Lindbuid, Secretary, Swedish Broadcasting Committee, 1960–65, containing a summary of the reports, made available to the author in manuscript form; reported in *EBU Review*, 92B, July 1965, pp. 15–18.
49. *Ibid.*, p. 17.
50. *Ibid.*, p. 18.

XIII

Finland: Broadcasting Link
Between East and West

FINLAND, because of historical and geographical realities, is related politically and economically to both the East and West. She trades with the countries of both areas, and is an active member of the Nordic Council and the United Nations.

As she is the only country belonging to both the European Broadcasting Union (EBU) and the International Radio and Television Organization (OIRT), Finland provides a link station for transmissions between the two networks. The EBU, with headquarters in Geneva, maintains Eurovision, the television network of the Western European countries. The OIRT, with main offices in Prague, is the sponsoring organization for Intervision which links the Eastern countries, including the Soviet Union, via television.

On two occasions, representatives of the EBU and the OIRT have met in Helsinki. The first joint meeting was held in 1957 and dealt with technical problems. In July 1964, the presidents and delegates of the two organizations met to consider other matters of common interest.

As in the other Norden countries, the official religion is Evangelical Lutheran, but every citizen is free to worship as he chooses. There is practically no illiteracy, and institutions of higher learning thrive throughout the country. Swedish, spoken by about eight percent of the people, is the second national language and along with Finnish has official sanction.

Radio Prior to the First World War

RADIO began in Finland during the early twenties. As was the case in many other countries, the first transmitters were built by amateurs. In 1923, radio listeners founded the Finnish Radio Society, and in 1924, this Society began to produce regular programs, transmitting them from a Helsinki station, then a part of the military establishment.[1]

In 1926, a special company, the *Oy. Suomen Yleisradio* (Finnish Broadcasting Company), was founded to expand the program service of the Finnish Radio Society.[2] The next fifteen years was a period of great growth in broadcasting. Before the outbreak of the war with the Soviet Union in 1939, there were seventeen stations with an accumulated transmitting power of 248.5 kilowatts.[3]

Postwar Growth

FOLLOWING the war, in February 1945, the Finnish Broadcasting Company (FBC) appointed a Committee to plan for expanding the facilities. Because of insufficient medium- and long-waves to meet the growing needs of radio, the Committee recommended the development of frequency modulation. Finland, along with Germany, was one of the first countries to develop a VHF system of FM transmission.[4] Presently, there are two FM networks consisting of thirty-four transmitters which provide nation-wide coverage. A third network with nine transmitters serves the Swedish-speaking regions of southwestern Finland.

Radio Programming

As reported in 1959, the FBC's objective in its program policy is threefold: "to convey news and information, to disseminate education and culture in programmes of high educational value, and to provide entertainment."[5]

Officials of the Company have further stated that, "contrary to experience gained abroad, the Finnish audience seems to favor talks and spoken programs in general to music."[6] Accordingly, it has been the deliberate policy of the Finnish Broadcasting Company to restrict the proportionate share of music in its programmes."[7] Music now occupies about forty-six percent of the total programming schedules. The remaining time is taken up by a wide variety of programs including radio dramas, reports, interviews, discussions, talks and religious broadcasts.

The FBC has its own news service with direct wire contacts with AP, AFP, Reuter, DPA, TASS, and the Scandinavian news agencies. Newscasts are broadcast practically every hour. Considerable time has been devoted to reporting international affairs. Correspondents, who serve both radio and television, are assigned to the major cities of the world, including Washington, D.C., New York (the United Nations), Moscow, London, Paris and Stockholm. The Company believes that "radio broadcasting is a valuable asset in furthering international understanding between the peoples of the world."[8]

To promote cross-cultural relations, outstanding foreign musicians and dramatists have been invited to participate in the Home Service broadcasts. The works of foreign authors have been featured on many programs.[9]

There is continuous radio transmission from six o'clock in the morning until midnight, seven days per week. On June 4, 1963, the "Melody Radio" program was initiated, and since September of that year this program has broadcast popular music for more than twelve hours each day. A Second Programme, emphasizing "cultural" broadcasts and designed to appeal to the more critical listeners, is being developed.

As reported by the FBC in June 1966, radio transmissions were divided into six Programmes: The Finnish First, the Finnish Second, the Swedish, the Short Wave, the Finnish Local and the Swedish Local.

Foreign Broadcasting

FINLAND operates five short-wave transmitters which beam programs to North and South America and Central and Western Europe. These programs consist mainly of Finnish and Swedish broadcasts selected from the Home Service and of news reports in English and French. Special programs are presented in Finnish and Swedish for the benefit of nationals who may be traveling on ships at sea or living abroad.[10]

Television

TELEVISION began in Finland in 1955. Engineering students of the Institute of Technology in Helsinki, financially supported by commercial firms, carried on limited experimental operations that year, and in the spring of 1956, a company known as *Tesvisio* initiated regular broadcasts. Its operations were financed largely through advertising and donations from nonprofit organizations.[11]

At the same time that it was developing FM broadcasting, the state-controlled FBC became interested in television and conducted experimental telecasts. In 1958, it launched a regular schedule of TV programs, twelve hours per week, half of which were on film.[12]

The FBC was faced with the question as to whether it should permit advertising or depend entirely upon government subsidies and license fees as was the practice in other Scandinavian countries. At first, the Finnish press displayed a certain reserve and some officials in the Broadcasting Company were opposed to it. Some felt that the cultural aspects of television would suffer if advertising should be permitted. On the other hand, the Government and Parliament favored commercial broadcasting from the beginning.[13]

A new company, *Oy. Mainos-TV Reklam,* was organized and the FBC sold a limited amount of air time to this Company which in turn contracted with commercial firms for advertising over the TV network. This Company is owned by the biggest advertisers in Finland and at the end of 1965 had more than two hundred shareholders. In 1966, *Mainos-TV* was responsible for about twenty-five percent of the total TV programming in Finland.[14]

By the end of 1959, a TV network had been established covering the southern part of the country, including the original stations in Helsinki and Turku and five new ones in Tampere, Lahti, Riihmäki, Tammela and Kotka. That same year Finland became a member of Eurovision which brought in a new supply of foreign programs. Public interest in the new medium was developing rapidly. There were more than twenty thousand licensed receivers in use—an increase of twelve thousand over the preceding year. Expenditures for television in 1958 amounted to one hundred and thirty million marks, fifty-one million of which were covered by income from license fees and advertising.[15]

By the beginning of 1967, the TV network of thirty transmitters had been built to cover about ninety percent of the country and reach ninety-five percent of the population. For the remainder of the country—parts of Lapland—facilities will be providing service by 1970. There are now more than eight hundred and twenty-two thousand licenses and about two-thirds of the homes have sets.[16]

In November 1962, Saara Palmgren, the head of program planning for Finnish Television, reported that programs were being presented from thirty to thirty-five hours weekly, including the transmission time sold to the *Mainos-TV* Company for advertising use. She pointed out that the schedules were composed of plays, documentaries (both live and on film), news commentaries, special telecasts for children, entertainment films, and "the light repertoire that we receive from Eurovision and Nordvision."[17] Presently, about seventeen percent of the total TV programming consists of news and actualities, thirty-one percent of documentaries and "factual programs," and the rest—approximately half—of entertainment, mostly films, sports and children's programs.[18]

A second network, which originated in *Tesvisio* but was bought by the FBC in 1964, is now in operation with a production center in Tampere about one hundred and thirty miles from Helsinki, and with transmitting facilities in Helsinki, Turku, Tampere and Lahti. Plans are under way to expand the facilities of the Second Channel (now received by only about forty percent of the people) and make it comparable in coverage to the

First. The average weekly transmission time is about forty-five hours for the first network and about twenty-two hours for the second.[19]

Educational Broadcasting

FINLAND has used radio to supplement classroom instruction since 1934. The FBC provides programs for both Finnish and Swedish schools. In 1964, about six hours of instructional radio were broadcast each week. Over sixty percent of the country's schools had receiving sets and were using the programs.[20]

In connection with this radio instruction, the Finnish Broadcasting Company publishes each year a number of program booklets in Finnish and Swedish. The State defrays two-thirds of the cost of these materials in rural schools and one-third in urban schools. The State also shares the costs of the radio receivers and loudspeakers used in the classrooms.[21]

Programs are designed to serve all levels of learning. Subjects which have been presented to the elementary grades have included religion, music and gymnastics. Some of the subjects for the higher grades have been sociology, geography, the natural sciences and history.[22] The school radio departments are also in charge of teaching foreign languages, which have included Swedish, English, German, Italian, Spanish, Russian and French.

Finland recently initiated a schools television program on the First Channel. Furthermore, in the field of adult education, the FBC has presented foreign programs such as the French language course, *"Les Française Chez Vous" (Radio Télévision Française)*, and the English language course, "Walter and Connie" (British Broadcasting Corporation).[23] In 1966, the Company introduced a series of telecasts dealing with "Modern Man and his Problems," which attracted a large audience.[24] Educational TV programming was presented about five hours per week in 1966.

The teachers have played an important part in the planning of classroom instruction via radio and television. An Advisory Committee of teachers and school officials gives continuing aid in the selection of subject matter, the arrangement of schedules and the production of broadcasts. The teachers and pupils are requested to criticize the programs and make suggestions for improvements.[25]

In line with the trend toward greater Nordic cooperation, reporters traveling in other Scandinavian countries make special recordings which are used in the Finnish schools broadcasts. Educational and dramatic scripts are exchanged with Sweden, Norway and Denmark, as well as with other European countries to the south.[26]

Research Activities

THE FBC considers research important to the development of programming. Kaarle Nordenstreng of the *Yleisradio* (FBC) recently stressed the importance of research and its function in the organization:

> In the newly reformed organization of the company, research is placed in a central organ of gathering and preparing information for decision-makers, the so-called "Section for long-term planning," which is directly responsible to the Director General. This kind of functionally committed but still formally independent role of research ensures an intimate and influential approach to the problem field: the researchers are informed of all the relevant, up-to-date questions, and their findings can be efficiently distributed among the policy-makers (big principle decisions), programming practicers (timing and coordination of channels) and, through professional schooling, producers and reporters (perception of programs, experimentation, etc.). The aim of the research is to provide a systematizing and stimulating contribution throughout the broadcasting activities to the administrative planning of the directors as well as to the creative work of the program-makers.

Mr. Nordenstreng further pointed out that research in Finland has developed along several lines. He referred to one as "the routine rating panel of the FBC." He also spoke of some "campaign surveys and studies on program experimentation conducted in cooperation with academic research." He states that the FBC's present policy is to maintain a variety of approaches, "so that the scope of broadcasting research will not be limited to audience research only, but will cover the rest of the communication aspects as well, i.e., communicator (individual producer and the whole programming system) and message (contents and style of programs)." He pointed out that broadcasting research in Finland is understood as "typically communication research from which only the purely 'technical' problems (studio acoustic measurements, development of electronic devices, etc.) are excluded. Consequently, in addition to audience ratings and influence studies, social organization theory as well as aesthetics of radio and TV will be relevant areas of research."

Mr. Nordenstreng concluded his statement by referring to specific studies now under way, and by indicating an interest in cooperating with the research organizations in other countries.

> The number of researchers permanently employed by the research center of the FBC, when fully staffed, will be relatively small, 5–7 persons. Their task will be preparing of research proposals, applying results and coordinating different studies rather than conducting them. Most of the original re-

search is done at different Finnish universities, sponsored by the FBC. This was made possible through the so called "research group of academic scholars," an informal circle of professors of psychology, sociology, education, political science and journalism (mostly chairmen of departments), who in 1965 first shared $20000 provided by the FBC for radio and tv research. This research group works in cooperation with the research center of the company, receiving annually about $30000 to be shared among the universities, employing researchers and supervising the projects. Presently, there are a dozen such academic studies (surveys and experiments) in progress. For instance there are studies on (1) the structure of audience (factor analyses of rating data over a long period of time), (2) psycho-sociological aspects of communication behavior, especially the choice of programs, (3) mapping of media images and credibility basis of news service, (4) influence of tv-programs on the norm formation and individuation process of youngsters, (5) consequences of the extension of tv to Lapland, and (6) for the possibilities of using tv as an effective aid to classroom instruction.

The Finnish broadcasting research—the research center at the FBC and the university institutions associated with it—are active in international contacts. Within Scandinavian countries there is a lot of natural cooperation. The contacts with other European broadcasting researchers will be assured by a newly formed association among them. Also research contacts outside Europe are being sought, among other things through active participation in the International Association for Mass Communication Research.[27]

Organization and Administration of Finnish Broadcasting

THE FBC is an autonomous, joint stock company which operates in accordance with a concession granted by the Government. This concession runs for five years and will be up for renewal in 1968 at the same time that the charter for the FBC is renewed. It contains rules setting forth the requirements for operation. The Ministry of Communications and Public Works has regulatory jurisdiction over Finnish broadcasting and is responsible for seeing that the FBC adheres to the contractual requirements.

The Finnish State owns ninety-three percent of the stock in the Company; various economic and cultural organizations and newspapers hold the remaining shares. There is an Administrative Council of twenty-one members elected by the Parliament. Their terms of office are for three years. The Council makes decisions on all important matters of policy, decides on the expansion or curtailment of facilities, and approves the annual budget.[28]

The Council appoints members of the Board of Directors, one of whom is designated Director General and serves as Chairman. Five of the Directors are in charge of programs: one for Finnish radio and television in general and especially for news and local programming, another for Swedish broadcasting (both radio and TV), a third for radio programs in Finnish, a fourth for television programs on the First Channel, and a fifth for television programs on the Second Channel.

There is a technical section divided into two departments—Production Engineering and Distribution Engineering—which are supervised by a Director of Engineering. One member of the Board is charged with the overall responsibility for personnel administration, while another oversees financial matters.

The Administrative Council has appointed three Programme Councils to assist it in supervising program activities: one concerned with Finnish-language television, a second with Finnish-language radio and a third with Swedish-language broadcasts. The members of these Councils are chosen to represent the various cultural and social groups and spheres of interest. All program schedules are scrutinized and approved by the Councils before being aired.[29]

The chart on the following page was prepared by the FBC and reflects the organizational structure of the Company.

Financing

THE radio operations are financed by license fees, collected by the Post and Telegraph Administration (PTA). The revenue from these fees goes into a fund, and, except for the part retained by the PTA to pay for the collection costs, is used by the FBC for operational expenses. The annual license fee is twenty Finnish marks for radio receivers and sixty for television receivers. These license fees account for about five-sixths of the total income, while about one-sixth is derived from commercial TV advertising.

As previously indicated, the FBC does not engage in commercial advertising itself. It sells broadcasting time and facilities to the *Mainos-TV* Company, which in turn sells time to business firms for commercials. In 1966, this advertising Company produced six hundred and eighty-six hours of network programming, about one-third of the total broadcasting time of the networks.[30] In 1966, a total of 13,822 commercials were broadcast on the national television network. More than fifty percent were fifteen seconds long. Two hundred and seventy-eight business firms advertised more than seven hundred and thirty products.

It should be pointed out that there are no "sponsored" programs. The advertising Company produces its own shows. Except for Finnish and foreign films, the Company uses its own personnel, actors and performers in its telecasts.

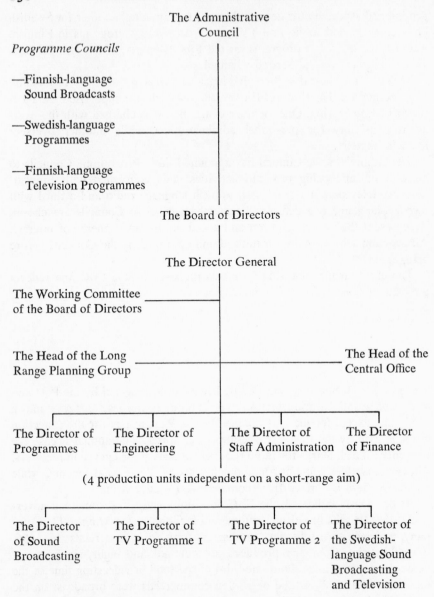

The Administrative
Council

Programme Councils

—Finnish-language
Sound Broadcasts

—Swedish-language
Programmes

—Finnish-language
Television Programmes

The Board of Directors

The Director General

The Working Committee
of the Board of Directors

The Head of the Long   The Head of the
Range Planning Group   Central Office

The Director of   The Director of   The Director of   The Director
Programmes   Engineering   Staff Administration   of Finance

(4 production units independent on a short-range aim)

The Director   The Director of   The Director of   The Director of
of Sound   TV Programme 1   TV Programme 2   the Swedish-
Broadcasting   language Sound
                                                        Broadcasting
                                                        and Television

Oy. Mainos-TV Reklam Ab.'s sales prices fluctuate considerably, depending on the season, day of the week and time of day, although the price agreement between it and the FBC prescribes one fixed price per minute for commercials. In 1966, this price was 2,380 marks per minute. The total income from advertising rose to 16.6 million marks in 1965 and was estimated to be twenty million in 1966, or approximately twenty-one percent of the FBC's income for the year.[31]

Advertising Restrictions

THE agreement between the FBC and the *Oy. Mainos-TV Reklam Ab.* contains some stipulations and restrictions regarding advertising. The agreement, for example, forbids the advertising of alcoholic beverages. The advertising Company has drawn up its own code and demands that TV advertising follow the principles recommended by the International Chamber of Commerce. There are special restrictions on the advertising of tobacco and medicines. Not more than fifteen percent of the broadcast time hired by the *Mainos-TV* Company may be used for direct advertising, and commercial spots may be inserted within a program only if the program exceeds twenty minutes. Also, definite limits are fixed as to the number of spots that may be broadcast in different time segments.[32]

All programs produced by the advertising Company are under the surveillance of the FBC's TV Programming Council. In 1967, *Mainos-TV* had two hundred and thirty-four permanent employees. In addition, it used a large number of temporary announcers, translators, program assistants and other employees.[33]

A Look to the Future

ON about thirty acres of land in Pasila, three miles north of Helsinki, the FBC is building a radio and television center. It is expected to be completed in 1980, and will include from five to six hundred thousand cubic meters.

The first unit of the center, Studio 1, was completed in 1961. A second building was constructed in 1964 and was taken over temporarily by the programming staff. However, it eventually will be used for "a decor workshop" (as was originally intended), when the thirty story office building is erected.

The third stage of center plans includes Studios 2, 3 and 4. Studio 2, with an area of about six hundred and fifty square meters, was ready for use in February 1966. It was planned so that color television can be developed. Studio 3 will be ready for use in a few years and Studio 4 will be constructed later; 1980 is the target date for completion of the center.

The final radio and television establishment will house a staff of three thousand, and will include all the production and transmission units for both radio and television, the office building, a transport center, a workshop, a training center and other necessary facilities. According to the

FBC, there will be forty production units for radio and several for television, each unit ranging in size from three hundred to one thousand square meters.[34]

More important, perhaps, than the expansion of facilities, are the long-range studies being made to improve program service to meet the future communication needs of Finland. In 1965, the *Oy. Yleisradio Ab.* appointed a Committee to conduct such studies and make recommendations. One of the group's main purposes is to suggest the lines of direction that Finnish broadcasting should take, based upon philosophical considerations, practical knowledge and scientific research. The first part of the Committee's study has been completed and a Report has been published. The second part is already in rough draft and the final section is being outlined.[35]

The first section defines the broad aims and tasks of broadcasting. It emphasizes the public service aspects of the media and warns against permitting the *Oy. Yleisradio Ab.* to become the instrument of any private group, be it commercial, political or otherwise. All attempts by radio and television to "create and form opinions" are to be avoided. On the other hand, it is the positive responsibility of broadcasting to present a wide range of information and ideas and provide "the building materials" to help the listener make up his own mind in an intelligent manner.

The Report further states that radio and television should be prepared at all times to experiment with new types of programs, even at the risk of mistakes. "It should be kept in mind," say the authors of this study, "that the public is not a compact, integrated mass, but is made up of many large and small groups, all of which have a right to be served by the broadcast media."[36]

Some of the main topics covered in the first part of the Report are:

1. Broadcasting and social change.
2. Problems and possibilities for programming in terms of Finnish interest and needs.
3. Diversified versus monopolistic control of broadcast media.
4. Freedom and independence for the broadcaster.

The second part of the Report, soon to be released, contains detailed plans and suggestions for future programming. The third and final phase will deal with special broadcasting problems, such as the technical, financial, managerial and research aspects.

NOTES

1. See discussion of the early history of radio in Finland in *Documentation and Information Bulletin,* OIR (International Broadcasting Organization), Prague, September 1956, No. 4/5 (58), pp. 191–192.

2. *Ibid.*, p. 191.
3. *Ibid.*
4. *Ibid.*, p. 192.
5. *Ibid.*, December 1959, No. 6 (77), p. 231.
6. *Ibid.*, pp. 231–232.
7. *Ibid.*, p. 232.
8. *Ibid.*
9. *Ibid.*
10. UNESCO, *World Communications: Press, Radio, Television, Film* (New York: UNESCO Publications Center, 1964), p. 279. Also, see *ibid.*
11. *EBU Review*, 71B, January 1962, p. 12, and 98B, July 1966, p. 14.
12. *Documentation and Information Bulletin,* December 1959, p. 232.
13. *EBU Review*, 71B, January 1962, p. 82.
14. Report of *Oy. Yleisradio Ab.*, Helsinki, 1966.
15. *EBU Review*, 58B, November 1959, p. 26. As of January 1968, the Finnish mark was equivalent to twenty-four cents.
16. Report of *Oy. Yleisradio Ab.*, Helsinki, 1966.
17. *EBU Review*, 58B, November 1959, p. 12.
18. Correspondence with *Oy. Yleisradio Ab.*, Helsinki.
19. Publication of *Oy. Yleisradio Ab.* (FBC), printed by *Uudenmaan Kirjapaino Oy.*, June 1966.
20. UNESCO, *World Communications,* p. 279.
21. See Helmi Palmén, Head of Finnish-language Schools Radio, and Nils Göran Engström, Head of Swedish-language Schools Radio, "Radio for Schools," *EBU Review,* 70B, November 1961, pp. 14–15.
22. *Ibid.*, p. 15.
23. See Valdeman Christensen, Head of School Broadcasting, Children's and Youth Programs, *Danmarks Radio,* "Scandinavian Prospects," *EBU Review,* 94B, November 1965, p. 34.
24. *Ibid.*
25. *EBU Review*, 70B, November 1961, p. 15.
26. *Ibid.*
27. Kaarle Nordenstreng, "Broadcasting Research in Finland," published by *Yleisradio,* Helsinki, January 1967. Mr. Nordenstreng's statement was made available to the author by the Finnish Broadcasting Company.
28. The organizational and administrative structure of the Finnish Broadcasting Company is described by Saara Polgren, Head of Program Planning, Finnish Television, in *EBU Review,* 58B, November 1962, p. 14.
29. See publication by *Oy. Yleisradio Ab.* (FBC), June 1966.
30. *Ibid.*
31. "TV Advertising in Finland," recent, undated publication by the Finnish Broadcasting Company.
32. *Ibid.*
33. *Ibid.*
34. See publication by *Oy. Yleisradio Ab.* (FBC), June 1966.
35. Eino S. Repo, Kari Ilmonen, N-B, Stormbom, Mauno Tamminen, Ville Zilliacus, *"Yleisradion suunta,"* (in Finnish), printed by Oy. Weilin + G885 Ab., Helsinki, 1967.
36. *Ibid.*, pp. 12–14.

· E ·

FRANCE AND THE
MEDITERRANEAN COUNTRIES

XIV

France: Radiodiffusion–
Television Française

TRADITIONALLY, the French Government has played an important role in the development and control of utilities and other industries clothed with the public interest such as transportation, telecommunications and broadcasting. In modern France, private enterprise has also been encouraged and, with a free press, has influenced the administration of these government functions while developing and controlling other industries essential to the national life. The present organization and operation of radio and television in the country are in keeping with these historical trends and behavior patterns in French society.

The Postal and Semaphore Systems of Communication

As was true in many other countries, the earliest kinds of long distance communication in France were operated and controlled by the State. From the beginning, the postal system was managed by the Government. Likewise, the semaphore system, which was developed later, was regarded by the French authorities as a government function, and the invention of the system and the apparatus were considered public property.[1]

Even before the French Revolution the utility of this visual medium of communication had been demonstrated, but the suspicions and fears of the populace that it might be used for subversive purposes delayed its development and actually provoked some mob violence in Paris.[2] But by 1793, the Revolutionary Government was convinced of its value (particularly for war purposes) and the Assembly took over the invention and ordered the construction of a line from Paris to Lille. At the end of the Napoleonic era, France had more than eleven hundred miles of semaphore facilities. King Louis Phillipe greatly extended the system and by 1844, France had more than five hundred stations and three thousand miles of service.[3]

The Development and Control of Wire Communication

FRENCH scientists were among the first to conduct successful experiments in telegraphic communication.[4] For example, a machine reported to be the first automatic telegraph was conceived and developed by the Frenchman, M. Amijot. In 1837, it attracted widespread attention in Europe. Amijot sent a model of his apparatus to Russia, where the Government, seeing it as a possible means of subversion, refused to permit its use and development. It was reported that Emperor Nicholas, during his reign, prohibited the publication of any information regarding it, including notices appearing in European journals.[5]

The French authorities also viewed the machine with some misgiving. They did not trust private operation; therefore, the Government was given the exclusive authority to operate and control such communication devices, as was the case with the postal and semaphore systems. A law to this effect, signed by the Minister of the Interior and King Louis Phillipe, was passed May 2, 1837, and any use of electrical telegraph apparatus was strictly forbidden without permission from the Government. Severe penalties were imposed for violating the law.[6]

The private use of telegraph facilities was not permitted until thirteen years later. The Government continued to operate the system, but a law, passed in 1850, made lines available for general use. Article k of this Act stated that properly identified persons might send messages and specified the tariffs to be charged. The statute declared, however, that private communication was to be subordinate to the paramount needs of the State. The Director of Telegraphs in the Ministry of the Interior was authorized to refuse to transmit messages if he felt they might offend public morals or incite public disorder.[7]

The growth of the postal and telegraph systems under government control led to the creation of the Ministry of Posts and Telegraphs in February 1879.[8] Five years later an administrative decree was issued extending its regulatory jurisdiction to telephone communication and authorizing it to establish rates and standards of service.[9]

The Advent of Radio

SOME of the earliest experiments in radio communication were carried out in France, and amateur operators were busy exploring the wonders of the "ether." As had been the case in telecommunications, the Government took an early interest in the development of the new medium. The statutes previously mentioned empowered the Government to operate and control telecommunications, including regulatory jurisdiction over radio.

On April 26, 1910, an administrative decree was issued establishing a special commission of representatives from several Ministries—Marine, War, Colonies, Foreign Affairs, Commerce and Industry, Public Works, Posts and Telegraphs—to make a broad study of radio *(la télégraphie sans fil);* to determine the role of the Government and private interests in the control and operation of stations, both domestic and foreign; and to conduct experiments for the improvement of transmission and reception.[10]

The construction of the famous Eiffel Tower in Paris (one thousand and six feet high) provided a valuable facility for experimentation. The Government began broadcasting time signals from the top of this structure. The first radio link between Paris and the United States was established in 1915 and, in 1916, the Administration of Posts and Telegraphs initiated a trans-Atlantic telephone service via radio waves.[11]

Postwar Developments

FOLLOWING the First World War, commercial interests, particularly the manufacturers of radio equipment, became interested in using the medium for advertising purposes. Several private stations were established. The duality of this system (with both the Government and private enterprise owning and operating broadcasting facilities) was reflected in an announcement of daily program transmission appearing in the March 24, 1923 issue of *Le Temps,* a leading Paris newspaper of that time. The schedules included two transmissions on different frequencies from the Eiffel Tower. One consisted of weather reports and a musical concert; the other was an educational program *(Station de l'Ecole Supérieure des PTT)* featuring a professor of political science conducting a conference. Also listed was a third station, operated by a manufacturer of receivers *(Radiola),* with a schedule of programs including stock reports, news and a piano concert.[12]

That same year, the Government reaffirmed its authority to cover all broadcasting, both public and private. On November 24, 1923, it issued an administrative decree providing for three classes of broadcasting stations: (1) those installed by government departments, local communes or public utilities to be used in connection with their official business functions; (2) government stations broadcasting programs for the general public; and (3) private stations with programs of similar purpose and design. The decree declared that all private operations had to be authorized by the Administration of Posts and Telegraphs upon the filing of written applications providing, among other things, information as to the identity, domicile and nationality of the applicant. Moreover, for the first time, it was ordered that private broadcasting stations would be required to pay the Government a license fee for the privilege of operating.[13]

Broadcasting Growth Continues

BROADCASTING growth continued. In 1924 and 1925, both government and private stations increased their hours of broadcasting. More informational programs of interest to the business community were added to the daily schedules. The teaching of foreign languages was introduced. Radio jazz made its debut. In late 1924, regular newscasts and live dramatic shows were initiated by the commercial *Radiola* station.

More time was allocated for political broadcasts and the coverage of election returns. The many French political parties, representing a wide range of opinion, have always valued broadcasting as a means of public persuasion, not only as an effective way of winning votes but also as an instrument for maintaining public support once a party is in power. A review of the program schedules of Paris stations during the twenties reveals many broadcasts by political candidates and public officials, particularly over government stations. For example, when the leader of the Radicals, Edouard Herriot, became Prime Minister, his whole inaugural speech on October 21, 1924, was carried by *Station de l'Ecole Supérieure des Postes et Télégraphes*.[14]

In addition to station operations, the Government was active in other important ways in the radio field. The Administration of Posts and Telegraphs published annual reports containing much information on the improvements in transmitting and receiving equipment, and summaries of significant research and experimental studies in France and elsewhere.

This office also took an active interest in the development of international communication. For example, in May 1925, at the invitation of the PTT Minister, eminent persons in the fields of letters, arts and sciences from France and other countries attended a conference in Paris. The main topic of discussion was the promotion of cultural exchange through the use of radio.[15]

Developing a Nation-Wide Radio Service

WITH the enlarged and improved program service, the radio audience increased rapidly. The sale of receivers became a profitable business. This accentuated the need for new facilities in Paris and other cities. The Government was pressed to sanction more channels for commercial operation. Consequently, under President Poincare's Administration,[16] the PTT authorized private stations in a number of cities and at the same time extended its own network operations.

A decree law dated December 21, 1926, stipulated the basic principles for the establishment of a national radio network. The decree provided for both government and private stations and authorized the broadcast of commercials.[17]

During the late twenties and early thirties, the government stations were financed mainly from appropriations made by the Parliament, although they did derive some revenue from advertising. In 1933, the PTT Minister reported to the Parliament that fourteen state-owned stations with studios and transmitting facilities were providing nation-wide service. He stated that, despite some income from commercials, maintenance of the system was costing the Government about forty-eight million francs per year. At the same time, he reported that ten private stations were operating commercially in Paris, Bordeaux, Toulouse, Nîmes, Lyon, Fécamp and other cities in France.[18]

The increasing costs of the state system prompted the Minister, in 1933, to sponsor a bill in Parliament that would levy an annual tax on owners of radio receivers and a sales tax on tubes. This precipitated a debate in which one senator contended that the PTT was competing with private stations and that it had become a monopoly in fact. The Minister, in support of the bill, stated that radio had become a marvelous means for education and propaganda, but that additional finances were needed to improve the facilities so that French broadcasting would measure up to the standards in other countries.

The bill was approved by a substantial majority and annual taxes on the use of receivers were established: fifteen francs for crystal receivers; fifty francs for other sets, if used privately; one hundred francs for sets used in public places (such as hotels) with no charge to the listener; and two hundred francs, if used by commercial establishments with charges made for listening.

State-owned educational institutions were exempt from the taxes. A proposed amendment to the bill would have relieved private schools from payment of taxes. However, after considerable debate, the amendment was defeated by a vote of one hundred and sixty-six to one hundred and twenty-two.[19]

Program Participation at Various Levels

FOLLOWING the passage of this law, the Government took steps to decentralize the control of radio programming and to permit more local participation. On February 13, 1935, Georges Mandel, the PTT Minister, decreed that each community having a state-owned station would hold an annual meeting to elect representatives to a community council of management. All persons who owned radio sets and could show certificates that they had paid the use tax would be eligible to participate in the meeting.

He further decreed that this council would be responsible for the station's programming. The PTT would provide a budget officer to keep the accounts for each station, and the Minister and his staff would coordinate programs for network stations. The decree also provided for the creation of a national program council to serve in an advisory capacity to the Minister.[20]

Subsequently, under the Minister's leadership, some interesting and important program developments took place at the national level. In January 1936, he announced that he would participate with a university professor in an administrative law course which would be broadcast over Radio Paris, the government-owned station in Paris.[21] That same month he arranged to have broadcast from Paris live comedy and opera for a trial period over the state network.[22]

In February, he announced that there would be daily television broadcasts from the Eiffel Tower.[23] That same month, Minister Mandel conducted an international conference on broadcasting and was officially commended by the conference for his leadership.[24]

During the election campaigns of 1936, the Socialists, Radicals and Communists combined to form what was called the "Popular Front." Radio, more than ever before, was used by the parties to discuss political issues and solicit support for their candidates.

Prior to the April national elections, the Paris newspapers reported radio speeches over station and network facilities by candidates of all the contending parties. The time was made available to the various parties and candidates by the PTT. Along with the press, the PTT network and its affiliated stations reported the local and national election returns and related news, including reports of public disturbances and incidents of violence caused in some communities by the elections.

As a result of the 1936 election campaign, the Government decreed a news broadcasting policy which still applies to all stations in France. Under the former arrangement, local associations were responsible for programs of a local character. The local committees, dominated by political groups (in some cases by Socialists and in others by reactionaries), often distorted or slanted the news in favor of their platforms and candidates. As a consequence, the PTT decreed that there would be no further local news reporting on the stations and that *Radio Journal de France,* a regular news feature of the network broadcast from Paris, would be solely responsible for the newscasts on all French stations.

By a decree dated October 27, 1936, a new organization, the *Conseil Supérieur des Emissions de la Radiodiffusion,* was created to carry on the expanded network operations in Paris. It consisted of six sections concerned with a broad range of programming: literary, musical, scientific, economic, social, news, sports, and recreation and tourism.[25]

War and the Demise of Private Broadcasting

WITH the outbreak of the Second World War, the local management committees were dissolved. The Government had been contemplating this action for some time since the legal validity of their operations was questionable. These committees were established with the idea that local citizens and groups would participate in the production and presentation of programs on a nonprofit basis. They were constituted as nonprofit organizations under a 1901 statute,[26] but by extending their activities to the sale of radio advertising, with some members deriving a substantial income, they became unlawful operations. This fact, plus the need to centralize broadcasting control in terms of the war effort, caused the Government to abolish the committees and to take over all program operations at the local level.

At the same time, the PTT Minister relinquished his authority over the state-owned network and its affiliated stations and the war agencies assumed complete control. The licensees of private stations continued to broadcast for a time, but the Vichy Government in 1941 cancelled their franchises and conscripted their facilities for military and propaganda purposes.[27]

At the end of the war, some of the stations that had lost their licenses were reimbursed by the new Government for the loss of their property. Others, suspected of collaboration during the war, not only were denied compensation for their property losses but, in some cases, their officials received prison sentences. In 1944, all private stations had ceased operation and the next year the Government withdrew all previously granted authorizations.[28]

Establishment of Radiodiffusion–Télévision Française

DURING the war, under the leadership of Général de Gaulle, a new radio organization had been created. As prescribed by a decree law dated October 1, 1941, it functioned under the authority of the Prime Minister or a member of the Cabinet to whom he might delegate the responsibility. Its organization consisted of a Board of Governors, composed of four or more members, and a Director-General, all appointed by the Government.[29] Following cessation of hostilities, it continued to function under the close scrutiny and control of the Prime Minister and the Cabinet. Called *Radio-diffusion–Télévision Française* (RTF) and subject to the supervision of the Government, it carried on all peace-time broadcasting activities in France, including television.

All staff members in Paris and affiliated stations throughout the country were employees of the national RTF organization. The various regional stations served as outlets for network programs, particularly for national newscasts from Paris. Local live shows were permitted, including some news reporting, and clusters of stations were authorized to work out the arrangements for some exchange of programs of regional interest.[30] Major policy and procedural matters, however, were handled by the RTF officials in Paris and the Prime Minister and his subordinates to whom these officials were responsible. And a large portion of the network programs emanated from the RTF studios in the nation's capital.[31]

Two Decades of Broadcasting Growth

THE late forties and fifties saw much progress in French broadcasting. Four separate networks and program services were established. *France-Inter* devoted its time largely to music (75.3 percent). Designed for wide appeal, its schedule included both popular and classical music and news reports. Among its broadcasts were live concerts by the RTF *Orchestre National,* recorded operas and symphony concerts from abroad and some dramatic and variety shows featuring outstanding French and foreign talent.

A second network (Parisian Programme) featured popular orchestra music, folk tunes, news reports, and generally light entertainment. The third "chain," the National Programme, was given over largely to serious music, drama, literature and other cultural broadcasts. A special program, consisting of classical music and other programs of aesthetic and intellectual appeal, was developed for a network of FM stations.

In 1955, as reported by the *Radiodiffusion–Télévision Française,* more than thirty thousand hours of programming were broadcast to the home audience on the four networks. This included seventy concerts by the *Orchestre National,* eighty concerts by the Paris Radio Symphonic Orchestra, one hundred and fifty-six broadcasts by the Radio Operatic Orchestra, two hundred and four concerts of light music, 1489 hours of "cultural" broadcasts, eight hundred and thirty-four original productions, twenty-one "first" performances, eighty-one transmissions of music festivals in France and sixty-one from foreign countries, as well as ninety-four broadcasts from theaters. In all, 15,065 musical recordings, including opera, operetta, symphonic, jazz, dance and other popular types, were prepared and presented.[32]

With a wider pattern of programming and expanded facilities, plus the sales promotion by manufacturers and distributors, the interest in radio programs greatly increased, and by 1960 more than ten million radio receivers were in use.[33] The RTF programs had achieved wide popularity not only in France but, through exchange arrangements, in other countries as well and often were internationally acclaimed for their quality.

Television also made a good start in France during the first decade after the war. As previously pointed out, the PTT had done important experimental work in television during the thirties. This, however, was interrupted by the war. When peace was restored, the RTF assumed the PTT's role. In 1948 regular television programming was provided on one channel for a few hours per week. By the end of 1955, expanded facilities included a network of ten stations, serving about fifteen percent of the country's area and about thirty percent of the population.[34]

One year later, the RTF reported that it was presenting about fifty hours of programming per week with the typical schedule running somewhat as follows: news, twenty-two percent; variety shows, twenty-five percent; theatrical performances, five percent; documentaries, twenty percent; films, fourteen percent; sports features, seven percent; special broadcasts for children, two percent; and miscellaneous, five percent. During 1955 more than two hundred live programs were telecast from outside the RTF studios—athletic contests, documentaries, and other programs of an educational and recreational character. In addition, eighty plays were broadcast, and instructional programs for classrooms were presented regularly two hours per week.[35]

The RTF took a leading role in the international exchange of television programs. Through Eurovision and film exchanges, it brought to its viewers many excellent foreign programs of a cultural and educational nature. At the same time, there was a growing demand for its programs in other countries.

The increasing popularity of TV programming in France is attested to by the increase in the number of receivers. Whereas only a few thousand sets were registered in the late forties, the number had jumped to almost one and one-half million by 1960.[36]

As the RTF expanded its radio and TV schedules, its financial and housing needs increased. Limited facilities, widely scattered offices and outdated studios and concert halls in Paris accelerated plans for a large radio and television center (conceived in 1935). A site was secured and construction of the *Maison de la RTF* began in 1955. Problems interrupted building progress from time to time, but these were overcome and, in 1963, the structure was officially dedicated. The magnificent *Maison de la RTF,* of functional, circular design, houses the offices, studios and concert halls for both national and foreign broadcasting in France.

As has been shown, by a succession of decrees and orders, the Government exercised strict control of broadcasting. Despite this, the RTF was able to build a large staff of experts and steadily expand and improve its service. But it felt increasingly handicapped by the strictures and vicissitudes of political supervision. It yearned for greater administrative and budget-making autonomy and more freedom to experiment with new types of programs—to develop a broadcast service more in keeping with the highest professional standards. Accordingly, the RTF pressed the Government for a written charter which would provide these things and spell out more clearly the range of RTF authority and responsibilities.

In February 1959, the Ministers of Information and of Finance and Economic Affairs submitted to the President of the Council of Ministers a proposed order which would clarify the RTF's status and functions and guarantee greater autonomy. It was approved and became effective the same month.[37]

This order provided that the Minister of Information have authority over all French radio and television, and that the RTF be constituted as a public establishment of the State, having an industrial and commercial character and budget-making autonomy.

It was further stated that the establishment was authorized: (1) to maintain, modify and manage the network system of broadcasting; (2) to broadcast its own programs or make them available to other broadcasting organizations; (3) to collect taxes on receivers; (4) to join with other government agencies or interested professional groups to study the technical standards and determine how these standards should be applied and enforced; (5) to provide to the public, from whatever source, programs of quality, either by direct broadcasting or jointly with the Administration of Posts, Telegraphs and Telephones over wire facilities exclusively controlled by that agency; and (6) to enter into agreements with other government agencies, particularly the PTT, for the transmission of programs to those areas in which the RTF operated.

Exceptions to these provisions could be made by the Government in the interest of scientific research and for limited periods, such temporary authorizations being revokable at any time. The order also provided that exceptions could be made by the Government in the interest of national defense.

Article II of the decree authorized the RTF to install and manage broadcasting stations outside the national borders and to negotiate agreements with foreign countries for this purpose.

Restrictions on the use of recordings were imposed in accordance with previous legislation protecting literary and artistic rights. Provisions were made for a Director-General, Associate Director-General and Assistant Directors for the RTF and, in accordance with previous directives, their responsibilities and prerogatives were defined. It was further stated that the order, countersigned by the Minister of Information and the Minister of Finance and Economic Affairs, would be issued prior to January 1, 1960, and would spell out the rules for appointment, remuneration and supervision of personnel other than the aforementioned Directors who held their positions at the pleasure of the Government.

Moreover, Article VII provided that the establishment would be conducted by a committee whose membership would be determined by executive order, and that budget estimates would be worked out by this committee and approved by the Minister of Information and the Minister of Finance and Economic Affairs. The RTF was to be reimbursed for the expenses incurred in making its facilities available to other departments of the Government in accordance with special agreements. The total costs of equipment, management and operation should be paid for out of the RTF's own resources, including particularly (1) revenue from the fees on the use of receivers and (2) proceeds from the sale of publications, recordings, films, and, in general, from any kind of activity in which it was authorized to engage, including public performances; from services rendered, proceeds from gifts, legacies, subsidies, investments and authorized profit-making loans; from liquid assets of the reserve fund; and from fines, settlements and other proceeds.

Article X stated that the fees for the use of radio and television receivers would be determined by the Council of Ministers, upon the recommendation of the Minister of Information and the Minister of Finance and Economic Affairs, and that the RTF was to be exempt from taxation on the revenue from these fees.

It was further declared in Article XI that the establishment was to be under the joint supervision of the Minister of Information and the Minister of Finance and Economic Affairs and that all rights and obligations of the State relating to French radio and television were to be transferred to the new establishment. The procedures for carrying out its work were to be determined by executive orders based upon reports of the two Ministers.

On February 5, 1959, pursuant to this mandate, the Prime Minister issued an order based upon the recommendation of the two Ministers. It authorized the RTF to make all arrangements and to enter into any contracts necessary to carry out its mission; to organize or have organized concerts or other performances and to acquire the right to broadcast all or part of these; and, in accordance with national and international copyright laws, to produce and acquire literary, musical, artistic and journalistic materials for broadcasting purposes.[88]

The RTF was also authorized to institute research studies designed to improve and extend broadcasting, and was directed to take the necessary measures to protect transmissions from atmospheric or industrial interferences.

It was further stated that the RTF in cooperation with the Minister of Foreign Affairs was authorized to deal with matters involving the direct working relations with foreign or international organizations, both government and nongovernment. The RTF was still further empowered, on request of or with the approval of the Government, to carry out missions of technical assistance in foreign countries.

The Board of Governors which had been previously created was continued. Specialized committees were to be responsible to the Director-General, and their composition and functions would be determined by the Minister of Information. The Chairman of each committee would be a member ex officio of the Board.

On January 9, 1960, a decree was issued providing that the Board had an obligation *tenu informé par directeur général* on matters pertaining to administration and finance, particularly as they related to the production, composition and distribution of programs. The Board was given the privilege of expressing its opinions and making recommendations regarding the programs to the Director-General. On all other matters, it was authorized to consult directly with both the Director-General and the Government.[39]

On February 4, 1960, acting upon the advice of the Minister of Information, the Government issued an order setting forth detailed regulations and conditions concerning the recruitment, working conditions, job classifications, remuneration, promotion and discipline of the RTF employees. This was the first detailed and comprehensive statement on the RTF's personnel procedures.[40]

New Progress in Programming

UNDER the 1959 Ordinance, the RTF achieved more independence in its operations. While subject to the general supervision of the Government, it was freer to make policy decisions and to function without the previous strict ministerial controls which many believed had an unsavory effect on its operations.

With this new organizational set-up, structural reforms in programming which had already been initiated were extended and accelerated. The program schedules were more diversified. Among the significant programs given new impetus were broadcasts directly from the National Library in Paris; regular discussions by various authorities on art, literature and philosophy; and talks by well-known scientists on subjects of current interest. An outstanding feature which aroused much interest was *"Analyse Sectrale de l'Occident,"* devoted to the problems and cultures of the Western World.

In late 1961, the head of the Educational and Cultural broadcasts of the RTF reported on the improved status of broadcasting. He stated that during the preceding year more than five thousand hours of educational programs had been presented. He spoke with justifiable pride of the "French Culture Hour," daily discussions on such topics as "Great Civilizations," "Men and Events," and "Science and Technology." Eminent scholars and specialists in France and other parts of the world had been brought before the microphone to present information and ideas on these subjects.[41]

Another important series of programs being carried was "International University of the Air" (URI), with lectures by educators and others representing more than thirty countries, dealing with such topics as "Scientific Research Throughout the World," "Great Writers' Views on Education," "Vocational Guidance," and "The Democratization of University Education."

Another noteworthy broadcast was "Knowledge of Man," with discussions of logic, ethics, aesthetics, metaphysics, psychology and philosophy. A regular feature, "Knowledge of Art," similar in format, presented enlightened comment and different viewpoints on architecture, music, dancing and literature.[42]

These and other programs such as "School Radio" (classroom instruction for primary and secondary schools) and "Theatre and University" (presentation of plays via radio for classroom study) reflected the new freedom of the RTF and the initiative and imagination of its staff.

Television, as well as radio, received a new impetus from the enterprising RTF leaders. While film productions received from outside sources constituted a large part of the 1960–61 broadcast schedules, these were carefully screened for quality by the administrative staff and the committee of program experts attached to the RTF.

Original broadcasts, prepared and presented by RTF talent, were on the increase. For example, in the year just mentioned, the national network produced and televised more than three hundred live shows as compared with two hundred and seventy-eight the year before.

That same year, the RTF and the National Institute of Education (*Institut Pédagogique National*) cooperated in producing and presenting live and film programs designed for use by primary, secondary and technical schools, for students enrolled in correspondence courses, and for adult listeners. Henri Dieuzeide, the head of the Audio-Visual Service of the National Institute and in charge of the school telecasts, was impressed with the utility of televised instruction based upon his experience in this joint undertaking:

> It appears that school television broadcasts add leaven to conventional education. Apart from increasing the child's store of knowledge, television can evoke an active response, whether individually or in groups, e.g., observation, self-expression, reading, research, etc. Far from forcing uniformity, it seems to stimulate considerable variety in teaching techniques. Indeed, apart from its direct impact upon the pupils, school television has sought to produce, and has generally obtained, a positive reaction from the teachers. They

readily agree that television provides them with new teaching formulae, original working tools for the benefit of their pupils, a fresh outlook, and some new tricks of the trade; in a word, it gives them a taste for the job or new taste, as the case may be.[43]

A year later, the RTF pointed out that a distinctive feature of school broadcasting in France was its close relationship and cooperation with the Ministry of Education. The RTF offered a wide place in its schedules for educational programs which it produced in its own studios with its own staff in cooperation with the National Institute of Education, and made available to the Ministry of Education a large number of its stations for the distribution of the broadcasts.[44]

Establishment of L'Office de Radiodiffusion–Télévision Française

THE Ordinance of 1959 had provided the autonomy and stimulus for improved broadcast service. But it was only an administrative decree and subject to change by any government of whatever political complexion which might happen to be in power at any given time. The RTF officials decided, with the support of the prevailing Government, that a bill should be proposed to the Parliament embodying the important principles of the Ordinance and adding the provisions necessary to make broadcasting more effective.

Accordingly, in 1962 the Prime Minister asked the Minister of Information to study the matter and consult with the Constitutional Committee to determine the form which the legislation should take.[45] The Government submitted a bill to the National Assembly in May 1964. After much debate in both the Assembly and the Senate, a law was enacted on June 25, 1964, establishing L'Office de Radiodiffusion–Télévision Française (ORTF) and prescribing its functions and responsibilities.[46]

As explained by the Minister of Information during the parliamentary debates, the main purpose of the new law was to give the RTF greater autonomy. The order of 1959 had established the RTF's freedom by decree; the law of 1964, adopted after full debate, reaffirmed it and gave it permanent, statutory sanction.

Provisions of the 1964 Law

THE new legislation created an establishment administered by an Administrative Council under the regulatory supervision of the Minister of Information. Acting jointly with the Minister of Finance and Economic Affairs, he approves the budget and exercises general supervision over the use which the ORTF makes of its resources.

An important provision of Article II gives the Administrative Council wide authority in determining policies of operation, subject only to the clearly defined and limited regulatory supervision of the Minister of Information, which had not been the case previously.

As provided in Article IV of the new law, the Administrative Council is composed of from fourteen to twenty-eight members, half of whom represent the State and the other half comprised of listeners, viewers and other qualified persons, the latter half being appointed from nomination lists submitted by representative organizations. It is further provided that the term for members of the Council shall be three years, except that the tenure of the state representatives may be terminated at any time. Members of the Council must be of French nationality, enjoy civil and political rights, and must not have been convicted of any serious crime.

The Council is authorized to elect from its membership a president and vice-president; determine general lines of procedure; control the execution of its budget; and be responsible generally for the quality and morality of ORTF programs and for the accuracy and objectivity of the newscasts. This group must assure that the broadcast facilities are used to express the principal trends of public thought and opinion.

Article V declares that the Government may, at any time, use the facilities of the ORTF to broadcast via radio or television any statement or communication which it deems necessary, but requires that they be announced as emanating from the Government. The proceedings of the Parliament may be broadcast, but only if approved by the particular house from which the broadcast is transmitted and supervised by the officers of that house.

Article VI provides for the appointment by the Cabinet of a Director-General and one or two Deputy Directors. These top officials are not appointed by the Administrative Council or selected by the Government from a list of nominees drawn up by the Council (as was favored by some members of Parliament), but are chosen by the Cabinet and serve at the pleasure of that political body. However, an important change was made by the 1964 law with respect to the authority of the Director-General. He, and *not* the Cabinet, is responsible for the appointment of all bureau personnel except the two Deputy Directors, which was not the case under the 1959 Ordinance.

The Minister of Information is required to make quarterly reports to the Parliament, and each year when appropriation bills are considered, on the basis of reports from the Assembly and Senate, the Parliament authorizes the collection of fees for the use of radio and television receivers. At the same time, the ORTF is under statutory mandate to submit to the

Parliament a financial statement covering its operations for the preceding and current year and a proposed budget for the following year. These statements must be appended to the finance bill.

Pursuant to the broad authority granted in Article X, the Government on July 22, 1964, issued a decree implementing the important provisions of the law.[47] Among other things, it was decreed that the ORTF Administrative Council should be composed of sixteen members named by the Cabinet as follows: eight members representing the State, one member chosen from lists nominated by listeners and viewers, one from lists submitted by representatives of the press, two members representing the ORTF personnel, plus four other qualified persons.

A detailed statement of regulations covering personnel administration in the ORTF was issued. This included job classifications and basic policies of remuneration, recruitment, promotion, discipline, hours of work, medical care and termination of employment.[48]

Special regulations were adopted relating to journalists and writers employed by the ORTF either permanently or temporarily. As provided in the Code of Practices of the national journalistic syndicate, all such employees working for the ORTF are obliged to respect the *"principes démocratiques de l'objectivité et de la liberté d'expression,"* and, in the presentation of domestic and foreign news, to be impartial, taking into account the various religious, political and philosophical convictions of listeners and viewers.[49]

Special attention should be called to three important changes in the ORTF operation. Previously, the control of the RTF expenditures was for the most part effected *a priori,* as is the prescribed practice for government agencies. At present, however, most of the ORTF expenditures are certified *a posteriori* which is the procedure prescribed generally for national public enterprises. This change was confirmed by Decree No. 64–737 of July 22, 1964,[50] which also sets forth the duties of the ORTF Director-General who, with the aid of an accountant, is responsible for keeping the accounts of the organization. Also prescribed are the duties and powers of the Administrative Council which, with the aid of a Financial Committee made up of members of the Council, must review regularly the ORTF administration.

Some parliamentary control of the ORTF and its operations is still retained, but there has been a change in the method. Under the 1959 Ordinance, a Supervisory Council, functioning within the Ministry of Information, was responsible for reviewing and evaluating the administrative, financial and technical operations of the RTF. Within this Council were representatives from the two houses of the Parliament. Article VIII of the 1964 law specifies that the Minister of Information is required to summon representatives of the two houses to a meeting with him at least quarterly. The Minister must initiate these meetings and must personally participate in the deliberations. Under this procedure, the Parliament is able to exercise continuous oversight of the ORTF by regular consultations with the Minister who is responsible for its general supervision.

Another change should be noted. As previously pointed out, under the 1959 decree, there was a Board of Governors concerned with programming operations. This Board was abolished. However, under the administrative decree of July 22, 1964, radio and television program committees were established to advise the president of the Administrative Council and the Director-General of the ORTF. One-third of the members of these committees represent public services and are chosen after consultation with the Government. One-third are persons with special knowledge in the arts, letters, the sciences, entertainment and radio and television. One-third are persons with special knowledge of and concern for social problems, including the welfare of the home, the family and the country's youth. These committees, it should be stressed, act in an advisory capacity only. Their function is to express opinions on the types and quality of programming presented via radio and television, and to counsel as to balance in terms of overall public interests and needs.

Present Facilities and Scope of Operations

OPERATING under this legislative authority and the regulations adopted to implement the law, the ORTF provides one of the largest and most important broadcast services in Europe. The *Maison de la RTF* in Paris which houses the administrative offices and central studios for network programs has already been mentioned. Plans for its construction were completed when television was largely in the experimental stage, and it was designed largely for radio transmission. Although it has been possible to convert some of the building space into television studios and to use the concert halls for television broadcasts (symphony concerts, for example), there is an acute shortage of space and facilities for the present program in television. Plans are under way to provide additional facilities to meet the needs of the expanded television service.

The ORTF is now operating three large national networks for radio transmission. These are *France-Inter, France-Culture,* and *France-Musique.* *France-Inter* operates twenty-four hours a day, and as the ORTF stated in June 1964, it provides a wide range of programming, consisting mainly of recorded music, dramatic serials, comedy and discussions of a practical nature.[51] Its twofold purpose is to entertain and inform, to reach as large an audience as possible, including both old and young listeners. Each evening, two distinct areas of programming are presented: *Inter-Varietes* with traditional dramatic shows and musical concerts designed for the older listeners and *Inter-Jeunesse* with broadcasts appealing to the younger generation.

News flashes, commentaries, documentaries, jazz, opera and a wide variety of informative programs dealing with the individual and his problems are included in the schedules of this network. It achieves nation-wide coverage by a large number of both AM and FM transmitters, with power ranging from less than one kilowatt to as high as five hundred kilowatts.[52]

France-Culture is a national network service which emphasizes programs appealing to intellectual and aesthetic tastes. The schedules include both French and foreign productions believed to have value for *"la civilisation et la culture françaises. En effet, si FRANCE-CULTURE est une chaine de grande création, elle est aussi celle de la recherche. Recherche dans le présent comme dans le passé: l'audace de ses programmes aurait peu de signification se elle n'était alimentée eticlairée par les richesses de la tradition."*[53]

Some examples of programs carried by this network are: *"l'Analyse Spectrale de l-Occident," "l'Heure de Culture Française," "Echos de Grand Siècle," "Soirées de Paris,"* literary, artistic, scientific and philosophical discussions, broadcasts based upon research relating to such problems as urbanism, leisure and wages, and concerts by the National, Philharmonic, Lyric and Chamber Orchestras which are attached to the ORTF and have achieved wide acclaim in the musical world. This cultural network, through a chain of both AM and FM stations, covers the nation, and many of its programs are recorded and made available to other countries for broadcasting.[54]

France-Musique, a third national network of FM stations, provides a musical program service. It might be described as a *Musée imaginaire de la grande Musique,* including all types—symphony, chamber, ancient, classical, romantic, modern, religious, grand opera, operetta, instrumental, vocal, jazz and folk.[55] The program design is to offer a wide range of music of the highest quality (including some stereophonic transmission) with informative and critical commentaries presented from time to time.

Foreign Broadcasting

As previously indicated, beginning in 1913, France has been a leader in short-wave, foreign broadcasting. Despite the damage and destruction of the Second World War, France still had five short-wave transmitters operating. Today, there are four times that many in service at Issoudin in the center of France. With a combined power of two thousand kilowatts, they beam programs in eighteen languages to all parts of the world. These broadcasts are varied, including commentaries, news bulletins, religious services, sports, French lessons, and relays of miscellaneous broadcasts of *France-Inter* and *France-Culture*.

Current Television Programming

FRANCE now has two television networks in operation. The First Programme broadcasts about sixty hours per week. Its programs are varied in content and designed to attract listeners and viewers in all age groups. As reported by the ORTF in June 1964, weekly broadcasting time on the First Programme was divided as follows: Information, news and commentaries, twenty-three percent; variety shows, twenty-one percent; documentaries relating to education, religion, art, literature and science, twenty percent; films, twelve percent; special programs for children, eight percent; sports, eight percent; music, one percent; dramatic shows, five percent; foreign programs, one-half percent; and regional transmissions, one and one-half percent.[56]

The ORTF continues to carry lessons for the classroom on the First Programme. In cooperation with the *Institut Pédagogique National,* it conducts the *Radio–Télévision Scolaire.* During the 1964–65 academic year, this school broadcast more than twelve hours of instruction per week in a variety of subjects, including mathematics, physics, technology, geography, literature, history, music, drama, elementary English and Latin. According to official reports, at that time as many as nine thousand French schools (secondary, elementary and technical) were using this television instruction.[57]

Drawing upon the knowledge of teachers and other experts, the *Institut* prepares and provides to schools helpful study guides which facilitate the use of the televised lessons and make them more effective in the classroom.

While comparatively little broadcasting has been used by French colleges and universities in the classroom (there has been some in Paris, Bordeaux and other places), considerable research and experimental work along that line has been carried on. An Audio-Visual Center at *l'Ecole Normal Supérieure de Saint-Cloud* in Paris, established in 1947 by the Director-General of Higher Education in France, has conducted such studies and produced considerable experimental programming for critical review. The operations of the Center are carried on by a committee of professors working with the Director-General. Among other things, the purposes of the Center are: (1) to familiarize universities with the techniques of audio-visual instruction; (2) develop specialized personnel; (3) prepare pilot films for study; and (4) evaluate the effectiveness of audio-visual techniques, including television, as aids to learning at the university level.[58]

The broadcasts of the First Programme achieve nation-wide coverage through a network system of more than thirty regional and almost one hundred local transmitters. Most of the programs for the network emanate from the Paris studios, are transmitted from the Eiffel Tower, and are picked up and relayed by the other stations. Some regional broadcasts, however, largely news and actualities, originate in local studios located in Bordeaux, Lille, Lyon, Marseilles, Rennes, Strasbourg and Toulouse.

On April 18, 1964, the Second Television network began operating in France. As is the case with the First, it attempts to provide a diversified service appealing to all important segments of society. At the same time, as its Director has pointed out, it avoids duplication as much as possible, to give the viewer a wider choice of programs:

> We who are in charge of the service try wherever possible to satisfy the audience's tastes, in so far as they are compatible with the organization's technical facilities and financial resources. Our aim is to please our audience but, conscious of television's educational and cultural role, we try to see that our programmes, after perhaps aiming a little too high, do not sink to the level of the facile, the banal or the vulgar.
>
> We attempt to strike a fair balance between what might be termed a widening of the audience's cultural horizon and television's essentially recreative role. In a word, we try at all costs to avoid either too high a degree of specialization, as this might tend to throw audiences back on the First Programme, which would inevitably come to be known as the "popular" programme, or too great a similarity between the two programmes, which would merely divide viewers between scarcely distinguishable alternatives. This synthesis between the wishes of the audience and the aims of those in charge was the determining factor behind my consideration of the various programme possibilities for the second service.
>
> We have tried to break the old moulds, and if we have sometimes been clumsy, it has always been with the intention of creating new styles. The old frameworks of drama, documentaries, variety and music have grown too rigid. . . .
>
> It is our new service's constant endeavour to be entertaining without abandoning standards. Variety broadcasts, the games and quizzes, the drama programmes (Labiche, Troyat, etc.) are all designed to maintain this spirit of gaiety and good taste.[59]

In June 1965, the Second Programme was on the air about fifteen hours per week. An analysis of the schedules for two weeks of that period revealed a wide range of programs—variety shows with emphasis on comedy and light entertainment, feature films (full length), continued dramatic serials, historical documentaries, sports via Eurovision, a concert by the ORTF National Orchestra, religious music, news reports and studio drama. While schedules for other weeks might vary in some details, these seemed to typify the program service on the Second network.

The programs of this Second service originate in the Paris studios, are transmitted from the Eiffel Tower and are relayed by transmitters in Lyon,

Lille and Marseilles. At the time of writing, plans were under way to construct eight additional ones, which, when completed, will provide network coverage for the nation.

Commercial Broadcasting

OVER a long period of time there has been intermittent agitation in France for the introduction of advertising on radio and television. Article LII of the 1961 Budget Appropriation Act, forbade the RTF to accept new sources of revenue such as advertising without legislative authorization. Proposals were made in the Parliament to incorporate this prohibition in the 1964 law which established the ORTF. These proposed amendments, however, were tabled. The Minister of Information assured the members that commercial broadcasting would not be initiated without their first having an opportunity to consider and debate the matter in Parliament.[60]

Some business and political interests in France, however, have continued to press the Government to authorize advertising, particularly on television. France's neighbors, Holland, Britain, Luxembourg, Italy, Spain and Switzerland, all permit commercials on some or all of their stations. Belgium has been making studies along this line.

When the budget for the ORTF was presented to Parliament in November 1964, the Minister of Information stated that the Government was continuing to study the possibilities of permitting advertising on television. He pointed out that the television deficit for 1964 was more than one hundred and forty million francs and that the development of the Second TV network was taking away much of the funds normally used for the program service on the First. While the taxes on receivers (the present source of revenue) could be increased, he thought this might be risky, and that it might reduce sales and actually diminish income.[61]

The Minister of Information pledged the Parliament that the most rigorous controls would be imposed on advertising if eventually it should be authorized, to avoid what he considered "intolerable abuses" in some other countries. He also promised that there would be no hasty action on the matter.[62]

NOTES

1. J. J. Fahie, *A History of Electric Telegraphy to the Year 1837* (London: E. and F. N. Spon, 1844), p. 498.

2. Alvin F. Harlow, *Old Wires and New Waves* (London and New York: D. Appleton-Century Company, 1936), pp. 19–20.
3. *Ibid.*
4. *Ibid.*, pp. 45, 51–56. Also, see Fahie, pp. 161–162.
5. Fahie, pp. 317–493. Also, see M. Amyot, *Note Historique, in Comptes Rendus*, French Academy of Sciences, December 26, 1937, p. 909.
6. *Bulletin des Lois de Royaume de France*, 1837, No. 495, Paris, pp. 261–262.
7. *Ibid.*, 1850, No. 2567, p. 685.
8. *Ibid.*, 1879, No. 7655, p. 15.
9. *Ibid.*, 1885, No. 15005, pp. 46–47; *Journal Officiel*, January 9, 1885.
10. *Bulletin des Lois*, 1910, No. 1506, pp. 1166–1167; *Journal Officiel*, April 30, 1910.
11. ORTF, *Paris Vous Parle*, No. 7, December 1964, p. 2.
12. *Le Temps* (Paris), March 24, 1923, p. 5.
13. *Bulletin des Lois*, 1923, No. 23582, pp. 3466–3474; *Journal Officiel*, December 14, 1923.
14. *Le Temps*, October 21, 1924, p. 6.
15. *Ibid.*, May 24, 1925, p. 5.
16. Poincare had been called back to national leadership in 1922, and in 1926, at the request of Parliament, formed a Government of National Union with the power to issue decree laws.
17. *Bulletin des Lois*, 1926, No. 29798, pp. 6135; *Journal Officiel*, December 31, 1926.
18. *Le Temps*, May 28, 1933, p. 4. In 1933, the franc was equivalent to 3.9 cents, but by 1948 its value had dropped to a small fraction of one cent. As of January 1968, the franc was equivalent to twenty cents.
19. Act of May 31 and June 1, 1933; Article CIX; *Recueil des Lois*, 1933, p. 261; *Journal Officiel*, June 8, 1933.
20. Decree dated February 13, 1935; reported in *Bulletin Législatif*, 1935, pp. 95–96.
21. *Le Temps*, January 6, 1936, p. 6.
22. *Ibid.*, January 11, 1936, p. 8.
23. *Ibid.*, February 18, 1936, p. 8.
24. *Ibid.*, February 18, 1936.
25. *Bulletin Législatif*, 1936, pp. 854–855; *Journal Officiel*, October 20, 1936,
26. *Recueil General des Lois, Décrets et Arrêtés*, 1901, p. 209. pp. 11280–11281.
27. Law of October 1, 1941, passed by the Council of Ministers, transferred all control over broadcasting, both public and private, to the Government, with the Vice-President of the Council exercising authority. *Journal Officiel*, December 6, 1941, p. 5270.
28. *Radiodiffusion–Télévision Française*, "Broadcasting in France," *EBU Bulletin*, September–October 1956, p. 639.
29. *Ibid.*, pp. 639–640.
30. *Ibid.*, p. 643.
31. *Ibid.*
32. *Ibid.*, p. 644. This report, prepared by the RTF, contains an excellent, detailed account of broadcasting developments in France until 1956.
33. *EBU Review*, 61B, May 1960, p. 14.
34. *EBU Bulletin*, September–October 1956, p. 721–722.
35. *Radiodiffusion–Télévision Française*, "Broadcasting in France," p. 646.
36. *EBU Review*, 61B, May 1960, p. 14.
37. Decree No. 59–273, February 4, 1959; *Journal Officiel*, February 11, 1959, pp. 1859–1860.

38. Decree No. 59–277, February 5, 1959; *Journal Officiel*, February 12, 1959, p. 1912.
39. *La Radiodiffusion en France (Historique)*, prepared by ORTF, undated.
40. *Ibid.*
41. Louis Foucher, "RTF Educational and Cultural Sound Broadcasts and the *Université de France*," *EBU Review*, 70B, November 1961, p. 16.
42. *Ibid.*, p. 18.
43. Henri Dieuzeide, "Ten Years of School Television," *EBU Review*, 69B, September 1961, p. 10.
44. *Radiodiffusion–Télévision Française*, "School Broadcasting," *EBU Review*, 74B, July 1962, p. 11.
45. *EBU Review*, 87B, September 1964, p. 33.
46. *Journal Officiel*, June 28, 1964; Law No. 64–621, June 27, 1964.
47. Decree No. 64–736, July 22, 1964.
48. *Journal Officiel*, July 23, 1964; Decree No. 64–738, July 23, 1964.
49. *Ibid.*, July 23, 1964; Decree No. 64–739, July 22, 1964.
50. Decree No. 64–737, July 22, 1964.
51. *Radiodiffusion–Télévision Française; Extrait de l'Annuaire Du Spectacle (Théâtre, Cinéma, Musique, Radio, Télévision)*, June 1964, p. 16.
52. *Ibid.*, pp. 65–66.
53. *Ibid.*, p. 17.
54. *Ibid.*
55. *Ibid.*, p. 18.
56. *Ibid.*, p. 37.
57. *Institut Pédagogique National, Bulletin de la Radio–Télévision Scolaire*, No. 11, June 22, 1964 (29, rue d'Ulm, Paris–V).
58. *L'Ecole Normal supérieure de Saint-Cloud. Fonctions et Activités du Centre Audio-Visuel* (undated), Paris. Also, see *Les Services Audio-Visuels, de Ministere de L'Education Nationale*, an extract from *"Les Techniques Audio-Visuelles au Service de l'Enserguement," Editions Bourrelier*, 1961.
59. *EBU Review*, 86B, July 1964, pp. 9–11.
60. *Ibid.*, 87B, September 1964, p. 35.
61. *Le Figaro* (Paris), November 9, 1964, p. 6.
62. *Ibid.*

XV

Italy: State Supremacy
in Broadcasting

B Y 1914 ITALY HAD BECOME AN IMPORTANT DEMOCRATIC NATION, but the First World War overwhelmed it. The hopelessness and chaos which followed were the seeds from which Fascism sprung and which gave rise to Mussolini and his totalitarianism. Out of this situation the original structure and pattern of broadcasting developed.

In October 1922, King Victor Emmanuel III invited Mussolini to Rome and asked him to form a cabinet. One of the basic features of Mussolini's policy was the unquestioned supremacy of the State in every important phase of the national life. This of course included all the communication media. He promptly made plans for the "organized use of propaganda, by the press, radio, and cinema, to dope the people at home, and to create abroad whatever impression was considered most desirable."[1]

A Royal Decree dated February 8, 1923, declared that radio was in the public domain and that no transmitting station could be operated without authority from the Government. The Ministry of Posts and Telegraphs, in consultation with the Ministries of War and Navy, exercised regulatory jurisdiction over all broadcasting.[2]

The Establishment of the URI

WITH *Il Duce's* sanction, on December 14, 1924, the Ministry granted a broadcasting license to a limited company, *Unione Radiofonica Italiana* (URI).[3] The decree which granted the license provided that the Company should have the exclusive authority to broadcast in the country for six years. It further provided that the Company should install a central transmission facility in Rome and regional stations in Naples, Palermo and Milan. The authority to establish additional stations in other cities, should the need for them arise, was also granted.

It was specified that these stations could broadcast musical concerts, theatrical performances, conferences, speeches, including sermons, educational lectures and news. Each station, however, was required to employ a state official who could censor any program not thought to be in keeping with fascist policies. All news programs not provided by *Il Duce's* press agency had to be approved by a local representative of the Party.

The Company started with a capitalization of one million and four hundred thousand lire, with the requirement that this would be increased to not less than six million within two months.[4] A majority of the stock had to be owned by Italian citizens; and the president of the Board, at least two-thirds of its members and at least three-fourths of the executive personnel were required to be Italian nationals.

The decree further provided that the Company should pay the Ministry of Communications an annual fee of fifteen thousand lire for each station in operation and a system of annual fees for the private and commercial use of receivers was established. Dealers engaged in selling receivers had to pay the concession company license fees in accordance with the number of retail establishments they owned and operated. Moreover, a tax was imposed upon the sale of radio parts, ten percent of which went to the State and ninety percent to the Company.

A daily program schedule was prescribed with the specification that the time from one to two o'clock in the afternoon and seven to eight o'clock in the evening be available for the broadcast of government messages. In case of emergency—and this was determined by the Government—the facilities could be requisitioned for official communiques at any time, day or night. Mussolini had set up a special agency which, together with the military authorities, was empowered to interrupt or suspend regular broadcast operations at any hour if such action was thought to be essential to national security.

The Company was required to deposit with the Government "caution money" in the amount of three hundred thousand lire as a guarantee of the fulfillment of its obligation under the concession. Failure to comply with all requirements, especially those pertaining to the broadcast of government communiques, made the Company subject to forfeitures and fines varying from one hundred to five thousand lire for each offense. Moreover, the decree provided that the Minister of Communications could revoke the Company's concession for violating any regulations. This sanction, plus the authority of the Minister of Communications to assess fines, assured compliance with Party policies and directives by all radio stations.

The Government Tightens Its Grip on Broadcasting

A SERIES of royal decrees followed in rapid succession, all designed to strengthen the power and influence of the Government over broadcasting.

Mussolini became increasingly concerned with foreign affairs and the expansion of his colonial empire. In line with this aggressive policy, he issued a decree in October 1925, tightening the Government's grip on broadcasting in all the Italian colonial possessions.[5]

Hearder and Waley have stated that "nothing reveals more clearly the grim and humourless determination of Mussolini to dominate every phase of national life, and to close every avenue of spontaneous initiative amongst the Italian people, than the working of the much trumpeted *Dopolavoro,* the association which controlled the recreation and pleasures of the people. Every form of sport and amusement had to be affiliated to a national organization, of which the presidents and secretaries had to be appointed by the Government."[6] In November 1926, Mussolini decreed that no public performance (this, of course, included all radio) given in Italy, including opera, drama, concerts, motion pictures and ballets, could be presented without the Government's prior approval.[7] Needless to say, this broadened the field of fascist propaganda and transformed entertainment and recreation into "moral and spiritual phenomena," inherently a part of Party discipline and practice.

The Beginnings of Educational Radio

ON August 13, 1926, a decree was published authorizing the Minister of Communications to grant licenses for stations operating solely for experimental and research purposes.[8] These stations were required to restrict their transmissions to scientific uses. Only Italian citizens without criminal records were eligible for such licenses, and the mayor of the town where he had his legal residence had to attest to the applicant's qualifications for this special type of broadcasting.

Universities, scientific institutes, law schools and public and private high schools could apply for licenses to broadcast for purposes of study and instruction and were relieved of paying the annual tax imposed on applicants not falling within these educational categories.

The Creation of the EIAR

BY the end of 1926, almost twenty-seven thousand radio receivers had been sold and registered. There was a growing interest in radio, and the Government wanted to expand the medium for political purposes. Accordingly, Mussolini appointed a Commission composed of representatives of the Government, industry and business, the arts and various professions to study broadcasting. All these appointees had to be registered, loyal members of the Fascist Party and unequivocally committed to Mussolini and his totalitarian policies and tactics.[9]

This study led to the creation by the Government in 1927 of a new broadcasting company. Replacing the URI and named *Ente Italiano Audizioni Radiofoniche* (EIAR),[10] this establishment started with a capitalization of eight million and two hundred thousand lire and a license to operate for twenty-five years. Like the URI, it was granted monopolistic privileges in broadcasting. It was prescribed by decree law that the appointment of the President of the Company, at least four other members of the Board of Directors and the manager of broadcast operations had to be approved by the Government. At the same time, the Government assumed no liability for damages to third parties which might be caused by the operation of any radio station owned by the Company.

The Company was guaranteed the same sources of revenue as its predecessor—license fees on receivers, taxes on the sale of radio parts and special contributions by municipalities. An additional source of income, however, was provided. Advertising, not to exceed ten percent of the total broadcast time, was authorized.

After being approved by a surveillance committee, programs were scrutinized by the Minister of Posts and Telecommunications who was authorized to require modifications, if, in his judgment, the public interest required. The stations were obligated to carry programs which the Government might prescribe as essential to the public interest and security. The censorship of news and public affairs programming was tightened, with government officials authorized to prohibit the broadcast of any program which they might consider out of line or inimical to Party principles.

It was specified that the Council of Ministers might interrupt, limit or even take over the operation of the Company and any of its stations, if the Council considered such action a military necessity or essential in any way to public safety.

Succeeding ministerial decrees provided for *vigilanza* committees to keep tabs on broadcasting in Rome, Milan, Naples, Turin, Genoa, Bolzano, Florence, Bari, Palermo in Sicily and Trieste. These committees evaluated and, if they thought necessary, restrained local radio programming, and were in direct communication with Rome at all times, keeping high government officials informed about program practices, and particularly any deviations from the Party line.[11]

Prewar Depression and Broadcasting

THE depression of the early thirties threatened the collapse of Italy's economic and financial structure. International conferences had assembled but had failed to alleviate the situation. Italy was therefore forced to pursue a policy of "self-sufficiency."[12] Mussolini sought by every means possible to increase production, accumulate raw materials and make Italy less dependent on foreign markets. He expanded the radio facilities, stepped up the transmitting power of stations and broadcast the message of "self-sufficiency" and the "battle of wheat," particularly to the farming and industrial areas.[13]

On June 15, 1933, he established the Radio Rural Agency *(Ente Radio-rurale),* which was to encourage the purchase of receivers and increase listening to radio in the rural areas. With regular informational and educational broadcasts he hoped to improve the farming methods and raise the cultural level of the farm population.[14]

The Agency was operated by a commission of nine members appointed by the Minister of Telecommunications upon the advice of the Ministers of Education, Agriculture and Forests, and representatives of the Ministries of Finance and Communications, and of EIAR. The original appointees consisted of the presidents of EIAR, the National Fascist Confederation of Industry and Commerce and the agricultural syndicates; two representatives of the Ministry of Finance, the Directors-General of the Ministries of Telecommunications, National Education, Agriculture and Forests; and the Chief, Radio and Telegraph Division of the Ministry of Telecommunications.[15]

Increasingly, *Il Duce* assumed dictatorial powers over all communication media. He established a Ministry of Press and Propaganda and transferred to it control over all broadcasting.[16]

Radio During the War

As the war approached, the Government continued to expand broadcast facilities and to increase the transmitting power of existing stations. A large installation for short-wave broadcasting at a cost of 15,910,000 lire was set up in Rome. Composed of five transmitters with effective radiated power ranging from forty to one hundred kilowatts, it had directional antennas designed to beam programs to strategic foreign areas, particularly the Italian colonies.[17]

In 1938, the so-called "Law of War and Neutrality" was enacted, authorizing Mussolini to censor all radio and, in addition, to determine what the people might and might not listen to.[18] In 1940, a Committee for Telecommunications, representing different departments of the Government, was established to coordinate and control all communication during the war. The Committee of course was under the direction of *Il Duce*.[19]

As the war was waged on numerous fronts, Mussolini continued to exercise strict control over the media until 1943 when his own Fascist Grand Council repudiated him and forced him to resign as Prime Minister. He was kidnapped and taken to Germany. Later he returned to northern Italy and set up a Fascist Republic, and on September 23, 1944, he ordered the nationalization of the EIAR and moved the head office for broadcasting from Rome to Turin.[20]

Following this action, King Victor Emmanuel III's son, Umberto, who had assumed the royal functions, signed a decree renaming the radio operation in Rome. It was called *Radio Audizioni Italia* (RAI) to avoid confusion with the EIAR facilities which had been taken over by Mussolini and the Fascists.[21] Shortly thereafter, a temporary commission was established in Rome to operate the RAI pending restoration of its normal functions.[22]

The war reached its climax in the spring of 1945. The Allies completed a successful offensive in northern Italy. Mussolini was executed by the partisans on April 28 of that year and the Germans surrendered a few days later.

Postwar Developments

IN the March 1946 referendum, the monarchy was rejected by majority vote and a democratic republic was established. After a prolonged debate, a constitution was adopted providing for a Council of Ministers and a legislature composed of the Assembly, or Chamber of Deputies, and the Senate, with the President of the Republic elected by the two chambers.

On April 3, 1947, a detailed legislative decree was adopted which established the legal and regulatory framework for the present operation of broadcasting in Italy.[23] This law provides that:

(1) The Ministry of Posts and Telecommunications exercise regulatory jurisdiction over the RAI, the concessionaire company; supervise technical operations; insure that no harmful interference is caused to other radio operations, and that efficient, up-to-date transmissions are maintained.

(2) The installation of new transmitting facilities must have the prior approval of the Ministry, which, after consultation with the military authorities, issues an opinion within thirty days after receiving the RAI requests for any construction permits.

The law further specifies that the Ministry carry out its regulatory functions through the appointment of special three member commissions: a program expert appointed by the mayor of the city where the commission is located, a listener designated by an association of radio listeners or by the Ministry itself and a technical official of the Government who serves as chairman. These commissions, responsible for making technical surveys and reporting to the Minister the need for any modifications and improvements in the service, are set up in cities where RAI stations are located.

As stated in Article VIII of the law, the Minister appoints a special national committee to prescribe the general principles and requirements for programming: cultural, artistic and educational. The committee members, whose two year appointments can be renewed, include representatives of the Ministries of Posts and Telecommunications and Public Instruction, and writers, editors, educators, experts in tourism and "private users" of radio. It is specified that the Prime Minister designate the chairman. Each quarterly schedule of programs, as proposed by the RAI, must have the prior approval of the Minister of Posts and Telecommunications after he receives the advice of this committee.

A special parliamentary committee was created to insure that "political independence" and "objectivity" in broadcasting are maintained. This regulation implicitly requires that the facilities not be used to espouse one political point of view to the exclusion of others, and that equal treatment be given to all bona fide political parties and candidates.

It is specified that this committee be composed of thirty members, fifteen from the Senate and fifteen from the House of Delegates, the appointments to be made by the speakers of the two chambers. The law further states that should any question be raised as to the RAI's adherence to the fairness and objectivity requirements, the committee, after study of the matter, is authorized to transmit its recommendation for remedial action to the Prime Minister, who, in turn, may issue directives requiring the RAI to change its policies and action to comply with his and the committee's opinion.

The RAI is under a statutory mandate to insure that its broadcasts do not discredit the nation or injure international relations. In this regard, should the Company have questions regarding the propriety of proposed broadcasts, it may seek the advice of the Council of Ministers. The Council, in such cases, responds with instructions which the RAI is then obligated to follow.

In accordance with Articles III and IV, the Minister of the Treasury and the Minister of Posts and Telecommunications oversee the bookkeeping and accounting operations of the Company. Moreover, the RAI belongs to a group of organizations which, under a recent decree, makes its bookkeeping functions subject to check by the State Auditing Office.[24]

In the event the Company does not fulfill its obligations under the concession, or does not observe the law and regulations, or should suspend or arbitrarily interrupt or, without due cause, should fail to maintain regular broadcast service, the Minister of Posts and Telecommunications is authorized to levy a fine which may range from a minimum of two hundred thousand to a maximum of five hundred thousand lire. The failure of the Company to comply with the law and regulations pertaining to political broadcasting may result in revocation of its license by the Council of Ministers. Prior to taking such action, the Council would receive the advice of the Minister of Posts and Telecommunications and the special parliamentary committee.

Likewise, the Council, upon the recommendation of the PTT Minister and upon the advice of the special committee on programming (provided for in Article VIII), may revoke the concessions for failure to meet other programming standards and requirements as provided by the law and regulations.

A legislative decree dated March 6, 1948, established a High Technical Council composed of the various government officials concerned with the technical aspects of communications, plus a number of experts outside the Government with recognized technical competency.[25] Through its engineering studies, this Council assists the PTT Ministry in acting on requests for new broadcasting installations or changes in existing ones. It is also concerned with the overall operation of telecommunications, conducts general and special research, and makes recommendations to the PTT Ministry for the improvement of the technical service.

The Development of Television

In January 1949, the Prime Minister appointed a special commission to study the problems relating to the establishment of television. The commission was composed of representatives of the various Ministries, the RAI and a number of outside educational and technical groups concerned with the development of the new medium.[26]

A few months later the first experimental TV operation was initiated by the RAI in Turin. About the same time, a number of demonstrations of TV apparatus were presented at the First International Television Exhibition in Milan.[27]

In March 1950, a plan for a national television network was published and in February 1951, the National Research Council recommended that Italy adopt the six hundred and twenty-five line system.[28] With the approval of the Technical Council for Telecommunications, the RAI began developing the first phase of the national television plan. With the renewal of the RAI's charter in 1952 (effective until December 15, 1972), on January 26, the President of the Republic signed a decree granting the RAI exclusive authority to operate both radio and television stations in Italy and to proceed with the building of a national network.[29]

By the end of 1953, the RAI was operating three television centers in Turin, Milan and Rome, providing service to more than fifty percent of the country, and broadcasting thirty-five hours per week. The initial weekly schedule consisted of six hours of programs designed for children and young people, eight hours of news and reports on current affairs, five hours of literature, plays, and operatic and symphonic music, six hours of variety programs and light entertainment. The remaining time was devoted to "cultural programs" and films.[30]

The formal inauguration of the television service was held on January 3, 1954, with appropriate ceremonies conducted in Rome, Milan and Turin, attended by representatives of the Government, local authorities and chief officials of the RAI.[31] The speeches made at these ceremonies stressed that television would bring the family together again around a new "fireside." The president of the RAI, Signor Ridmi, spoke of television as *"focolare del nostro tempo,"* which was freely translated by the editor of the *EBU Bulletin* at the time as "Television, household god of today."[32]

With television added to its domain, the RAI's name was changed in April 1954, to *RAI-Radiotelevisione Italiana.*[33] With a combined monopoly in radio and television, the Company moved rapidly to expand its operation.

An Era of Rapid Growth

THE progress during the next four years far exceeded the objectives and plans announced in 1954. In 1958 three radio networks, using more than one hundred and ten standard (medium-wave) and more than four hundred FM transmitters, provided excellent broadcast coverage throughout the nation, including Sicily and Sardinia. Nine short-wave installations beamed programs to foreign areas. Also, a television network *(Programma Nazionale)* spanned the nation, operating more than two hundred and seventy transmitters, twenty-seven of which were main installations and the remainder relays and repeaters.[34]

The RAI reported that during the fiscal year 1956 it had broadcast 35,490 hours of radio programs, with a weekly average of more than six hundred and seventy-eight hours. The three networks presented three levels of programming to meet the varied interests of the domestic audience. In addition, almost one thousand hours of transmission in more than thirty languages were provided during the year.[35]

Television programs reached an annual total of more than two thousand hours, or about thirty-nine hours weekly. Two-thirds of this time was devoted to "recreational and cultural" programs, with the remainder in the so-called "informative" category (news, *telegiornale,* current events and sports).[36]

The RAI's 1957 report referred to its audience studies during the year, including personal interviews with twenty thousand selected persons, more than nineteen thousand post-broadcast telephone calls eliciting reactions to the programs, and correspondence with eighteen thousand licensees of radio and television sets.[37]

In this same report, the RAI stated that there were 6,235,377 licensed radio and television receivers, and as many as eighteen million regular listeners. As many as eleven million listened during the peak evening periods and never fewer than one million during the day.[38]

To take care of this rapidly expanding broadcast service, the RAI, as of December 31, 1956, had 5,668 persons on its payroll, an increase of more than five hundred during the preceding twelve months. It had a gross annual income of 26,002,660,228 lire with a gross profit of 1,716,971,306 lire.[39] The income from the radio license fees was more than fifty percent of the total, about fifteen percent came from television fees, and advertising contributed the rest.[40]

As reported by the RAI, the Company spent its money during 1956 as follows:[41]

Program production	9,282,373,664 lire
Technical services	5,837,529,201
Administration	7,084,023,781
Taxes, etc.	1,708,310,899

Present Broadcasting Dimensions

THE RAI has experienced continued growth during the past decade. The 1964 *Annuario* of the RAI reported that medium-wave transmitters numbered one hundred and twenty-seven, with a total transmitting power of 1,446 kilowatts; that there were 1,288 FM transmitters in operation (more than three times as many as in 1958) with a combined power of 222.3 kilowatts and ten short-wave transmitters with five hundred and fifty-five kilowatts.[42] Wired radio *(La Filodiffusione),* which was initiated in 1958, has been extended and now provides service in Milan, Naples, Genoa, Bologna, Bari, Venice, Florence, Palermo, Gagliari and Trieste. Subscribers to this service can receive clearly all the radio network programs. Stereophonic transmission is provided, and the wired transmission is "compatible" and can be received by the owners of standard monaural sets.[43] The RAI also continues to operate *Giornale Radio Telefonico,* a subscription service on telephone wires, providing short, periodic news bulletins during the day. Initiated in Turin in 1952, the service now operates in twenty-three Italian cities.[44]

As of 1964, there were more than nine million registered radio receivers in the country, an increase of almost three million over the number in 1957.[45] Licensees pay an annual fee of 2,450 lire for the use of the radio set and ten thousand lire for a television.[46]

Two television networks are now in operation. The first one, initiated in 1954, has thirty main and almost six hundred VHF auxiliary transmitters, capable of reaching ninety-seven percent of the population. The second one, started in 1961, now has more than thirty main transmitters linked together in an extensive chain served by fifty repeaters and relays. More than four million licenses have been issued for television receivers and the number is steadily increasing.[47]

The second network operates on UHF channels and all transmitters and repeaters are equipped for compatible color. The RAI is now experimenting with color TV and, according to informed sources, could go on the air with regular broadcasts, but the Government's policy is to delay regular programming until 1970.

Production Centers and Regional Offices

THE RAI currently maintains separate program production centers for radio and television in Rome. It also operates a single center (for both media) in Turin, Milan and Naples. The central planning and coordination of the programming is done in Rome, but the other centers produce some programs for local as well as network distribution in accordance with the directives of the RAI programming departments in the capital.[48]

There are regional establishments in Ancona, Bari, Bolzano, Cagliari, Cosenza, Florence, Genoa, Palermo, Perugia, Pescara, Potenza, Trieste and Venice. Except for those in Bolzano and Trieste, these establishments do not produce programs but, along with the production centers, have important technical and administrative responsibilities. Each is in charge of the maintenance and operation of transmission facilities in its area, and, among other things, carries on publicity work and attempts to increase the number of licensees of radio and TV receivers. In Bolzano and Trieste, in addition to the regional offices which oversee the technical and administrative matters there, the RAI maintains production studios where special programs are prepared and transmitted for the German and Slovene ethnic groups living within the coverage area.[49]

Administration and Personnel

IMPLEMENTING the 1947 law on broadcasting and in accordance with its charter, the RAI operates as a joint stock company with a monopoly in radio and television. As reported in 1964, it had a capitalization of eight and one-quarter billion lire, with a majority of the stock owned by the *IRI-Istituto per la Ricostruzione Industriale* (Institute for Industrial Recovery), a government authority which administers a large part of the State's shares in many industrial and business enterprises in Italy.

While some private investment is permitted, the RAI is essentially a government operation with the Institute holding a majority of the stock and the Minister of Posts and Telecommunications acting in a regulatory capacity. The General Assembly of stockholders determines basic policies. There is a Board of Managers with sixteen members, ten of whom are appointed by the Assembly and six by state offices such as the Office of the Prime Minister, and the Ministries of Foreign Affairs, Internal Affairs, Treasury, Public Revenue and Posts and Telecommunications.[50]

The Board of Managers elects from its members a president and vice-president. It appoints a Director-General and Deputy Director subject to the approval of the Minister of Posts and Telecommunications and the Council of Ministers.[51]

There is a Board of Auditors consisting of five members (and two substitutes or alternates) appointed by the Ministry of the Treasury. It is presided over by a representative of the State Accounting Office and serves as a watchdog over the financial affairs of the organization.

Operating under the supervision of General Management, numerous departments are concerned with general administration, radio and television programming, technical operations, buildings, research, training, general affairs and foreign relations.

The Department of General Affairs is responsible for a multiplicity of services—publicity, public relations, legal matters, including copyright restrictions, program coordination, audience survey, documentation and overall research activities.

Personnel in the Department of Foreign Relations maintain contact with international and foreign broadcasting organizations and conduct program exchanges with other countries. The RAI Corporation, established by this Department in 1960, has main offices in New York to foster exchanges of programs between Italy, the United States and Canada. The RAI also has offices in Montevideo to arrange for similar exchanges with the Latin American countries. The *Italia Prize Secretariat,* attached to this Department, has, since 1948, promoted international competitions in radio and television programming and the annual prizes provided by the organization are among the most coveted by producers and artists in broadcasting.

As reported by the RAI in its 1964 *Annuario,* there were 9,277 employees in the total organization. Of these, 2,917 were concerned with the production of programs; 1,873 were connected with administration; 2,816 had technical jobs; 879 were classified as "auxiliary personnel"; and 668 were hired on a temporary basis to perform special production assignments.[52] These figures do not include a large number of free-lancers who perform varied services for the RAI.[53]

Annual income and expenditures are also reported in the 1964 *Annuario*. The following figures reflect the RAI's income for 1963:[54]

Subscription fees for radio and TV	53,659,496,145 lire
Radio advertising	9,243,207,776
Television advertising	11,063,625,105
Miscellaneous income	2,154,770,202
Total	76,121,099,228 lire

Expenditures broken down into general categories were:[55]

Program production	27,182,319,173 lire
Technical operations	17,075,451,419
Administration, public relations, (both domestic and foreign), surveys, personnel training, etc.	17,607,297,695
Taxes and State participation in RAI income	8,798,334,869
Interest payments and miscellaneous expenses	449,803,538
Total	71,113,206,694 lire

It will be noted that the income for 1963 exceeded expenditures by 5,007,892,534 lire. Also, this income was over eight billion lire more than that for the preceding year, whereas the increase in expenses was only a little more than seven billion lire. The profit for 1963 was 721,085,765 lire more than that for 1962.

Radio Programming

RADIO programs are distributed over three national networks. The AM transmissions over the First (national) chain are varied and include a wide range of both classical and popular music, plays, news, literary and scientific discussions, documentaries, instruction for schools and religious broadcasts.[56]

The Second network, while providing a variety of programs, emphasizes entertainment, with news, popular music, quiz shows and other light features making up the bulk of the schedules. The design is to reach the larger and less sophisticated audience.[57]

The schedule of the Third network is geared to the more highly educated listener. A review of its offerings for the second quarter of 1965 revealed a great number of historical, literary and scientific discussions and much classical music.[58] Listeners with cultivated tastes in music, literature, drama, or with an interest in scholarly, critical lectures in philosophy, science, and in current affairs and news analysis in depth, find the Third network to be a rich source of programming.

A fourth channel *(Rete Quettro)* carries programs emanating from Bolzano and designed for the German-speaking population in the Italian Alps.[59]

It was reported in 1964 that the RAI's domestic programs were being broadcast about three hundred hours per week, with music (classical and light) making up about fifty-five percent of the total output.[60] A substantial portion of the remaining time was devoted to informational programs including news and "cultural" features. More than two hundred hours of school broadcasting were presented during the year for use in the elementary and secondary schools.[61]

In addition to the national network offerings, there are those emanating from the various regional centers. These are cultural and informative programs of particular interest to the local areas. The total number of these run almost as much as the total number of transmissions on the networks.[62]

Short- and medium-wave broadcasts designed for foreign reception are presented more than twenty-five hours per week. A large portion of these are short-wave transmissions beamed to all parts of the world in more than thirty languages and dialects.[63]

Television Programming

AT the time of this writing, the RAI was broadcasting about seventy hours per week on its First TV network, and more than twenty-two hours on its Second network. The following figures, as reported in its 1964 *Annuario,* suggest the general pattern of the RAI's TV programming.[64]

	DIVISION IN PERCENTAGES		
	First	Second	
Culture and Entertainment	Program	Program	Total
Symphony and chamber music	1.3	3.1	1.7
Lyrical music and ballet	0.6	2.7	1.1
Opera, theatre	2.4	11.2	4.5
Original drama and adaptations	2.	5.8	2.9
Feature films and telefilms	5.2	17.	8.
Variety shows	3.	8.8	4.3
Musical comedy	—	0.6	0.2
Popular music	1.8	3.3	2.1
General cultural	6.6	10.3	7.5

DIVISION IN PERCENTAGES

Culture and Entertainment	First Program	Second Program	Total
Programs for special audiences	2.3		1.8
Religious programs	2.6	0.3	2.
Programs of children	10.1		7.7
School Programs	27.8		21.3
Informative Programs			
News	11.5	7.1	10.5
Special features, documentaries, discussions, etc.	6.2	6.4	6.2
Sports	8.8	15.6	10.4
Other programs, including announcements, advertising and station calls	7.8	7.9	7.8

Telescuola

THE RAI devotes more than one-fourth of its time on the First network to programs for the classroom. *Telescuola,* now a unit in the Television Programmes Department, began in 1958. Initially, its purpose was to provide children who had finished primary school with the opportunity to continue their studies, particularly in those areas still without intermediate schools *(scuola media inferiore)*. The courses of study stressed vocational training to help youngsters no longer in school to acquire skills for gainful employment. Italo Neri, the former director of the *Telescuola* Center, stated that the overall aim of the program, as originally conceived, was "to use television's capacity for mass communication to provide compulsory education prescribed by the Italian Constitution for children up to the age of fourteen."[65]

By 1960, the RAI was broadcasting four courses on a regular basis, three concerning vocational training for industrial jobs and one for agricultural work. These courses were transmitted for four hours each afternoon (except Sunday) from October 3, 1960, to June 24, 1961. They were presented in the form "of two half-hour lessons a day on the main subjects with a ten or fifteen minute break devoted in turn to lessons on auxiliary subjects such as religion, music and singing, domestic science, caligraphy and physical education."[66]

For supplementary reading, the RAI's publishing house, *Edizioni Radiotelevisione Italiana* (ERI), every four months printed and distributed brochures containing exercises and illustrative materials relating to the subjects taught.

Through the cooperation of private and public organizations and with the support of the Ministries of Education and Labor, *Telescuola* listening posts were set up in various parts of the country. In areas where there were no secondary schools, groups of young people gathered in halls where television sets had been installed. As Signor Neri reported, they were assisted by a coordinator, a voluntary helper willing to instruct and direct the group's activities. In 1960–61, there were almost two thousand registered listening posts, more than forty percent of which were located in southern Italy, where the number of schools is limited and the need for skilled labor has been acute.[67]

The initial success of the project is attested to by the fact that of those who presented themselves for final examinations in the telecourses only fifteen percent failed. Some completed the full three year program, passed all their examinations at a state school and secured certification for employment and the opportunity to continue their studies at vocational and technical institutes and apply for civil service status.

In addition to *Telescuola*, the RAI, in 1960, developed a special program in adult education for illiterates. This was a six month course, "It's Never Too Late," arranged and presented in cooperation with the Ministry of Education's Central Service for Adult Education. Impressed with the effectiveness of this course, Signor Neri reported in September 1961:

> The purpose of this service is to develop and coordinate the different initiatives that have helped to halve the number of illiterates in Italy. (Thanks to the different types of adult education courses organized by the Ministry of Education the number has fallen from 5,000,000 in the 1951 census to 2,000,000 at the present time.) The idea of using television springs from the conviction that this means of attraction, by combining education with entertainment, would succeed in "bringing out of their lairs" the illiterates living in psychological isolation. Experience has shown that this conviction was justified; in other words, the television medium—thanks to the experience gained from the vocational training courses—is considered to be not only a valid teaching tool but also a stimulus to overcome the psychological resistance of older and isolated people and to penetrate to corners where the irreplaceable live voice of the teacher has been unable to obtain any reaction.[68]

In order to get and hold the attention of the illiterates, entertainment elements were injected into the telecasts. The teacher's instruction was supplemented by materials such as short dramatic scenes presented by professional actors; cartoons and interviews aroused interest and increased intelligibility.

As was the case with *Telescuola*, listening posts were set up by the Ministry of Education. In 1960–61, more than two thousand of these were in operation, a majority of which were in southern and central Italy and the islands nearby, where the illiteracy rate is still comparatively high.[69]

Telescuola and the educational program for illiterates have continued to expand and have attracted the interest of educators throughout Europe and other parts of the world. In February 1964, it was reported that during the school year, courses were televised on an average of seven hours per day as follows: secondary education, adult education, pre-university science courses, refresher courses for teachers and professional orientation programs.[70] The instruction was presented by a highly trained professional staff and the production facilities compared favorably with those of other European countries.

In 1961, the RAI organized an International Congress on School Broadcasting under the auspices of the European Broadcasting Union. The Congress assembled in Rome in December of that year. Sixty-four countries in Europe, North and South America, Asia and Africa were represented at the meeting. The proceedings of the conference, published in 1962, contain an excellent collection of papers on the developments in educational broadcasting throughout the world.[71]

Every year, between October and June, the RAI conducts informational courses and institutes for the benefit of foreigners wishing to study *Telescuola,* its aims, methods and accomplishments. In 1963, more than one hundred experts from thirty-four countries visited Italy and participated in these programs.[72]

Television Expeditions Abroad

SPECIAL mention should be made of the RAI's broadcast expeditions abroad. Luca di Schiena, the former Chief Television Editor of the RAI, reported on these activities in the May 1965 issue of the *EBU Review.*[73] Recent examples include the coverage of Pope Paul's trip to the Holy Land. To accomplish this, on Christmas Day, 1963, an auxiliary vessel of the Italian Navy unloaded at Beirut twenty-seven vehicles for use in Jordan, and four days later landed fourteen vehicles in Haifa for operations in Israel. About two hundred engineers, cameramen, producers, organizers and reporters flew to their assignments, for the most part by charter flights sponsored by the RAI.

The problems of providing coverage for this historic pilgrimage and the success with which it was achieved were dramatically reported by Signor Schiena:

> . . . The first impressions gave rise to some anxiety; not only was there as yet no regular television service in either country but they also presented certain difficulties from the point of view of sound broadcasting, the most serious problem being that of circuits to Italy. Further, the political situation prevented the rapid exchange of men and material along the frontiers. Nor

did the confined spaces on the sites, the roads and inside monuments simplify the work of the installation or the business of getting about; and, moreover, the strange surroundings and the uncertainty of the final programs added to the difficulties of the preparatory work.

. . . .

. . . When the uncontrolled enthusiasm of the crowds exploded on the Pope's arrival at the Damascus Gate it was really a baptism of fire, and more than hundred of us found ourselves in the front line. . . . Reporters, cameramen, motorcyclists, drivers and organizers all had to get to the posts allocated to them, turn up on time at the rendezvous, hand over the reels of film and the commentary notes, collect the material and dash to the airport where the aircraft, engines running, would be waiting for the signal to take off.

. . . .

A carload of cameramen and radio reporters at the head of the Papal procession ensured the coverage of all visits and any unforeseen detours. In another car, the head of the journalistic services preceded the Papal procession by a few minutes in order to coordinate the work of the reporters, supervise the operation of the fixed positions and arrive on the spot ahead of the procession. Another group was kept busy collecting the films and rushing to the airport by fast car (on the day of the visit to Israel even by helicopter) to dispatch them to Italy. Transport was effected by jet aircraft of the Italian Air Force which touched down at Athens almost at the limit of their flying capacity and, so as not to lose time in refuelling, handed over the material to a second jet standing ready for the final dash to Rome. Scheduled airline flights were only rarely used, and then for films of less urgency.

. . . .

It will be readily understood that the whole operation demanded a rigid adherence to the timetable, not only in respect of flight departures, drawn up with an eye to the Italian and European programme plans, but also taking into account the distances to be travelled by the vehicles in order to cover all the proceedings in rapid succession.[74]

Much the same procedure was followed in the RAI's coverage of the Pope's visit to Bombay. In addition to the problems of transporting equipment, India had limited communication lines and facilities for pickup and transmission. Other expeditions abroad have included televising the celebration of King Constantine's marriage in Greece, and providing technical assistance to the Maltese Government for transmission of the country's independence celebrations.

The following words of Signor Schiena express pride in these foreign projects and his supreme confidence in the RAI's ability to engage in much more difficult exploits abroad and above:

. . . Our engineers, producers and reporters have now acquired such vast experience in the field of television "expeditions" abroad that if Werner Von Braun were to place the slightest trust in them they could even manage to organize a trip to the moon in a matter of a few days.[75]

NOTES

1. H. Hearder and D. P. Waley, *A Short History of Italy* (London: Cambridge University Press, 1963), p. 205.
2. Royal Decree, No. 1067, February 8, 1923; *Official Gazette* (Rome), No. 125, May 29, 1923.
3. Royal Decree, No. 2191, December 14, 1924; *Official Gazette*, No. 11, January 15, 1925.
4. As of January 1968, one lira was equivalent to 0.16 cents.
5. Royal Decree, No. 2128, October 15, 1925; *Official Gazette*, No. 288, December 12, 1925.
6. Hearder and Waley, pp. 210–211.
7. Royal Decree, No. 1848, November 6, 1926; *Official Gazette*, No. 257, November 8, 1926.
8. Royal Decree, No. 1559, August 13, 1926; *Official Gazette*, No. 216, September 16, 1926.
9. Royal Decree, January 27, 1927; *Official Gazette*, No. 23, January 29, 1927.
10. Royal Decree, No. 2207, November 17, 1927; *Official Gazette*, No. 287, December 13, 1927.
11. Ministerial Decree, January 23, 1932; *Official Gazette*, No. 30, February 6, 1932.
12. Hearder and Waley, pp. 219–220.
13. *Ibid.*, p. 223.
14. Ministerial Decree, No. 791, June 15, 1933; *Official Gazette*, No. 162, July 14, 1933.
15. Ministerial Decree, August 7, 1933; *Official Gazette*, No. 189, September 16, 1933.
16. Royal Decree, No. 1829, September 26, 1935; *Official Gazette*, No. 252, October 27, 1935. The organization and powers of the Ministry of Press and Propaganda were set forth in Royal Decree, No. 1834, September 24, 1936; *Official Gazette*, No. 246, October 22, 1936.
17. Ministerial Decree, January 31, 1937; *Official Gazette*, No. 98, April 28, 1937.
18. Royal Decree, No. 1415, July 8, 1938; *Official Gazette*, No. 211, September 25, 1938.
19. Decree Law, No. 281, dated January 29, 1940; *Official Gazette*, No. 102, April 30, 1940.
20. Ministerial Decree, September 23, 1944; *Official Gazette*, No. 253, October 28, 1944.
21. Royal Decree, No. 457, October 26, 1944; *Official Gazette*, No. 22, February 20, 1945.
22. Ministerial Decree, January 20, 1945; *Official Gazette*, No. 43, February 10, 1945.
23. Legislative Decree, No. 428, April 3, 1947; *Official Gazette*, No. 131, June 12, 1947.
24. *This Is RAI*, edited by the Office of Documentation and Studies (arranged for printing by Sergio Raffolo), July 1963, p. 5.
25. Legislative Decree, No. 433, March 6, 1948; *Official Gazette*, No. 111, May 14, 1948.

26. Decree of the President, Council of Ministers, No. 013322, dated January 10, 1949.
27. *EBU Bulletin*, March–April 1954, p. 227. This article lists important dates in the history of Italian television.
28. *Ibid.*
29. *Ibid.*
30. *Ibid.*, pp. 228–234. This report contains a detailed account of the television situation in Italy as it developed during the early fifties with charts showing location of stations, their transmitting power, and other data regarding transmission, coverage and programming.
31. *Ibid.*, p. 227.
32. *Ibid.*, p. 233.
33. *This Is RAI*, p. 3.
34. See *RAI Annuario*, 1964, edited by the Office of Documentation and Studies, Rome, July 31, 1964, pp. 270–293; lists all radio and TV stations on the air as of 1958.
35. *EBU Review*, 47B, February 1958, p. 21.
36. *Ibid.*
37. *Ibid.*
38. *Ibid.*
39. *Ibid.*
40. *Ibid.*
41. *Ibid.*
42. See *RAI Annuario*, 1964.
43. *Ibid.*, pp. 21–22.
44. *Ibid.*, p. 22.
45. *Ibid.*, p. 5; also p. 418.
46. *This Is RAI*, p. 23.
47. See *RAI Annuario*, 1964.
48. *This Is RAI*, p. 10.
49. *Ibid.*
50. See *RAI Annuario*, 1964, p. 443; also, *This Is RAI*, pp. 1–2.
51. *This Is RAI*.
52. *RAI Annuario*, 1964, p. 445.
53. *This Is RAI*, p. 9.
54. *RAI Annuario*, 1964, p. 445.
55. *Ibid.*, p. 444.
56. See RAI, *Schema dei Programmi Radiofonica*, Second Quarter, 1965, Rome, February 1965, pp. 19–100.
57. *Ibid.*, pp. 103–122.
58. *Ibid.*, pp. 133–179.
59. *Ibid.*, pp. 125–130.
60. *RAI Annuario*, 1964, pp. 30–31.
61. *Ibid.*
62. *This Is RAI*, p. 14.
63. *RAI Annuario*, 1964, pp. 26–27, 35–36.
64. *Ibid.*, p. 146.
65. Italo Neri, "Educational Television," *EBU Review*, 69B, September 1961, p. 14. Also, see English translation of *School Broadcasting in Italy*, a publication of *Servizio Propaganda*, RAI, edited by Pino Tovaglia, Rome, December 3, 1961. This contains an excellent discussion of the history, aims, procedures and accomplishments of *Telescuola* until late 1961.
66. *School Broadcasting in Italy*.

67. *Ibid.*, pp. 14–15.
68. *Ibid.*, p. 16.
69. *Ibid.*
70. See *This Is Telescuola*, edited by the *Servizio Documentazione e Studi*, RAI, Rome, February 1964.
71. See *Proceedings at the International Conference of Broadcasting Organizations on Sound and Television School Broadcasting* edited by the *RAI Documentazione e Studi Servia*, Rome. This conference was held from December 3 to 9, 1961, and this seven hundred and twenty-two page document (printed in English) contains the statements of outstanding leaders in educational broadcasting from Europe, Africa, Asia, and North and South America. It also includes the stenographic, edited reports of seven working groups dealing with various phases of the Conference subject. The book should be a must for students interested in the status of educational broadcasting throughout the world as of 1961–62.
72. *This Is Telescuola*, p. 19.
73. Luca di Schiena, "Television Expeditions Abroad," *EBU Review*, 91B, May 1965, pp. 18–20.
74. *Ibid.*, p. 18.
75. *Ibid.*, p. 20.

XVI

Greece: Anxiety and Instability

THE NATURE OF THE BROADCASTING SYSTEM IN GREECE and its present pattern of operation are understandable within the context of Grecian history and the basic values and feelings of the people. For example, the Government operates and controls a substantial portion of the radio facilities. The willingness of the people to entrust the Government with these important media stems to a large extent from a traditional respect for the Government and its function in enterprises so vitally related to the national interest. While they may deplore the irresponsibility and corruption of some officials, the populace has been conditioned to respect authority and the Government's role in national and international affairs.

Another characteristic of the Greeks which affects the pattern of broadcasting is their interest in and respect for learning. While there is still a comparatively high degree of illiteracy (particularly in the remote, mountainous areas), in the urban centers such as Athens, the people generally possess high intellectual and aesthetic tastes. This has been true throughout the country's history. Its early experiments with democracy, the ideas of its ancient philosophers and rhetoricians, the creative works of its jurists, architects, poets, dramatists and literary scholars—all constitute a cultural heritage of which the nation may be justly proud.

It is not surprising, therefore, that the educational aspects of radio are emphasized. Although the average Greek listener is interested in light entertainment, studies have shown that he feels that the dissemination of knowledge is the more important function of broadcasting.

Most Greeks have an intense interest in national and international affairs. Homes, offices and coffee houses buzz with conversations about the vital issues of the day. There is anxiety about what is happening abroad, and a desire to keep informed, particularly regarding foreign political and military activities. Considering Greece's long history of suffering from foreign aggression and particularly its recent, agonizing experiences in two world wars, the people's concern for events outside their own borders and the possible recurrence of an ordeal more devastating than any yet experienced is understandable. Broadcast schedules contain a large number of news reports and discussions of important international events relative to the security of the nation.

The broadcast facilities of Greece are comparatively limited. While plans were well advanced, as of 1965, there was still no television in the country. Because of the limited resources and a history replete with periods of poverty and starvation, the Government has been economy-minded. As will be pointed out later, radio network facilities now span the nation, but quantitatively they do not compare with those in some other European countries where material resources are more abundant. The Government has considered establishing television for a number of years, but the large cost of providing nation-wide coverage, particularly in view of Greece's mountainous terrain and sparsely settled areas, has been a delaying factor.

Early History of Grecian Radio

BROADCASTING in Greece started on an experimental basis during the early twenties. The first significant demonstrations of transmitting and receiving equipment were conducted by representatives of a Swedish company. At that time Greek scientists were interested in the possibilities of using electromagnetic waves for regular broadcasts to the general public. In 1924, a physics professor in Athens and a technical school carried on experimental transmissions.[1]

The first broadcast station in Greece to provide regular programs was established in Thessaloniki in 1928. Christor Tsinguirides, who had studied electronics at the University of Stuttgart, used his own resources to construct a modest facility which he continued to operate privately for more than twenty years. His first broadcasts consisted mainly of news, recorded music, lectures by professors and interviews with authors and other celebrities in the community.

The programs of this Thessaloniki station and the experimental transmission in Athens, plus broadcasts reaching Greece from other countries, awakened the interest of the Greeks in the "wonder of the ether" and the market for radio receivers expanded. From 1921 to 1926, the Ministry of the Navy exercised limited regulatory jurisdiction over radio in Greece, and all transmission and receiving installations had to be authorized by this Ministry. Owners of radio sets were required to pay annually to the Government five hundred drachmas as license fees.[2] Failure to pay these fees subjected the offenders to fines and possible jail sentences.

In 1926, the control of broadcasting was vested in the Radio Electric Service Section of the Ministry of Posts, Telegraph and Telephone (PTT). For a number of years thereafter, the PTT made periodical broadcasts from Piraeus for the service of Coast Guard ships and for hospital patients.

In the latter part of 1929, the Greek Government contracted with a private foreign company for the establishment of radio stations, with the understanding that the company might exploit the facilities for commercial purposes. The operating rights under this arrangement were later transferred to the Telefunkin Company. The contract, however, was never consummated and was abrogated by law in November 1935.[3]

In early 1936, after considerable experimental broadcasting, the Greek Government decided to set up and operate its own system.[4] Accordingly, in July of that year, the PTT called for bids for the construction of stations and the Telefunkin Company was given the contract to provide the facilities and build a one hundred kilowatt medium-wave station in Thessaloniki, but persisting financial crisis and political instability prevented the execution of the construction plans. This second contract was never fulfilled, and the new Government, under the leadership of General John Metaxas, decided to proceed with the building of radio facilities on a more modest basis.

New bids were invited for the construction of a fifteen kilowatt transmitter in Athens. The Telefunkin Company again was the successful bidder, and a third contract was made with the Company in November 1936, for the purchase and installation of the transmission facility. The equipment was delivered to Greece in 1937 and in January 1938, after further negotiations with the Government, the Company completed the installation. About two months later, King George II participated in the inaugural broadcast of the new government station.

The Second World War brought changes in the control and operation of Greek broadcasting. In February 1939, a special division of Press and Radio created by the Government took over the Athens facility. Later, in April 1941, under German control, the station became an instrument for Nazi propaganda.

The Establishment of the Hellenic National Broadcasting Institute

IN 1943, by decision of the Cabinet, a new private organization, the Society for Radio Broadcasting, was created and granted a charter with an exclusive monopoly for broadcasting in Greece.[5] After the liberation of the country, the Society broadcast programs for about a year under the regulatory jurisdiction of the Division of Radio Service in the PTT. However, in 1945, the Government established a new, autonomous organization, the Hellenic National Broadcasting Institute (HNBI).[6] The Institute acquired the title to all radio installations previously owned and operated by the Society.

In 1953, a law was passed which established the legal framework within which the HNBI now operates.[7] The statute declares that the Institute is a public service agency, created by public law and subject to state control. The law also grants an exclusive franchise for broadcasting to the HNBI.

With central offices located in Athens, the HNBI possesses administrative and financial autonomy under certain conditions and restrictions as set forth in the law. It is provided that the technical operations and the financing thereof are subject to the control and supervision of the Ministry of Communications. In all other respects, including programming, regulatory control is vested in the office of the Minister to the Prime Minister.

Article II of the law specifies that the HNBI has the exclusive right to establish, maintain and exploit all technical means for the broadcasting of both domestic and foreign programs.

Article VII provides for an Administrative Council of nine members. Some are officials of various government ministries with special interests in radio, others are private citizens whose knowledge and qualifications contribute to the determination of HNBI policies. These private members are appointed by the Minister to the Prime Minister. The Director-General of the HNBI is appointed by the Cabinet upon the nomination of this Minister.

Article XII prescribes the technical standards and requirements for the maintenance of stations and networks, and provides for an advisory technical committee to be appointed by the Minister of Communications in collaboration with the Undersecretary of the Minister to the Prime Minister. This committee is composed of the technical director of the HNBI and representatives of the Ministry of Communications, the Army and other government establishments and institutions of higher learning.

The law, as originally adopted, provided for a Supreme Advisory Council, which was obliged to receive reports twice a year from the HNBI regarding past performance and future program plans. The Council was made up of the Archbishop of Greece, the President of the Academy of Athens, the deans of the universities and polytechnical schools, the chief of the general staff of the Army, the Governor of the Bank of Greece and representatives of the various ministries. However, in 1961, the Government decided the Council was no longer needed and its operations were terminated.

Article XVIII specifies that no one in Greece may own a radio receiver without payment of a license fee. The current fee is one hundred and sixty drachmas per year. Manufacturers and dealers are required to report monthly to the HNBI all sales of receivers with the names and addresses of purchasers. Fines may be imposed for failure to report sales or pay license fees. Police are authorized to "seal" sets if this tax is not paid.

In 1951 a law was passed allowing for the operation of military broadcasting stations. This statute provided:

> The National Defense Staff shall be authorized to install and operate stations for sound broadcasting, television or other applications of radio, or call stations, for the purpose of informing, instructing, entertaining and generally raising the educational level of the armed forces, and, in wartime, of strengthening the morale of the nation at war, due respect being paid to the obligations assumed in the international sphere with regard to power and wavelength.[8]

From May 1948 to April 1950, the Army operated a medium-wave and a short-wave station in Athens. Later, additional facilities were built in Thessaloniki. These stations and others constructed later were established primarily for the entertainment, education and training of the armed forces, although their programs have come to have wide appeal among civilian listeners.

Quantitative Dimensions of Broadcasting

THE Government's plan to establish a nation-wide network was interrupted by the Second World War. By the time the war had ended, the only Greek station had been almost completely destroyed. The first task of the HNBI, therefore, was to repair the fifteen kilowatt transmitter in Athens and to build additional transmitters which would provide coverage for the more densely populated areas of Greece. By 1957, the HNBI was broadcasting three programs and had increased its facilities to include a one hundred and fifty kilowatt medium-wave transmitter in Athens and a five kilowatt one in Salonica, Komotini, Rhodia and Chania. A five kilowatt and a two kilowatt transmitter in Athens and low-power (less than two hundred and fifty watts) transmitters in Volos and Patras were also in operation. The establishment of a fifty kilowatt station in Corfu the same year provided coverage for the northwestern part of Greece.[9]

Today, the HNBI and the Armed Services operate nineteen medium-wave broadcast stations. The HNBI controls twelve of these, using transmitters with a combined power of two hundred and eighty-two kilowatts. These are located in Amalias, Athens (three), Salonika, Patras, Volos, Komotini, Canea, Corfu, Rhodes and Zante. The HNBI also broadcasts overseas with two short-wave transmitters in Athens, each with a power of twelve kilowatts.

The Armed Services has seven medium-wave stations located in Athens, Salonika, Kavalla, Florina, Tannena, Tripolis and Larissa. These stations use six transmitters with a combined power of 37.25 kilowatts. In addition to domestic broadcasting, the Services operate six short-wave transmitters for broadcasts to foreign listeners.

Private Stations

WHILE no precise figures are available, there may be as many as one hundred private stations in Greece. Operated by municipalities, local trade unions and other private groups, they use low power (two hundred and fifty to three hundred and fifty watts) and cover small areas. Some are located in remote, mountainous regions far removed from the surveillance of the Government in Athens. A large number have not been duly authorized by the Ministry of Communications. The increase in these clandestine stations, much like the situation in Spain, has caused problems of interference and has adversely affected radio reception. According to recent reports, the Ministry has become increasingly concerned, and has intensified its efforts to prohibit these unauthorized operations.[10]

George A. Koumantos, the legal adviser to HNBI, writing in the January 1966 issue of *EBU Review,* referred to the situation:

> ... One cannot fail to notice the appalling number of infringements of the HNBI's monopoly. Wholly illegal low-power private stations abound throughout the country, ranging from the child's toy to the organized transmitter with regular programmes and even commercial broadcasts. The Institute possesses no legal means whereby it could effectively try to stamp out these stations, and its monopoly, being unprovided with sanctions, is in effect a *lex imperfecta.* The Institute is reduced to talking about the administrative action which the Government ought to take, but governments have so far preferred to seek refuge behind certain legal uncertainties as to the manner of their intervention, rather than enact measures which they consider may be unpopular.[11]

Financing

THE HNBI is financed exclusively by the income from license fees on radio receivers, from the sale of advertisements in its weekly radio magazine and from commercials broadcast on its Second program. It has not been the general policy of the Government to provide subsidies. However, Professor Koumantos wrote in January 1966 that "a large proportion of the revenue from subscriptions will be impossible to raise, and the Government is having to make good the deficit out of its own funds."[12]

In 1964, there were approximately eight hundred thousand licensed receivers in Greece. With each owner of a radio set paying one hundred and sixty drachmas, the total income from these fees would be about four million and eight hundred thousand dollars. However, it has been estimated that a substantial number of people do not pay these fees, and that the actual revenue for 1964 ran only about two million dollars. The income from the fees was supplemented by some revenue from commercials on the Second program and from the weekly radio magazine.

In April 1965, a new law was under consideration in Parliament, which, if passed, would abolish the license fee and substitute a monthly charge of ten drachmas, to be paid by every consumer of electricity, except for residents in towns with a population less than five thousand and for electricity consumers whose monthly bills run less than sixty drachmas.

The Armed Services, which operates a tape network with central studios in Athens, finances its network and affiliated stations with Army funds, and revenue from broadcast advertising. The private stations are self-supporting and some derive revenue from broadcast advertising.

Programming

IN July 1959, the HNBI reported that the number of licensed radio receivers had reached six hundred thousand, or one for every thirteen inhabitants. The main goal of the Institute, said the report, was the "education of the listeners. The programs are planned not only for recreational purposes and for the information of listeners about everyday events, but also to make known the cultural tradition of the nation as well as contemporary spiritual and social problems as they stand in relation to those of other countries, in order to demonstrate the mutual influence of the Greek and international civilizations."

Based upon information supplied by the HNBI at that time, the *EBU Review* reported further details regarding the program service of the Institute:

A series of programmes presents: (a) the problems and ideas which set the world's spiritual life in motion; (b) achievements in science and art; (c) personalities from the world of art, letters and science who express their views on subjects of vital interest. These broadcasts are presented in various forms ranging from simple talks to discussions.

The Institute presents 3 plays each week of which one is Greek, another chosen from the classical or the contemporary repertoire and the third an adaptation of a well-known work in contemporary Greek or foreign literature. Three symphony concerts are also broadcast every week, one given by the Athens State Orchestra, one by HNBI's own orchestra and the third by the New York Philharmonic Orchestra specially recorded for the HNBI. In addition to the above broadcasts the HNBI transmits serial programmes from the outstanding works in Greek literature. There is also a daily programme covering art, science, philosophy, history, Greek folklore and customs of the Greek people and of those in foreign countries.

Special attention is paid by the Institute to its broadcasts for children and young people for whom about 14 appropriate programmes of 15 to 20 minutes' duration are given each week. There are also daily broadcasts for farmers which, as well as covering subjects of immediate interest to them, give useful advice on hygiene, cleanliness, the rearing of the young, odd jobs about the home, etc. A daily programme for women not only covers subjects of primary importance to housewives, working women, young wives and mothers, but also gives talks on the activities of women from all walks of life, on home economy, the upbringing and education of children, home decoration, etc.

A special glance in the HNBI's programmes is reserved for religious broadcasts of which there are six each week. The purpose of these broadcasts is: (a) to strengthen religious feeling by explaining the Gospel and other holy texts and by relaying processions from churches; and (b) to obtain the widest possible diffusion of the Christian way of life.

In sending us this information of their service the HNBI stresses that there is an almost complete balance between broadcasts of socio-political education, those of an instructive nature and those which are purely recreational.[13]

While there have been some additions and changes since this 1959 report, the general purposes and pattern of programming today are much the same. The HNBI now broadcasts three programs from three transmitters in Athens. The First Program (Athens National Program) is broadcast more than one hundred hours per week and is mainly informative. Forty percent of its broadcasts go out over the national network.

The Athens Second Program emphasizes entertainment and is broadcast about ninety-five hours per week, with about twenty-five percent of its time used for network transmissions. The Athens Third Program (about thirty-five hours per week) is not carried by the network and consists largely of classical and serious music. The National and Third Programs do not broadcast advertisements; the Second Program, however, is heavily commercial.[14]

An analysis of the three Programs for the summer period of 1964 revealed average hours of programming per week as follows:

Type of Program	Hours	Percent
News	20.55	10
Serious Music	14.55	7
Greek Music		
Folk and popular	49.55	24
Foreign music		
Light and popular	60.40	30
Variety		
Dramas, serials, etc.	50.45	25
Miscellaneous		
e.g., programs for		
children, housewives, etc.	6.45	3

A subsequent analysis of weekly program schedules as reported in January 1966 reflects the following percentage breakdown of total broadcasting time (two hundred and thirty-nine hours) for all three operations, with programs classified somewhat differently by a professor at the University of Athens:[15]

1. *Spoken word broadcasts*
   (a) News-current events   9.50 percent
   (b) Cultural   2.40
   (c) Drama   2.10
   (d) Children's and school
        broadcasts   1.50
2. *Musical programs*
   (a) Greek music   28.00
   (b) Serious music   20.50
   (c) Foreign light music   26.00
3. *Variety*   7.00

The Ministry of Education cooperates in the preparation of school programs which are carried over the national network. This instruction, including history, mythology, folklore and physics, is broadcast regularly three times per week.

In addition to carrying the network offerings from Athens, affiliated stations originate some programs, mainly music and literary and historical discussions.

From time to time, foreign language courses have been broadcast by the HNBI. Series in English and French have been made available by the British Broadcasting Corporation in London and the *Radio Télévision Française* in Paris and have been popular with Greek listeners.[16]

Through its "Voice of Greece," the HNBI transmits via short-wave from its Athens studios for about seventy hours per week programs designed for countries in the Near and Middle East, the Balkans and Western Europe. The programs, presented in Greek, French, English, Turkish, Serbian, Albanian, Bulgarian, Rumanian and Russian, consist largely of music and news, with some special broadcasts (for example, church services) for ships at sea.

The Armed Services Radio stations emphasize news and popular music. Greek folk music with wide appeal gets a large play in the general programming. While the stations generally prepare their own broadcasts, they do make regular use of news and other types of taped programs prepared in the Armed Services studios in Athens.

The programs of the private commercial stations consist mainly of news bulletins and popular music with occasional informational broadcasts, including historical, literary and religious discussions of local interest.

Recent statistical reports indicate that eighty-eight percent of the families in Athens and seventy percent in Salonica listen regularly to radio broadcasts. Forty-four percent of the listeners prefer the National Program, fifty-two percent the Second Program, and four percent the Third.[17]

Political Broadcasting

POLITICAL broadcasting in Greece is a problem which deserves special mention. Section 15, sub-section 1 of the Act governing broadcasting provides that "the Institute is obliged to transmit government communications and those arising out of general or special decisions of the Minister to the Prime Minister's Office." However, as Professor Koumantos has pointed out, the "politicization" does not stop here:

> The legal nature of the director-general's function, whereby he is allowed to plan programmes free of any supervision either from the Administrative Council or another body which might be called upon to ensure the political impartiality of the radio and especially its news broadcasts, is another factor which confers on Greek broadcasting the "governmental" character with which it has been burdened ever since its inception under a dictatorial regime in 1937. The opposition parties protest against this, but their protests are forgotten as soon as they come to power. It seems as if the broadcast eulogy is too attractive a weapon for the governing party to do without. The malady is chronic and the variations only quantitative, depending on the mentality of the particular government and the tact of the director-general in office.[18]

FM and Television Broadcasting

As of January 1966, frequency modulation broadcasting and television had not yet been initiated on a regular basis. The Institute was broadcasting experimental television programs, consisting largely of films, in Athens two hours per week. The transmitter and studios, built by HNBI technicians, are located in Athens. The low-power facility is used mainly for training personnel.

In the late fifties, the Government considered using the fifteen million dollars in war reparations paid by Italy to establish television stations.[19] Bids for the construction of facilities were invited but in view of critical financial needs in other important areas, the Government decided, for the time being, against the expenditure of money for television construction.

In 1953, experimental television was carried on briefly in Athens by private interests. That year, bids for construction of stations were invited by the Government, and the Director of the Institute reported that the Government had decided to erect a network of seventeen television stations which would serve four-fifths of the Greek population. He further reported that the Government had announced that a FM network would be installed, that two new one hundred kilowatt short-wave transmitters would be put in operation, and that a center which would house all radio and television services in Athens was to be built. It was stated that the project was to be developed in two stages and would cost up to thirty million dollars.[20] As of February 1966, contracts for the construction of these new facilities had not been made, and the outlook for FM and television was still uncertain.

NOTES

1. *Elliniki Radiofonia*, Radio Karayanni, Athens, 1952. Much of this early history of Grecian radio is based upon translations of this book.
2. As of January 1968, one drachma was equivalent to 3.4 cents.
3. *Journal of Government*, No. 581, November 20, 1935, Athens.
4. *Ibid.*, No. 95, 1936.
5. *Ibid.*, No. 63, May 17, 1943.
6. *Ibid.*
7. G. A. Koumantos, "Broadcasting in Greece," *EBU Review*, 95B, January 1966, p. 53.
8. *Ibid.*, p. 56.
9. *EBU Bulletin*, January–February 1957, pp. 53–54.
10. Based upon discussions the author had with government officials in Athens in March 1965.
11. *EBU Review*, 95B, January 1966, p. 56.
12. *Ibid.*, p. 55.
13. *Ibid.*, 56B, July 1959, pp. 19, 20.
14. *Ibid.*, 95B, January 1966, p. 56.
15. *Ibid.*
16. *Ibid.*, 75B, September 1962, p. 14.
17. *Ibid.*, 95B, January 1966, p. 56.
18. *Ibid.*, p. 57.
19. United States Information Agency, Research and Reference Service, *Greece: A Communications Fact Book*, November 19, 1962.
20. *EBU Review*, 79B, May 1963, p. 32.

· F ·

THE MIDDLE
EUROPEAN COUNTRIES

XVII

Germany: Cultural
and Political Conflicts

ERMANY, with an estimated population of more than seventy-five
million, is presently comprised of two units: The Federal Republic
(West Germany) and the German Democratic Republic (East Germany). Since the Second World War, both areas have developed extensive broadcasting systems which are organized and controlled quite differently. In West Germany, the control is decentralized, residing largely in the various states *(Länder)*, whereas, in East Germany it is centered in agencies attached to the Council of Ministers.

Early Days of Radio

GERMAN scientists played an important role in the early development of radio communication. As early as 1887, toward the end of Bismarck's regime, Henrich Hertz, a physicist of Karlsruhe, demonstrated conclusively that electromagnetic waves could be transmitted through space and received at distant points.[1] Four years later a law was enacted giving the State the exclusive right to carry on both wire and wireless telegraph and telephone operation.[2] The German military establishment under William II was quick to realize the utility of wireless communications, particularly in naval operations.

To alleviate the problems of technical interference in the "ether," in 1906 Germany conducted a conference in Berlin. Twenty-seven countries were represented at the meeting and signed an international agreement regarding the allocation and use of electromagnetic waves for radio-telegraphy.[3]

The years leading up to the First World War were ones of experimentation. In 1913, scientists such as Dr. Hans Bredow had succeeded in transmitting music and speech via radio waves. And, at the beginning of the war in 1914, the Germans as well as the English were broadcasting entertainment programs to the troops on both sides of the western front.[4]

Postwar Years

AT the end of the First World War, Dr. Bredow, who had contributed so much to the technical development of radio, accepted the position as Chief of the Department of Wireless Communication, in the Ministry of Posts. Under his leadership broadcasting experienced tremendous growth during the next fifteen years.

With the establishment of the Weimar Republic, Bredow undertook to develop a "nonpolitical" broadcasting system. While he wanted to preserve the sovereign rights of the Government in broadcasting, he was eager to set up a structure that would be free of partisan influence. Accordingly, under his direction, the Ministry of Posts built the transmitters, but private companies were licensed to provide the programming. The system was financed by an annual tax on receivers and the revenue was about evenly divided between the Government and the private broadcasting companies.

The first license for broadcasting was granted in 1923 to the Radio Hour Company in Berlin. Eight additional companies were authorized to provide programs in 1924, with studios in Leipzig, Munich, Frankfurt, Hamburg, Stuttgart, Breslay, Konisberg and Cologne. These stations were conceived as regional nonpolitical operations, and the broadcasts of each were designed to serve the educational and cultural interests and needs of a particular area.

Appreciation for radio increased rapidly and by the end of 1925, about one million receivers had been licensed for use in Germany. As the industry expanded, the importance of radio as an informational medium and its impact upon public opinion were being increasingly realized by both the Federal and Provincial Governments. A national broadcasting company was established in 1926 in which the Ministry of Posts held fifty-one percent of the stock, with the remainder held by private interests. This company established a station in Berlin with programs designed for nation-wide reception. It also assumed economic control of all broadcasting stations in the Republic. Regional Governments appointed so-called "cultural committees" to advise on programming. Also, since the Federal regulations specified that broadcasting could serve no political parties, a "supervisory committee" of three members (one representing the Federal Government and the other two the region) was appointed to scrutinize program content and prohibit the broadcast of any material believed to be of partisan character. News was provided by DRADAG, a company in which the Federal Government held the majority of the stock.

The Rise of the Third Reich

WHILE the "supervisory committees" were insuring that no political messages were emanating from the radio stations, the National Socialist Party, under the leadership of Hitler, was using every promotional means possible and was fast gaining popular favor. The Party zealously strove for the centralized control of all broadcast media for the propagation of its revolutionary doctrines. In 1932, an important move in this direction was made when the Papen Government appointed a "second commissioner" to work with Dr. Bredow, who had been appointed as the first Commissioner of Broadcasting in the Ministry of Posts in 1926. This new Commissioner was responsible for political broadcasting, for news and for all program exchanges. The supervisory committees in the provinces were replaced by national commissars. While the controlling stock of the national broadcasting company was retained by the Ministry of Posts, private investors were compelled to sell their stock to the *Land* Governments which were increasingly the puppets of the Federal Government.

On January 30, 1933, Hitler was appointed Chancellor. One month later Dr. Joseph Goebbels, who was soon to become the Minister of Propaganda, wrote in his diary:

> I talk over the beginning election campaign in detail with the Leader. The struggle is a light one now, since we are able to employ all means of the State. Radio and Press are at our disposal. We shall achieve a masterpiece of propaganda. Even money is not lacking this time.
>
> The only difficulty lies in the organization of the contest. We decide that the Leader is to speak in all towns having their own broadcasting station. We transmit the broadcast to the entire people, and give listeners a clear idea of all that occurs at our meetings. . . .
>
> The Radio causes me some trouble. All the important positions are still held by the same old-System profiteers. They have to be got rid of as soon as possible, that is before the fifth of March, lest they endanger the election.
>
> The Propaganda Department of the Reich is moving to Berlin, in order to be able to direct the contest with all its forces concentrated.[5]

And, on March 1, Goebbels was ready to purge the Radio staff:

> I am just about to take over the vast sphere of the Radio. I shall have to get rid of many of the inefficient members of the staff. Essential reconstruction must be carried out, especially in the personnel of the management. Final decisions will be taken about this matter once the elections are over.[6]

The election of March 5 was a victory for the Nazis. Out of about thirty million votes cast, the Nazis received about seventeen million (forty-four percent). Each of the other four parties received from three to seven million. Although the Nazis had a plurality, the election was far from a mandate for Hitler. Three days later, Goebbels had completed plans for his Ministry to be made up of the following departments: Press, Film and Radio Propaganda, and Theatre. He was sworn in as Minister of Propaganda on March 14 and, in accordance with pre-election plans, he proceeded immediately to fill many important posts in the departments with National Socialists.

Before the year had ended, all the provincial radio companies had been dissolved and the National Government had taken over all radio facilities in the country with Dr. Goebbels and his Ministry in complete charge of broadcast operations. The Post Office Department continued to collect the taxes on receivers; the Ministry of Propaganda used fifty-five percent of the proceeds to finance its work.[7]

All broadcast programs, without exception, were designed to promote the aims of the Third Reich. The schedules were loaded with biased and often false news reports, propaganda exhortations and broadcasts of huge political rallies, with frenzied crowds exclaiming *"ein Volk, ein Reich, ein Führer."* Entertainment programs—music, comedy, drama—were all adapted to the service of "national will building." Only the music of the German masters such as Beethoven and Wagner was broadcast, while the works of composers such as Mendelssohn were strictly prohibited.[8]

Not only did the Ministry of Propaganda strictly limit and control what the people could hear on German stations, but at the beginning of the war in September 1939, the Ministry forbade listening to any broadcasts emanating from foreign stations. Any "clandestine" listening was made subject to severe penalties.[9]

As the German Wehrmacht invaded the countries of Europe, the broadcasting stations of each country were taken over and became largely relay facilities for the propaganda messages emanating from the Ministry of Propaganda in Berlin. Before the war ended, Dr. Goebbels and the Nazi war machine controlled a large part of the communications apparatus in both Western and Eastern Europe. Toward the end of hostilities, as the Nazis withdrew from the countries which they had taken over—Luxembourg, Belgium, Czechoslovakia, to mention only a few—they destroyed many of the radio installations in these countries as part of their "scorched earth" policy. Germany suffered greatly from Allied attacks, but surprisingly enough, much of the broadcasting system in Berlin—housing, transmitters and towers—remained intact, and was quickly converted to peacetime uses after the war.

Postwar Developments

IN 1945, the Allies took possession of the broadcasting facilities in Germany. Zone commanders were in charge while Germany recovered from the

Nazi collapse. General Lucius O. Clay, in November 1947, stated that the U.S. military administration favored the wide distribution of the print and broadcast media and freedom from government control.[10] This was the pattern which evolved in West Germany and which characterizes its operation today.

After the withdrawal of the occupation forces in 1948–49 and the dissolution of the High Commission which exercised control over broadcasting until 1955, the Federal Republic of Germany assumed the responsibility for broadcasting.

Henning Wicht, the Director of Sound Broadcasting, *Hessischer Rundfunk,* stated in the *EBU Review* for March 1963:

> The German radio service's present organizational structure was developed in the years immediately after the war, from 1945 onwards. The people whose duty it was to prepare a fresh start in broadcasting after the end of the Hitler dictatorship still had a vivid recollection of the way in which this important medium of mass communication had been debased by the National Socialists into a political tool of the totalitarian state and misused for propaganda purposes. They accordingly strove from the outset—and with some measure of success—to safeguard broadcasting against any possibility of being exploited either by the government or by political and business interests for purposes of their own. On the strength of this policy there were established in the various federal Länder (sometimes by several Länder acting in concert) the Norddeutscher Rundfunk (Hamburg), the Westdeutscher Rundfunk (Cologne), the Hessischer Rundfunk (Frankfurt), the Südwestfunk (Baden-Baden), the Suddeutscher Rundfunk (Stuttgart), the Bayerischer Rundfunk (Munich), the Sender Freies Berlin in West Berlin and Radio Bremen; later, when the Saar territory was reincorporated in the Federal Republic, the Saarlandischer Rundfunk joined the list.

> All these purveyors of broadcasting services in the Federal Republic and West Berlin are *Anstalten des öffentlichen Rechts,* the English equivalent of which is chartered corporations; thus they are neither government agencies nor private companies, a fact which has been of decisive importance for their programming up to the present time and will continue to be in the future.

> The broadcasting corporations in the Federal Republic are consequently independent of the government and of any social pressure groups. This of course does not prevent them from giving appropriate opportunities to the Federal Government, the Land Governments and naturally the Opposition as well to expound their views, explain their measures and thereby utilize the potentialities of sound broadcasting for the formation of enlightened public opinion.[11]

Present Administrative Structure

EACH broadcasting system in West Germany elects a general director *(Intendant),* who is responsible for its overall operation. He is aided by a board of directors usually composed of seven to nine men, with some elected by the local broadcast council[12] and others holding membership on the board by virtue of public office, such as a chief justice of a state court or members of a state legislature. The general director usually appoints the administrative staff—director of personnel, technical and financial officers, and program directors.

These chartered broadcasting corporations are loosely banded together in an association, *Arbeitsgemeinschaft der Öffentlich-rechtlichen Rund-funkanstalten der Bundes-republik Deutschland* (ARD), an alliance established in August 1950. The ARD provides a mechanism for cooperation among the state systems in programming, technical and legal matters. Mr. Wicht has described its main functions:

> The ARD's chief interest in matters of programming is to achieve a rational coordination of their programmes, since in many parts of West Germany their effective reception areas overlap. Questions of programme exchanges are discussed and arrangements made for joint cultural or sporting transmissions such as relays from festivals or live broadcasts from Olympic games and world football championships in the regular conferences of the programme directors. In the technical field the ARD has done the bulk of the work for the coordinated establishment and extension of the West German network of transmitters both in sound broadcasting and in television, and it also conducts a common programme of research and development activities.[13]

Through ARD, the members cooperate in legal matters, in the financing of overall operation and in other areas where common interests will be served. For example, for a number of years the members have maintained a revenue adjustment contract. The effect is that corporations having smaller receipts because of a lower population density in their fee-collection areas receive supplementary grants-in-aid from the richer ones.

While there is some cooperation among the members, the largest part of broadcasting is done independently by the state corporations, since the Constitution of the Federal Republic stipulates that the *Länder* are responsible for cultural affairs. Broadcasting has been judicially construed to fall within this category.

The importance which these state corporations attach to their independence was explained by Franz Reinholz of *Norddeutscher Rundfunk* at the International Conference of Broadcasting Organizations on Sound and Television School Broadcasting, held in Rome in 1961. He stated that although the broadcasting companies of West Germany are represented in the European Broadcasting Union through ARD, and although they have interests in common, they are independent in their operations.

> I come from Hamburg where today my colleagues are meeting to decide on the programmes for the fourth and fifth week in 1962. The colleagues in Stuttgart or Munich or in any other of the broadcasting stations do not have the slightest idea of the programmes being broadcast today in Hamburg.

There is no such thing as a common policy. This may seem rather extraordinary to you. For this reason I would therefore like to say to you that we are very proud of this profound difference that there is between us and that we shall defend it bitterly against every attack. The memory of the broadcasting company of the Reich, that was an expedient of the Minister dealing with Propaganda, Josef Goebbels, is still much too vivid to us. And we also remember that this rigidly centralized organization of the German Radio was an exceptionally efficient instrument of the German dictatorship. And this centralized radio, moreover, carries a large portion of the responsibility of the catastrophe that, starting from Germany, involved the whole world. Do not shake your head therefore if we of the German Radio do not insist on what we have in common but on what divides us. We have had our lesson and we defend our Federation bitterly against any influence on the part of the central power. So long as we carry on like this, we deserve your approval.[14]

Radio Programming

EACH German station broadcasts a first and second program. An attempt is made to appeal to different interests and provide a balanced program structure. For example, if light music is featured on one network, there is likely to be something of a more serious nature on the other. In fact, the tendency has been to earmark one program for the majority audience and the other for the minority, one being more general and entertaining in format, and the other more specialized and appealing to cultivated tastes.

A few of the larger systems provide a third program. For example, special broadcasts of *Bayerischer Rundfunk* (Munich) and *Westdeutscher Rundfunk* (Cologne) plus a joint transmission of *Norddeutscher Rundfunk* (Hamburg) and *Sendes Freies* (Berlin) provide a third service, which presents programs with intellectual appeal, featuring outstanding scientists, dramatists and writers.

A large component of the schedules of West German stations consists of music, both classical and popular. Numerous music festivals, including German jazz, are broadcast. Each of the corporations maintains its own symphony orchestra, with outstanding conductors and soloists.

Radio plays still attract large audiences, although they admittedly are competing with television drama with its added optical dimension. Added to these are programs dealing with literature, art and current affairs.[15]

Educational Radio

A GREAT deal of school broadcasting is carried on by the various state systems. The ministers for public education in the various *Länder* work only as advisors to planning instructional broadcasts. The companies' script writers and other programming personnel, who consult with these officials and with teachers, determine the content and format of instructional transmissions. Special series of broadcasts for the schools have included instruction in science, history, language and public affairs. School broadcasts such as "A Continent in the Making," a study of Africa, broadcast by *Hesischer Rundfunk,* frequently appear in the program schedules.

It has been estimated that roughly one-half of the corporations' broadcast time is devoted to "instructive and educational" programs, including those dealing with public affairs and those designed to influence public opinion.[16]

Foreign Broadcasting

Since more than ninety percent of the population in East Germany is able to hear three or more programs from the Federal Republic, all the state systems in the West devote considerable time to programs counteracting the propaganda broadcast from the communist regime in the East. In addition, programs are beamed across national boundaries by *Deutschlandfunk* and *Deutsche Welle,* two stations licensed to corporations established under Federal law. *Deutschlandfunk* is a long-wave station whose function is to "arrange broadcasts for (East) Germany and the other countries of Europe and in this way to present a comprehensive picture of Germany to listeners in other continental countries."[17] It gives special attention to the preparation of programs for reception in the German Democratic Republic, "in order to set up a truthful picture of life in the Federal Republic to counteract the slanted propaganda put out by the state-run communist radio in that zone."[18]

The *Deutsche Welle* provides a short-wave service for overseas listeners. It broadcasts programs in German and other languages to the Far, Near and Middle East, Africa and the Americas.

Television

The British occupation forces permitted *Norddeutscher Rundfunk* (Hamburg) to begin experimental television in 1948. In December 1952, this corporation put two TV transmitters in operation in Cologne and Hannover. And, in March 1953, the ARD initiated plans by which individual member stations could share time and facilities.

Until recently, only two television programs were broadcast: the First, *Deutsches Fernsehen* (DFS), a so-called "pool" program on VHF, and the Second, *Zweites Deutsches Fernsehen* (ZDF), broadcast by an autonomous public corporation established in April 1963. This second program is financed by a thirty percent levy on license fees collected by the regional broadcasting organizations.

Both these programs are carried on nation-wide networks and are jointly produced by the nine state corporations, through the Association of Broadcasting Corporations (ARD). Each of the stations contributes programs in terms of its income from license fees on receivers within the area it serves. As reported in 1964, the percentage contributions to the two television networks were roughly as follows: *Westdeutscher Rundfunk* (Cologne) twenty-two and one-half; *Norddeutscher Rundfunk* (Hamburg) twenty-two and one-half; *Bayerischer Rundfunk* (Munich) seventeen; and *Hessischer Rundfunk* (Frankfurt), *Süddeutscher Rundfunk* (Stuttgart) and *Sender Freies* (Berlin), each eight percent. Radio Bremen and *Saarländischer Rundfunk* are entitled to contribute as much as three percent each if they desire to do so.[19]

According to a UNESCO survey in 1964, television programs were being transmitted about forty-five hours per week. About twenty-five percent of the time was given over to news and discussion programs. Sports occupied more than twelve percent; plays, films and light entertainment took up more than thirty percent; special broadcasts for women and children accounted for fifteen percent; Eurovision had ten percent; and religious programs had one percent.

A third television program was initiated in 1964 in the states of Bavaria and Hesse. In September of that year, Bavaria's *Bayerischer Rundfunk* began its "study programs," complementing the teaching already being done on the second network. These programs consisted of daily telecasts (Sundays excluded) with instruction in such subjects as science, political economy, music and languages. Programs of general cultural import included "Education and Society," "Ancient Greek Civilization," discussions of the basis and background of German politics and a variety of scientific and literary programs.

In Hesse, a third program which began about the same time had as its aim, as stated by *Hessischer Rundfunk,* the broadcasting of programs for "qualified" minorities and courses in adult education. It was proposed that programs would fall into three categories: (1) those dealing with regional affairs; (2) special instruction for adults such as courses in Russian, mathematics and modern art; and (3) programs with special appeal, dealing with fine arts, medicine and agriculture.[20]

Egon Wagner, the legal adviser to the *Südwestfunk,* writing in the *EBU Review* of May 1965, predicted that this third program would soon be initiated by other companies and be available throughout the country. He stated that the programs would have a similar content and format throughout West Germany, but would be produced by the individual broadcasting organizations to meet the interests and needs of the different *Länder*. "In the news and information on cultural events, in the field of the documentaries as well as in the cultural programmes, it is intended to achieve what is described as a 'self-portrayal of the Land and its scenery.' "[21]

Financial Support for Broadcasting

ALL the broadcast corporations receive financial support from the license fees assessed against radio and television receivers (twenty-four Deutsch marks per year for radio and seventy-four for television).[22] These fees are collected by the Federal Post Office *(Bundespost)* which keeps a portion of the proceeds to cover costs of collection, to maintain lines and cable connections for the various stations, to detect unlicensed sets and insure that technical interference from the various transmissions is avoided. Each station receives a share of the license proceeds in accordance with the population of the state where the station is chartered.

In addition to license fees, all the radio and TV stations allocate some time for commercials (the average time is about eight percent). These commercials are presented in time blocks separate from the programs. They are prepared by subsidiary companies which determine their own budgets, take care of all sales and production costs, and reimburse the stations for the use of the technical facilities.[23]

Struggle for Media Control

As presently constituted, the Federal Government's authority with respect to television and radio is limited to the technical aspects of operation. Since the Second World War, it has not exercised any regulatory jurisdiction over programming. This authority has been taken over by the *Länder*. The broadcasting companies and their association, the ARD, have enjoyed much freedom and autonomy in their operations. However, in 1960 Chancellor Adenauer gave his blessing to the proposed establishment of a national television company and plans were announced for the beginning of a Federal nation-wide service on January 1, 1961. In August 1960, the Provincial Governments of Hesse and Hamburg protested that any such undertaking by the Federal Government would violate the basic law pertaining to broadcasting in the Republic and, among other things, infringe upon the rights of the provinces which, they alleged, had exclusive authority in the field of programming. They appealed to the Federal Constitutional Court for a decision. In the meantime, the Federal Government was temporarily enjoined from proceeding with plans for the construction of facilities pending a decision of the Court.[24]

On February 28, 1961, the Court handed down its decision, holding that the Federal Government, through the establishment of the German Television Company, had indeed violated the basic broadcasting law. Among the numerous reasons stated in support of its decision, the Court declared that freedom of information through radio and television was guaranteed by law and that control of the media should not be vested in one single authority or one social group. This halted any further attempt by the Federal Government to move into the broadcasting business and left the field open for the *Länder* and the existing corporations to expand their operations.

A recent campaign to break up the present pattern of control and operation has been launched by the newspapers in West Germany. Mr. Wagner has described the situation:

The fight of the newspaper publishers to gain access to television is being carried out in several rounds. We are still in the middle of the controversy, and the end seems a long way off. . . .

The Second German Television Programme would be entrusted to a company of newspaper publishers. It is true that the chartered corporation, the Zweites Deutsches Fernsehen, would remain as a cover, but the entire programme, according to this proposal, would be produced by the company of newspaper publishers and financed exclusively by means of advertising. . . .

The broadcasting organizations themselves, as well as the churches and the trade unions, have publicly protested against such a scheme. Eminent experts in constitutional law have pointed out that the implementation of such proposals was irreconcilable with the decision of principle reached by the Federal Constitutional Court in the well-known television dispute. The Federal Constitutional Court laid down in this decision that, in the first place, a broadcasting enterprise in the Federal Republic must have the form of its organization defined by legislation and that, on the other hand, broadcasting must not be entrusted to an individual economic or political group.

In the meantime, doubts have also been expressed in the political field. Access to television is chiefly sought by the Springer concern. The publishers of the smaller and medium newspapers are to a large extent uninterested. They know that they do not possess the financial means to become genuine business partners in a commercial television system. However, Springer has already achieved a concentration of power in the German press such as is without parallel in Germany: out of the total number of newspapers which are published in the Federal Republic (21.79 million copies), a good third, or to be exact, 36.35%, is controlled by the Springer concern. The breakdown is of interest in this connection. Of the daily newspapers with a more than regional circulation, amounting to a total of 4.8 million in the whole of the Federal Republic, 4.2 million are published by the Springer concern. . . .[25]

Mr. Wagner states that thirty-seven percent of the West Germans rely heavily upon the Springer press for news and says that "if they obtained the rest of their news over the television screen from the same source, this would create a monopoly of mass influential media without parallel, a monopoly which cannot be controlled or regulated, but would be exploited exclusively according to the principles of economics and power politics."[26]

On the other hand, the newspaper publishers take the position that they can provide a quality news service, that the overall programming will be better balanced, and that the income from advertising on television would make the newspaper business more financially secure. Some publishers look upon the commercials now carried by the corporation stations in the *Länder* as a competitive threat to newspapers which do not benefit from license fees but which must rely largely upon advertising revenue for their maintenance and survival.

In 1964 the Federal Parliament appointed a committee to determine whether there is "distorted competition between press and broadcasting and whether the economic existence of the newspapers is endangered by television advertising."[27] At the time of writing the issue had not yet been settled. Informed sources in Germany state that the committee was scheduled to make its report in October 1967. If and when Parliament does act on the Springer request, the matter probably will be reviewed by the High Court, as was the case when the Federal Government attempted to establish a competitive commercial television service.

Broadcasting in East Germany

WHEREAS the control and operation of broadcasting in West Germany after the war was decentralized among the various *Länder,* the opposite pattern was established in East Germany. All authority over radio and television was vested in the State Broadcasting Committee attached to the Council of Ministers, and the management and operation were modeled after the Soviet system.

According to UNESCO reports in 1964, there were at that time four domestic radio networks in East Germany. Equipment consisted of more than twenty long-, medium- and short-wave transmitters with a combined power of eighteen hundred kilowatts. More than twenty FM transmitters were in operation.[28]

A major part of the program schedules of the networks is devoted to music and news. The Broadcasting Committee maintains correspondents in Moscow, Peking, Warsaw, Prague, Budapest, Stockholm, Paris, London, Geneva, Cairo and Baghdad. Frequent news reports are presented on all the networks. As is true in other Eastern European countries, many programs are designed for farm and industrial workers and educational programs make up a heavy component of the schedules. This includes considerable propaganda broadcasting designed for listeners in West Germany.

The international section of East German Broadcasting is one of the most important. Programs for foreign listeners are broadcast more than thirty-five hours a day to Europe, the Near East, Africa and Latin America. These are transmitted in English, French, Danish, Italian, Arabic, German, Swedish, Spanish and Portuguese. UNESCO has reported that the Russian Military Administration operates a station in Potsdam which relays Radio Moscow to the German area twenty-four hours a day.[29]

The East German Broadcasting System is financed by license fees on receivers. The country has developed a sizable industry which produces most of the receiving sets which are sold and used.

Television

EXPERIMENTAL television was initiated in East Berlin in 1952 and regular telecasting, using a six hundred and twenty-five line system, began in 1954. Today, more than a dozen main stations and twice as many relay transmitters provide East Germany with television programs. In 1964, it was reported that television programs were being broadcast sixty-five hours per week. News and drama are emphasized, with many adaptations of plays and some original TV films featured regularly. Much time is devoted to school programs and adult education.[30]

East Germany is affiliated with Intervision and carries a large number of its programs. It also uses some Eurovision broadcasts on a highly selective basis.

East Germany manufactures its own TV transmitters and receivers and the number of receivers has greatly increased in recent years. As reported in March 1966, there were, as of the end of 1965, 3,216,421 licensed television receivers and 5,743,036 radio receivers. This was considerably less than in West Germany where there were 11,379,049 combined radio and TV sets in addition to 6,498,871 separate radio sets. It is interesting that more than one-third of the licenses for radio receivers and about twelve percent of those for TV receivers in East Germany were granted free of charge. In West Germany, however, only about eight percent of the separate radio and less than one percent of the joint radio and TV licenses were granted without charge.[31]

NOTES

1. Orrin E. J. Dunlap, *The Story of Radio* (New York: The Dial Press, 1935), pp. 21–22. Also, see Gunter Pipka, *Broadcasting and Politics (Rundfunk Und Politik), Funkhaus Hannover des Norddeutschen Rundfunks* (Hannover: 1961), p. 1.
2. Pipka.
3. *Ibid.*
4. *Ibid.,* p. 13.
5. Joseph Goebbels, *My Part in Germany's Fight* (Plymouth: The Mayflower Press, 1938), p. 211.
6. *Ibid.,* p. 223.
7. Pipka, p. 22.
8. *Ibid.,* pp. 22–23.
9. *Ibid.*
10. *Ibid.,* p. 23.
11. *EBU Review,* 78B, March 1963, p. 25.
12. These local councils consist of from sixteen to forty members who represent the audiences in the different areas. In some cases the members are chosen by the *Land* Parliaments; in others, by social institutions such as churches, schools, and workers' organizations. The councils advise on programming and approve the budgets of the broadcasting organizations.
13. *EBU Review,* 78B, March 1963, p. 26.
14. RAI, *Radiotelevisione Italiana, Proceedings of the International Conference of Broadcasting Organizations on Sound and Television School Broadcasting,* Rome, December 3–9, 1961, p. 88.
15. *EBU Review,* 78B, March 1963, pp. 25–26.
16. *Ibid.*
17. *Ibid.,* p. 27.
18. *Ibid.*
19. UNESCO, *World Communications: Press, Radio, Television, Film* (New York: UNESCO Publications Center, 1964), pp. 288–289.
20. *EBU Review,* 88B, November 1964, p. 43.
21. *Ibid.,* 91B, May 1965, p. 69.
22. As of January 1968, one Deutsch mark was equivalent to twenty-five cents.
23. *EBU Review,* 78B, March 1963, p. 27; also, see *Broadcasting in the Federal Republic,* news release published by *Hessischer Rundfunk,* Frankfurt, October 18, 1963, p. 4.
24. Pipka, p. 36.
25. *EBU Review,* 91B, May 1965, pp. 69–70.
26. *Ibid.*
27. *Ibid.*
28. UNESCO, *World Communications,* p. 291.
29. *Ibid.*
30. *Ibid.*
31. *EBU Review,* 96B, March 1966, p. 37.

XVIII

Austria: Compromise between Centralism and Federalism

FOLLOWING THE FIRST WORLD WAR, amateurs or "ham" operators played an important part in the technical development of radio in Austria. It was not until the early twenties, however, that broadcasting there got its start. The initial organization and operation are explained in part by the existing financial and political misfortunes.

Although some progress was being made, the country in the early twenties had by no means recovered from the ravages of the First World War. What had once been an Austro-Hungarian Empire with more than fifty million people was suddenly reduced to an area about the size of Scotland with a population less than that of London. In September 1924, the Financial Council of the League of Nations reported that "Austria was undoubtedly one of the countries of Europe which seemed nearest to ruin."[1]

The democratic republic which was formed after the war represented a compromise between centralism and federalism. The Constitution, which was adopted in 1920, reinforced this compromise by dividing legislative power between the Federal and the nine Provincial Governments.

Beginnings of Broadcasting

FROM the beginning, the postwar Government was faced with a critical financial situation. It was difficult enough for the country to secure food, housing and jobs for an impoverished people, let alone spend precious money to build radio stations, especially when most people viewed radio largely as a novelty without much promise of social value.[2]

Despite this, there were some who had faith in broadcasting's future as an educational and commercial medium and were willing to invest some capital to get it started. In 1923, the Ministry of Posts, Telegraph and Telephone authorized a private company to build a station and conduct experimental transmissions in Vienna. The station, Radio Hekaphon, although short-lived, awakened the public's interest, particularly in Vienna, in the entertainment and cultural values of radio programs.[3]

Following the Hekaphon experiments, a joint stock company was established in 1924 to broadcast on a regular basis in Vienna. The capital stock was held by the Federal and Provincial Governments and private interests, including an advertising agency, electric equipment companies, banks and other commercial concerns in Vienna.[4] This cooperative undertaking was a microcosm of Austrian society, in which both public and private interests combined their efforts and shared responsibility in the development of an enterprise intended to provide benefits to all the people.

The new company, *Osterreichische Radioverkehrs A. G.* (RAVAG), was granted a license by the Administration of Posts, Telegraph and Telephone (*Post-und Telegraphenverwaltung*), which had exercised regulatory jurisdiction over telecommunications and extended its authority to all wireless broadcast transmissions. The company was granted a monopoly in broadcasting and its license specified that the station should provide "news, weather forecasts and musical, literary, educational and children's programs."[5]

Pursuant to this requirement, some of the station's first programs included opera, live drama, orchestra concerts and sports, plus frequent news reports. To promote listener interest, the company published a magazine, *Radio Wien,* which reported regularly the program schedules of the station.

Facilities and Programs are Expanded

As A. Hartner has pointed out, "The programs, which had early been limited to a few hours a day, were extended, and prominent performers, whose attitude toward the new medium had originally been skeptical or even frankly negative, realized that broadcasting offered them opportunity to reach every individual and communicate intellectual and cultural treasures. The ranks of those who placed their intellectual, scientific, artistic or musical talents at the disposal of the new medium swelled constantly."[6] Interest in the programs increased rapidly; people bought many more receivers. It was evident that radio was destined to play an increasingly important part in the life of the nation.

During the next decade broadcasting facilities and service were extended and improved. As early as 1925, RAVAG was receiving and retransmitting programs from stations in other European countries. That same year, it inaugurated a regular series of adult education broadcasts and brought to its listeners a wider variety of entertainment programs.[7]

By 1935, a one hundred kilowatt transmitter had been constructed in Vienna. Transmitters had been installed in the provincial capitals, the PTT had completed the construction of cable links, and mobile transmitting units were in operation. Experiments in FM broadcasting were being conducted, and the station was broadcasting by remote control programs such as important athletic events and the Salzburg Festival.[8] A School of the Air had been instituted and more than seventeen hundred schools were using these instructional broadcasts.[9] The amount of programming on the station had been increased to sixteen hours per day.[10] In 1924, the number of registered radio sets was about thirteen thousand; by 1934, the number had increased to five hundred thousand.[11]

The broadcasting operations of RAVAG from the beginning had been financed by private capital and by receipts from the license fees on radio sets collected by the Government. To supplement this income, *Radio Wien,* in April 1937, began accepting paid announcements. To attract advertisers, the station established a special department to produce entertainment programs with wide listener appeal. By 1938, a national network had been established with transmitters located in the provincial capitals, and the new *Funkhaus* in Vienna, one of the finest broadcasting centers in Europe, was ready for occupancy.[12]

The War Years

BUT progress was interrupted. In the first official broadcast of RAVAG in Vienna fifteen years before, the then Chancellor of Austria had expressed the hope that the new medium "would promote international understanding and peace and open the way for freer communication among the people of the world." Little did he realize that a few years later, quite the opposite would be true—that not only in Austria but throughout much of Europe, access to the microphone would be largely limited to the Nazis and their agents and radio would become an instrument for the promotion of international strife and war. Hitler and his armies moved into Austria and seized the just completed broadcasting house. RAVAG was dissolved and the technical facilities of the Vienna station and its network were taken over by the German postal authorities and made a part of the Reich broadcasting system.[13] Radio in Austria became a military and propaganda medium.

Toward the end of the war in 1945, the Vienna *Funkhaus* was hit by bombs. Fortunately, however, most of the important studios and transmitting facilities survived and were available for use when the war was over.

Postwar Developments

AFTER the war, the control of broadcasting was decentralized and vested in the Allies. Prior to the war, the management had been exercised by one company; it was now distributed among the various *Länder,* with the British, French, Americans and Russians exercising supervision in different zones.

In accordance with the Austrian law known as the *Verwaltergesetz,* the Government set up in Vienna the *Oeffentliche Verwaltung* (Public Administration).[14] At first, the *Oeffentliche Verwaltung fuer das Oesterrichische Rundspruchivesen* functioned only in the Vienna zone with the Russians in command, but eventually its jurisdiction was extended to broadcasting in other zones: *Sendergruppe West* (Tyrol and Vorarlberg) in the French zone; *Sendergruppe Rot-Weiss-Rot* (Salzburg and Upper Austria) in the American zone; and *Sendergruppe Alpenland* (Carinthia and Styria) in the British area. Studios were constructed in each division so that each broadcasting system could produce its own programs. License fees imposed on all owners and receivers were collected by the postal authorities and divided among the various stations in accordance with the number of registered sets in each zone.

In 1945, the transmitters in the various provinces were joined together in a network for the broadcasting of a national program. Shortly thereafter, a second program, emphasizing broadcasts with an aesthetic appeal, was instituted. The establishment of a new School of the Air followed in February 1946.[15]

The extension of the program facilities and services demanded additional finances. The Government, therefore, authorized an increase in the license fees on radio sets. Commercial broadcasting, which had been discontinued during the war, was reinstituted to provide additional income.[16]

A report of *Radio Wien* on April 1, 1950, indicated the types of programs, as classified by the station, carried on Vienna I and Vienna II (First and Second Programmes) during 1949, together with the percentage of time devoted to each type:[17]

Type of Program	Percentage
Music	
Serious	10
Light	42.2
Science	8.7

Type of Program	Percentage
Literature	
Plays	2
Talks	4.3
Russian Hour	6.3
News	6.3
Communiques	6
Gruss an Dich	4.3
Official broadcasts	2.4
Advertisements	1.1
Social Gossip	1
Sports	0.9
Commentaries	0.7
Vienna–Paris	0.5
Chain of Happiness	0.2
Miscellaneous	3.3

About this time there was a resurgence of interest in educational broadcasting for the schools. In May 1949, the national School Broadcasting Committee formed a working group in each of the Austrian states to develop radio for classroom use. By the end of the year, five hundred and seventy-six school broadcasts had been presented and eighteen hundred schools had made regular use of these broadcasts.[18]

Communications Act Adopted

UNDER the supervision of the occupying powers, the Government had been regulating broadcasting in accordance with the earlier statutes relating to postal service and telecommunications which had been adopted before broadcasting had achieved such large dimensions. New legislation was needed. On July 13, 1949, the Parliament passed the Communications Act giving the Federal Government jurisdiction over wire and wireless communication, and specifically including broadcasting. The new law authorized the Government to grant licenses for broadcasting stations and to regulate the operation of all technical facilities for "the transmission, and reception of signals, scripts, pictures, sound waves or communications of any kind, be it wire or wireless, by optical means or any other electromagnetic system."[19]

The Act specified that the Federal Ministry of Transportation and Communications was to determine the conditions for granting licenses. It was further provided that the fees for such licenses would be set by that same Ministry and the Federal Ministry of Finance.

The Federal Government was authorized to take action to prevent interference among stations and to close down temporarily or permanently, or curtail the use of, any broadcasting operations, if, in the opinion of the Government, the public interest required and if appropriate compensation was paid to the owners of the facilities for any losses incurred.

The law stated that regulatory jurisdiction over all broadcasting stations was to be vested in the Federal Ministry of Transportation and Communications. The Director-General of the Postal and Telegraph Administration of this Ministry and its regional offices were to enforce the regulations regarding the issuance and revocation of licenses, operational requirements, license fees and the use tax on receivers.

Included in the statute were the usual prohibitions against broadcasts which might endanger the security of the State or which were contrary to law, or which might unduly disturb the peace or offend public morality. The Ministry was empowered to assess prescribed penalties for violation of the regulations or for the nonpayment of fees.

During the early fifties, as the occupying powers gradually relaxed their hold on broadcasting, moves were made to establish a national, unified system. A national radio advisory committee representing the various provinces continued working with the Director-General to develop plans for an integrated service.

Since there was a legal question as to whether, under the Constitution, the Federal or the Provincial Governments had regulatory jurisdiction over broadcasting, a petition was filed by one of the Provincial Governments with the Austrian Constitutional Court, requesting adjudication of the matter. On October 5, 1954, the Court decided in favor of the Federal Government.[20] All the provinces turned over their broadcasting facilities to the Federal Government, thus completing the unification of the service in Austria.

The Establishment of the Austrian Radio Company

THE Austrian State Treaty was concluded in May 1955, and after a brief period of interim operation, the National Cabinet assumed the control of broadcasting. In July 1957, a limited liability company, *Osterreichischer Rundfunk Gesellschaft, M. b. H.,* was created, and all responsibilities for radio and television were transferred to this organization.[21]

The Company began with a capitalization of 82.2 million schillings, eighty million of which came from the Federal Government and 2.2 million from the provinces.[22] The voting shareholders consisted of the Chancellor, the Vice-Chancellor, the Minister of Education and the Minister of Transport and Electricity, all representing the Federal Government, and a representative from each of the provinces.[23]

On December 28, 1957, the Director-General of the Postal Administration granted a license to the new Company. Four days later the control of all broadcasting in Austria was transferred from the Public Administration to this licensee, thus ending a transitional period of multiple and undefined authority and technical difficulties which had existed since the reconstitution of the Republic in 1945.[24]

As prescribed in paragraph two of the charter, the purpose of the new organization was threefold: (1) to prepare and disseminate radio and television programs of all kinds, including news, destined for reception by the general public; (2) establish and operate recording and taping installations; (3) establish and operate radio and television transmission and receiving facilities.

At the founders' day meeting on December 11, 1957, the principals representing the Federal Government and the states of Burgenland, Carinthia, Lower Austria, Upper Austria, Salzburg, Styria, Tirol, Vorarlberg and Vienna unanimously approved the following program directives for the operation of the Company:

1. The broadcasts of Osterreichischer Rundfunk were to be arranged "independently and responsibly in the spirit of democracy," showing regard for the interests of Austria as well as other countries. Moreover, these broadcasts were not to serve unilaterally any one political party or organization, any special interest group, any religious group or any particular ideology. All programs were required to conform as far as possible "to the desires of the radio and television listeners" and "advocate peace and social justice."
2. Broadcasts were specifically prohibited which would contravene basic constitutional rights or run contrary to law and social order. Also prohibited were broadcasts which would endanger domestic or international security, or which would grossly offend decency and good taste.

As constituted, the organization consisted of a General Assembly of shareholders representing the Federal Government and the nine provinces, a Board of Control elected by the Assembly, various directors and sixteen departments to carry on the work.

Furthermore, a national advisory committee was established to assist the Board and its staff. As set up, the committee consisted of forty-eight members representing the Federal Government, the provinces, Catholic and Protestant churches, the Ministry of Education, the universities, adult education groups, the Austrian Trade Union Federation, and chambers of commerce, agriculture and labor.

Thus a national autonomous agency was created. The Company was granted a broadcasting license by the Ministry of Communications and Electric Power on December 19, 1957, with exclusive jurisdiction over broadcasting, but so constituted as to give broad representation to the Federal Government, to all Provincial Governments, and to a wide variety of private groups, both commercial and noncommercial.

Broadcasting Growth Continues

PRIOR to the creation of this Company, the program exchange among the various networks had been expanded, regular FM broadcasting had been initiated, and experimental short-wave transmissions were being carried on. *Osterreichischer Rundfunk* continued this expansion program. New studios and transmitting facilities were provided to establish more complete and effective service. Network facilities were extended.

More variety in programming and special features excited the interest of radio listeners. For example, in 1958, the world champion skiing matches in Bad Gastein were broadcast to eager sport fans throughout the nation. The Olympic Games in Squaw Valley and Rome in 1960 were carried by the network. The Krushchev-Kennedy meeting in Vienna in June 1961, was transmitted for world-wide reception. Other important national and international events were broadcast over facilities which, by the end of 1962, consisted of a number of high-powered transmitters in the vicinity of some of the larger cities in Austria. Programs spanned the nation and were heard by about seven million people in more than two million households.

Present Radio Facilities and Programs

STUDIO facilities are now located in Vienna, Graz, Klagenfurt, Linz, Salzburg, Tirol and Vorarlberg. In December 1964, the broadcast facilities had been increased to include eighty-three medium-wave transmitters with a total power of 686.1 kilowatts, twenty-eight FM transmitters with a total power of 745.6 kilowatts and nine short-wave installations with a combined power of 75.2 kilowatts. Three national programs were being broadcast simultaneously, two on medium-wave and one on FM.

Radio Vienna, which emanates a large number of programs carried by the national network, has expanded its schedules to include more than two hundred and seventy-six hours of programming per week. A large number of its broadcasts are carried by the provincial stations and can be heard by more than eighty percent of the nation's population. As recently classified and reported by the Austrian Broadcasting Company, the allocation for the various types of programs on the medium-wave stations is:

Classical music	13 percent
Light, popular music	53
News	12
Educational (general)	3

School broadcasts	2
Advertising	4
Miscellaneous	13

The fortieth anniversary report shows that about sixty-one percent of all the national network programs are produced in the Vienna studios, with the remainder fairly equally divided among the provincial stations.

In 1964, there were more than two million registered radio receivers in Austria. With a population of about seven million, it appears that radio has reached the saturation point.

A short-wave service has been operating since 1955. It is beamed to Europe, North and South America, the Near East, India, Japan, Australia and North and South Africa.

Television

TELEVISION started comparatively late in Austria. During the early fifties there were some sporadic experiments. Toward the end of 1954, the Government made a grant of forty-five million schillings for experimentation. Subsequently, this was supplemented by a grant of about ten million.[25] In 1955, the first TV studio and transmitter in Vienna were constructed and began experimental telecasts. In January 1957, *Oesterreichischer Rundfunk* initiated regular service, transmitting programs six days per week.[26]

With the signing of the Austrian State Treaty and the restoration of freedom to the nation, the TV facilities were expanded rapidly. During the next decade, transmitters were built in Graz, Jauerling, Innsbruck, Vorarlberg and Linz, and regular transmissions were extended to seven days per week. Commercials were introduced on January 1, 1959.[27] At the beginning, these were limited to short spot announcements, arranged in time blocks during the evening hours, and separated from the programs.

A second program was introduced. Austria became a member of Eurovision and televised to the world programs of international interest such as the Salzburg Festival, the Kennedy-Khruschev meeting in Vienna and the Olympic Games in Innsbruck. In July 1962, moving pictures of the famous Spanish Riding School in Vienna were carried via Telstar and seen by millions of television viewers in many parts of the world.

Today, there is one originating TV station in Vienna providing that city with two programs on Channels 5 and 24. Twelve other channels serve the other areas. Eleven relay stations and about forty-eight converters make it possible to provide good coverage for the First Programme to about seventy-five percent of the nation and coverage approaching fifty percent for the Second Programme. All TV programs in Austria are produced in the Vienna studios and relayed to the country by the network facilities.

The six hundred and twenty-five line system is used. As of June 1965, the First Programme was transmitting eleven and one-half hours per week, and the Second Programme, eleven hours. The First Programme, as a general rule, begins at half past six in the evening and concludes about eleven, depending on the length of the final broadcast for the day. Exceptions are the school programs and special telecasts for adults who work in the evening which are presented during the morning and afternoon hours. On Saturdays and Sundays, there are special programs for children starting at half past four in the afternoon.

The Second Programme, which is broadcast on Tuesday, Wednesday, Friday and Saturday evenings, consists largely of "repeats" of program material carried on the First Programme, including films and kinescopes. The stress in general is on programming with an intellectual and aesthetic appeal.

Television plays are an important part of the First Programme. For reasons of economy, the Austrian stations cooperate with the stations in West Germany and Switzerland in the production of drama. Also, Austrian Television is provided with tape recordings and films produced by *Telepool G. m. b. H.,* a company founded by *Bayerischer Rundfunk, Osterreichischer Rundfunk* and *Schweizerische Fundspruchgesellschaft,* with main offices in Munich.

The First Programme also includes many discussions of national and international affairs. Eminent personalities are regularly featured on these programs.

Special attention is given to the telecasting of important sports events, and as a member of Eurovision, Austrian Television frequently receives and transmits live athletic contests of national and international interest.

According to a 1964 report, about twenty percent of the total time on television is devoted to news, more than eleven percent to "youth and family" programs and about two percent to popular educational and cultural broadcasts. *Forty Years of Broadcasting in Austria* shows a variety of types: programs dealing with traffic problems, hints on cooking, cabaret shows, debates and panel discussions dealing with controversial subjects of public importance, all sorts of athletic events, including boxing, skiing, weight lifting and football, to mention only a few.

Financing

THE operation of *Osterreichischer Rundfunk,* including both radio and television, is financed from a number of sources. In 1964, the organization's total income was 60,311,000 schillings, 22,557,000 of which was radio revenue and 37,754,000 television revenue. More than sixty-three percent of the total income was derived from the annual license fees on radio and TV receivers. Twenty percent of the money from these fees (now seven schillings per month for radio and fifty for television) goes to the Administration of Posts for collection expenses.[28] Radio and TV advertising provided 28.9 percent of the Company's 1964 income. Receipts from loans amounted to 2.9 percent. The Government granted a subsidy of 1.6 percent for short-wave broadcasting. Other miscellaneous revenues amounted to 2.4 percent.[29]

New Developments in Radio and Television Programming

AT a press conference on January 15, 1965, the Director of Austrian Television announced that beginning April 1, 1965, additional emphasis would be given to newscasts, with news highlights broadcast at the beginning and end of each program. He also stated that a regular 6:30 evening newscast would be rescheduled for 6:50 P.M. so that it could be viewed by a larger audience.

He further reported that during the summer months a full schedule of TV programs would be maintained, rather than the previously curtailed one, and that the schedule of the experimental Second Programme would be extended from three to four days. The Second Programme now operates on a limited schedule duplicating telecasts on the First Programme, but the Director of the state TV system envisions a substantial increase in the broadcasting time on the experimental channel by 1969.

The Director expressed the hope that TV exchanges of programs between Austria and countries of Eastern Europe might be intensified, especially uncensored political discussions broadcast live for simultaneous reception in the countries involved.

Negotiations were under way in early 1965 for an exchange of programs between Austria and Czechoslovakia, Hungary and Poland. A report from a Vienna newspaper, *Die Presse,* dated February 13, 1965, read in part:

> Liberalization has shifted to the air. If one likes, this can be described as a phenomenon of ideological softening, or presumably more aptly, as an indication of growing tolerance. Fact is that the European Communist countries no longer seriously impede Austria's efforts to be a bridge between West and East also by means of radio and television. Quietly and outside the sphere of official politics, preparations are being made for genuine cooperation. The first and more striking success was the arranging of (Vienna-Prague TV) *Stadtgespraeche* (City Talks) in Prague. A radio quiz contest between the cities of Gyoer and Kapfenberg is now planned. The program will be staged by Austrian experts, but from Budapest.
>
> . . . .
>
> The Poles, on the other hand, will establish closer contact with Austria through television, notably through a program which is to be produced by Dr. Helmut Zilk. It will be similar to the (radio) *Stadtgespraeche,* but the

framework will be narrower. Representatives of the universities of Krakow and Vienna, presumably of the philosophical faculties, will have a discussion in front of the TV cameras. The date has not yet been fixed, but the Poles have expressed their willingness to participate.

A (TV) *Stadtgespraeche* is to be staged also in Budapest, perhaps after the pattern of the program which was telecast from Prague. It must not be forgotten that also a "return talk" with Prague is on the agenda, to be conducted in Vienna. The projected film exchange with the Soviet Union rounds off a picture which is gratifyingly positive. "To Get Better Acquainted"—that is the motto. It does not matter whether this will be achieved by quiz or by "City Talk." The success will be decisive, and let us hope that there will be such success.[30]

A report from a Slovak newspaper, dated March 14, 1965, read in part:

> Should the negotiations with Austria take a satisfactory course, the Bratislava studio is likely to be of more importance than previously, considering its geographic location in relation to Vienna . . .[31]

After pointing out the possibility of improving the Czech programming, the article went on to say that it would be desirable to draw more upon the radio and TV program resources of Austria and other western countries. It was implied that a cooperative exchange of programming would be mutually advantageous to the western and eastern countries participating in such arrangements.

At the time of this writing, Austria appeared to be taking the lead in this broadcast exchange and East European countries were responding in a sympathetic and constructive manner.

NOTES

1. Julius Brounthal, *The Tragedy of Austria* (London: Victor Gollancz, Ltd., 1948), p. 44. For a full discussion of the financial and political crises in Austria after the First World War, see pp. 30–53.
2. A. Hartner, a member of the administrative staff of *Osterreichischer Rundfunk* in Vienna, discusses these early attitudes in *EBU Review*, 87B, September 1964, p. 6.
3. *Forty Years of Broadcasting in Austria (40 Jahre Rundfunk in Osterreich), Chronik 1924–1938*, published by *Osterreichischer Rundfunk*, 1964, p. 3. Also, see *EBU Bulletin*, July–August 1954, p. 352.
4. Hartner.
5. *Ibid.*
6. *Ibid.*
7. *Forty Years of Broadcasting in Austria, Chronik 1924–1938.*
8. *Ibid.*
9. *EBU Bulletin*, July 15, 1950, p. 179.
10. *Forty Years of Broadcasting in Austria, Chronik 1924–1938.*

11. *Ibid.*
12. *EBU Bulletin,* July–August 1954, p. 179.
13. Based upon conversations in Vienna in 1965 with former employees of RAVAG. Also, see *EBU Bulletin,* September–October 1957, p. 573, for good discussion.
14. The *Verwaltergesetz* had been enacted to enable the Government to appoint temporary administrators with machinery to reinstate organizations and institutions which had lost their legal status during the war and to restore to them properties and assets which had been taken over by the invading Nazis.
15. *Forty Years of Broadcasting in Austria, Chronik 1945–1964,* p. 1.
16. *EBU Bulletin,* September 15, 1950, p. 276.
17. *Radio Wien,* April 1, 1950; reported in *EBU Bulletin,* May 15, 1950, p. 82.
18. *Ibid.*
19. *170. Bundesgesetz vom 13. Juli 1949, betreffend das Fernmeldewesen (Fernmeldegesetz—FG); Bundesgesetzblatt fur die Republic Österreich,* August 1949, 36. Stuck, p. 799.
20. *Forty Years of Broadcasting in Austria, Chronik 1945–1964,* p. 1.
21. *EBU Bulletin,* September–October 1957, p. 573.
22. As of January 1968, one schilling was equivalent to 3.9 cents.
23. *Ibid.*
24. *Forty Years of Broadcasting in Austria, Chronik 1945–1964,* p. 3.
25. *EBU Bulletin,* March–April 1952, p. 198.
26. *Ibid.*
27. *EBU Review,* 52B, December 1958, p. 15.
28. Information provided by officials of *Osterreichischer Rundfunk* in Vienna.
29. *Ibid.*
30. *Die Presse* (Vienna), February 13, 1965.
31. *Pravda* (Bratislava), daily newspaper of the Slovak C.P. Central Committee, No. 72, March 14, 1965.

XIX

Switzerland: Confederation
and Neutrality

O N AUGUST 1, 1965, the small country of Switzerland celebrated six
hundred and seventy-four years of independence. It is one of the
oldest and purest democracies in the world, in which the local community is the most important unit in the political structure and in which the
individual citizen plays an active and important role in public affairs.

Although it has been necessary in the course of time to give increased
powers to the Federal Government, the cantons and communes still jeal-
ously guard their rights and resist undue encroachment upon their authority.
They insist on running their own Governments in terms of local and regional needs, but where the national interest requires they willingly work
together through the Confederation to attain common goals.

They have been able to do this despite linguistic and cultural differences. Four languages are spoken in Switzerland: German (including numerous Swiss-German dialects), French, Italian and Romansch. According
to the 1960 census, 3,764,000 Swiss spoke German, 1,025,000 spoke
French. Italian was the language of 514,000, and Romansch the language
of 51,000. All these are national tongues recognized by the Government.
German, French and Italian are used for official purposes as there is no
common written Swiss-German language. Despite this linguistic multiplicity
and the cultural diversity associated with it, more than six centuries of
common experiences have given the Swiss a basic unity of mind and spirit.
One writer has put it this way:

> . . . The growth of nationalism in Europe in the 19th century took place
> very largely on the basis of a community of language which the nations then
> identified with a common racial origin in order to justify the wars of conquest
> which then afflicted the world. That Switzerland with her multiplicity of lan-
> guages took no share in this movement shows clearly that doctrines of such
> a kind cannot stand the test of reality, and that it is neither language or race
> which goes to make a nation. . . . in Switzerland no matter what a man's
> mother tongue may be, he is first and foremost Swiss, and not German,
> French or Italian.[1]

There are religious as well as language differences in Switzerland. The 1960 census showed that of every one thousand Swiss, five hundred and twenty-six were Protestant, four hundred and fifty-six Catholic, and eighteen belonged to other denominations or professed no religious faith at all. This religious diversity, however, has not worked against national solidarity. What religious strife there once was has mostly disappeared. The Constitution guarantees freedom of worship. There is no official religion and the Government as well as its citizens generally respect a man's right to profess and practice whatever faith he prefers.

This tolerance and respect for linguistic, religious and cultural differences at the domestic level has influenced Switzerland's relationships with other nations. The country has officially maintained a policy of neutrality since 1815 when, at the Congress of Vienna, it was declared that "the neutrality and inviolability of Switzerland and her independence from all foreign influence were in the true interests of Europe."[2]

Switzerland, in line with this policy, has been careful to avoid taking sides in the Cold War. She has entered into no military alliances and is not a member of the United Nations, although she is affiliated with all its technical agencies. Despite her traditional policy of neutrality, she has shown concern for the needs of humanity regardless of political alignment or geographical location. Switzerland has often been a haven for foreigners in distress and has frequently offered asylum to political refugees.

By not taking sides in international disputes, Switzerland has been able to play an important role in world affairs by placing her diplomatic offices at the disposal of other countries. During the Second World War, she served thirty-five countries in this capacity and now carries the responsibility of eleven diplomatic representations for seven nations on four continents. Switzerland serves as the headquarters for a number of international institutions: the Universal Postal Union in Berne, the European Office of the United Nations, the International Telecommunication Union, the World Health Organization, the International Bureau of Education, the International Labor Organization, the International Union for the Protection of Intellectual Property and the World Council of Churches, all located in Geneva. The International Red Cross, founded over one hundred years ago in Geneva, represents one of the most constructive achievements in the area of international cooperation.

In an attractive brochure published by the Swiss National Exhibition in 1964, this statement appears: "Swiss neutrality is not an end in itself, but is designed to serve as a guarantee of our continuing sovereign rights. By means of this determined position, we have avoided becoming a political pawn in the hands of the great powers. Without it, we could have maintained neither our own inner diversity nor our close relationships with the rest of the world—for our basic cohesion as a nation would have been jeopardized time after time."[3]

Early History of Broadcasting

OFFICIAL reports indicate that as early as 1911, watchmakers in Switzer-land were constructing receivers to pick up the time signals being trans-mitted via radio from the Eiffel Tower in France.[4] By 1914, there had been considerable development in radio transmission.[5] Further expansion, how-ever, was interrupted by the First World War. Following cessation of hostilities, newspaper reports of sensational broadcasts in the United States (*"emmissions sensationnelles aux Etats-Unis"*) stimulated interest in radio transmission, and by 1920, there were seventy radio license holders in Switzerland.[6]

On August 22, 1922, the first official broadcast station began operation in Lausanne. Its transmissions consisted mainly of weather reports and recorded music. On October 14, 1922, the Federal Assembly passed a law authorizing the Federal Council (*Bundesrat*) to regulate and suspend, if necessary, radio communication throughout the country.[7]

The success of the experimental operation in Lausanne led to the founda-tion in 1923 of a private organization, *Utilitas,* which applied for and was granted a concession to provide the first regular broadcast service in French-speaking Switzerland.[8] This was followed by the establishment of regional broadcast societies and stations in other cities: *Radiogenossen-schaft* in Zürich (August 23, 1924), *Radiogenossenschaft Bern* (November 19, 1925), *Société des Emissions de Radio-Genève,* Geneva (February 1925), *Radiogenossenschaft Basel* (February 3, 1926), and *Ostschweiz-erische Radiogesellschaft,* St. Gall, and *Società Cooperativa per la Radio-diffusione Nella Svizzera Italiana,* Lugano, both established in 1930.[9]

On February 24, 1931, the Swiss Broadcasting Corporation (+SBC)* was constituted as a confederation of the regional broadcast establishments. A General Assembly at the national level made up of representatives of the various regions allowed all the linguistic groups—French, German, Italian and Romansch—to have a voice in determining the overall policies of the +SBC. The Corporation was designed to provide grass-roots partici-pation as opposed to centralized, bureaucratic control, but also supplied the mechanism for a cooperative, associated effort among diversified groups to achieve, on a national basis, the most economical and efficient service.

The original concession granted to the +SBC in 1931 was revised and continued in force on November 30, 1936.[10] The development of short-

---

* The official title in 1931: Swiss Broadcasting Corporation (+SBC) = *Société Suisse de Radiodiffusion* (SSR)/*Schweiz Rundspruchgesellschaft.* The new titles since 1960: Swiss Broadcasting Corporation (+SBC) = *Société Suisse de Radiodiffusion et Télévision* (+SSR), *Schweiz Radio und Fernsehgesellschaft* (+SRG), *Società Co-operative per la Radiotelevisione Nella Svizzera* (**CORSI**).

wave broadcasting in other countries influenced the Government to establish such a service in Switzerland. Accordingly, in 1938, after a number of experimental short-wave transmissions, the Federal Assembly authorized the expenditure of one hundred and eighty thousand francs to build a short-wave transmitter at Schwarzenburg.[11] Experimental operations were being conducted at the new installation when, on July 6, 1939, it was completely destroyed by fire.[12]

Hitler declared war on Poland September 1, 1939, precipitating the Second World War. On September 2, 1939, the Federal Council, in accordance with the authority previously granted by the Federal Assembly, suspended the concession and transferred the control of broadcasting to the Department of Posts and Railways. A new organization, *Service de la Radiodiffusion Suisse,* was established to conduct broadcasting during the war under the regulatory jurisdiction of this Department.

In September 1940, the short-wave transmitter at Schwarzenburg was rebuilt and regular foreign broadcasting was initiated. These transmissions were carefully designed to avoid offending any of the belligerents and to comply with Switzerland's policy of neutrality.

Postwar Growth of Broadcasting

FOLLOWING Hitler's defeat, on June 13, 1945, the Federal Council abolished the war-time agency for broadcasting and normal operations were restored.[13] The annual tax on radio receivers which had been fifteen francs was increased to twenty francs to provide additional funds for expanding the broadcasting facilities.[14] By 1949, there were more than one million licensed receivers in the country.

The Federal Post, Telephone and Telegraph Services (PTT), responsible for the erection and operation of transmitters and for the collection of the license fees on receivers, paid the +SBC 12,822,545.50 francs at the end of January 1950. Because more receivers were purchased than had been anticipated, this represented 628,545.50 francs more than the estimated income for 1949. Over two million and three hundred thousand francs were allocated to the head offices of the +SBC and short-wave services in Berne while the balance was divided among the linguistic regions as follows:[15]

4,812,700 francs—Beromunster	47.5 percent
3,394,220 francs—Sottens	33.5
1,925,080 francs—Monte Ceneri	19.0

As reported by the +SBC, the percentages of time devoted to the different types of programs (as classified by the +SBC) carried on the regional stations were:[16]

	Sottens	Monte Ceneri	Beromunster
Serious Music	29.40 percent	19.36 percent	27.30 percent
Light Music	22.15	37.03	27.30
Mixed Broadcasts	8.37	5.35	7.24
Spoken Broadcasts	16.58	18.53	13.51
Topical Broadcasts	13.60	13.04	13.37
Special Broadcasts (school, religious, agricultural, young peoples', foreign languages, etc.)	9.90	6.69	11.41

About the middle of 1950, it was announced that the PTT would soon begin TV tests near Zürich where an experimental transmitter was to be set up. It was also announced that, as is the case with sound broadcasting, the PTT would be in charge of technical TV operations, while the +SBC would be responsible for programs. It was not expected that home television would be available for four or five years.[17]

In June 1950, the Director-General of the PTT reported that tests were being conducted, and that "we firmly intend to adopt the international 625 line system as this is the definition adopted by three out of four countries on our borders and by other parts of the continent of Europe and of the world." He further stated that television would be developed on a national basis, that it would be a Swiss service respecting the historical and cultural characteristics of the country, and that the PTT would handle the engineering and the +SBC the programming. The Director-General also announced that the plans for experimental installations had been approved by the Federal Council on February 27, 1951, and that the matter was pending in Parliament.[18]

The 1951 annual report of the +SBC provided the following information about radio programming trends. In the Sottens area more programs using local live talent were being presented. It was reported that the Geneva and Lausanne studios were working closely together, with the former featuring opera and symphonic and chamber music, and the latter providing dramatic shows and "actuality broadcasts" such as *"Le Micro dans le vie"* and the *"Forum de Radio-Lausanne."*

In the Monte Ceneri region, there were numerous commemorative broadcasts during the year such as the fiftieth anniversary of the death of Verdi, and the one hundred and fiftieth anniversary of Ticino's entry into the Swiss Confederation. In *cultura e vita* there were fifty-two broadcasts covering varied aspects of intellectual life, many news reports and analyses. Music, both light and serious, was broadcast regularly in this Italian-speaking area.

Closer and more effective collaboration between the three studios in Zürich, Berne and Basle were reported. The Zürich studio varied its offerings with serial plays, commentaries, discussions of social and economic questions, and school broadcasts. Commemorative programs were featured —the six hundredth anniversary of Zürich's entry into the Confederation and the thirteen hundredth anniversary of the death of Saint Gall, patron of the town of that name. The Berne studio varied its programs but gave special attention to broadcasts in the Bernese dialect dealing with Bernese customs. The Basle studio did special programs commemorating its twenty-fifth anniversary and the four hundred and fiftieth anniversary of Basle's entry into the Swiss Confederation. Classical music was featured.[19]

The short-wave service for foreign listeners reported receiving, in 1951, 3,050 letters from Great Britain, 1297 from Switzerland, 1221 from the United States and 421 from Japan. The aim of the programs was to "cultivate the ties between the Swiss abroad and their home country and, above all, to interest the foreign listener in Switzerland and Swiss affairs."[20] While spoken broadcasts were emphasized, regular concerts of serious music were presented by Swiss soloists and ensembles.

New License Approved

ON June 30, 1952, the Ministry of Posts and Railways made public the text of a new broadcasting license which had been approved by the Federal Council. The new authorization, issued for a five year period, called for some changes in the organization and operation of the +SBC.

One of the most important changes was a provision that thereafter the Federal Council would issue the license instead of the PTT. Article IV of the concession stated: "The Federal Council, which is the licensing authority, shall designate the department to be entrusted with the supervision of the licensee." Regulatory powers, therefore, were to be vested in a Federal Department which was to be designated. The PTT, however, was to have charge of all technical equipment and the +SBC was to be responsible for programming.

A second modification provided for the addition of two societies to the seven existing affiliates: *Innerschweizerische Radiogesellschaft,* Lucerne, and *Cumunanza Radio Rumantsch,* Coire, both founded in 1946. These new groups gave representation in the +SBC to central Switzerland and the Romansch-speaking Grisons. No additional studios, however, were to be added. Programs would continue to emanate from the stations in Lausanne, Geneva, Zürich, Berne, Basle and Lugano.

New Organizational Structure

As authorized by the concession and implemented by the By-Laws of the +SBC adopted November 29, 1952, the following organization was established. A General Assembly of eighty-seven members replaced the former Assembly of twenty-one delegates. It was made up of six delegates (previously the number was only three) from each of the regional societies, and four delegates from each of the four new program committees representing the three linguistic areas and the short-wave service. Completing the total of eighty-seven delegates was a Central Committee of seventeen (the administrative body of the +SBC), eight of whom were nominated by the Federal Council plus one chosen by each of the nine regional societies.

The By-Laws provided for the appointment of a Director-General, an administrative director and a director of the short-wave service. The appointment of the directors of regional studios was made subject to the approval of the Central Committee.

As reported by the *EBU Bulletin,* the new By-laws of the +SBC were designed (1) to emphasize the democratic character of broadcasting; (2) to give listeners a more active part in the enterprise; and (3) while recognizing the need for centralized administration, to pay due respect to the varying interests and needs of the regional societies.[21]

Following the adoption of the new By-Laws, on October 13, 1953, the Federal Council delegated regulatory authority over broadcasting to the Ministry of Posts and Railways which was assigned the *"autorité de surveillance"* for the +SBC. The Federal Post, Telephone and Telegraph Services, a department within the Ministry, would continue to be in charge of the construction and maintenance of transmitting facilities and the Corporation would be responsible for programming. On the same day the Council granted the +SBC its new license which was to become effective January 1, 1954, and run for ten years.

Radio Expansion

BROADCASTING in Switzerland experienced a remarkable growth during the next decade. By the end of 1956, an FM network had been established providing a second program for all areas of the country.[22] A survey conducted by the Swiss Public Opinion Institute (ISOP) in 1958 showed that there was a growing interest in radio programs. The number of radio sets in use had risen to one million and seven hundred thousand and about eighty percent of all homes had at least one set.[23]

Each of the societies developed its own pattern of programming designed to serve the interests and needs of its coverage area. A wide variety of programs was presented on the First Programme, including much classical music, news and commentaries, dramatic shows, educational and religious broadcasts, children's programs, literary and scientific discussions, and variety shows. The Second Programme tended to be similar in format, although there was more emphasis on music.

The twenty-fifth anniversary of school broadcasting in French-speaking Switzerland was celebrated in November 1958. Switzerland was one of the first European countries to recognize the value of radio as a teaching tool. In November 1961, Rene Dovaz, then the Chairman of the Swiss Central Committee of School Broadcasting, reported on the status of school broadcasting. He stated that each community with a production center had a local group of educators responsible for the production and administration of school broadcasts. In each of the linguistic regions a committee coordinated the program to avoid overlapping or incongruity in the choice of subjects. The Central Committee made up of representatives of all the regions dealt with educational matters of concern to all the regions and the distribution of the funds made available for instructional broadcasts by the Swiss Broadcasting Corporation. In his discussion of the development of school broadcasts, Mr. Dovaz said:

Experiments carried out over a number of years, searching inquiries among the teachers, studies of the practical results obtained among the pupils, information supplied by the parents after repeats of the main programmes for their benefit—these are the things that have helped school programmes to achieve stability by adopting subjects and forms designed to obtain the maximum response from the child.

Three very important facts have emerged that are worth noting. First, it is *music* that has played a predominant part in school broadcasts, entailing to a certain extent a veritable initiation into the art by the use of vivid resources that had never before penetrated the majority of our schools. Secondly, it is the dramatised form of presentation that is more successful than all the others, and the straight-forward talk—even accompanied by sound effects— is tending to disappear completely. And lastly, the subjects broadcast to schools may be classed as follows in order of interest (at any rate according to statistics drawn up in recent years):

French-language Switzerland: music 32 percent, literature 21 percent, history 16 percent, science 16 percent, geography 13 per cent, miscellaneous 2 percent.

German-language Switzerland: music 20 percent, science 19 percent, history 17 percent, geography 17 percent, literature 15 per cent, fine arts 5 percent, miscellaneous 7 percent.

Italian-language Switzerland: literature 32 percent, social studies 20 percent, history 16 percent, science 12 percent, geography 12 percent, and music 8 percent.

Can any other conclusion be drawn than that which forms the fundamental principle underlying schools broadcasts: school broadcasting should open a window on the outer world by providing teachers with the additional material that will enable them to impart a richer quality to their teaching in sympathy with their own desire to escape from routine and conventionality, two of the most redoubtable enemies of the school?[24]

The +SBC's annual report for 1967 showed the percentages of broadcast time devoted to the following categories:[25]

	First Programme	Second Programme
Total Speech Programs	43.93	26.77
Drama	3.74	4.25
Drama (dialect)	0.67	0.44
Conferences, debates	8.43	10.07
International news	6.52	2.33
National news	13.13	5.03
Religious broadcasts	1.72	0.50
Agricultural broadcasts	0.68	0.02
Emissions pour les malades	0.54	0.08
Sports	2.86	1.82
Broadcasts for women	1.56	0.55
Broadcasts for children and young people	2.50	1.64
Broadcasts to schools (*radioscolaire*)	0.68	0.03
Miroir du temps	0.90	0.01
Total Musical Programs	45.55	61.97
Lyrical works	1.95	6.80
Symphonic music	10.23	16.01
Chamber music	5.20	11.40
Religious music	1.01	1.89
Light music, jazz	23.62	23.75
Popular music	3.54	2.12
Total Special Broadcasts	10.49	11.26
Varieties	9.78	5.84
Romantche broadcasts	0.16	1.06
Foreign broadcasts	0.19	4.04
Choral music	0.36	0.32

The 1967 report also indicated the portions of the total amount of time devoted to the broadcasts by the various orchestras.

	First Programme	Second Programme
Beromunster Orchestra	15.98 percent	7.66 percent
Lugano Symphony Orchestra	20.34	10.06
Lausanne Chamber Orchestra	9.18	19.70
Swiss Romande Orchestra	17.70	26.78
Beromunster Light Orchestra	11.89	10.51
Orchestre léger Radiosa	18.07	12.32
Orchestra léger suisse romande	6.84	12.97

Special mention should be made of the recent developments in programs for children. Otto Pünter, the former head of the +SBC Information Department, in the March 1964 issue of the *EBU Review,* stated:

> What is true of Swiss radio and television is particularly true of the services which are responsible for children's programmes. Theirs is not just a job to be done but an undertaking accepted in an attempt to awaken in the child a spirit of tolerance, a sense of fairness, the notion of brotherhood within a democracy, and the feeling of a national community despite the diversity of the country's four languages and its different religions, to say nothing of the inevitable cultural influences of the surrounding countries. It is a difficult task, full of responsibility but not without its satisfactions.[26]

Mr. Pünter stated that radio in French-speaking Switzerland "addresses itself to all age groups with broadcasts of stories, legends, literary works (mostly in the form of serials) and documentaries."[27] Music is also featured. The aim is to "entertain, inform and educate."[28] For example, *Radio-Genève* and *Radio-Lausanne* present the half hour program, "Hello, Children," on Wednesday and Saturday afternoons. These broadcasts include stories for very young children, documentaries on such subjects as geography, zoology and current events, songs and rhyming games.

Mr. Pünter further reported that radio in German-speaking Switzerland conceives as one of its tasks the establishment of a link between the modern child ("affected by the feverish age of the motor car") and the world of the fairy-tale, the song, the poem and other literature. The Beromünster station broadcasts three half hour programs in dialect each week. Programs emphasizing the heritage of the Grisons are broadcast in Romansch for the children by *Radio Zürich* every Friday and Sunday afternoon at five o'clock.

The Monte Ceneri transmitter in the Italian area of Switzerland sends out programs for children every Wednesday afternoon from five to half past five. The broadcasts are "specially adapted to the child's imaginative powers and emotional reactions and offers a variety of items including stories of adventure, discovery and invention, and current affairs likely to interest young people."[29] The programs are presented by a team of actors in the Lugano studio and by young people who have had special training in speech.

Foreign Broadcasting

THE Swiss short-wave broadcasting which was initiated in 1938 has already been mentioned. Since the Second World War, this service has been expanded. The +SBC reports that there are now four one hundred kilowatt and two two hundred and fifty kilowatt directional transmitters and two two hundred and fifty kilowatt non-directional transmitters operating in Schwarzenburg and in Beromunster.[30] Programs designed for reception in Europe and North Africa are presented regularly in German, French, Italian and Esperanto. The overseas service includes broadcasts in English, Spanish, Portuguese, French, Italian, Swiss-German and Arabic which are beamed to Africa, Ireland, Spain, Portugal, Japan, China, Australia, New Zealand and Southeast Asia, India, Pakistan, the Near and Middle East and North, Central and South America.

The United Nations owns and operates a short-wave facility in Geneva. The station, which has no official connection with the +SBC, transmits with a power of twenty-five kilowatts, and programs are presented regularly in English, French, Russian and Arabic. Sessions of the General Assembly are broadcast daily. The program, *"Le Tour du Monde des Nations Unies,"* is transcribed and made available to more than twenty French-speaking countries for rebroadcasting.

Television

TELEVISION, like radio, is operated by the +SBC. As is the case with radio, the technical facilities for TV are operated and controlled by the Swiss PTT. The development of Swiss television was no easy task. An official statement of the +SBC in 1958 reported the major difficulties encountered:

> There is hardly another country in which the introduction as well as the development of television have encountered such heavy obstacles as in Switzerland. In the Helvetic Confederation not less than three large linguistic groups live closely together—German, French and Italian—to which must be added a fourth, smaller group: the Romanche. They all have their own claims and needs which must be met, for Switzerland's existence depends entirely on the equality of rights that its citizens enjoy in all political and cultural fields. Though almost three quarters of the whole population belong to the German dialect-speaking part of Switzerland—which because of its alemmanic origin distinguishes itself distinctly from our German neighbors—a public service, like television, is to satisfy all inhabitants alike. That signifies that at least three television services have to be installed in our country. One each for the German dialect-speaking, the French-speaking and the Italian-speaking regions. This was aimed at from the beginning, and if we are not yet quite as far as that today, considerable progress has been made.[31]

The statement also mentioned the small population and the comparatively limited resources in Switzerland. Added to this was the strong opposition of most newspaper publishers, concerned about the competition for advertising which commercial TV would provide.

Despite these obstacles, the Swiss Broadcasting Corporation applied for and was granted in 1952 a concession for an experimental TV operation.

The Parliament appropriated money for the new service. The first telecasts were initiated in Zürich on July 20, 1953, for the German-speaking area. In 1955, French programs were transmitted from studios in Geneva and in 1958, the Tessin operation was connected to the Swiss network. The PTT took care of the planning and construction of network facilities for nation-wide coverage and established connections with Eurovision.

After much soul-searching it was decided that the only way in which television could be adequately financed was to permit commercials. The newspapers were greatly alarmed and, through the Swiss Association of Newspaper Publishers, offered to make an annual grant of two million Swiss francs to the +SBC for the construction and operation of TV stations with the assurance that no commercials would be broadcast. The Swiss Government as well as the Parliament agreed to this proposal. In addition, the Swiss Broadcasting Corporation was granted a Federal loan of up to eight million and four hundred thousand Swiss francs repayable at the rate of three percent interest.[32] With these combined resources, the Corporation expanded its facilities and increased its hours of telecasting. By 1961, there were nine main transmitters and five TV boosters operating in the German, French and Italian areas plus eight gap-filling transmitters owned by local authorities or viewer associations. The viewers in French- and German-speaking Switzerland were receiving about twenty-four hours of programming per week and the Italians only slightly less.

In 1961, the +SBC transmitted one hundred and ninety-six hours of foreign programs provided by Eurovision, and supplied that organization with more than one hundred hours of programming for world-wide distribution.[33] The European TV program exchanges within the framework of the EBU were established on the initiative of Marcel Bezencon, the +SBC Director-General and the president of the EBU TV Program Committee. The first Eurovision program exchanges took place on June 6, 1954.

The number of licensed TV receivers increased from nine hundred and twenty in 1954 to more than one hundred and seventy-six thousand in October 1961. This latter number had more than doubled by 1963.[34] In the meantime, the annual license fees had been set at eighty-four Swiss francs for home receivers and one hundred and sixty-eight francs for receivers in public establishments.[35] By February 1967, the total number of television licenses in Switzerland had increased to 785,211, almost one-half of the 1,678,480 radio licenses. Ninety-seven percent of all Swiss homes had a radio set and nearly fifty percent had television.[36]

Present TV Facilities and Programming

THE +SBC now has seven main transmitters and thirty-seven low-power boosters in the German-speaking area. There are seven main transmitters and nineteen boosters in the French section. Two main transmitters plus nineteen boosters serve the Italian viewers. There are three microwave links providing nation-wide network service. Studios are located in Zürich, Geneva and Lugano.[37]

The +SBC has reported on the types of TV programs and percentages of time devoted to each type, based upon program log analyses for 1964:[38]

	French	German	Italian
Total hrs. of broadcasting	1720 h., 20 min.	1660 h., 12 min.	1313 h., 25 min.
Telejournal (excluding ATS news)	8.5 percent	9.1 percent	5.8 percent
Information and actualities (news debates, commentaries, direct broadcasts, chronicals, etc.	15.7	13.2	14.2
Sports	19.3	19.3	25.7
Documentaries	8.5	14.1	12.4
Theatre and Ballet	5.5	9.2	1.4
Variety shows	5.5	7.8	8.4
Film features, animated cartoons, etc.	15.2	7.6	15.7
Programs for the family (women, children), music (symphony, chamber, choir)	1.2	0.5	2.2
Religion	3.7	3.2	3.3
Continuity, intermissions	5.6	6.6	4.4

Two areas of TV programming in Switzerland deserve special mention: children's programs and adult education. In the March 1964 issue of the *EBU Review,* there is a special report on telecasts for children and young people in the three linguistic areas. In the French-speaking area, a fifteen to twenty minute program, "The Magic Screen," addressed to children from four to seven and presented each Wednesday afternoon, consisted mainly of puppet shows, simple games and child handwork. Also, a fifty minute broadcast, "Junior Television," designed for children in school, was presented the same day. It was made up of exciting stories and reports of life in foreign lands, interesting scientific experiments, handwork and "how to do it" features, and adventure stories.[39]

On Saturday afternoons, from its studios in Geneva, the French service broadcast a program for teenagers, including an adventure story and a forum in which they might express their views on controversial subjects.[40]

In the German-language service, with studios in Zürich, a variety of programs for children at different age levels is offered—children's theater, illustrated stories, cartoons, puppets, ballet, pantomime, handwork with various "how to do it" programs, music, documentaries concerned with history and current affairs, educational programs in science, literature and civics, plus purely entertainment features with clowns and conjurers and films such as the American-produced "Lassie."[41]

As reported by those in charge of the German service, attempts are made to encourage young viewers "to take an active part in the programs, either by suggesting practical work or by appealing to their imagination or intelligence. What it tries to avoid above all is the risk of turning them into passive, superficial viewers."[42]

The Italian programs emanate from studios in Lugano. Three types of programs for the young are presented. There is *"Girotondo"* for the smallest children with animated cartoons, filmed stories, news items and the puppet Bongo bobbing up from time to time as a link between the various sequences.

"Ribalta della Gioventu" (replaced in 1964 by *"Anni Verdi"*), designed to appeal to children from eleven to fourteen, presented filmed items made available by other Eurovision countries, with local commentaries adapted to the interests of the adolescent viewers. Also, as is true in the other linguistic zones, programs concerned with handcrafts are emphasized.

"Club dei Giovani," broadcast once a month for young people in their late teens, deals mainly with the problems of social adjustment, vocational and professional opportunities, and features filmed documentaries of educational and recreational value.[43]

In the field of adult education, Swiss television is doing some outstanding programming. Dr. Pünter recently reported regular features in the French area such as "Choose Your Own Future," designed to help school drop-outs and other young people decide on careers. In German-speaking Switzerland, broadcasts dealing with a wide range of subject matter in the natural sciences are presented regularly. All three linguistic areas receive health programs providing information on how to prevent disease. Other typical programs which have been broadcast in one or more of the areas are those dealing with the conquest of space, traffic problems, art and literature, civics and public affairs, and the teaching of English. Courses in ballroom dancing have been featured frequently on Swiss TV and have been extremely popular.[44]

Television Advertising

THE Society for Swiss Television Advertising is in charge of all TV advertising in Switzerland. Forty percent of the Society's capital stock is owned by the Association for the Development of Television (the newspaper group which previously provided the two million franc subsidy); forty percent by the +SBC; eight percent by the Committee of the Swiss Association of Commerce and Industry; and four percent each by the Swiss Press Association, the Swiss Farmers Association and the Swiss Trademen's Union.

The net proceeds from TV advertising are passed on to the +SBC (21.2 million francs in 1965, 26.5 million in 1966, and about twenty-eight million in 1967). This income is used by the +SBC to finance its TV programming.

The basic advertising rate for advertising (network) was originally set at six thousand francs per minute. On January 1, 1967, this was increased to seven thousand francs per minute. The commercials are separated from the programs. Only spot announcements are broadcast and no programs are sponsored.

The commercial spots run twenty, thirty, forty or sixty seconds and are presented in several time blocks. As of January 1, 1968, these blocks were: in German-speaking Switzerland, 7:00, 7:20, 7:50 and 8:15 P.M.; in French-speaking Switzerland, 6:50, 7:20, 7:55 and 8:15 P.M.; and in Italian-speaking Switzerland, 7:10, 7:40, 8:10 and 8:35 P.M.

Total commercial continuity was originally limited to twelve minutes per day. This was increased to fourteen minutes on July 1, 1967 and to fifteen minutes in 1968. No advertisements of alcoholic beverages, tobacco or medicines are permitted on Swiss television and no commercials of any kind are allowed on radio.

Reorganization of the +SBC

IN 1964, the Federal Council approved a reorganization of the +SBC and on October 27 of that year granted a new radio and TV license for ten years (valid until December 31, 1974). The By-Laws of the Corporation, as ratified in 1964, provide that the +SBC be composed of three regional organizations:

1. *La Radio und Fernsehgesellschaft der Deutschen und der Räto-romanischeu Schweiz* (SRG), composed of the following members: *Radiogenossenschaft* in Zürich, Berne and Basle, plus *Ostschweizerische Radiogesellschaft, Innerschweizerische Radiogesellschaft,* and *Cumüanza Radio Rumantsch,* with three radio studios in Zürich, Berne and Basle, one TV studio in Zürich, three small radio and TV program centers in St. Gall, Lucerne and Coire; and with radio headquarters in Basle and TV headquarters in Zürich.

2. *La Société de Radiodiffusion et de Télévision de la Suisse Romande* (SSR), composed of the following members: *Fondation de Radiodiffusion et de Télévision à Lausanne* and *Fondation de Radiodiffusion et de Télévision à Genève,* with two radio studios in Lausanne and in Geneva; one TV studio in Geneva; and radio headquarters in Lausanne and TV headquarters in Geneva.

3. *La Società Cooperative per la Radiotelevisione Nella Svizzera Italiana* (CORSI) with studios for both radio and television located in Lugano.

In addition, the +SBC runs a radio and TV program center in the Parliament Buildings in Berne, enabling on-the-spot reporting by political correspondents from the capital. These broadcasts are carried by the network to the whole of Switzerland.

As presently constituted, the General Assembly, the supreme policy-making body of the +SBC and its constituent organizations, is composed of delegates representing the regional groups as follows:

German- and Romansch-speaking	42
French-speaking	18
Italian-speaking	12
Each regional program committee (2 members)	6
National Television Program Committee	4
National Short-wave Program Committee	4
Central Committee	17

As was true prior to the reorganization, the Swiss Government reserves the right to appoint the Chairman and seven members of the Central Committee. Moreover, it nominates its representatives in the general assemblies of the new regional organizations, nine in German-speaking Switzerland, eight in the French area, and it is represented at the general assemblies of the CORSI in Lugano.

The Central Committee is in charge of the general administration and its responsibilities, among others, are (1) to represent the +SBC in Switzerland and foreign countries, particularly before the courts and other official bodies; (2) to conduct the general business affairs of the organization and approve the by-laws of the regional societies to see that they are in accord with the provisions of the concession; and (3) to name three permanent committees: financial, legal and one concerned with housing and construction. Furthermore, it is empowered to appoint other committees for special purposes. Subject to the approval of the Government, it appoints the Director-General who is responsible for the conduct of the day-to-day business affairs of the +SBC and its program service, both domestic and foreign.

The By-Laws provide for the establishment of a national TV program committee.[45] In addition to the Director-General it is made up of eighteen members and eight deputies, chosen to represent the *"milieux culturels, politiques et economiques"* and linguistic areas of the country. One-half of the members and deputies are designated by the Government and the other half by the Central Committee from nominations submitted by the regional societies. Its functions include the study and evaluation of program service and the submission of reports and recommendations to the Central Committee and the committees of the regional organizations.

There is a program committee for short-wave broadcasting made up of the Director-General, eight members and four deputies chosen to provide a balanced representation of the cultural, political and economic interests and the linguistic regions of the country. Its main task is to advise and make recommendations to the Director-General for the improvement of the foreign broadcasting service.

The program committees are presided over by the Director-General of the +SBC. The committees meet in regular session every four months. In the absence of the Director-General, a vice-president elected by each committee presides at the meetings.

The Central Committee distributes +SBC income to the various regional societies after deducting necessary sums to defray expenses of the Director-General's offices and overall operations of the organization, and to maintain a central reserve fund as required by Article XXII of the concession.

As stated by the +SBC, its organizational and administrative "structure is in keeping with the cultural and political federalism of Switzerland. In all the national bodies of Swiss radio and television, and especially in the general assembly, the highest organization of SBC, democratic representation is given to the linguistic, denominational, cultural, economic and political groupings of Switzerland. In this way, the SBC does its best to uphold and foster the country's cultural values, and to contribute to intellectual, ethical, religious, civic and artistic life and ideas."[46]

Current Status of Swiss Broadcasting

In the June 14, 1967 issue of the *Christian Science Monitor*, Frank Shaw reported from Zurich that the broadcast media have become "powerful factors" in the social structure of Switzerland, with networks (both radio and television) transmitting in French, German and Italian. He stated that the estimated total income from TV advertising and from license fees on radio and TV sets would be more than twenty million dollars in 1967.[47]

The importance that the Swiss people attach to local autonomy and their traditional aversion to Federal controls are suggested by the public controversy which resulted from the recent elimination of a popular satirical radio program, *"Mini Meinig–Dini Meinig"* (My View and Your View). Some members of the Parliament alleged that this program was discontinued because of government pressure, and that "secret dossiers on radio and TV programs were being kept by the Administration in Berne, the federal capital."[48]

The allegations were denied by the Swiss broadcasting officials. In fact, the Director-General of the national broadcasting service went on the air to deny the charge that a recent meeting between broadcasting officials and government authorities in Berne was called to put the +SBC "on the carpet." His version was that the broadcasters had asked for the meeting with the Government "in order to invite national leaders to take part in televised debates with journalists."

With considerable concern over the alleged censorship expressed by newspapers and other segments of the Swiss public, there was a five hour debate in the National Council in which Rudolf Gnaegi, the Minister of Transport, Communications and Energy, participated. He stated, among other things, that there should be "freedom for broadcasting, but it should be within limits."

In his report to the *Christian Science Monitor,* Mr. Shaw said:

> In the course of the debate it became clear that there are two sides to the medal of broadcasting freedom. In regard to the disputed radio program, it emerged that complaints had been edited in such a way that the opinions expressed were distorted. To meet this point, the journalist producing the show had been asked to submit his tapes to the studio director before broadcast. This he had refused to do, and the program therefore came off the air.
>
> Gnaegi promised at the conclusion of the debate that the broadcasting concession would in any case be studied again by the Federal Council, to see if the guarantees of independence could be strengthened. It was, in a sense, one of those moments in which one feels that history of a kind is being made.[49]

Perhaps one should be cautious in attaching too much emphasis to the *"Mini Meinig–Dini Meinig"* affair. As one Swiss official put it, "it was just an incident which had its echo in German-language Switzerland only."

The controversy as to whether the Government did, does, or should interfere in +SBC program matters has induced the Ministry of Transport, Communications and Energy (the regulatory authority for the +SBC) to take up again the idea of a constitutional amendment to enable the Confederation to pass laws touching the whole field of broadcasting. The existing laws cover only the technical operations and not programming. Such an amendment was proposed in 1956 but was rejected by a plebiscite in March 1957, by a vote of 427,859 to 319,634. The renewal of public concern will probably cause the Swiss Parliament to reconsider the issue and the problem.

NOTES

1. Hans Bauer, *All About Switzerland: A Short Survey* (Zürich: Swiss National Tourist Office, 1963).
2. William E. Rappard, *The Government of Switzerland* (New York: D. Van Nostrand Company, Inc., 1936), p. 133.

3. *Switzerland*, published by the Swiss National Exhibition (Lausanne: 1964), p. 7.
4. *Quel ques dates Importantes de l'évolution de la radiodiffusion en Suisse, Le 25 ème Anniversaire de la Société Suisse de Radiodiffusion*, published by *Société Suisse de Radiodiffusion* (Berne: February 22, 1956), p. 2.
5. *Ibid.*
6. *Ibid.*
7. *Recueil Officiel des Lois et Ordannances de la Confederation Suisse*, Berne, XXXIX, 1923, 14.
8. *Quel ques dates Importantes*, p. 2.
9. *Ibid.*, pp. 2–3.
10. *Recueil Officiel*, LV, 1939, 822.
11. *Ibid.*, LIV, 1938, 202–203. As of January 1968, one Swiss franc was equivalent to 22.9 cents.
12. *Quel ques dates Importantes*, p. 2.
13. *Recueil Officiel*, LXI, 1945, 498.
14. *Ibid.*, LXII, 1946, 838. In 1956, the annual tax on a radio receiver was increased to twenty-six francs; in 1966, to thirty-three francs. The +SBC receives seventy percent of the revenue from the license fees; the Federal Post, Telephone and Telegraph Services (PTT) receives thirty percent.
15. *EBU Bulletin*, July 15, 1950, pp. 168–169.
16. *Ibid.*, p. 181.
17. *Radio Actualités*, June 25, 1950; reported in *EBU Bulletin*, July 15, 1950, pp. 196–197.
18. *EBU Bulletin*, September 15, 1951, pp. 503–504.
19. *Ibid.*, July 15, 1952, pp. 403–404.
20. *Ibid.*, p. 406.
21. *Ibid.*, September 15, 1952, p. 502, and January 15, 1953, p. 57, for discussion of concession and the +SBC statutes implementing it.
22. *Ibid.*, March-April 1957, p. 152.
23. *EBU Review*, 53B, February 1959, pp. 8–9.
24. *Ibid.*, 70B, November 1961, p. 41.
25. *Emissions de la Radiodiffusion Suisse 1966*, tabulation published by the +SBC and supplied the author by letter.
26. *EBU Review*, 84B, March 1964, p. 23.
27. *Ibid.*
28. *Ibid.*
29. *Ibid.*, p. 24.
30. Information received from the +SBC, Berne, October 1967.
31. *Société Suisse de Radiodiffusion et Télévision*, "Television in Switzerland" (Berne: July 1, 1958), p. 1.
32. *Ibid.*, p. 3.
33. UNESCO, *World Communications: Press, Radio, Television, Film* (New York: UNESCO Publications Center, 1964), p. 329.
34. *EBU Review*, 85B, May 1964, p. 29.
35. *Ibid.*, 92B, July 1965, p. 38.
36. *Société Suisse de Radiodiffusion et Télévision, Documentation*, March 1967.
37. *1966 World Radio TV Handbook* (20th ed.; Sundvej 6, Hellerup, Denmark: World Radio-Television Handbook Company, Ltd., 1966), p. 257.
38. *Société Suisse de Radiodiffusion et Télévision*, "Statistique de Programme-TV," January 1 to December 31, 1964.

39. *EBU Review*, 84B, March 1964, p. 25.
40. *Ibid.*
41. *Ibid.*, pp. 25–26.
42. *Ibid.*, p. 25.
43. *Ibid.*, p. 26.
44. *EBU Review*, 94B, November 1965, p. 36.
45. *Statuts de Société Suisse de Radiodiffusion et Télévision*, undated publication by the Society.
46. *Société Suisse de Radiodiffusion et Télévision, Press et Documentation*, undated.
47. *Christian Science Monitor*, June 14, 1967, p. 8.
48. *Ibid.*
49. *Ibid.*

· G ·

THE IBERIAN PENINSULA

XX

Spain: Franco and Private Enterprise

THE SYSTEM OF BROADCASTING in Spain is unique. It is an outgrowth of institutional and social forces which have controlled the Iberian Peninsula for many centuries. As in many other European countries, the Government has played an important, positive role in the development of the broadcast media in Spain, and today exercises a large measure of authority over their operations. Business interests also operate many stations in the country and have helped to shape the general pattern of broadcasting.

Moreover, the Catholic Church, the national religion to which most Spaniards have been traditionally committed, has operated many radio stations through its national organization and many local parishes, and continues to control a network of medium-wave stations. Church doctrines and practices not only are the main subject matter of the programs of many of its stations, but they directly or indirectly influence the content and format of other broadcast operations.

The national syndicates, representing multiple business enterprises and their workers, have been potent forces in the national life since the close of the Spanish Civil War in 1939. Closely allied to the syndicates, the *Movimiento,* now the only official political party in Spain, also wields great influence. Both the syndicates and the party have their own national radio networks over which they promote public acceptance of their ideas and programs.

In 1964, Spain celebrated twenty-five years of peace. Under the leadership of Generalissimo Franco, the Government in Madrid, with the support and advice of these interests and organizations plus the military establishment, has been able to maintain a social order largely free of major tensions and strife. For more than a quarter of a century, there has been steady economic and educational progress.

The standards of living for the average citizen, while not high, are considerably better than they were in the late thirties and early forties. Unemployment and illiteracy have been reduced. Although Spanish workers have recently demonstrated to express their dissatisfaction with wages and working conditions, and students have protested against alleged government restraints of free speech and assembly, the people generally appear satisfied with the present conditions.

Early Regulation of Communications

TODAY, there are almost two hundred radio stations in Spain. A television network covers the nation. The *Radio Nacional de España* broadcasts to foreign countries in more than twenty languages. There are more than eight million radio receivers and about 2,550,000 television receivers in the country. The development of broadcasting into such an important aspect of Spanish life is a fascinating story.

From the beginning, wire and wireless communications in Spain have been looked upon as public functions subject to state control. At the same time, Spain has encouraged private enterprise and, with government authorization, business interests have been allowed to operate these media for profit.

The growth of wire communication before and during the First World War prompted the Government to announce in 1917, by Royal Decree, that all scientific investigation for weather observations would be subject to inspection by the Director-General of Posts and Telegraphs. The Decree further stated that the purpose of the inspections would be to see that the regulations and the conditions of each concession were complied with and that the public interest was served.

Article VI of the Decree declared that applicants for licenses to operate radiotelegraphic stations would be required to state the purposes of and justify the proposed operations, and to provide information as to location, operators to be used, and qualifications of operators. Article VII stated that stations operating without authorization or in violation of regulations would be closed by the Director-General, the property confiscated, and the owners held criminally liable.[1] This was supplemented and reaffirmed by a decree dated January 13, 1920.[2]

Don Antonio de Castilla, an outstanding pioneer in Spanish broadcasting, developed a wireless receiver and demonstrated the transmission of radio waves from fixed to moving points. With the support of financial entrepreneurs in Spain, in 1917, he helped to establish the Iberian Telecommunication Company (*La Compañía Ibérica de Telecomunicación*) for the manufacture of transmitting and receiving equipment. The Company was located in Madrid. Its production was limited at first because of a lack of raw materials, but it was destined to become one of the most important manufacturing concerns in Spain.

The Government became increasingly interested in the development of broadcasting. In 1920, it arranged a series of discussions and demonstrations under the direction of Castilla which was concluded with the transmission of a concert from the Exhibition Palace *(Palacio de la Exposición)* to a single receiver at Valencia University.

The following year, the Government authorized Castilla's Iberian Company to operate a small experimental broadcasting station. Its first programs consisted of lectures and transmissions of opera from the Royal Theatre. At the same time, amateurs ("ham" operators) and other radio fans were stepping up their activities and in 1922 organized the *Real Club de España,* popularly called *radiomaniáticos* (radio maniacs), to promote their interests.[3]

In the meantime, the general public became more interested in purchasing receivers and *La Compañía Ibérica de Telecomunicación* increased its production. For example, on April 17, 1923, the Company announced in *La Correspondencia de España,* a Madrid newspaper, that it had made fifteen hundred radio receivers and could easily produce more. It advertised the prices of receivers: crystal sets, sixty pesetas; sets with tubes, four hundred and ninety pesetas; short-wave sets (five tubes) capable of receiving programs from Paris and London, 1,650 pesetas.[4]

In March 1923, the Director-General of Posts and Telegraphs established a Commission to prepare a code of regulations for radio, as authorized by Royal Decree the month before.[5] On June 2, the Government announced the adoption of the code based upon the recommendations of the Commission. Stations were classified into five categories: (1) those established by "centers of learning," (2) those designed for investigation, research and study by Spanish nationals; (3) transmitters for point-to-point communications; (4) broadcast stations; (5) safety and special service stations (including weather and aviation).

The order defined "broadcasting stations" as those transmitting to the general public. To secure and maintain their licenses, the Government required them to provide the following types of programs: (1) official information of interest to the general public such as items from the official government bulletin, reports on sessions of Parliament, market and mercantile information and "other services deemed important to the State"; (2) programs designed to promote culture, education and recreation such as reports of educational conferences, musical concerts, discussions regarding business and industry and sermons. The broadcasting of commercial advertising was specifically authorized.

It was further stated that these stations would be under the regulatory jurisdiction of the Telegraph Division *(Cuerpo de Telégrafas)* in the Ministry of the Interior, and that the frequencies and transmitting power would be determined by the Director-General of the Division. For Class A stations, a network service would be established and operated by the State under the direction of the Telegraph Division. Other stations (Class B) were to be licensed to societies, corporations and individuals, "if for some reason the State could not use them."

Applications had to be filed, purposes of station operation stated, and equipment to be used specified. Licenses were limited to not more than ten and not less than two years.[6]

The Growth of Commercial Radio

THE State did not see fit to establish its own stations at that time and commercial interests were permitted initially to take over the field. Some experimental broadcast transmissions were authorized under the new regulations but these did not prove to be financially successful.[7] One of these was initiated by Don José Guillén García in Montjuick. After a short period of unsuccessful operation, it merged with *La Compañía Ibérica de Telecomunicación* station in Madrid. According to Mr. Anibal Arias Ruiz, this merger led to the establishment of *Radio Ibérica,* and was the first broadcasting station in Spain to provide regular program service.[8]

Operating on a limited schedule during the evening hours, *Radio Ibérica* broadcast mainly concerts and lectures. It introduced advertising and promoted the sale of receivers on its programs. With high transmitting power, it achieved wide coverage and became one of the best known stations in Europe.

On July 14, 1924, the Government issued more detailed and definitive regulations covering broadcast stations. Transmitting power was limited to a maximum of eight kilowatts. As much as five minutes of commercial continuity could be included in each hour of broadcasting. Public service programs had to be presented regularly. The regulations further specified that licensees had a responsibility to observe moral standards and promote cultural growth.[9]

Radio Ibérica was given the call sign EAJ-6. José Guillén García, in the name of the *Associación Nacional de Radiodifusión,* applied for and was granted a concession for a station in Barcelona. It was granted the call sign EAJ-1, and came to be known as *Radio Barcelona.* Subsequent concessions were granted as follows: *Radio Cádiz, Radio Castilla, Radio San Sebastian, Radio Bilbao, Radio Catalana de Barcelona, Radio Málaga, Radio España de Madrid, Radio Asturias, Radio Sevilla, Union Radio de Madrid, Radio Salamanaca, Radio Madrileña* and *Radio Cartagena.*[10]

By order of the Government, on January 1, 1930, an annual tax for the use of radio receivers was imposed. The tax was set at five pesetas for private use and fifty pesetas for public establishments.[11]

Early Radio Programming

ALTHOUGH listeners were delighted with the broadcasts of these early stations, the programs at first were necessarily limited. For example, the Barcelona station (EAJ-1), established in November 1924 by a number of business interests in that city, carried mostly piano music and phonograph recordings. There were occasional orchestra and band concerts, and on June 23, 1925, the station broadcast by remote control some night festivities held in the ancient *Paseo del Rey*.[12]

Union Radio, EAJ-2 (later called *Radio Madrid*), went on the air as a commercial station in the late twenties. On January 1, 1929, *ABC,* a Madrid newspaper, reported EAJ-2's programs for that day. The schedule began at a quarter to noon with comments on cooking, followed by market reports. Classical music, presented by a live orchestra, at two o'clock in the afternoon, was followed by the news at a quarter to four. Beginning at seven o'clock in the evening, a variety of vocalists were broadcast, and the remainder of the schedule, running until half past midnight, consisted of market reports, popular music and a resume of the day's news.[13]

Five days later, on January 6, the station featured, during the early evening hours, recordings of dance music, including a number of popular American melodies of that period. In the late evening, religious music, commemorating the Adoration of the Three Kings, was broadcast.[14]

The programs of the Barcelona and Madrid stations and others mentioned above, plus broadcasts from France, England and other parts of Europe, became increasingly popular with Spanish listeners during the late twenties and early thirties. The market for receivers expanded. In 1933 there were more than two hundred registered radio manufacturers and dealers in the Spanish capital alone and more than one hundred and fifty thousand receiving sets had been sold and licensed.[15]

In addition to the stations already mentioned, a sizable number of low-power (two hundred and fifty watts) installations were established. These had been authorized by the Government on December 8, 1932, with special regulations covering their operations.[16] These new community stations plus the older, high-power ones still in operation (a few had gone out of business because of financial difficulties) brought the total number of stations in 1934 to more than sixty, and paved the way for regional and national networks.[17]

By 1935, *Union Radio,* EAJ-2 in Madrid, had expanded its operating schedule to seventeen hours per day. In the meantime, another Madrid station, *Radio España,* had started regular broadcasting from two o'clock in the afternoon until midnight, presenting mainly recorded popular music, but doing some instructional programs such as "Lessons in Latin," one of the first efforts in educational radio in Spain.[18]

Other large markets were served by stations in Seville and Valencia. *Radio Sevilla,* more than two hundred miles south of Madrid, had a daily schedule from half past eight in the morning to half past ten in the evening, consisting principally of popular recorded music, market reports, sports news, and national and world news supplied by wire twice daily by *Union Radio* in Madrid. This cooperative news arrangement between the two stations foreshadowed the development of a network to be known as *Sociedad Española de Radiodifusión,* with numerous stations operating in the larger cities of Spain.

The manufacture and sale of radio sets continued to increase and in 1935 a number of American companies—Philco, Atwater Kent, RCA and Zenith —as well as several large European companies, such as Phillips and *Ibérica de Electricidad,* were active in the Spanish market.

Plans for a National, Integrated Broadcast Service

UNTIL 1929, private and commercial interests dominated broadcasting. On June 26 of that year, however, a Royal Decree authorized the establishment of a state-owned and operated system. The Government attempted for a number of years to implement the Decree but encountered difficulties in working out a plan that would satisfy both private and public interests. It was not until June 26, 1934, that a law was passed providing for the establishment of a national chain consisting of central broadcasting facilities in Madrid and regional operations in the provinces. This statute also provided for the creation of a foreign broadcasting service, with programs to be beamed from Madrid via short-wave to America and other parts of the world.

National and regional planning boards were to be set up to advise the Government on the technical and programming phases of the broadcast operation. These boards would be made up of members representing a wide range of interests—artistic, literary, scientific and educational. The plan envisioned the continued operation of the older commercial and private stations as well as the newly authorized local ones. The private stations were to be subject to government regulations, with censorship imposed on all newscasts and all political and religious programs.

It was ordered that stations for the national network would be located in Madrid, Barcelona, Valencia, Seville, La Coruna, Vizcaya and the Canary Islands. Relay installations were to be established in Murcia and Oviedo.

A maximum of three years would be allowed for the construction of all facilities in the national system.

On November 22, 1935, a decree was issued by the Ministry of Public Works creating a Department of Broadcasting in the office of the Undersecretary of Communications. The decree further provided that the office and the National Broadcasting Service would be financed with income from a tax on the sale of radio equipment, license fees on receivers, advertising, publications, and from voluntary contributions and endowments.[19]

Civil War

THE political situation in Spain prevented the fulfillment at that time of the plan for a national broadcasting service. In fact, during the early thirties there were more than twenty-five different government administrations. In 1936, the "leftist" parties united in the "Popular Front" and overwhelmed the conservatives and moderate liberals in the national election. The first few months after the election saw violence of the worst sort. Two hundred and forty-nine murders; burnings of one hundred and seventy churches, sixty-nine political clubs and ten newspapers; and over three hundred general or partial strikes were reported to the Cortes during the first four months of "Popular Front" rule.[20]

War broke out with agonizing fury. The "Nationalists," including the more conservative groups plus the Spanish Army, were pitted against the "Loyalists," made up largely of the newly elected "Popular Front" Government, labor groups and a mixture of republicans, socialists, anarchists and communists. The vital energies and resources of the nation generally were consumed by the war. Radio facilities were conscripted and used on both sides for military and propaganda purposes.

On January 14, 1937, all authority over radio in the "Nationalist" zone was assigned to a war-time agency in charge of press and propaganda. Under the direction of General Francisco Franco, this agency established a number of new stations, including high-power ones which could be heard over wide areas in both fighting zones. Of particular importance was the inauguration of *Radio Nacional España* on January 19, 1937. Operating with twenty kilowatts of power, it became an effective weapon for the "Nationalist" cause, and following cessation of hostilities continued to function as an important agency of communication for the Government.[21]

Postwar Developments

AN office of Undersecretary of Popular Education was established after the war and took over the control of *Radio Nacional España* and other stations

which had been created by the "Nationalists" during the military operations.[22] The private and commercial stations which were still financially
stable were permitted to continue operation under government surveillance.
In 1941, the number of broadcast stations in Spain totaled more than
eighty.[23]

Union Radio, which had started the first network operation in Spain in
the late twenties, changed its name to *Sociedad Española de Radiodifusión*
(SER). Although its broadcasting activities had been disrupted, it reorganized, acquired new properties, and by 1945, had broadcasting facilities
in several large cities including Madrid, Barcelona, Bilbao, Valencia, Seville
and San Sebastian. By 1963, it had extended its network operations to a
large number of local stations widely distributed in the country.[24]

In 1964, the SER had more than three thousand employees. A magazine,
Ondas, which *Union Radio* started publishing in the late twenties, had more
than eighty-six thousand subscribers in 1964 and was widely read in the
larger cities of Spain.

News reports make up an important part of the SER's programming.
The network maintains a full editorial staff in its central offices in Madrid
and has correspondents in all of its subsidiary and associated stations plus
more than twenty reporters abroad.[25]

Establishment of a State-Owned Network

THE outbreak of hostilities in 1936 suspended plans for the creation of a
state-owned and operated network, but these plans were revived after the
war. In 1942, the *Red Española de Radiodifusión* (REDERA) was created,
including stations in Madrid and several other large cities. The Under-
secretary of Popular Education delegated authority to REDERA to operate
these stations as well as those which had been built during the war under
the auspices of the Falange Movement *(Falange Española),* the only political
party then officially sanctioned by the Franco regime, which aggressively
supported the General's cause during and after the war.

For administrative purposes, the Spanish Broadcasting Authority was
created on February 15, 1942.[26] Shortly thereafter, the Authority started
the construction of a radio center at Arganda del Ray within the environs
of Madrid, including a standard broadcast transmitter with one hundred
and twenty kilowatts of power and a short-wave transmitter with forty
kilowatts. These were connected with the program studios in Madrid by an
underground cable.[27]

Two years later, the state broadcasting complex was given a new name,
Radio Nacional de España. Its central studios and standard and short-wave

transmission facilities in the capital city and seven regional stations (Barcelona, Valencia, Seville, Cuenca, La Coruña, Huelva and Málaga) furnished an extensive broadcast service both at home and abroad.

On July 27, 1945, the delegation of authority to REDERA was cancelled. The organization was dissolved and the national broadcast services were made an integral part of the Ministry of National Education, with a new undersecretary in charge of the broadcast operations. A Director-General, responsible to the undersecretary, was appointed to administer the state system.[28]

A New Era in National Broadcasting

A new era in Spanish broadcasting began in 1951. On July 19, the Ministry of Information and Tourism was created and given control over all print media and publications, public performances both dramatic and recreational, radio and television, and "tourism."[29] Although regulatory authority was transferred from the Ministry of Education, it set up a Secretariat for Cultural Extension and continued to prepare and provide educational programs for both public and private radio stations.

The new Ministry began to reclassify stations and systematize the nation's broadcasting facilities. On November 15, 1952, it issued a decree dividing broadcasting stations into three categories: (1) *national,* including the high-powered, state-owned and operated stations (twenty kilowatts or above); (2) *regional,* covering those with power limited to five kilowatts, which might be state-owned and operated, or licensed to commercial interests who would undergo competitive selection tests to acquire the privilege; (3) *local,* the low-powered stations broadcasting in the small communities which would be permitted to operate under special regulations to be adopted by the Ministry of Information and Tourism. At the same time, the Spanish Broadcasting Authority, which had been created by a decree of February 15, 1942, was made responsible for the operation of the state stations in the first category.[30] It was declared that the regional stations would be considered government property but that licenses would be granted to commercial concerns for a period of twelve years, subject to the approval of the Director of Broadcasting and a review board appointed by the Ministry to pass on the qualifications of applicants.[31]

To provide for more flexibility and efficiency in administration and speed up the development of broadcasting, the Ministry took steps to give independent status to the Spanish Broadcasting Authority. It was decreed, therefore, on October 3, 1957, that the Authority would continue to function under the regulatory jurisdiction of the Department of Radio and

Television in the Ministry *(Dirección General de Radiodifusión y Tele-visión)*, but that it should enjoy full corporate status with administrative and financial autonomy.[32] Its functions were to be:

(a) the operation, upkeep and maintenance of the national stations owned by the State which are entrusted to it by Ministerial Order, or those which the Spanish Broadcasting Authority plans and installs on its own behalf, with the authorization of the Ministry of Information and Travel;
(b) the exclusive broadcasting of bulletins of home and foreign news, pro-grams intended for abroad and foreign broadcasts relayed to Spain;
(c) the exclusive broadcasting of television stations and the technical de-velopments of the Spanish television service;
(d) the direct management of radio and television advertising over the State transmitters operated directly by the State, and those authorized by the Ministry, for the making of contracts for such advertising;
(e) the pursuit of such other activities connected with broadcasting or tele-vision as may be considered needful or desirable for the accomplishment of the purposes mentioned above.[33]

In January 1958, the Ministry of Finance issued a decree with regula-tions covering the State's share in revenue from advertising broadcast over radio and television stations, both public and private. It was prescribed that the Government's share would be twenty percent of the gross income. It was specified that, thirty-six hours in advance, a daily schedule of adver-tisements to be broadcast and charges to be made should be forwarded to the provincial offices of the Ministry of Information and Tourism. Deliberate failure to comply with this regulation was made subject to severe penalties.[34]

Because of the rapid growth of radio and television during the late fifties, the Government felt the need for more effective coordination of the various broadcast services and for more centralized control of the media. Accord-ingly, in 1960, the Department of Radio and Television in the Ministry of Information and Tourism was reorganized, the autonomous character of the Spanish Broadcasting Authority disappeared and its functions were made part of the new organizational structure of the Department.[35] On October 11, 1962, a new National Broadcasting Service, directly controlled by the State, was established and officially took over the operation of the network and the state-owned stations.[36]

Following this reorganization, the National Broadcasting Service of the Ministry started the operation of a new transmitter with two hundred kilo-watts at Majadahonda. With this new facility and other improvements in the national network, the Ministry of Information and Tourism hailed 1963 as *"el año de la radio"* (the year of radio) because of the fulfillment of the plans for a national chain of stations that had their inception in the years prior to the Civil War.[37]

At the beginning of 1965, the facilities of the national network *(La*

Cadena Nacional de Radiodifusión) included three stations in Madrid with fifty, one hundred and twenty, and two hundred kilowatts; and one station in each of the following cities: Valencia, twenty-five kilowatts; La Coruña, one hundred kilowatts; San Sebastian, twenty kilowatts; Oviedo, five kilowatts; Málaga, six kilowatts; Seville, two hundred and fifty kilowatts; Cuenca, five kilowatts; and Huelva, five kilowatts.[38]

The National Service now owns and operates a commercial station in Madrid (the fifty kilowatt one mentioned above). Until 1960, all operations of the state-owned network (excluding the regional stations licensed to commercial interests) were noncommercial. That year, however, the fifty kilowatt operation, *Radio Peninsular,* was joined to the complex of *Radio Nacional de España.* It started regular broadcasts from Majadahonda, featuring popular music and news and carrying commercial advertising. Selected programs are broadcast by other network stations and are heard throughout the country.

Until recently, the Government continued to assess annual license fees on all radio receivers, but with substantial advertising income from its own operation as well as that from other commercial stations, it found that these fees were not needed to maintain operations and abolished the tax.

Other Networks

BESIDES the state network and that of the SER previously discussed, other networks have developed in Spain since the Civil War. All have been authorized by the Government and are licensed for commercial operation. One of these is *Radio España de Barcelona* (REBSA), which provides a program service in the Barcelona area. Established in the early thirties, it now includes stations *Radio España de Barcelona, Radio España de Gerona, Radio Lerida, Radio Manresa* and an associated station, *Radio Popular de Figueras.*

On January 9, 1947, *La Compañía de Radiodifusión Intercontinental,* with studios in Madrid, was granted a concession and authorized to operate with a power of ten kilowatts. By 1951, it had linked up with a number of domestic and foreign stations and was broadcasting an international program service. In 1955, the Government extended its concession for twelve years and today, through informal negotiations, it exchanges programs with stations in other areas, including Andorra, Gibraltar, Monte Carlo and Luxembourg. It has impressive studios in Madrid and superior transmitting equipment. Its programs featuring popular music and newscasts have attracted a large audience in Spain and adjacent areas.

A third network of regional character, *Rueda de Emisoras Rato* (RER), began in 1948 when *Radio Toledo* was established and was featuring sportscasts. These and other broadcasts of regional interest have become increasingly popular and today the RER, through an association of five affiliated stations, is heard by a large audience in southern Spain.

During the Civil War, a number of short-wave stations, operated by amateurs, made their facilities available to the "Nationalist" forces. For military reasons, their transmitting power was increased and they performed useful propaganda purposes in General Franco's crusade. When peace was restored, they were grouped in a network called *La Red de Emisoras del Movimiento* (REM). Their main purpose has been to support the Falange Movement which had its inception prior to the war. In November 1954, by order of the Ministry of Information and Tourism and the Secretary General of the Movement, the REM stations were integrated with the state-owned network.[39] Its stations, which previously had been transmitting mainly via short-waves, were assigned frequencies in the standard broadcast band. The total transmitting power was increased considerably, achieving much wider and more effective coverage.

Cooperating and working closely with the *Radio Nacional de España*, the REM has featured many informational and educational programs designed to promote emotional solidarity among the Spanish people and to improve the national culture. Of special note is its sponsorship of music festivals and other creative activities in the arts. In 1964, Spain celebrated twenty-five years of peace. The REM dedicated many of its programs during that year to General Franco and the accomplishments of his Administration. That same year, it sponsored a national poetry contest *(Justas Poeticas de la Paz)* which stimulated many creative minds in Spain and attracted widespread interest.

Almost fifty stations now make up this Movement combine and, being harmoniously associated with the state-owned network, constitute a valuable educational and propaganda medium for the National Government.

In June 1941, a small two hundred watt station, founded by the Spanish University Union, started operating in Madrid. It developed into a system of school stations, *La Cadena Azul de Radiodifusión* (CAR), sponsored by the Youth Front, an organization established to stimulate interest and support among the young people of the nation for the Movement and its causes. In addition to educational broadcasts the CAR sponsors training programs and workshops for persons preparing for careers in radio and television. The network now includes more than sixty stations and provides both commercial and noncommercial programs to listeners in all sections of the country.[40]

Another network, *La Cadena de Emisoras Sindicales* (CES), comprising about sixty stations, is owned and operated by the trade unions, or syndicates. Its operation is separate from the Movement networks and is administered by an independent board composed of representatives of its affiliated stations. Its main purpose is to provide information and entertainment for the workers and various industries of the nation and to serve their interests and needs.[41]

The Catholic Church continues to be active in the radio field. Based upon records of the Director of Radio and Television in the Ministry of Information and Tourism, COPE (Network of Spanish Popular Waves), operated by the Church, now has fifty stations. Individual parishes throughout the country were operating more than one hundred additional stations, with power ranging from less than one hundred watts to as much as two kilowatts. Most of them were transmitting with less than one hundred watts, had meager installations, and were largely the instruments of parish priests.[42] However, these small parish stations have been required to cease operations, because many were unauthorized and were conjesting the radio spectrum.

Frequency Modulation Broadcasting

FM broadcasting got its start in Spain in March 1957, when the *Radio Nacional de España* established an experimental station in Madrid. Shortly thereafter, this station was providing a regular program service from four to half past four in the afternoon and from half past nine to midnight. The following year, the RNE began a second FM operation in Barcelona. By 1964 there were nine FM transmitters (governmental and commercial) in major cities with a combined power of fifty-nine kilowatts.[43] As will be more fully explained later, the Government, by administrative decree, has acted to accelerate FM development in the country. It is expected that this will eventually result in a nation-wide network service.

Foreign Broadcasting

BEFORE and during the Civil War, short-wave transmissions conducted by amateurs and private interests were received by foreign listeners. The fighting forces conscripted their use for military purposes. During and after the hostilities, the Franco regime broadcast via short-wave to Spanish outposts and to other parts of the world. It was not until 1942, however, that the Government initiated a systematic schedule of programs designed especially for foreign listeners. That year, as previously mentioned, the *Radio Nacional de España* constructed a forty kilowatt short-wave transmitter at the Arganda Center near Madrid, and began beaming programs to America and other distant lands.[44] Since then, the RNE has expanded its short-wave facilities and now operates a network for Spanish outposts in Africa, the

Atlantic and Mediterranean areas, and beams programs in more than twenty languages to Asia, Africa, the Middle East, Europe and South America.[45]

Problems of Mushroom Growth

OFFICIAL reports in 1964 showed about thirty domestic broadcast stations classified by the Director-General of Radio and Television under the category, *Situación Especial*.[46] A number of these stations had not been officially authorized by the Government. At the beginning of 1965, more than five hundred stations were on the air. The proliferation of Spanish stations resulted in a chaotic situation. Multiple, and in some cases, unauthorized operations militated against quality programming and often interfered with good reception in some areas. As a corrective measure, the Government announced on December 22, 1964, a "transistory plan" to reduce the number of medium-wave stations. The plan authorized, without change, the continued operation of the government network and its affiliates, and the nine state-owned but privately and commercially operated stations. But it proposed to reduce the number of stations of the National Movement, limiting their power to two kilowatts, and permitting only one such station to operate in each province. An exception was made in the case of Madrid, where two Movement stations would be allowed, each with a maximum power of twenty kilowatts. Limitations, likewise, were to be imposed on Church stations. Only one, with a maximum power of twenty kilowatts, would be authorized in Madrid, and only one with two kilowatts in each of the provinces.

The decree further stated that the Ministry of Information and Tourism, within thirty days, would publish in the *Boletin Oficial del Estado* the list of authorized stations and these stations would be required to file applications for temporary permits to continue operation. The procedures for closing unlicensed stations were also set forth in the government order.

It was announced that each of the companies and enterprises receiving the authority to continue medium-wave broadcasting would be required to construct, within eighteen months, a frequency modulation station and operate it simultaneously during the hours of medium-wave transmission. The construction of these new facilities, as prescribed by the Government, was officially considered to be an important step in the development of nation-wide FM and stereophonic broadcasting.[47]

Radio Programming

A study of the Spanish Institute of Public Opinion contains detailed information regarding the programs presented by radio stations in Madrid during the time of December 2–18, 1963.[48] Conferences with knowledgeable persons in Madrid plus considerable monitoring of programs in the early part of 1965, suggested that the broadcasts for December 1963, were still fairly typical of station offerings in that city, although there were some changes in 1964.[49]

An analysis of the schedule revealed that *Radio Nacional,* on its First Programme, devoted approximately ten percent of its broadcast time to news. More than twenty percent was taken up with informational discussions on labor, industry, agriculture and economic subjects, plus reports on the weather and other subjects of interest to the public. Sports occupied about six percent of the schedule. Classical music (symphonic, chamber, opera, musical comedy) ran about twenty percent, while light music topped all categories with more than thirty percent.

Other program types with divisions of time were: interviews and conferences, 1.73 percent; serials, 0.77 percent; literary adaptations, 3.54 percent; drama, 0.88 percent; programs for women and children, 2.06 percent; and a general category labeled "cultural," 8.05 percent.

It is interesting to compare the programs of *Radio Nacional,* which is state-owned and operated, with those of five privately and commercially operated stations in Madrid. For example, the average time of these commercial stations for news was only three percent as compared with the ten percent for the national network. Whereas *Radio Nacional* devoted twenty percent to "informational" programs, the commercial stations averaged only twelve percent. Also, they devoted more than forty percent of their time to "light music," including popular records played on request shows.

These private stations used seven percent of their time for quiz and audience participation shows whereas the schedule of *Radio Nacional* revealed none of this kind of programming. They devoted about fifteen percent of their broadcasting to commercial advertisements with one station running as high as twenty-seven percent.

It should be mentioned that the broadcast format of *Radio Peninsular,* the state-owned and operated commercial station in Madrid, varied considerably from that of *Radio Nacional.* More than eighty percent of its time in 1964 was taken up with popular music, less than five percent was devoted to classical numbers and less than four percent to news. The schedules, however, showed a comparatively small portion of time, four percent, used for broadcast advertising.

Note should be taken of a program schedule of *Radio Nacional* for the last week of April 1964, as reported by the Institute of Public Opinion.[50] In some program categories, there was little change from the December 1963 schedule just analyzed. The percentages for news and symphonic music remained about the same but the total time for all other types of "classical" music was almost two-thirds less and "information, cultural" programs had been reduced by one-half. At the same time, "light" music had been increased almost nine percent, with more emphasis on Spanish melodies.

In addition to *Radio Nacional's* First Programme which is varied in content and designed for a wide audience, the Government broadcasts a separate schedule of programs, consisting mainly of classical music and "cultural" offerings, to appeal to the intellectual and aesthetic interests of the radio audience. Moreover, its FM transmissions are largely musical. More than one-half of the time is devoted to popular music, about thirty percent to classical, especially symphonic, and the remainder to news and "informational" and "cultural" programs.

Radio Advertising

RADIO advertising has become a prosperous business in Spain, particularly in the Madrid and Barcelona markets. The total income for broadcast advertising in these markets for November 1963, as reported by the Institute of Public Opinion, was 14,196,944 pesetas. Of this total, the stations realized the following incomes for that month: *Radio Madrid* and its network, 7,467,628 pesetas (fifty-three percent); *Radio Intercontinental,* 3,445,600 pesetas (twenty-four percent); *Radio España,* 690,770 pesetas (five percent); The Voice of Madrid, 622,916 pesetas (four percent); *Radio Juventud,* 151,035 pesetas (one percent); and *Radio Peninsular,* 1,818,995 pesetas (thirteen percent).

Manufacturers of food products spent the most for radio advertising during this period, 11.94 percent of the total. Drugs and perfumes came next with 8.58 percent. Other products and percentages were: garments, 7.14 percent; wines and liquors, 5.72 percent; pharmaceuticals, 6.28 percent; assorted department store goods, 5.12 percent; electrical appliances, 5.26 percent; soaps, 4.53 percent; household goods, 2.02 percent; clothing and ready-made goods, 7.14 percent; watches and jewelry, 1.86 percent; automobiles and accessories, one percent; *"espectáculos,"* 2.97 percent; advertising agencies, 0.37 percent and *"varios y guias commercials,"* 35.36 percent.[51]

Instructional Broadcasting

A small number of instructional programs were carried by private stations in Spain during the early days. Not until the fifties, however, were any systematic schedules set up and broadcast over wide areas. The Ministry of National Education created the Cultural Extension Commission *(Comisaría de Extensión Cultural)* which for many years has supplied Spanish stations with "cultural and educational" programs on a variety of subjects, including poetry, theater, music, history, religion, art, literature and languages. Moreover, in the early sixties, the Commission became interested in the development of systematic, sequential instruction by radio and began an experimental program called *Radio Reválida* (School Diploma by Radio). The success of this experiment prompted the Commission to expand the operation. Cooperating with the Director-General of Secondary Education *(Dirección General de Enseñanza Media)*, the Commission set up Radio Baccalaureate *(Bachillerato Radiofónico)*. This school provides, through the facilities of more than two hundred stations in Spain, daily instruction at the elementary and secondary levels. It has proved to be especially useful to working people and to those who live in sparsely populated areas far removed from teaching centers. The Commission supplies each registered, tuition-paying listener with reading materials related to the broadcasts and, if he desires, he may submit written papers for review and correction, take final examinations and, if successful, receive a diploma certifying completion of the courses.[52]

The *Bachillerato Radiofónico* programs are prepared and recorded in special studios owned by the Commission. Outstanding instructors are chosen to present the lessons. In 1964, the Commission reported that more than ten thousand persons had registered for the courses, not to mention the large number of unenrolled listeners who benefitted from the instruction.

Recently, the *Bachillerato Radiofónico* service has been extended to Spaniards living abroad. The programs have been taped and sent to schools in Germany, Switzerland and France, where Spanish nationals may listen to the tapes and, with the help of teaching aids, acquire the knowledge necessary to pass the courses. Examiners are sent to these schools in other countries to conduct final examinations, grade the papers, and certify passing marks for those students registered for academic credit.

Television

TELEVISION started in Spain on an experimental basis in 1951; regular programming was initiated in 1956. All facilities are owned by the State and *Televisión Española* (TVE) is operated by the *Dirección General de Radiodifusión y Televisión* in the Ministry of Information and Tourism. The total investment in these facilities has been estimated by network officials to be over seven hundred million pesetas.

There are nine central studios in Madrid (five new ones have just been constructed), four studios in Barcelona and one in Las Palmas in the Canary Islands. National network service is provided by an extensive system of relay transmitter centers located in the following cities: Chamartin–

Madrid (two kilowatts), Navacerrada–Madrid (two hundred and fifty kilowatts), Barcelona (one hundred and twenty-five kilowatts), Santiago de Compostela–La Coruña (sixty kilowatts), Sollube–Vizcaya (sixty kilowatts), Guadalcanal–Sevilla (sixty kilowatts), Aitana–Alicante (sixty kilowatts), La Muela–Zaragoza (ten kilowatts), Izañan–Tenerife (three hundred kilowatts), Alpicat–Lérida (three kilowatts), Gomoniteiro–Oviedo (three kilowatts), Altabia–Baleares (three kilowatts) and Sierra Lujar–Granada (two hundred kilowatts).

Programs are produced in both the Madrid and Barcelona studios and are transmitted over the network, with the major portion emanating from Madrid. Thus far, the station in the Canary Islands has broadcast only programs coming from the mainland, except for one informational feature which originates in the local studio.

The 1964 Report of the Institute of Public Opinion revealed that there were five hundred and sixty regular employees in the national network system including three hundred and thirty-four in Madrid and sixty-eight in Barcelona. The remainder were technicians distributed among the other relay centers.[53] In addition, according to the Report, there were from six to seven hundred actors engaged in one or more performances on the network in 1964.

Excluding executive and administrative personnel, the Report listed twenty-four university graduates as regular employees, including six "technicians," six engineers, one lawyer, three industrial experts and one doctor of philosophy.

Informed sources in Madrid report that as of October 1967, the total number of employees in TVE had increased to more than twelve hundred. Two hundred and thirty were engaged in the production of programs; six hundred and fifty-eight were performing technical services; one hundred and ninety-seven were doing administrative work; seventy-eight were stage carpenters and sign painters; and ninety-eight were subaltern employees.

Nature of TV Programming

In 1963, eighty-one percent of the television programs emanated from the studios in Madrid, eighteen percent from Barcelona and two percent from Eurovision. Twenty-four percent of the total broadcast output from these three sources was of an "informational" and "cultural" character, two percent related to religion, four percent to sports, six percent to variety shows, four percent to quiz programs, thirteen percent to Spanish and North American telefilms (serials), nine percent to live dramatic shows, five percent to children's programs, two percent to "home" features, and two percent to feature films (Spanish, Italian, French, English, Mexican and U.S., a majority being from the United States). The remainder of the time was classified as *"carta de adjuste y signo de Inversion."*[54]

Special TV Programs for Children

IN September 1965, the Information and Publications Commission for Children and Young People in Spain reported on some new developments in television programming. The TVE was making a special effort to provide regular high-quality programs for children and adolescents. An expert in child psychology was placed in charge of these broadcasts. He had the assistance of an advisory committee of specialists on different aspects of child behavior.

Careful studies and critical discussions led to various conclusions and program criteria established by those in charge of the telecasts. One important conclusion was that educational programs for the young should be "explicitly recreational and implicitly cultural and instructional." "What must be found," said the head of this new service, is a "hero" or protagonist "who is exemplary in a constructive way, while the programmes must be adapted to the child's psychological world, paying special attention to age groups." Other conclusions related to the hours chosen and the duration and selection of the programmes, as well as to their subject matter, with special emphasis on meeting the psychological, political, religious, social and cultural needs of children.[55]

Short "filmlets" were presented daily. For example, a short program each evening, "Let's Go to Bed," had a large audience among Spanish children. "Kids," presented from six to seven o'clock on Thursday evening for children under twelve years of age, attempted to appeal to the fancy of the child by scenes "depicting little heroes, fantastic figures and clowns." A second regular feature, "Only For Young Persons," broadcast from five to half past five each Saturday evening, was intended for adolescents. On Sunday evening from five to six o'clock a variety show for children of all ages was presented. This broadcast included comic films and cartoons, puppet shows, and various competitions of interest to young people.

Jésus Mario Vázquez, the head of this new television service, suggests the emphasis now being placed upon television as a means of influencing Spanish children:

> The social phenomenon of television, in relation to children and young people, is one of the subjects being intensively studied by TVE. Ever more frequent meetings, studies of increasing depth, more and better trained specialists in each aspect, all converge in the effort to plan, construct, complete and present children's programmes commensurate with the great importance of this delicate and indispensable task.[56]

Instructional Television

THE *Comisaría de Extensión Cultural* of the Ministry of National Education, working with the *Dirección General de Enseñanza Media* (Director of Secondary Education), prepares and provides video tapes which are broadcast by the TVE and which complement the *Bachillerato Radiofónico* radio programs previously discussed. The subjects which have been televised in this experimental project include the natural sciences, geography, history, mathematics, languages, drawing, physical education, chemistry and religion. Lessons thirty minutes in length are televised three times per week, and are illuminated with pictures, dioramas and other audio-visual aids.[57]

Television Advertising

Televisión Española is authorized to carry commercials and a substantial portion of its revenue comes from this source. In 1963, the gross proceeds from network advertising amounted to 521,267,945 pesetas. Out of this amount, thirty-nine agencies were paid commissions of 39,439,757 pesetas. The same year the State contributed an additional forty-two million pesetas to the television enterprise.[58] Recent reports indicate that the income from commercial TV advertising during the past several years has substantially increased. In 1966 it was about one and one-half billion pesetas.

Television sponsors in 1963 included: food industry, fifteen percent; beverage companies, seventeen percent; assorted goods, seventeen percent; electrical appliances, seven percent; amusement enterprises, six percent; cosmetic concerns, six percent; drug companies, three percent; toilet articles, two percent; magazines and periodicals, three percent; and home furnishings, ten percent.[59]

Televisión Española does not prepare commercials but sells blocks of time to agencies who in turn contract with individual companies for the advertisements. All commercials, however, must be approved by network officials before they are broadcast.

The Government continued for several years to collect an annual tax on television receivers (three hundred pesetas for those with small screens, five hundred for the larger ones). However, the increasing revenue from advertising made it possible to abolish this tax and presently there are no license fees on radio or television sets.

The Outlook for Television

As previously stated, there are now more than 2,550,000 television receivers in Spain, but viewers have been limited to one program. In early 1965, *Televisión Española* started experimental transmissions foreshadowing a second program that will run simultaneously with the first. This new service will use UHF channels and eventually is expected to be nation-wide.

As stated by *Televisión Española,* the purposes for the experimental transmissions now being carried on are: (1) to train technicians to take charge of transmitters to be installed in the future for a nation-wide service; (2) to help Spanish industry to adapt television receivers to the UHF channels and transmission; and (3) to study the technical problems in UHF transmission.

The Government announced in late 1964 that experimental transmissions would be conducted from two to three hours per day and would consist of programs already broadcast over the VHF network.

Following the experimental period, it was expected that UHF transmitters would be built in Barcelona, Zaragoza and other principal cities in Spain. The ultimate goal is a network of thirty-four UHF stations, the building of which the Government anticipates will require at least three years.

NOTES

1. Royal Decree, February 8, 1917; *Gaceta de Madrid,* February 9, 1919, pp. 322–324.
2. Royal Decree, January 13, 1920; *Gaceta de Madrid,* January 14, 1920.
3. Anibal Arias Ruiz, *La Radiodifusión Española, Publicaciones Españolas,* No. 453, 1964, Madrid. This is a discussion of the history of broadcasting and its control in Spain by a government official who has been concerned for many years with the regulatory aspects of radio and television in Spain. He is Director-General of the REM, the national network of Movement Stations. The author is indebted to Mr. Ruiz for making this excellent paper and other helpful materials available for study. Much of the historical data in this chapter is based upon a translation of his study.
4. *La Correspondencia de España,* April 17, 1923, p. 5. As of January 1968, one peseta was equivalent to 1.4 cents.
5. Royal Decree of February 27, 1923.
6. *Gaceta de Madrid,* No. 153, June 2, 1923, pp. 897–900.

7. Ruiz, p. 8.
8. *Ibid.*
9. *Ibid.*
10. *Ibid.*, p. 8.
11. *Ibid.*, p. 9.
12. *Sociedad Española de Radiodifusion, Radio Barcelona, Sus Mensajes Llegan a Todos Los Hogares,* Publication No. 3, 1964, pp. 3–4.
13. *ABC* (Madrid), January 1, 1929, p. 48.
14. *Ibid.*, p. 61.
15. Ruiz, p. 9. Also, see *ABC*, January 4, 1929, pp. 40, 44 for advertisements of *Telefauken* and *Radio Saturno* radio sets.
16. Ruiz, p. 9.
17. *Ibid.*
18. *ABC*, March 1, 1935, p. 51.
19. Order of Ministry of Public Works, dated November 22, 1935.
20. See William C. Atkinson, *A History of Spain and Portugal* (Baltimore: Penguin Books, 1961), p. 330.
21. Ruiz, p. 11.
22. *Ibid.*, p. 12.
23. *Ibid.*
24. *Instituto de la Opinion Pública, Estudio sobre los Medios de Comunicación de Masas en España,* Second Part, 1964, pp. 625–627.
25. Ruiz, pp. 25–26.
26. *Boletin Oficial del Estado, Gaceta de Madrid.*
27. Ruiz, p. 12.
28. *Boletin Oficial del Estado, Gaceta de Madrid.*
29. *Ibid.*
30. *Boletin Oficial del Estado, Gaceta de Madrid.*
31. *Boletin Oficial del Estado, Gaceta de Madrid.*
32. *Boletin Oficial del Estado, Gaceta de Madrid,* No. 285, November 13, 1957.
33. *Ibid.*
34. *Boletin Oficial del Estado, Gaceta de Madrid.* Also, see *EBU Review,* 47B, February 1958, pp. 24–25.
35. Ruiz, pp. 22–23.
36. *Boletin Oficial del Estado, Gaceta de Madrid.*
37. Ruiz, p. 24.
38. *Ibid.*, p. 23.
39. Also, see Ruiz, p. 29.
40. *Ibid.*, p. 31. Also, see *Instituto de la Opinion Pública,* pp. 628–629.
41. *Instituto de la Opinion Pública,* p. 630–631.
42. *Ibid.*, pp. 633–640.
43. Ruiz, p. 16.
44. *Ibid.*, p. 21.
45. See *Servicio de Programas en Onda Corta Para el Esterior, Radio Nacional de España,* No. 27, *programación,* December 14–27, 1964.
46. *Instituto de la Opinion Pública,* pp. 641–642.
47. *Boletin Oficial del Estado.*
48. *Instituto de la Opinion Pública,* pp. 679–726.
49. Based upon study of program schedules, select monitoring of stations by the writer and interviews with selected program directors and listeners.
50. *Instituto de la Opinion Pública,* pp. 701–702.

51. *Ibid.,* p. 620.
52. Data supplied the author by Ministry of Education in January 1965.
53. *Instituto de la Opinion Pública,* pp. 738–741.
54. *Ibid.,* pp. 749–762.
55. *EBU Review,* 93B, September 1966, p. 37.
56. *Ibid.,* p. 38.
57. Printed materials of the Ministry of Education.
58. *Instituto de la Opinion Pública,* pp. 762–776.
59. *Ibid.,* p. 763.

XXI

Portugal: A State Monopoly

T HE STATE HAS ALWAYS ASSUMED LARGE AND IMPORTANT POWERS in the life of Portugal and her people. From time to time there have been public reactions against authoritarianism. Attempts have been made to democratize the State and subordinate the Government's role, but these attempts have often been accompanied by violent social disorder and unrest. While no doubt there are some dissident elements in Portugal today, it seems clear that the people are generally content with the prevailing regime of Antonio de Oliveira Salazar who has kept the country free of wars and has realized new economic, educational and cultural benefits.

While political rule has been firm, there has been close cooperation with business and industry. Private enterprise and commercial practices have been encouraged, and so long as they have not interfered with what the Government considers the higher interests of the State, they have received full official sanction. Closely linked with this combine is the Catholic Church whose doctrines and practices over a long period of time have strongly affected the thinking and behavior of the people. Added to this triumvirate is the new force of education with its programs for reducing illiteracy, building and improving schools, and spreading knowledge.

Historic Social Patterns and Broadcasting

THESE basic social patterns have influenced the broadcasting system of the nation. As was true in most European countries, Portuguese radio was started during the twenties by amateurs curious about radio phenomena, and by private groups interested in the commercial possibilities of the medium.

A review of the newspaper files reveals that, for the most part, the only broadcasts heard regularly in Portugal during that early period emanated from foreign countries, including Spain, France and England. But by the end of the twenties, domestic broadcasting had made a start. For example, the January 26, 1929 issue of *Seculo,* a Lisbon newspaper, carried a program schedule of Station CTIAA in Lisbon which included recorded music, short talks, a piano recital, operatic arias, a 'cello concert and a duet. About the middle of the same year, another station, CTIBO, started operating in the capital. A short-wave station, CTIBO broadcast regularly on Tuesday and Thursday nights and Sunday afternoons with programs of recorded music, recitals by Portuguese artists and newscasts. Advertisements in the newspapers and public exhibitions of transmitters and receivers indicated a number of stations on the air and a growing market for radio equipment. Some of these early stations eventually banded together and formed the *Emissores Associados de Lisboa,* a commercial combine which is operating today.

Early Regulation

WHILE no general regulations had yet been adopted by the Government, stations were receiving assignments of frequencies and call letters from the Administration of Posts and Telegraphs in the Ministry of Commerce and Communications, in accordance with the agreements made in 1926 at the Washington conference on international radio communication to which Portugal was a signatory.[1] The Government had already taken the position that the radio spectrum was a natural resource clothed with the public interest and that its use should be subject to state control. In the light of Portuguese history and the dominant position assumed by the Government in other important areas of the national life, it is not surprising that Portugal followed the same course in the control of radio.

On January 27, 1930, referring with approval to the articles of agreement at the Washington conference, the Government decreed that all radio communication throughout Portugal was subject to state control. The law charged the Ministry of Commerce and Communications, through the Administration of Posts and Telegraphs, with the regulation of broadcasting on the continent, the Atlantic islands and the overseas colonies. It also authorized other ministries to use and control radio in governmental areas for which they were responsible.

Article V provided that the Ministry of Commerce and Communications, on proposal of the Postmaster General, might grant licenses for the establishment and operation of amateur stations on a trial basis. Operations unauthorized by the Government were strictly prohibited.[2]

During the next few years, the interest in radio increased rapidly. The Government, sensing the possible use of the medium to promote national solidarity and establish closer ties with its colonies, initiated plans for the building of a network and the expansion of its short-wave facilities. On June 29, 1933, in a new decree law superseding the one of 1930, the Government announced that a new state agency to be known as *Emissora Nacional de Radiodifusão* was to be created which would be responsible for national network operations and short-wave transmissions to outlying territories.[3] Article I reaffirmed the concept that radio is clothed with the public interest, constituting a state monopoly except that the Government might grant concessions and licenses to private concerns for commercial and noncommercial use.

The Ministry of Public Works and Communications was given the job of establishing short-wave facilities and the network system. The network was to consist of at least one medium-wave station in Lisbon and one in Oporto and was to be operated directly by the State or by some concessionaire under its control. The Administration of Posts and Telegraphs was given regulatory jurisdiction over the network as well as over other broadcast operations in the country. The Colonial Minister was authorized to establish stations in the overseas territories to relay the programs broadcast by the national network.

Article XI provided that valid sources of revenue for financing the network would be: (1) state subsidies; (2) taxes on station licenses and receiver license fees on the continent; (3) gifts from private parties subject to approval by the Government; (4) subsidies granted by official bodies; (5) twenty to fifty percent of the income derived from taxes on receiving sets in the overseas territories; and (6) income from publications.

A decree law of the same date stated that concessions for the operation of radio stations were to be granted by the Minister of Public Works and Communications subject to advice from the Director of Radio Services in the Administration of Posts and Telegraphs (*Administração Geral dos Correlós e Telégrafos*).[4]

The same decree imposed a small annual tax of six escudos on radio receivers, with additional fees assessed for sets used in cafes, clubs or other public places.[5] Taxes were also imposed on stations. Amateur operators were to pay ten escudos per year, private stations from twenty to one hundred, and broadcasting stations from forty to two hundred. All stations were obliged to secure licenses from the Minister of Public Works and Communications, based upon written applications. Call letters were assigned in accordance with the international conventions then in force.

Twenty-Five Years of Growth

OPERATING under the 1933 regulations, by 1940 the national network had expanded its facilities to include two medium-wave transmitters in Lisbon with a total transmitting power of thirty kilowatts, a short-wave facility with forty kilowatts, and two regional transmitters in Oporto and Coimbra for the relay of national programs. Along with this network development there was a marked increase in the number of radio receivers in Portugal. In 1933, the year the network started operations, there were only 15,973 radio sets in use. By 1940, the number had risen to eighty-nine thousand and three hundred.

During the Second World War, Portugal remained neutral, thereby avoiding the heavy drain on its resources which was experienced by many other European countries. The radio industry benefitted from the economic growth during and after the war. The number of radio receivers in Portugal doubled between 1937 and 1947 and had jumped to five hundred and thirty-four thousand by 1957. Meanwhile, the *Emissora Nacional* had expanded its facilities to provide wider and more effective service, and by 1957 had twenty stations with a total of six hundred and fifty kilowatts of power in operation.

Organizational Structure. During this time the network, with some minor modifications, had operated with the basic organization established in the thirties. There was need to improve its structure and more clearly define its functions in terms of new conditions. Accordingly, in 1957, a new decree law was adopted.[6] It restated the broad objectives of the *Emissora Nacional* —to provide educational and entertainment programs for home and foreign audiences. In addition, it authorized the organization to promote by its own means or by outside institutions the training of artists and technicians in the radio field, and under conditions set by ministerial order, to subsidize authors and other creative persons whom it determined to be worthy of such aid. Furthermore, it was to represent the nation in international radio conferences.

The statute further provided that the network agency, subject to the approval of the Government, could prepare and administer its own budget and collect its own income. Authorized sources of revenue were listed as government subsidies, license fees on radio receivers, ten percent of the proceeds from taxes on television receivers as collection expenses, private loans or contributions if authorized by the Government, and the income from public or private organizations for services rendered.

The *Emissora Nacional* was made an autonomous body with a Board of Directors, its chairman serving as Director-General and working directly with the Prime Minister; an administrative council composed of the Director of Administrative Services as chairman and the heads of bureaus concerned with general administration, accounts and budgets; a program council of six members composed of two administrative heads in the Department of Program Services and of four other persons of "proved competence," one of whom was to serve as chairman; and program committees to serve the regional broadcasting centers. All members of the Board of Directors, the councils and the committees were to be appointed by the Government.

The agency was made responsible for the collection of annual taxes on television and radio receivers used on the mainland. The decree prescribed an annual tax of one hundred escudos for radio sets and three hundred and sixty escudos for TV receivers. For nonpayment of the radio tax, the set owner could be fined from one hundred to one thousand escudos. Penalties for failure to pay the television tax could run as high as one thousand escudos, plus confiscation of the set.

Present Scope. Operating within this legal framework, the *Emissora Nacional* now provides a nation-wide radio service with two main studios and two transmitters each in Lisbon and Oporto and with relay stations in Coimbra, Faro, Guarda, Covilha, Viseu, Portalegre, Elvas and Ponta Delgada, and in Portugal's major provincial centers. In addition to its medium-wave service, it operates numerous high-power short-wave transmitters, beaming programs in various languages to its overseas territories and to many other parts of the world.

Using two different channels and one hundred and thirty-five kilowatts of power, the network broadcasts two separate program schedules, Lisbon I and Lisbon II. Parts of these programs are relayed by the regional stations and are received in all sections of the country.

The two broadcast schedules are essentially different. As described by network officials, Lisbon I, which runs from seven o'clock in the morning until one o'clock in the morning, emphasizes "informational" and "recreational" features, while Lisbon II stresses the "cultural." Among the recreational and entertainment programs appearing in recent schedules were popular music, light dramatic serials, frequent short news reports including sports reviews and commentaries and the "Daily Journal" which provides interpretations and depth analyses of important events in Portugal and other parts of the world.

Included in the informational offerings were stock quotations, weather forecasts, helpful household hints and reports on industrial and agricultural activities, fishing, mining and other important Portuguese pursuits, and talks on literature, history, art and science. Live orchestras and small musical groups presented varied types of popular music, including Portuguese folk songs. A number of choral groups and individual artists employed by the *Emissora Nacional* performed regularly over the network.

A part of the Lisbon I schedule consisted of school broadcasts designed by the Ministry of Education for use at the primary level. There were also special programs for teenagers. As pointed out by the Director of Program Services, an attempt is made on the first program to provide a service with wide appeal which is also sufficiently diversified to serve the informational and entertainment needs of different social classes.[7]

Lisbon II, which runs from noon until midnight, is geared to the intellectual and cultural interests of the listeners and includes both recorded and live symphony concerts, chamber music recitals, opera excerpts, and light music for the younger people. Some drama with a romantic flavor is included and cultural broadcasts from other countries are often presented. The second program also carries newscasts of important events at home and abroad and provides regular reports on public lectures, concerts, art exhibits and other cultural affairs. Drama with an aesthetic appeal and serious music (symphonic, chamber and opera) make up a large portion of Lisbon II's schedule.

Under the auspices of the Ministry of Education, an organization of university students broadcasts one hour per day (three hours on Sunday) over Lisbon II. The *Emissora Nacional* gladly makes its facilities available for "University Radio," since it offers valuable training for those wishing to do professional work in broadcasting and provides a type of educational entertainment service which has become quite popular among many radio listeners in Portugal.

The regional stations, while carrying a part of the network offerings, also originate broadcasts. These consist mostly of light music, news and information of local and regional interest.

Emissora Nacional also presents a late-evening third program over three FM transmitters. This consists mostly of symphonic and operatic music, with some news reports and occasional high-quality dramatic shows.

Overseas Radio

PORTUGAL has an extensive system of overseas broadcasting. Broadcasts are transmitted in a variety of languages including English, French, Italian, German, Spanish and Koncani. These programs are beamed to Africa, Europe, Southeast Asia, North and South America, the Far East and other parts of the world.

In the various overseas territories, including the Azores, Madeira, Angola, Mozambique and Guinea, the *Emissora Nacional* has its own facilities for transmitting and relaying programs from the mainland. In Angola, for example, with a land area of 481,351 square miles and a 1965 population of almost five million, broadcast coverage is provided by a short-wave station in Launda, the capital. Programs are received and re-broadcast by twelve local medium-wave stations distributed over Angola. Plans are under way to establish a network of FM transmitters which will duplicate and extend good program service throughout the territory.[8]

In 1965, the *Emissora Nacional* was supplying eight hundred hours of transcriptions per month to the stations in the various territories and to more than eighty stations in foreign countries. The overseas broadcasts emphasize the common interests of the nation and the colonies and a continuing effort is made to strengthen political and cultural unity.

Commercial Broadcasting

THE first regular commercial broadcasting in Portugal was provided by the *Radio Clube de Portugues,* first licensed on April 21, 1931. This station, formerly owned by a private club, was later taken over by a cooperative association.[9] It is still operating today with studios and transmitters in both Lisbon and Oporto.

Radio Renascenca, another commercial operation in Lisbon which started operating in the early thirties, is owned by the Catholic Church. Six small independent stations in the city also carry commercials. All operate in their own names with their own studios, but are associated in an organization known as *Emissores Associados de Lisboa* and share transmitting facilities.

Three small commercial stations operate in Santarem, Covilha and Regua. Five others are located in Oporto. These eight stations share transmission facilities and are associated in an organization known as *Emissores Reunidos de Norte.*

The technical operation of all private stations is regulated by the Administration of Posts, Telegraphs and Telephones (PTT) and the programming of the stations is under the jurisdiction of the National Secretariat for Information, Popular Culture and Tourism.

Radio clubs own private stations in the provinces of Madeira, Angola, Mozambique, Sal Tome, the Cape Verde Islands and Macao. For example, in Angola more than fifteen such clubs transmit programs. Licensed by the provincial PTT agency, they finance their operations in part by advertising.

The general format of these continental and provincial stations consists of light recorded music, short news reports and advertisements, supplemented by tapes prepared and supplied by the *Emissora Nacional* in Lisbon.

Television

IN 1953, the Emissora Nacional began planning a television service for Portugal. On January 27 of that year, the Government appointed a Television Study Committee consisting of representatives of the *Emissora Nacional,* private broadcasting stations and the Post, Telephone and Telegraph Administration.

Acting upon the recommendations of this Committee, in October 1955, the Government issued a decree setting forth the principles governing the grant of an exclusive license for operating a public television network for twenty years, with a provision for extending it by consecutive periods of ten years, and with an option of purchase by the Government after the first ten years of operation. It was specified that the transmission standards of the Portuguese television service would consist of the six hundred and twenty-five line system (CCIR) used by most countries in Western Europe. The concession was granted to the corporation, *R. T. P. Radiotelevisão Portuguesa S A R L* (RTP). As prescribed in the decree law, the corporation began with a minimum capital of sixty million escudos with the Government holding one-third of the shares (twenty thousand), private commercial stations in Portugal and in several of the provinces owning one-third, and banks and other private interests the remaining third. On November 17, 1958, the total capital was increased from sixty to one hundred million escudos and the additional forty thousand shares were subscribed by the Government.

As provided by the law, the organization of *Radiotelevisão Portuguesa* consists of a Board of Directors made up of five members of Portuguese nationality, two of whom are appointed by the Government with one designated as chairman. A general meeting of all the share-holders elects the other three to represent nongovernment interests. As of 1965, two of these three represented the commercial radio stations and the third represented the banks and other private interests holding shares in the corporation.

There is also a Fiscal Board of three members, one appointed by the Government, the other two elected by shareholders having no connection with the State or anybody representing it. This Board has the privilege of advising the Directors and of making recommendations to the general meetings of the shareholders. The members of the Board of Directors and the Fiscal Board are elected for three years and are eligible for re-election. Disputes between the Government and the RTP, should they occur, are settled by a Court of Arbitration of three members, one chosen by the Government, one by the RTP and one by the Supreme Court.

The law provides that the technical operations are to be regulated by the Post, Telegraph and Telephone Administration and that the television network and its operations are to be financed by a tax on receivers, receipts from commercial advertising, and ten percent of the taxes on radio receivers collected during the first ten years of the network's operation.[10]

The corporation, as authorized, has conducted a program promoting the sale of receivers. In fact, it has stores in both Lisbon and Oporto where it sells receivers at moderately low prices. Many private dealers are also engaged in the business. In early 1965, there were almost one hundred and fifty thousand sets in use in Portugal as compared with only seventeen thousand and five hundred in 1958, shortly after the RTP began operating.

The RTP started television broadcasting in Lisbon in August 1956. The network has been expanded and now operates stations in Lisbon, Oporto, Coimbra, Montejunto and Monchique with a number of auxiliary transmitters distributed to provide wide coverage.

Television Programs. To stimulate interest and encourage the purchase of receivers, the RTP has carried programs with a broad appeal. In October 1964, it announced the following divisions of time for various program categories as typical of its program service: current news and commentary, 14.53 percent; actualities, 3.95 percent; sports, 5.56 percent; dramatic productions, 17.19 percent; classical music, 1.60 percent; light music, 5.43 percent; specials, 16.96 percent; cultural programs, 9.00 percent; educational, 8.43 percent; advertising, 6.39 percent; and subsidiary, 10.96 percent.

"Special programs" included daily summaries of national and international news, commentaries by experts on important national and foreign events and informational features dealing with subjects of general concern, such as "accidents on the highways" and other topics related to the health and welfare of the nation. In addition, there were weekly sports reports. The RTF was linked with the Eurovision network on January 1, 1966, thus enabling direct broadcasts of events such as the Olympic Games.

During 1964 there were four hundred and seventy-nine broadcasts of dramatic shows, including films, and live production of plays by well-known national and foreign playwrights. Such American shows as "Bonanza," "Beverly Hillbillies," "Mr. Ed," "The Lucille Ball Show," and Walt Disney productions were featured. British programs from the British Broadcasting Corporation and Independent Television were carried, and for a time "Cinema Museum" showed older American films featuring Charlie Chaplin, Douglas Fairbanks and Rudolph Valentino, as well as pioneer European productions.

Music of the finest quality was presented by both national and foreign groups. Outstanding Portuguese artists, Italian opera, symphony orchestras from Paris, Munich and Rome, popular jazz, folk songs and other types of music consumed one hundred and twenty-five hours of network time during 1964.

Programs for different groups—farmers, homemakers, children, teenagers and schools—were broadcast. The schedule included course offerings in mathematics, physics, music, physical training and Portuguese history. There were broadcasts on literature, sculpture, painting, ballet and other arts. The listeners' religious interests were served by regular features such as "meditations," "our Lord's Day," "Tomorrow is Sunday" and the mass.

A report received from *Radiotelevisão Portuguesa* regarding TV programs since 1966 read, in part:

> . . . In 1965 and 1966, studies on the composition of the TV audience have been made as well as an analysis of their preferences.
>
> Over this period, we did not fail to offer, in acceptable proportions: serious music and ballet; light entertainment; interviews and cultural speeches; film series and long films; newsreels; programs for children, for the youth and for women; sport newsreels and sport events live coverage, etc.
>
> In 1966 the total transmission time has reached 2,930 hours, 38 minutes, 55 seconds, exceeding by 571 hours, 21 minutes and 16 seconds the 1965 production.

Being a comparatively small country with limited economic resources, Portugal does not provide the quantity and variety of television programming seen in the United States and some European countries. Viewers cannot make program choices, but must listen to the one transmission coming over the network. But this will not always be the case. Studies are now well advanced in Lisbon for the introduction of a second TV channel, for coverage of the Madeira and Azores Islands, and for the building of a new production center. Some experiments with color television are being carried on but it has not yet been decided whether to adopt the French (SECAM) or German (PAL) system.

Television Advertising. Unlike *Emissora Nacional, Radiotelevisão Portuguesa* is authorized to sell and broadcast commercials. At first it used its own staff for this purpose, but subsequently it was decided to assign the task to a firm of advertising experts. Accordingly, exclusive monopoly rights have been granted to Movierecord, an advertising agency which handles all the business, supplies all the commercials and shares the income with the network.

Advertising rates for Class A time (half past eight in the evening to sign off) range from three thousand and five hundred escudos for a fifteen second spot to as high as 10,750 escudos for a full hour. At these prices, the advertisers secure full network coverage, including the large markets of Lisbon and Oporto; since there is no competing television service, they are assured of the entire television audience, whatever it may be at a given time.

The Future of Portuguese Broadcasting

WHILE its present facilities are fairly adequate, *Emissora Nacional,* now in its thirty-fifth year, is in serious need of more studio space and improved equipment. Its expanded domestic and overseas operations now include two domestic medium-wave services and one FM, plus extensive short-wave transmissions to its provinces and to foreign countries throughout the world. To provide the needed facilities, plans have been made to construct a large broadcasting center in Lisbon which, when completed, will be one of the finest in Europe.

Although television is comparatively new in Portugal, its present studios are not adequate. With the increasing interest in television programs, more elaborate facilities will be needed to provide the high-quality, diversified service which will be demanded by the public. Officials of the RTP and the Government are aware of this and have long-range plans for meeting the need as it arises.

On January 7, 1965, the Minister of Education announced that an Institute would be established by decree law to promote the instructional uses of radio and television as well as other audio-visual aids. He also stated that a "teleschool" would be set up to provide supplementary teaching materials to the schools and general public. The plans included the systematic broadcasting of vocational instruction and informational programs of a literary, scientific, economic and civic character, for the benefit particularly of those who have had little formal education.

The Minister stated that the Institute would provide broadcasts on the arts, the technical and social sciences and other subjects with an intellectual and aesthetic appeal for the educated viewer.

The Minister announced that special reception and teaching halls would be provided in various sections of the country for those wishing to enroll in the "teleschool," and that teaching permits would be granted by the director of the Institute to those qualified and wishing to participate in the nation-wide program of instruction.[11]

This TV school was initiated on October 11, 1965. The RTP, working with the Institute for Audio-Video Means of Teaching in the Ministry for National Education, now carries on sequential instruction in languages, geography, the natural sciences, mathematics, drawing, and other subjects. Students may enroll in the courses and obtain certificates which permit them to continue their education in classical or technical schools. These instructional programs are produced in the Oporto studios and are telecast daily from three o'clock in the afternoon to seven in the evening.

NOTES

1. *Diario do Govêrno*, January 29, 1930, p. 194.
2. *Ibid.*
3. Decree Law No. 22:783, *ibid.*, June 29, 1933, pp. 1206–1208.
4. Decree Law 22:784, *ibid.*, pp. 1208–1212.
5. As of January 1968, one escudo was equivalent to three and one-half cents.
6. Decree Law No. 41:484, *Diario do Govêrno*, pp. 1481–1500.
7. See Jose Luis Da Silva Dias, *Director dos Servicos de Programs, Emissora Nacional de Radiodifusão, Plano do Programs para 1964*, November 1963.
8. *Ibid.*
9. Information supplied by officials of *Emissora Nacional*.
10. For full text of the law see Administrative Decree No. 40:341, *Diario do Govêrno*, October 18, 1955, pp. 891–895.
11. See *Diario do Noticias* (Lisbon), January 7, 1965, p. 2. Also, see *TV in Portugal*, booklet published in 1967 by *Radiotelevisão Portuguesa, S. A. R. L.* (Rua de S. Domingos (à Lapa), 26, Lisboa 3). This is the latest report on current TV programming in Portugal and is written in both English and Portuguese.

· H ·

THE SOVIET UNION
AND EASTERN EUROPE

XXII

The Union of Soviet Socialist
Republics (USSR): Statism Supreme

THE UNION OF SOVIET SOCIALIST REPUBLICS is a federation of fifteen
Republics. The Russian Soviet Federated Socialist Republic (RSFSR,
or Soviet Russia proper) contains more than fifty percent of the
USSR's total population and more than seventy-five percent of its territory.
Its capital is Moscow and it is here, in the Kremlin, that the basic national
policies for broadcasting, both domestic and foreign, are formulated and
executed.

All means and instruments of production in the USSR constitute state
property or are subject to collective ownership. State property includes
land, minerals, waters, forests, factories, mines, transportation facilities,
banks, large agricultural enterprises, most dwelling houses and communications, including broadcasting.

Early Broadcast History

ONE of the first radio stations to be operated in the Soviet Union was the
Khodyne station, built in Moscow in 1914. Operating with a power of one
hundred kilowatts, it was used by Soviet authorities during the Civil War
and came to be known as "The October Revolution Radio Center."[1]

The Soviet Government established a radio laboratory in 1918 to conduct
experiments in radio telephony and radio broadcasting. These experiments
had the enthusiastic support of V. I. Lenin, who wrote the director of the
laboratory:

> . . . I am taking this opportunity to express to you my deepest gratitude
> for the work you have accomplished in the field of radio research. The newspaper without paper and "without boundaries" you are devising will be a
> brilliant achievement.[2]

Until 1922, experimental broadcasting was carried on in Moscow,
Gorkij, Kazan and in other locations. In August of that year, however, the

first Soviet broadcasting station, operating on a regular schedule, was initiated. On September 17, 1922, the first all-Russian radio concert was presented. This marked the beginning of outstanding musical programs which became increasingly popular with Russian listeners.

From the beginning, Russian radio was viewed as an important political instrument. The recorded speeches of Lenin were being broadcast as early as December 1922. A Soviet radio official reported that "a mighty step forward in Soviet broadcasting was recorded in 1924 when Moscow Radio started regular transmissions of talks and lectures, news from journals, and later broadcast concerts, theatre performances, reports of demonstrations of workers on Red Square in the Soviet Capital, etc." Radio had found its way into the everyday life of the Soviet people.[3]

By 1924, the Government was broadcasting over its Moscow facilities with one hundred and fifty kilowatts of power, and in 1926 it set up a short-wave radio link between Moscow and other cities.[4]

During the next decade, an extensive radio network was constructed. At the end of 1934, there were two and one-half million listeners.[5] As Alex Inkeles has pointed out, there was much stress on group listening.[6] In 1936, for example, in one city, Kharkov, of twelve hundred radio receivers, one hundred were located in "houses of culture," stores and dormitories, and it was estimated that there were from four to five thousand radio listeners in the city.[7]

Postwar Developments

As in other countries, broadcasting facilities were conscripted largely for military purposes during the Second World War. At the end of the fighting there were fewer than six million radio sets. However, once peace was restored, Soviet authorities gave special attention to developing the national broadcasting system. They built new research institutes and laboratories and stepped up the production of transmitters and receivers. The central broadcasting facilities in Moscow were greatly expanded and many stations were built in other regions.

By 1956, it was reported that twenty-five million radio sets were in use, and as many as one hundred million Russians were listening daily to the programs of Soviet Radio. In addition, the wired systems of transmission had reached almost national proportions and were bringing through loudspeakers the message and music of communism to hordes of farmers and millions of citizens in towns and villages throughout the USSR.[8]

Not only were the Soviets pushing the spread of these communication systems in every part of the Union, they were extending technical aid and facilities to neighboring communist countries. Broadcasting officials in

Rumania, Poland, Hungary and North Korea, to mention only a few, have acknowledged the Soviets' help and participation.[9]

The dimensions of broadcasting in the USSR in 1956 were explained by the then Deputy Chairman of Soviet Radio, I. Andreyev:

> The organizational structure of the Soviet radio tends towards satisfying the demands of listeners living in different parts of the country and speaking different languages.
>
> At present the average daily air time is 125 hours. Three parallel programmes are broadcast for the inhabitants of the Soviet Union. Apart from that, special programmes are devised for listeners living in the Far East, Siberia, Ural and in Central Asia. . . .
>
> Broadcasting is carried on in more than 85 languages spoken in the USSR and abroad. Not only in the union and autonomous republics but also in small national districts and areas, programmes are broadcast in languages spoken in the respective areas. . . . Even such numerically small nationalities as the Evenks, Sakha and others who until the October revolution had no written language of their own now hear programmes in their mother tongue.
>
> The activities of the Soviet Radio are extensive and varied in character. It informs listeners about the most significant events of home and international life, disseminates the great ideas of Marxism-Leninism, the most important decisions of the CP of the USSR, reports on experiences of outstanding workers and farmers and on achievements in culture, science and art. . . .[10]

Increased Emphasis on Political Propaganda

As previously mentioned, the Russian Government has always viewed broadcasting as a strong, effective tool for political propaganda. This political emphasis was greatly increased in the decade following the Second World War, as the Communist Party grew and extended its influence and power in all important areas of Soviet life. The increasing use of radio for discussions of the Communist Party's policies has been described by Mr. Andreyev:

> An important place in the programme of the Soviet Radio is occupied by talks given by commentators on various problems concerning international problems and questions of foreign politics, by talks analysing the decisions of the XXth Congress of the CP of the USSR which ratified the Leninist principles of foreign politics: the policy of peaceful coexistence and development, of the reinforcement of mutual confidence and of the development of international collaboration. Concrete examples and facts prove the peace-loving foreign politics of the Soviet Union, tending towards relaxation of tension in international relations. Exhaustive analyses are presented revealing the attitude of the Soviet government towards problems of inter-

national concern such as: the cutting of armament, ban of atomic weapons, the establishment of a collective security system, the solution of the German problem, the development of East-West contacts, restoration of legitimate rights of the Chinese People's Republic . . . . A number of transmissions deal with problems of peaceful coexistence of states with differing social systems, with the establishment of friendly political, economic and cultural relations between the USSR and the countries of Asia, with the national liberation movement in colonial, semi-colonial and dependent countries, with the peace movement, and with the situation of workers in the capitalist countries.

   The Soviet Radio regularly broadcasts popular talks analysing the internal situation of the USSR and the directives for the Sixth Five-Year Plan given by the XXth Congress of the CP of the USSR. In articles and lectures discussing important political, economic and cultural problems, the gigantic organizational work of the Communist Party of the USSR is demonstrated and its role as the leading and directing force of the Soviet society is revealed. . . .[11]

Following the war, the Government stepped up its technological research in many areas. Carefully calculated plans were carried out to stimulate widespread interest in technology and the study of science. Discussions by renowned scientists and specialists in a variety of fields were broadcast regularly. An important subject which was frequently aired was "the infinite technical possibilities of atomic energy . . . in a way comprehensible to the masses. . . ."[12]

In 1956, in line with the directives of the Twentieth Congress of the Communist Party, programs, designed to promote agricultural production and strengthen the national economy, were broadcast regularly to the farm population.

As reported that same year, over half the programs of Soviet Radio were musical. More than fifty concerts, presenting more than four hundred pieces of music with more than one hundred soloists, were broadcast.[13] Russian officials stated that a large component of the schedules consisted of folk and contemporary music, recorded by soloists and orchestras in forty countries, including the Chinese People's Republic, Poland, Czechoslovakia, Hungary, Rumania, Bulgaria, Albania, the German Democratic Republic, Yugoslavia, North Korea, Vietnam, Finland, India and Indonesia. Some of these countries reciprocated by broadcasting Russian music. These exchanges were apparently designed to strengthen inter-cultural ties and promote friendship for the USSR.

A wide variety of other programs—dramatic, literary, educational and artistic—made up the remainder of the schedules. As in all communist countries, many broadcasts designed for young listeners emphasized the ideals of communism and its progenitors, Marx and Lenin. It can be accurately said that the overriding purpose of all areas of Soviet broadcasting during the late fifties was "directed towards the most successful popularization of the historical decisions of the 20th Congress of the

Communist Party of the USSR and of the Directives of the Sixth Five Year Plan."[14]

Present Organizational Structure and Dimensions
of Russian Broadcasting

THE Center for International Studies at the Massachusetts Institute of Technology reported that there were, as of April 1963, forty-seven long-wave, sixty-two medium-wave, sixty-one short-wave, and eighty-six FM broadcasting stations in the USSR.[15] These stations were distributed throughout the Union with a heavy concentration of facilities in the western part where the bulk of the Russian population resides. Transmitters operate at three levels. The highest of these are operated by Central Broadcasting in Moscow and provide long- and medium-wave and wire service to Moscow and its suburbs and to networks in close proximity to the capital. Central Broadcasting also transmits programs via short-wave to isolated and distant networks.

The second level of transmission is carried on by networks operating in the various Republics. Interconnected by wave or wire, or both, with Moscow Central, they carry many of the Moscow broadcasts and originate some of their own for radio and wire distribution to listeners within their coverage areas.

The chief function of the lowest level of broadcasting, the radio diffusion exchange (*radio translyatsionniy uzel*), is to receive programs, usually by wave transmission, from Moscow or regional centers, and transmit them via wire to receivers in homes, factories, or public address systems in a variety of locations. In some cases, the exchange may add programs of local interest.

The receivers in these local wire systems consist of a transformer, speaker, volume control and a switch. And, until recent years, as listeners were limited to the one program carried by the radio-uzel system, the receivers had no selection apparatus. In the early sixties, however, multi-programming was introduced in some areas.[16] Special selector devices which could be attached to an ordinary loudspeaker became available, making it possible to receive more than one program. The report of the MIT Center for International Studies has pointed out that "Moscow, possessing the largest wired network in the country, with over 1,500,000 radio-points, was the first locality to receive the new system on a large scale, though it has been used in Riga, Latvia, in Ashkhabad, Turkmenia, and in the Uzbek Republic. The extension of the system is planned to cover eventually the whole of the Soviet Union, thus providing some power of program selection even for those who do not own wave sets."[17]

The number of radio receivers has greatly increased in recent years. In 1953, there were only half as many such receivers as there were wired speakers. According to 1963 data, there were about thirty-three million wired and thirty-two million radio receivers.[18] There are now more than forty million individual radio receivers, twenty-four million of which are equipped for short-wave reception. The number of wired speakers has increased to about thirty-eight million.[19]

With the growth of networks and the vast increase of reception points in recent years, the maintenance of wired systems has become increasingly expensive. Moreover, the reception quality of the wired loudspeakers now in use is comparatively low. Soviet authorities, therefore, probably will not push for further expansion of the wired systems, but more likely will emphasize the development of multiple channel broadcasting and the use of improved radio sets. As will be shown later, in the rural areas the wired receivers still far outnumber radio sets, but the latter are increasing steadily.

Growth of FM

As has been the case in many European countries, FM broadcasting has had an accelerated growth in Russia in recent years. A partial explanation may be found in the following statement by a former chairman of the Russian State Committee on Radio and Television:

> FM broadcasting is to a large degree free of the inadequacies which are inherent in AM broadcasting on the long, medium, and short-wave lengths, since it is almost entirely free of static interference. . . . A large scale development of ultra short wave broadcasting is one of the ways to improve and expand local broadcasting inasmuch as, with the broadcast of the Central program, it permits the organization of high quality broadcasts by the oblast and republic radio without interfering with the central programs.[20]

According to the report of the MIT Center for International Studies, eighty-six FM transmitters were operating in the USSR.[21] Because of the increasing interest the Soviets have shown in providing, at the local level, more broadcast facilities and a wider range of programming, the number of FM stations has since increased to over one hundred.[22]

Rural Radio

SPECIAL mention should be made of the use of radio in rural communities. In 1957, more than four thousand collective farms had wired radio systems, with about seven and one-half million plug-in sets; the number of radio and TV receivers grew from nine hundred thousand in 1954 to 2,223,000 in 1958.[23] Since then, there has been a substantial increase in all types of receivers. For example, in 1960, in the rural areas of the Russian Republic, there were 8,620,000 plug-in sets and 1,877,000 radio sets.[24]

The report of the MIT Center for International Studies describes the service provided by rural radio:

> . . . The example which we have at our disposal is that of a collective farm of "average" size, located in the Ukraine near the town of Dnepropetrovsk. The farm covers an area of about 3,000 hectares (approximately 7,200 acres). On the farm live and work 1,100 persons in 600 separate households. Since there are only 12 trucks for the use of the farm workers and two cars for the exclusive use of the farm chairman, the use of mass media becomes an especially important means of communicating with the community outside of the farm.
>
> Because of the size of the farm, radio is also used as a means of communication between the administration of the farm and its members. The farm has its own radio-diffusion exchange, which receives broadcasts from the local network in Dnepropetrovsk and broadcasts them to the home speakers, of which there is one in almost every household. At the diffusion network the farm sometimes adds local features having to do with farm production, goals, and so forth; the farm chairman frequently speaks to members of the farm over the exchange. There are radio sets in about half of the farm households. An exact proportion of the number of television sets to population was not obtained. Indications were that there were quite a few sets on the farm, but "not, of course, enough to go around." This is probably a fairly unusual farm in this respect. Television is still a fairly rare phenomenon on most farms. Programs are transmitted from Kiev and Dnepropetrovsk; often programs from Moscow can be seen via the Kiev stations, but this is not done on a regular basis.[25]

Radio Programming

IN 1964, Radio Moscow was broadcasting four separate programs in sixty-four languages for a total of five hundred and forty-five hours per week. Music took up more than fifty percent of the time. Sixteen percent was devoted to news, more than ten percent to socio-political items, nine percent to literature and drama, about seven percent to special programs for children and a fraction more than two percent to other programs.[26]

Stations in other Republics, territories and regions were broadcasting more than six thousand and five hundred hours per week in their native languages, and providing a variety of programs of local interest.[27]

Programs for listeners abroad are transmitted by Radio Moscow on short- and medium-waves in more than forty languages. In addition, programs are broadcast in as many as eight languages spoken by various national groups in different parts of the Soviet Union.[28]

Foreign Broadcasting

THE foreign broadcasts of Radio Moscow are beamed by high-power transmitters to all parts of the world for more than one thousand hours per week. In response to a request in 1960 for information about the history of Radio Moscow, Victor Kuprianov, formerly associated with "Moscow Mailbag," a regular feature of the station, wrote that "Radio Moscow broadcasts in foreign languages date back to the autumn of 1920 when the first program was beamed to Germany. . . ."[29]

He further stated that in November 1927, a number of foreign groups visiting the Soviet Union to participate in the Tenth Anniversary of the Socialist Revolution were permitted to broadcast their impressions from Moscow. Thereafter, Radio Moscow periodically broadcast in foreign languages, and in 1929 a regular foreign service was initiated. Mr. Kuprianov explained the nature of the initial service and the circumstances leading to its establishment:

> This was the period of the first 5-year Plan. The country had repaired the damage caused by World War I, by the Civil War and Intervention. The Soviet people started overcoming their century-old economic and technical backwardness and launched on a gigantic industrialization program. Radio Moscow's mail pouch kept growing and growing. Many requests came from abroad asking for information about the world's first socialist country. To cope with these requests a foreign broadcasts service was inaugurated. The Foreign Service Broadcasts Department was organized in October, 1929. At first, Radio Moscow broadcast in German every other day, twice daily. Beginning with November 7th, Radio Moscow started broadcasting in French, and one month later—in English. In 1930 these broadcasts became regular daily features.[30]

Mr. Kuprianov also pointed out that by 1933 Radio Moscow was broadcasting in English, German, French, Hungarian, Spanish, Italian, Swedish, Czech, Turkish and Portuguese. By the middle of 1941, the station was transmitting programs in eleven languages regularly and in others periodically.

The station became an important propaganda medium during the Second World War and transmissions were expanded to reach countries under the Hitler yoke—Slovakia, Greece, Iran, Poland, the Netherlands and Norway. Special broadcasts were designed for the Jews then subject to the persecution of the Nazis.[31]

Mr. Kuprianov reported that after the war "Radio Moscow's main object became promoting world peace and friendship between the nations, and describing the progress made in building a communist society in the Soviet Union."[32] In 1960, daily broadcasts in foreign languages amounted to one hundred and twenty-eight hours, twelve of which were beamed in English to the United States.[33]

New York consultant Chester Burger, formerly the National Manager of CBS Television News, stated in the Spring 1966 issue of *The Public Relations Quarterly* that Radio Moscow had attained a high level of effectiveness in its propaganda broadcasts. He referred specifically to the program "Moscow Mailbag" as one of "the most listenable and impressive programs on communist radio." His description and evaluation of the program are as follows:

> The program format is simple, nothing more than questions sent in by listeners in the United States, plus answers provided by commentator Joe Adamov. Several factors account for its remarkable success. For one thing, the names, street addresses, and cities of the questioners are always given: these are not "planted" questions. For another, the program producer generally tries to select questions which are hostile rather than those which are sympathetic to the Soviet Union. This turns out to add considerable interest and credibility to the program.
>
> The answers, of course, represent the Soviet viewpoint. The Red view of the world is generally presented with quiet understatement, avoiding strong or extreme language. While Americans would not accept the communist opinions expressed, the facts generally are accurately presented, at least insofar as they can be readily checked by U.S. sources.
>
> Many questions ask about particular aspects of Soviet life, and they are answered equally factually. There is little or no attempt to embellish, moralize, or to propagandize heavily. When criticisms of United States policies, conditions, or activities are made, they are given matter-of-factly, rather than in a name-calling or hostile manner.
>
> But these low-key techniques do not fully explain the power of "Moscow Mailbag." In my observation, two additional factors are responsible. The first is the consistent use of the "third-person endorsement" so familiar to public relations practicioners and also used by the Voice of America. . . .
>
> To validate its statements, "Moscow Mailbag" invariably cites United States sources. Assuming the listeners know Moscow has a communist axe to grind, "Moscow Mailbag" quotes not Pravda or Izvestia but The Wall Street Journal, The New York Times, Business Week, and The Chicago Tribune, along with many others. Names and dates are given so carefully that a public relations man instinctively assumes that the Moscow radio station must subscribe to a U.S. press clipping service. For skeptical American listeners, these quotations carry credibility.
>
> The major reason for the program's impact, however, is the commentator himself, Joe Adamov. Mr. Adamov speaks in impeccable English, without the slightest trace of any accent. It is not schoolbook-English, or even Berlitz-

English, it is ordinary conversational English. Adamov is relaxed; he is idiomatic; he is friendly without being syrupy; he is factual without arrogance or condescension. He reminds you of the intelligent and well-informed fellow who lives next door, and who has dropped in on a Sunday evening for a drink and a stimulating conversation.

I don't know if Mr. Adamov ever lived in the United States, but I suspect he did. I don't know how anyone could acquire his easy fluency in English without prolonged residence in the United States.

But more than that. Mr. Adamov obviously prepares his program by gathering notes and background information about the questions asked, and then adlibs his answers to a tape recorder. He sometimes hesitates, corrects himself, emphasizes, repeats. But he never reads a script, as many other international broadcasters have yet to learn.[34]

Television Programming

ACCORDING to UNESCO reports, experimental telecasts in the Soviet Union were first made in 1931. TV stations were on the air in Moscow and Leningrad in 1938; a third station began broadcasting in Kiev in 1951. In 1964 ninety-three main stations and numerous relays made programs available to half of the Russian population.[35]

In 1964, Moscow, Kiev and Riga had stations operating on two channels. Other cities had telecasts on only one channel. Moscow I was broadcasting five hours on weekdays and seven hours on Sunday. Moscow II was on the air only two hours per day, not including Sunday. Informed sources report that experimental color television, using the French system, is occasionally broadcast in the Kremlin. At the time of this writing, regular color telecasts have not yet been presented.

The administrative and organizational structure of Moscow Central Television is illustrated by the chart on the following page.[36]

The Moscow Central Television station (on the air more than sixty-five hours per week) was providing programs as follows in 1964: films, twenty-two percent; literature and drama, nineteen percent; music, eighteen percent; news, seventeen percent; programs for children and young people, fourteen percent; socio-political items, eight percent; and miscellaneous broadcasts, about two percent.[37]

TV stations in other cities carry many of the programs transmitted by Moscow Central, and also produce in their own studios programs of regional and local interest. The Moscow operation is linked by cable to Kiev, Minsk, Riga, Rostov-on-Don, Tallin, Leningrad, Sverdlovsk, Bukhara and Tashkent.[38]

The Russians have emphasized the educational uses of television. One program, the "People's University," consists of three faculties—science

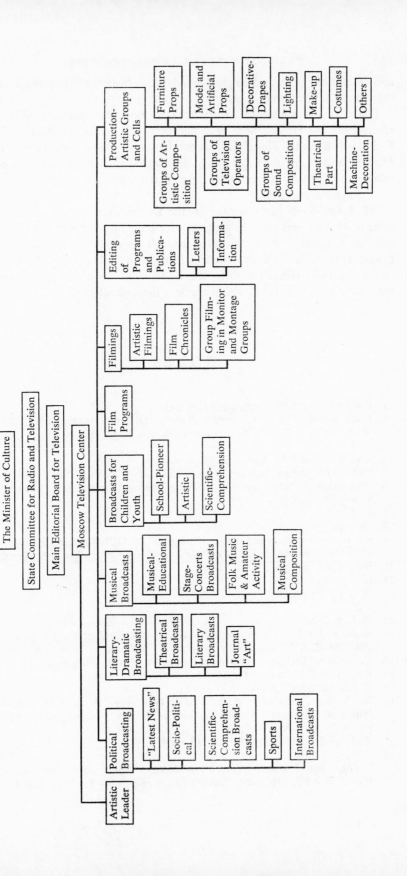

and technology, arts and English—and presents instructional programs in these areas several times a week.

It has been estimated that there are now more than nineteen million TV receivers in the USSR, more than half of which are in the Russian Soviet Federated Socialist Republic. More than two million of these are in Moscow and its environs. Many sets are located in clubs, social centers and other public places, where many persons not owning receivers are able to view programs regularly.

All Soviet television operates on the six hundred and twenty-five line system. The stations provide programs for both Intervision and Eurovision, and, on a selective basis, receive, through these international networks, programs from Eastern and Western Europe and other parts of the world. According to UNESCO reports, the USSR also has exchange agreements with more than twenty television services throughout the world.[39]

NOTES

1. *EBU Bulletin,* July–August 1955, p. 395.
2. *Documentation and Information Bulletin,* OIR (International Broadcasting Organization), Prague, September 1956, No. 4/5 (58), p. 239.
3. *Ibid.*
4. *EBU Bulletin,* July–August 1955, p. 395.
5. Ziglin, "Radio Broadcasting in the Soviet Union," p. 71.
6. Alex Inkeles, *Public Opinion in Soviet Russia* (Cambridge: Harvard University Press, 1958), p. 275.
7. *Ibid.*
8. *Ibid.,* p. 333.
9. See *Documentation and Information Bulletin,* OIR, for reports on postwar radio developments in the Soviet Union and the Eastern European countries.
10. *Ibid.,* pp. 239–249.
11. *Ibid.,* p. 239.
12. *Ibid.,* pp. 240–241.
13. *Ibid.*
14. *Ibid.,* p. 242.
15. *Radio and Television in the Soviet Union* (Cambridge: Center for International Studies, Massachusetts Institute of Technology, June 1965), p. 101.
16. V. Belikov, "Welcome Innovation," *Izvestia,* May 7, 1962, p. 4.
17. *Radio and Television in the Soviet Union,* p. 2.
18. *Ibid.,* Appendix I, p. 96.
19. See *National Economy of the USSR; Transport i Sryaz USSR.* Also, see James W. Markham, *Voices of the Red Giants* (Ames: Iowa State University Press, 1967), p. 85.
20. *Radio and Television in the Soviet Union,* p. 5.
21. *Ibid.,* p. 6.
22. Foreign Broadcasting Information Service, *Broadcasting Stations of the World,* Part III, Frequency Modulation Broadcasting Stations, June 1, 1966.

23. B. Kuibyshev, "Speed Up the Radiofication of the Farm," *Pravda*, July 18, 1958, p. 2.
24. A. I. Popov, "On the State of Cultural Service to the Population and Measures to Improve Them," *Pravda*, October 26, 1960, p. 2.
25. *Radio and Television in the Soviet Union*, p. 18.
26. UNESCO, *World Communications: Press, Radio, Television, Film* (New York: UNESCO Publications Center, 1964), p. 367.
27. *Ibid.*
28. *Ibid.*
29. *Journal of Broadcasting*, IV, No. 4 (Fall 1960), 337.
30. *Ibid.*
31. *Ibid.*
32. This is of course Mr. Kuprianov's opinion. Many students of mass media and politics in other parts of the world would take issue with him (see Markham, pp. 248–257).
33. *Journal of Broadcasting*, Fall 1960, p. 338.
34. Chester Burger, "Short Wave Lessons in Credibility," *The Public Relations Quarterly*, Spring 1966, pp. 11–12. Mr. Burger's special interest in propaganda broadcasts began with service in the CBS International Shortwave Division in 1941–42.
35. UNESCO, *World Communications*, p. 368.
36. This chart, prepared by F. Gayle Dunham, appears in *Radio and Television in the Soviet Union*, p. 109.
37. UNESCO, *World Communications*, p. 368.
38. *Ibid.*
39. *Ibid.*

XXIII

Hungary: Voice of the Proletariat

SOME HUNGARIAN OBSERVERS have stated that Radio Budapest, under communist control, played a major role in the uprising of 1956. They have recalled that some of the first shots were fired by soldiers defending the station against a crowd which appeared to protest the regime's broadcasts. The station's continued reports aggravated the populace and, according to these observers, was an important precipitating factor in the revolt.

The resistance was put down and broadcasting in Hungary continued to prohibit any criticism, literary or otherwise, questioning the ideals of communism or the policies of the Government. The mass media are completely dedicated to the propagation of the Marxian philosophy and the building of a communist state. The present Hungarian broadcasting system and its programs are rigidly controlled and structured to help accomplish these ends.

History of Radio

SOMETHING like radio communication got an early start in Hungary. In 1893, through a system of telediffusion invented by a Hungarian engineer, Tiradar Puskas, programs were transmitted by wire to receivers in homes and public places. These transmissions originated in a small studio in a wagon. News, presented five or six times daily, constituted the bulk of the first programs.[1]

Originally, the enterprise was experimental. With favorable response from subscribers, the schedules were expanded to include music, drama and informational programs. Encouraged by the success of the project, the founder of the system contracted with the Ministry of Posts, Telegraph and Telephone (PTT) to supply these programs regularly to telephone subscribers for a monthly fee. Studios and transmitting equipment were enlarged and improved. Theatrical and operatic shows and other quality performances were presented. The service became well established and was widely used in the Budapest area.

Experimental broadcasting in Hungary followed the First World War but not until the middle twenties was radio established on a regular basis as a state enterprise. The PTT, which had exercised regulatory control over the wire service, continued to supervise broadcasting. Following the pattern of some other countries, a private corporation with shareholders was formed in the early thirties and granted a concession by the Government to engage in commercial broadcasting. This corporation was given an exclusive franchise but was subject to regulation by the PTT.

During the Second World War two large transmitters and several smaller relay stations were operating, subject to control of the Government and occupying military forces. After the war, the commercial system was abandoned and an exclusively state-owned system was established.

Expansion Since the War. Under government control and operation, new radio transmitters were built, a nation-wide network service was established and the production of radio receivers was greatly increased.[2] Until the early fifties broadcasting in Hungary was highly centralized, with programs emanating largely from Budapest. Under the Five Year Plan, some local radio outlets were established. These centers provided the entertainment programs with local talent. Informational programs regarding the production of mines and factories and other matters of local and regional interest were included in these schedules.

Many of the best writers were enlisted to describe and dramatize the achievement of the Five Year Plan. Programs of special interest to the workers were presented. A literary department was formed "to make use of the best works of the past, both Hungarian and foreign, and of Russian literature, of which it has a very well-stocked library."[3] One series of discussions, "The Soviet Union—The Country of Socialism," described the life and work of the peoples of the USSR. There were some satirical broadcasts about America and the problems of colonial peoples. In accordance with agreements made with Czechoslovakia and Poland, the exchange of programs was increased in an effort to strengthen the bonds among the Eastern European countries.[4]

Hungary also expanded its foreign broadcasting. By 1950, it was transmitting in nine foreign languages six hours per day. Music and news were featured. Special programs in English and Magyar designed for North American listeners were also included in the schedule.[5]

As was true of many countries in both the East and the West at that time, Hungary stepped up its propaganda broadcasts to foreign countries. The *EBU Bulletin* reported that the postwar days had not brought about "the expected disappearance or decrease" in broadcast propaganda. On the contrary, it was "becoming the *raison d'etre*" of more and more broadcasting services. "Perhaps the most striking example," reported the *Bulletin,* "of the building up of foreign language services for purposes of radio propaganda," was "the case of broadcasts directed to Yugoslavia."

In 1946, the USSR broadcast to Yugoslavia less than nine hours per week; in September 1950, the total was more than fifty-five hours. In 1948, Hungary transmitted about three hours per week to its neighbor to the south; by 1950, this had increased to almost fifteen hours.

By 1962, the number of licensed radio sets had increased by almost two million, reaching more than two million and three hundred thousand, or approximately one receiver for every four persons. By 1967, there were almost two and one-half million radio sets in use.[6]

Television

THE State, with the help of the Hungarian Workers' Party, took the initiative in developing television. Experimental work began in the early fifties. The USSR provided much technical aid and equipment in the beginning. In 1953, plans envisioned the immediate establishment of a key station with studios in Budapest and an eventual network with transmitters located in the various provinces to bring television from Budapest to the entire nation.

Official 1953 reports stated that "activities at the Hungarian Television Office have reached fever pitch, particularly in respect of the coordination of planning and manufacturing of television equipment which will devolve on various factories and kindred institutions."

> Towards the end of next year, television will be fully available in factory clubs, social centers and so forth. During the next five-year plan period, mass production of television receivers will begin. Finally, large-scale introduction of receivers linked by cable to a central television receiver will make it possible to popularize television still further. This reception method is based on a recent discovery made by Soviet engineers. Television will thus provide the means of familiarizing workers even more with the achievements of soviet culture.[7]

Regular telecasting made its debut in 1958. At the beginning only one regular program per week was presented, but by 1962 the number had increased to six, supplemented from time to time by special programs.

To accomplish the State's objectives in broadcasting, the Office of Hungarian Radio was established in 1950. In 1952, jurisdiction was transferred to the Government Information Office. In 1958, authority was vested in a new agency, the Hungarian Radio and Television Service (*Magyar Radio es Televizie,* MRT), which is now responsible for all broadcasting.[8] Transmission facilities, excluding studios and accessory equipment, are owned and controlled by the Ministry of Posts, Telegraph and Telephone.

Administrative Structure

PRIOR to the establishment of the MRT, both radio and television operated under a single administration. Under the present organization, they function as separate, independent establishments. Both services, however, report to the president of the MRT, who is appointed by and responsible to the Council of Ministers.

The state broadcasting organization has four vice-presidents, two for radio and two for television. One of the radio vice-presidents is charged with administrative responsibilities for finances and personnel. The other vice-president is concerned with program planning and production and the use of the medium for the attainment of social, political, educational and cultural objectives. The two television vice-presidents have similar responsibilities.

In addition to the organizational units concerned with personnel administration and technical matters, both the radio and television divisions have four departments concerned with program areas as follows: political, musical, literature, and youth and children. Furthermore, each division is served by a central programming committee representing these different departments. The committee's primary function is to help achieve and maintain program balance. It regularly reviews programs which have been presented during the preceding week and each month prepares a statistical report on percentages of broadcast time devoted to the various types of programs.

Radio has a separate department for foreign broadcasts, including a central section for program planning and an operating branch for each language area. The central section prepares and furnishes the various branches with broadcast materials, news reports and commentaries, musical and literary programs. While a major portion of the program material comes from the central section, the language branches do some independent broadcasting.

Although radio and television have separate staffs and operate independently, they maintain close relationships. At the top administrative level, activities are coordinated through an advisory council of seven members: the president of *Magyar Radio es Televizie,* the two vice-presidents of each division, the secretary of the Hungarian Socialist Workers' Party and the secretary to the president of the MRT.

In addition to this council, a joint advisory group of key staff members, representing the different departments of the two divisions, coordinates the MRT's total program service. This group receives and discusses reports from the various departments in radio and television, considers problems of common concern, evaluates the broadcasting service as a whole and provides counsel on effecting the basic broadcasting objectives to which *Magyar Radio es Televizie* is committed.

Broadcasting Dimensions

As of May 1965, twelve medium-wave transmitters with a combined power of six hundred and thirty-six kilowatts were operating in Hungary. The transmissions from these facilities provide nation-wide coverage and reach into foreign countries. Six one hundred kilowatt short-wave transmitters beam programs to Europe, the Near East, and North and South America. Two FM installations, each with two kilowatts, serve limited areas.

The MRT operates six main television transmitters (six hundred and twenty-five line definition) in Budapest, Pecs, Miskolc, Szentes, Sopron and Kabhegy. Two auxiliary relays complete the system. With the building of the largest transmitter in Kabhegy in 1962, programs from Budapest are relayed over a radius of one hundred kilometers in the trans-Danubian section and from eighty to eighty-five percent of the country is now able to receive programs.

The MRT is a member of Intervision and regularly transmits and receives television programs through this Eastern European network. From time to time, it also connects with Eurovision, the Western network, and transmits programs considered to be of special interest to the Hungarian people.

In 1967, Hungarian authorities estimated more than two and one-half million radio and almost one million television receivers in use.[9] In addition, more than two hundred and sixty thousand wired sets received selective sound programs over telephone lines for which subscribers paid a monthly fee.

The Hungarian broadcast industry appears to be thriving. Receivers, transmitters and other broadcast equipment are manufactured in great variety. For example, a Hungarian publication recently reported that more than two hundred and ten thousand television sets were produced in 1962, and it was stated that "in the course of the second Five-Year Plan," the output of television sets was to be increased by seventy percent.[10]

Radio Programming

IN 1965, the total time for domestic radio exceeded thirty-six hours daily. From seventeen to eighteen hours per day are devoted to foreign transmission. Hungarians generally are music lovers and more than sixty percent of the programs are devoted to music, both popular and classical. Hungarian Radio organizes and promotes many music festivals which are broadcast domestically and are frequently relayed by systems in other countries.

Radio, as a state function, is considered an important educational medium. Programs on communist ideals and the building of a socialist state are emphasized. The schedules often include informational broadcasts and discussions on the interests, needs and problems of the agricultural and industrial workers. Numerous transmissions from Budapest treat the rich

Hungarian heritage in science, art and literature, although censorship imposes certain limits. Programs dealing with agricultural science, problems of health, Hungarian history, geography and literature, to mention only a few, have appeared in recent schedules.

In every important area of Hungarian life, the training, indoctrination and education of young people is stressed. The administrative structure of the Hungarian radio system has a special department concerned with youth, and includes regular broadcasts designed to influence the thinking of young people.

Some emphasis is placed upon programs for the schools. In 1964–65, regular transmissions available for the secondary schools covered a variety of subjects: physics, chemistry, geography, biology, music, history and language instruction in English and Russian. Also, a special program in elementary science was offered for children between the ages of six and ten.

Instructional broadcasts have been presented occasionally for more than ten years, but in 1962 a special radio school with systematic, sequential instruction was instituted as an experiment. The Minister of Education selected one hundred schools to participate in the program. According to Hungarian radio officials, the response of the educators and students was favorable and the service was established on a regular basis. Recent surveys indicated that about one-fourth of all the secondary schools in Hungary were using these broadcasts.

As of April 1965, the foreign broadcast service (both medium- and short-wave) was transmitting programs in English, German, Greek, Hungarian, Italian, Spanish, Arabic and Turkish. These programs consist largely of news, commentaries and music, both light and serious, with Hungarian folk tunes featured on some programs.

Television Programming

HUNGARIAN television, as reported in April 1965, was operating five hours per day four days a week, and nine hours on Sunday. About twelve percent of the time was devoted to news and commentary and about fifteen percent to live telecasts from theaters. In 1962, thirteen percent of the time was devoted to sports but this has since been increased to twenty percent.

The most marked increase in the past few years has occurred in educational programming, including television instruction for classroom use. In 1962, only 2.6 percent of the total television time was used for such programs; this has since been increased to twenty-five percent.

A television science program designed for school children is in an experimental stage but is expected to become a regular service. A large number of Hungarian schools have receivers and are already using this telecast.

The State provides television receivers to schools wishing to use the service but lacking funds to purchase the sets. This is not always necessary, however, since parents, parent-teacher associations and other community groups often are sufficiently interested to pay for the equipment.

The remainder of the programming is varied. Feature films, live drama (both light and serious), variety shows and a considerable number of Intervision and Eurovision programs make up a large portion of the schedules.[11]

Financing

THE Hungarian Radio and Television Service is financed largely by funds derived from license fees on receivers. The present monthly assessment is ten forints for radio, and fifty forints for television.[12] In 1964, with about 2,450,000 licensed radio sets and about 650,000 licensed television receivers in use, the monthly income from fees was more than one and one-half million dollars.

In addition, the state system derives some revenue from radio and television advertising. Small weekly portions of time are devoted to marketing information. These commercials, presented in time blocks separate from the programs, take the form of recommendations of products made by the Hungarian Radio and Television Service on the basis of quality and price. For this service, the manufacturers and dealers pay the rates set by the authorities of the state broadcasting system.[13]

NOTES

1. The data on the early history of broadcasting in Hungary were provided by MRT officials in Budapest.
2. *Bulletin de Presse de la Radiodiffusion Hongroise,* December 27, 1949, and January 16, 1950; reported in *EBU Bulletin,* May 15, 1950, p. 78.
3. *OIR Bulletin,* July 15, 1952; reported in *EBU Bulletin,* November 15, 1952, p. 636.
4. *Ibid.*
5. *EBU Bulletin,* October 15, 1950, p. 317.
6. Reports of MRT officials in Budapest; also, *Statistical Handbook of Hungary,* 1967, p. 11.
7. *EBU Bulletin,* September 1953, p. 603.
8. Information regarding organizational and administrative structure of MRT received from government officials in Budapest.

9. *Ibid.; Statistical Handbook of Hungary*, 1967, p. 196.
10. *Ibid.*
11. Data obtained from MRT officials.
12. As of January 1968, one forint was equivalent to four cents.
13. Data obtained from MRT officials.

XXIV

Yugoslavia: Regional Diversity

Y UGOSLAVIA HAS a population of about twenty million with five principal nationalities (Serbian, Croatian, Slovenian, Macedonian and Montenegrin) and a dozen minority groups, including Albanians, Turks, Hungarians, Rumanians, Gypsies, Vlacks and Slovaks. In this cultural mosaic there are two alphabets (Cyrillic and Latin) and three religions (Orthodox, Catholic and Moslem; Protestants form a tiny minority).

The Socialist Federal People's Republic of Yugoslavia *(Federationa Narodna Republika Jugoslavya)* consists of six republics: Slovenia, Croatia, Bosnia-Herzegovina, Serbia, Montenegro and Macedonia. There are also two autonomous regions administratively related to Serbia: Voivodina, north of Belgrade, and Kosmet, mainly inhabited by Albanians.

A unique feature of the political system is the Worker's Councils,[1] consisting of the personnel in the various industries called the "working collectives." Each of these Councils cooperates with the directors of the enterprise in the management of the business.

The broadcasting system of Yugoslavia has been developed to conform to both the country's cultural complexity and her communist institutions. The first radio transmissions in Yugoslavia were made in 1904 when an experimental station was put into operation on Volujica Mountain on the Adriatic Coast. The ceremonies opening this station were attended by Guglielmo Marconi himself and marked the beginning of an important era in radio communication in that part of the world. Subsequently this station became an important link between Yugoslavia and European countries to the west and east.

During the First World War, the original station was destroyed. New ones were established for military purposes, but they suffered the same fate. However, after the occupation forces withdrew, a number of other stations were built and used largely by postal authorities and by military and police establishments.

Following the war, radio amateurs became increasingly active. Because of their great contributions to a wider application of radio techniques in Yugoslavia, these enthusiasts may well be called the pioneers of the civilian sound and telegraph service.[2]

Early Regulation of Radio

FROM the beginning, radio channels were considered a part of the public domain and subject to government regulation. The Ministry of Postal, Telegraph and Telephone Service (PTT) exercised jurisdiction over radio communications, as well as over telephone and telegraph.[3] With the development of broadcast stations in other countries and the accelerated activities of amateurs at home and abroad, the PTT, on July 23, 1923, promulgated a regulation forbidding the use of receivers without a license from the Ministry.

The first attempt at regular broadcasting for home reception was made by an engineer who was authorized by the PTT to "broadcast a concert lasting one hour three times a week" over a station located near Belgrade. However, this operation was soon closed down because the Ministry did not feel that the quality of the programs merited the Government's continued support.

Broadcasting by Entrepreneurs. Other trial operations were carried on briefly in other parts of the country during the middle and late twenties. Radio clubs were organized and, despite high costs, radio receivers were imported in increasing numbers. One of these clubs applied to the Ministry for authority to operate a station in Zagreb. The license, issued on August 5, 1925, specifically stated that the station was to broadcast news, weather and stock reports, music and programs on the sciences and arts.

To obtain capital for the construction and initial operation of the station, the club secured government approval to organize a limited stock company which assumed the operation of the station. The permit guaranteed the shareholders one hundred and fifty dinars a year from each subscriber in Zagreb and the surrounding area.[4] By the first night of broadcasting, May 15, 1926, only two hundred and ninety had paid the fee. In less than ten years, however, the number had increased to almost nineteen thousand; broadcasting had become a profitable business.

During the same period, private enterprisers established two additional stations in Ljubljana (1927) and Belgrade (1929). A fourth station, built in Skoplje in January 1941, served mainly as a relay station for Radio Belgrade, although it did originate some programs in its own studios.

Radio Facilities Nationalized. As early as 1936, the Central Press Bureau in the Prime Minister's office had established a foreign language, short-wave station. Four years later, with the approach of the Second World War, the Government nationalized all broadcast facilities and assumed control of their operations. Most of these facilities were destroyed or taken over by the invading armies. During the later period of the war, some stations, including one called "Free Yugoslavia," were operated by the Supreme Command.

After the war, the older stations were restored to full operation. Several new ones appeared in different parts of the country, such as Radio Dubrovnik and Radio Rijeka in the Croatian Republic.

Under the Government's reconstruction program the commercial radio companies were dissolved and plans were initiated for a nation-wide network. The power of the stations in Belgrade, Zagreb, Ljubljana, Skoplje, Sarajevo and Novi Sad was increased. Under the new Tito regime, special attention was given to developing a system which would provide each nationality and its language with an outlet for expression. The *1963 Yugoslav Radio and Television Yearbook* (JRT) stated:

> This inviolable right was guaranteed to all Yugoslav nationalities including the minorities. This is what constitutes the special feature of the Yugoslav broadcasting programme. Apart from programs in Serbo-Croat, Slovene and Macedonian, the Yugoslav radio gave regular broadcasts in Italian, Hungarian, Czech, Rumanian, Slovak, Albanian, Ruthenian and Turkish.[5]

As social, economic and political conditions were stabilized under Tito's leadership, broadcasting facilities expanded rapidly. In addition to new stations, new relay transmitters were built to provide wider and more effective coverage. With over two-thirds of the country covered by mountain ranges, this was a serious problem. While the configuration of the Yugoslav terrain has continued to present difficulties, persistent efforts with the application of new scientific knowledge and techniques has made it possible to provide quality reception and service in most areas of the country. Plans are under way to increase the power of some main transmitters and establish additional low-power facilities to extend coverage to those sections not now adequately served.

Present Dimensions of Broadcasting

YUGOSLAVIA's domestic networks now consist of eight main regional and seventy local stations. The main stations are located in the capitals of the six constituent republics, Belgrade, Zagreb, Ljubljana, Sarajevo, Skoplje, Titograd, and in the capitals of the Serbian provinces of Novi Sad and Pristina. Of the local stations, twenty-eight are in the Republic of Croatia, eighteen in Macedonia, thirteen in Slovenia, six in Herzegovina and five in Serbia.

In 1939, on the eve of the Second World War, Yugoslavia had only three medium-wave and one short-wave radio transmitters with a combined power of forty-five kilowatts. As of January 1966, the country had one hundred and thirteen medium-wave transmitters with a combined power of more than six hundred and sixty-seven kilowatts. In addition, eighty-four VHF transmitters with a total power of six hundred and eighty kilowatts linked the main stations and provided means for broadcasting programs where medium-wave transmission was not available.

There is no central radio system in Yugoslavia. Because of the variety of distinctive cultures, nationalities and languages, the broadcasting leaders have encouraged the development of regional and local systems with indigenous programming. However, administrative machinery has been set up to facilitate program exchanges. The PTT provides transmission links by which the main stations share broadcasts with one another and with stations in other countries. Some stations have built their own high-quality connections for cooperative programming and improvement of reception in certain areas.

In 1939, there were only 155,133 licensed radio receivers in Yugoslavia. In 1966, there were over three million, the majority of which were in the more populous, urban areas such as Serbia, Croatia and Slovenia. Within recent years, however, National and Regional Governments and the radio industry have encouraged the purchase of receivers in the smaller towns and rural communities.

Radio Programming

ALL the regional radio stations operate from the early morning hours to midnight or later. Belgrade, Zagreb, Ljubljana and Novi Sad stations all have two programs running simultaneously part of the day. The first and more varied program is broadcast from eighteen to twenty hours on weekdays and from twenty to twenty-three hours on Sundays. The second broadcasts news, music and some entertainment five to ten hours daily. In the interest of providing more variety, a third program was introduced in 1965 and is carried by the Belgrade and Zagreb stations.

Officials of the Yugoslav Radio and Television Association (JRT) have reported on the programs transmitted by the eight regional stations in 1966:

> Classical music, 20.70 percent; popular music, 30.66 percent; folk music, 12.37 percent; news, 9.45 percent; foreign affairs, 1.87 percent; home affairs, 2.70 percent; economy, 1.90 percent; agriculture, 0.70 percent; sports, 1.43 percent; arts and culture, 3.55 percent; general education, 3.11 percent; special transmissions, 4.40 percent; popular transmissions, 2.10 percent; and economic publicity (advertising), 5.06 percent.

The JRT reported in 1966 that the regional stations then devoted more than forty percent of their broadcast time to informational and educational programs. An objective of paramount importance, they say, is to keep the listening audience informed about important "social and political events." At the national level, in 1963, the emphasis was on the preparation, adoption and "carrying out" of the new constitution of Yugoslavia; in 1964, "the stress was on the Eighth Congress of the League of Yugoslav Communists (SKJ) and the problems it considered." At the same time, stations generally reported activities of the "working collectives," efforts toward "strengthening of self-management, as well as material, financial and social progress in the communes."[6]

Special attention was given to events of international importance—President Tito's visits to Latin America, Finland, Poland and Hungary, President Kennedy's assassination, the Cairo Conference of Nonaligned Countries and the International Economic Conference, to mention only a few. Many broadcasts for domestic and foreign reception were designed to promote "the international labor movement and the development of the socialist countries."[7]

A perusal of Radio Belgrade's 1963 and 1964 schedules revealed a wide range of subject matter. Regular programs included:

"Tribune of the Socialist Alliance," a weekly broadcast with speakers from the League of Communists and other political workers; "Marxism Today," which elaborated the Marxist theory based upon the Yugoslav experience; "From Industry to Industry," with talks by economic leaders, the Federal Executive Council, the Chamber of Industry, trade unions and bankers; "Transmissions for the Countryside," with discussions by experts and social-political workers designed to stimulate and inspire agricultural production; "We in Society and at Home," including lectures and discussions by physicians, pedagogues, psychologists, civil engineers, economists, public officials, social workers and others expressing views on individual and community problems; "From the Glorious Days of the Peoples' Liberation War," a weekly broadcast presenting recollections of participants in the Second World War. Other program titles which appear to be typical are: "Natural Beauties of Our Country," "From the UN," "Through Our Enterprises," and "Red Signal' (traffic safety).

Chosen at random from the schedules of stations in other cities were such programs as "Panorama of Modern Poetry" and "Talks on Language," carried by Radio Ljubljana; "Man and His World" and "Literary Cabaret" on Radio Sarajevo. "Advice for Farm Producers," "Meeting on Sunday," "From the Life of Communes," "Physical Training and Sports" and "Practical Advice for Women" appeared in the schedules of other stations. Similar programs appear in 1966 schedules.

Drama occupied an important position in the cultural program category. In 1963 and 1964, the eight principal stations presented almost one thousand plays. Of these, one hundred and five were original Yugoslav dramas, forty-seven were premieres of adaptations; ninety were foreign plays and one hundred and three were premieres of adapted works by foreign writers. The *1966 Yugoslav Radio and Television Yearbook* indicates a similar emphasis on drama.

Adult Education. Special mention should be made of "Radio University," a program of adult education covering the sciences, the humanities and the arts. Another feature is "Radio School" with regular instruction available for classroom use. During the school year, educational authorities prepare and present over the stations a wide variety of subject matter, including geography, history, the natural sciences, art and foreign languages. It has been estimated that in 1964–65 more than eleven thousand elementary and secondary schools used this sequential instruction to supplement their regular curricula.

The stations present a variety of musical programs, including folk, jazz, classical, modern symphonic and operatic works. While recordings and tapes are used, many of the musical broadcasts are presented live.

To stimulate creativity in popular music, the stations sponsor musical contests and festivals which attract nation-wide interest. Prizes are awarded and members of the radio audience are permitted to participate in the selection of winners.

The leading radio stations conduct an extensive program exchange with foreign broadcasters. According to the *1966 Yearbook,* Yugoslav stations used roughly five hundred and seventy-four hours of recorded and taped music from forty foreign stations and supplied stations abroad with about six hundred and fifty hours of Yugoslav music.

Foreign Broadcasting

SINCE its first foreign broadcasting station was created in 1936, short-wave transmissions have come to occupy a central position in Yugoslav radio. Short-wave broadcasts for foreign audiences originate in the studios of Radio Belgrade and are prepared and administered by that station's Department of Foreign Programs. In 1966, more than ten hours of such programming was broadcast each day in Albanian, Arabic, Bulgarian, Czech, English, French, German, Polish, Russian and Spanish.

The stated purpose of the foreign transmissions is to provide listeners with an "objective and complete picture of Yugoslav reality, as well as the idea about the role and place of Yugoslavia in the current events of the world and her contribution to the international rapprochement and understanding among people."[8]

The *1963 Yugoslav Radio and Television Yearbook* has described the types of programs:

> All the broadcasts are generally composed in such a way that their first part represents the daily current material from Yugoslavia and abroad, and the second part consists of the material about Yugoslavia.
>
> The editorial offices of the broadcasts in individual foreign languages make the daily programme on the basis of weekly schemes which provide what the most important material is to be transmitted each particular day. The weekly schemes take care of the specific characteristics of the individual regions for which the broadcasts are intended. There are also broadcasts transmitted only in one or several languages and broadcasts which are common for all the transmissions.
>
> Broadcasts of 15 minutes are for the greater part composed of news from Yugoslavia and abroad. Sometimes, after the news, the corresponding com-

mentary on the most important home or foreign event or the home and foreign press review is broadcast.

In the broadcasts of 30 minutes, the bulletin of home and foreign news takes on an average 30 to 40 percent of the programme. Besides the news, the current commentaries are transmitted on home and international themes. The second part of the broadcasts consists of the material about Yugoslavia according to determined schedule. The material about Yugoslavia is very often illustrated with music which takes about 5 to 8 minutes of the broadcast.[9]

The general nature of the programs is illustrated by the following titles logged in the weekly schedules: "Seven Days in Yugoslavia," "From Yugoslav Republics," "Economic Chronicle," "Through the Yugoslav Press," "Tourism," "Yugoslav Schools," "Science and Technology," "Cultural Panorama," "Yugoslav Foreign Policy," "From the International Workers' Movement" and "Youth Broadcast."

The foreign programs of Radio Belgrade are financed by funds received from the Federal Government. Accordingly, the Federal Executive Council maintains an active interest in the technical and program operations of the short-wave service.

Through their medium-wave operations, some regional and local stations carry on broadcasting designed for national minorities in other countries. Special programs are beamed by Radio Novi Sad to Hungarian, Rumanian and Slovak listeners. Radio Koper has reported that it receives about one hundred thousand letters a year from its listeners in Italy. Radio Skoplje presents programs for Turkish and Albanian listeners. Radio Pristina does programs in Shiptar and Turkish. Yugoslav emigrants abroad may hear special programs from Radio Osijek and Radio Murska Sobota. Radio Zagreb does some regular broadcasts in Esperanto.

Radio Belgrade maintains a special service for contacts with foreign listeners and regularly solicits reactions to programs with expressions of opinion as to how the station can serve their interests more effectively. In 1966, the Foreign Program Department reported that it had received letters from seventy countries.

Radio Program Research

ALL the principal radio stations in Yugoslavia have conducted systematic studies to determine audience reaction and the effectiveness of programs. One of the first important studies of this kind, made by Radio Zagreb in 1959, attempted to find out from listeners something about the quality of its signal reception. Shortly thereafter, a program research department was established at Radio Belgrade and in most regional stations.

A second survey of Croatian listeners conducted by Radio Zagreb in the spring of 1962 showed that listeners in that area were as follows:

Housewives and office employees, twenty-seven and twenty-five percent respectively; elementary school pupils and workers, about fifteen percent; craftsmen, seven percent; high school students, five percent. At the time the survey was conducted, farmers constituted only four percent of the listeners to this station, although they owned twelve percent of the receivers. University students made up only a little more than one percent of the audience.[10]

A survey by Radio Belgrade in 1962 covering radio subscribers in eight towns and twelve villages in Serbia revealed data on the numbers of listeners at different periods of the day. It showed that from seven to nine o'clock in the evening, one and one-half million persons were tuned to the station, and from three to four in the afternoon there were about one million. About nine hundred thousand listened from six to eight o'clock in the morning. On the basis of the 1962 population figures for Serbia, about two-fifths of the persons above ten years of age were tuned to programs during the peak listening periods.[11]

A study conducted by the Ljubljana Institute of Sociology in which more than twelve thousand persons over fourteen years of age were polled (roughly one percent of the total population of Slovenia), showed that musical programs were much more popular than commentaries, and that national folk music was highest on the listening scale, followed by light music and jazz. Chamber and symphony music had the smallest audience (six percent).[12]

As might be expected, the more highly educated listeners preferred classical music. The same was true of discussion programs concerned with social, economic and political subjects. Despite the high rate of literacy in Slovenia, over fifty-five percent of the respondents stated that radio was their chief source of information, while only twenty-eight percent named newspapers and periodicals.[13]

While these surveys are not without significance in the areas where they were conducted, they do not necessarily reflect conditions throughout the country. Continuing efforts, however, are being made by broadcast leaders at national, regional and local levels to ascertain the distinctive interests of listeners and to evaluate the effectiveness of radio programs. In fact, the *1966 Yearbook* (the latest available to the author) reports considerable increase in research; for example, recent studies have been made as to the relative importance of the third program introduced in 1965 and carried by stations in Belgrade and Zagreb.

Television

TELEVISION got a much later start in Yugoslavia, relatively, than did radio, and sound broadcasting greatly influenced the pattern of television growth and control.

The Phillips Company made the first practical demonstrations of television in Yugoslavia in 1939. At that time, this Dutch company exhibited closed circuit operations at fairs in Belgrade and Zagreb. Interest was aroused but the war delayed development; television did not become a reality in Yugoslavia until twelve years later. In 1949, the Institute for Electro-Communications studied television techniques and two years later put into operation experimental equipment in Ljubljana. This developmental work was followed by joint studies of the electrical industry, Radio Belgrade, the PTT Ministry and the League of Yugoslav Radio Amateurs. At the same time, the Yugoslav Radio and Television Association (JRT), interested in promoting the medium, sponsored a number of regional meetings, one of which was held in Zagreb in December 1954.

On the basis of studies and reports made by the leaders of radio stations and other experts, the Federal Executive Council (FEC) set up a study commission to consider the introduction of television.

With the aid of French experts, Radio Zagreb took the initiative in establishing experimental facilities. By the end of 1958, with the promotional efforts and financial support of the JRT Association, stations were established in Belgrade and Ljubljana. Two transmitters in the Belgrade area and two in the environs of Zagreb and Ljubljana, together with a number of relays, made it possible for the three stations to exchange programs, as was the pattern in radio, and to provide television coverage to about four million people.

On November 28, 1958, the first Yugoslav television broadcast originated in Ljubljana. It carried the sessions of the Seventh Congress of the League of Yugoslav Communists and evoked widespread interest.

Current TV Dimensions. As of the end of 1966, there were thirty-five television transmitters in operation. A large number of TV links and repeaters extended coverage over wide areas. Studios are now located in Belgrade, Zagreb, Ljubljana and Skoplje. Plans for expanding studios and technical facilities are well under way. As of 1966, television was reaching more than eighty-five percent of Yugoslavia's area with service available to more than ninety-two percent of the people.

In 1957, shortly after the initial telecasts of the Zagreb Television Center, there were only four thousand television sets in Yugoslavia. By 1962 the number had reached one hundred and twenty-six thousand. In 1966 there were about seven hundred and seventy-seven thousand licensed receivers, and, with the completion of present plans and the realization of nation-wide coverage, it is expected that the number of licenses will increase substantially.

Television Programming. Television programs are now jointly provided by the large broadcasting establishments in Belgrade, Zagreb and Ljubljana. Sarajevo, Titograd and Skoplje, while lacking transmitting facilities, do contribute some telecasts.

In 1966, joint programs were aired seven days per week, with an average of more than twelve hours of broadcasting per day and a total of about three hundred and twenty-four hours for the month. In 1964, more than sixty percent of the total time was used to telecast domestic materials and the remainder was divided among programs imported from Germany, Italy, Bulgaria, Russia and the United States. A sizable number were secured from Eurovision and Intervision.

The broadcast schedules from February 27 through April 16, 1965, showed that about twenty percent of the time was devoted to sports programs, including international hockey, ice skating, skiing, table tennis and numerous other athletic events. About ten percent was devoted to local, national and international newscasts. A wide variety of musical programs occupied a little less than ten percent of the schedule—live concerts of folk melodies, light and popular tunes and classical music, including symphonic and operatic performances.

In the entertainment category there were feature films from the United States and Russia, serial dramas such as the American shows, "Lassie" and "Naked City," quiz programs, puppet shows and cartoons for children, and some light comedy.

Educational broadcasts included regular informational programs for the farm population, scientific and literary discussions, reports on sessions of the Communist Party and Congress, and other regular features such as "Man and His Work," concerned with such topics as the self-management system; "TV Platform" for the discussion of important public issues; "Cultural Platform," with varied expressions of opinion in the fields of art and literature, and "Discoveries," typified by one broadcast which told the story of the discovery and development of electricity.

Instructional telecasts, during the period mentioned above, included language courses in Russian and English for general reception and two periods each week of instruction for classroom use. Plans are under way to enlarge the educational television service. In 1963, JRT, the association which has played a major role in the development of Yugoslav television, stated:

> The educational program is only in its initial stages, partially as a result of the fact that a large-scale program of extending the TV network is now under way in this country. In the transition period, there was no need for larger numbers of specialized transmissions, and the aim was to meet the interests of the largest possible number of subscribers, the more so as the TV program is financed largely from their subscriptions. Consultations are now in progress with the institutions concerned to ensure the necessary technical equipment and funds for educational television, so that a systematic work may start also in this field in the near future.[14]

A review of the 1964–65 schedules revealed a large number of regular programs for classroom use, including considerable language instruction.

Audience Research for Television. The JRT and the three large television centers have conducted some studies to ascertain audience size and composition and to evaluate the effectiveness of programs. For example, a 1962 research study of RTV Zagreb showed that about one hundred and fifty thousand people in the Socialist Republic of Croatia viewed its telecasts daily. The structure of the audience was:

Workers	3.56 percent
Office employees	44.27
Craftsmen	3.43
Housewives	20.90
Elementary pupils	15.67
Secondary pupils	4.99
University students	1.95
Children under 7	5.22

The same study showed percentages of viewers in terms of education:

Those with elementary school education	7.60 percent
Those with lower secondary school education	16.15
Those with full secondary school education	60.10
University graduates	16.15

The audience was about equally divided between men and women.[15]

More recent studies have been made to ascertain the interests and needs of the people in terms of a second TV program to be introduced in 1969. Radio–Television Zagreb has reported some recent research as follows:

In the course of the past years besides regular daily programme control, the Office for Programme Research based its work, on the analysis of the quantity of reception and the effect of radio and television programmes. Large-scale inquiries were carried out on a mass scale including as many as 10,000 people. . . .

. . . In 1966 mass quantitative inquiries were carried for television programmes. The result of these inquiries were taken to a certain degree, as the basis for drawing up a programme scheme for 1966. What did the inquiries show? First, considerable changes in the publics' attitude toward the programme. A televiewer becomes more demanding and critical. Second, there is the differentiation of the listeners' interest. . . . The televiewer is no longer "dazzled" by television as was the case at its beginning, he is becoming critical and selective. Third, the most popular programmes are those for which the desks have the least "merit," features films and serials. Fourth, political-informative programmes have asserted themselves in full and justly. Many viewers give priority to these features, which was not formerly the case.

Among the inquiries which, to some extent, classify the successfulness of programme with regard to quality, some of the most important were:

I. Analysis of appraisal of a week's programme by a sample of tele-viewers in the constituent Republic of Croatia.

II. Inquiries about the views of students'

III. The effect of television on children aged to 12

IV. Comparison of the reception of the programme by municipal radio stations, district radio stations (Osijek, Rijeka, Pula, Split, Dubrovnik), and by the first, second and third programme of Radio Zagreb.

. . . The students' attitude toward the programme, apart from being more critical, does not differ from that of the general public. . . . The inquiry about the effect of television on the children up to 12 was of a purely scientific character. . . . The inquiry covered several thousand children from the most varied backgrounds and environment, children who differ in their school work and general abilities. The results showed that besides an undoubtedly good effect on the educational development of a child in general, there are no signs of any negative influence of television whatsoever, unless, of course, some other points are taken into consideration, such as: wasting time and the like. . . . (*1966 Yearbook*, pp. 212–213.)

Organization and Administration

THE 1955 law covering both radio and television stations defined all broad-casting in Yugoslavia as a public service function. The law states that all stations are obliged to broadcast programs of an artistic, scientific, educational and cultural nature, designed to serve the general public interest. Broadcasters are charged with the responsibility of popularizing the country's social achievements and are under a mandate to cooperate with institutions and organizations concerned with educational and cultural growth. The 1965 law reaffirms these obligations.

As previously pointed out, Yugoslavia has no single broadcasting system with centralized control. Nevertheless, some organizational unity is assured by the Yugoslav Radio and Television Association (JRT). This association was organized in 1952 as a voluntary organization. Although the 1955 law made membership of all the republican and provincial stations compulsory, the 1965 law made membership optional. While local stations are not affiliated, their interests are represented in the Association by the principal stations.

The Association is composed of representatives of members elected for two year terms. As a Board of Management they determine basic policies and issue general directives for the conduct of the Association's work. The Board carries on the activities of the Association in accordance with its articles of agreement and the general directives of the members.

A general secretary, appointed by the Management Board, has a staff to carry on the day-to-day work of the Association in accordance with the basic policies laid down and directives issued by the Board. This secretary represents the Association in business matters and executes contracts as authorized by the Board.

Four standing commissions—program, legal and administrative, technical and financial—complete the organizational structure. These groups make continuing studies in the particular areas for which they are responsible and serve in an advisory capacity to the Management Board.

Tasks of the Association. The Association serves as a planning and coordinating agency for all radio and television stations. As stated in the articles of agreement, its specific tasks are to consider and determine:

1. Plans of development of broadcasting networks relating to the entire broadcasting network in the country and its connection with foreign networks.

2. Questions of mutual cooperation in the field of broadcasting and undivided coordinated participation of members of the Association in international broadcasting organizations.

3. Questions connected with preparation and transmission of common radio and television programs.

4. Realization of cooperation between the members of the Association concerning programs, technical and other questions of common concern.

5. Representation of members of the Association in the matters of common concern before competent organs of the socio-political communities, working and other organizations.

6. Proposals to the organs of socio-political communities of plans of establishment and development of broadcasting networks and financing thereof, based on the plans of individual members of the Association.

7. Conclusion of contracts with foreign broadcasting organizations on program and other cooperation in the field of broadcasting.

8. Participation at international meetings discussing the questions of broadcasting.

9. Establishment of permanent cooperation with the organizations in the fields of information, telecommunications and radio techniques in the country and abroad and with the domestic radio industry.

10. Control of utilization of the wave lengths allocated to various broadcasting institutions, members of the Association, proposing of revised plans of distribution of wave lengths; offering proposals for utilization of the existing wave lengths and undertaking of appropriate measures for protection of the existing wave lengths in the country and against foreign countries.

11. Creation of a technical base for common needs of members of the Association.

12. Preparation and proposing of draft regulations and enactment of the necessary measures in the field of broadcasting.

13. Ensurance of foreign exchange from the competent state organs.

14. Organization of common exploitation of the materials obtained from reporters of members of the Association in the country and abroad.

15. Arrangements for exchange of experience relating to the matters of education and promotion of the cadres of broadcasting institutions; arrangements of various advance programs of professional training and specialization of such cadres.

16. Arrangements for exchange of materials and experience concerning

programs, organization, financial management and distribution, and regular collection and publication of information, and issuance of the Yearbook JRT and of other publications in the field of broadcasting.[16]

Government Controls

UNDER the 1955 law[17] a broadcasting station could be established by the Federal Executive Council (FEC) or by an executive council of any republic or province, acting on authority of the FEC. Accordingly, the existing main stations operated by the republics and provinces had permits from the Federal Government. The FEC, while having the legislative authority to establish broadcasting facilities, did not choose to exercise this privilege and, for all practical purposes, transferred the right and responsibility for broadcasting to the republics and provinces.

In recent years, in accordance with the general laws providing for the establishment of production enterprises, some local organizations including newspapers, economic groups and communes have been granted permits to operate local stations.

Article XLVI of the 1955 law provided that the republican executive councils were responsible for supervising the operations of broadcast stations, including relays, but the FEC, through its Secretariat for Information, exercised overall regulatory authority. No station could operate without its premises, wave length, power and antenna installation being in accordance with the international regulations to which the Federal People's Republic of Yugoslavia adheres. All regulations of stations regarding election of councils, management boards, directors, financial operations, sources of income and distribution thereof, methods of remuneration for employees and discipline were subject to approval by the Secretariat of Information of FEC. Article X authorized the Secretariat to order all stations to broadcast a program which it considered in the general interest of the Federal People's Republic.

Station Management

As provided in Article XXI each station had a council of nine to seventeen members appointed by the founder and holder of the station authorization. Two-thirds of these members had to be appointed from the ranks of public workers and one-third from the station's so-called "working collective." The council, as stated in Article XXV, determined basic policies, regulations and procedures regarding management of personnel, programming, budget, distribution of funds and other important areas of station operation.

Assisting the council was a Management Board composed of five to nine members selected by the "working collective" from among its own members. The principal function of this Board was to implement the council's decisions and directives, and, among other specified duties, draft the budget, draw up annual financial reports, oversee the fiscal affairs of the station, propose investment programs to the council, and insure that rules and procedures pertaining to working conditions were applied. In carrying out these tasks, the Board was obliged to consult with the station's "working collective" and solicit its views on important decisions to be made or actions to be taken.

Each station had a director appointed by the holder of the station authorization. His job, as defined by the 1955 law, was to insure that the station operated in accordance with the law and regulations, and the policies, procedures and directives of the Management Board and the council. While it is true that all regulations and procedures of the stations were subject to the approval of the Federal Executive Council in Belgrade, the independent status of the stations made it possible for them to vary modes of operation to fit particular regional and community interests and needs.

The 1955 law was replaced by the Basic Law on Radiobroadcasting Institutions promulgated on April 1, 1965. Numerous changes were made. Of special note is the provision for greater autonomy for the stations and less control by the Federal Government. For other changes see complete text of the new law in Appendix X.

Personnel

As reported by the JRT Association in 1966, there were 7,236 full- and part-time employees in all radio and television staitons. There were 1,936 in the Belgrade operation, 1,691 in Zagreb, 840 in Ljubljana, 533 in Sarajevo, 725 in Skoplje, 5 in Titograd, 406 in Novi Sad and 211 in Pristina.

In all seventy local stations, there were only seven hundred and two employees. Most of these stations operate for only a few hours per day, or as little as three or four hours per week. Some are used largely to relay broadcasts of the main stations. Since their operating schedules are limited, their personnel needs are not great. More than two-thirds of the employees are administrators and technicians, with a comparatively small number engaged in programming.

Financing

BROADCASTING in Yugoslavia is financed with proceeds from a number of sources. The largest amount of income is derived from the subscription fees which all owners of receivers are required to pay. The amounts of these fees are determined by the broadcasting organizations and are paid directly by the set owner to the regional station in the republic or province where the set is located and used.

The 1966 subscription fees for television receivers, as classified and prescribed by Radiotelevision Belgrade, were:

Private sets	2,000 dinars per month
Schools and hospitals	2,000 dinars per month
State administrative offices, business concerns, social institutions, etc.	80,000 dinars per year

The subscription fees for radio receivers, as classified and prescribed by Radiotelevision Belgrade, were:

Private sets	600 dinars per month
Schools and hospitals	600 dinars per month
State administrative offices, various social organizations	29,000 dinars per year
Economic organizations, catering establishments, shops, etc.	29,000 dinars per year
Automobile receivers	600 dinars per month
Economic organizations engaged in production, sale and repair of receivers	29,000 dinars per year

According to the *1966 Yugoslav Radio and Television Yearbook,* the license fees for radio and TV receivers as set by the broadcasting organizations in other parts of the country were substantially the same.

Income of Yugoslavian stations in 1966 was more than thirty-six million dollars. This included all types of revenue—license fees, advertising, etc.

A large source of this revenue is "economic publicity," or advertising. These commercials are presented in time blocks. Occasionally, news stories about economic and business enterprises are broadcast during the evening hours in conjunction with recorded musical programs. Radio and TV Belgrade devotes several periods per day to these commercials. Approximately six percent of the total time is devoted to this type of broadcasting. Other main stations devote from four to seven percent of their time to commercials and "economic publicity." Producers and distributors of chemicals, foods, textiles, metals, cosmetics, electronic equipment, tobacco, soaps, plus publishing enterprises and various other business concerns paid the broadcasting stations over one million dollars for advertising in 1961. In 1964, the amount increased to more than two million dollars. This figure grew substantially in 1966. Additional sources of income include government subsidies for television broadcasts and programs for minority groups and the sale of programs to foreign stations.

NOTES

1. Federal Institute for Statistics, *Statistical Pocket-Book of Yugoslavia 1965* (Belgrade: March 1965), p. 160. This annual publication contains a wealth of information regarding the social, economic and political structure of Yugoslavia. More than one hundred thousand copies of the 1965 edition were printed in three Yugoslavian languages and in English, French, German and Russian.

2. Yugoslav Radio and Television and Yugoslav Institute of Journalism, *Yugoslav Radio and Television Yearbook 1963*, ed. Dr. Irko Pustisek, Secretary General of Yugoslav Radio and Television (JRT), 1964, p. 9. This document (English edition) contains a detailed history of Yugoslavian broadcasting and much information regarding its operation and control. The author is indebted to Dr. Pustisek and the *Yearbook* for much of the factual material which appears in this chapter. Later editions contain additional useful information.

3. Jean Gantelme, "From Private Enterprise to the Idea of Public Service Broadcasting," *EBU Bulletin*, May 15, 1950. This article contains a very helpful explanation of the shift from private to public control of broadcasting during the twenties by Yugoslavia and some other European countries. Also, see George A. Codding, Jr., *Broadcasting Without Barriers* (Paris: UNESCO, 1959), pp. 36–38.

4. As of January 1968, one dinar was equivalent to eight cents.

5. *Yugoslav Radio and Television Yearbook 1963*, p. 23.

6. *Ibid., 1964*, p. 57.

7. *Ibid.*, pp. 57–59.

8. *Ibid., 1963*, p. 123.

9. *Ibid.*, pp. 123–124. The *1966 Yearbook* (p. 199) stated that the programs that year "included information on Yugoslavia's foreign policy—on its policy of non-alignment, coexistence and international cooperation, as well as on her initiative and general efforts to remove the trouble spots in the world, constituting a threat to peace, to prevent military intervention, to eliminate aggression and war operations—of which there were many instances in 1966. The idea was to describe as realistically as possible the support Yugoslavia was extending to the peoples fighting for their freedom and national independence. The development of Yugoslavia's bilateral relations with other countries was a constant and gratifying topic on the programme, for it offered ample opportunity to talk about the factors which inspire international cooperation, and are a positive contribution to strengthening world peace."

10. *Ibid.*, pp. 130–131.

11. Information supplied the author by JRT officials in Belgrade, May 1965.

12. *Yugoslav Radio and Television Yearbook 1964*, pp. 150–151.

13. *Ibid.*, and information supplied the author at the offices of JRT in Belgrade, May 1965.

14. *Ibid., 1963*, p. 113.

15. *Ibid.*, pp. 130–131.

16. *Yugoslav Radio and Television Yearbook 1966*, p. 289.

17. This law was passed by the Federal People's Assembly and published in the *Official Gazette* of the Federal People's Republic of Yugoslavia, No. 52, 1955, Belgrade. It also is reproduced in English in the *Yugoslav Radio and Television Yearbook 1964*, pp. 197–205.

· I ·

THE MIDDLE EAST

XXV

Turkey: Relief From
Bureaucratic Formalities

IN 1964, the Radio–Television Association of Turkey (TRT) was
reorganized, as provided for by an Act passed by the Turkish Grand
National Assembly in December 1963. In an article for the November
1964 issue of the *EBU Review,* Sedat Tolga, the Under–Secretary of State
for Tourism and Information and President of the TRT, explained the
provisions of the new law and discussed the purposes and functions of the
Association. Ali Ihsan Göğüs, the Minister of Tourism and Information, in
the January 1965 issue of the *Review,* described the Association's objectives as Turkish broadcasting faces the future. With the permission of the
magazine and the authors, both articles are reprinted in full.

LEGISLATION SETTING UP THE RADIO–TELEVISION

ASSOCIATION OF TURKEY (TRT)*

The Act setting up the Radio–Television Association of Turkey (TRT),
bearing the number 359, passed by the Turkish Grand National Assembly
on 24th December 1963 and published in issue No. 10596 of the Official
Gazette, came into force on 1st May 1964.

This Act, generally known as "the TRT Act," provides that the radio
and television services shall be organized in the form of an autonomous
and independent economic establishment incorporated under public law.

Before the Act came into force, the Turkish broadcasting service had
been under state control since 1938. In accordance with the provisions of
Act No. 5392 of 24th April 1949, the service came under the authority of
the Prime Minister, as a department of the Directorate-General of the Press,
Broadcasting and Tourism. Later, when Act No. 265 was passed on 2nd

*Article by Sedat Tolga, Under-Secretary of State for Tourism and Information
and President, TRT, *EBU Review,* 88B, November 1964, pp. 48–52. Reprinted by
permission.

July 1963, it became the Broadcasting Department of the Ministry of Tourism and Information. The departments concerned were subject to the fiscal and administrative regulations. Since this system did not favour the development of the broadcasting service, the question of reorganizing it was often mooted. Efforts were made to give it a more flexible status, in keeping with its requirements.

However, the TRT Act cannot be considered to have stemmed solely from these efforts. The real reason which induced the Turkish Government to lay the TRT Bill before Parliament lies in the 1961 Constitution and in the principles contained in the State Economic Development Plan. Article 121 of the Constitution of 9th July 1961 (Act. No. 334) provides that the administration of radio and television stations, as autonomous bodies corporate, shall be governed by legislation, that all broadcasts shall conform to the rule of impartiality, and that the radio and television service shall be endowed with the powers it requires to fulfil its function of contributing to the dissemination of culture and the education of the masses.

In the provisional Article 7 of the Constitution, it was furthermore stipulated that, by 25th October 1963 at the latest, legislation should be drawn up on the creation and operation of the establishments provided for in the aforementioned constitutional Act.

These provisions originate in a reaction to the attitude adopted by the party in power which, during the political events leading to the revolution of 27th May 1960, did not hesitate to make unilateral use of the state broadcasting service for propaganda purposes, and in the aim of ensuring that the principle of keeping the information media, and particularly broadcasting, politically neutral was constitutionally guaranteed. A provision to the same effect is to be found in Article 26 of the Constitution and reads as follows:

> Persons and political parties shall be entitled to make use of information media other than the press, owned by establishments of public law. The conditions and form of such use shall be laid down by law, in accordance with democratic principles and the demands of justice. The law may not formulate prohibitions which would hamper the dissemination of information by these media, the free conception of ideas, and the formation of personal opinions and of public opinion.

This provision was intended to prevent unilateral and biased broadcasts of an essentially political nature. Another provision stipulates the right of reply and rectification both with regard to the press and to programmes broadcast by the radio and television services. The relevant passage reads as follows:

> The right of reply and rectification laid down by the law shall be recognized only in cases where the honourable reputation of citizens is damaged or where a broadcast concerning them personally is untruthful. In the event

of refusal to make public the reply and rectification, the judge shall decide whether they shall be punished or not.

In addition to the above-mentioned constitutional provisions, the importance attached to the education of the people in the Five-Year Development Plan made necessary certain structural alterations to the radio and television services, so as to enable them to make a substantial contribution to the education of the masses and to the proposed cultural reforms.

Until the TRT Act came into force, the aims of the broadcasting service had never been clearly defined, and the principles governing them had never been the subject of legislation. From this standpoint, the TRT Act, which has now laid down the functional principles governing broadcasting, has brought about a fundamental change in the service. For this reason, the law may be said not only to "reorganize" the service, but also to "reform" it.

Having thus briefly outlined the reasons which induced the legislature to draw up the Act in question and the circumstances which attended its preparation, we must now consider the nature of the organization thus established and the legislative principles to which it is subject.

Legal Status

THE Radio–Television Association of Turkey (TRT) is a state economic establishment *sui generis*. It is therefore a publicly-owned autonomous institution having legal status, and its functions may be defined as being those of a public service. It has a monopoly of broadcasting in Turkey.

From the financial angle, the Association does not come under the general budget. Nor is it subject to supervision by the Audit Office in the same way as the various government departments. Its finances and accounts are governed by the much more flexible system laid down in the law applying to state economic establishments. It should be noted that the latter legislation is in the nature of a general law applicable to all wholly and partly state-controlled undertakings in the business sector.

It should not be deduced, however, that the organization is a typical state economic enterprise, which is completely and unreservedly subject to the provisions of the relevant legislation. The composition of its Administrative Council, the character of a public service inherent in its functions, the subsidies it receives from the state budget, the fact that its associations are not considered as state economic undertakings, and the further fact that its staff is prohibited from engaging in any form of political activity, are all features which lend it the character of a nationalized institution, guarantee it administrative autonomy and independence as far as its broadcasts are concerned, and therefore imbue it with certain very special characteristics which widely distinguish it from ordinary state economic enterprises. This is why we have no hesitation in describing it as a state economic organization *sui generis*.

It should likewise be noted that the special features of this Association are not restricted to its autonomous nature and legal status and to the fact that it lies outside the governmental hierarchy. Its functions and powers are limited rather by considerations of public interest and by the aim of safeguarding national affairs.

The Association has its seat at Ankara. Its title is commonly abbreviated to "TRT".

Functions and Powers

THE functions and powers of the Association, according to the law, may be summed up as follows: to operate the broadcasting service, to set up new broadcasting stations and to improve existing stations, to carry out research, and to take appropriate steps to extend the reception area of broadcasts.

It was specifically with a view to enabling the service to fulfil these functions that it was endowed with legal status and granted the monopoly it enjoys in respect of the aforementioned functions on the national territory. This monopoly therefore includes the installation and operation of all radio and television broadcasting stations in Turkey.

Furthermore, the Association has been granted the right to lay down the basis of the programmes sent out over the schools' transmitters and to take responsibility for broadcasts of all kinds.

The TRT is authorized to set up and run the telecommunications installations required for the operation of the entire radio and television system, to set up factories for the manufacture of apparatus and equipment for use in radio and television, to embark on financial and commercial ventures in the field of radio and television, and to enter into relations with international organizations and foreign broadcasting services. However, the Ministries of Foreign Affairs and of Tourism and Information lay down the procedure to be followed in the matter of relations with international organizations and foreign broadcasting services.

The organization is entitled to take expropriation measures in the interests of the state, in accordance with the regulations in force, and enjoys priority in respect of the use of postal, telephone, and telegraph communications as well as a preferential tariff.

Executive Organs and Management

THE Association is run by an Administrative Council composed of nine persons, as follows:

1. the director-general,
2. one member appointed by the Council of Ministers at the instance of the Minister of Education,
3. one member appointed by the Council of Ministers from among the officials of the Ministry of Tourism and Information, at the instance of the competent Minister,
4. one member elected by the teaching staff of a technical university having a radio and television department, and attached to one of these universities,
5. one member attached to a Faculty of Law, Economics' or Social Science elected by the teaching staff of these Faculties,
6. one member elected by the following procedure: the boards of the lecturing staff of the Faculties of (a) Literature and Modern Languages, and (b) History and Geography, of the universities and of the Academy of Fine Arts shall, at the invitation of the Rector of the University of Ankara, select from among their number two groups each composed of three members of the teaching staff, who shall, in their turn, elect five persons, not chosen from among their electors, who will have distinguished themselves by their services or their works in the fields of literature, ideas or art. These five will then, in collaboration with the aforementioned groups, select a person of great prominence in the fields of literature, ideas or art,
7. one person who has performed services or produced works of note in the field of music and the figurative arts, selected by a committee composed of the director-general of the state theatres and of two representatives of each of the following bodies: the boards of teaching staff of the state Academies of Music, the teaching staff of the Department of Oriental Music of the Academy of Music of the City of Istanbul, the actors of the State Theatre, the actors of the Istanbul Municipal Theatre, and the musicians of the Philharmonic Orchestra of the President of the Republic—either from their own number or from outside, in Ankara, at the invitation of the Minister of National Education,
8. and 9. two persons, one of whom will carry out the duties of administrator and the other those of senior electrical or electronics engineer, shall be appointed, by the members of the Administrative Council, at the invitation of the Minister of Tourism and Information, from the staff of the organization who have been appointed to a permanent post and have held this post for a period of at least one year.

The members of the Administrative Council, other than the director-general and the representatives of the government, shall hold office for a period of five years. Should they be legally prevented from carrying out their duties or be absent from the meetings of the Council on three consecutive occasions without adequate reason, they will be removed from office, subject to the approval of the Minister of Tourism and Information.

Members of the Administrative Council may not belong to any political party or engage in any form of political activity.

The Administrative Council is legally entitled to set up consultative committees for the purpose of discussing matters relating to the sound radio and television services. Furthermore, the director-general is personally authorized to set up regional consultative committees, of limited scope, in order to determine local requirements in the various reception areas more exactly.

Administration

THE director-general of the Association has three assistants, one of whom must be a senior electrical or electronics engineer.

The director-general is appointed by decree, issued by the Council of Ministers, in accordance with a proposal submitted by the Administrative Council to the Ministry of Tourism and Information and at the instance of the Minister concerned. The director-general's assistants are appointed following a proposal by the director-general and a decision of the Administrative Council.

In order to carry out the duties of director-general or of his assistant, nominees are required by law to have received higher education in economics, political science, news and information, radio and television, or programmes, and to have acquired the knowledge and experience demanded of a senior civil servant.

The director-general's appointment may be terminated only on receipt of written notice from the Administrative Council and by decree issued by the Council of Ministers, with a view to the security of the country, the preservation of law and order, and the consolidation of the government's relations with foreign countries. In the event of any dispute arising, the matter may be settled only by the Council of State.

The administration of the TRT, matters concerning executive staff, and the remuneration paid to such staff are laid down in a set of regulations which comes into force after having been submitted to the Minister of Tourism and Information for approval.

When persons are selected for appointment to the executive staff, the Ministry of Tourism and Information must first obtain approval to appoint them from the Government Personnel Department and from the Ministry of Finance.

Remuneration paid to staff is considered, as a matter of principle, within the framework of the remuneration paid to staff employed by publicly-owned economic establishments. With regard to any special services required by the organization, arrangements have been made for the TRT to pay an indemnity or to employ specialists under contract, for this purpose.

Like the members of the Administrative Council, the executive staff of the TRT may not engage in any form of political activity and may not have any other type of employment, except in the Ministry of National Education.

Sources of Income and Financial Provisions

THE Association's nominal capital amounts to three hundred million Turkish pounds. By decree issued by the Council of Ministers, this capital may be increased by up to two thirds. The sources of this capital are the current amounts of all kinds of assets made over to the organization by virtue of the Act, and the credits made available under the general budget.

The sources of income of the TRT comprise the fees paid for the use of all kinds of radio and television receiving sets and fines imposed in this connection, the sums paid for all types of advertising on radio and television, the income derived from public events arranged by the organization, such as concerts, dramatic performances, and so on, the income accruing from the sale of publications dealing with broadcasts, such as books, anthologies and records, the profits and gifts resulting from all kinds of commercial operations undertaken in the field of radio and television, and state subsidies.

The scale of fees charged comes into force by virtue of a decree issued by the Council of Ministers. Both the fees for the use of receiving sets and any fines, for which provision is made in the Wireless Act No. 3222, are collected by the post office authorities, which deduct 10% from the sums in question to cover the costs of collection.

The organization receives a subsidy to meet operation and installation costs incurred as a result of programmes which it is obliged to broadcast for educational purposes or for broadcasts to foreign countries. It may benefit from credits opened by the State Investment Bank in order to finance its installations. In accordance with its declared aims and within the framework of the principles stressed in the decree of the Council of Ministers, the organization is authorized to set up limited-liability associations under civil law with both Turkish and foreign physical persons or bodies corporate. The TRT supervises, checks and takes responsibility for programmes broadcast by stations set up by these associations.

The Principles Governing Broadcasts

THE Administrative Council ensures that the tasks assigned to the Association by law are carried out and lays down the principles governing broadcasts. To this end, it sees to it:

1. that the public is supplied with programmes of a completely impartial nature,

2. that the programmes are prepared having regard to the basic ideas and principles underlying the Constitution and to the aims of the Atatürk revolutions as well as to the new ideas and way of life which they introduced into the country,

3. that the sources of news reports should be stated accurately, rapidly, and in conformity with the procedure followed at present in the matter of the communication of news,

4. that a clear distinction is made between news and commentaries,

5. that the programmes are prepared by competent experts and are satisfactory from the standpoint of culture, education and social development,

6. that operation of the broadcasting stations reaches the required technical standard and is adapted to present-day requirements.

However, the Administrative Council is not authorized to lay down the principles governing broadcasts to foreign countries and broadcasts made by schools. The principles and methods to be followed in the case of broadcasts made to foreign countries are laid down by joint agreement between the Foreign Ministry and the Ministry of Tourism and Information. The principles and methods governing sound radio and television programmes broadcast as a teaching aid by schools and universities with technical facilities, and which are in the nature of experiments, are laid down jointly by the TRT and the Ministry of National Education.

The Act also contains a number of clauses defining the liability involved in the case of offences and illegal acts committed through the medium of broadcasting. The staff actually directing and supervising the broadcast concerned assume liability for any offences and illegal acts committed as a result of broadcasting and, in the case of a live broadcast, the person having committed the illegal act constituting the offence is held responsible; in cases where the live broadcast was based on a text or a recording, the person who wrote the text or whose voice was recorded assumes liability. Announcers responsible for reading a text in the form in which it is submitted to them are not held liable for any offences or illegal acts committed as a result of the broadcast in question, unless they were specifically instructed to check and supervise the broadcast.

On the other hand, the Association and its staff assume no liability for statements and communiqués issued by the government and the political parties at election time in the form of recorded broadcasts, the special nature of which has been clearly announced before the broadcast.

Charges concerning offences and illegal acts which have not been preferred within two months of the date of the broadcast will not be considered. The preliminary investigation will be carried out by the Public Prosecutor, even in cases where the action is the result of a charge preferred by an individual. However, the name of the TRT station which was responsible for the broadcast as well as the day and exact time of the broadcast must be clearly indicated in the petition or indictment.

Relations with the Executive Organs

WHEN the relations between the executive organ and the TRT were defined in the Act, this organ was not granted any official authority over the TRT, but, in consideration of the facts that the latter is a publicly-owned body corporate and that the service it supplies is of a public nature, the executive organ was granted specific powers in the following cases:

the definition of the principles and methods applying to broadcasts to foreign countries, the obligation to obtain the views of the Ministry of National Defence before setting up radio and television installations, the right to prohibit the broadcasting of news and information or of any other programme in the interests of national security (with the exception, however, of party political broadcasts at election time), the removal of the director-general from office in the interests of national security and law and order and to consolidate the country's external relations, the definition of the principles and methods to be followed by the TRT in its relations with foreign broadcasting organizations, the provisions relating to staff regulations, the licence fees charged for the use of radio and television receiving sets, the preparation of the installation programme, and the approval of the annual budget.

The Association is legally entitled, however, to appeal to the Council of State against any arbitrary decision reached by the executive body.

Relations with the Political Parties

THE political parties have a legal right to avail themselves of broadcasting facilities in accordance with the conditions, principles and procedure laid down in the legislation on elections.

In addition, they are legally entitled to avail themselves of broadcasting facilities in the following cases:

(*a*) the Association must broadcast any comments on the general budget, as a whole, made by the spokesmen of groups of political parties on behalf of the Senate of the Republic and the National Assembly, provided that each commentary of this type does not exceed the prescribed maximum duration of half an hour;

(b) during sessions of the Grand National Assembly and live transmissions from Parliament, the TRT must accord equal treatment to the speeches of the government representatives and to those made by the political parties, with regard both to form and duration;

(c) any political party which has not joined the government and which has at least ten members in the Grand National Assembly, is entitled to express its views in cases where it considers that its opinions on a subject under discussion have been disputed or criticized by the government or by one of the parties forming the government.

Should any dispute arise, the Association is bound to lay the matter before the Arbitration Committee for political broadcasts, at the request of the political party concerned. The Arbitration Committee is convened at the invitation of the director-general of the TRT in accordance with the procedure laid down by law and reaches a decision whether the political party concerned shall be granted the right of reply.

Furthermore, the Administrative Council must ensure that political broadcasts are so conceived as to give expression to all shades of political opinion (so that the parties in power and the opposition parties shall have an equal chance) and that the TRT serves the public with absolute impartiality.

Relations with Private Persons

No provision is made in the 1961 Constitution for the granting to private persons of the right to broadcast.

However, the TRT may form associations with physical persons or bodies corporate, with the approval of the Council of Ministers and provided that the organization has sole responsibility for the planning of broadcasts.

In order to determine the wishes and requirements of public opinion more exactly, the TRT may set up consultative committees. It is the duty of the Administrative Council or, in the case of regional broadcasting stations, of the director-general, to convene the consultative committees, and they are completely free to decide on their composition.

Finally, both physical persons and bodies corporate have a legal right of reply and rectification as far as radio and television broadcasts are concerned. They may avail themselves of this right in cases where damage is done to their good reputation or where a broadcast concerning them personally is untruthful. The judge decides whether the reply or rectification shall be made public or not, and such a reply or correction should be forwarded to him by the person concerned, in accordance with the procedure laid down by law, within seven days of the date of the broadcast in question.

Inspection

THE Association is subject to inspection by the Higher Council of Inspection. This inspection concerns administrative, financial and technical matters as a whole.

The Higher Council of Inspection is obliged to draw up an annual report on the activities of the TRT, which it then submits to the Grand National Assembly, the Ministry of Tourism and Information, and the other ministries concerned. Furthermore, the Ministry of Tourism and Information may request the Higher Council of Inspection to examine a specific question.

We expect this reorganization of the Turkish broadcasting service to be of great benefit to the country, and we trust that our hopes will not be disappointed.

TURKISH BROADCASTING FACES THE FUTURE*

The Radio-Television Association of Turkey (TRT), a founder member of the EBU, has just undergone a reorganization and is pleased to have this opportunity of making its voice heard. As regards its legal position, this has already been described in the *EBU Review* by Mr. Sedat Tolga, Under-Secretary of State and president of the Administrative Council of the Turkish broadcasting organization.

I will endeavour to explain what we expect from this new organization, now relieved of the bureaucratic formalities of a state administrative and fiscal system, and able to maintain a well-paid staff.

We are looking for a new type of broadcast; the underlying principles of this are explained in Article 5 of the Act. Everyone, we hope, will listen to these broadcasts with confidence and keen interest. They will open up wider horizons and aid in unifying the people and in promoting a new joy of living.

To achieve this end the following are obviously necessary: (1) sources of income, (2) a qualified staff, (3) an organization with a sense of values, (4) permanent supervision and control. Let us consider these problems one by one.

Sources of Income

THE financial resources of this organization are already by no means negligible. Advertisements and commercial broadcasts contributed 16 million Turkish pounds to its finances in 1963.

*Article by Ali Ihsan Göğüs, Minister of Tourism and Information, *EBU Review*, 89B, January, 1965, pp. 16–17. Reprinted by permission.

The expense involved in our expansion will certainly be enormous, since the existing installations are less than adequate. Programmes of good quality necessitate considerable expenditure, as does also the training of staff. To skimp on costs will not produce the results hoped for. High-class artistic and intellectual creations have to be amply remunerated.

The organization can increase its financial resources by publishing reviews, books and records and by rationalizing and developing its commercial broadcasts. It could organize concerts, charging an admission fee.

For the broadcasting network alone, many millions would be required, but the support of the state is ensured since, in a sense, it feels obliged to back up the efforts of the broadcasting organization, on which the education of the masses depends.

To accomplish this difficult task an approach could be made to those towns or districts which want to have their own stations and wish to work in association with the TRT. The network would thus be rapidly ramified and the weight of the state's responsibilities would be correspondingly lightened. In the economically prosperous areas, commercial radio and television can be organized in association with private Turkish and foreign undertakings.

Since television entails great cost, it should in the beginning be used only to complement mass education and school instruction. The studies and research on this subject will have to be rapidly completed, and the next step will then be the training of staff and trial broadcasts according to established principles. Television, for the education of the Turkish people, is more than a need, it is an absolute necessity.

Qualified Staff

HERE there is a shortage which it is not easy to make good. However, no time must be wasted. Advantage must be taken of the possibility of sending trainees abroad, and fellowships must be created, as well as a training centre for staff under the supervision of carefully-chosen teachers. We must recruit staff with great care and then train them systematically. As to specialists, obviously much more time and concentrated effort is required; as they are at present practically non-existent, the services should be enlisted, outside radio circles, of all intellectuals, writers, sociologists, performers, philologists and thinkers who can contribute their experience.

We hope that, even before our broadcasting service is enriched by these new additions, those who are at the head of this organization will not fail to take the necessary steps to secure every possible improvement and to open the door on the western world, that they will not neglect the exchange of programmes through the agency of the EBU and its members, that they will bring us into close contact with foreign cultural and artistic centres, and that they will establish links with other broadcasting organizations throughout the world. All this will not only play a part in the development and training of the personnel, but will also contribute to the enrichment and improvement of the programmes.

An Organization with a Sense of Values

WHAT does this mean? In establishing services and recruiting staff, special account must be taken of the functioning of the TRT. The signposts which lead the trainee to full competence must be discerningly placed, and a fair salary system established. While observing a strict discipline, a serious professional attitude must be developed without reducing personal initiative.

How are these results to be obtained under present conditions with a staff which is inadequate both in quality and number? By turning to well-informed persons and to foreign experts, for example to the members of the Near East Institute of Public Administration in Ankara, to experienced administrators, and to all thinking persons who are ready to make a personal sacrifice.

Supervision and Control

THE organization, now independent, will itself maintain an internal supervision and control. Being conscious of its goal, and of the needs and inclinations of the people from the cultural, artistic, social and moral point of view, the radio must seek the most direct means of making itself heard. Statistics and surveys will point out the road to follow in the education of the people, taking into account their various psychologies and tendencies. The TRT will be guided by careful planning, by the social, cultural and legal principles of the country, and by the programmes of well-established radio stations in other countries.

Advisory committees must therefore be created as quickly as possible. It is especially important to enlist the cooperation of the people themselves and to set up radio clubs. Any bodies of this kind will be invaluable to us and will contribute to the development of our broadcasting.

We shall cooperate not only with the Ministry of National Education but also with all cultural and art establishments and with leading figures from these circles. The short-wave broadcasting activities of the Turkish radio have the support of the government.

These are all the things we expect from this organization whose course is laid out by the new Act. We shall endeavour to serve the people by raising their intellectual and cultural standard according to an established order and in awareness of our duty.

The EBU will have at its side a new member broadcasting organization; we hope to strengthen our links with the Union and cooperate with our fellow-members for the expansion of culture in the free world.

· J ·
AFRICA, ASIA
AND AUSTRALIA

XXVI

Africa: An Overview*

I T IS MILDLY IRONIC THAT, as evidence accumulates to support the theory that man originated in Africa, there should also be evidence to suggest that until recent years the greater share of mankind was leaving Africa behind in the climb toward a brighter future for the human race. Various reasons have been advanced for this state of affairs; the one perhaps most often put forward by Africans themselves is that during the Industrial Revolution, virtually the entire continent was exploited by various colonial powers. They claim that generations of Africans knew only what their colonial rulers wished them to know of the outside world. The few Africans fortunate enough to receive a formal education were schooled in the manner of the colonial power under whose rule they lived, which means that they left the educational institutions more as black Frenchmen, Englishmen or Portuguese than as Guineans, Nigerians or Angolans, and were thus ready to identify themselves with the purposes of France, England or Portugal, rather than with their own birthplaces.

In short, Africans individually and collectively were woefully ill-equipped to communicate with one another about problems of mutual concern. Furthermore, this situation extended to the means of communication themselves. Where newspapers existed, where there were radio stations, these served generally to reinforce the ties between the particular African country and the colonizing power. A newspaper was often a pale reflection of *France-Soir* or of the *London Daily Mail,* the radio service a miniature British Broadcasting Corporation or *Radio Télévision Française* (often relying heavily, in fact, on transcriptions from these services). Many African languages have no printed form, so the lack of newspapers in the vernacular could perhaps be excused; but few of the radio services attempted to broadcast in anything other than the language of the colonial power (the Gold Coast, however, was a notable exception). The content of both the press and radio was heavily European, from the news to the entertainment features, and, for radio, the music.

As independence came, the situation changed—radically for some countries, little for others. A set of growth figures for radio set ownership reveals something of the increased popularity and availability of the

*Prepared by Donald R. Browne, Professor of Speech, University of Minnesota.

medium: in 1957 (the year the Gold Coast—now Ghana—received its independence, thus initiating a "decade of independence" throughout Africa), there were some three million radio sets in the entire continent; ten years later, there were approximately twelve million. To take a more particular example, in 1956 the British Crown Colony of Kenya (which, incidentally, is the pioneer among African broadcasters, with a station dating to 1926) registered some twenty-four thousand radio receivers; today, the figure stands at over four hundred thousand. Television did not exist in the Africa of 1957, save for a furtive attempt to establish a service in Morocco; presently, there are between seven hundred thousand and eight hundred thousand television sets in use (including some four hundred thousand in the United Arab Republic).

Just as impressive is the growth of mass media institutions, radio stations and printing plants in particular. Many African nations now possess modern, spacious, well-equipped broadcast operations, and no independent African nation is without its own radio service. Several have printing plants with the latest equipment. In 1961, the Guinean Government dedicated *both* a one hundred thousand watt radio transmitter and one of the largest printing plants in Africa. Ghana opened a new Television Centre in 1965, and, to judge by the photographs and physical descriptions, it compares favorably with many American operations. Throughout Africa, the means of mass communication are on the increase, and radio and television are leading the way.

The Advantages of Mass Communication

There are several explanations for the increased emphasis on the mass media in Africa. One school of thought contends that the African nations are anxious to imitate their colonial mentors in the outward signs of civilization; therefore, it becomes necessary to have large, well-equipped mass media operations simply because the more advanced nations have them. Another school holds that, because most African nations are under a strong one-party, or even one-man, rule, it follows that the party or man in power will wish to perpetuate itself-himself, and the mass media afford an excellent vehicle for so doing, as long as they are kept firmly under control. Still a third school feels that the African nations, faced with the problem of modernizing their political, economic, social and educational systems as rapidly as possible, have turned to the mass media because they seem to represent the swiftest means of overcoming the centuries of neglect and backwardness.

As it happens, all three contentions are correct—at least, each of the three seems to have been a motivating factor in the decision of various African nations to expand their mass media activities. Henry Cassirer, the

Director of Radio and Television for UNESCO, has stated, however, that in the past some of these factors were more important than others. His remarks to this effect, although dealing with television alone, seem to apply to all of the media. In an article for the *Telecommunications Journal,* Cassirer wrote:

It appears that only rarely is the employment of television to solve the major tasks faced by society the dominant motive for its introduction in these countries. Frequently, the driving force seems to be a mixture of national prestige, commercial venture, thirst for escape and entertainment, and of the all-pervading "spirit of the time" which is hard to resist in any corner of the world.[1]

Quite aside from the question of what the various African nations see in the mass media, however, there is the matter of suitability: how well or poorly is each of the media equipped to serve African needs? What are the advantages and disadvantages of newspaper, film, radio and television?

The newspaper has the advantage of requiring no physical machinery of reception, aside from the natural faculties of most human beings. For this same reason, it has great portability, and can be "used" any time, any place. Finally, since it is tangible, it can be referred to again and again. Its one chief disadvantage is that it does require the ability to read—and in a continent where the literacy rate runs ten percent or less in over half of the nations, this is obviously a disadvantage of major proportions if the press is to serve as an instrument of *mass* communications.

Widespread illiteracy is no problem for film, which also retains the advantages of "reusability" and portability, but cost of equipment—both for the original filming and for projection—is high, and transporting the projection apparatus from village to village, especially during the rainy season, which in Africa turns such roads as exist into mud, is difficult. And even if each village had its own projection equipment, the films themselves would still have to be transported from place to place. Moreover, film tends to deteriorate rapidly in the humid areas which are abundant in Africa.

There remain radio and television, the two mass media for which the strongest claims have been advanced in the search for a solution to Africa's problem of catching up with the more developed nations. Radio and television share one advantage with film: the illiterate can understand them, at least to a degree. They also have an advantage over film in that they need not be concerned with transportation of projection equipment and film footage from village to village. And the frequently impassable roads—where roads exist—are no barrier to either medium.

Yet, if radio and television are free of many of the disadvantages of film and newspaper, they fare no better in regard to cost. The millions of dollars that are required to establish and maintain a nation-wide broadcast network must be measured against the miniscule budgets of many African nations, where fifty million dollars a year is relative abundance. With this in mind, it is surprising that every independent African nation possesses its own radio service, and that over a dozen are active in the much more costly field of television.[2]

In the final analysis, however, it is not the mere presence of radio and television in Africa that count, but rather how they are being used. This, quite naturally, is of strong interest to those who feel that in these media lies hope for more rapid modernization of Africa. There is, indeed, a very real danger that whatever potential radio and television might have for playing a significant role in national development will be largely dissipated if these media are not used in a skillful and purposeful manner from the very start, or near start. If the bulk of the populace receives little but pure entertainment or political harangues from the media, it will be all the more difficult in future years to get people to listen or watch with the expectation of profiting from the activity.

Not that it is ever particularly easy to get people to listen or watch purposefully. After serving as head of the BBC Colonial Service and working with African broadcast operations, J. Grenfell Williams observed:

> It is a comparatively simple matter to arouse interest. It is a very different matter to sustain it. Busy, tired people who have worked all day in the fields —and in most underdeveloped countries the whole community works very hard—will not easily be persuaded to come together at regular times every day unless there is something pretty powerful to attract them. And if they are persuaded to listen, conditions are often too difficult to make listening easy or pleasurable. There is indeed a real danger of this kind of listening doing positive harm to broadcasting, which may well be ignored after the first novelty of it has worn off, and become merely another voice added to the voices of the country.[3]

This should help to explain the earlier contention that the media should be used both skillfully and purposefully; purpose alone does not suffice. The desire to improve their individual and collective lots is not so strong among Africans that *any* program designed to contribute to cultural, social or economic progress is automatically guaranteed of success; the form in which it is cast and the skill with which it is presented are just as important as its underlying purpose.

Radio, Television and National Development

In an examination of the various ways in which radio and television are being used in the continent-wide movement to "catch up with the twentieth century," certain classifications are useful. The set of three categories suggested by Lucian Pye and Wilbur Schramm are especially appropriate for the African nations.[4] These are: creation of a national spirit, improvement of the educational system, and modernization of the economic system.

Creation of a National Spirit. The heart of the dilemma facing most African governments is how to make their people aware of the newly independent nation. This is doubly difficult because of a common colonial power pattern of behavior: both Great Britain and France found it useful to encourage the ancient tribal divisions as an antidote to nationalism. Thus, most African nations have acquired legal independence, but without an accompanying awareness on the part of the population-at-large as to what this might mean.

But radio and, where it is available, television, have been pressed into service to fill this void. And here the advantages of being able to reach all parts of the nation simultaneously (transmitter power allowing) and to speak to a largely illiterate audience seem especially pertinent.

The Republic of Guinea, which received its independence from France in 1958, was even more lacking in a "sense of nation" than most of her neighbors, partly because of the French policy of encouraging tribalism and discouraging any sort of indigenous national movement. This state of affairs was also helped along by the mass media themselves. Before independence, Guinea had both a radio station and a daily newspaper. Each, however, was run largely by and for the resident French population. Little news transmitted by either medium concerned Guinean affairs.

Independence changed all of this rather swiftly. The newspaper was soon withdrawn from circulation and replaced by a mimeographed bulletin for government employees and political party functionaries. The radio schedule was completely revamped to the point where eventually all "western" music (including jazz) was replaced by the tribal music of Guinea and other African countries. News broadcasts changed just as radically, and now began to stress developments within or concerning the Republic, especially those in which President Sekou Toure and his Democratic Party figured. Although many of the items were written by inexperienced reporters and often came out in a long-winded, heavy-handed manner, they provided the Guinean people with their first exposure to the concept of the "Republic of Guinea," simply by telling them what the nation was doing. Finally, in order to reach as many ears as possible, Radio Guinea increased the number of languages in which it broadcast to cover the major and chief minor tribal dialects; also, in 1961, it installed a one hundred thousand watt transmitter.

Broadcasts of the music of various tribes have also been used to develop a sense of nation. The spoken copy for these programs occasionally emphasizes the fact that the diversity of tribal music is simply another aspect of the entire nation's rich and varied cultural tradition, and that the heritage of the tribe belongs to, and should be shared by, all of Guinea.[5]

Nationhood has also been promoted through various radio programs dealing with the rights and duties of citizens under national law. A case in point is a series, "Aminata's Home," in which women are informed of their rights under the Guinean legal system. Through narration and dramatic vignettes, women are told about individual laws and how to seek protection under them. Although the Guinean woman in the post-independence era is often just as leery as she ever was of seeking legal redress when wronged by her husband, an increasing number of women in court cases seems to indicate that the message is coming through, however slowly, and that traditional tribal customs are giving way to national institutions.

Other African nations have used radio and television in much the same fashion in their attempts to give the people a stronger sense of nation, as opposed to tribe, or, in some cases, as opposed to the institutions of the former colonial government. A few have even gone beyond this to concentrate on promoting an awareness of what is specifically African, as opposed to non-African. Ghana, while under the rule of Kwame Nkrumah, made much of its efforts to promote Pan-Africanism, and the effect of this philosophy on the nation's mass media seems evident in a statement made by Mrs. Shirley DuBois, the Director of Ghana Television:

> Television will disseminate the true history of African society, so that this society may guide and direct our nations; we shall revive and make alive the chronicles of our people; teach the language and symbolism of our dances and replace the cheap and maudlin tunes of the West with the rich and powerful music which has sustained Africa through its centuries of pain and travail. Television will lift the African personality before the world in all its true beauty and dignity.[6]

Improvement of the Educational System. In perhaps no other single respect is Africa so obviously attempting to catch up with the present as she is in education for both children and adults. There are the usual shortages of schoolrooms, books (especially those appropriate for the *African* situation) and qualified teachers. Crash programs and heavy investments in educational facilities are the order of the day in many African countries, and new schools have sprouted in profusion in the most remote areas.

A crash program is probably a satisfactory way of building schools, but writing textbooks to fit the African scene and training qualified teachers are both longer term propositions. It is quite likely that, if traditional means are relied upon, a number of years, even decades, will pass before the deficit is made up. More than one African official has therefore asked whether radio and television might not be of help in speeding up the process. These media would make it possible to "revise" or supplement traditional textbooks immediately, even in vernacular languages for which no written form exists. They would also permit the talents of any nation's few well-qualified teachers to be shared by all.

These answers represent vast over-simplifications. The ephemeral nature

of broadcast messages hardly makes for the ideal "revised" or supplementary textbook, and not all "master" teachers are masterful over radio
and television. But the current state of educational affairs in most African
nations often causes officials there to be somewhat less critical of the im-
perfections of educational radio and television, and several nations have
already begun to use these media in their quest for more rapid educational
development.

One of the newer and faster growing educational broadcast systems is in
one of the newer African states, Zambia. Zambia (formerly Northern
Rhodesia) has had radio facilities since 1941 and television since 1961,
but it was not until the summer of 1965 that an Educational Broadcasting
Unit was set up within the Zambian Broadcasting Corporation.

Educational broadcasting in Zambia is carried on at nearly all levels:
elementary, secondary, adult, and for teacher training colleges. Radio
predominates, but educational television, at present confined to the "Copper-
belt" (northern region), is growing. Many of the broadcasts now carried are
provided by the British Broadcasting Corporation and the Independent
Television Authority; these programs at least have the virtue of presenting
English life and culture in something other than the half-comprehended
form in which these subjects have been traditionally taught in Zambian
schools.

But the Educational Broadcasting Unit is increasingly turning to programs which will serve specific Zambian needs, often in subjects where no
text of any sort exists. In July 1965, it initiated a five day a week series of
one-half hour radio broadcasts for adults. The subjects included personal
hygiene, Zambian history, basic French (the French-speaking Republic of
the Congo lies immediately to the north of Zambia) and instruction in better
expression in English.

Programming for the current school term reflects some of the same considerations: a weekly fifteen minute series for radio on Zambian history
(sixth grade level), a series of similar length and frequency on current
affairs as seen "through Zambian eyes." Still another series for various
educational levels features reports by the Ministries of Agriculture and of
Health on current projects.

Educational television in Zambia is considerably more modest: five and
one-half hours per week, which is still a considerable increase over the 1966
average of three and one-half hours a week. Much of the programming,
"An Age of Kings," "Discovering Science" and "G.C.E. Geography," was
originally intended for British audiences. However, the Zambian Educational Television Service is now beginning to produce a modest number of
programs, particularly in the field of teacher training ("Teaching Science,"
"Teaching Mathematics" and "Teaching English," all currently for seventh
grade teachers) and in subjects of general interest ("Pottery Making" and

"The Ministry Speaks," a five program series in which senior members of various Ministries discuss with a panel of teachers the work they are doing to develop the country).[7]

Zambia's record in educational broadcasting can be matched and even surpassed by a number of other African nations, notably Nigeria and Ghana. The Nigerian Broadcasting Corporation, with the aid of a Ford Foundation grant, undertook in 1961 to provide a regular educational radio service to schools throughout Nigeria. The approach was thorough, with numerous preliminary trips through the country to consult with teachers, administrators and pupils. Once the programs were on the air, the Nigerian Broadcasting Corporation kept in touch with its audience by creating an advisory council on educational broadcasting and by soliciting regular reports from teachers and students, for which a form was provided. According to the feedback received, the service is proving both popular and useful.[8]

However, precise measurements of success are generally lacking in these African ventures into educational broadcasting. The one exception is in the area of "literacy by radio," where relatively complete documentation exists for experiments undertaken in Cameroun in 1957–59 and in Niger in 1961. Both experiments were moderately successful, at least to judge from the number of students (all adult) completing each course—approximately sixty percent in Cameroun and forty percent in Niger—but neither experiment has been followed up on anything approaching a national scale.[9] A common criticism of both experiments, however, was that the respective Governments failed to provide the "new literates" produced by the programs with suitably simplified and useful reading matter, with the result that most of the students soon lapsed back into illiteracy. The Ivory Coast has recently conducted an experiment involving the use of television in literacy instruction in which roughly two-thirds of a class of twelve hundred workmen passed the final examination for the course of study.[10] Several other nations have indicated a strong interest in similar projects.

The real impact of educational broadcasting in Africa can only be estimated. To judge from the number of countries currently using radio and television for educational purposes—at least sixteen—there appears to be a widespread feeling that this approach holds promise, even with the lack of concrete evidence to confirm this faith.

Modernization of the Economic System. The African economy is characterized by agriculture and mining. There are few industries that turn out finished products, except on a modest local or regional basis. It is not surprising, therefore, that when African officials speak of economic modernization, they generally mean a modernization of agricultural methods.

There is little doubt that agriculture in Africa is badly in need of modernization. A French agricultural specialist, Réné Dumont, has observed:

The agricultural system practiced (in the 14th and 15th centuries)—working the soil with a hoe after having burned it off, and letting it lie fallow for long periods of time—is still found today, rarely modified . . . agricultural progress has been considerably hampered by the absence of the cart, the wheel and animal power to pull them . . . the only ready source of energy was, and generally remains to this day, that of men and especially women, both much weakened by illnesses and parasites, as well as by malnutrition.[11]

Certainly the African agricultural situation differs little from that prevailing in India and in some parts of Japan, where radio and television have been used in the attempt to modernize centuries-old practices.[12] In fact, broadcasters from several African countries have attended meetings at which the experiences of these and other countries in this field were discussed.

Basically, most plans for the modernization of agricultural methods with the assistance of broadcasting rely upon the forum concept: a group of people gathers to hear the broadcast, then discusses it, often with the aid of printed materials furnished by the Ministry of Agriculture, occasionally with the guidance of a field agent from the Ministry.

Ghana appears to lead in this form of broadcasting in Africa. The Ghana Radio and Television Corporation has had a separate Rural Broadcasts Section since 1962, and in 1965 initiated a special training program in farm radio forum operations for representatives from the Ministries of Health and Education, the United Ghana Farmer's Council Cooperatives, and several other groups which were in one way or another connected with rural development programs.

The principle agricultural program broadcast by Radio Ghana, *"Adwuma Adwuma O"* ("Congratulations for Work"), is broadcast for thirty minutes each Saturday evening in the Akan language, spoken by about half of Ghana's people, and is repeated on Sunday afternoons. It includes a rural news segment, a talk on vocational problems, and a dramatized instructional serial about a rural Ghanaian family. Polls conducted by the Sociology Department of the University of Ghana and reports submitted by listener panels throughout the country indicate that the broadcasts are popular, although there is as yet no evidence to show how effective they might be in bringing about change.

Other programs for rural audiences in Ghana include *"Fifiri ne Ahoto"* ("Sweat and Happiness") and "Farmer's Questions and Answers." The former deals with improvements in farming and living conditions in rural areas, while the latter, broadcast in six languages, seeks to furnish farmers with a common and easily accessible source of answers to their questions.

Radio Ghana's hopes that these programs will have some impact on the life of the entire nation are evident in a remark made by one of the Rural Broadcasts Section staff:

This kind of programming (Adwuma Adwuma O), like all our programmes at the moment, goes out to all listeners at the same time—to the rural as well as the urban listener. So while the rural listener has practical interest in the programme, the urban listener hears it and keeps himself informed about what his brothers in the "bush" are doing.[13]

Several other African countries have undertaken similar projects in rural broadcasting, although none of these has involved a true forum concept. Radio Cotonou (Dahomey), for example, broadcasts a thirty minute radio program for rural audiences entitled "Under the Palaver Tree," which attempts to duplicate the ancient tribal custom of gathering under a large shade tree in the village for discussions of serious matters. In the broadcast, a young man explains to a group of village elders some of the newer agricultural methods. Radio Malgache has reported some success with a series of programs designed to encourage reforestation and prevention of forest fires. And Radio Senegal has in the past carried a daily fifteen minutes program entitled "Conversations with Mr. X," in which rural dwellers could freely express their opinions on rural development projects proposed by the Government.[14]

The success of many of these broadcasts for rural areas—in those few instances where success can be measured—seems in part due to the fact that they are set in the various principal dialects of the country, and not in the so-called "national language," which is often English or French and which few farmers can speak. J. Grenfell Williams pointed out in a study for UNESCO on radio's use in adult education[15] that he found it necessary while in Ghana as adviser to the broadcast service to take great care to catch the essence of the dialect forms; a mere translation from English into dialect was not enough, and it was often necessary to use proverbs and songs in order to get the point across. This should only serve to point out once again the need on the part of African broadcasters for a careful understanding of the indigenous forms of culture, particularly in the rural areas, and an equally careful assessment of the suitability of broadcast forms and materials from other countries for their own situations.

Problems and Prospects

All of this would seem to add up to an impressive picture of the purposeful use of radio and television in Africa. In practice, however, the impressiveness is often somewhat diminished. To begin with, this purposeful use of the media may account for a very modest percentage of the total daily output. In several African radio operations, music accounts for nearly two-thirds of each broadcast day, and there are few African countries where it occupies much less than half of the schedule. Furthermore, the music may not even be predominantly African.[16] Even the in-school broadcasts, as in the instance of Zambia, may devote more time to various facets of European culture than to African culture. Where television exists, it may be given over largely to American, British and French programs, with light entertainment predominant.

Systematic research could provide some indication of the present and potential effectiveness of broadcasting in changing the patterns of African life, and thus perhaps influence officials to devote more time, money and effort to this activity. A few organizations, such as Tunisian Radio and Television and the Ghana Radio and Television Corporation, have research units, but they lack the money and the trained personnel to do a thorough job. A number of research institutes serving various regions of Africa, rather than individual nations, would seem to be one way to make the most of often meager resources—if the nations concerned could get together, which they rarely seem able to do.[17]

There are other problems, of course. For example, with the introduction of television to Africa, various unforeseen situations are developing in an area which might be called "visual semantics." The more Westernized African broadcasters are at times discovering that their less sophisticated audiences often will not accept black-and-white images as valid representations of what they are accustomed to seeing in natural colors; will not perceive a close-up of a malaria mosquito as merely an enlarged view of the same insect that plagues their sleep, but instead think of it as a giant mosquito, the likes of which they have never seen; and, finally, will not transpose the two-dimensional television image into the three dimensions it represents, but will believe it to be a sort of compressed three-dimensional image and will marvel at the sight of a man (foreground) who is as tall as a house (background). There are indications that "visual sophistication" is acquired quite rapidly, but as yet there has been no serious research into this area.

There is also the overall problem of the increasing gulf between the sophisticated town-dweller and the resident of the "bush." Broadcasters have often become so well-adapted to urban life that they have lost contact with the rural areas they largely serve. This was pointed out by the Director of Broadcasting for Sierra Leone, Mr. John Akar, at a recent Commonwealth Broadcaster's Conference:

> Too often producers, once again because they are resident in cities, become out of touch with the bulk of their listeners except city and town folk. They hardly go to the country, to the farming communities, to rural areas. The result is that they do not understand the country folk, a fact which is sorely reflected in their programs, and the country folk in turn cease either to appreciate, understand, or even listen to the programs.[18]

Still other problems revolve around the general question of providing: providing the means for villages, if not individuals, to obtain radio and television sets; providing further training for broadcast personnel, who will be called upon to meet the increased demands being placed on the media;[19] providing up-to-date studios and equipment for those nations still lacking these things; providing further broadcast services in the many tribal languages in which nearly all African nations abound; providing increased transmitter power to overcome the heavy atmospheric interference common during certain seasons in tropical Africa. All of this, of course, ultimately means more money. Broadcasting in Africa is variously supported by the governments, by license fees on receivers, by advertising—none of which is by itself sufficient. It seems that, for some time to come, African broadcasting will have to rely heavily on the generosity of the "have" nations (in particular, the former colonial powers, the United States and the Soviet Union) whose motives for this generosity may not always be purely philanthropic, and of various supranational organizations, such as UNESCO, EBU, OIR, and the International Telecommunications Union.[20]

Even after taking due notice of these problems, however, radio and television seem not only destined to play a leading role in the development of Africa, but are even now accomplishing much along these lines. Africa is perhaps the last great testing ground of the thesis that broadcasting can be used purposefully to uplift society. Henry Cassirer has said of television (and it can apply with equal force to radio):

> It will be possible to find (the) funds, to liberate skilled personnel, to train new cadres and to organize the constructive use of television, if its importance is fully appreciated and recognized. If television is seen as a source of relative luxury, if its role in education is supplementary and incidental, if governments believe that commercial television will bring them "something for nothing," its cost in a developing society will always be prohibitive. But if it is placed on a position where it can make a major contribution to social, economic and educational development, it may turn out to be among the cheapest, the most effective and the fastest means to obtain rapid advances.[21]

NOTES

1. Henry Cassirer, "Television in Developing Countries," *Telecommunications Journal*, December 1963.
2. Admittedly, many of these operations are the result of generous aid given by the two chief ex-colonial powers in Africa: France and Great Britain. But much of this financial aid has been used, not to make a broadcasting operation possible, but to improve on what the nation had already decided it could afford on its own resources.
3. J. Grenfell Williams, *Radio in Fundamental Education* (Paris: UNESCO, 1950), p. 139.

4. Lucian D. Pye, ed., *Communications and Political Development* (Princeton: Princeton University Press, 1963).

5. But several friends of the author who had spent some time in the Somali Republic noted that certain Somali tribes actually lost a certain amount of faith in the national radio service because the service had had the bad judgment to play the music of some (in their eyes) "worthless" tribe in another part of the country!

6. Cited in *Contrast*, III, No. 4 (Summer 1964), 234.

7. For details on the structural aspects of educational broadcasting in Zambia, see P. G. Delahunty, "Educational Broadcasting in Zambia," *EBU Review*, 102B, March 1967, pp. 33–35.

8. Also, see Adekunle Salu, "Educational Broadcasting in Modern Nigeria," *EBU Review*, 95B, January 1966, pp. 25–27. This is a fairly thorough critical evaluation of educational broadcasting in Nigeria by a member of the Nigerian Broadcasting Corporation.

9. Detailed discussion of both experiments may be found in Andre Celarie, *La Radiodiffusion Harmonisee au Service du Developpement* (Paris: Creations de Presse, 1962), pp. 76–79, 85–86, 112–115.

10. See Jean Meyer, "Learning to Read by Television?" *EBU Review*, 94B, November 1965, pp. 53–55.

11. Réné Dumont, *L'Afrique Noire est Mal Partie* (Paris: Editions de Seuil, 1962), p. 21 (author's translation).

12. See *Rural Television in Japan* (Paris: UNESCO, 1960); J. C. Mathur and Paul Neurath, *An Indian Experiment in Farm Radio Forums* (Paris: UNESCO, 1959); *Social Education Through Television*, UNESCO Reports and Papers on Mass Communication, No. 38 (Paris: UNESCO, 1963).

13. Bekoe Mfodwo, "Ghana's Experience," *Rural Broadcaster*, Spring 1962, pp. 5–6. The author is indebted to Mr. J. Bernard Murphy of Wayne State University for much of the information on Ghana's rural broadcast activities.

14. See Celarie, pp. 89, 106, 118 for further discussion of rural broadcasting in these countries. Senegal has also recently initiated an experimental television service, thanks in part to the cooperation of UNESCO. Early reports on the impact of a series of programs on hygiene are encouraging. See "Television and the Social Education of Women," UNESCO Reports and Papers on Mass Communication, No. 50 (Paris and New York: UNESCO, 1967).

15. Williams, *passim*.

16. It certainly was not when the author was in Africa in the early 1960's and heard the latest popular music from France played for several hours daily over Radio Abidjan and Radio Senegal, although the situation may have changed since then.

17. In fact, some African nations, such as Guinea, and, prior to Nkrumah's fall from power, Ghana, have attacked their fellow African states regularly through radio broadcasts. However, for a more encouraging picture of cooperation in the area, see UNESCO Report MC/51, November 3, 1964, entitled "Meeting on the Introduction and Development of Television in Africa."

18. John J. Akar, "Programming for African Stations," paper delivered to the 1963 Commonwealth Broadcasters Conference, Toronto, Canada, p. 5.

19. For a discussion of the sometimes sensitive area of training personnel for mass communications, see Donald R. Browne, "Do We Offer Good Instruction to Mass Communication Students From Africa?" *NAEB Journal*, XXV, No. 6 (November–December 1966), 55–64.

20. For further discussion of some of the problems facing broadcasting in Africa, see Cassirer; Celarie, pp. 167–179; Harald Voss, *Rundfunk und Fernsehen in Afrika* (Cologne: Verlag Deutscher Wirtschaftsdienst, 1962), pp. 13–15; Francis Bebey, *La Radiodiffusion en Afrique Noire* (Paris: Editions St. Paul, 1963), pp. 151–187; Don R. Browne, "Radio in Africa: Problems and Prospects," *NAEB Journal*, XXII, No. 6 (November–December 1963), pp. 32–35; UNESCO, "Developing Information Media in Africa," Reports and Papers on Mass Communications, No. 37 (Paris and New York: UNESCO, 1962).

21. Cassirer.

XXVII

India: A Synthesis of
the East and the West*

ACCORDING TO THE 1961 CENSUS, India has about four hundred and thirty-nine million inhabitants, second only to Communist China. The society is predominantly agrarian; eighty-two percent of the people still live in villages and rural areas. India's population is diverse, containing multiple linguistic and religious groups, with many people living at low social and economic levels. According to the 1961 census, there are fifteen major languages and three hundred and forty-five dialects. The Indian Constitution recognizes fourteen regional languages, the most widespread of which are Hindi, Teluja, Marathi, Tamil, Bengali, Gujrati and Kannada.

The religious groups in India include eighty-five percent Hindus, ten percent Moslems, about two percent Christians and about two percent Sikhs, plus minority groups of Jains, Buddhists and Zoroastrians.

According to the 1961 census, only twenty-four percent of the population is literate. These linguistic and religious diversities, combined with a predominantly agrarian and illiterate population, have had an important effect on the Indian broadcasting system and have presented a serious challenge to the system in its task of helping to build a unified nation.

Since independence in 1947, the objectives of the State's economic policy have been to secure for the common good, an equal distribution of ownership and control of material resources, and to ensure that the operation of the economic system did not result in an undue concentration of wealth and means of production in the hands of the few. However, these goals were not to be achieved by revolutionary means, but by democratic processes. Both public and private enterprises have played an important role in the overall economic development of the nation.

Thus the Indian economic system was designed to involve the people, individual enterprise and the State. All were to be active in the attempt to

*Prepared by Dr. Dharam P. Yadav while pursuing graduate studies at Michigan State University.

[*451*]

bring about, as quickly as possible, an improvement in the national economy. It was within this social framework that the broadcasting system was to develop. The system in turn was expected to serve as a means of information and education, and to implement the Five Year Plans by mobilizing the people's participation.

Broadcasting under British Rule

ORGANIZED broadcasting in India began in 1926 when the Government authorized a private concern, the Indian Broadcasting Company, to set up two medium-wave radio stations in Bombay and Calcutta. These stations began transmitting on July 23 and August 26, 1926, respectively.[1] Due to financial difficulties, the Company was liquidated in 1930 and the Government assumed direct control of the operation, which was renamed the Indian State Broadcasting Service. In 1936, the Service was redesignated as All India Radio (AIR).[2]

The first important phase of development, from 1936 to 1939, was marked by installations of medium- and short-wave stations in six major cities, Delhi, Bombay, Calcutta, Madras, Tirvelie and Lucknow. During the Second World War, high-power transmitters were built in Delhi for broadcasts to West Asia, Southeast Asia, Europe and South Africa. At the same time, stations were established in the states of Mysore, Baroda, Hyderabad and Travancore and operated by the Indian Government, then subject to British rule.

Broadcasting after Independence

AFTER India achieved independence in 1947, the broadcasting facilities were adjusted to meet the needs of the various linguistic zones. By 1950, several pilot stations had been built and All India Radio was presenting programs in all of the regional languages.[3] The total number of radio stations increased from six in 1947 to twenty-one in 1950. During the first Five Year Plan, 1951 to 1956, high-power transmitters were installed and a few additional stations were established to ensure that each language area was served effectively by at least one transmission facility. By 1955, the number of stations had increased to twenty-six.

The chief aim of the first Five Year Plan was to set up high-power medium- and short-wave transmitters at Delhi, Calcutta, Bombay and Madras to provide nation-wide radio coverage. The main objective of the second Five Year Plan was not so much to establish new stations as to extend the coverage of the existing facilities.[4] It also provided for an expansion of the listening facilities in the rural areas and for the initiation of television.[5]

The third Five Year Plan, which began in 1961, was intended to improve domestic coverage by expanding the medium-wave facilities, and by further improving the foreign short-wave services.[6] By the end of the second Five Year Plan, only thirty-seven percent of the country and fifty-five percent of the population were covered effectively by medium-wave. The design of the third Five Year Plan was to reach more than sixty percent of the area and more than seventy percent of the population.[7]

By 1964, ninety-four transmitters, thirty-three principal radio stations, thirteen auxiliary centers and seventeen Vividh Bharati Centres (a light music program broadcast via short- and medium-wave) were in operation.[8] It was expected that by the end of the third Five Year Plan, there would be one hundred and twenty-nine transmitters, thirty-six principal stations, twenty-two auxiliary centers and thirty-three Vividh Bharati Centres.[9]

Diffusion of Radio Receivers

THE purchase of radio receivers by people in a developing society such as India is conditioned by domestic production, availability and cost, as well as by other factors such as literacy, public education, increase in per capita income and electrification. Table I reflects the rate of diffusion of radio sets from 1927 to 1961.

TABLE I.[10] *Number of Domestic Radio Receivers per Million Population, 1927–1962.*

YEAR	NUMBER OF SETS OWNED	RADIO SETS PER MILLION POPULATION
1927	3,594	13*
1931	80,562	29
1936	37,797	128*
1941	147,121	468
1946	232,368	626*
1951	635,026	1,776
1956	1,075,909	2,703*
1961	2,080,780	4,285

*The populations for 1927, 1936, 1946 and 1956 are estimated by taking into account the average net increase in population per year.

Table I shows that the rate of diffusion has been quite rapid, especially during the two Five Year Plan periods from 1952 to 1961. Increases in the domestic production of radio sets, in electrification, in literacy and in per capita income seem to have been important factors stimulating the purchase of radio receivers. Table 2 gives the number of radios imported and produced domestically.

TABLE 2.[11] *Imported and Domestically Produced Radio Sets in India*
1947–1960

YEAR	SETS IMPORTED	SETS PRODUCED
1947–51	293,741	151,008
1952–56	72,222	418,099
1957–60	4,393	871,752

These years of rapid radio diffusion were also marked by record progress in electrification. About fifty-eight percent of the towns having populations of from five thousand to ten thousand, and 93.7 percent of the towns having populations above ten thousand were electrified. However, rural electrification lagged far behind: only 2.8 percent of all the villages in India were electrified from 1951 to 1961.[12]

Based on official census figures, it has been estimated that literacy increased from 16.6 percent in 1951 to 23.7 percent in 1961. It is also significant that per capita income rose from two hundred and sixty-six rupees in 1951 to three hundred and twenty-six in 1961.[13]

When compared with many other countries, it appears that radio diffusion in India has been relatively slow. India is far below the UNESCO standard which says that a nation has inadequate communication facilities if she has less than five radio receivers per one hundred inhabitants.[14] In 1960 there were only 0.5 radio sets per one hundred Indians.[15] However, the inadequacy in the overall development of broadcasting in India is expected to change with the economic improvement of the country.

Government Aid

SOME radio diffusion in small towns and rural communities has resulted from projects sponsored by the Government. Receivers are provided free of cost to the communities to encourage group listening and discussion of programs. Community listening sets were originally introduced in the villages by the British Government during the Second World War. Following independence, the program was expanded into a nation-wide venture. The pace with which the diffusion of community receivers has progressed over the past three decades is apparent from Table 3, which also includes the number of Indian schools utilizing radio.

TABLE 3.[16] *Number of Community Radio Sets and Schools with Radio Installation, 1937–1962.*

YEAR	NUMBER OF COMMUNITY SETS	NUMBER OF SCHOOLS WITH RADIO
1937	Nil	Nil
1939	100	—
1942	1,050	—
1947	2,039	—
1952	6,613	2,972
1957	29,100	10,165
1962	72,577	16,623
1965	145,000	Not available

The data in Table 3 indicates the increase in community receivers but it will be noted that the use of radio in schools is still very limited. Based on these statistics, about one-fourth of the villages had been provided with community receivers by 1965.

This induced program of diffusion by the Government entered a new phase in 1959 when All India Radio, in collaboration with the Ministry of Community Development, launched a nation-wide movement to organize Rural Radio Forums in which villagers listen to educational programs, discuss them in a group and then take action to improve their farms, homes and communities.

Radio Programs

ALL India Radio's major objectives[17] are to provide (1) *entertainment* consistent with the cultural heritage of the different groups in the Indian society; (2) *information* on current events in the form of news bulletins, newsreels, commentaries, talks; and (3) *education* in the widest sense of the term. The percentages of the various program types presented in 1962 are shown in Table 4.

National programs feature talks, discussions and dramas intended to promote a general understanding of national issues and a climate of receptivity for national integration. No political party, including the one in power, is permitted to use All India Radio for promoting its policies and programs. News bulletins, containing both national and international news, are broadcast in the various languages from All India Radio's central

TABLE 4.[18] *Composition of Home Programs 1962*

PROGRAM	PERCENTAGE OF TIME BROADCAST
Regional Services	
Indian music	45.0
Western music	1.9
Talks, discussions	5.3
Dramas and features	4.8
News	21.4
Special broadcasts—children, women, rural, educational, etc.	21.6
	100.0

studios in Delhi and are relayed by the regional radio stations. These regional stations, however, enjoy a fair amount of autonomy in broadcasting local and regional news. All India Radio has correspondents in the different state capitals and in the Press Trust of India and a monitoring unit in Delhi.[19] The system averages about eighty-five news bulletins each day in about thirty different languages and dialects.

Foreign Broadcasting Service

THE primary aim of All India Radio's foreign broadcasts is to create an awareness and understanding among the peoples of other countries regarding Indian life and to provide information about national and international affairs. These foreign programs are aired in seventeen languages, twenty-four hours a day, for listeners in Asia, Australia, New Zealand, Africa and Europe. Broadcasts for Indians living abroad are directed to Southeast Asia, East and Central Africa, Aden, Mauritius and Fiji and are in four languages, Hindi, Gujrati, Konkani and Tamil. Other programs are transmitted in Arabic, Burmese, Cantonese, English, French, Indonesian, Konyu, Nepali, Persian, Portuguese, Pushto, Swahili and Tibetan. These foreign broadcasts generally include music, news bulletins, talks and discussions. About thirty-five news reports are presented daily.

Educational Radio Programs

THE programs for special audiences, women, children, rural people and industrial workers, are primarily informative and educational, although some elements of entertainment are included. Special broadcasts for students in secondary schools are carried by more than twenty stations for twenty to thirty minutes, from four to six days per week. There are some programs for university students consisting of talks and discussions on subjects of academic interest. University speech contests and plays are carried regularly in all major dialects. Some programs on the objectives and the progress of the Government's Five Year Plans are carried by both national and regional stations.[20]

Rural Radio Forum

AFTER independence, Rural Radio Forum received considerable attention and an attempt was made to reach a large portion of India's village population. These broadcasts deal with all important aspects of rural life and provide useful information to villagers through dialogues, discussions, plays and news, weather and price reports. The problems of agriculture, education, health and hygiene are dealt with by experts and are broadcast for about thirty minutes a day by thirty stations in all the major Indian languages and fifty dialects. The Government made a major effort to promote the use of the programs and, as previously mentioned, provided receivers to the rural areas on a nation-wide scale. It was realized, however, that the mere distribution of sets was not enough. Rural people were assisted and encouraged to listen to programs, to discuss them, and then take community action. As B. P. Bhatt and P. V. Krishnamoorthy have pointed out, radio is not a self-sufficient medium, but when it is coupled with group reception and discussion, and when it is systematically built into an overall plan for rural development, it can be a major factor in effecting needed changes.[21] This is the underlying principle motivating the Rural Radio Forum.

UNESCO Assistance

GUIDED by the success of the Radio Farm Forums in Canada,[22] UNESCO, in collaboration with the Government of India, in 1956 initiated a pilot project establishing Radio Farm Forums in one hundred and fifty villages in the State of Bombay. The organization of the forums closely followed the Canadian pattern. Each forum had twenty members, a chairman, and a secretary to maintain records of group discussion, decisions and actions taken. The radio programs dealt with specific agricultural, health and community problems and were broadcast twice a week for about three months.

The effectiveness of these Radio Farm Forums in increasing knowledge and motivating members to adopt improved methods was evaluated by Paul Neurath who compared villages not having the forums with those that did.[23] The success of the forums is shown by the data in Table 5.

TABLE 5.[24] *Knowledge Gain by Literate and Illiterate Members of Forums and Non-Forums.*

TREATMENT	RESPONDENT-TYPE	MEAN KNOWLEDGE PREBROADCAST	POST BROADCAST	GAIN
Forums	Literates (n = 266)	7.1	12.2	5.1
	Illiterates (n = 43)	3.1	9.4	6.3
Non-Forums	Literates (n = 194)	5.3	6.5	1.2
	Illiterates (n = 60)	2.1	3.1	1.0

The forum groups showed an impressive gain in knowledge over the non-forum groups, but more important is the remarkable improvement of the illiterates. The success of this project indicated that India might modernize a large percent of her rural population, now predominantly illiterate, if long-range, well-coordinated plans for Radio Farm Forums were effectively expanded and implemented.

Radio Farm Forums have been conducted in India since 1959. All India Radio and various Ministries have coordinated their efforts at regional and local levels to organize and promote these rural forums.[25]

Figures 1 and 2 represent the basic framework within which Radio Rural Forums function. According to 1964 estimates, the total number of forums was about ten thousand. Although the forums' utility thus far has been well demonstrated, more research is needed to determine their precise value and to make them more effective in terms of community and national development.

Television in Education

TELEVISION was introduced on an experimental basis in 1959. Since then, a number of pilot projects have been carried on by All India Radio to evaluate the potentialities and effectiveness of the medium as a tool in formal and informal education.

These projects were greatly facilitated by UNESCO, when, at a general conference in New Delhi in 1956, it passed a resolution to assist member countries in setting up experimental TV centers designed to promote educational and community development. Experiments sponsored by UNESCO in 1954 in France[26] had demonstrated television's potential as an effective means of adult education.

The first experimental TV center began operating in Delhi on September 15, 1959. Transmission was limited to a fifteen mile radius. Since the primary object was adult education, tele-clubs were organized at twenty community centers, each of which was provided with a television set. Each tele-club had from twenty to twenty-five viewers who were expected to engage in group discussion after every broadcast in a manner similar to Radio Farm Forum. The programs were broadcast during the evening hours, twice a week. From December 1960 to May 1961, twenty special telecasts were directed to members of the tele-clubs on the general theme, "Responsibilities of Citizenship." More specifically, the programs were designed (1) to increase the members' knowledge by communicating new information on selected subjects, (2) to influence the members' attitudes on certain important issues, and (3) to suggest leads for follow-up activities.

A study was conducted to evaluate the effects on attitudes and behavior. The findings, documented in a UNESCO publication,[27] clearly established television's importance as a medium for social education and made clear the way for a further expansion of its use for this purpose.

Television in Schools

IN January 1960, the Ford Foundation invited a team of U.S. media specialists to assess the potentialities of television as an instructional tool in the schools of Delhi State.[28] Upon the recommendations of this team, the Foundation sponsored a four year grant, providing a program of educational television for the Delhi school system. In October 1961, in-school programs were telecast from All India Radio TV Center. The subjects taught were physics, chemistry, English and Hindi.

The following year, the project was broadened to include both the higher and lower grades. Each TV transmission was twenty minutes long, half of the total class period. All the topics taught conformed with the regular curriculum and selected syllabi prescribed by the schools. According to latest reports, the project is still under way and has been successful in two hundred and forty-seven of the three hundred and fifty-six higher secondary schools in Delhi.[29]

Future of Television in India

TELEVISION'S importance as a medium of social education for adults and as an instructional tool in school systems has been amply demonstrated. Since August 15, 1965, All India Radio Delhi has been providing regular television programs three days a week. These telecasts include newscasts, documentaries, music, drama, children's and women's programs. It may be noted, however, that Indian television remains restricted to Delhi and its suburbs. Further expansion is badly restricted because there is no television manufacturing industry in India and there is an acute shortage of foreign exchange.

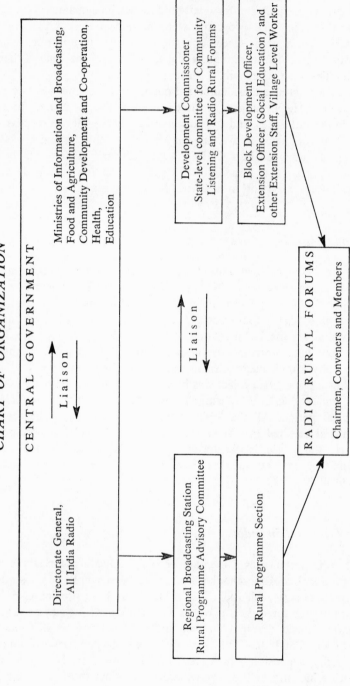

CHART OF ORGANIZATION

CENTRAL GOVERNMENT

Directorate General, All India Radio

Ministries of Information and Broadcasting, Food and Agriculture, Community Development and Co-operation, Health, Education

Liaison

Liaison

Development Commissioner State-level committee for Community Listening and Radio Rural Forums

Block Development Officer, Extension Officer (Social Education) and other Extension Staff, Village Level Worker

Regional Broadcasting Station Rural Programme Advisory Committee

Rural Programme Section

RADIO RURAL FORUMS

Chairmen, Conveners and Members

FIGURE I:

Adapted from: *RADIO BROADCASTING, SERVES RURAL DEVELOPMENT*, PARIS, UNESCO, No. 48, 1965.

THE LINES OF COMMUNICATION

Radio outflow to Rural Forums

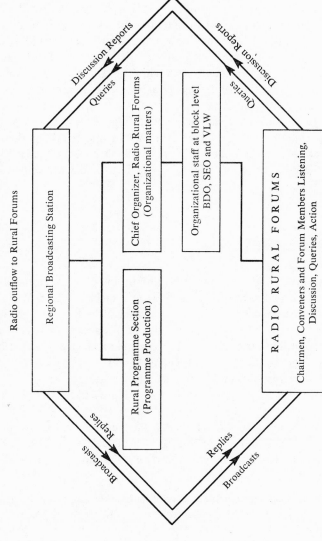

FIGURE 2:

RADIO BROADCASTING, SERVES RURAL DEVELOPMENT, PARIS, UNESCO, No. 48, 1965.

Adapted from:

The recommendations of the Chanda Committee on Information, appointed by the Government to suggest means for redefining and improving the functions of broadcasting, include the establishment of a national TV network and a TV manufacturing industry.[30] The Committee recommended that, by the end of 1976, television stations be established in all Indian cities with a population of one hundred thousand or more, providing coverage to about forty-seven percent of the country's total area. The Committee also suggested that government ownership of Indian broadcasting be abandoned, and that radio and television be carried on by separate and autonomous corporations.

What the future holds for Indian broadcasting remains to be seen. The Committee's report is hopeful. There is no doubt that television does have great potential for education, and in view of India's predominantly illiterate population, the disposition of Indian leaders is to make full and effective use of the medium.

Organizational Structure

ALL broadcasting in India is now controlled by the Government. All India Radio, the sole broadcasting organization, is attached to the Ministry of Information and Broadcasting. The executive head is the Director General who reports to the Ministry of Information and Broadcasting. The Director General is responsible for executing the broad plans and policies set by the Ministry. Regional stations of All India Radio are headed by station directors, who are responsible to the Director General.

Although the broadcasting system is controlled by the State, the press is free. Considering the multi-language, multi-religious, multi-racial, predominantly rural and illiterate character of the Indian society, perhaps there is good reason to have state control of broadcasting, with a free press catering primarily to the comparative few who are educated. Wilbur Schramm has written:

> The amount of freedom which India permits is quite unusual among the developing countries. Indeed it is probably wrong for us to expect a country which is trying to gather together its resources and mobilize its population to permit the same kind of free, competitive and sometimes confusing communication to which we have become accustomed in this country. . . . We must be prepared to sympathize with this point of view and to expect that as these countries grow toward economic strength and political stability, they will be more likely to encourage communication freedom.[31]

Thus, as literacy increases and political institutions become more stable, it is expected that Indian broadcasting will enjoy more flexibility and freedom. The findings of the Chanda Committee point out this trend.

Several advisory committees have been constituted by All India Radio to study public opinion and tastes and to obtain suggestions for improving program content and quality. A Central Program Advisory Committee, composed of members of Parliament, writers, poets and educators, advises the Ministry of Information and Broadcasting on general principles of planning and presenting programs. A Central Advisory Board of Music consisting of musicologists and musicians determines AIR's music policies. Also, at each regional station, there is a Program Advisory Committee, Rural Advisory Committee, Advisory Committee for Industrial and Tribal Programs, and a Consultative Panel for Educational Broadcasts. The establishment of these committees indicates the AIR's concern to provide a national broadcasting service that meets the interests and needs of all the people.

Financial Support for All India Radio

THERE is no commercial broadcasting in India. In addition to the regular appropriations made by the Government under the Five Year Plans, All India Radio derives revenue form a licensing system as follows:

1. Licenses issued to individuals owning radio receivers in their homes—15 rupees per year.
2. Licenses issued to business firms for such receivers used for commercial purposes—50 rupees per year.
3. Licenses for demonstration sets used by radio dealers—15 rupees per year.
4. Licenses for community radio receivers—10 rupees per year.
5. Licenses for use of receivers in schools—3 rupees per year.
6. The individual license fee for a TV receiver is 30 rupees per year; for a school TV set, 10 rupees; and for a commercial license, 120 rupees.[32]

The licenses are issued and the fees collected by the Post and Telegraph Department which serves as an agent for All India Radio.

NOTES

1. Government of India, *India 1952—A Reference Annual* (New Delhi: Research and Reference Division, Ministry of Information and Broadcasting, 1957), p. 165.
2. G. C. Awasthy, *Broadcasting in India* (Bombay: Allied Publishers Private Limited, 1965), p. 9.
3. *Ibid.*, p. 13.
4. Government of India, *Second Five Year Plan* (New Delhi: Planning Commission, 1956), p. 498.
5. *Ibid.*, p. 498.
6. Government of India, *Third Five Year Plan: A Draft Outline* (New Delhi: Planning Commission, 1960), p. 253.

7. Government of India, *Third Five Year Plan* (New Delhi: Planning Commission, 1961), p. 572.
8. Information Service of India, *India 1964* (London: 1964), pp. 105–106.
9. *Ibid.,* p. 106.
10. Compiled and estimated from Government of India, *India 1955—A Reference Annual* (New Delhi: Research and Reference Division, Ministry of Information and Broadcasting, 1955) and all subsequent publications for 1956, 1957, 1958, 1959, 1960, 1961 and 1962.
11. Compiled from *India 1955—A Reference Annual* and subsequent publications to 1961.
12. *Third Five Year Plan,* p. 188, and *India 1963—A Reference Annual,* p. 243.
13. *India 1963—A Reference Annual,* p. 145. As of January 1968, one rupee was equivalent to ten and one-half cents.
14. UNESCO, *Mass Media in the Developing Countries* (Paris: UNESCO, 1961), pp. 16–17.
15. UNESCO, *World Communications: Press, Radio, Television, Film* (New York: UNESCO Publications Center, 1964).
16. Compiled from Awasthy, pp. 261–262; *The Times* of India, *Directory and Year Book 1964–65* (Delhi: Times of India Publication, 1965), p. 182; and B. P. Bhatt and P. V. Krishnamoorthy, *Radio Broadcasting Serves Rural Development* (Paris: UNESCO, No. 48, 1965), p. 1.
17. Information Service of India, *India 1964,* p. 106.
18. *India 1963—A Reference Annual,* pp. 125–126.
19. Awasthy, p. 121.
20. *India 1963—A Reference Annual,* p. 127.
21. Bhatt and Krishnamoorthy, p. 1.
22. John Nicol, Albert A. Shea and G. J. P. Simmins, *Canada's Farm Radio Forum* (Paris: UNESCO, 1954).
23. Paul M. Neurath, *Radio Farm Forum in India* (Delhi: Government of Inida Press, 1960), pp. 135–155. For more information, see J. C. Mathur and Paul M. Neurath, *An Indian Experiment in Farm Radio Forum* (Paris: UNESCO, 1959).
24. Mathur and Neurath, p. 155.
25. Bhatt and Krishnamoorthy, p. 14.
26. Joffre Dumazedier, *Television and Rural Adult Education* (Paris: UNESCO, 1956).
27. UNESCO, *Social Education Through Television* (Paris: UNESCO, 1963), pp. 35–38.
28. Douglas Ensminger, *TV Goes to Schools in Delhi,* Ford Foundation Program Letter, India, Report No. 126, May 8, 1962, p. 1.
29. L. S. Chandrakant, "An Indian Cast Study," a paper presented to Ditchley Foundation Conference on Aid to Developing Countries through New Educational Technologies, February 1966.
30. The Committee, headed by A. K. Chanda, was appointed in December 1964. Cited from Borra Ranjan, "TV in India," *Television Quarterly,* V, No. 4 (Fall 1966), 54–55.
31. Wilbur Schramm, "Communication Process and the Development Process," *Communications and Political Development,* ed. Lucian W. Pye (Princeton, New Jersey: Princeton University Press, 1963), p. 55.
32. *India 1955—A Reference Annual,* p. 268.

XXVIII

Communist China:

Politics Above All*

OMMUNIST CHINA HAS BEEN STRUGGLING for nearly two decades to transform the social, economic and political conditions of her seven hundred and fifty million people. Considering the vast territories of the country, the third largest in the world, inhabited by more than one-fifth of the entire human race and characterized by diverse ethnic and linguistic groups, it seems an impossible task to indoctrinate the masses in communist ideology and secure their participation in nation building. But the extensive and vigorous manipulation of mass communications in Communist China, as a means of transforming the entire society, is a startling new phenomenon —new both to China and to world communism.

The Communist Political System and Broadcasting

EVER since the Russian Revolution, the Communists have consciously sought to exploit every potential of the mass media in the service of propaganda. In the struggle first for existence and then for power, Communist Parties have always tended to believe that the secret of politics is locked in the power of agitation and propaganda[1] and that the realization of power requires an absolute monopoly over all communications. A unique feature of their approach is the attempt to eliminate the gap between the mass media and more personal and informal methods of communication. In Communist China, these face-to-face communications are channelled into highly controlled and organized forums as follow-ups of mass media messages.[2]

The basic doctrine, "thought determines action," is the basis for the role which has been assigned to the mass media in the People's Republic. An editorial in the *People's Daily* explained this doctrine:

*Prepared by Dr. Dharam P. Yadav while pursuing graduate studies at Michigan State University.

Work is done by man and man's action is governed by his thinking. A man without the correct political thinking is a man without a soul. If politics does not take command, there can be no direction. In every work we undertake, we must always insist that politics take command and let political and ideological work come before anything else. Only when we are both thorough and penetrating with our political and ideological work can we guarantee the accomplishment of our task.[3]

Thus the supreme goal of the communist political system is to indoctrinate the masses through persuasive communication. Wilbur Schramm has stated that in this system, there is not a theory of state and a theory of communication; there is only one theory.[4]

Frederick Yu has summarized three aspects of the Chinese Communist ideology which are especially important in the realm of mass communications.[5]

Class Consciousness. The Chinese Communist Revolution is a class struggle and the entire course of propaganda and agitation stems from one fundamental concept: class consciousness. According to Marx, the central purpose of communications propaganda is to awaken, heighten and sharpen the class consciousness of the masses from which the real strength of the revolution is supposed to be generated. Lenin further developed the idea that class consciousness must be awakened and brought into the battle under the leadership of the professional revolutionaries.

The Mass Line. Like class consciousness, the mass line has acquired sacredness in China. The Communists talk fervently about the harmonious unity within the masses, the viewpoint and wisdom of the masses. The mass line principle means that the Party's policy and methods are supposed to originate with the masses. Under this concept, communication feed-back is important in the process of mass persuasion and education.

Unity of Theory and Practice. According to Chairman Mao Tse Tung, all truths are obtained through direct experience. Thus a Chinese peasant worker shows that he has benefited from the wisdom of Marxism–Leninism–Maoism by "accusing," "attacking" or eliminating reactionary elements and participating actively in tasks assigned by the Party cadres. The ideology must be practiced and the entire process of mass persuasion is always built around one central task or another. The policy of communication is synchronized with every task of the Party and it is through this means that major propaganda objectives are achieved.

National Broadcasting System

IN spite of a relatively high peasant population (about seventy percent of the total) coupled with an illiteracy rate of about sixty percent,[6] Communist China has developed an efficient communication system which reaches almost every segment of the population. Radio broadcasting was utilized by the Communists even before they assumed power in 1949 and has since become a most important medium of propaganda and indoctrination.

Franklin F. Houn has provided an historical analysis of broadcasting by the Chinese Communists.[7] The first transmissions by the Communists were on September 5, 1945, when they established a radio station in Yenan. This station, located at a small temple, had a power of three hundred watts and was on the air for a short time each day. A second station in Kalgan quickly followed. By the end of 1948, there were sixteen stations broadcasting in the so-called liberated areas.

After conquering the Mainland, the Communists took over all stations formerly operated by the Kuomintang regime and converted them into "people's stations" owned and operated by the new Government. In April 1950, there were fifty "people's stations" and thirty-three privately owned and operated installations. Shortly thereafter, the Communists imposed strict control over the private stations and prohibited them from broadcasting any program of a political nature. The owners of private stations were required to submit daily written reports on the content of their broadcasts and were not allowed to communicate with other stations or transmit by short-wave. They were required to rebroadcast certain programs, mostly political, originated by the communist stations.

During the year 1952–53 the Government nationalized all the privately owned radio stations and brought them under state control. Since then the number of radio stations has steadily increased. A marked expansion began in 1958, the year of the Great Leap Forward. The number increased from ninety-seven in 1958 to one hundred and forty-one in 1963.

Structure of Broadcasting System

BROADCASTING in Communist China is structured like a pyramid. At the summit is the Central People's Broadcasting Station, located in Peking and supervised by the Bureau of Broadcasting Affairs of the State Council. The nerve center of the entire radio network, it plays a role similar to that of the Central Broadcasting Stations of the Soviet Union located in Moscow. Since 1950, the Central People's Broadcasting Station has used two separate installations for domestic and foreign broadcasts. The domestic programs, aired in all the major languages and dialects spoken by the Hau Chinese and other ethnic groups, are directed toward the entire Chinese listening public, either directly or by network hookups. According to Chao Tse-Jeng,[8] in 1963, twenty-five medium-wave and seventy-eight short-wave stations were broadcasting domestically and three medium-wave and ninety-four short-wave stations were transmitting foreign programs. The Central People's Broadcasting Station has twenty-four broadcasting studios, and a Russian-made three hundred kilowatt transmitter claimed as the biggest medium-wave transmitter in Asia. The provincial and municipal stations, in addition to transmitting local programs serve as relaying stations for Radio Peking to the thousands of wired broadcasting stations in counties and communes. This organizational network has been schematically represented by Alan Liu:[9]

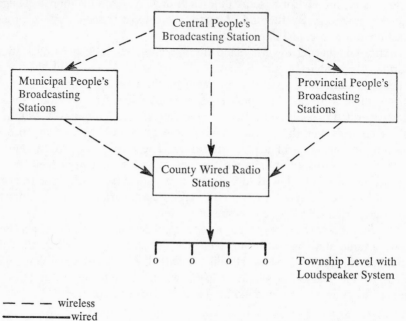

The provincial stations, located in each of the provincial capitals, are used primarily to announce decrees and regulations and to broadcast news of concern to the province. The main task of the municipal stations, which exist in some important cities, is to conduct "social education," essentially a form of propaganda and agitation. These stations transmit the national and international news as well as other programs emanating from the Central People's Broadcasting Station in Peking.[10]

Political and Administrative Control Over Broadcasting

THE Chinese Communists believe that the solidarity and advancement of a society depends upon ideological unanimity; communications transmit the model with which everyone is expected to conform.[11] The mass media are the most important instruments of mass persuasion and ideological indoctrination in Communist China. To achieve ideological consensus and mass mobilization, complete control is exercised by the Department of Propaganda of the Party's Central Committee. The network is supervised by a dual hierarchy of party and government organs. Government agencies in charge of cultural and educational affairs execute most of the policies formulated by the Party. This dual system of control operates all the way from the Central People's Broadcasting Station to provincial, municipal and county radio stations. And, as previously indicated, one of the unique features of the Chinese Communist broadcasting system is its direct link with organized media forums or collective listening groups, controlled by local Party committees such as rural communes and factory production teams. The Party, therefore, has complete control over the broadcasting system.

Patterns of Broadcasting Stations

The Radio Broadcasting Monitoring System. In April 1950, the now defunct Information Administration issued a document, "Decision on the Establishment of Radio Broadcast Monitoring Network," to help promote collective listening in factories, mining plants, enterprises and even in the armed forces. This decision required that all the county and municipal governments appoint appropriate persons to be monitors.[12] Monitors were appointed in the People's Liberation Army, factories and schools, and were registered with the Central or Provincial People's Broadcasting Stations. In essence, their duties were to monitor important political newscasts, distribute the news through pamphlets or blackboard bulletins and organize the local people for collective listening.

As of January 1956, there were eleven thousand monitoring teams in the offices of county and district governments; another seventeen thousand and seven hundred were active in industrial fishing and in agricultural co-operatives. Still another twenty thousand teams were attached to the armed forces.[13] This monitoring system was designed to achieve the goal of total politicization and indoctrination among government, industrial and military personnel.

Wired Broadcasting Systems. The Communist Party continued the "Radio Broadcast Monitoring Network" from 1950 to 1955, after which the regime switched the emphasis to wired broadcasting. Wired systems had been initiated early in 1950, but due to technical limitations and political considerations their development had been rather slow. Wired broadcasting was already operating in the Soviet Union under the name of "radio diffusion exchange," described by Alex Inkeles:

> The equivalent of the radio station in the system of wired reception is the diffusion exchange. The exchange has a powerful aerial receiver that picks up

the broadcasts from the central or local stations. The broadcasts picked up by the receiver as well as those brought in directly over the inter-city telephone lines, as in an ordinary radio hook-up are intensified and strengthened. They are then sent over a system of wires radiating in all directions from the exchange to the home of the subscriber. There the subscriber's wired radio speaker transforms the electrical signal into the usual sounds.[14]

In Communist China radio diffusion exchanges were not constructed in rural districts and in medium- and small-size towns until 1952. Even then the exchanges were placed chiefly in industrial and mining plants, in schools and in units of the armed forces.[15] It was not until the latter part of 1955 that the construction of radio diffusion exchanges was speeded up. By 1959, wired broadcasting systems were operating in Kwantung, Kiangsu, Chebiang, Hupeh, Anheuei, Kirin, Liaoning, Fukien and Heilunkiang Provinces. In the Kwantung and Heilunkiang areas, eighty-four percent of the rural cooperatives had loudspeakers.[16] By 1959, every county in the provinces of Kirin, Liaoning and Fukien had a wired broadcasting station and most of the townships had been equipped with loudspeakers.[17] Thus the great industrial centers in Manchuria, the fertile river delta in Kwantung and almost all the coastal provinces, where the population is most easily exposed to foreign broadcasts hostile to the regime, were now covered by the wired network.

The phenomenal growth of wired broadcasting stations in Communist China is evident from the following data.[18]

Year	Number of Wired Stations	Loudspeakers
1949	8	500
1950	51	2,200
1951	183	6,100
1952	327	16,200
1953	541	31,800
1954	577	47,500
1955	835	90,500
1956	1,490	515,700
1957	1,700	993,200
1958	6,772	2,987,500
1959*	11,124	4,570,000

*Reports indicate there has been a large increase since 1959.

In addition to being an instrument of propaganda and indoctrination, the wired broadcasting system, especially in the rural areas of China, was considered essential to speeding up the modernization of a predominantly illiterate peasantry.

The Chinese Communists believe that radio diffusion exchanges are valuable for agitating for higher labor productivity, for carrying on socialist education among workers and peasants and keeping them informed as to current national and international affairs, for transmitting and explaining policies and decrees of the Party and Government, and for popularizing advanced agricultural and industrial methods.[19]

Franklin Houn has evaluated the advantages of the wired system of broadcasting:

1. It is more economical. More speakers can be installed with limited financial resources.
2. Programs can be originated at the exchanges. This makes possible the utilization of radio for mass communication of a purely local nature or for conducting agitation in industrial and mining plants or on cooperative farms.
3. The radio diffusion exchange can broadcast without actually going on the air. The authorities can make special pronouncements to the population on matters they want to keep secret from foreign listeners.
4. Finally, program content can be controlled because the listener can tune in only to the programs carried by the wired system.[20]

The wired broadcasting system has become the core of the Chinese Communist mass media network, especially in the rural areas. Even though the majority of the peasants are illiterate, verbal symbols such as "socialism," "communism" and "imperialism" flow daily from the media to the masses. Peking now speaks directly to the villagers, for every wired radio station in rural regions is required to rebroadcast in full the national and international news programs of the Central People's Broadcasting Station. According to the latest information, county diffusion stations generally broadcast three to four hours a day. Collective units like production brigades and teams in the rural areas can all be reached by the wired broadcasts.[21]

Program Content

IN Communist China, the Party determines the content of broadcasting. A statement issued in 1958 by the Department of Propaganda of the Chinese Communist Party described the policies:

> Broadcasting is to relay quickly the Party's political task to the audience. Knowledge should be selectively disseminated among the masses. At present broadcasting should promote the propaganda of the "Great Leap Forward." Radio broadcasting must carry out propaganda for industry and agriculture. Broadcasting is allowed to criticize but its job mainly is to encourage. . . . Broadcasting should put more emphasis on implementation of the goals rather than on goals themselves, more on previous experiences, on model workers and on masses' creativeness.[22]

Radio broadcasting is supposed to adjust to shifting Party policies; therefore, the composition of the programs aired by the Central People's

Broadcasting Station, or the provincial and municipal stations, changes often. Generally, the Central People's Broadcasting Station devotes about fifty percent of its time to news and political broadcasts, twenty-five percent to "social education" and the remaining twenty-five percent to cultural and recreational subjects.

News and political programs are designed to indoctrinate the masses in communist ideology, to familiarize them with important events in the nation and the world, to announce major decrees and regulations of the Party and the Government, and to transmit official explanations and clarifications of established policy.

The Central People's Broadcasting Station presents series of lectures by leading communist theoreticians on the history of social development, imperialism, theory of state, people's dictatorship, and political economy. Each of these series usually lasts for several months and some segments of the population are virtually compelled to listen collectively in "radio auditoriums." These lectures, a direct form of political and ideological indoctrination, are relayed through the provincial, municipal and wired broadcasting networks. News broadcasts are characterized by the predominance of reports and feature stories on factory, mine and farm production, on the regime's diplomatic and cultural plans and achievements, and on developments in other communist states. Domestic affairs of the United States and other Western countries are less frequently featured, but when they are, it is often with distortion or for the purpose of criticism. As Franz Schurmann has pointed out, a belief system expressing basic social and human values has been replaced by an ideology reflecting values and goals of socio-political action and achievement.[23]

National and International News Content. The source of national and international news in China is the New China News Agency (NCNA) controlled by the Party's Central Committee. In addition to its domestic news bureaus, the New China News Agency has more than thirty in foreign countries.[24] The NCNA also records the news broadcasts of stations such as All India Radio, the Voice of America, the British Broadcasting Corporation and Radio Moscow. The NCNA selects the items to be transmitted to the people through national newspapers, Radio Peking, and the central, provincial and municipal radio stations.

At the national level, the key link in the national system is *Jen Min Jih Pao (People's Daily)*. The news for this paper is exclusively selected by the NCNA which owns and publishes the paper on behalf of the Communist Party. The news reports of the *People's Daily,* in turn, are carried by the People's Broadcasting Station in Peking, relayed by stations in the provinces, and finally transmitted by the wired broadcasting networks to collective listening groups. The NCNA also publishes selected news items in the *NCNA Bulletin* which is distributed to international agencies and provides information to the outside world. Furthermore, the NCNA prepares

Reference Material which is specifically designed for Party officials and other approved individuals.

Distribution of News Sources

THE distribution of news sources utilized by the three NCNA publications in six issues (February 4, 5, 6, 10, 13, 21, 1960) was analyzed in a study reported by Henry Schwarz.[25] Table I summarizes this data.

TABLE I. *Distribution of Primary News Sources (domestic and foreign) in* People's Daily, NCNA Bulletin *and* Reference Material *by Nationality*

NEWS SOURCES REPORTED FROM	PEOPLE'S DAILY % OF TOTAL STANDARD UNITS	NCNA BULLETIN % OF TOTAL STANDARD UNITS	REFERENCE MATERIAL % OF TOTAL STANDARD UNITS
U.S.	1.5	1.3	28.0
U.K.	—	—	12.7
India	—	—	8.4
France	—	—	8.5
Hong Kong	—	—	5.2
Western Germany	—	.006	4.1
Nationalist China	—	—	3.7
Indonesia	—	.003	2.2
Other Non-Communist Countries	2.0	4.4	10.3
Communist China	69.0	70.0	11.3
U.S.S.R.	19.1	7.4	—
Other Communist Sources	8.6	15.6	5.5

Trends in National and International News Content. National and international news transmitted to the Chinese people by the broadcasting stations is primarily drawn from the *People's Daily,* the official organ of the Communist Party. An analysis of data compiled by Alan Liu[26] based upon his study of sample issues of that paper for 1950, 1955, 1960 and 1965 reflect the trends in news content. Graphs I, II, and III illustrate the changes in news patterns.

Some reasonable hypotheses for the changes in news patterns can be suggested. For example, from 1950 to 1955, China was involved in the Korean War and the Government was more concerned about building anti-American feeling than about the domestic economy. Thus the news content was more international. One strong evidence of this was the direc-

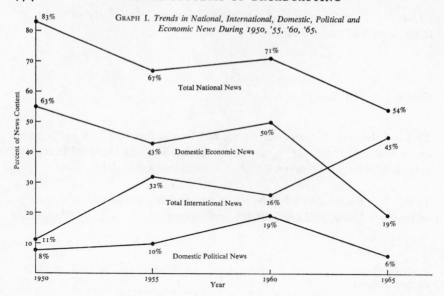

GRAPH I. *Trends in National, International, Domestic, Political and Economic News During 1950, '55, '60, '65.*

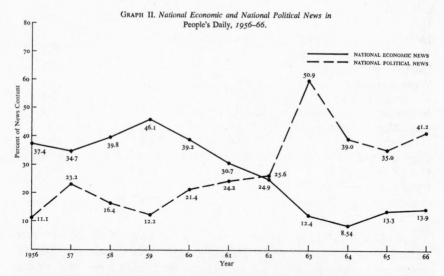

GRAPH II. *National Economic and National Political News in People's Daily, 1956–66.*

tive issued in 1952 by the Department of Propaganda of the Party's East Bureau and summarized by Frederick Yu: "At present our propaganda efforts are mainly to develop continuously the Resist America Aid Korea Protect Home Defend Nation Movement and to elevate the consciousness of masses in anti-imperialism."[27]

It is quite evident that the increase in national economic news during 1956 to 1959 was due to the greater emphasis placed on the Great Leap Forward. When the Leap did not succeed, it was only natural that the Government should shift the news emphasis from economic failures to

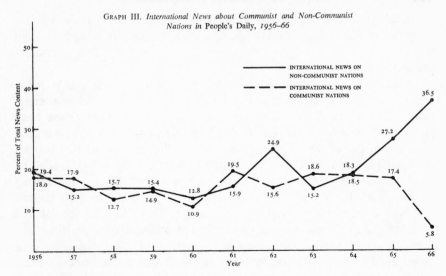

GRAPH III. *International News about Communist and Non-Communist Nations in* People's Daily, *1956–66*

political matters. Chou En-lai, in a 1961 address to the National People's Congress, said: "In order to cope with the situation created by the three year 'Great Leap Forward,' it is necessary to adjust not only the economy but the political life of the state."[28] An editorial in the *People's Daily* about the same time was in the same vein:

> The "mass line" is being redefined. It is not so much a matter of mobilization and launching "mass movement" regardless of conditions as it tended to be during the "Great Leap Forward," it is now a matter of listening to the masses, explaining the Party's policy to them one by one if necessary and always using persuasion.[29]

After 1965, a great effort to combat "revisionism" and cope with the aftermath of the unsuccessful Leap Forward was made. This no doubt explains to a large extent the increase in national political news and the decrease in news about other communist countries.

Penetration of International Broadcasts in Communist China

SOME Chinese owning short-wave radio sets receive the programs beamed to them by foreign stations such as the Voice of America (VOA), the British Broadcasting Corporation (BBC), the Voice of Free China (VOFC) and Radio Moscow. The Communist Party and the Government have attempted to jam these outside broadcasts. Moreover, while no official order prohibits listening to a foreign broadcast, the penalties are severe for anyone discovered doing so. In spite of these preventive measures, broadcasts from foreign stations do penetrate Communist China.

From the estimated production of radio sets in the late 1950's, Vincent King has provided approximate figures on the availability of radio sets in the country.[30] According to his estimates, about 8,850,000 sets were produced in 1962.

In spite of these estimates, it is still difficult to determine how many radio sets on the Mainland can receive foreign broadcasts and how many people tune in on them. The VOA and the Voice of Free China have powerful transmitters which can reach the whole Mainland and their broadcasts can be picked up by ordinary sets. According to information obtained from refugees, some special groups regularly listen to the foreign broadcasts. These include: government and Party cadres responsible for monitoring programs, intelligence, defense, propaganda and foreign affairs departments, and the New China News Agency and *People's Daily* (monitoring for and by these groups is always carried out in the presence of more than one person); senior Party cadres such as secretaries of Party committees or propaganda directors who listen to keep themselves informed to counteract "rumors" and anti-communist propaganda; Party members in charge of collective listening groups who listen to foreign broadcasts secretly although not officially permitted to do so; and certain elite groups (as reported by Liu[31]) such as managers of factories and stores, technicians, physicians and other professionals.

Television

TELEVISION tests were started in China in 1956, and regular telecasting was initiated in 1958.[32] Recent data were not available when this chapter was being written. However, newsmen associated with Japanese broadcasting who visited China in August 1960, reported that eighteen Chinese television stations were on the air, located in Peking, Tieutsin, Shanghai, Canton, Wuhan, Nanking, Shenyang, Changehun, Harbin, Anshan, Tsingtao and in other unidentified cities. According to these observers, "to elevate the moral standard of the masses, education programs were provided and, in addition, operas, theatrical performances and dances were also on the air."[33]

They further reported that there were ten thousand receivers in the neighborhood of Peking and about twenty thousand sets in the whole country. The majority of these sets were purchased in large quantities by "collective bodies like the people's communes."[34]

Much emphasis is placed upon using television for formal instruction. With the help of Soviet experts, the teaching and research personnel of the Peking College of Posts and Telecommunications established a TV station in 1957–58.[35] The "Peking Television University" was formally initiated in March 1960. Hsu Mei-li of Peking Normal College taught the first lesson in "advanced chemistry."[36] The nature of the TV university has been described by officials:

> Peking Television University is a spare-time university established jointly by the Education Bureau of Peking municipality and the Peking television station of the Bureau of Broadcasting enterprise under the leadership of the CCP Peking Municipal Party Committee. The mode of study consists mainly of self-study by correspondence with television teaching as its supplement; the unit to which the students belong also helps to organize their members to study. A proper course and a preparatory course are set up in the school. At present, more than 6,ooo students are enrolled. Most of the proper course students are the working personnel of factories, mines, enterprises, government organs, army units, associations and schools with the cultural level or the equivalent of senior middle school. The students of the preparatory course have to go through a preparatory stage before they are promoted to the proper course. Three departments of mathematics, physics and chemistry, are set up in the proper course. Basically, the teaching of every subject is undertaken independently. Eight hours of study are required in a week, four for self-study and four for lessons before the TV receivers. The classes are conducted two times and each time covers two periods of one lesson; every lesson is rebroadcast once more on the next day. In the course of teaching, films on science and education are also shown, guidance and tests are organized to enrich the pedagogic contents. Meanwhile, the students are organized to do experiments and to finish their assignments according to the needs of the curriculum.
>
> The teachers of all departments or subjects of this university are provided by Peking University, Peking Normal University and Peking Normal College. These three higher educational institutes sent experienced professors and leading cadres of administration to be concurrent heads of various departments. The part-time teachers sent from the three higher educational institutes have all made up their minds to teach well the courses of the television university; they prepared their lessons and compiled their teaching materials in advance passionately. To make the contents of the lectures more suitable for the practical needs of the students, the teachers and students of the TV university working groups of the chemistry department of Peking Normal University went to the various units to find out conditions of the students and re-compiled once more their outlines for teaching.
>
> During the preparatory period, this university had undertaken four trial teaching broadcasts through television and organized the television receiving in the factories, mines, enterprises and schools. The results were excellent.[37]

Shanghai Television University also started classes in 1960 with an enrollment of more than eight thousand. This was followed by the establishment of the Harbin Television University with more than eleven thousand workers, cadres of government agencies and teachers enrolled. Although no current reports are available, the indications are that Chinese television has grown considerably during the past seven years with the same kind of emphasis on education and indoctrination that have characterized radio.

NOTES

1. Lucian W. Pye, "Alternative Patterns of Development," *Communications and Political Development,* ed. Lucian W. Pye (Princeton, New Jersey: Princeton University Press, 1963), p. 254.
2. *Ibid.,* p. 255.
3. *Jen Min Jih Pao (People's Daily,* Peking), editorial, November 11, 1960.
4. Wilbur Schramm, *Responsibility in Mass Communication* (New York: Harper, 1957), p. 81.
5. Frederick T. C. Yu, "Communications and Politics in Communist China," *Communications and Political Development,* ed. Lucian W. Pye (Princeton, New Jersey: Princeton University Press, 1963), pp. 261–262.
6. *Communist China Digest,* Joint Publications Research Service, No. 20, 1960, pp. 50–56.
7. Franklin W. Houn, "Radio Broadcasting and Propaganda in Communist China," *Journalism Quarterly,* XXXIV, No. 3 (September 1957), 366–377.
8. Chao Tse-Jeng, "Study on Communist Broadcasting System," *Ta-Lu Fei-Chin Che-Pao (Quarterly Report on Communist Mainland,* Taipei), October 1962, p. 1.
9. Alan P. L. Liu, *Radio Broadcasting in Communist China* (Cambridge: Center for International Studies, Massachusetts Institute of Technology, 1964), p. 19b.
10. Houn, p. 370.
11. Frederick T. C. Yu, *Mass Persuasion in Communist China* (New York and London: Frederick A. Praeger, 1964), p. 3.
12. Liu, *Radio Broadcasting in Communist China,* p. 3.
13. *Ibid.*
14. Alex Inkeles, *Public Opinion in Soviet Russia: A Study in Mass Persuasion* (Cambridge: Harvard University Press, 1958), pp. 239–240.
15. Houn, p. 373.
16. Chu Ching-Kwei, "The Development of Broadcasting for the National Minorities," *Hsin-Wen Chan-Hsien (News Front,* Peking), No. 11, 1959, p. 25.
17. *Ibid.,* p. 25.
18. Alan P. Liu, "Growth and Modernizing Function of Rural Radio in Communist China," *Journalism Quarterly,* XLI, No. 4 (Autumn 1964), 574.
19. Chen-Yen Wang, "Intensifying Propaganda and Agitation for the Fulfillment of the Five Year Plan," *People's Daily,* February 22, 1956.
20. Houn, p. 375.
21. *China News Service,* Peking, August 5, 1963.
22. Chou Tang, "Two Roads and Two Ways to Do Work," *New China Fortnightly,* No. 11, 1958, pp. 118–119.
23. Franz Schurmann, *Ideology and Organization in Communist China* (Berkeley and Los Angeles: University of California Press, 1966), p. 8.
24. Vincent S. King, *A General Study of the Channels of Communication between Communist China and the Western World* (Cambridge: Center for International Studies, Massachusetts Institute of Technology, May 1964), p. 21.

25. Henry G. Schwarz, "The T'San-K'ao Hsiao-hsi: How Well Informed are the Chinese Officials about the Outside World," *The China Quarterly*, No. 27, July–September 1966, pp. 54–84.
26. Liu, *Radio Broadcasting in Communist China*, p. 82.
27. Yu, *Mass Persuasion in Communist China*, p. 85.
28. Cited from W. A. C. Adie, "Political Aspects of the National People's Congress," *The China Quarterly*, No. 11, July–September 1962, pp. 78–82.
29. *People's Daily*, January 13, 1962.
30. King, p. 44.
31. Liu, *Radio Broadcasting in Communist China*, pp. 56–57.
32. *Television and Radio* (OIRT), No. 6, 1962, pp. 7–8. Also, see *Ta-Kung Pao*, Hong Kong, September 4, 1960, p. 1; *Union Research Service*, XXIII, No. 12 (May 12, 1961), 189, published by Hui Shun Chi (71–B Waterloo Road, 6–B F1, Kawloon, Hong Kong).
33. *Union Research Service*, p. 189.
34. *Ibid.*
35. *Ibid.*, p. 185.
36. *Ibid.*
37. *Ibid.*, p. 187.

XXIX

Japan: The Search for Expression*

THE HISTORY OF JAPANESE BROADCASTING can be split into two distinct periods—the era prior to and including the Second World War, and the period from the end of the war, including the Allied Occupation, to the present. Broadcasting from its inception in 1926 until 1945 was characterized by increasing central control. General laws were interpreted by administrative action as restrictions on the mass media. Article XXIII of the Press Law (*Shimbunshi Ho*), enacted in 1909, read:

> The Home Minister may prohibit the sale or distribution or if necessary seize a newspaper when it is deemed that articles disturbing to the peace and order or injurious to public morals are contained therein. . . .[1]

Such a broad charge left the execution of the law to administrative actions which fluctuated according to the temper of the times. Indeed, as Japan became embroiled in militaristic action and citizen sacrifice became necessary, the interpretations were increasingly restrictive.

Since 1945, broadcasting has been characterized by a minimum of control and the insuring of legal clarity. The attempt to establish workable norms is still going on. In the meantime, with the advent of television in 1953, coverage has grown to unprecedented size, and the problems of broadcasting philosophy are often submerged by the *fait accompli* of practices shaped to meet the demands of an increasing audience.

The Period from 1925 to 1945

JAPANESE broadcasting began in 1925, when radio stations were established in Tokyo, Osaka and Nagoya by various interests, principally local newspapers. In 1926, these three stations were merged into a single corporation, the predecessor of the present Japan Broadcasting Corporation (NHK). Although later events seemed to point toward the NHK as a government-run institution, legally this has never been the case. The original corporation was organized under the provisions of the Japan Civil Code.[2]

*Written by Dr. Hideya Kumata, Professor of Communication and Director of the International Communication Institute, Michigan State University.

However, radio's potential was recognized early, and broadcasting was made subject to the Ministry of Communications under provisions of the 1915 Wireless Telegraph Act. It is difficult to justify the inclusion of radio broadcasting as part of the Wireless Telegraph Act. The peculiarity of the Japanese Government, under the 1889 Constitution, was the attribution of legislative power to executive units. This meant that, in addition to acts passed by the Diet, the legislative branch, various executive agencies could, in effect, make laws. Thus, the interpretation placing radio under the rubric of the Wireless Telegraph Act was made by the Minister of Communications.[3]

The Corporation was a monopoly and its expansion was an extension of a single voice. Major decisions were submitted to the Ministry of Communications for approval. In addition, broadcasters were guided by a number of standing committees, including the Ministries of Communications, Education, and Home (Interior). The Ministry of Home included the national police system.[4]

As Japan moved toward militaristic rule, the responsibility for policy formation was placed upon a special board of information instead of the Ministry of Communications. As the Second World War progressed, the president of the board operated virtually as a minister without portfolio.[5]

Broadcasting, however, was only one of the institutions affected by Japan's militaristic drive. Almost all aspects of Japanese life were put under rigorous surveillance and control. Thus, the prospect of a free broadcasting system was slim. Broadcasting was a valuable arm of citizen socialization, indoctrination and mobilization, and therefore could not be allowed to experiment with programs which might put different alternatives for action before its audience.

The other mass media were subjected to similar control and restrictions. The Japanese press, for example, had a history dating to the late nineteenth century, but the 1909 Press Law and several Peace Preservation Laws made it quite clear that if necessity demanded, newspapers could come under direct government control. The motion pictures were subject to censorship after production until 1939, when the National Mobilization Law stipulated that films would be controlled before production to ensure that proper themes and portrayals would be filmed.[6]

It is difficult to believe that such measures would be tolerated unless the nature of Japan's modernization is taken into account. The Meiji Restoration of 1868 has often been referred to as the date from which Japan entered into a deliberate act of modernization. And, the actions taken at that time, such as the establishment of universal education, a conscript army rather than an elite professional warrior class and a constitution, were steps congruent with a move toward modern times. But the Restoration was not a revolution, it was not a popular uprising against feudalistic rule. The signs were favorable for a populist movement but the official action was one of granting privileges on a wide scale. Thus, although the society was reshaped, the power of those in control was preserved.

The Restoration, in spite of words to the contrary, did not alter the basis of sovereignty, which continued to reside with the Emperor and not with the people. It also became clear that the executive arm of the Government was responsible to the Emperor and not to any other agency including the legislative body.

It is not surprising that broadcasting became an agency of the Government. The precedents for a free communications environment had never been established. Until 1937 when an extremely restrictive policy was applied, the era could be characterized as accordion-like with respect to the mass media. More liberties could be taken at certain times and less at others. The prevailing mood of the Government was reflected in the severity or laxity of the measures to control the mass media.

The year 1937 marked the start of totalitarian control. That year the people were asked to gird for sacrifices to further the Japanese military effort in China. In 1937, at the initial meeting of the Movement for National Spiritual Mobilization, a movement calling for unquestioning sacrifice, the then Premier of Japan made the following speech.

> The conception that the State is not a promiscuous association for purposes of profit, but a community having a definite cultural mission, while the subject is not a profit-seeking materialistic entity but a spiritual entity whose purpose is to make certain contributions to humanity through the structure of a nation-State, is attracting serious attention today among thinking people who are not satisfied with the materialistic aspects of Western culture. We in Japan are certainly witnessing a rising tide of such a conception and a strong desire for its realization. This conception is inherently materialized in the national structure of Japan which orientates itself around the Throne occupied by a single dynasty from time immemorial. When therefore our consciousness of this definite fact about our State has been intensified, national spiritual mobilization will be achieved of its own accord.[7]

Murky though the words were, the Premier sounded the future course of Japanese life wherein everything would be subjugated to the will of the State. Broadcasting became an essential part of this thrust toward spiritual mobilization.[8]

The following presents the major activities which affected broadcasting prior to 1945, and provides some idea of the mass communication environment in Japan during the prewar era:

Brief Chronology of Major Actions Affecting Broadcasting Until the End of World War II

1889   Article XXIX, Japanese Constitution. "Japanese subjects shall, within the limits of law, enjoy the liberty of speech, writing, publication, public meetings and association."

1909 Press Law. Set forth qualifications for publishers and editors and the conditions under which publication would be allowed. Articles XXIII, XXIV and XXVII provided the basis for seizure of newspapers and gave such authority to the Home Ministry primarily, but also to the Ministries of War, Navy and Foreign Affairs.

1915 Wireless Telegraph Act. Set out the provisions for the operation of telegraph and telephone enterprises. Broadcasting was brought under the supervision of the Ministry of Communications through interpretation of this Act.

1924 Ministry of Communications Directive. Article VI decreed that program content and other details be reported before broadcasts. Article VII extended the provisions of the Press Law to broadcasting. This directive was in anticipation of the start of broadcasting activity in Japan.

1925 Ministry of Communications Directive. Forbade the broadcast of speeches and discussions about political issues.

1925 Peace Preservation Law. Updating of a law from 1887 which gave the Home Ministry, through its police arm, the power to suppress anything which threatened the peace and order of the nation.

1928 Wireless Telegraph Law. Article VIII empowered the Ministry of Communications to stop any communication which might incite disorder or affect morals.

1933 Ministry of Communications Directive. Forbade the broadcast of ideas supporting extreme views. Also banished any persons in broadcasting who supported such views. Forbade the use of inflammatory language in broadcasts.

1936 Establishment of a Commission of Information. A coordinating body under the Prime Minister's office which established provisions for the regular broadcasts of government policy.

1937 Commission enlarged to the Bureau of Information. Duties included not only broadcast time and schedules for government policy declarations but operations in collecting and disseminating pertinent items to the mass media.

1939 Ministry of Communications Directive. Article VIII gave additional powers to the Ministry by which it could order broadcasters to disseminate items necessary for national welfare and could, if necessary, specify format, direction and treatment.

1940 Bureau of Information enlarged to the Board of Information. Took over the content direction of the 1939 Directive, leaving to the Ministry of Communications matters concerning broadcast facilities. Also took over the direction of newspapers, motion pictures and the stage.

1941 Board of Information Directive. Forbade the broadcast of any item relating to war unless released by Imperial Headquarters (armed forces).

1943 Creation of policy planning body within the Board of Information. Membership on this body was composed of members from the Army, Navy and the Headquarters of the Greater East Asia Co-Prosperity Sphere. It determined basic policy on information and propaganda matters.

The End of the War

AUGUST 1945, marked the first time that an Emperor of Japan was heard by the populace. Radio carried the recorded speech announcing Japan's capitulation. This unique event also marked the beginning of a period of turmoil for Japanese broadcasting. The Japanese Government was convinced that most of its institutions would undergo great change during the Occupation. Those concerned felt that the nature of broadcasting would be radically changed, with most predicting the end of the Japan Broadcasting Corporation's monopoly.

Anticipating the end of monopoly broadcasting, the Board of Information submitted a plan to the Allied authorities immediately after the war in which privately owned radio stations would be allowed along with the Japan Broadcasting Corporation. The Allied response seemed encouraging and the Japanese Government informed various interests that there would be air space available to private interests. As a result of this, applications to set up broadcasting stations were submitted as early as December 1945.[9]

The Allied action to permit private broadcasting did not occur. Instead, the recommendation was that the present monopoly system be continued. Directives from Allied General Headquarters, however, ordered the reorganization of the Japan Broadcasting Corporation separating the Corporation from government control. Several other directives stated the principles of free speech to be followed. However, mass communication was to be monitored for materials deemed deleterious to the Allied Occupation. Although the first steps had been taken to free broadcasting from tight authoritative control, in essence the Allied Powers became the rulers over the mass media.

Article XXI of the new Constitution, adopted in 1947, stated that "Freedom of assembly and association as well as speech, press and all other forms of expression are guaranteed. No censorship shall be maintained, nor shall the secrecy of any means of communication be violated." Thus, what had been ordered by Allied directive, became a legal basis for broadcasting.

The Constitution, however, did not solve all the thorny problems. Indeed, the Allied authorities and the Japanese Government spent much time trying to establish: (a) the form and nature of the Japan Broadcasting Corporation, (b) the regulation and coordination of broadcasting, and (c) the basis for commercial broadcasting.[10]

The future course of Japanese broadcasting became set, after prolonged discussion and debate, with the passage of three laws in 1950. These statutes established a broadcast regulatory commission patterned after the Federal Communication Commission in the United States; made the Japan Broadcasting Corporation a public juridicial person independent in large part from government control; and laid the basis for the entry of commercial stations.

Present Operations

Two systems, private and public, exist in Japan. The public system is financed primarily through the collection of fees (called contracts) levied on each radio and television set. The fees are collected by the administrative arm of the Japan Broadcasting Corporation. In recent years, the fees for radio receivers have been reduced and in cases of portable sets are not collected at all. Thus the main income is from fees on television receivers.

The money collected is solely for the use of the Japan Broadcasting Corporation. Commercial broadcasters are financed through time sales even though people who are serviced by their programs pay a fee to the Japan Broadcasting Corporation. The law provides, however, that the money be allocated by the NHK only after budget approval by the legislative arm of the Government. Further, the Government's audit body inspects the NHK's books annually. Fees were collected under the old system before the Second World War but government action could be taken by the executive arm. Moreover, direct interference in programming could be and was often done. Now, aside from the review of financial matters, government action is restricted by law.

The NHK is also authorized to borrow money up to three times the net property value of the Corporation for capital improvement. The NHK pays no taxes on its operations but commercial broadcasters are subject to tax.

The NHK is specifically directed by law to provide coverage to all of Japan. Since the advent of television, a massive construction program to insure the availability of signals has been undertaken with relay stations, community antennas, and other means to reach remote areas receiving top priority. This, in turn, has caused a phenomenal increase in the number of television sets. As they are under no such dictate, commercial broadcasters cluster their stations around the most lucrative market areas.[11]

The NHK is also charged with responding to the needs and wishes of the citizens. To meet this responsibility, the Corporation has established a research department. The results of this research are made public but the main emphasis is on analyses of NHK programs so that commercial broadcasters may glean some information for their own purposes but are dependent upon commercial research agencies for their decision making purposes.

Both NHK and commercial broadcasters must apply through the broadcast regulatory body for air space. Although there have been no cases of NHK and commercial broadcasters competing for the same allocation, this is theoretically possible and raises an interesting question. As in other countries, the applications must include programming intent and the regulatory agency scrutinizes intended program balance as one of the criteria for making an award.[12]

No obligations are placed upon the commercial broadcasters except a stricture against monopoly arrangements with respect to program sources. The law allowed for commercial or private broadcasting but did not stipulate much beyond that. Recently, self-regulation has been attempted in order to prevent criticisms of low-quality programs. Evidently this has not succeeded and there is a move to enact some form of measure to curb excesses in broadcasting.

Scope of Operations

JAPAN presents an outstanding example of the growth of broadcasting. Although recent figures on the size of the radio and television audiences are available, comparable statistics for past years are hard to obtain. A more conservative figure in terms of coverage is the number of contracts (or fee payments) made each year. There is a good estimate of the number of television households, as the NHK does a thorough job in getting all television owners meshed into the fee apparatus.[13]

In 1925, one radio station had 5,455 contracts, roughly one-tenth of one percent of households. In 1945, at the end of the war, there were eighty-five radio stations with over seven million contracts. This was 50.4 percent of all households with one or more radios. Radio stations increased to four hundred and forty-four in 1966, one hundred and forty-five of which were commercial. Probably ninety percent of the homes now have radios, although this can only be estimated because radio and television contracts are combined for those who own both. In 1966, there were 2,361,046 radio contracts which means that approximately ten percent of the families had radio only.

Television, which started with one NHK and one commercial station in 1953, is now at 1,239 stations, four hundred and fifty-six of which are commercial. There are over eighteen million contracts, about eighty-four percent of all households.[14]

Of the two hundred and ninety-nine NHK radio stations, one hundred and twenty-nine are for educational purposes. Of the eight hundred and forty-two NHK television stations, three hundred and eighty-six are educational. One commercial station in Tokyo, underwritten by various industries, attempted to become an educational station primarily for industrial training, but failed. The NHK is the only system now transmitting educational programs. The rest of the NHK stations are classified as general cultural programming although this rubric includes sports coverage, daytime serials and variety shows.

Programs—Types and Content

PROGRAM content in Japan is indistinguishable from broadcasting elsewhere. Except for the educational stations, both the NHK and commercial systems carry a high degree of entertainment, about 25.4 percent of the NHK programs. News accounts for about 29.2 percent, educational programs 11.5 percent and cultural programs 33.9 percent. On the educational stations, the NHK breaks down its programming into 76.3 percent classified as educational, 23.3 percent cultural and 0.4 percent news.

In its early days, television carried many U.S. features. It still does so, but more and more of the programming is being produced in Japan. Most U.S. features are dubbed in Japanese, with only an occasional program with subtitles.

Numerous critics have criticized the nature of the programs. For a while, the term "masu-comi," a Japanese contraction of "mass communications," was a topic for heated discussions. Most of the dire warnings about the effects of broadcasting, notably television, on social values which have been voiced in the United States, have also been raised in Japan. Yet, the programs against which voices have been raised manage to draw high audience ratings.[15]

Broadcasting Audiences

EXPOSURE to television and radio is extremely high in Japan. A recent study on leisure time activities revealed that the Japanese spend about twenty-one hours a week viewing TV and another three hours a week listening to radio. Reading newspapers and magazines accounts for slightly over one-half hour per day. The figures for TV viewing rise each time a survey is taken. Increased leisure time and increased economic affluence seemingly results in an increase in broadcast attention, notably television.[16]

This high amount of viewing is apparently universal. There are very little differences among occupations, between sexes, and among various age groups in the time spent with television. If one couples this high exposure with the amazing diffusion of television sets, one can readily see why some people are so concerned about the effects and the role of broadcasting in Japan.

Over eighty-eight percent of the urban and sixty-nine percent of the rural households own television sets. In comparison, sixty-six percent of all urban families own a washing machine, less than forty percent own a refrigerator and less than thirty-eight percent own a vacuum cleaner. Clearly, televisions are purchased before any labor saving devices are considered.

The audience consistently puts sports, comedy programs, mystery dramas and westerns at the top of their preferences. Except for special events, such as the first political debates ever televised, the Japanese viewing patterns seem to be much like those in the West. Although the NHK stations, because of their ubiquity, are dialed frequently, audiences seem to choose the entertainment programs even though more educational and cultural programming is available through the NHK. When audiences are analyzed for educational television viewing, young people between the ages of sixteen and twenty seem to comprise the largest segment.

Research in Broadcasting

JAPAN probably has one of the most comprehensive research operations in broadcasting. In keeping with the law reorganizing the NHK, that system has supported a far reaching research program in both technical experimentation and audience investigation.

The NHK's nontechnical research is conducted by two agencies, the Radio and TV Culture Research Institute and the Public Opinion Research Institute. Both Institutes engage in research intended to guide programming policy. However, basic research in the field of communication is sometimes carried out, although the justification for such research must include its possible use in actual operations.

The Public Opinion Research Institute conducts nation-wide surveys, not only program ratings but also special studies on social and political conditions and problems. Its main effort is to ascertain audience response. The data is used in two ways—as a source of information for program planners and as a source of data for social scientists investigating audience behavior.[17]

The Radio and TV Culture Research Institute conducts research on program content, language usage in broadcasting, maintains historical data connected with broadcasting and supports a theoretical research center. This last group, which undertakes relatively involved social research, comes closest to an academic operation. Its primary purpose is to advance broadcasting research as a science.

In addition to the NHK research operations, a number of commercial research organizations exist, mainly in the form of marketing and advertising agencies. There are also audience rating agencies for commercial purposes.

A great number of publications from the various research agencies are available. A look at this output is both encouraging and discouraging to the student of mass media. On the one hand, research on specific program items, which seems to contribute little to a better understanding of broadcasting, abounds. Often, however, significant items appear which illuminate the effects of communication upon an industrialized society.

The first splurge of studies on broadcasting which appeared shortly after the end of the Second World War and continued until 1960 seems to have abated. In that period, the concern with the implications of free speech and the fear of past authoritarian trends, produced historical research on the mass media which had never before been attempted. Further, the period of recovery which carried Japan to previously unknown heights of prosperity, brought with it a vast resurgence of the mass media. The advent of television and its popularity added to this boom. Research took on all manner of exciting problems deemed worthy of analysis.[18]

But breakthroughs in communications theory did not result from this flurry of research. Instead, the nontheoretical basis of many of the studies caused the scholars to re-evaluate mass media research as perhaps a diversionary effort. Thus the initial interest was followed by a decrease in the numbers seriously investigating broadcasting.

A truly Japanese viewpoint on the mass media is yet to come. Most theoretical writings have taken American research as the starting point, usually seeking Japanese analogues to American writings. The diffusion of American research results to Japan is both rapid and widespread. Each new theoretical twist is known and discussed in Japan almost simultaneously with its release in the United States. But the results have been somewhat disappointing.

Future Trends and Growth

JAPANESE broadcasting has experienced two dramatic periods. It suffered under authoritarian control as an agency of the Government. Having passed from a period when administrative action became law to one where safeguards for freedom are written into the law, broadcasting is now subject to minimum control.

In this reversal, Japanese broadcasting along with Japanese society has had to reorient itself drastically. The memory of past experiences is still strong, however, and the mass media, broadcasting in particular, will fight to guard the freedom it has been given. But freedom entails some responsibility. The exact nature of this responsibility is still being debated in Japan. The moves to amend the broadcast laws reveal some concern about the future of Japanese broadcasting. The extent to which freedom of speech in broadcasting should be curbed is a pressing question in Japan.

The scope of Japanese broadcasting with respect to audiences has about reached the saturation point. As early as 1963, Japan was second in the number of TV sets owned, exceeded only by the United States. Perhaps the pattern in the United States will follow—the resurgence of radio as it finds its role in an increasingly TV-dominated environment.

Commercial broadcasting still has room to grow in Japan, and probably it is in the commercial field that the greatest expansion will come in the near future. This poses some problems for the NHK. The NHK's role seems to be similar to that of the British Broadcasting Corporation. The NHK second network, emphasizing educational and cultural programming, will probably cater to a more restricted audience. The NHK general service may begin to emulate its commercial competitors with an increasing number of programs which get high ratings.

NOTES

1. H. Kumata and W. Schramm, *Four Working Papers in Propaganda Theory* (Washington, D.C.: USIA, 1955).
2. NHK, *The History of Broadcasting in Japan,* 2 vols. (Tokyo: NHK Press, 1965).*
3. Y. Uchikawa, Y. Arase, *et al.,* "Study of the Process of Communication Control under Japanese Fascism," *Institute of Journalism Bulletin,* University of Tokyo, 1959;* Y. Uchikawa and S. Kochi, "Study of Media Control under Japanese Fascism, Part I," *Shiso,* July 1961.*
4. "Conforming to the New National Structure," *Tokyo Gazette,* No. 14, 1940.
5. "Enlargement and Reorganization of the Government Agency for Information," *Tokyo Gazette,* No. 7, 1941.
6. N. Takagi and K. Fukuda, "Study of Mass Media Control under Japanese Fascism," *Shiso,* July 1961.*
7. Fumimaro Konoye, "Concerning the New National Structure," *Tokyo Gazette,* IV, No. 4, 1940.
8. Fumimaro Konoye, "Confronting the Crisis," *Tokyo Gazette,* IV, No. 5, 1940; "On the National Mobilization Law," *Tokyo Gazette,* No. 11, 1938; "On Publicity and Information," *Tokyo Gazette,* No. 4, 1937; "Policy Activities in the Present Emergency," *Tokyo Gazette,* No. 16, 1938; "Concerning National Spiritual Mobilization," *Tokyo Gazette,* No. 24, 1939.
9. NHK, Radio and Television Culture Research Institute, *Studies of Broadcasting* (annual volumes on research in Japan printed in English).
10. National Association of Commercial Broadcasters, *A Decade of Commercial Broadcasting in Japan 1951–1961* (Tokyo: Nihon Minkan Hoso Renmei, 1961).*
11. T. Sato, *et al.,* "A Historical Review of Television Development in Japan," *Chosa Joho,* LXXII, 1965.*
12. Y. Nomura, "Japan's System of Broadcasting and Its Characteristics," *Studies of Broadcasting,* I, 1963.
13. K. Kojima, "Recent Trends in Radio Listening," *NHK Institute Monthly Report,* XXII, No. 4, 1962;* NHK Radio and Television Culture Research Institute, *Annual Reports;* NHK Radio and Television Culture Research

Institute, *Bunken Geppo* (monthly research reports);* NHK Radio and Television Culture Research Institute, *Hosogaku Kenkyu* (monthly research reports).*

14. Y. Takagi, "Television Networks in Japan," *Chosa Joho,* 1966.*
15. Yutaka Arase, "Television and the Printed Media," *Shiso,* November 1958;* Kanji Hatano, "Television and Education," *Shiso,* November 1958;* K. Sasaki, "What is Television Culture?" *Shiso,* November 1958;* Ikutaro Shimizu, "The Television Era," *Shiso,* November 1958.*
16. K. Hirota and C. Nagai, "A Study of Exposure Habits in Television," *Kansai University Shimbun-gaku Kenkyu,* No. 9, 1962;* K. Hirota and C. Nagai, "A Study of Exposure Habits in Television—No. 2," *Kansai University Shimbun-gaku Kenkyu,* No. 10, 1963;* Hidetoshi Kato, "Television and Entertainment," *Shiso,* November 1958;* Yomiuri Television, "Survey on Exposure to Mass Media," *YTV Report,* No. 38, 1965.*
17. Takeo Furu and Teruo Kondo, "Radio and Television Surveys," *Lecture Series on Applied Social Psychology,* Kobunsha, II, 1957.*
18. Takeo Furu, "The Functions of Television for Children—A Cross–Cultural Study," *Studies of Broadcasting,* NHK, V, March 1967; J. Hino, "The Effects of Television on Housewives and Children," *Minkan Hoso Kenkyu,* No. 9, 1957;* Hajime Ikeuchi, K. Okabe, *et al.,* "Urban Residents: Their Daily Lives, Leisure-time Activities, and Attitudes toward Urban Life," *Institute of Journalism Bulletin,* No. 10, University of Tokyo, 1960;* Newspaper Readership Survey Committee, *Mass Media and the Audience,* Nihon Seisan-sei Honbu, 1965.

* In Japanese

XXX

Australia: Partnership of Public and Private Enterprise

THE MOST RECENT REPORTS INDICATE that Australia now has 2,357,-642 radio and 2,457,300 television receivers. With a population of little more than 11,537,000, almost half of which is located in the southeast, a relatively small part of the vast island continent, this represents a high degree of saturation in set ownership. This remarkable growth in broadcasting has taken place in a democratic society which emphasizes the public interest aspects of broadcasting with the Government playing an important role, but which affords private enterprise the opportunity of participating.

Early Broadcast History

As was true in many other countries, there was little regulation of broadcasting in Australia during the early period of its growth. In 1905, Parliament passed the Wireless Telegraphy Act authorizing the Postmaster General to establish and operate apparatus for the transmission and receipt of wireless messages, and to grant licenses to others for such terms and under such conditions, including payment of fees, as he might prescribe. However, he exercised comparatively little control over broadcasting stations once they were on the air.[1]

The twenties was definitely a decade of *laissez faire*. Ian Mackay has written that "there was no desire on the part of the government to extend the range of state activities, but rather a tendency to avoid responsibilities that could be left to private enterprise; government excursion into the field of private enterprise was regarded as a threat to the liberal traditions of the day."[2]

But private interests naturally established stations in the more populous eastern cities and avoided the large arid and mountainous areas with comparatively few people, where broadcast coverage was expensive and commercially infeasible. As early as 1924 the Postmaster General called a conference of the radio industry, which adopted new regulations dividing stations into two classes: "A" stations financed by listeners' license fees, and "B" stations financed by advertising. In 1929, the Government announced its intention to nationalize all the "A" stations.[3] The following year, bids were invited for the supply of programs for a national broadcast service with technical facilities provided by the Postmaster General. The Australian Broadcasting Company was the successful bidder and by 1932 was operating, under contract with the Government, twelve stations in different parts of the country.[4] However, wanting to extend the national service to areas not yet covered, the Government terminated the contract with the Company and introduced in Parliament legislation to set up the Australian Broadcasting Commission. The Australian Broadcasting Act was approved on May 17, 1932. The Commission, consisting of a Chairman, Vice-Chairman and five Commissioners, all appointed by the Governor General, was granted the following powers:

(1) To appoint a General Manager and "such other officers and servants as it thinks necessary."

(2) To provide and broadcast adequate and comprehensive programs and to take in the interests of the community all such measures as, in the opinion of the Commission, are conducive to the full development of suitable broadcast programs.

(3) To compile, prepare, issue, circulate and distribute magazines, periodicals, books, pamphlets and circulars as it thinks fit.

(4) To collect news in such a manner as it thinks fit and to subscribe to news agencies.

(5) To establish and utilize in such manner as it thinks desirable in order to confer the greatest benefit on broadcasting, groups of musicians for the rendition of orchestral, choral and band music of high quality.

(6) To appoint committees to advise it on any matter.

(7) To determine to what extent and in what manner political speeches might be broadcast.

The Act imposed certain limitations and special responsibilities on the Commission:

(1) The Commission could not acquire any property, or dispose of any property exceeding 5,000 pounds or enter into a lease exceeding 5 years without the approval of the Minister in charge of communications.

(2) The Commission was not permitted to broadcast commercials.

(3) An annual report and balance sheet had to be supplied the Minister for presentation to Parliament.

(4) The Minister retained the right to order or prohibit the broadcast of any matter.

(5) The salaries of the General Manager and the next six most highly paid officers had to be approved by the Governor-General.[5]

On July 1, 1932, the Commission started operating eight metropolitan stations in the larger cities and four regional ones for wide coverage in the

smaller towns and rural areas. These operations were financed by a small
license fee on receivers, half of the license revenue going to the Commission
for program services, about one-third to the Postmaster General for maintaining technical facilities, and the remainder for patent rights.[6] In addition,
there were more than forty commercial stations totally financed by advertising. These continued to operate on a private basis under licenses granted
by the Postmaster General, whose authority to grant such licenses was
derived from the Wireless Telegraphy Act of 1905 which was still in effect.

As Ian Mackay has pointed out, the problems facing the new Commission
were many, varied and peculiar to Australia:

> There was a great deal to be learned from the experience of other
> countries, but the overall plan had to be Australian in design and execu-
> tion. The cities and towns were widely separated and, with Tasmania,
> covered seven widely differing states, each with a varying background,
> tradition and interest. The time factor across the continent involved
> broadcasters in special problems, with a variation of two hours between
> Sydney and Perth. The A.B.C. was called upon to devise a broadcasting
> system which would link this continent into one big community so that all
> radio-equipped homes would know what was going on elsewhere. This
> national system was expected to provide the same programmes for the
> outback as for the major cities and the concert platform was to cover the
> entire continent. The objectives of any national service are similar but
> it is the methods of carrying them out that vary.[7]

He has listed the Commission's major objectives:

1. To provide the best possible programme service for listeners throughout
Australia.
2. To inform, educate and entertain the Australian people by satisfying
a wide variety of tastes and requirements in fields of drama, music, variety, news and information.
3. To cater to specialized needs in children's programmes, religious,
institutional, political and school broadcasts, rural and women's interests.
4. To reflect, in programmes, all aspects of Australian life and provide a
forum for the discussion and a balanced view of public affairs.
5. To foster and sustain Australian talent in speaking, music, drama, and
writing.
6. To contribute to Australian nationhood and unity and safeguard the
national heritage.
7. To bring to Australia programmes from other countries.

Mr. Mackay has further pointed out that "the successful attainment of
these objectives would result in an informed democracy, but the problems
they posed were many and varied. The service had to be developed on a
national scale and additional transmitters were required before a nation-
wide audience was possible. New studios and a co-ordinated centralized
control system depended on the availability of capital while the overall
results depended on the wisdom of the Commissioners and staff and the
degree of idealism that would characterize operations."[8]

Broadcast Expansion

UNDER the auspices of the Australian Broadcasting Commission, the national service was greatly expanded during the next ten years. Sixteen new ABC stations were built and put into operation. Network facilities were extended; program services were enlarged; and school broadcasts were initiated in 1933. In 1936, studio orchestras were established in all states and subscription concerts were introduced in various regions where stations were operating. In 1939, with the use of mobile units, news coverage was enlarged and improved. That same year, the ABC took over the overseas, short-wave service and stepped up its broadcasts.[9]

In 1941–42, the number of commercial stations increased to ninety-seven. Only fifty-three of these, however, were making a profit; the remainder were struggling to keep alive.[10] Since the Broadcasting Act of 1932 pertained only to the national ABC service, Parliament felt that a study of all broadcasting in Australia and specific legislation covering commercial stations were needed. Accordingly, in 1941, a Joint Parliamentary Committee of Inquiry was appointed to review all aspects of the industry.[11]

New Broadcast Legislation

IN 1942, this Committee reported its findings which served as a basis for the passage that same year of a new Broadcasting Act replacing the 1932 law and covering all phases of broadcasting.[12] One of the most important features of the new legislation was that it provided the statutory base for commercial radio; it specified that licenses for such stations were to be granted for a period not exceeding three years, as might be determined by the Minister; that license renewals were to run for one year; and that a service fee was to be charged for the licenses and renewals. The charge was specified as twenty-five pounds for an original license and the same amount plus one percent of the gross annual earnings of the station for each renewal.[13]

Furthermore, the Minister was authorized to revoke licenses for violations of the Act or regulations, if he concluded such action would serve the public interest. Abdication of licensee responsibility was made unlawful and no transfer of control could be made without the Minister's prior written consent.

The law contained a number of provisions regarding programs. All matter, including advertisements, to be broadcast by commercial stations, was made subject to censorship as the Minister might determine; no programs of another station could be rebroadcast without the consent of the originating station and the Minister; nor could news or information published in a newspaper be broadcast without the newspaper's permission.

At least two and one-half percent of the ABC stations' total broadcast time devoted to music was required to consist of works by Australian composers, produced either on sound records made in Australia or by artists actually present in the studio. The same rule applied to every commercial station. The Minister was authorized to vary all or any of the conditions of a license during the license period, expenses, if any, to be borne by the licensee.

Finally, Part IV of the Act specified the establishment of a Parliamentary Standing Committee of nine members, three chosen by the Senate and six by the House of Representatives, with the Minister of State, President of the Senate, Speaker of the House, and the chairmen of committees ineligible for appointment. This Committee was given a mandate to make continuing studies of broadcasting and, before the commencement of each session of Parliament, to submit a report to the Governor General and to each house of Parliament with recommendations for action.

The next five years were an unhappy period for commercial broadcasters who complained that they were "tired of being lectured to by politicians on alleged failures to raise cultural standards as if culture could be turned on by a tap."[14] They demanded that a new regulatory body be created which would be able "to appraise judicially the services rendered by both national and commercial stations. . . ."[15] They hoped that the new agency would differentiate between the functions of the Commission and commercial stations and not expect the latter to "become a pale imitation" of the former.

Australian Broadcasting Control Board Established

RESPONDING to this situation, the Government, on September 28, 1948, introduced legislation providing for the establishment of a special board "to control broadcasting, television and other like services." After some debate, Parliament passed the Australian Broadcasting Act of 1948, establishing the Australian Broadcasting Control Board with regulatory authority over all broadcasting.[16]

This 1948 law made some changes in the ABC. The number of the Commissioners was increased to seven. It was also specified that one Commissioner was to be an officer of the Treasury and one an officer in the Postmaster General's Department, both to hold office at the pleasure of the Governor General. An additional proviso was that the Commission should prepare annual estimates of expenditures and be financed by parliamentary appropriations.

By 1950, the national ABC network had more than fifty affiliated stations, and the number of licensed listeners was over two million. Interest in the development of television was increasing, and Parliament was being pressed to provide for the establishment of stations. In 1953, Parliament passed a law authorizing the Postmaster General to make TV stations available for the national TV Service and to issue licenses for commercial TV stations.[17]

At the same time a Royal Commission was appointed to inquire into the number of TV stations to be established, the areas to be served, conditions of establishment, program standards, advertisements, periods of broadcasts and special conditions relating to certain broadcasts such as political and religious matters.[18]

Broadcasting and Television Act Adopted

THE following year, upon the recommendation of the Royal Commission and under the authority of the 1953 law, the ABC was appointed as the national television authority.[19] Subsequently, Parliament passed the Broadcasting and Television Act of 1956 which confirmed the ABC's authority to provide national TV programs.[20]

This law further provided that Post Office representation on the Commission should be discontinued; that the Commission's authorization for expenditures should be raised to twenty thousand pounds (since 1932 it had been only five thousand pounds); that the percentage of Australian music required on ABC programs be raised to five percent; and that the Parliamentary Standing Committee be abolished.[21]

The Broadcasting and Television Station License Fees Act of 1956 continued the annual license fee of twenty-five pounds plus one percent of the gross earnings derived from advertisements during the preceding year, and made it applicable to television as well as radio. The total amount of license fees paid by commercial radio and TV stations in 1958–59 was 83,902 pounds; in 1959–60, it rose to 92,795 pounds.[22]

Further Amendments to the Act

THE Broadcasting and Television Act was amended further in 1960, 1961, 1962 and 1963 to provide additional regulatory controls for television which was expanding rapidly. The Broadcasting and Television Act 1942–63, which is the 1942 Act with all amendments to date, governs broadcasting in Australia today.[23]

The law provides for the continuation of the Australian Broadcasting Commission with seven members, one of which must be a woman. Any Commissioner who may have a substantial financial interest in any contract made or proposed by the Commission, must disclose the nature of the interest, and is prohibited from taking part in any consideration or decision on the matter by the Commission.

Section 59(1) of the statute states that the Commission "shall provide, and shall broadcast or televise from transmitting stations made available by the Postmaster General, adequate and comprehensive programs and shall take in the interests of the community all such measures as, in the opinion of the Commission, are conducive to the full development of suitable broadcasting and television programs."

It is further provided in Section 60 that the Commission "may compile, prepare, issue, circulate and distribute, whether gratis or otherwise, in such manner as it thinks fit, such papers, magazines, periodicals, books, pamphlets, circulars and other literary matter as it thinks fit (including the programs of national broadcasting stations and of other broadcasting and television stations), provided that, prior to publication, a copy of the program is made available on equal terms to the publishers of newspapers, magazines and journals in Australia."

The Commission may provide offices and studios as necessary to carry out its functions, but the location must have the Minister's approval, and no agreement involving an expenditure of more than twenty-five thousand pounds or extending for a term of more than five years may be entered into without his consent.

Specific Program Requirements for National Stations

NONE of the Commission stations is permitted to broadcast commercials, but all must make available, on demand, free of charge, time to the Government for the broadcast of messages which the Government deems to be in the public interest.

The law imposes a number of specific program requirements on the national stations:

1. They must present national and international news daily, and maintain an adequate staff for this purpose.
2. They must provide groups of musicians for the broadcasting of "orchestral, choral, and band music of high quality."
3. They must refrain from broadcasting any program which the Minister deems improper or not in the public interest, provided the Minister gives written notice prior to the broadcast.

Granting, Renewal, Transfer and Revocation
of Commercial Licenses

LICENSES and renewals thereof for commercial stations are granted by the Minister after review by and recommendation of the Broadcasting Control

Board. The initial licenses are for five years, renewals for one year only. If the Minister concludes there are grounds for refusing a license or renewal, he may direct the Board to conduct a formal inquiry. If such a hearing is held, the Board must make a report of its findings and recommend appropriate action to the Minister.

The Minister may, by notice in writing, suspend or revoke a license if the licensee has (1) failed to pay a license fee required by the Broadcasting and Television Stations License Fees Act of 1956; (2) failed to comply with the law or regulations; (3) not complied with conditions in the license; or (4) if it appears, for specified reasons, that the public interest would not be served by permitting the licensee to continue operations. No license may be revoked finally, however, until the Board has conducted a formal inquiry and has made a recommendation to the Minister. And, any revocation action of the Minister may be appealed in the Commonwealth Industrial Court which has the authority to confirm the action or order that the license be restored.

No license may be assigned or control of the station transferred without the Minister's written consent. Nor can a person own or control more than one metropolitan commercial broadcasting station* in any state, more than four such stations in Australia, or more than eight commercial broadcasting stations (regardless of type or location) in the country.

Ownership of commercial television stations is limited to one in a territory or not more than one within a radius of thirty miles from the General Post Office in the capital city of a state, and not more than two in Australia. And, no more than twenty percent of the stock in any licensee company may be owned by persons not residents of Australia.

Subject to the direction of the Minister, the Board determines the location of commercial stations, their frequency assignments and transmitting power, their hours of operations, and sets the standards for their technical operation.

Board Control over Programs

THE Board has considerable authority with regard to programs. It is authorized to establish standards and to require all commercial stations to comply with them.

The Commission is required to make available to commercial television stations, in areas where there are no national television stations, programs of the Commission as specified by the Minister. Both Commission and com-

---

*A metropolitan commercial broadcasting station is defined as one situated within a radius of thirty miles from the General Post Office in the capital city of a state.

mercial stations, "as far as possible," are required to use Australians in the production and presentation of programs.

Political Broadcasting

SPECIAL sections of the law pertain to political broadcasting. The Commission itself, subject to certain limitations, determines to what extent and in what manner political or any controversial matter will be broadcast by the Commission. There is a statutory prohibition against all stations dramatizing any political matter "which is then current or was current at any time during the last five preceding years." Licensees are required to provide equal opportunities to all political parties contesting in an election for seats in Parliament, if such parties were represented in either house of Parliament at the time of its last meeting before the election period began, but no station in Australia may broadcast political matter of any kind on election day. Licensees may sell time for political broadcasting and are not required to give free time for such transmissions. The law requires that speakers on political subjects and current affairs, and the parties, if any, they represent, be clearly identified over the air, and a record of their names, addresses and occupations must be kept and made available, on written request, to the Board.

Indecent Programs Prohibited

SECTION 118 of the law prohibits the broadcasting of blasphemous, indecent or obscene matter. It is unlawful for any person to submit such programming or for a station to present it over the air. Offenders of this law are subject to criminal prosecution, although an offense of this kind may not be prosecuted without the written consent of the Minister.

Broadcasting Growth Since the War

BROADCASTING in Australia has shown a marked growth since the Second World War. In 1950, for example, there were only fifty-one ABC radio stations and fifty-six commercial ones.[24] The Australian Broadcasting Commission reported in June 1965, that the number of ABC stations had increased to eighty-three and the number of commercial stations had practically doubled.[25] Added to these medium-wave facilities were ten short-wave stations providing domestic service to the island continent and six such stations broadcasting programs overseas. Transmission hours for ABC radio had increased from 288,507 in 1950 to 522,147 in 1965.[26]

The ABC formerly operated only two radio networks, but in 1963 a third one was added. Frank Watts, the ABC Director of Education, reported this development in the May 1964 issue of the *EBU Review* and explained the different patterns of programming to be provided by the three networks:

In the cities the ABC operates two radio networks. Until the reorganization in 1963, one of these networks contained light and service material, the other more serious material and parliamentary broadcasts when the Australian Federal Parliament in Canberra was in session. For some time it had been a matter for regret to the ABC that when Parliament was being broadcast—which is on three days and nights for about 23 weeks of each year—the amount of fine music and the number of serious talks and discussions, radio features and plays that could be broadcast were very greatly reduced.

When an assessment was made of the effect of television on the radio audience, it became obvious that television was pre-eminent in the field of straight entertainment, although of course it had a great deal to offer in the way of information and instruction too. But it was just as obvious that there were some things that radio could still do better, and it was in this area that the ABC had most to offer, in the more serious types of broadcasting.

Consequently the two city networks, redesignated the First Network and the Second Network, were so arranged that the First should carry lighter types of programmes and, when the Federal Parliament was in session, should broadcast Parliament proceedings; and the Second should carry service material—most news bulletins, the "Country Hour," school broadcasts, etc.—and the more serious types of programmes: the recitals and orchestral concerts, operas, the discussions and talks series, plays and radio features. Without the interruption of parliamentary broadcasts, the Second Network can broadcast a great deal more of such material than has been possible in the past.

While working on the reorganization of the metropolitan networks, ABC planners took the opportunity of improving the programmes for country listeners as well. Because there are transmission facilities for only one programme outside the range of the city transmitters, the single Regional Programme must be a compromise, containing essential elements, like the service-type units, as well as a balanced selection of the best light and serious units. The ABC programmes for country listeners were redesigned as the Third Network and organized to operate largely independent of the two metropolitan programmes. In this way greater flexibility was obtained and a better balanced output made possible.

This reorganization of the ABC's radio programmes into three networks was given the identification of "Newrad." Since it came into operation its effects have been carefully studied and a number of modifications made. This has been in line with the declared policy that the programme organization must be at all times dynamic. After the initial discomfort of finding their listening habits disorganized, listeners have reacted favourably to the changes, the greatest approval being for the Second Network with its increased output of serious material. Further appraisals are planned and, where necessary, further changes will be made in the Newrad layouts.[27]

Current Patterns of Radio Programming

FOR the year 1964–65, the ABC reported percentages for the different types of national programs:[28]

	Metropolitan Stations PERCENTAGE	Regional Stations PERCENTAGE
Classical Music	24.61	11.27
Light Music	6.43	3.47
Light Entertainment (dance music, musical comedy, cabaret music, etc.)	21.34	20.01
Drama and Features	3.69	5.31
Children's Programs	2.53	4.94
Education	3.53	7.01
Parliament	3.77	—
Talks (stories, talks, discussions, news commentaries, topical actualities, magazine programs, political broadcasts, election results)	6.96	8.21
Religious Programs	3.14	3.84
News (national, state, regional BBC, and Asian)	8.01	12.05
Sports	5.86	9.84
Rural Programs	1.63	4.83

As the above figures indicate, ABC radio is designed to provide a wide variety of programs and to serve the majority as well as the minority interests and tastes. As will be noted, musical programs make up a large component of the broadcasts. In recent years, particular attention has been given to contemporary works by Australian composers, including indigenous folk music. Distinguished overseas conductors are increasingly featured, and American entertainers such as Sammy Davis, Jr. and Danny Kaye have received top billing on network shows.

Comprehensive coverage of domestic and foreign news is maintained. Full-time correspondents are stationed in Southeast Asia, the United States and other parts of the world.

Education has always received major radio attention. As early as 1955, instructional programs were being featured. The ABC reported that school broadcasts that year were used by 7,981 Australian schools, or eighty-three percent of the total in the country.[29] In 1964–65, more than five hundred hours of instructional radio were presented and were used by almost one thousand schools (ninety-eight percent of the total) throughout the country.[30]

Radio Australia

RADIO Australia, the ABC's overseas service, operates four short-wave transmitters in Victoria. This service was started during the Second World War and has been expanded to include a wide variety of programs—news, music, documentaries and language instruction, to mention only a few. It originally broadcast nine hours a day, using only European languages. Today, it operates around the clock and, in addition to the European languages, broadcasts in most of the major tongues of Southeast Asia. It transmits more than forty-four news bulletins each day. These are presented in English and seven other languages and are heard in almost every part of the world.

English lessons for Indonesians have become increasingly popular. In 1965, more than thirty thousand copies of Thai/English textbooks, prepared by the ABC's Education Department, were distributed in Thailand.[31]

Programs in French broadcast to Asia are increasingly emphasized. Mr. Paul Ormode, the Publicity Officer of Radio Australia, has explained the reasons for this: ". . . Basically, it is because of the large French-speaking community in South-east Asia, particularly in Vietnam, Cambodia and Laos, as well as French speaking in the former French territories of Africa and the Pacific (which are all within Radio Australia's strong signal area). The short-wave enthusiast in Paris can hear the French Service too— and he will notice the emphasis in news bulletins and commentaries on events in Asia and the Pacific. Tell *him* that Australia is part of Asia, and he will probably be inclined to agree."[32]

ABC Television

TELEVISION was instituted in September 1956. Beginning in Sydney and Melbourne, it was later expanded to other capital cities, Brisbane, Adelaide,

Perth and Hobart. The next step was to establish facilities in the larger inland centers, followed by stations in the more sparsely populated areas. As of June 1965, the ABC was operating twenty-seven transmitters. These, plus the commercial TV facilities now in operation, bring more than ninety percent of the country within range of one or more high-power television stations. Plans are under way to fill in the gaps and improve marginal reception by using large numbers of low-power translators.[33]

Australians took a quick fancy to television. Whereas it took more than thirty years for radio to reach its present dimensions with about two million and four hundred thousand licensed receivers in use, television, which is little more than ten years old, has achieved virtually nation-wide coverage, and the number of licensed TV receivers already about equals the number of radios.[34]

An analysis of the program logs for 1964–65 shows the following percentages of time devoted to different TV program categories:[35]

	Percentage
Music	3.04
Light Entertainment (music, variety and character comedy)	7.20
Drama (adventures, mysteries, Western, situation, literary adaptations, screen plays, studios productions, etc.)	21.29
Children's session	8.72
Education (kindergarten, school, extension)	14.62
Talks (interviews, documentaries, election talks, women's programs, etc.)	18.17
Religion (studio and outside broadcasts)	2.61
News	6.41
Sports	10.72
Rural	2.22
Non-Departmental	5.00

In January 1964, an Advisory Committee on Educational Television Services was appointed to advise the Australian Broadcasting Control Board on the contribution television might be able to make to education in Australia. The director of the Commonwealth Office of Education was appointed Chairman, and the membership comprised a panel of distinguished educators from various states.

The Committee held hearings and made its report at the end of the year. The Board passed on the Report with comments to the Minister and the Postmaster General, who presented it to the House of Representatives in May 1966. Among other things, the Committee recommended:

(1) that instructional television should be developed as an integral part of the educational systems in Australia;

(2) that the need exists for total teaching by TV at pre-school and adult

levels and in teacher education for supplementing instruction at the primary and secondary levels of learning; and that one VHF channel should be reserved for educational purposes in each established service area;

(3) that control and operation of the educational TV services be vested in a separate authority constituted for that purpose, and

(4) that the costs of establishing and operating the educational TV services should be paid by the Government from loan funds and consolidated revenue.[36]

While the Postmaster General supported the Committee's view that instructional television ought to be an integral part of the Australian systems of education, he thought that the "first and essential" step should be to consult with the State Governments as to their educational needs and priorities and the extent to which they would be willing to help finance the program. He and the Government, therefore, did not agree with the Committee that a separate network should be provided for educational television, "holding that a new network of stations exclusively for instructional purposes would be unused for varying periods of each day and, at the same time, there would be unused capacity in the national and commercial transmitters."[37] Accordingly, it was decided that the ABC, in association with state authorities, should continue to present instructional programs.[38]

Commercial Television

AUSTRALIA has had commercial television for more than ten years. A. S. Cowan, the general manager of the Federation of Australian Commercial Television Stations, has pointed out that "this decade has seen commercial television firmly entrenched in the lives of the community and as a potent force in selling goods and services of its many advertisers."[39]

As of March 1967, there were forty commercial TV stations with programs transmitted from thirty-one centers. Fifteen stations are located in the capital cities (three each in Sydney, Melbourne, Brisbane and Adelaide, two in Perth and one in Hobart) and twenty-five in the provincial cities (eleven in New South Wales, six in Victoria, six in Queensland and one each in South Australia and Tasmania). These plus the ABC stations make a total of seventy-eight television stations in the dual service. Recent studies show that on an average day in 1967, 4,503,000 people in the five mainland capitals watched commercial television at some time, an increase of more than two hundred and fifty thousand over the preceding year. It has been reported that, on an average, Australians view commercial TV programs three hours and twenty-two minutes a day.[40]

Australia, in terms of population, ranks high among the nations of the world in TV set saturation. There are two hundred and twenty-nine sets for every one thousand persons and the dual system (commercial and non-commercial) gives the viewer programs on four separate channels in each of the four capitals, three in Perth and two in other areas.

The programs of commercial TV stations consist mainly of drama, variety shows and music, with about four percent of the total broadcasting time devoted to news. More than sixty percent of the time of these stations is used to broadcast filmed material produced in the United States.[41] This has been criticized by the Australian Broadcasting Control Board, particularly the tendency of commercial stations to replace live programs designed for children with imported films produced for general audiences.[42]

The ABC and commercial stations cooperate in broadcasting important events. For example, all seventy-three stations (national and commercial) were linked to provide simultaneous coverage of President Johnson's recent tour through Australian cities.

Both the ABC and the Federation of Australian Commercial Television Stations are associate members of the European Broadcasting Union and draw upon and contribute to the program resources of Eurovision.

NOTES

1. *The Acts of Parliament of the Commonwealth of Australia,* 1905, IV, No. 8, pp. 10, 11.
2. Ian K. Mackay, *Broadcasting in Australia* (Melbourne: Melbourne University Press, 1957), p. 3.
3. The Australian Broadcasting Commission, *The History and Development of the A. B. C.,* undated, p. 1.
4. *Ibid.*
5. *The Acts of Parliament,* Act of May 17, 1932, XXX, No. 14, 43–53.
6. *Ibid.,* p. 48.
7. Mackay, p. 38.
8. *Ibid.,* p. 38.
9. *The History and Development of the A. B. C.,* pp. 4–5.
10. *Eleventh Annual Report of the Australian Broadcasting Control Board for the Year 1959–60,* p. 9.
11. *The History and Development of the A. B. C.,* p. 5.
12. *The Acts of Parliament,* Australian Broadcasting Act of 1942, Act of June 12, 1942, XI, No. 33, 78–102.
13. As of January 1968, one Australian pound was equivalent to $1.13.
14. Mackay, p. 185.
15. *Ibid.*
16. *The Acts of Parliament,* Australian Broadcasting Act of 1948, December 6, 1948, XLVI, No. 63, 336–346.
17. *Ibid.,* Television Act of 1953, March 20, 1953, No. 5, pp. 15–16.
18. *The History and Development of the A. B. C.*
19. *Ibid.*

20. *The Acts of Parliament,* Broadcasting and Television Act of 1956, June 20, 1956, No. 33, pp. 403–428.
21. *The History and Development of the A. B. C.*
22. *Eleventh Annual Report of the Australian Broadcasting Control Board, 1959–60,* p. 9.
23. Commonwealth of Australia, *Broadcasting and Television Act 1942–1963* (Canberra: A. J. Arthur, Commonwealth Government Printer, 4642/63–2).
24. European Broadcasting Union, *Documentation and Information Bulletin,* III, No. 15 (September 15, 1952), 497; also, see ABC, *33rd Annual Report,* 1964–65, p. 27.
25. *List of Stations,* published by Australian Broadcasting Commission, October 1965.
26. ABC, *33rd Annual Report,* 1964–65, p. 27.
27. *EBU Review,* 85B, May 1964, p. 31.
28. ABC, *33rd Annual Report,* 1964–65, pp. 28–29.
29. *EBU Bulletin,* July–August 1955, p. 385.
30. ABC, *33rd Annual Report,* 1964–65, pp. 28, 42.
31. *Ibid.,* pp. 20–21.
32. *EBU Review,* 102B, March 1967, p. 33.
33. *EBU Review,* 95B, January 1966, p. 30.
34. *Ibid.*
35. ABC, *33rd Annual Report,* 1964–65, pp. 29–30.
36. Commonwealth of Australia, *Report of the Advisory Committee on Educational Television Services to the Australian Broadcasting Control Board* (Tasmania: Government Printer, 1964), pp. 59–60.
37. *EBU Review,* 99B, September 1966, p. 26.
38. *Ibid.*
39. *EBU Review,* 102B, March 1967, p. 32.
40. *Ibid.*
41. *Ibid.*
42. *Ibid.*

PART II

International
Broadcasting

XXXI

International Organizations Concerned with Broadcasting Across National Boundaries

The International Telecommunications Union (ITU)

RADIO WAVES DO NOT STOP at national boundaries. Without cooperation and agreements among nations regarding the allocation and use of radio frequencies, effective international broadcasting would be impossible. To avoid intolerable interference and chaos in the airways, there must be regulations and a recognized international organization to administer them. The International Telecommunications Union (ITU), with headquarters in Geneva, Switzerland, serves this purpose. One hundred and twenty countries are members of the Union and subscribe to its rules and regulations.

The Union was established in 1865 to provide for the orderly development of telegraph service across national boundaries. Since that time, its regulatory jurisdiction has been extended to include all international wire and wireless communications.

In carrying out its main objectives—to harmonize the actions of nations and promote the development of technical media and the improvement of telecommunication services throughout the world—the Union is required to (1) allocate frequencies and provide for the registration of their assignments to the various countries; (2) coordinate national efforts to eliminate objectionable interference among stations and achieve maximum utility of the radio spectrum; and (3) in the area of common carrier communications, to foster collaboration among Union members to maintain reasonably low rates consistent with efficient service.[1]

Another important duty of the Union is to aid emerging countries in the development of improved means of communication, especially by participating in appropriate programs of the United Nations, to which the ITU has been attached since 1947.[2]

STRUCTURE OF THE INTERNATIONAL
TELECOMMUNICATION UNION

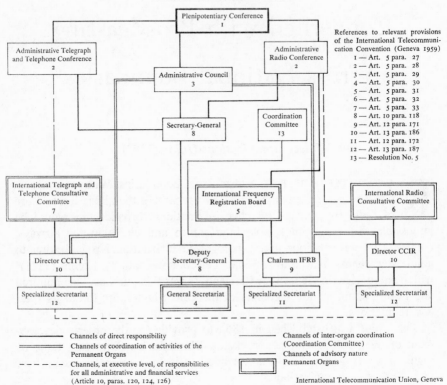

References to relevant provisions
of the International Telecommunication Convention (Geneva 1959)

1 — Art. 5 para. 27
2 — Art. 5 para. 28
3 — Art. 5 para. 29
4 — Art. 5 para. 30
5 — Art. 5 para. 31
6 — Art. 5 para. 32
7 — Art. 5 para. 33
8 — Art. 10 para. 118
9 — Art. 12 para. 171
10 — Art. 13 para. 186
11 — Art. 12 para. 172
12 — Art. 13 para. 187
13 — Resolution No. 5

——————— Channels of direct responsibility
═══════ Channels of coordination of activities of the
         Permanent Organs
— — — — Channels, at executive level, of responsibilities
         for all administrative and financial services
         (Article 10, paras. 120, 124, 126)

——————— Channels of inter-organ coordination
         (Coordination Committee)
— · — · Channels of advisory nature
▭ Permanent Organs

International Telecommunication Union, Geneva

The preceeding chart, prepared by the ITU, reflects the organizational structure of the Union.[3]

The *Plenipotentiary Conference,* the highest authority of the ITU, makes broad policies which are embodied in the International Telecommunication Conventions, determines the budget, elects members of the Administrative Council, appoints the Secretary-General and the Deputy Secretary-General, represents the Union in agreements with other international organizations and determines the formula for annual contributions of member states to defray the costs of Union activities.

The *Administrative Conferences* are responsible for drawing up and revising, as occasion may require, regulations covering radio, telegraph and telephone communication. The Administrative Radio Conference elects the members of the International Frequency Registration Board (IFRB). This group also provides for *extraordinary administrative* conferences which may deal with certain parts of the regulations and/or special problems such as the allocation of frequencies for broadcasting stations in a particular region. For example, such a meeting was held in Geneva in 1963 to allocate frequency bands for space radio communications.

The *Administrative Council* (twenty-nine member countries chosen to represent all parts of the world) is responsible for coordinating the Union's activities between the Plenipotentiary Conferences which normally are held every five years.

The *Consultative Committees* make studies and recommendations on technical matters. Mr. Namurois has described their functions:

Participation in the work of the International Consultative Committees is open not only to all members and associate members but also to certain recognized private operating agencies. The committees are required to draw up a list of questions for consideration. Each item is thereupon referred to a "study committee" composed of a limited number of experts from administrations which have expressed a desire to take part in the discussion; these experts have an exchange of views either by correspondence or in interim meetings and report back their findings to the Plenary Assemblies of the Consultative Committees which are generally held every three years. The Consultative Committees do not frame regulations; they merely express advisory opinions on technical, operating and tariff questions, and quite a number of these opinions are taken as the basis for the revision of the Telegraph Regulations, the Telephone Regulations or the Radio Regulations respectively at the following Ordinary Administrative Conferences.

An important function of the Consultative Committees lies in the organization of the Planning Committee and its three regional Subcommittees for Latin America, Asia and Africa respectively, which coordinate the development of national telecommunications systems with a view to ensuring good international connections. It should be noted that the deliberations of the Planning Committee and its Subcommittees are of very great importance for the new and developing countries which are trying to develop their telecommunication service.[4]

Mr. Namurois has pointed out in a footnote that much of the technical progress due to the Union is the result of the deliberations of these Committees, since special studies are made at an early date of practically all technological innovations in telecommunications. Moreover, these Committees are important in "standardizing the working of equipment and the method of operating it," a vital function, because equipment may come from many different countries and it must be capable of working as an integral part of international telecommunications systems.[5]

The *International Frequency Registration Board* of five members is chosen by the Administrative Radio Conference to achieve broad geographical representation. The Board's function is to maintain an orderly record of frequency assignments made by the various countries in accordance with the procedure set forth in the Radio Regulations. It keeps up to date a Master Register (a punched-card form) on which it enters data on the use of frequencies, and, periodically, publishes this data along with the *International Frequency List,* containing over five hundred thousand frequency assignments.

The Board publishes *Monthly Summaries* of information received from international monitoring stations, and four seasonal, short-wave broadcasting time tables and provides assistance to countries in finding suitable frequencies for this type of radio transmission. The Board also compiles and makes available to the Administrative Radio Conferences technical data essential for the preparation of frequency allocation plans.

Finally, the Union staff, headed by the *Secretary-General,* directs the *General Secretariat* and is responsible for the administrative and financial operations of the Union. One section of the General Secretariat, the *Department of Technical Cooperation,* in cooperation with the United Nations, makes experts available to the various countries to assist governments in training technicians and developing communication facilities.

Important regulations pertaining to radio communication are annexed to the International Telecommunication Convention. The Convention has established the principle that each government holding membership in the ITU is responsible for applying these regulations and securing their observance by all stations operating within the territorial borders of the particular country. As Mr. Namurois has pointed out, any member of the ITU "will be at fault if a station within its jurisdiction provides international service in breach of the international regulations, or if such a station causes harmful interference to radiocommunication services in other countries."[6]

Since the radio spectrum is not unlimited it has been necessary for the ITU to adopt conservation measures. The International Telecommunication Convention states that "members and associate members recognize that it is desirable to limit the number of frequencies and the spectrum space used to the minimum essential to provide in a satisfactory manner the necessary services."[7] In this connection, the Union has adopted a Frequency Allocation Table which represents an agreement among member countries on the sharing of the spectrum and the allocation of frequencies for the various services, including broadcasting, in the different parts of the world.

The General Secretariat of the ITU and its offices are located in Geneva. It has many duties, the most important of which is its contribution to the preparatory work, as well as the follow-up activities of the many ITU conferences. A large staff is occupied with the publication of many documents. In fact, the list of current Union publications comprises about two hundred separate items. The *Telecommunication Journal,* the ITU's official monthly journal, is issued in English, French and Spanish, and has a worldwide distribution and reputation. The magazine contains a variety of information—technical progress reports, articles dealing with the Union's many activities, book reviews, a calendar of the ITU conferences, to mention only a few—and has been in continuous publication since 1869.

In a centenary volume published in 1965, the author, Dr. Anthony R. Michaelis of London, described the ITU offices and the spirit of internationalism:

> At the *Place des Nations,* opposite the older *Palais des Nations,* stands the modern glass and aluminum mansion of the International Telecommunication Union. It is a worthy outward symbol of the modern spirit of the Union. Throughout its hundred years of history the Union has not only kept pace with changing times but has often been well in advance of them, and yet it has never neglected to heed the lessons of its own tradition.
>
> Any sensitive visitor to this building can feel these two influences at work. From the outside, array of dipole antennae on its roof shows its links with the rest of the world; its amateur radio station was the gift of the United States of America. A modern system of internal inter-office communications is also a gift by the same government, and its magnificent automatic telephone exchange was presented to the I. T. U. by the Federal Republic of Germany on the occasion of the inauguration of the new building. The Kingdom of the Netherlands contributed to the efficient working of the I. T. U. with two sets of simultaneous interpretation equipment for the Council Chamber and the Committee rooms.
>
> The traditional influence on the Union is shown by the splendid gifts which adorn its halls and passages, gracefully arranged between exotic plants, themselves a gift of Monaco. An ancient amphora from Cyprus, two traditional stools from Ghana, a bronze statue of Lord Krishna from the Republic of India, three glass vases—2,000 years old—from Nazareth, the gift of Israel, silken tapestries from Japan, these antiques and many modern works of art and tasteful furniture—all gifts from Members of the Union —adorn the inside of the building. Outside stands a two meter high bronze statue, the present from the Soviet Union, symbolizing man's striving for a better future. . . .[8]

The European Broadcasting Union (EBU)

BROADCASTERS in different parts of the world have joined together in organizations to promote program exchanges and have developed international networks for this purpose. One of the most important of these is the European Broadcasting Union (EBU), founded in Torquay in the United Kingdom in 1950, but with administrative offices now located across the street from the ITU headquarters in Geneva and a technical center in Brussels, Belgium. Article II of the *Statutes of the European Broadcasting Union* provides that it shall be noncommercial and that its purposes are:

(a) to support in every domain the interests of broadcasting organizations which have accepted these Statutes and to establish relations with other broadcasting organizations;

(b) to promote and coordinate the study of all questions relating to broadcasting, and to ensure the exchange of information on all matters of general interest to broadcasting services;

(c) to promote all measures designed to assist the development of broadcasting in all its forms;

(d) to seek the solution, by means of international cooperation, of any differences that may arise;

(e) to use its best endeavours to ensure that all its members respect the provisions of international agreements relating to all aspects of broadcasting.[9]

To carry out these objectives, the *Statutes* state that the EBU may employ adequate means of study or action and, in particular, (1) have at its disposal permanent services; (2) set up committees and study groups for the examination of particular problems; (3) acquire housing and other facilities to achieve its purposes; and (4) carry on research and undertake publications related to subjects concerned with broadcasting.[10] The Union publishes the *EBU Review* which deals with current developments and problems of national and international broadcasting. The magazine, published in two parts, one technical, the other concerned with legal and programming matters, has a wide circulation in many parts of the world.

EBU membership is restricted to duly authorized organizations or groups of such from a country that is a member or associate member of the ITU. There are three classes of membership: active, supplementary active and associate. Only broadcasting groups from a country situated in the European Broadcasting Area, as defined by the European Broadcasting Convention currently in force, which "provide in that country a broadcasting service of a national character and national importance" may be *active members,* and they may not be admitted in any other capacity.[11] No country may have more than two active members, although additional organizations which qualify under paragraph 4 of the *Statutes* not associated with the active members may be admitted as *supplementary active members*. Broadcasting organizations or groups thereof situated outside the European Broadcasting Zone may be admitted only as *associate members*.

As of early 1967, broadcasting systems in twenty-five countries of Western Europe and Yugoslavia held active membership in the EBU. Broadcasting organizations in thirty other countries were associate members. The active and associate members and the countries they represent, as of October 1967, are listed in Appendix V.

The supreme body of the EBU is the *General Assembly* which possesses all the powers necessary to achieve the Union's objectives. It is made up of all members, although only active members have voting rights. Ordinary sessions of the Assembly are held annually. Extraordinary sessions may be called as circumstances require.

The *Administrative Council* of eleven active members is chosen by the General Assembly. A representative of one of these is elected by the Assembly to serve as President and representatives of two others as Vice-Presidents. Its powers and duties are set forth in Paragraph 7 of the *Statutes* which states that the Council:

    (a) holds, between the ordinary sessions of the General Assembly, and subject to subsequent ratification by the latter, all the rights and powers of the General Assembly except those which the Assembly reserves for itself by an explicit decision;

    (b) ensures that the decisions of the General Assembly are carried out;

    (c) reports on the activities of the E.B.U. to each ordinary session of the General Assembly and after each of its own meetings sends an account of its work to all the active members;

    (d) takes the necessary steps for the admission and withdrawal of members, and proposes to the General Assembly the expulsion of members;

    (e) considers and recommends to the General Assembly the establishment when necessary of Committees additional to those established by the General Assembly, and sets up any Study Groups which it considers useful;

    (f) receives and considers the reports of the Committees and Study Groups and decides what further actions should be taken on them;

    (g) prepares the provisional programme of activities and drafts the budget for the following financial year; draws up and arranges for the auditing of the acounts of the last financial year in accordance with Article 17 of these Statutes;

    (h) makes proposals to the General Assembly for the appointment or dismissal of the Directors and for the amount of their salaries and additional allowances within the limits of the budget; the Council may, however, delegate all or part of these latter prerogatives to the Directors in their respective spheres as defined in Article 15;

    (i) performs within the limits of the budget all legal acts, both in respect of disposal and of administration, necessary to achieve the objects of the E. B. U. but with power to delegate day-to-day business to the Directors in their respective spheres as defined in Article 15; and

(k) fixes the amount of the subscriptions of active members.[12]

Three Directors are chosen by the Council. One is in charge of the General Administrative Office in Geneva; the other oversees the Technical Center in Brussels. At the General Assembly and Council meetings, however, the Director of the Administrative Office serves as Secretary General, and between sessions is responsible for coordinating the administrative activities of the Geneva and Brussels offices.

The financial obligations of active and supplementary active members, whose revenue is derived mainly from license fees paid by users of receivers or from government subsidies, are determined in accordance with the number of licenses issued on January 1 preceding the beginning of the fiscal year in question.

An associate member's annual contribution to the EBU's expenses is set by the Administrative Council, in terms of specific services rendered and the financial resources of such member.

Probably the EBU's most well known activity is Eurovision, a network of stations in the northern, western and southern parts of Europe which provides for an international exchange of television programs. What began as a bilateral exchange over the English Channel soon grew into a regular network service when eight nations established television links on June 6, 1954. Today, many countries in Europe and other parts of the world participate in this service. With the recent technological developments, Eurovision has now achieved world-wide coverage and has recently been instrumental in linking all the continents in dramatic displays of satellite transmission.

It was no easy technical task to initiate Eurovision. The EBU has explained some of the early difficulties:

> The problems that had to be solved, before Eurovision could function satisfactorily were rather formidable. First of all, it was necessary that in each participating country there would exist an adequate network of radio or cable links. This, of course, is a national problem inherent in the normal development of the television service. Then it was necessary to join these national networks together, but on different sides of the frontiers there are often different television standards . . . France, the French-speaking part of Belgium, Luxembourg, and Monaco have pictures composed of 819 lines, the United Kingdom and part of Ireland have 405 lines, while the rest of Europe uses 625-line systems. Television pictures originating, say, in the United Kingdom cannot be reproduced directly on French receivers. The signals have first to be "converted," that is to say, changed from 405 to 819 lines. Standards conversion, of which this is one example, is one of the important problems in planning Eurovision operations.[13]

But the most difficult technical problems had to do with the transmission of sound. The EBU has pointed out:

It is necessary in general to transmit both the local sound (for example, the noise made by the crowd during a sports event) and the explanatory commentaries. The first-mentioned, the local or "international" sound, is of interest to all the participating services, and it is broadcast in all the countries where the pictures are broadcast. Each commentary, however, is broadcast in a more restricted area, according to the language in which it is given. For every one of the languages in which a commentary is required (there are at least fourteen languages spoken in Western Europe), there must be the the same number of commentators and the same number of sound-programme circuits, each with its control circuits, all connecting to the stations in the countries using the particular languages, which immensely complicates the planning and operational tasks. For each programme, then, there are needed a vision circuit linking all the countries concerned, as must also the international-sound circuit, plus the several commentary circuits, to which must be added the control circuits running alongside the programme circuits and the coordination circuits linking the E. B. U. Centre. . . .[14]

It was recognized at the beginning that a "nerve center" for effective transmission would be necessary. That task is performed by the International Technical Control Center in the *Palais de Justice* in Brussels. The Center's primary job is to supervise and switch the programs coming from various sources, and thus serve as a master control mechanism for incoming and outgoing programs.

The statistics indicate that sports makes up a large part of Eurovision's program schedules. The exciting, visual aspects of competitive games lend themselves admirably to television. About thirty percent of the programming consists of news. Music and ballet, "because of their spectacular and universal appeal," have attracted large audiences. Some plays are televised over the network. However, this presents some problems since plays must be transmitted in the language of the country where the programs are being received.[15]

Many events of international importance have been presented, and as satellite technology becomes more fully developed, the EBU is destined to play an increasingly important role in intercontinental television.

Olof Rydbeck, the former president of EBU, in 1964 on the EBU's tenth anniversary, wrote:

Ten years ago, it was an adventure to bridge the English Channel by television. Today, through the united efforts of different countries, we have even crossed the frontiers of Eurovision by means of transatlantic transmissions via satellites. Undoubtedly, this is but the beginning, and as Eurovision celebrates its tenth anniversary we stand on the threshold of the next great achievement—world-wide television. This is a past and a future for which many of those who have worked in Eurovision can take well-deserved credit.

A system of communications is neutral, that is to say the system itself does not dictate how it should be used. It is we, the broadcasters, who have to make that decision, and to do that we must know what it is that we wish to show the world via an intercontinental communications system. When the whole world can see and hear our programmes, our responsibilities will be even greater. . . .[16]

The International Television and Radio Organization (OIRT)

THE counterpart of the European Broadcasting Union is the International Television and Radio Organization (OIRT), which was established in 1946. As early as 1925, the International Broadcasting Union (UIR), the OIRT's predecessor, had served as a medium of radio program exchange in Europe. Following the Second World War, in 1946, because of the shifts in European political power, the UIR was dissolved and the International Broadcasting Organization (OIR) was established with headquarters in Brussels. In 1949, a group of broadcasting organizations in Western Europe withdrew from the OIR to form the European Broadcasting Union (EBU) and the OIR moved its headquarters to Prague. During the fifties, the OIR became concerned with the development of television as well as radio in Eastern Europe and in 1959 changed its name to International Television and Radio Organization (OIRT).[17]

Articles II and III of the *OIRT Statutes* state the aims and purposes of the Organization. It is noncommercial, nonprofit and, as specified in Article II, is concerned with:

(a) establishing links between the various organizations ensuring radio and television service, and having accepted the present Statutes;

(b) securing, as completely as possible, mutual exchange of information amongst members of the O.I.R.T. on the technical progress of sound and television broadcasting, on different schemes purporting to improve these techniques and, in general, on all measures taken in broadcasting activities;

(c) all-round protection of the interests of radio and television in every sphere;

(d) seeking a solution of broadcasting problems by means of international co-operation;

(e) studying and working out all measures generally directed toward the development of radio and television, especially the development of the broadcasting technique;

(f) studying and working out of measures important for rapid development of radio and television broadcasting techniques in insufficiently electrified regions, and regions with specific climatic conditions.[18]

Article III provides that, in carrying out its objectives, the OIRT:

(a) ensures that all its members strictly observe their mutual commitments;

(b) concentrates all information relating to radio and television;

(c) forms commissions and study groups entrusted with investigation of problems peculiar to radio and television;

(d) ensures that all its members rigorously respect the provisions of international agreements relating to radio and television;

(e) intervenes with all possible means to compel all radiocommunication services, non-members of the O.I.R.T., to honour international agreements on radio and television and those concerning the branch of radiocommunication relating to radio and television;

(f) co-operates with all governmental services entrusted with telecommunications and all those on whom radio and television services and organisations, in every country, depend, and also with the International Telecommunication Union, all official international bodies which take an interest in broadcasting problems, and all other bodies, companies, groups and persons whose co-operation may assist the O.I.R.T. to attain its aims;

(g) may eventually become one of the specialised agencies as provided for in Article 57 of the United Nations Charter, or join one of these agencies;

(h) issues monographs, reports, magazines and bulletins;

(i) may resort to any adequate means of action and study.[19]

Article V sets forth the qualifications for and classes of membership:

1. Only the following organisations may be members of the O.I.R.T.:
   (a) State organisations which ensure directly radio and television service;
   (b) organisations of a civilian character which under Government authorisation ensure a radio and television service;
   (c) national organisations of a civilian character grouping organisations which fulfil the conditions defined in items "a" and "b" of this paragraph.

2. Members of the O.I.R.T. are those organisations defined in the first paragraph of the present article which have taken part in the constitution of the Organisation, as well as those organisations which will be accepted as members in the future.

3. The members of the O.I.R.T. are subdivided as follows:
   —active members
   —associate members

4. Only active members enjoy full social rights.

5. There may be only one active member in any one country.
   (a) When in any country there is only one Government radio and television service, or only one private Government authorized radio and television service, this organisation can, by right, be the active member for the country.
   (b) Whenever in any country several Government radio and television services fulfil the necessary conditions for becoming members of the O.I.R.T., these organisations may try to reach an agreement among themselves as to which one shall be the active member of the O.I.R.T.

for that country. They may also form an organisation of a civilian character which might be the active member of the O.I.R.T. for the respective country. In any case, the qualified national administration is, in the last resort, responsible for nomination of the active member of this country.

(c) Whenever in any country there exist simultaneously a Government radio and television service or a group of Government radio and television services, and one or more private radio and television organisations, or Government authorized ones, or groups of private organisations, the status of active member belongs by right to the Government organisation or group of Government organisations of that country.

(d) Whenever in any country there exist only private radio and television organisations fulfilling the necessary conditions for membership of the O.I.R.T., these organisations may come to an agreement among themselves for the appointment of an active member to the O.I.R.T.; they may also constitute one or several groups of a civilian character; these groups may come to an agreement among themselves regarding the appointment of an active member to the O.I.R.T.; if an agreement is not possible between the organisations or groups, the active member is appointed from among these organisations by the competent authority of their country.

6. Associate members may be those radio and television organisations or groups of radio and television organisations which, although they fulfil all conditions for active membership, do not qualify as the organisation or the group of organisations to represent their country as active members. The associate members enjoy none of the social rights of the active members, particularly the right to become members of the Administrative Council or the right of a deciding vote at the sessions of the General Assembly; they may, however, attend the sessions of that Assembly with a consultative vote; moreover, they may resort to the services of the O.I.R.T.

7. Each member is represented at the sessions of the O.I.R.T. by a delegate of his choice; this delegate may be accompanied by experts.[20]

By 1959, broadcasting organizations from the following countries were active members of the OIRT: Albania, Bulgaria, Byelorussian Soviet Socialist Republic, Cuba, Czechoslovakia, Democratic People's Republic of Korea, Democratic Republic of Vietnam, Estonian Soviet Socialist Republic, Finland, German Democratic Republic, Hungary, Iraq, Latvian Soviet Socialist Republic, Lithuanian Soviet Socialist Republic, Mali, Moldavian Soviet Socialist Republic, Mongolia, People's Republic of China, Poland, Rumania, Ukranian Soviet Socialist Republic, the Union of Soviet Socialist Republics and the United Arab Republic. Recent press reports indicate that the People's Republic of China and Albania, having withdrawn because of differences in political ideology, are no longer active members.[21]

The highest OIRT authority is the General Assembly composed of all members. Between sessions of the Assembly, the OIRT's affairs are ad-

ministered by an Administrative Council. There is a General Secretariat at
the administrative headquarters in Prague and a Technical Center located
nearby.

There are three commissions (technical, programming and television)
and numerous study groups which meet from time to time, reports of which
appear in the magazine, *Radio and Television,* the OIRT's official publication. This periodical was initiated in 1960, replacing *Documentation and
Information Bulletin* which had been published for a number of years.
Radio and Television is supplemented by a monthly publication, *O.I.R.T.
Information,* containing news about the activities of member organizations.

As is the case with the EBU, one of the OIRT's most important activities
is international broadcasting and exchange of radio and television programs.
OIRT's members are affiliated with Intervision, the television network
which, in the countries of Eastern Europe, is the counterpart of Eurovision,
whose service area is largely in Western Europe. The network was established in February 1960, with Czechoslovakia, Hungary, the German
Democratic Republic and Poland as the original members. Subsequently,
they were joined by the USSR. Still later Rumania and Bulgaria came in.
In 1966–67, thirteen countries were affiliated with Intervision, including
Byelorussia, Estonia, Finland, Latvia, Lithuania and the Ukraine, plus the
others mentioned.[22]

Intervision is directed by the Intervision Council, consisting of representatives of members and the OIRT Secretariat General. The Chairman of
the Television Program Committee is the Chairman of the Council. Program and technical coordination centers organize all Intervision relays and
implement the Council's decisions.[23]

Intervision, Eurovision and other television networks, through the use of
satellites, are occasionally linked for the broadcasting of programs with
global appeal. Such events as the World Olympics, the Kennedy–Khrushchev meeting in Vienna, and other events of international significance have
been televised to millions of people in all parts of the world. Conflicting
political ideologies, however, have militated against the frequent participation of Intervision in world hook-ups, and its service area has been limited
largely to Eastern Europe and the Soviet Union.

The Asian Broadcasting Union (ABU)

On July 1, 1964, the Asian Broadcasting Union was founded as a result of
statutes adopted at the Fifth Asian Broadcasters Conference held in Seoul
in September 1963.[24] The resolution to establish the Union was adopted at
the Fourth Conference in 1962 held in Malaysia.[25] As reported by the
ABU in 1967, the following countries were members:[26]

Full Members

Radio Afghanistan
Australian Broadcasting
   Commission
Broadcasting Corporation of
   China
All India Radio
Nippon Hoso Kyokai
Korean Broadcasting System
Radiodiffusion Nationale Lao
Radio Malaysia & TV Malaysia
Department of Broadcasting,
   Radio Nepal
New Zealand Broadcasting
   Corporation
Radio Pakistan

Philippine Broadcasting
   Service
Radio Thailand
Turkish Radio & Television
   Association
UAR Broadcasting Corporation
Radio Viet-Nam
Samoan Broadcasting Service
Ceylon Broadcasting Corporation
Radio–Television Singapura
Tonga Broadcasting Commission
Radio Republik of Indonesia/
   Televisi Republik Indonesia
Radio Iran/National Iranian
   Television

Associate Members

Federation of Australian Commer-
   cial Broadcasters
Radio Brunei
Canadian Broadcasting Corpora-
   tion
Fiji Broadcasting Commission
Office de Radiodiffusion-
   Télévision Française
Radio Hong Kong
British Broadcasting Corpora-
   tion
Columbia Broadcasting System
   (USA)
National Broadcasting Company
   (USA)
International Broadcasting
   Service—Voice of
   America
Arbeitsgemeinschaft der Offentlich–

Rechtlichen Rundfunkanstalten der
   Bundesrepublik Deutschland
   (ARD, Germany)
Zweites Deutsches Fernsehen
Pacific Broadcasting Corporation
   (Guam)
Hong Kong Commercial Broadcasting
   Company
Munhwa Broadcasting Corporation
   (Republic of Korea)
Mindanao Broadcasting Network
   (The Philippines)
Independent Television Authority/
   Independent Television Companies
   Association (UK)
American Broadcasting Company
   (USA)
National Educational Television
   (USA)

The statutes of the organization provide for a General Assembly, which elects a president and two vice-presidents from among those broadcasting systems holding full membership. The seal of the Union and its headquarters are located in Tokyo, and its official language is English.

The General Assembly, hosted by the Australian Broadcasting Commission, had its first meeting November 23, 1964, in Sydney, Australia. Officers were elected and four committees were established—General, Programs, Engineering and Finance. Among other things, plans were made for staff training projects, joint production and exchanges of radio and television programs and publicity materials regarding the broadcast media in the various countries.[27]

The third meeting of the Assembly was held in Taipeh in October 1966. Sixty-two delegates from twenty-four broadcasting organizations as well as numerous observers from other national and international groups attended the meeting. Primary attention was given to space communications. Other subjects discussed were the establishment of a training institute in Asia and the further development of commercial broadcasting throughout the area. Most of the ABU members already have, or are planning, some type of commercial service.

A 1967 project of the Union involved a joint effort in the production of educational films for circulation and for world-wide distribution.[28]

Union of National Radio and Television Organizations
of Africa (URTNA)

IN September 1962, delegates from radio and television organizations of twenty-three African countries met in Lagos to ratify the statute providing for the establishment of the Union of National Radio and Television Organizations of Africa (URTNA). An Administrative Council was elected, composed of representatives of the broadcasting systems in Guinea, the Ivory Coast, Cameroun, Ghana, Nigeria, Senegal, Togo, Tunisia and the United Arab Republic. Three permanent commissions were created: Technical, Program Exchange, and Administrative and Legal.

The organization passed a resolution recommending that all national television services adhere to the six hundred and twenty-five line definition which had been adopted in Nigeria, Senegal and the Ivory Coast.[29]

Inter-American Broadcast Association

FOR many years countries of the Western Hemisphere have been working together in the Inter-American Broadcast Association. The Association has been concerned with program exchange, technical developments in radio and television including satellite transmission, and cooperative plans for achieving maximum utility from the radio spectrum. Since most stations in North and South America are commercial, member nations share information and exchange ideas on advertising methods and marketing techniques. Legal matters, such as copyrights, also receive attention. In October 1965, the Association met in Rio de Janeiro, Brazil. More than two hundred delegates attended, representing Argentina, Bolivia, Brazil, Canada, Chile, Cuba, Ecuador, Honduras, Mexico, Nicaragua, Panama, Peru, the United States, Uruguay and Venezuela. Observers from the United Nations, the Organization of American States and UNESCO were also present.

The *EBU Review* reported that the agendas of the committees and the plenary session included items regarding the Association's financial condition, the continental campaign for free enterprise, anti-democratic infiltration and activities in the radio and television news agencies, tax exemption for broadcasting stations, satellite communication, color television, and the President's proposal that radio and television stations devote more time to educational broadcasts.[30]

The plenary session approved the setting up of a committee to study methods of defending private enterprise, the establishment of an inter-American market for radio and TV talent, the granting of an award for the station doing the most to promote free enterprise, and the creation of an inter-American Exchange Center. It was further recommended that the various associations work toward the enactment of legislation limiting government controls of broadcasting, and that the associations, in their respective countries, use their influence to prevent over-commercialization.

The former president of the Association was Felix Cardona Moreno of Venezuela. In 1967, Herbert E. Evans, the President of the Peoples Broadcast Corporation, Columbus, Ohio, was elected to this position.

British Commonwealth Broadcasting Conference

As early as 1945, members of the British Commonwealth were holding conferences to discuss broadcasting matters of mutual concern. Recent meetings have involved working sessions on copyright problems, program exchanges, production techniques and staff training. A Secretariat in London facilitates continuity between conference meetings in the fields of engineering, programming and administration.

Community of French Language Radio Programs

IN 1955, representatives of *Radiodiffusion–Télévision Française* and the French sections of Belgian and Swiss Broadcasting established the Community of French Language Radio Programs. Shortly thereafter, the French service of the Canadian Broadcasting Corporation joined the group.

Sessions of this organization, together with meetings of subcommittees, are held each year to study the problems of radio, to compare experiences and share ideas and "to harmonize the guiding principles governing broadcasts in order to offer to their vast audiences (about 60 million listeners) programs satisfying every need and taste."[31]

The Community sponsors a competition, *Le Beau Voyage,* in which thousands of school children in all four countries have the opportunity to learn more about their native lands. The "Paul Gibson Grand Prize," ten thousand Swiss francs, is awarded annually by the Community for the best dramatic or literary work. A prize of four thousand Swiss francs is also presented for the best news story of the year. Joint production of programs has been encouraged and a wide range of programs is made available to the French-speaking republics of Africa, Asia and America.[32]

International Radio-Television University (URI)

THIS organization, founded in 1949, in 1965 had a membership of forty-five countries, including representatives from every continent. Its function is to provide to all member broadcasting organizations an international pool of quality recordings and films dealing with cultural and educational topics. Many outstanding scientists, philosophers, artists, men of letters, statesmen and others are heard via the URI by millions of listeners in many countries.

The permanent secretariat is located at the ORTF headquarters in Paris. The ORTF finances the URI's work, including the meetings of its General Assembly held every two years.[33] The ORTF maintains an archives service —a collection of texts and a film reference library—for the benefit of URI members. More than four thousand texts and a variety of films are available. A catalog has been compiled which lists the names of leaders in the sciences, literature, philosophy and the arts.

Through the URI's facilities, more than three thousand talks were broadcast in 1964 by organizations in all parts of the world. Up to the beginning of 1965, there were two hundred and sixty-seven orders for films which had been selected for showing by the organization's permanent committee.[34]

International Catholic Association for Radio
and Television (UNDA)

THE Catholics have an international broadcasting organization which began in early 1927 when Church leaders met for the first time in Cologne to exchange views and plan for "permanent collaboration." The original organization was called International Catholic Radio Bureau, but in 1945 its name was changed to UNDA, Latin for "wave."

In 1928, there were six member countries: Austria, Belgium, Czechoslovakia, France, Germany and the Netherlands. Today, the International Catholic Association for Radio and Television (as it is generally known) comprises seventy-two Catholic radio and television centers.

The organization has a controlling legislative body, the General Assembly. An executive bureau of twelve members and a permanent executive organ, the Secretariat General, are responsible for documentation and information.

The purposes as stated by the organization's statutes, adopted in 1962 and approved by the Holy See, are:

(a) to favour collaboration between national Catholic radio and television organizations in the various countries, duly recognized by their respective episcopates, so as to enable these organizations to become better aquainted, to help each other, and to pool the knowledge each of them has gained through study and experiment;

(b) to stimulate and coordinate the activities of these organizations in order to undertake, in agreement with them, tasks which go beyond the national sphere;

(c) to represent the interests of its members in the international sphere;

(d) to the extent and in the manner desirable in view of the objects of the Association, to collaborate with the institutions which, in the cultural, technical and economic fields, pursue aims similar to its own.[35]

To carry out its mission, UNDA proposes study and the exchange of information and mutual aid, having in view the work which Catholics have to accomplish throughout the world in sound broadcasting and television; regular contacts with members of the Association, and the organization of international congresses for the purpose of working out joint directives and recommendations on the basis of the experience and scope of the various national organizations; and publication of the Association's official bulletin, *UNDA*.[36]

The Association, whose Secretariat General is in Fribourg, Switzerland, held its ninth International Television Meeting from February 14 to 19, 1966, in the *Palais des Congres* in Monte Carlo. There were more than one hundred participants from Austria, Belgium, Canada, Denmark, France, West Germany, Indonesia, Ireland, Italy, Monaco, the Netherlands, Spain, Sweden, Switzerland, the United Kingdom (England and Scotland) and the United States. Mr. J. E. Reymond, the Principality's Minister of State, took the chair at the opening session and, in an impromptu speech, "stressed the power of television and expressed the wish that the UNDA prizes, the 'doves,' would go through the world, spreading a message of peace, joy and beauty."[37]

Much of the meeting was concerned with the viewing of films submitted as entries in the international competition sponsored by UNDA and the presentation of awards for the best productions.

Radio Vatican

AT the UNDA meeting in Monte Carlo, His Excellency Monsignor Rupp, the Bishop of that city, in his address, referred to the Second Vatican Council, and mentioned that one of the Council's documents was devoted to radio and television.[38] Since the early days, papal authority has enthusiastically supported the use of broadcasting to spread the Church's message. Radio Vatican, with studios and transmitting facilities in the Leonine Tower overlooking the Palace Gardens just back of St. Peter's, now broadcasts, via short-wave, in thirty languages, and reaches millions of people in all parts of the world.

The Voice of the Vatican, as it is called, began on February 12, 1931. As a part of its inaugural broadcast, Marconi, who had planned and constructed the station, introduced Pope Pius XI. The Pope, responding to the introduction, stated that "being the first to be able to avail ourselves from this place of the wonderful Marconian invention, we address ourselves at the start to all things and to all mankind. . . ." He continued by stressing the historical nature of the occasion and by referring to the immense communicating power of radio and its great utility for the promotion of world peace.[39]

The initial broadcast occurred on the second anniversary of the Lateran Treaty in which the Italian State had recognized the Vatican City's right to have direct links with the various states by means of telegraphic, telephonic, radiotelegraphic and radiotelephonic services.

The station began its transmissions from a building in the middle of the Vatican Gardens. It operated via short-wave on two frequencies with ten kilowatts of power. The facilities, however, were enlarged in 1937 with a twenty-five kilowatt short-wave transmitter and additional towers and directional antennae. And, following the Second World War, the Dutch Catholics, on the golden jubilee of Pius XII's priesthood (April 3, 1949), donated a Phillips one hundred kilowatt transmitter.

At the same time, the original ten kilowatt transmitter was replaced by a fifty kilowatt one. Other technical improvements were made, including new studios, transmission halls and a more spacious auditorium. Two mobile broadcasting units were secured, making possible on-the-spot coverage of important meetings and events of interest to the Church.

In October 1957, Pius XII inaugurated the new transmitting Center of Santa Maria di Galeria. A hexagonal building housing powerful medium- and short-wave transmitters was built in a large enclosed area which formerly belonged to the German College near Cesanna. An array of towers stands outside the building with a vast system of twenty-one directional antennae which "makes it possible to direct towards any part of the globe a sufficiently intense beam of electromagnetic waves and of a frequency suitable to the ionospheric conditions of the moment and at an angle of inclination suitable to the distance to be reached."[40]

Further expansion in 1959 included new offices and studios in a building previously used for the Petrine Museum. The offices for the news department and the Director of Programs, plus studios for recording and some regular broadcasting, are located in these facilities.

In 1960, Radio Vatican acquired an additional one hundred kilowatt transmitter, a gift from the Archbishop of Cologne. On November 6, 1961, this transmitter was inaugurated at Santa Maria di Galeria and began daily broadcasts to the people of Africa.

On Radio Vatican's thirtieth anniversary, three one hundred kilowatt transmitters were presented to the Pope by the Episcopate of Australia and New Zealand, the Knights of Columbus in the United States and Cardinal Spellman, the Archbishop of New York. These gifts were put into operation in 1962.

Originally, the station was conceived mainly as an instrument for the transmission of papal ideas. The service, however, was gradually expanded to provide programs such as "Catholic Information Service." During the Second World War, it was used to relay "news and reaffirm principles which would guide listeners and enable them to evaluate conflicting reports of the tragic events."[41]

After the war, programming was expanded, the object being "to render the Vatican Radio a living and concrete expression, as it were, of the universality of the Church." By 1962, programs were being broadcast in thirty languages, seventeen of which are spoken in countries behind the Iron Curtain. Those in charge of Radio Vatican have had a special concern for peoples in the emerging countries. "The delicate phase of the rapid evolution," Vatican officials have said, "towards full political and social status through which so many countries of Africa and Asia are going, an evolution which is being followed by the Holy Father with special attention and interest, has rendered all the more necessary a service from the Vatican Radio. It is a service that has been requested for a long time by the faithful and by the Hierarchies of these continents. The remarkable number of radio stations in Latin America which link themselves daily with the Vatican Radio to relay its programmes, shows the utility and the interest that these have for the Catholics of the entire continent."[42]

News about the Church and its activities throughout the world makes up a large part of the daily program schedules. Religious services such as the Holy Rosary and mass on feast days are included. Symphonic and chamber music of high quality, inspired by religious themes, are broadcast regularly.

"The Quarter Hour of Tranquility," now extended to thirty minutes, is dedicated to the sick.[43]

World Association for Christian Broadcasting (WACB)

THE World Council of Churches began to implement plans for the international development of religious broadcasting in 1961. A committee for this purpose was established, but was replaced in May 1962, by the World Association for Christian Broadcasting with headquarters in Geneva.

The Association's Secretary for Work in the Field of Broadcasting has stated that WACB "provides church and missionary agencies on the one hand, and broadcasting on the other, with a forum for the discussion of both Christian and secular matters of mutual concern."[44] He explained that the Association is concerned with training technical and broadcasting personnel, research, and the exchange of information and programs, all in accordance with WACB's purpose as stated in its Constitution: "to provide a working fellowship of churches, agencies, organizations and persons concerned with the use of radio and television to proclaim the Christian Gospel in its relevance to the whole of life, and with the role of these media in society."[45]

There are three classes of membership: corporate, personal and associate. The first group includes such organizations as the British Broadcasting Corporation, the Independent Television Authority, *Sveriges Radio* and the Nigerian Broadcasting Corporation, to mention only a few. In those cases where broadcasting groups, for legal reasons, may not join as corporate members they may be admitted as associates. All persons who are engaged in Christian broadcasting, whether or not employed by religious groups as such, are eligible for personal membership.

UNDA cooperates with the World Association for Christian Broadcasting in sharing ideas and experiences in the production of religious programs and for this purpose has sent representatives to WACB conferences. WACB officials have, in turn, reciprocated by attending UNDA meetings.[46]

Furthermore, WACB maintains relations with other international broadcasting organizations such as the European Broadcasting Union, and is now attempting to extend its activities and influence in every part of the world.

International Christian Broadcasters

THE World Conference on Missionary Radio (WCMR) has been active since 1954. It has sponsored many world conferences and promoted the cause of missionary radio throughout the world. Its publication, *Foreign Missionary*, has been distributed widely to religious leaders concerned with using broadcasting to spread the Christian gospel.

However, to attain more effective coverage, the Conference federated with the National Religious Broadcasters of the United States to form the International Christian Broadcasters (ICB). In 1966, the ICB was incorporated and the WCMR was dissolved.

According to Reverend Richard Wolff, the Executive Secretary, ICB activities have been significant.[47] The *ICB Bulletin* has been enlarged and sent free of charge to all who request it. A useful list of missionary radio stations is published and recently a study of radio-television evangelism was conducted in Japan. The ICB sponsors an annual day of prayer on the second Sunday of June. In 1966, more than one hundred radio stations cooperated in the observance of this day.

The ICB has been particularly concerned with research into the effects of religious broadcasting on listeners and viewers. Costa Rica and Arubu have been selected for pilot studies.

Members of the ICB are classified as corporate, associate and individual. Corporate members include the Evangelical Radio Alliance of Great Britain (ERA), representing a cross section of British broadcasters. Associate membership is granted to individual stations such as HCJB in Quito, Ecuador. Individual memberships are granted on a broad basis to persons concerned with the promotion of missionary radio.

The by-laws state the ICB's main purposes:

> . . . to aid and strengthen the Christian church world-wide through mass communications; to provide an international service organization for those who use radio and television to proclaim the Gospel of our Lord Jesus Christ, and to encourage the use of these media throughout the world for the furtherance of the Gospel. The training of leaders, global strategy, research, to encourage the formation of missionary radio and television stations and studios in strategic areas throughout the world, to promote the improvement of Christian programmes, these and other related activities are part and parcel of the total outreach of the ICB.[48]

NOTES

1. See International Telecommunication Convention, Article IV, No. 18–26; also, see Albert Namurois, *The Organization of Broadcasting: Problems of Structure and Organization of Broadcasting in the Framework of Radiocommunications*, Legal Monograph 2 (Geneva, Switzerland: European Broadcasting Union, December 1964), p. 12. This excellent monograph by a distinguished legal scholar contains a description of the organizational and administrative structure of typical national systems of broadcasting,

analyzes important principles governing telecommunications (including broadcasting) at the international level, gives an account of the important role played by the ITU and the laws and regulations which govern global broadcasting. It constitutes important source material for all students of the organizational and regulatory aspects of foreign and international broadcasting.

2. Namurois, p. 12.
3. *Ibid.*, p. 14.
4. *Ibid.*, pp. 16–17.
5. *Ibid.*
6. *Ibid.*, p. 26.
7. International Television Convention, No. 299; quoted by Namurois, p. 27.
8. International Telecommunication Union, *From Semaphore to Satellite*, Geneva, Switzerland, 1965, p. 207. This volume, published by the ITU on the occasion of its centenary, contains information on the development of communications from the earliest times and the evolution of international regulations and the important role the ITU has played in this history.
9. *Statutes of the European Broadcasting Union*, Article II, p. 1, published by the EBU in both English and French, Geneva, Switzerland, 1961.
10. *Ibid.*, pp. 1–2.
11. *Ibid.*, p. 2.
12. *Ibid.*, p. 6–7.
13. European Broadcasting Union, *This is the EBU*, Geneva, Switzerland, undated publication, p. 28.
14. *Ibid.*, p. 29.
15. *Ibid.*, pp. 33–55.
16. Olof Rydbeck, "Ten Years of Television," *EBU Review*, 85B, May 1964, p. 7.
17. See Kenneth H. Harwood, "The International Radio and Television Organization," *Journal of Broadcasting*, V, No. 1 (Winter 1960–61), 61–72. This excellent, well-documented study covers the origin, development, organization and operation of OIR and reports data gathered by Dr. Harwood on a trip to Eastern Europe in the summer of 1960.
18. International Radio and Television Organization, *OIRT Statutes*, sanctioned on June 26th, 1946, by the Constituent Assembly, Brussels; modified by the General Assembly at its extraordinary sessions in Brussels on October 31, 1946; in Prague, on December 21, 1951; in Goowaldov, on April 27, 1952; in Leipzig, on December 1, 1955; and in Helsinki, on July 20, 1959. The *Statutes*, as revised, appeared in a document dated June 1962, published by the OIR General Secretariat, Prague, Czechoslovakia.
19. *Ibid.*, pp. 2–3.
20. *Ibid.*, p. 5.
21. Although the Chinese have recently appeared at meetings of other communist world organizations, Communist China did not send delegates to the October 1966 meetings of the Administrative Council in Vilva USSR. See "Activities of the Communist World Organizations," published by the International Documentation Centre (Van Stolkweg 10, S'Gravenhage, Netherlands), 1966, p. 17.
22. International Radio and Television Organization, *General Information*, 02330, 1966–67, pp. 2–3.
23. *Ibid.*, p. 4.
24. *EBU Review*, 87B, September 1964, p. 28.
25. *Ibid.*, 77B, January 1963, p. 18.

26. Asian Broadcasting Union, *Proceedings of the Fourth General Assembly,* Singapore, October 23–30, 1967, pp. 9–12, 43.
27. *EBU Review,* 87B, September 1964, p. 28.
28. *Ibid.,* 101B, January 1967.
29. *Ibid.,* 78B, March 1963, p. 35.
30. *Ibid.,* 96B, March 1966, p. 38.
31. *Ibid.,* 86B, July 1964, p. 30.
32. *Ibid.,* 92B, July 1965, p. 32 and 95B, January 1966, p. 30.
33. *Ibid.,* 92B, July 1965, p. 32.
34. *Ibid.*
35. *Ibid.,* 97B, May 1966, p. 74.
36. *Ibid.,* p. 73.
37. *Ibid.,* 96B, March 1966, pp. 38–39.
38. *Ibid.,* p. 39.
39. *Thirty Years of the Vatican Radio,* 1931–1961, undated publication by Radio Vatican, Vatican City, pp. 1–2.
40. *Ibid.,* p. 20.
41. *Ibid.,* p. 9.
42. *Ibid.,* p. 11.
43. *Ibid.,* p. 13.
44. *EBU Review,* 97B, May 1966, p. 70.
45. *Ibid.*
46. *Ibid.,* p. 75.
47. *Ibid.,* 101B, January 1967, pp. 20–21.
48. *Ibid.,* p. 21.

XXXII

American Broadcasting Overseas

International Broadcast Stations

SEVERAL INTERNATIONAL BROADCAST STATIONS are authorized to operate in the United States. These stations, as defined by the Rules of the Federal Communications Commission, are those whose transmissions are intended to be received directly by the general public in foreign countries. Seven discrete bands of frequencies between 5,950 and 26,100 kilocycles have been allocated by the FCC for this service.[1]

Section 73.788 of the FCC Rules provides that these stations "shall render only an international broadcast service which will reflect the culture of this country and promote international good will, understanding and cooperation. Any program solely intended for, and directed to an audience in the continental United States does not meet the requirements of this service."[2]

FCC Form 309 is used to apply for a construction permit to build one of these international broadcast stations.[3] This is followed by the submission of FCC Form 310 which requires proof that the construction has been satisfactorily completed and requests a license for operation.[4]

The Commission has stated that a license will be issued only after the applicant has satisfactorily shown that:

(1) there is a need for the service;

(2) necessary program resources are available;

(3) directive antennas and other technical facilities will be used to deliver maximum signals to the "target" area or areas for which the service is designed;[5]

(4) competent personnel will be used;

(5) the applicant is technically and financially qualified and possesses adequate facilities to carry forward the service proposed; and finally,

(6) the public interest will be served by the proposed international broadcast operation.[6]

Such stations are licensed for unlimited time operation. However, certain stations receive frequency authorizations four times a year with hours for operation and target areas specified.[7] International stations must operate with not less than fifty kilowatts of power and their signals must have a strength of at least one hundred and fifty microvolts per meter fifty percent of the time in the distant target area.[8]

Assignment of Frequencies. Section 73.702 of the Rules says that frequencies in the bands allocated to the international broadcast service will be assigned to authorized stations for use at certain hours and for transmission to stated target areas.[9] Licensees may request the use of specific frequencies for particular hours of operation by filing informal requests in triplicate with the Commission six months prior to the start of a new season.[10] These requests are honored to the extent that interference and propagation conditions permit.[11]

Not more than one frequency is authorized for use at any one time for any one program transmission except in instances where a program is intended for reception in more than one target area and the intended target areas cannot be served by a single frequency.[12]

In 1955, the World Wide Broadcasting Company, the former licensee of international broadcasting station WRUL,[13] petitioned the Commission to reconsider its prohibition against using more than one frequency for transmitting programs to the same area. The station contended that other nations, particularly Russia, employ multiple frequencies to transmit programs to the same area causing interference to certain frequencies used by U.S. international stations, making it necessary for the latter to use more than one to insure reception in a particular area.

The Commission denied the petition on the grounds that such multiple frequency transmission to the same area is inconsistent with Article XLIII of the Convention of the International Telecommunications Union which requires the Commission to limit the number of frequencies and spectrum space to the minimum necessary to render satisfactory service. The Commission said, however, it would "take appropriate action" to protect the station from harmful interference caused by foreign stations operating in violation of international agreements.[14]

The Commission has stated that "all specific frequency authorizations will be made only on the express understanding that they are subject to immediate cancellation or change without hearing whenever the Commission determines that interference or propagation conditions so require and that each assignment of 'frequency hours'[15] for a given season is unique unto itself and not subject to renewal, with the result that completely new assignments must be secured for the forthcoming season."[16]

Section 73.792 of the Rules describes the geographic areas to be served by an international broadcast station.[17] Licensees sending programs to several of these areas must specify one as *primary,* and state the reasons for the choice, with special reference to the nature and special suitability of the proposed programming.[18]

Commercial Programs Permitted. International broadcast stations are permitted to carry commercial or sponsored programs provided no more than the name of the sponsor and the name and general character of the commodity or service is advertised.

Section 73.788 of the Rules gives several other restrictions on advertising: (1) a commodity advertised must be one regularly sold or being promoted for sale on the open market in the foreign area to which the program is directed; (2) commercial continuity advertising an American utility or service to prospective visitors must be particularly directed to such persons in the foreign countries where they reside and to which the program is directed; and (3) where an international attraction such as a world fair or resort is being advertised, the oral continuity must be consistent with the purpose and intent of the provisions in this Section.[19]

Operational Requirements. The FCC Rules contain specific requirements regarding the equipment and operation of international broadcast stations. These technical requirements, relating to power, frequency control, antenna design, auxiliary and alternate main transmitters, changes in equipment and keeping and preserving logs, are in many ways substantially the same as those governing other broadcast stations. However, some differences are necessary because of the service's special character. For example, antennas must be so designed and operated that the field intensity of the signal toward the specific country served will be 3.16 times the average effective signal from the station.[20] Moreover, station identification, program announcements, and oral continuity must have international significance and be communicated in a language suitable to the foreign areas for which the service is primarily intended.[21]

Licenses for international broadcast stations are issued for one year only.[22] Unless otherwise directed by the Commission, each renewal application must be filed at least ninety days prior to the expiration date of the license.[23] FCC Form 311 is used in applying for the renewal.[24] A supplementary statement must also be submitted showing the number of hours the station has operated on each assigned frequency, listing contract and private operations separately,[25] and reporting reception, interference and conclusions regarding propagation characteristics of assigned frequencies.[26]

The Voice of America (VOA)

THERE are only three private international broadcasting stations operating in the United States under the regulations discussed above: WINB, Red Lion, Pennsylvania; WNYW, Scituate, Massachusetts; and KGEI, Belmont, California. The Voice of America, however, an instrument of the United States Information Agency (USIA), is the official U.S. Government radio, and, as such, operates a large number of high-power stations beaming programs to many parts of the world.

Section 305(a) of the Communications Act of 1934 states that radio stations belonging to and operated by any agency of the United States Government are not subject to the regulatory powers of the FCC as set forth in Sections 301 and 303 of the Act.[27] The only exception is that government stations (not including those on government ships beyond the continental limits of the United States) when transmitting a radio communication or signal relating to government business must conform to Commission regulations designed to prevent interference with other radio stations and the rights of others.[28]

Accordingly, the President, through delegated authority, assigns the frequencies to the USIA for the Voice of America transmissions. The VOA's program policies and pattern of operation are determined by the USIA. The Director of the Agency reports to the President through the National Security Council. Since one of the Voice's chief functions is to report and interpret to foreign peoples policies and actions of the U.S. Government and promote national security, its activities are closely coordinated with the White House, the State Department, the Office of Civil and Defense Mobilization, the military establishment and other government organizations concerned with the country's position and participation in world affairs.[29]

The Voice, with headquarters and central studios in Washington, began on February 4, 1942. On the first day of its operation, with the Nazis on the rampage in Europe, a VOA announcer broadcast in German via shortwave these words: "Daily, at this time, we shall speak to you about America and the war. The news may be good or bad—we shall tell you the truth." This, say the VOA officials, has continued to be the guiding principle of all programming.[30]

After the war, the program services were expanded. Statesmen, educators, artists, writers, businessmen and laborers were brought before the microphones to express their ideas about the American way of life and world affairs in general. News reporting was greatly increased. Other program features were added. Since the operation was financed by the Federal Government and programs had to be approved by officials in Washington, convenience and economy dictated that headquarters be moved there. In 1954, the offices and studios were moved into the Health, Education and Welfare Building. Subsequently, new transmitters were built and the old ones improved. Overseas program centers were built, and a world-wide network of correspondents was established.

The Voice has grown rapidly since 1954 and now has thirty-eight transmitters in the United States and fifty-four abroad, with a combined output of more than fifteen million watts. Programs are sent via microwave and telephone lines from Washington to the domestic broadcasting sites where they are relayed by short-wave to overseas relay stations which in turn boost them to the intended reception areas. The VOA operates transmitters in Greenville, North Carolina; Marathon, Florida; Dixon and Delano,

California; and Bethany, Ohio. The Greenville operation is said to be the world's largest broadcasting facility, having an output of almost five million watts, equal to the transmitting power of nearly one hundred of the largest commercial stations in the United States.

The overseas establishment of the Voice includes transmitting installations at Woofferton, England; Munich, Germany; Tangier, Morocco; Thessaloniki and Rhodes, Greece; Okinawa; the island of Luzon in the Philippines; Colombo, Ceylon; Monrovia, Liberia; and Hue, Vietnam. New transmitters are being built in northern Thailand, northern Greece and the Philippines.

In addition to the overseas booster stations, there are more than five thousand foreign-owned and operated stations in many parts of the world that carry programs produced and supplied by the Voice. In fact, about thirteen thousand hours of its programs are carried each week by these stations.[31]

The VOA now broadcasts more than eight hundred and fifty hours weekly in thirty-seven languages to an overseas audience estimated in the tens of millions.[32] The programs are varied, with about fifty percent devoted to up-to-the-minute news and commentaries on current developments throughout the world.

In addition to the straight news, the Voice prepares and broadcasts many commentaries, analyzing and interpreting important national and international events. In preparing these commentaries, it has access to a wide variety of informational services, including the White House, the State Department, other government agencies, the commercial news services and its own reporters.

The VOA's charter states the following guiding principles for news analysis and reporting:

1. VOA will establish itself as a consistently reliable and authoritative source of news. VOA news will be accurate, objective and comprehensive.

2. VOA will represent America, not any single segment of American society. It will therefore present a balanced and comprehensive projection of significant American thought and institutions.

3. As an official radio, VOA will present policies of the United States clearly and effectively. VOA will also present responsible discussion on these policies.[33]

Another important component of Voice programs is music. A brochure published by the VOA contains the following discussion of its musical broadcasts:

Music, considered as the greatest common denominator in attracting and holding a radio audience, occupies an important place in VOA programming. Music is one of the few genuine American products which can be offered to foreign listeners first hand. Music is not thought of solely in terms of entertainment but also as an important means of conveying a message, telling a story. The Voice has created programs that cut across historical, educational, cultural and religious lines. For example, by projecting a series of programs called *Music in Our Schools,* VOA also reflected the activities and interest of American youth in cultural fields. Another series, *Musical Folkways,* used music to relate the entire history of the founding and development of the United States and its democratic principles.

There are some 600 symphony orchestras in the United States. The world is generally familiar with the Big Three—the New York Philharmonic, and the Boston and Philadelphia symphony orchestras—but the Voice of America records concerts by many other orchestras representative of various sections of the country. It covers numerous music festivals: the Aspen Music Festival in Colorado, the Berkshire Festival in Massachusetts, the Newport Jazz Festival in Rhode Island, and the Folk Festival in North Carolina.

Popular music and jazz fill the widely-listened-to program, *Music USA.* Music selections are often accompanied by interviews with leading personalities in the jazz and popular fields on various aspects of style, development and history of American music.

• • •

In most musical programs of the Voice of America, music, with its universal message is an end in itself. But music is also used in many narrative programs to add diversity and interest. In both cases, whether used incidentally or as the principal ingredient of a program, music displays an aspect of living culture in the United States and the creative people who contribute to it.[34]

Various other types of programs are presented. Well-known statesmen, scientists, philosophers, authors, clergymen and others discuss a wide range of important topics and public issues in forums which reflect, in general, contemporary thinking in the United States. Also, some of the finest dramatic, artistic and literary talent is brought before the microphones to give the world a balanced view of American culture.[35]

The Soviet Union stopped jamming VOA programs in 1963. Although it is costly and not very effective, Communist China, Bulgaria and Cuba continue to jam the VOA's programs. Nevertheless, the response to Voice programs is reported to be good. For example, in replies to announcements during a single week, in 1964, the Voice received thirty-five thousand letters from listeners in Latin America, including fifteen hundred from Cuba. Over twenty-five thousand Brazilians responded, and broadcasts in English brought in over eighty-five thousand replies from almost every country in the world including Communist China.[36] Total audience mail now runs over two hundred thousand letters a year.

In 1965, the Voice spent $28,819,536 to finance its operations, and the expenditures for 1966–67 were over thirty-two million.[37] In addition, more than twenty-six million dollars was requested from Congress in 1966 to construct new and improve existing facilities.[38]

While the Voice is concerned with radio, the USIA provides many television programs for stations overseas. Regular series have been produced by the Agency for countries such as Japan, Nigeria, Thailand and Latin America. Some USIA programs have been carried by more than eighty stations throughout Latin America. Broadcasts such as "Let Us Continue" (how democratic life continues even if a President is assassinated),"Some of Our Voices" (new cultural developments) and "Adventures in English" are a few of the USIA television programs which have been widely seen in other countries.

Radio in the American Sector (RIAS)

RIAS, a radio station in West Berlin owned and operated by the United States Information Agency, began as a wired radio system in early 1946, sending out news and recorded music to several hundred telephone subscribers. Its audience grew rapidly and it soon took to the air with a larger variety of entertainment and educational broadcasts.

It now provides two separate programs. Its principal program (RIAS I) is broadcast twenty-four hours daily by one three hundred kilowatt and one one hundred kilowatt medium-wave transmitter, plus one twenty kilowatt short-wave facility at night. All these facilities are located in West Berlin. Two FM stations there also carry this program. RIAS also uses one VOA one hundred kilowatt transmitter in Munich. In Hof, in Bavaria, RIAS also maintains a forty kilowatt installation and one FM station.[39]

The second program (RIAS II), on the air during the evening and other select times, repeats some RIAS I broadcasts, including those that may have special political or cultural significance and musical programs that appeal to a more sophisticated audience.

With its two programs, RIAS broadcasts thirty-three hours each weekday, thirty-five hours on Saturday and forty hours on Sundays and holidays.[40]

The station, with a staff of almost five hundred, presents a wide variety of programming—straight news, educational broadcasts, music (chamber, choral and orchestral, ranging from classical to modern), drama, religious programs, light entertainment such as quiz shows and situation comedies and other special features. Ninety percent of all these programs are produced by the RIAS staff and facilities.

Officials of the station have stated:

> RIAS is today, more than ever, the bridge between the Free World and the people of the Soviet Zone of Germany. When Walter Ulbricht began the erection of the Wall the morning of August 13, 1961, the manifold contacts between East and West came abruptly to a halt. . . . Radio, and to a lesser extent, television, remain the only media of exchange between the Free World

and the unwilling inmates of the "German Democratic Republic." RIAS now carries an even heavier responsibility than before in informing the East Berliners and the East Germans of the true nature of events in their own country and in the world, and in providing continuing cultural contacts with the West.[41]

In this connection, RIAS provides regular political commentaries. The station has explained its pattern of broadcasting in this regard:

> While the basic philosophy of RIAS is that the facts speak for themselves, it is imperative that RIAS expresses its own opinion on the significance of particular events in the public eye at the moment. When RIAS takes a stand on such an issue, it is clearly labeled as commentary. Thus, its main political commentary is introduced with the words, "And now, our evening commentary," followed by the author's name. When comments on developments outside Germany are necessary, the commentary may be written in Berlin, or by the RIAS correspondent in the country indicated. This correspondent is generally a German journalist with an international reputation, also representing a major German newspaper. In this case, the commentary is by the individual concerned, and carries his name. All commentaries are succinct; rarely do they exceed 6 minutes.[42]

In addition to the two or three daily commentaries, RIAS supplements its hourly newscasts with analysis and interpretation designed to help put current events in perspective for East Germans. On RIAS I, the news commentaries and analyses are interspersed with popular music nine hours each day. On RIAS II, the news and commentaries are often presented in much greater depth for more discerning listeners.

RIAS has further stated that "roundtable discussions are frequently used to present divergent but basically free opinion on matters of political and cultural interest. The traditional European political cabaret is not used to make fun of the problems of the people in the Soviet Zone, but rather to point out in a light vein the understanding and sympathy of the free peoples for those problems. . . ."[43]

Radio Free Europe

THE early operations of RIAS and its broadcasts to East Germany were influential in the development of plans for Radio Free Europe (RFE), a private American network of five stations broadcasting to the communist East European countries. While he was the U.S. Commander in Germany in 1948–49, General Lucius D. Clay was greatly impressed with the RIAS broadcasts. Upon his return to the United States, he proposed a similar operation "to break the Communist monopoly of communications in the satellite states of central Eastern Europe."[44] This led to the organization of the National Committee for a Free Europe in 1949 by a group of distinguished American citizens. The Committee, now called Free Europe, Inc., is a private, nonprofit organization incorporated under the laws of New York and managed entirely by U.S. citizens and organizations. Almost one hundred organizations in the United States make financial contributions to the operation. Solicitations for funds are made over the national networks and contributions come in from many individuals over the country.

The RFE's main offices in New York City are maintained by a staff of about ninety-seven. Its operations include the publication of *East Europe,* a monthly journal of information and opinion regarding affairs in the communist world which is circulated in eighty countries. Another of the Committee's functions is to provide liaison with national and international organizations established by exiles from nine communist countries in Eastern Europe.

The most important function is Radio Free Europe, initiated July 4, 1950. Its studios in Munich and thirty-one transmitters (combined power of over 2,260,000 watts) in Portugal and West Germany make up one of the largest broadcast operations in the world. In 1966, the RFE averaged about nineteen hours of broadcasting a day to Poland, Czechoslavakia and Hungary, twelve hours to Rumania and about seven and one-half hours to Bulgaria.[45] Only the languages of these countries were used in its programs.

That same year, news reports occupied about seventeen percent of its broadcast schedules with politically significant programs running to forty-four percent. Music took about twenty-five percent of the total time. The remaining fourteen percent consisted of religious programs representing all faiths, educational and cultural features, dramatic shows (some satirical) and special programs for farmers and other labor groups.[46]

RFE programs have included reports on outstanding cultural events in the West, including interviews with well-known personalities. Direct coverage of a European music festival, transmission from backstage at an American jazz concert, and live broadcasts of important dramatic and operatic performances typify the many special programs which RFE has carried.

As a basis for preparing the news commentaries, radio stations in communist countries are extensively monitored and hundreds of communist publications are studied. Information derived from the reports of western observers and interviews with travelers and refugees from the Eastern European countries are also useful in the analysis and interpretation of news reports from foreign stations and news agencies.[47]

Exiles from the communist countries within the station's coverage area make up the personnel of the broadcast departments. They write and broadcast the programs under the direction of an American director who is assisted by a staff of specialists in East European affairs.

It has been estimated that eighty-four million people live in the five countries covered by the RFE and that more than half the families in these countries have sets capable of receiving its programs. RFE surveys have indicated that about thirty-eight percent of the persons in Bulgaria, forty-one percent in Czechoslovakia, forty-five percent in Rumania, fifty-two percent in Hungary and fifty-six percent in Poland listen to its programs at least twice a week. There are no laws *per se* against listening to the RFE, although the radio stations and the press in the reception countries frequently attack its operations. RFE has also reported that there is a large amount of jamming of the Czechoslovak and Bulgarian programs but states that, through imaginative engineering techniques and transmission of the same program on multi-channels, ninety percent of the RFE signals reach the target areas unimpaired.[48]

A West European Advisory Committee (WEAC) of prominent citizens counsels the RFE on matters of policy. In May 1967, this Committee held its eleventh session. Eminent political and intellectual leaders from eleven West European countries held discussions with Free Europe officials on "Building Bridges to East Europe," and the RFE's role in East–West communication.[49]

RFE's Philosophy of International Broadcasting

THE Free Europe Committee's philosophy of broadcasting, the mission of RFE and its criteria for programming have been presented in various materials published by the Committee. One of the RFE's important principles, that all peoples have a right to secure pertinent facts and opinions concerning world developments, is confirmed by Article XIX of the Universal Declaration of Human Rights. RFE believes that a free flow of information across national boundaries is essential to individual and national freedom everywhere. Since Eastern European countries do not accept this principle, RFE feels it has a moral responsibility to broadcast to these countries.

A second tenet of its philosophy is that people ultimately can reach intelligent decisions if they have access to the important facts. And it conceives as a major task the making of public opinion in East Europe more enlightened and a more effective force for democracy.

Moreover, the station views the communist governments as unpopular with the people and believes they will continue to be so as long as these regimes suppress individual liberties. And, while totalitarianism may compel obedience for a time, the yearning of the people for freedom will ultimately prevail and they will insist on a return of their rights.

RFE officials look upon the communist regimes of East Europe as quite different from other types of authoritarian governments to which the station does not broadcast. The Communists, it is said, are hostile to the "free world" and determined to remake it in the Marxist image. As a part of an international "camp," they are committed to aggressive action and force, if necessary, to attain their goals.

In carrying out its mission, RFE seeks to break the news monopoly exercised by the East European governments and to provide citizens in these countries with full information about important developments within as well as outside their national boundaries. It hopes to convince these peoples that the communist system must fail since it is antipathetic to human aspirations, and that their destiny is more logically and properly linked with the democracies of the West.

RFE Criteria for Selection of Broadcasting Materials

IN a July 15, 1964 statement regarding the sources for RFE newscasts, the RFE staff said:

> RFE newscasts must be accurate, objective, truthful and complete as possible. In general, unconfirmed, opinionated, or interpretive material will not be used in newscasts. Newcasts must carefully avoid slanting or taking material out of context. Primary responsibility for newcasts lies with the individual broadcasting departments, whose selection and presentation of newscast material is guided by the needs and interests of their audiences and the general objectives of RFE.[50]

Another important aspect of the RFE operation is the separation of the news reports and editorials. While the station does broadcast editorials, they are always labeled as such and may not be included as integral parts of newscasts.

RFE officials wish to create an image of credibility. Accordingly, they insist that news be carefully checked for accuracy, that the commentaries be as objective as possible, and that the program schedules be well balanced, even to the extent of presenting views which are contrary to those held by the station. For example, one program, "Press Review," which covers a wide spectrum of national and international opinion on important current topics, is especially designed for this purpose.

Radio Liberty

THE American Committee for Liberation, like the Free Europe Committee, is a private organization of prominent U.S. citizens. It was incorporated

January 18, 1951, under the laws of New York. Its expressed purpose is to promote democracy in the Soviet Union. Those who shape the Committee's policies state that their main purpose is to help bring about the "liberation" of peoples in the Soviet Union and the "establishment of a genuine representative government responsible to the will of the people."[51]

It is financed by private interests in the United States and receives no revenue from foreign countries. The President and his high-level staff direct the varied activities of the organization from the New York offices.

One of its principal functions is research which is conducted through its Institute for the Study of the USSR. The Institute maintains a library of more than fifty-five thousand volumes, including a large number of books and periodicals dating to Imperial Russia. And through microfilm processes it has developed a complete file of the Russian publications, *Pravda* and *Izvestia,* dating to 1917.

The Committee has a large research staff of Soviet scholars, many of whom left the USSR for political reasons. With the aid of these scholars and other specialists, it publishes authoritative materials on the Soviet Union in English, Russian, French, German, Spanish, Turkish, Arabic, Ukrainian and other languages.

Other activities have included sponsoring international symposia with world-renowned experts discussing important current developments in Russia, and schools for the study of the Russian language attracting students from the United States, Canada, Europe, Africa, Asia and Australia. The Institute has also provided facilities for research by scholars who have fellowships with universities and other educational organizations.

The Committee's most important activity is the operation of Radio Liberty with studios in Munich. This station broadcasts twenty-four hours a day, over seventeen transmitters in West Germany, Spain and Formosa with a combined output of 1,840,000 watts. Whereas RFE directs its programs to five countries in Eastern Europe, Radio Liberty beams its programs largely to the Soviet Union and the Soviet armies in East Germany, Poland and Hungary. These programs are broadcast in seventeen languages spoken in the USSR.

Radio Liberty's programming center is a reconstructed former airport building at Oberwiesenfeld on the outskirts of Munich. The staff consists mostly of former Soviet citizens—more than two hundred officials, writers, scientists, teachers and political leaders—representing more than a dozen nationalities in their homeland.

Two programs are presented over the station. The First Program begins at seven o'clock in the evening, Moscow time, and runs for two hours. This two hour segment is repeated around the clock. The Second Program begins at nine o'clock in the evening, runs for one hour, and is repeated throughout the evening and most of the next day.

A review of one week's broadcasts in 1965 (said to be typical of the station's operation) on the First Program showed the following schedules for Sunday and Monday of that week.[52]

Sunday: 7:00 P.M.—News; 7:15—Newsmagazine; 7:30—Suggested by a Listener: Russia Yesterday, Today and Tomorrow—Present-day Soviet Society in a Historical Perspective; 7:50—Paths to Peace—An Analysis of Practical Approaches to Peace and Ways to Insure It; 8:00—News; 8:15—Panorama; 8:30–9:00—Discussion: The Youth Show—Life, Travel, Recreation, Student Affairs, Education, and Opportunities in the Free World.

Monday: 7:00—News; 7:15—News Features; 7:30—Doctor's Talk; 7:40—Listeners Present Their Views: Answers to Letters; 8:50—A Service for the Consumer: Technology in Everyday Life; 9:00—News; 9:15—News Features; 9:30—Book-of-the-Week Program—The Bookshelf—Books Banned in the USSR or Unknown Fiction and Nonfiction; 9:40—A Cultural Critic Looks at Soviet Literature and Art; 9:50–10:00—Africa–Asia–Latin America: The Developing World—Reports from Radio Liberty Correspondents.

Other First Program features which appeared later in the week included an analysis of "Problems of Stalinism"; reports on "The United Nations at Work"; a variety show with interviews, music, verse and commentary, and a panel discussion involving a clergyman, historian, journalist and economist, discussing religion and ethics, problems of ideology, life in the USSR and Soviet and world economy.

News and commentary constitute a large part of Radio Liberty's programming. The network devotes much attention to reports of events and affairs within the Soviet Union and the communist bloc. Radio Liberty's officials have stated that RL "discloses what the Soviet rulers would conceal. It reports accurately what the Soviet media distort. No less important, it lifts to a level of significance many events, within or outside the USSR, which the Kremlin buries in a few lines."[53]

The schedules on the Second Program for the same week were designed for special audiences. The programs for Sunday were: 7:00 P.M.—This is Jazz—interviews with top musicians—new trends in serious jazz—original Soviet music banned in the USSR, arranged and played by leading U.S. artists; 7:30—News; 7:45—Topical Feature—discussion of where Communism is being built; 7:55–8:00—Topical Commentary.

On Monday the Second Program included: 7:00—Analysis of Soviet Communist Party Affairs; 7:30—News; 7:45–8:00—Topical Features. Some of the offerings later in the week were discussions of cultural trends, science, art, literature, and economic theory and practice. A thirty minute period was devoted to drama, in which plays and literature which had been banned in the Soviet orbit were presented and analyzed.

In connection with its program preparation, Radio Liberty monitors more than sixty Soviet radio stations and screens more than two hundred

Soviet publications. It also has its own research unit as does RFE, the wire services of UPI and Reuters, and numerous publications in the West.[54]

In his Annual Report to the Board of Trustees of the Radio Liberty Committee, dated November 30, 1964, the President said:

> Radio Liberty's chief purpose is to give the Soviet citizen that information and that view of the world that he would get if the press, radio, and TV of his country were not controlled by a dictatorship. Although the Soviet citizen is primarily interested in what is going on inside his own country, he is still very much concerned about what is happening to the rest of the world, especially when those happenings have particular relevance to himself. The VOA and the BBC, of course, attempt to satisfy his curiosity in this respect, but they are limited to the extent that they are the official voices of governments. In addition to its heavy emphasis on the internal Soviet scene, Radio Liberty devotes a great deal of energy to filling out the Soviet citizen's knowledge of the free world.[55]

The Communications Satellite Corporation (COMSAT)

THE growth of satellite communication in recent years has been spectacular. Experimentation in the United States, Russia and other countries has greatly improved the technology in a relatively short time. Outer space was first penetrated by man-made vehicles less than twelve years ago, and as John Johnson, the Vice-President of the Communications Satellite Corporation, has said: "The simultaneous development of rocket propulsion and advances in electronic technology opened up a totally new resource for economic exploitation. For the first time man was able to place mechanisms of considerable size far above the earth's atmosphere, to control their position and movement with amazing precision, and to utilize them to serve his scientific and economic interests."[56]

Early in 1961 the FCC and Congress became seriously concerned with these new developments. It was apparent that some systematic regulatory plan would have to be devised to provide for the orderly growth of satellite communications at both the domestic and international level. The FCC appointed an ad hoc committee to study the problems. Both the House and the Senate conducted protracted hearings, exploring frequency allocation needs and considering various regulatory proposals. Some witnesses urged that the Government should own and operate the satellites. Others contended that a monopoly should be granted to communication carriers such as the American Telephone and Telegraph Company, subject to limited control by the Government. Still others urged the adoption of a compromise plan—the establishment of a private corporation with a limited amount of stock owned by communication carriers and the rest by the general public.[57]

The last plan won the support of Congress, and on August 31, 1962, the President signed the Communication Satellite Act authorizing the establishment of a corporation with the authority to develop a communications satellite system in the United States.[58]

In establishing this law, Congress stressed the international aspects of satellite communication, stating that "it is the policy of the United States to establish, in conjunction and in cooperation with other countries, as expeditiously as practicable a commercial communications satellite system, as part of an improved global communications network, which will be responsive to public needs and national objectives, which will serve the communication needs of the United States and other countries, and which will contribute to world peace and understanding."[59]

"The new and expanded telecommunication services," said the Congress, "are to be made available as promptly as possible and are to be extended to provide global coverage at the earliest practicable date. In effectuating this program, care and attention will be directed toward providing such services to economically less developed countries and areas as well as those more highly developed, toward efficient and economical use of the electromagnetic frequency spectrum, and toward the reflection of the benefits of this new technology in both quality of services and charges for such services."[60]

In order to achieve the objectives and carry out the purposes of the Act, Congress provided that the President should:

(1) aid in planning and development and foster the execution of a national program for the establishment and operation, as expeditiously as possible, of a commercial communications satellite system;

(2) provide for continuous review of all phases of the development and operation of such a system, including the activities of a communications satellite corporation authorized under title III of this Act;

(3) coordinate the activities of governmental agencies with responsibilities in the field of telecommunication, so as to insure that there is full and effective compliance at all times with the policies set forth in this Act;

(4) exercise such supervision over relationships of the corporation with foreign governments or entities or with international bodies as may be appropriate to assure that such relationships shall be consistent with the national interest and foreign policy of the United States;

(5) insure that timely arrangements are made under which there can be foreign participation in the establishment and use of a communications satellite system;

(6) take all necessary steps to insure the availability and appropriate utilization of the communications satellite system for general governmental purposes except where a separate communications satellite system is required to meet unique governmental needs, or is otherwise required in the national interest; and

(7) so exercise his authority as to help attain coordinated and efficient use of

the electromagnetic spectrum and the technical compatibility of the system with existing communications facilities both in the United States and abroad.[61]

The Act also provides that the National Aeronautics and Space Administration (NASA) should cooperate in research and development; consult with the Corporation with respect to the technical aspects of the communications satellite system; and, upon request, provide satellite launching and associated services.[62]

This legislation gives the FCC overall regulatory authority over the Corporation to insure effective competition in the procurement of equipment and services; to see that all authorized communications carriers have nondiscriminatory use of and access to the facilities of the satellite system and under reasonable regulations and charges; to institute, through appropriate proceedings,[63] new service to a particular point upon advice from the Secretary of State and NASA that will be technically feasible and will serve the national interest; to prescribe accounting regulations, approve technical characteristics of the operational system and terminal stations; and to "grant appropriate authorization for the construction and operation of each satellite terminal station, either to the Corporation or to one or more authorized carriers or jointly to the Corporation and carriers, basing the grants upon the public interest without reference to either the Corporation or carriers."[64]

Furthermore, the law empowers the FCC to authorize the Corporation to issue new shares of stock and negotiate loans, if the FCC determines such to be in the public interest. Finally, the Act specifies that no substantial additions to the facilities of the system or satellite terminal stations may be made without the FCC's approval in terms of the public interest. Moreover, subject to procedural requirements in Section 214 of the Communications Act of 1934, as amended, the FCC may, on its own initiative, require that such additions be made if it finds the public interest will be served.[65]

The law provides that the President should appoint the incorporators, by and with the consent of the Senate, to serve as the initial Board of Directors until the first annual meeting of the stockholders and that these incorporators should arrange for an initial stock offering and take the necessary action to establish the Corporation, as approved by the President.[66]

Section 303 (a) states that there shall be a Board of Directors made up of fifteen U.S. citizens, three appointed by the President, subject to Senate approval, six elected annually by the common carriers and six by other stockholders. The terms of the three presidential appointees run for three years except, to provide for a staggered arrangement, the terms of two of the original appointees were limited to one and two years.[67] If a vacancy occurs, the replacement gets only the unexpired part of the term of the Director he succeeds.

Congress defined the purposes and powers of the Corporation:

(1) to plan, initiate, construct, own, manage and operate itself or in conjunction with foreign governments or business entities a commercial communications satellite system;

(2) furnish, for hire, channels of communication to United States communications common carriers and to other authorized entities, foreign and domestic; and

(3) own and operate satellite terminal stations when licensed by the Commission under Section 201 (c)(7).

(4) conduct or contract for research and development related to its mission;

(5) acquire the physical facilities, equipment and devices necessary to its operations, including communications satellites and associated equipment and facilities, whether by construction, purchase or gift;

(6) purchase satellite launching and related services from the United States Government;

(7) contract with authorized users, including the United States Government, for the services of the communications satellite system; and

(8) develop plans for the technical specifications of all elements of the communications satellite system.[68]

To carry out these purposes, the Corporation is given the usual powers conferred upon stock corporations doing business in the District of Columbia by the D.C. Business Corporation Act.[69]

Section 404 of the COMSAT law requires that the President make an annual report to Congress describing the activities and accomplishments of the communications satellite system. It also calls for annual reports to Congress from the Corporation and the Federal Communications Commission. Pursuant to this mandate, on March 17, President Lyndon Johnson submitted his report for 1967. He referred to the creation of the International Telecommunications Satellite Consortium (INTELSAT), and the recent progress in satellite communications that has been made at the domestic and international level through the cooperative efforts of various agencies of the Federal Government and more than fifty-five countries that are now members of INTELSAT. His complete report appears in Appendix VII.

The American Forces Network—Europe*

From Wasserkuppe, a tiny remote village, to Munich, a sophisticated metropolitan city, and from a lonely patrol along the Czech border to a

*The American Forces Network in Europe is one of the best known radio services in the world. Although programmed by and for Americans, its activities and scope are nearly unknown to most people living in the United States. Major Ovid L. Bayless, who worked as a consultant with AFN during the summer of 1966, and at present is Associate Professor of Speech and English at the United States Air Force Academy, is the author of this article, which appeared in the Spring 1968 issue of the *Journal of Broadcasting*. It is reprinted with the permission of the author and the *Journal*.

full-scale field operation in southern Bavaria—regardless of where the G.I. serves, he can twist his radio dial and listen to the American Forces Network (AFN). As a significant part of the Overseas Military Information Program, AFN provides entertainment, news, and special events to literally hundreds of thousands of American military personnel and their families; it has done so for the more than 20 years that the American military has been present in Europe.

The network went on the air for the first time on July 4, 1943, broadcasting from London to five 50-watt transmitters located throughout the British Isles, using space and equipment loaned by the British Broadcasting Corporation. When the Allied invasion force crossed the channel on June 6, 1944, AFN followed immediately as "mobile broadcasting units attached to U.S. First, Seventh, and Ninth Armies."[70] After Germany surrendered, AFN's headquarters was located in the *Schloss,* a 14th Century Von Bruening Castle in Hoechst, a village just outside Frankfurt. The headquarters remained there until June 1966, when it moved into an ultramodern $2 million facility located adjacent to *Hessicher Rundfunk,* the German radio station in downtown Frankfurt. This present AFN,[71] its personnel, organization, facilities, and programming bring the American serviceman in Europe closer to home, and, incidentally, provides Europeans with an additional American "voice."

Personnel and Organization. The AFN Headquarters assigns personnel, on a permanent basis, to seven different studio-transmitter locations in West Germany. Frankfurt is the network's key station and headquarters; other stations are located in Berlin, Munich, Stuttgart, Kaiserslautern, Nuremberg, and Bremerhaven. Most local productions originate from Frankfurt, where nearly half the network's approximately 232 engineers, announcers, newsmen, and so forth, are located. Both Army and Air Force personnel man the network, with the Army providing roughly 85% of the people. Since AFN is not an orthodox military unit, and since it has a unique function, it has a large portion of civilian employees. Over half of AFN's authorized manpower spaces are civilian, either American or local nationals, who mainly work in either programming or engineering.

The organizational structure of the network compares with most military units in that it has an officer-in-charge and staff heads for personnel, administration, logistics, engineering, and programming. The officer-in-charge, an Army lieutenant colonel, is responsible to the Public Affairs Division, Headquarters U.S. Army Europe, though he maintains close liaison with Headquarters U.S. Air Forces Europe.[72] Military officers are in charge of personnel, administration, and logistics, while civilians head engineering and programming. The station manager is the ranking man at each outlying station, and he is responsible to the network officer-in-charge.

Facilities. The network has thirty AM transmitters compared with only six FM. Twenty-nine AM and five FM transmitters blanket central and southern Germany. Berlin, situated in the heart of East Germany, operates both an AM and an FM transmitter. Berlin required an FM transmitter because a portion of the city's American Sector was unable to get adequate AM reception, according to Lt. Col. Victor Bloecker, former officer-in-charge.

The most powerful transmitter in the network is located at Frankfurt; it has 150,000 watts of power, which is three times the maximum authorized in the U.S., and operates on a frequency of 872 kc; Munich (1106 kc) has a 100,000-watt transmitter. Four other studio-transmitter locations, Berlin (935 kc), Kaiserslautern (611 kc), Nuremberg (611 kc), and Stuttgart (1142 kc) have 10,000-watt transmitters, and Bremerhaven (1142 kc) has 5,000 watts. Besides the Berlin station, AFN has FM transmitters at Augsburg, Frankfurt, Stuttgart, Pirmasens, and Illesheim. The network installed these FM facilities primarily because of the increased number of FM receivers owned by Americans in these areas of troop concentration.

Twenty-three well-situated AM repeater-transmitters insure primary coverage for the U.S. serviceman in the less populated areas of Germany. In addition to these, the network also operates three FM repeater-transmitters in the Netherlands. Engineering personnel of the studio-transmitter station nearest the repeater facility are responsible for routine maintenance on the repeater-transmitters. Engineers dispatched from the headquarters in Frankfurt handle more serious trouble on a call basis.

The network is presently negotiating for transmitter locations for Belgium in order to provide broadcast support to the NATO and SHAPE headquarters which were moved from Paris in the Spring of 1967. AFN ceased broadcasting in France in the fall of 1967 when its Bel Manior transmitter, near Paris, went off the air at the end of September. AFN's outlets in France were the last U.S. elements to be withdrawn from that country.

Programming and Audience. The AFN programming format is much like traditional network radio in the U.S. "before television." The normal broadcast day runs nineteen hours, from 6:00 a.m. until 1:05 a.m. Record and variety shows, both local and transcribed from Armed Forces Radio and Television Services (AFRTS) in Los Angeles, are presented throughout the day aimed primarily at the serviceman's wife and off-duty personnel. Most of the shows originate in the Frankfurt studios, since most of the program material is located there and since the network reserves only three hours each day for programming by the local outlet.

The Frankfurt music library contains 1,500,000 music selections and 250,000 complete shows, enough material to program regularly for six years without repeating; AFN boasts that this is the largest radio library in the world. A typical morning schedule includes a "request" show to start the day, followed by the Ira Cook show, Don McNeill's "Breakfast Club," and Arthur Godfrey. The afternoon format includes more request music, "Musical Heritage," and the "Jim Ameche Show." The programming shifts to country music at 4:05 p.m., with a 55-minute request show from Frankfurt. The evening schedule includes a 55-minute block of uninterrupted instrumental music of the David Rose variety, followed by a 55-minute block of drama, such as *The Whistler,* and *Suspense.* The typical total broadcast week, classified by program type, is presented in Table I.

TABLE I

Program Classification

Program Type	AFN Program Schedule	AFRTS Recommended Program Schedule
News	14.5%	11.3%
Information	5.1	10.0
Education	2.3	3.6
Variety	11.2	7.3
Sports*	3.1	2.6
Drama	5.4	1.4
Religion	3.0	2.6
Music	55.4	61.2

*During football and baseball season this increases to nearly 8%.

The most important aspect of AFN programming is its news, which is presented every hour (five minutes) except when three major newscasts (thirty minutes) are aired at 7:00 a.m., 6 p.m., and 10:00 p.m. Through the facilities of AFRTS in New York and Los Angeles, AFN has more news input sources than any other single mass communication medium. In addition to wire service from Associated Press and United Press International, the network obtains news feeds via shortwave from all four major radio networks in the United States. Furthermore, AFN has two correspondents[73] of its own, located in the German cities of Bonn and Frankfurt. Greater dimension is provided AFN's current events coverage by its own special events production crew which interviews noted personalities when they visit Europe; *On the Scene* and *Eucom* (European Command) *Report* are two of the shows that give AFN a personality of its own in terms of local coverage.

The central programming axiom is that AFN will air no show that has propaganda overtones. The news programs are "straight" news presentations that are free of editorializing. Any news in depth show normally is taken from one of the major radio networks and involves a respectable journalist. For example, programs like *David Brinkley Reports* are quite often aired during one of AFN's major newscasts.

Since most G.I.'s are sport fans, AFN has a heavy sports format which runs throughout the year. To avoid preempting regular shows, the network broadcasts professional baseball only on the weekend, Saturday and Sunday evenings. The games are taped earlier and aired regularly during the season at 9:05 p.m. Network policy is to broadcast one National League game and one American League game every weekend if possible, and also to broadcast games involving teams that are in contention for the pennant. AFRTS relays these regular season games to AFN via shortwave, but for the World Series AFRTS uses a transatlantic cable to insure that AFN gets satisfactory reception. Atmospheric conditions often limit or prohibit broadcasting special events from the United States and costs and higher Signal Corps priorities prevent using the cable on a regular basis.

The network broadcasts college and professional football and basketball each Saturday and Sunday during the season. AFRTS does an excellent job of feeding AFN with highly attractive contests. For example, during the fall of 1965 AFN aired such college games as Notre Dame and Army, Texas vs. Arkansas, Air Force vs. Army, Michigan State vs. Notre Dame, and Army vs. Navy. The 1965 Professional Football contests included Green Bay vs. Baltimore, Cleveland vs. Dallas, and Chicago vs. Baltimore. The season was climaxed with the championship games of both the National and the American Football Leagues, plus the Cotton Bowl and the Rose Bowl. For the 1966 basketball season, AFN carried games such as Boston College vs. Providence, Army vs. Navy, Kentucky vs. Tennessee, Detroit Pistons vs. Cincinnati Royals, and Boston Celtics vs. Philadelphia 76ers. To supplement the AFRTS sport schedule, the AFN sports staff covers important sports events on the Continent, such as service football championships and the races at *Le Mans*.

The heavy emphasis on American news and sports no doubt means that AFN's most loyal listeners are the quarter of a million or so American servicemen and their families; the entire AFN programming schedule aims specifically for these people. Nevertheless, AFN has a large non-American audience; with signals beaming "from Scandinavia to Italy and from Ireland to Austria"[74] an indigenous audience of millions could hardly be denied. Just how many millions is not known though estimates range from 20 million[75] to 50 million.[76]

For Europeans desiring to learn English, listening to AFN is an excellent instructional device. The younger Europeans have grown up with AFN and it has provided adjunct instruction for those engaged in studying English in the classroom. Other Europeans, those not particularly interested in learning English, listen to AFN mostly for entertainment. Jack Gould of *The New York Times* suggests that many Europeans dial AFN because it has an established credibility, nurtured over the past 20 plus years.[77]

The AFN listening audience is increased considerably by Americans residing in Europe who are not associated with the Department of Defense.

These include State Department personnel, employees of large U.S. companies, and tourists. During the summer months especially, the large influx of Americans who flock to the Continent greatly swells the audience. Hundreds of cards and letters from tourists indicate that AFN not only keeps them posted on the latest news and special events from home, but that it entertains them as well.

Conclusion. As long as United States foreign policy requires that a substantial number of American troops be stationed in Europe, no doubt the American Forces Network will continue to provide entertainment, news, and special events. During the serviceman's normal three year tour in Europe, he will keep track of the happenings at home through several different avenues; AFN radio is one of the most important. Throughout his stay he knows he can hear many familiar programs, the stateside news immediately, and the nation's most exciting sports events; AFN links the serviceman and "back home." And Europeans will continue to listen to AFN for entertainment, to learn English and to get objective news. For these reasons AFN will not only remain an integral part of the Overseas Military Information Program, but it will also be what Gould calls "an admirable ambassador on the airwaves."

NOTES

1. Section 73.701(a), FCC Rules and Regulations; 1 RR 53:851. Section 73.2(c); 1 RR 53:853.
2. Section 73.788(a); 1 RR 53:869.
3. Section 73.711(a); 1 RR 53:857.
4. An FCC requirement, but apparently not covered by a regulation.
5. A target area, as defined by Section 73.701(m); 1 RR 53:851, is a geographic area in which the reception of particular programs is specifically intended and in which adequate broadcast coverage is contemplated.
6. Section 73.731; 1 RR 53:859. Also, see *Report of Commission,* 13 RR 1501.
7. Section 73.761; 1 RR 53:865.
8. Sections 73.702(d) and 73.751; 1 RR 53:853, 861.
9. 1 RR 53:852.
10. *Ibid.* Four seasons are defined by the FCC Rules: March and April; May, June, July and August; September and October; and November, December, January and February.
11. *Ibid.*
12. Section 73.702(f); 1 RR 53:854.
13. Station WRUL is now owned by the Church of Jesus Christ of Latter Day Saints and is known as Radio New York World Wide, Inc., WNYW.
14. FCC Docket No. 10962; 13 RR 1510a.
15. The term "frequency hour," as defined by Section 73.701(b); 1 RR 53:851, means one frequency used for one hour.

16. Section 73.702(a); 1 RR 53:852.
17. 1 RR 53:873.
18. Section 73.702(b); 1 RR 53:852.
19. Section 73.788; 1 RR 53:869.
20. Section 73.753; 1 RR 53:861.
21. Section 73.787(b); 1 RR 53:868.
22. Section 73.718; 1 RR 53:859.
23. Section 1.539; 1 RR 51:267.
24. Section 1,539(d)(2); 1 RR 51:268.
25. "Contract operations," as defined by Section 73.701(n), means any non-government operation of an international broadcast station pursuant to a contract with an agency of the U.S. Government and subject to government control as to program content, target areas to be covered, and time of broadcast. These operations no longer exist. "Private operation," as defined by paragraph (o) of the same Section, is any operation not of a contract character. See 1 RR 53:852.
26. Section 73.791; 1 RR 53:872.
27. 48 Stat. 1083.
28. *Ibid.*
29. See *United States Government Organization Manual*, 1959–60, pp. 506–510; also, see *Annual Reports* of the USIA, 1954–59.
30. *VOA*, published by the Broadcasting Service of the United States Information Agency, 1964, p. 7.
31. *Facts About the USIA* (Washington: U.S. Government Printing Office, 1964), p. 6.
32. Radio Moscow leads in foreign broadcasting with 1,620 hours per week. Radio Peking presents twelve hundred hours and the United Arab Republic nine hundred and twenty hours weekly. The British Broadcasting Corporation, with eight hundred hours a week, follows the VOA.
33. *VOA*, p. 15.
34. *Ibid.*, p. 17.
35. *Ibid.*, p. 7.
36. *Facts About the USIA*, p. 7.
37. Committee on Appropriations, Congress, House, Committee on Appropriations Hearings, Departments of State, Justice, Commerce, the Judiciary and related agencies, Appropriation for 1967, 88th Congress, 2nd Session, 1966, p. 625; also, 90th Congress, 1st Session, 1967, p. 651.
38. *Ibid.*, 1967, p. 764.
39. *RIAS, the Free Voice of the Free World*, published by RIAS, West Berlin.
40. Information received from RIAS in West Berlin as of October 23, 1967.
41. *RIAS, the Free Voice of the Free World*, p. 3.
42. *Ibid.*, pp. 10–11; also, more recent reports from RIAS.
43. *Ibid.*
44. *Radio Free Europe, What It Is—What It Does*, Radio Free Europe (One English Garden, Munich, Germany).
45. *Thumbnail Sketches of Radio Free European Programs*, Radio Free Europe (Two Park Avenue, New York), p. 1; this has been updated by October 1967 correspondence.
46. *The Job Ahead*, Free Europe, Inc., 1965, published in 1966, p. 4; updated by October 1967 correspondence.
47. *Ibid.*, p. 9.
48. *Radio Free Europe.*

49. *The Job Ahead,* p. 10.

50. Statement supplied the author by RFE when he visited the Munich operation in 1965.

51. American Committee for Liberation, *The Most Important Job in the World,* undated, p. 1.

52. The author received this weekly program schedule from officials at Radio Liberty in Munich when he was visiting there and studying RL's operation in May 1965.

53. American Committee for Liberation, p. 5.

54. *Radio Liberty Russian-Language Program Schedule,* with informational notes, published by Radio Liberty (30 East 42nd Street, New York, N.Y., 10017).

55. Radio Liberty Committee, *The President's Annual Report to the Board of Trustees,* November 30, 1964, p. 14.

56. John A. Johnson, "Satellite Communications: The Challenge and the Opportunity for International Cooperation," *Federal Communications Bar Journal,* FCC Bar Association, XIX, No. 3 (1964–65), 89. This is an excerpt from a speech Mr. Johnson gave before the Washington World Conference on World Peace Through Law; Working Session II—Section II, September 14, 1965.

57. See Hearings before the Committee on Commerce, United States Senate, 87th Congress, 2nd Session, on S. 2814, *A Bill to Provide for the Establishment, Ownership, Operation, and Regulation of a Commercial Satellite System, and for Other Purposes;* April 10, 11, 12, 13, 16, 24 and 26, 1962 (Washington: U.S. Government Printing Office, 1962). Also, see Hearings before the Committee on Interstate and Foreign Commerce, House of Representatives, 87th Congress, 1st Session, July 25, 26, 27, and 28, 1961 (Washington: U.S. Government Printing Office, 1962).

58. *U.S. Statutes at Large,* 87th Congress, 2nd Session, Vol. 76, 1962, pp. 419–427.

59. *Ibid.,* p. 419.

60. *Ibid.*

61. *Ibid.,* p. 421.

62. *Ibid.*

63. *Ibid.,* p. 422.

64. *Ibid.*

65. *Ibid.,* p. 423.

66. *Ibid.*

67. *Ibid.*

68. *Ibid.,* p. 425.

69. *Ibid.*

70. "The Servicemen's Voice in Europe," *Army in Europe,* USAREUR Pamphlet 360–43, July, 1966, p. 6.

71. In the course of this investigation the author received the assistance of a great many people; he is especially grateful to Lt. Col. Victor Bloecker, Lt. Col. William Ellington, former officers-in-charge, and Lt. Col. Henry L. Cody, present officer-in-charge. He specifically acknowledges the help of Mr. Robert J. Harlan, present Program Director. Several members of the AFN staff were also most helpful: Capt. Eugene Bickley, Chief Warrant Officer Robert Moore, Mr. George Kaso, Mr. Harry Bean, Mr. Frank Mortensen, Mr. Jimmy Lunsford, Mr. Shelby Whitfield, and Sergeant Major Samuel Summer.

72. The U.S. Air Forces in Europe operate the only Armed Forces television

on the continent, three stations in Germany: Ramstein, Spangdahlem, and Berlin. The Ramstein program is relayed to Wiesbaden and Rhein Main Air Base which in turn rebroadcasts it over low-powered translators.

73. Until recently the network also had correspondents in London, Paris, and Berlin.
74. Jack Gould, "A Voice that Europe Trusts," *The New York Times,* April 17, 1966.
75. *Ibid.*
76. *This is AFN Europe.* (Undated), p.1. This publication is available at the Headquarters, American Forces Network, Bertram Strasse, Frankfurt, Germany.
77. Gould, *op. cit.*

XXXIII

The "Pirate" Stations

PIRATE" STATIONS, unlicensed transmissions from ships in international waters, have been mentioned in the discussions of broadcasting in Luxembourg and the Netherlands. Chapter VIII on Dutch broadcasting describes a television station which operated on an artificial island in the North Sea. Ship stations featuring light programs, primarily popular music interspersed with commercials, have attracted increasingly large audiences in various parts of Europe. Since 1958, ten of these stations have been on the air, although most of them have recently been forced to discontinue operations because of government action in the Netherlands, the Scandinavian countries and Great Britain.

The first "pirate" station, set up in 1958, broadcast from a vessel anchored outside territorial waters in the Sund between Sweden and Denmark. The programs were beamed particularly to the Copenhagen area. Another, Radio Mecur, installed on a ship in waters of the Great Belt, began transmitting in February 1961, with programs designed for Danish listeners. A year later, Radio Nord took to the air, transmitting from a ship anchored in the archipelago not far from Stockholm. This was followed a few months later by *Danmarks Commercielle Radio* in the Sund area.

Other "pirate" operations include Radio Veronica and *Till Eulenspiegal,* the first sending programs not far from the Dutch Coast and the second (until it floundered in a storm) invading the Belgian territory with heavy doses of the top forty tunes interspersed with commercials.[1]

Other "clandestine" stations have operated near British territory. Two of them, Radio Caroline North, located on a ship anchored off the Isle of Man, and Radio Caroline South transmitting off the Essex Coast, claimed a combined audience of nine million and a monthly advertising revenue of two hundred and twenty-five thousand dollars.[2] Radio London, moving in international waters, emphasized popular music. These three operations have shut down because of a law passed by Parliament in 1967 which made it illegal for British citizens to be employed by such a station.

It was recently announced in the American press that a group of entrepreneurs were planning to purchase a ninety foot vessel on which they would operate a transmitter off Long Beach, California, outside the three mile limit in Pacific waters. Lawrence Tipton, one of the principals in the enterprise, was quoted as saying the ship would fly a foreign flag which, he said, would make it immune to U.S. Maritime regulations. He was further quoted as saying that the station would broadcast eighteen hours a day, and, unlike the European "pirates," whose programs consist mainly of "teen-oriented rock and roll music," would include a variety of programs—dramatic shows, satire, humor, news, music and discussions of important public issues on which the management would take definite positions. The proposed station is to be financed by advertising and Mr. Lipton stated that the owners would seek financial support from foundations and would solicit funds from the general public.[3]

Should this station go on the air, like existing "pirates," it will operate without a government license of any kind and on a frequency of its own choice without regard to the established allocation procedures and regulations of the International Telecommunications Union.

These operations on ships at sea have raised serious legal questions and many licensed broadcasters in Europe, the European Broadcasting Union, the ITU and other organizations are giving serious study to means by which these "clandestine" transmissions can be terminated. Albert Namurois, the legal adviser to the *Radiodiffusion–Télévision Belge,* and Karel Remes, the legal adviser to the Dutch Broadcasting Organization (VARA), both authorities in this field, have discussed at some length the problems of preventing broadcasts from "pirate" stations and artificial islands. Also, E. C. Robbins, the legal adviser to the British Broadcasting Corporation, has recently reported actions by the British Government to suppress transmissions which invade the United Kingdom. The first two of these discussions appeared in the March 1965 issue of the *EBU Review* and the third in the March 1967 issue. Because of the current, world-wide interest in this subject, all three are reproduced in full with permission of the magazine and the authors.[4]

THE PREVENTION OF THE ACTIVITIES OF "PIRATE"

BROADCASTING STATIONS

A EUROPEAN AGREEMENT (STRASBOURG, DECEMBER 1964)*

The Facts

EACH country shall have the sovereign right to regulate its telecommunication.[5] This is laid down in the preamble of the International Telecommunication Convention.

* By Albert Namurois, the legal adviser to the *Radiodiffusion–Television Belge.* Reprinted by permission of the *EBU Review* and the author.

A number of countries, particularly on the continent of Europe, have placed sound and television broadcasting in the hands of governmental or quasi-governmental services, the activities of which are financed, whether directly or indirectly, by means of the license fees paid by the owners of receiving sets. It is not my intention to attempt to discover the reasons which have led the governments of the countries concerned to make broadcasting an organic public service; it will suffice to point out that, in many countries, the authorities have been reluctant to authorize the establishment of private broadcasting stations financed by income derived from advertising. When it is considered that this system is in force for the most part in countries made up of zones with an extremely dense population, it is not surprising that financial groups, sometimes international and frequently of considerable size, have considered the possibility of setting up private broadcasting stations in such zones, but outside the sovereign jurisdiction of any given country—consequently, outside territorial waters.

Experiments of this nature had already occupied the attention of European countries between the two world wars and, at the present time, the system seems to be gaining momentum; the fact is that it is profitable and is often looked on in a favourable light by public opinion, which fails to realize the disadvantages and even dangers it may involve.

The procedure is to equip a vessel on board which a broadcasting station is installed; the vessel must next be given a nationality and the government of some distant country is then approached to secure the entry of the vessel in its register of shipping. Under the flag of this country, the vessel is anchored close to the zone for which the broadcasts are intended, but outside territorial waters. It leaves the spot where it is anchored only in cases of *force majeure,* since in a port it runs the risk of being seized. Supplies are brought from the land, whether they are required for the operation and maintenance of the ship and the broadcasting station (mechanical or magnetic recordings of programmes and advertising material, spare parts and fuel) or provisions for the staff living on board. The supplying country is usually that for which the broadcasts are intended, and the company frequently has its head offices there.

At the present time, approximately ten "pirate"[6] broadcasting stations have been established, of which several have already ceased their activities.

• • • •

Other projects are at present under consideration, but it is not possible to go into them in detail here. It would not appear that there is any intention to install "pirate" stations on board aircraft, although this is technically feasible, since they would have to land frequently and it would thus be easy to take action against them. Furthermore, such activities would involve operational costs that would undoubtedly be out of proportion to the income likely to be derived from them.

The Dangers Resulting from the Activities of "Pirate" Stations

IN a legal opinion given on 22nd August 1960, on the activities of "pirate" stations in relation to the precepts of international law,[7] Mr. Jens Evensen, barrister, principal officer of the Norwegian Ministry of Foreign Affairs, quoted a passage from a memorandum drawn up by the United Nations Conference on Freedom of Information, held in Geneva in 1948, which states the problem most aptly. This memorandum, which deals with broadcasting and its relationship to freedom of information, draws special attention to the following:

> The universal propagation of radio waves which ignore national frontiers, the limited number of available frequencies and the danger of mutual interference between radio stations require legislative measures if the proper functioning of services is to be ensured. Nothing prevents the publication of an unlimited number of newspapers or the production of an unlimited number of motion pictures. . . . The limitation of the frequency spectrum, however, makes it impossible to establish an unlimited number of radio stations. Frequencies must be allocated to the different radiocommunication services (fixed, mobile, land and maritime mobile, aeronautical fixed and mobile, radio direction-finding, radionavigation, maritime and aeronautical radionavigation, standard frequency station, meteorological aids, amateurs, broadcasting including television) and to the stations in the different regions and countries. It is often necessary to limit the power of the stations, in order to reduce their service area, and to limit the transmission time in order to enable another station to use the same frequency. (Cf. United Nations Memorandum, Social and Economic Council, E/Conf. 6/30, 19th March 1948, pp. 3–4.)

After drawing attention to the disastrous overcrowding of the frequency spectrum, Mr. Evensen in his legal opinion goes on to point out that the availability of frequencies is strictly limited and must, therefore, be closely controlled. Radio waves are, by their very nature, international and strict international regulations must be maintained.

In order to avoid complete chaos in the air, the various countries and organizations have been working painstakingly and systematically for the past 50 years on the preparation of a law of the air and have been willing to find compromises and make sacrifices in the interests of mankind. Thus, world legislation on radio communications, based on conventions and agreements of international application and on the general priniciples of international law, made its appearance as early as the beginning of the 20th century.

The next important development was the preparation of regional plans for the allocation of frequencies to the broadcasting stations. Here, mention can be made of the Copenhagen Conference, held in 1948, which dealt with the question of the use of hectometric waves in sound broadcasting, and of the Stockholm Conference of 1961, which had on its agenda the use of metric and decimetric waves in sound broadcasting and television. Needless to say, no provision was made for "pirate" stations in the Plans appended to the Copenhagen Convention and the Stockholm Agreement.

The provisions of these Conventions and their Plans are, consequently, singularly restricted in scope through the very existence of these stations; this is all the more true if the country whose authorities have registered the vessel, and which is therefore responsible, in principle, for the operation of the broadcasting station, is not situated in the area concerned and thus played no part in preparing the Plans.

Countries are bound by the International Telecommunication Convention to oblige radiocommunication services coming under their jurisdiction to take all practicable steps to prevent harmful interference.[8] This brings us to a second kind of nuisance, and even danger, resulting from the activities of "pirate" radio stations. The fact is that the technical level of the broadcasts made by these stations usually fails to reach the standards laid down in the International Telecommunication Convention, either because of lack of suitably qualified staff or because the equipment used is of poor quality. These factors lead to harmful interference such as that caused by a "pirate" station transmitting in frequency bands allocated to a mobile aeronautical service.

It should be noted that if the "pirate" stations at present operating in Europe on metric waves do not cause much obvious harmful interference, this is because a number of the stations provided for in the Plans appended to the Stockholm Agreement have not yet been put into operation, but there can be little room for doubt that, as these stations are opened one by one, the situation will get out of hand if the "pirate" stations continue to operate. The dangers of such a chaotic state of affairs will become increasingly serious when it is considered that this harmful interference may affect radio-determination stations, aeronautical and radionavigation stations, or authorized transmitters broadcasting in the interest of the safety of ships at sea.

The Basis of the Campaign Against "Pirate" Stations

IN international legislation the states have a very broad basis for the preparation of national regulations aimed at putting an end to the activities of "pirate" broadcasting stations. In a note submitted to the Council of Europe,[9] the International Telecommunication Union sums up the present state of this legislation as follows:

The present international radio legislation was codified in Geneva (1959) by the ITU Plenipotentiary and Radio Conferences; the first of these Conferences reviewed the Buenos Aires International Telecommunication Convention (1952), and the second the Atlantic City Radio Regulations (1947). This legislation is embraced in the International Telecommunication Convention (Geneva, 1959) and in the Radio Regulations (Geneva, 1959) which are annexed thereto and are binding on all members and associate members of the ITU . . .

The present law of the sea is embodied in the Conventions drawn up by the United Nations Conference on the Law of the Sea (Geneva, 1958 and 1960), and especially in the Convention on the Territorial Seas and the Contiguous Zone (1958 and 1960) and in the Convention on the High Seas (1958). Eighty-six countries were represented at the Conference held in 1958 and eighty-eight at the Conference of 1960.

In addition, we might refer to the Convention on International Civil Aviation (Chicago, 1944), which contains regulations applying to aircraft from the point of view of nationality and registration.

By way of completing his list of the international legislation on which countries might base their campaign against the activities of "pirate" broadcasting stations, Mr. Evensen drew attention to two general principles of the laws of nations, namely the principle of abuse of rights and the principle of *bon voisinage,* which, he added, were closely connected with the question of the exercise of rights and the fulfilment of obligations in good faith, whether these rights and obligations have their origin in treaties and conventions or in the general precepts of the law of nations.[10]

Among the international laws on radiocommunication, mention should be made in particular of the provision contained in No. 422 of the Radio Regulations (Geneva, 1959), which prohibits the establishment and use of broadcasting stations (sound and television) on board ships, aircraft or any other floating or airborne objects outside national territories, and that contained in No. 962, which prohibits the operation of a broadcasting service by mobile stations at sea or over the sea.[11]

International legislation therefore affords a broad basis for the preparation of national regulations. However, we should not deceive ourselves in this matter since these provisions, as a whole, cannot take full effect unless all the states actually have the will to implement them in accordance with the principle of *bon voisinage.*[12] This fact was realized by the Administrative Radio Conference (Geneva, 1959) when it adopted Recommendation No. 16.[13] It was fully aware that it would be difficult to ensure that the provisions it had just drawn up, on the subject of broadcasting stations on board ships and aircraft outside national territories, were observed.

In May and October 1960, the EBU Administrative Council in its turn adopted two series of recommendations, in consideration of the fact that the operation of "pirate" stations was gravely prejudicial to the interests of broadcasting. The EBU made a point of recommending that its members should endeavour to draw up national legislation making it an offence to assist in the operation of such stations, whether by supplying goods or provisions, technical services, capital, advertising or programmes or by offering services.

Mention should also be made of the action taken in June 1962 by the International Frequency Registration Board (IFRB),[14] which sent a circular letter to the administrations of the member states of the ITU inviting them to see to it that the services which entered the vessels in the register of shipping should inform the vessels thus registered that it was prohibited to make broadcasts, in any place whatsoever, and that they should henceforth register no vessel without having informed the applicant of this prohibition.

At the same time, the IFRB drew attention to Article 5 of the Convention on the High Seas which stipulates:

> each state shall fix the conditions for the grant of its nationality to ships, for the registration of ships in its territory, and for the right to fly its flag. Ships have the nationality of the state whose flag they are entitled to fly. There must exist a genuine link between the state and the ship; the state must effectively exercise its jurisdiction and control in administrative, technical and social matters over ships flying its flag.

Making reference to this Article, and to Article 6 of the same Convention, which stipulates that

> ships shall sail under the flag of one state only and . . . shall be subject to its exclusive jurisdiction on the high seas . . . ,

the IFRB pointed out that, in its view, any state which granted its nationality to a ship was responsible to the other states for seeing that the obligations incurred under the International Radio Regulations, including those implied in the provisions contained in Nos. 422 and 962 of the Radio Regulations and those concerned with the solution of problems of harmful interference, were observed on board the ship in question.

Should it be concluded from the recommendations adopted in 1959 and 1960 by the two international organizations best qualified in broadcasting matters that national legislation is silent on the subject? Not so, since each state possesses its own set of radio regulations which, in pursuance of the International Telecommunication Convention, are everywhere subject to the proviso that authorization shall be obtained, accompanied by conditions which take this Convention into account as well as any special situations existing in each territory.

Moreover, it should be borne in mind that before licences are issued, enquiries are usually made and the future installations visited. In many ports and shipyards, attempts have been made to equip ships with broadcasting stations with a view to making transmissions outside territorial waters. It has often been possible to unmask such a state of affairs by paying a visit to the site, and authorization has generally been refused. Special attention should be drawn to a decree issued in Sweden in 1961 prohibiting foreign vessels passing through Swedish territorial waters from carrying, without Royal approval, a wireless installation intended for use in violation of international radiocommunication regulations.

Reference should also be made to a decree issued in France on 27th October 1961, which makes it an offence for vessels and aircraft situated in French ports, roadsteads and anchorages, or in French territorial waters, to transmit broadcasts.

At the beginning of 1962, and in pursuance of the existing legislation, the British Postmaster General decided to suspend radiotelegraph and radiotelephone services to ships from which broadcasts were being transmitted, except in cases where the safety of persons and navigation were concerned.

While it can be said that the handful of regulations briefly referred to above is already a step forward in the campaign against "pirate" stations, it must be admitted that they are inadequate and do not appear to meet the new commitments assumed by states which have ratified the Radio Regulations (Geneva, 1959). Some of them have accordingly already amended their radiocommunication regulations, with a view to fulfilling the new obligations resulting from the provisions contained in Nos. 422 and 962 of the Radio Regulations, introduced by the Radio Conference of 1959.

Mention should first of all be made of the Scandinavian states; special legislation came into force as early as 1st August 1962 in Sweden, Denmark, Finland and Norway. The main features were laid down by the Nordic Council; it was a question of combating illegal broadcasts made to Scandinavian countries, as an area or individually, and also broadcasts causing harmful interference in these countries. Scandinavia thus forms a single region, so that any reprehensible action affecting it must be suppressed in each of the separate countries, even in cases where there is no other factor such as nationality or territoriality to link the offence with the country concerned. The main act consisting in the establishment and operation of "pirate" stations, as well as the usual forms of direct and indirect assistance, are punishable under national legislation.

The Belgian Parliament next passed special legislation on "pirate" stations, on 18th December 1962. This legislation makes it an offence for Belgian nationals, whether in or outside the national territory, to carry out or to assist, whether directly or not, in the carrying out of any act connected with the operation or activities of "pirate" stations, even if they are installed on board ships or aircraft of foreign nationality. The same prohibition applies to non-nationals when the act is committed on the national territory and even outside it, but in the latter case the non-national concerned must have worked with a Belgian national in one of the punishable activities.

There can be no doubt that, when they come to ratify the Radio Regulations (Geneva, 1959), other states will realize the necessity of amending their radiocommunication legislation to fit the new provisions introduced by the Geneva Conference.

The European Agreement for the Prevention of the Activities of "Pirate" Stations

THE WORK OF THE LEGAL COMMITTEE ON BROADCASTING AND TELEVISION

SINCE the recommendations formulated in 1960 the EBU has continued to devote serious attention to the problem of "pirate" stations. At the EBU General Assembly held in Copenhagen in June 1961, the Netherlands delegate, Mr. Broeksz, expressed the view that an effective way of conducting the campaign against "pirate" stations would be to convene an international conference on the law of the sea. This suggestion was not followed up, since it was considered in some quarters that it was likely to lead to considerable difficulties. However, the administrative conference of Scandinavian broadcasting organizations, held in Oslo in April 1961, put forward the idea that the Council of Europe should deal with the problem. This idea was taken up by the EBU, which requested the Legal Committee on Broadcasting and Television of the Council of Europe to put the question of "pirate" broadcasting stations on its agenda.

Under the chairmanship of Professor G. H. C. Bodenhausen (Netherlands), assisted by two vice-chairmen, Dr. Filippo Pasquera (Italy) and Judge Torwald Hesser (Sweden), the Legal Committee began to study the question during its seventh meeting (June 1962) at the Maison de l'Europe in Strasbourg.

The seventh report of the Committee of Ministers, drawn up by Mr. Maurice Lenoble, the General Rapporteur of the Legal Committee, drew attention to the fact that this study was carried out on the basis of a preliminary draft convention for the prevention of radio broadcasts made from international waters, submitted by the Swedish experts. It was in fact agreed from the start that the Council of Europe should deal with the problem of "pirate" stations. The question of the competence of the Council of Europe in the matter was raised in some quarters, but the ITU representative at once admitted that his organization had met with serious difficulty in taking steps to ensure that international telecommunication regulations, which made no provision for repressive measures, were adhered to, and he therefore expressed the hope that action would be taken along other lines. The authority of the Council of Europe to fill this legal gap was thus recognized by the international organization most qualified in the matter. The view had also been expressed that it would be sufficient to lay down certain principles. The argument against this method was that it would prove inadequate, and reference was made in this connection to the recommendations formulated by the ITU and the EBU, which had had no effect. Thus it was unanimously agreed within the Legal Committee that it was essential for a convention to be drawn up under the auspices of the Council of Europe.

A European Agreement was drafted and forwarded to the Committee of Ministers which referred it back to the Legal Committee for further examination, after amendments and comments had been made by several governments. These proposals were reviewed by the Legal Committee at its eighth session held in June 1963, when Mr. Torwald Hesser was elected chairman in succession to Mr. G. H. C. Bodenhausen, who had in the meantime been appointed to the high post of director of BIRPI. Mr. Hesser was replaced in his office of vice-chairman by Mr. Léon Schaus, Councillor of State, Luxembourg. The second draft Agreement drawn up by the Committee during this eighth meeting was also laid before the Committee of Ministers. However, a new development had occurred in the meantime: there were grounds for belief that a television station was about to be installed on an artificial island off the Dutch coast.

Since no provision had been made for such a situation in the draft Agreement, the Legal Committee took advantage of the occasion and of a few final comments to draw up, at its ninth meeting in May 1964, the draft European Agreement for the Prevention of Broadcasts transmitted from Stations outside National Territories, which was ratified, not without difficulty, by the Ministers' deputies, in the course of their session in December 1964.

The Ministers' deputies actually held a number of meetings to deal with this question, during which they studied the comments, requests for interpretation of the text, and proposed amendments submitted by several governments (Netherlands, United Kingdom, Denmark, Switzerland). We shall henceforth use the term "Agreement" when referring to the treaty thus ratified.

ANALYSIS OF THE TEXT OF THE AGREEMENT

General Notes

The aim of the Agreement is to oblige the contracting states to take appropriate steps in accordance with their domestic law, to introduce standard regulations into their legislation; until the latter has been amended to bring it into line with the standard regulations the undertaking given by the state will be unfulfilled and the Agreement will remain without practical effect.

An attempt was made to define the means to be employed at national level to ensure that the provisions contained in Nos. 422 and 962 of the Geneva Radio Regulations[15] could be effectively implemented. It was in fact useful, and even indispensable, that governments should be informed of the repressive measures considered essential to call a halt to the activities of broadcasting stations operating from ships or aircraft outside national territories, while recognizing the power of the governments to increase the severity or scope of these measures or to extend their application to stations installed on objects affixed to or supported by the bed of the sea. This is the reason why, in the preamble to the Agreement, mention is made of Nos. 422 and 962 of the Radio Regulations, as being the main foundation on which the Council of Europe's action rests in this particular case.

Broadcasting Stations Coming Within the Scope of the Agreement

Article I[16] of the Agreement defines the stations concerned.

(a) First of all the stations in question must be broadcasting stations. The General Rapporteur noted in the seventh report submitted to the Committee of Ministers that the Legal Committee had not considered it essential to give a definition of the term "broadcasting station", in view of the fact that such a definition is contained in Nos. 28 and 29 of the Radio Regulations.

It must therefore be understood that the provisions of the Agreement only apply to stations transmitting sound radio or television broadcasts intended for *direct* reception *by the general public,* which excludes any other type of radiocommunication service, whether fixed or mobile, such as the church/hospital ship coming under the jurisdiction of the Netherlands, whose broadcasts are made for a specific purpose.

(b) Moreover, the stations in question must be broadcasting stations installed or in operation[17] *aboard ships, aircraft* or any other floating or airborne object.

The General Rapporteur took note of the fact that the Legal Committee intended to exclude from the scope of the Agreement broadcasting stations which might be installed *on board space ships;* the problems raised by broadcasting from outer space fall completely outside the scope of the Agreement.

However, during its ninth meeting, in May 1964, the Legal Committee was apprised of the novel situation referred to above. The new development was the imminent opening of a television station installed outside territorial waters *on an island* specially constructed for this purpose and supported by the sea-bed, a type of installation not covered by the draft Agreement. Mr. C. E. Lovell, the eminent United Kingdom delegate who had made an active and valuable contribution to the preparation of the Agreement, requested that it should obligatorily be made to apply to broadcasting stations installed on artificial islands. If such a proposal had been accepted, the legislation of certain countries would have had to be amended before they ratified the Agreement. Owing to the urgency of securing ratification by as large a number of states as possible, the Legal Committee considered it preferable to adopt a solution which did not put them under any obligation but left it open to them to apply the provisions of the Agreement to broadcasting stations installed or in operation on objects affixed to or supported by the bed of the sea. This point is dealt with in Article 4 (b) of the Agreement.[18]

(c) A further requirement if the activities connected with broadcasting stations are to come within the scope of the Agreement is that their broadcasts must be made *outside national territory,* i.e. outside the national territory proper, the territorial waters and the air space over this territory and these waters. It was considered that the national and international regulations in force were adequate to put an end to the activities of broadcasting stations located inside national territory.

(d) The Agreement covers the stations referred to above, viz. broadcasting stations transmitting from outside national territory, when such broadcasts are *intended for reception on the territory of a contracting state, or are capable of being received there, wholly or in part.*

It should be noted that the scope of the Agreement is limited to cases where the broadcasts are intended for reception or are capable of being received on the territory of one or several contracting parties only. This geographical restriction has a dual purpose, first, of encouraging the adhesion of the greatest possible number of states desiring to avail themselves of the advantages of the Agreement, and secondly, of ensuring that the Agreement is applied on a fair and reciprocal basis.

It may be as well to point out here that the member states of the ITU may become parties to the Agreement, in addition to the members of the Council of Europe, once the instrument has come into force (Article 10).

(e) The Agreement also covers the stations referred to above under (a) and (b) if they are a source of harmful interference to a radiocommunication service[19] provided this service is operated with the authorization of one of the contracting parties and in accordance with the Radio Regulations.

The Legal Committee first of all felt that it would be advisable to make the Agreement apply to all stations of any kind causing harmful interference, without distinction as to their location or the destination of their broadcasts, since interference in itself constitutes such a serious violation of international regulations that any form of territorial restriction would appear to be unjustified. A number of governmental delegates drew attention to their governments' reluctance to put an end to such activities, even in cases where the interference was caused to services which were perfectly lawful but operated under the jurisdiction of states not parties to the Agreement. The United Kingdom delegate furthermore pointed out that it would not induce member states of the ITU to adhere to the Agreement if the European countries agreed to be wholly responsible for the attempt to put an end to the harmful activities of "pirate" stations. Thus, action should be taken only in the case of interference with services operated with the authorization of one of the contracting parties. It is clear, however, that a state could make it an offence to participate in any way in the activities of a "pirate" station which was causing harmful interference to a radiocommunication service coming under the jurisdiction of non-contracting states, provided that this service was operating in conformity with the Radio Regulations; this possibility is all the more evident since, as will be seen later on, Article 4 of the Agreement clearly indicates that the prescribed measures constitute only a minimum beyond which countries may go when drawing up their national regulations.

(f) It should be understood that the reference made in Article 2 of the Agreement to "stations" applies not only to transmitters but also to the ship, aircraft or other object on which the station is installed. This is made clear in an interpretative declaration submitted by the United Kingdom Government to the Council of Europe and approved by the Ministers' deputies.

(g) To sum up, the Agreement applies to the following types of broadcasting station:
—those which broadcast from outside national territories
   and
—which are installed—
     either on board ships or aircraft, but not space ships (optional); or on
     objects affixed to or supported by the bed of the sea,
provided that their broadcasts
—are either intended for reception on the territory of one of the contracting
   states, or are capable of being received there, wholly or in part,
—or cause harmful interference to a radiocommunication service operated
   with the authorization of one of the contracting parties, in accordance with
   the Radio Regulations.

While such stations are generally described as "pirate" stations, the Legal Committee was unwilling to adopt the term "pirate station" which, as I have pointed out above, has an exact meaning in international law, which would not always cover the stations concerned.

The Acts to be Prevented

By the fact of becoming parties to the Agreement countries give an undertaking, in pursuance of Article 2,[20] to take the necessary steps to prevent as a punishable act, first, the establishment or operation of "pirate" stations and, secondly, certain acts of collaboration carried out for this purpose.

(a) It is clear that the states will have to take the necessary steps only in conformity with their domestic law. However, the Legal Committee made this point in order to show that it was not only a question of legislation properly speaking, but also of other administrative instruments such as decrees, ordinances, etc. The Committee thus wished to draw the attention of the contracting parties to the fact that they were entirely free to adapt the preventive measures to their own domestic legal system, both as regards procedural matters and the penalties inflicted.

(b) The term "offence" had been used in the first instance, but it was later considered preferable to use the word "infringement" instead, in order to make clear the intention to leave it to the discretion of the contracting parties to describe the acts according to their own penal system. It is common knowledge that the legislative authorities in each country usually divide offences into three categories, according to the harm they cause to society; thus, the most serious are known as crimes, and at a lower level we have what are described as "offences" and "minor offences" or "infringements" which are in the main infringements of police regulations.

(c) The acts which are to be prevented by the contracting parties are, first of all, the establishment and operation of "pirate" stations. Then come acts of collaboration in establishing and operating such stations, carried out knowingly, since it is obviously essential that the author of the act, to be liable to punishment, should be aware that he is assisting in committing a specific infringement.

(d) With regard to acts of collaboration, the Legal Committee had first of all adopted a text containing a list of examples of such acts. It was indeed pointed out by some that this procedure was permissible even in criminal law, provided that the list merely served to illustrate a general prohibition, as in this case. The contrary view was expressed that, at least in states where a ratified treaty had the force of a domestic law, such a non-restrictive list would be incompatible with the principles of criminal law. Another difficulty then arose regarding Scandinavian legislation relating to "pirate" stations.

Mr. Jens Evensen, in this case the valued adviser of the Legal Committee in his capacity of expert on international law, pointed out that a restrictive list containing the examples quoted might possibly result in the Scandinavian countries being regarded as having violated the Agreement; in his view, international treaties could not normally be interpreted as constituting minimum standards beyond which the contracting parties were free to go. The Legal Committee solved this tricky problem by making the list of cases of collaboration a restrictive one, after having given further information, however, in certain cases, particularly as regards advertising. Moreover, the Committee supplemented the text of the Agreement by adding the provision contained in Article 4 (a) to the effect that the Agreement does not prevent the contracting parties from taking measures to repress acts of collaboration other than those of which a restrictive list is given in Article 2.

(e) It may be considered that the list contained in the said article is comprehensive enough to cover the majority of cases of participation in the establishment and operation of "pirate" stations, and that such participation constitutes a major aid of a nature to make the person responsible a co-author, or a subsidiary aid making him simply an accomplice.

Among the acts listed in Article 2 (see footnote) attention should be drawn to contributions to the production or financing of advertising programmes. It was the Legal Committee's intention to strike a blow at the main sources of the "pirate" stations' revenue, namely any kind of programme containing advertising material or sponsored programmes. It should also be noted that, in referring to the supply of means of transport, the Committee had in mind mainly the shipping agencies, while in referring to the production of advertising material it was thinking of advertising agencies. Not only advertising activities carried on by means of broadcasts should be prevented, but also advertising on behalf of the stations, by means of newspapers, printed matter, or other methods.

(f) It was agreed that the acts of collaboration listed in the Agreement could be of a technical, artistic, economic or financial nature. These acts will be punishable whether carried out on behalf of the broadcasting station itself or on behalf of the ship, aircraft or floating island on which the station is installed. They involve, in particular, the provision and transport of equipment and supplies, the maintenance and repairing of equipment and the transport of staff. They also cover supplies in bulk, such as diesel oil, but not sales of goods which would not be material to the continued operation of the stations in the sense referred to above (cf. 15(e)).

(g) In connection with artistic services, performances given by *performing artists* as part of the production of programmes intended for transmission do not necessarily have to be suppressed, except in cases where they are given on "pirate" stations. In accordance with the terms of Article 5, "the Contracting Parties may elect not to apply the provisions of this Agreement in respect of the services of performers which have been provided elsewhere than on the stations referred to in Article 1".

The wish was expressed in some quarters that this option should be abolished, while in others it was desired to extend its application to persons other than performers. It was then pointed out that the sole purpose of the provision was to enable the Agreement to be ratified by states which had just drawn up domestic legislation providing for a similar exception. The Legal Committee therefore refused to broaden the scope of Article 5 so as to include *the authors* or their assigns, since it considered that it was the responsibility of the competent courts to judge whether the authorization given to "pirate" stations to use copyright works did or did not constitute an act of collaboration coming within the scope of the Agreement.

(h) It may be as well to draw attention to the further indications requested by one government to enable countries to make certain acts punishable offences; these related to the command of a ship or an aircraft known as a "carrier" and the supply, maintenance or repair of equipment on behalf of the carrier. It is clear that the adoption of the interpretative declaration submitted by the United Kingdom Government (cf. 15(e)) meant that the Minister's deputies no longer needed to deal with this request.

The U.K. declaration also recommended that the question of the supply of foodstuffs to the station should be excluded. Since this request was not accepted by the Ministers' deputies, it must be considered that even the supply of such goods should be regarded by the contracting states as an act of collaboration.

(i) Before bringing this section on punishable acts in the field of "pirate" stations to a close, I should add that, in deference to the general principles of the law of the sea and the law of the air, the Legal Committee introduced into the Agreement a provision stipulating that these acts cannot constitute an infringement if they are carried out with certain humanitarian aims in view. It is laid down in Article 6 of the Agreement that "The provisions of Article 2 shall not apply to any acts performed for the purpose of giving assistance to a ship or aircraft or any other floating or airborne object in distress or of protecting human life". It follows that repressive measures cannot be taken against "pirate" stations on account of such acts if they are carried out with one of these aims in view, as, for example, in the case of the broadcasting of SOS messages.

Criteria for the Applicability of the Agreement: Nationality (Partly) and Territoriality

The definition of the criteria whereby "pirate" stations' activities may be linked to the contracting parties is all the more difficult in that these activities spring from radio broadcasts which ignore national frontiers.

(a) The Scandinavian countries realized this when they enacted legislation on "pirate" stations in such a way that Scandinavia is henceforth treated as a single area; the result is that any offence committed in the area must be suppressed in each of these countries, even if there is no other link between the offence and the country concerned.

When it started its work, the Legal Committee had contemplated a similar solution by creating a certain solidarity between the contracting parties in preventing acts contrary to the common interest. The argument had been advanced that each state had the sovereign right to estimate the interests the violation of which would make it necessary for its courts to take repressive action and that, furthermore, states were at liberty to introduce new rules of international law applicable between themselves. However, it was not possible for the Committee to pursue its intention of creating such an interrelationship between contracting states, since the delegates of several countries explained that such a procedure would not fit in with their legal system and that no ratification of the Agreement on their part could be expected.

The objection made by these delegates to the argument put forward above was that a contracting state could be obliged to exercise its penal jurisdiction against the nationals of non-contracting states in respect of acts which did not concern it either with regard to the place where the acts had been carried out, the interests thereby harmed, or the offender's place of residence.

(b) The Legal Committee then adopted the solution of making the obligation for contracting states to prevent the punishable acts depend only on the criteria of nationality and territoriality. It followed that this obligation existed for each of the parties only as far as its own nationals were concerned, whatever the place where the act had been carried out, and, as far as non-nationals were concerned, if the act had been carried out on its national territory.

Even this system was not universally accepted; some governments urged that repressive measures should be taken against the nationals of any given state only in cases where the punishable act was carried out by them either on the territory, ships or aircraft of the state or outside the national territory, on board any ship, aircraft or other carrier.

This was the solution finally adopted by the Committee; it is contained in Article 3 of the Agreement. [21]

(c) It will be noted that this provision entirely adopts territoriality as the criterion of applicability of the Agreement, since action should be taken as a contracting state against both non-nationals and the state's own nationals when they carry out a punishable act on its national territory. The criterion of nationality has been partly abandoned since a national of a contracting state should not be proceeded against by that state when he commits a punishable offence on the territory of another state, but only where he commits such an offence on board ships, aircraft and, at the discretion of the state concerned, on an artificial island situated outside the national territory. Thus, for example, country X should enact the necessary legislation to be able to proceed against any of its nationals who carry out an act of collaboration on behalf of a "pirate" station, whether on its national territory, or on board a ship, aircraft, or possibly an artificial island outside its national territory.

The same country X will have to enact the necessary legislation to take action against foreign nationals who commit a punishable offence on its national territory,[22] but not in cases where they carry out such an act on board a ship, aircraft or artificial island not coming under its jurisdiction.

(d) However, the Legal Committee had to deal with the case of states which had already enacted legislation having a broader scope. Thus, for example, the Belgian Act of 1962 makes it possible to proceed against Belgian nationals wherever they have committed the offence; it likewise enables action to be taken against foreign nationals who have either directly or indirectly assisted a Belgian national to commit a punishable offence outside the national territory. As far as Scandinavian legislation is concerned, we have already pointed out that each country takes action against the nationals of Norway, Denmark, Finland or Sweden, even if the offence was not committed on the territory of the country of which the culprit is a national, but on the territory of one of these other countries. Attention was drawn in this respect to the argument advanced by the Norwegian delegate when a solution was chosen which involved giving a restrictive list of acts of collaboration,[23] namely, that international treaties cannot normally be interpreted as constituting minimum provisions which the contracting parties are free to go beyond.

In order to obviate this difficulty, the Legal Committee adopted a dual resolution during its ninth meeting in May 1964. It first of all requested its General Rapporteur to indicate in his report to the Committee of Ministers that it was considered desirable that the contracting parties should punish their own nationals, provided their legal principles were not opposed to such action, wherever such offence was committed. The Committee also decided to introduce a new provision into the Agreement; this provision is contained in Article 4 (a)[24] and is intended to stress the fact that the regulations provided for by the Agreement constitute a minimum level of protection of the public interest and that there is nothing to prevent states from adopting in their legislation standards exceeding those laid down therein, as regards both punishable offences and persons.

One may wonder whether Article 4 (a) satisfies expectations when, by making it possible for states to treat as an offence not only the acts of collaboration covered by the Agreement, but also other acts added by the national legislative authorities, it enables the latter to proceed against persons other than those referred to in Article 3. Strictly speaking, the Legal Committee is not referring to "other persons," but to the same persons, namely, the country's own nationals and non-nationals, who commit an offence in a place other than those referred to in Article 3. This point is not of great importance, however, if one considers the interpretation given by the General Rapporteur of the provision under fire.

The Prohibition Against Introducing Reservations

While the Agreement makes it possible for countries to increase the number and severity of the repressive measures to be taken and to put them into effect in a greater number of situations, by virtue of the provision contained in Article 4 (a), it is further stipulated in Article 7 that it is not permissible to make reservations. The contracting states are, consequently, not allowed to make provision in their national legislation for measures less strict than those mentioned in the Agreement, in their efforts to put an end to the activities of "pirate" stations.

A state wishing to become a party to the Agreement will in any event have to take the necessary steps to proceed against both its own nationals and foreign nationals in cases where they establish and operate a "pirate" station or commit one of the acts of collaboration mentioned, on its own national territory (in the broadest sense of the term) and even, in the case of its own nationals, on a ship, aircraft or other carrier situated outside its national territory, whatever their nationality.

The state concerned will have to take the necessary measures with regard to "pirate" stations both in cases where they transmit broadcasts intended for reception or capable of being received, wholly or in part, on the territory of one of the contracting states, and in cases where their broadcasts cause harmful interference to a radiocommunication service duly authorized by one of these states.

The Contracting Parties. Entry into Force

The member states of the Council of Europe can become parties to the Agreement by one of the following methods: by signature with reservation in respect of ratification or acceptance or by ratification or acceptance. Other states may become parties to the Agreement, from the time of its entry into force, provided they are members or associate members of the ITU; it is however, necessary to obtain the prior agreement of the Committee of Ministers. The instruments must be deposited with the Secretary-General of the Council of Europe (Articles 8 and 10).

The Agreement comes into force one month after three member states of the Council of Europe have become parties to it. As regards other states which become parties to it subsequently, it will come into force one month after the date of signature or of deposit of the instrument (Articles 9 and 10).

Other Clauses

No special features distinguish the few remaining clauses, which deal respectively with overseas territories (Article 11), with the indefinite duration and the denunciation of the Agreement (Article 12) and with the notifications to be made by the Secretary-General of the Council of Europe (Article 13). These clauses are purely formal and their text does not differ from that of the other treaties of the Council of Europe.

Final Considerations

IT has been shown in this survey that the operation of "pirate" stations runs counter to the rational use of frequencies and is likely in the long run to create an extremely confused situation, especially as this activity takes place completely outside the jurisdiction of the member states of the ITU and thus makes the direct application of national legislation a more difficult matter. Moreover, the situation is particularly difficult when "pirate" stations operate on board ships or aircraft that have not been registered in the proper manner in any country. This is why the Geneva Administrative Radio Conference held in 1959 introduced, into the Radio Regulations, Nos. 422 and 962 to which reference has frequently been made in these notes.

However, neither these Regulations nor the legislation on the high seas contains provisions relating to repressive measures. In order to fill this legal gap, which discouraged quite a few governments, the Legal Committee on Broadcasting and Television of the Council of Europe took up the suggestion put forward by the EBU, with the backing of the ITU, that a regional agreement should be drawn up which would oblige the contracting parties to enact the necessary legislation to prevent and, in any event, to eliminate the activities of "pirate" stations.

The Agreement is based mainly on Nos. 422 and 962 of the Geneva Radio Regulations of 1959 and constitutes a minimum degree of protection of the public interest and the security of radiocommunications. It does in fact recognize the contracting parties' right to take more severe preventive measures, in particular, by making it possible for them to broaden the list of acts of collaboration in the activities of "pirate" stations and to proceed against their own nationals and non-nationals, wherever the offence has been committed.

The reason why the Legal Committee has adhered in the Agreement to a text which is fairly limited in scope is that it was intended to make the Agreement form a common denominator of existing legal systems. As Dr. Georges Straschnov commented in his report to the EBU Legal Committee, there can be little room for doubt that a treaty going beyond the bounds of international law and practice would have been ratified by few countries; it was a better policy to draw up an instrument which, while less ambitious, was more realistic, even if it had to be licked into final shape at a later stage.

It was feared in some quarters that the activities of the Council of Europe in respect of "pirate" stations might hamper the work being carried out in the field of submarine research into mineral deposits, or even weaken the implementation of the Convention on the Continental Shelf (Geneva, 1958) which was mainly based on the principle of exploitation by the national territory as well as on the desire of the coastal states to secure at the present stage the exclusive benefit of such exploitation.[25] The Committee made a point of requesting its General Rapporteur during its ninth meeting (May 1964) to counter this objection in his report to the Committee of Ministers. It is therefore stated in this report that the Agreement cannot prejudice the right of contracting countries, so far as concerns the high seas, to take legal action and institute regulations which have no connection with broadcasting. It was again pointed out that the Agreement applies to radio broadcasts, i.e. broadcasts intended for direct reception by the general public, whereas submarine research stations make use of other types of radio-communications such as radio-location, radar or, more frequently, radiotelephony and radiotelegraphy.

While the European Agreement for the Prevention of Broadcasts transmitted by Stations outside National Territories is in fact a regional agreement, it is as well to stress the fact that from the time it comes into force any member state of the ITU may accede to it, even if it is not a member of the Council of Europe. In this respect, and also as the first international instrument indicating the steps to be taken to put an end to the activities of "pirate" radio stations, the Agreement constitutes a pilot treaty.

I hope I have amply demonstrated why it is a matter of urgency to convince governments of the necessity for their countries to become parties to the Agreement, so that a vast area may be formed within which the harmful and even dangerous activities of "pirate" stations can be prevented, and, in cases where they already exist, eliminated.

PREVENTION OF BROADCASTS TRANSMITTED FROM

ARTIFICIAL ISLANDS

DUTCH LEGISLATION ON INSTALLATIONS ON THE HIGH SEAS*

While the legislators and the lawyers were devoting attention to the question of sound radio transmissions from ships outside territorial waters, a new phenomenon appeared: television broadcasts from an installation, generally known as an "artificial island," supported by the bed of the sea.

This event naturally raised a number of new legal problems. The solution found by the Dutch legislature cannot be said to lack originality. Moreover, this is the first time, as far as I am aware, that a state has taken direct preventive measures against a transmitting station situated outside territorial waters. It seems to me that the importance of this question for broadcasting calls for a review of the events concerned, a broad outline of the legal aspect of the problem, and an account of the legislation enacted by the Dutch Government in the matter.

It was in September 1963 that the press first drew attention to the existence of plans to broadcast commercial television programmes from an artificial island to be situated outside Dutch territorial waters. The promoters of the plan set up a limited company known as Reclame Exploitatie Maatschappij (REM). Although the REM made quite sure that it received daily publicity, it nevertheless remained shrouded in mystery. At the beginning, it merely stated that the undertaking was financed exclusively by Dutch capital. Not until April 1964, when work on the installation had already been completed in the Irish shipyards, did the names of the two Dutch promoters become known, whereas the third, a foreign national, remained anonymous. At the same time, the REM announced that the artificial island was foreign property and that the REM was merely a tenant. I dwell on this question of ownership because it was an important factor in the legal disputes.

In the meantime, the question aroused the interest of the lawyers, lively discussions were held on the legality or illegality of such an undertaking, and well-known scholars expounded their arguments for and against. The Government announced that it would not hesitate to take action against the station. On 9th May 1964, a Bill on the subject was actually laid before Parliament, which discussed the matter immediately.

On 4th June a start was made on the construction of the artificial island on the site itself, and the transmitter was delivered by RCA. Experimental

* By Karel Remes, the legal adviser to the Dutch Broadcasting Organization, VARA. Reprinted by permission of the *EBU Review* and the author.

broadcasts began on 15th August 1964, and on 1st September "TV Noord-zee" started regular transmissions. The 214 m. wavelength was used for sound broadcasting, and band 11, assigned to the Netherlands for broadcasts in connection with aeronautical navigation, was used for television.

A short while before, in August, the REM had founded another limited company, known as the Volks Aandelen Trust (VAT), as the sole proprietor of the REM. The VAT's capital consists of 350,000 shares worth 20 florins each, and of preference shares amounting to a total of 5,000,000 florins. The latter are in the hands of the two Dutch promoters of the REM and of an unknown foreign national, the supposed owner of the artificial island. The REM also announced that it was insured at Lloyds against any material hindrance preventing it from making broadcasts, under any national legislation of any country whatsoever. The underwriter was bound to pay, if the occasion arose, the sum of 9,000,000 florins to the owner of the artificial island, while the latter would pay compensation to the "tenants."

The Bill was passed by the Chamber of Deputies on 17th September 1964, with 114 votes for and 19 against, and by the Senate on 1st December 1964, with 57 votes for and 9 against. The REM let it be known that the responsibility for running the installation had been transferred to High Sea Television Ltd., which was set up for this purpose in London on 13th November 1964.

According to this communication, the owner of the artificial island was Excomar S.A. of Panama, an assertion which was, however, disputed by the Government of that country.

These are the facts of the case, although I cannot claim to have given an entirely complete picture.

It is quite clear that the REM's transmissions were addressed to the Netherlands and intended for reception by Dutch viewers. There can be absolutely no doubt that the installation of the broadcasting station outside Dutch territory was aimed at removing it from the state monopoly of telecommunications, thus getting round the legislation prohibiting commercial television. In other words, the promoters' intention was to place themselves outside the Dutch jurisdiction. Unlike a ship, which comes under the jurisdiction of the state whose flag it flies, an installation set up on the bed of the sea does not come under the jurisdiction of another state because such installations cannot fly a flag.

The question therefore arose whether the Netherlands should accept this situation or whether, on the contrary, they were entitled to take action and, if so, by what means. It should be noted that the matter fell entirely within the competence of the government authorities and not within that of the broadcasting organizations. The latter have no broadcasting monopoly and have played no part in this affair.

There can be no question that the legislation in force in any given country is, as a general rule, considered to take effect on the territory of that country; any extension of its field of application outside that territory involves the law of nations. The question therefore arises of establishing to what extent it is permissible, within the framework of the law of nations, for a country to extend the scope of its legal system to cover acts which have taken place outside its national territory, and to what extent and by what means this state is entitled to use force to ensure that its legislation is respected.

In this particular case, it is a question of acts committed in installations affixed to the sea-bed, and of the power exercised over them. The term normally used, namely "artificial island," may possibly give rise to confusion. Such installations cannot be treated in the same way as natural islands. It is explicitly stated in Article 5, §4, of the Convention on the Continental Shelf that such installations shall not possess the legal status of islands. Ownership is not a decisive factor inasmuch as the state of which the owner is a national cannot link them in any way with its territory. Nor is it permissible for a coastal state to annex them to its territory.

The earth is not the only place where men can engage in their activities: the sea also provides a suitable field. It follows that human relationships must be subject to legal regulations both at sea and on the land. It would be an intolerable state of affairs if men were not held responsible for acts committed at sea and if each state were able arbitrarily to exercise its power over the high seas. Thus, the necessity arose for the establishment of certain rules of the law of nations, rules both of common law and of written law.

The codification of the law of the sea, at the 1958 Geneva Conference, is of fundamental importance in this respect. Four Conventions, signed on 29th April 1958, emerged from the conference:

(a) The Convention on the High Seas
(b) The Convention on the Continental Shelf
(c) The Convention on the Territorial Sea and the Contiguous Zone
(d) The Convention on Fishing and the Conservation of the Living Resources of the High Seas.

With the exception of that referred to under (d), the Conventions have already come into force and bind a large number of states. The Netherlands have yet to ratify them, but a Bill to this end has already been laid before Parliament.

However, this does not mean that the Netherlands are not concerned with the standards laid down in these Conventions, since, in the majority of cases, they merely serve to codify principles of common law already in existence.

The law of the sea makes a distinction between the high seas on the one hand and the territorial sea on the other. The term "high seas" means all parts of the sea that are not included in the territorial sea or in the internal waters of a state (Article I of the Convention on the High Seas).

However, the Convention contains no definition of the term "territorial sea" and merely refers to it as a belt of sea adjacent to the coast of a country. The reason for this is that it did not prove possible, either at the 1958 Geneva Conference or at the Second Conference on the Law of the Sea to obtain unanimous agreement on the usual delimitation of a three-mile zone.

The distinction between the territorial sea and the high seas is of prime importance, because the two are governed by two opposite principles: that of the sovereignty of the coastal state in the first case, and that of the freedom of the seas in the second.[26,27] The freedom of the high seas is intended to guarantee and protect freedom of navigation, freedom of fishing, freedom to lay submarine cables and pipelines, freedom to fly over the high seas and "others which are recognized by the general principles of international law" (Article 2). It is important to note that the freedom of the high seas is recognized in favour of states and not of individuals. While excluding the exercise by states of any sovereignty over the high seas, the principle of the freedom of the high seas is not in any way intended to rule out the application of legal regulations governing human activities on the high seas. For a long time, such activities could be exercised, apart from a few exceptions, only on board ship. The logical conclusion is that the law of the sea was concerned mainly with the legal position of ships. In general, ships are subject to the jurisdiction of the state whose flag they fly, which is not necessarily the state of which the owner of the ship is a national. The jurisdiction in question applies to all persons on board the ship, regardless of their nationality; it is therefore not restricted to the nationals of the country concerned.

The exploration and exploitation of the natural resources to be found in the subsoil of the sea introduced a new factor into the question of the use of the high seas and led to the appearance of new constructions on the surface. It became necessary to adapt and add to the provisions of the law of the sea. The Convention on the Continental Shelf, referred to above, made adequate provision for this new situation by creating special regulations for that part of the high seas known as the "continental shelf."[28] This shelf is not considered to belong to the territory of the coastal state but, on the contrary, to continue to form part of the high seas, although the coastal state is granted certain sovereign rights.[29] Both the construction of drilling installations and all activities carried out on such installations come under the jurisdiction of the coastal state, regardless of the ownership of the installation or the nationality of the persons concerned. However, the sovereign rights exercised by the states are expressly restricted to the exploration and exploitation of the natural resources of the high seas and cannot therefore be extended to cover installations erected for other purposes. The regulations governing the continental shelf are, consequently, not applicable to installations used as a base for a television station. An installation of this type constitutes a new form of use of the high seas, for which no provision is made in the conventions on the use of the high seas. The only relevant provision contained in international law is to be found in the International Telecommunication Convention. However, the provision in question (Article 7 of the Regulations) applies only to radio-communications and, even in this respect, refers only to broadcasts made from ships or other floating objects. There is, therefore, a gap in the legislation on the subject, and the question arises who is called upon or authorized to fill it.

The most satisfactory and desirable solution would be the adoption by an international conference of a regulation forming part of the law of the sea. However, the procedure to be followed in drawing up such a regulation would take years and meanwhile the chaotic situation could develop beyond repair. May a country affected by the problem take the initiative in the meantime? If so, which one—the coastal state or some other country? Should such action be taken according to the criterion on territoriality or that of the persons involved?

The measures taken in the past may give us some guidance. From the legal standpoint, the continental shelf is at present governed by the provisions of a convention, but at the beginning the regulations arose out of unilateral action taken by a single country on its own initiative.[30]

Is it not advisable to follow this example? The law of nations is largely common law and, in the nature of things, common law springs from unilateral action taken by the states.

I have endeavoured to sketch the broad outline of the legal position, while at the same time following the considerations that occupied the attention of the Dutch Government. The discussions in Parliament and the various articles dealing with the question have shown that the problems of the law of nations are extremely complex and that the law of the sea is in many respects controversial. The very basis of the law of the sea, namely, the freedom of the high seas, would appear to lead to diametrically opposite conclusions. Whereas, in some quarters, it is taken to mean the freedom to erect installations and use them without any interference from the states, the same acts are considered in other quarters to constitute a violation of the freedom of the high seas, which the states have an obligation to repress. My own view is that there are no grounds whatsoever to support the argument that broadcasts made from an installation on the high seas should be regarded as the exercise of the other freedoms "which are recognized by the general principles of international law" (Article 2 of the Convention on the High Seas).

The legal problems connected with the "REM island" have particularly exercised the minds of the lawyers. In addition to a hundred references to the subject in the press, there have been about 20 scientific studies.[31] The fundamental principles of common maritime law have been discussed and their drift examined with a view to ensuring that they should be applied in an equitable manner. There is no call for me to add my own voice to this concert of soloists. It would be completely beyond the scope of this article, which is solely intended to supply a little general information on the new Dutch legislation on the subject, to reproduce and analyse all the arguments advanced by the various parties.

It was possible to envisage a number of different repressive measures. All of them were taken into consideration by the Government and thoroughly discussed in Parliament.

The simplest solution, which was suggested in several quarters, would have been simply to inflict penalties on the spot. The Ministry of Justice shared the view that there was nothing in international law to prevent such a course being taken and that, from this standpoint, the state would be within its rights in acting along these lines. However, under Dutch domestic legislation, there remained a possibility of the state being held liable, and any action which did not have a sound basis in domestic legislation might, in the Government's opinion, be regarded as an offence committed by the state.

Another suggestion was that the scope of the relevant legal provisions (in particular, Article 20 *et seq.* of the Telegraph and Telephone Act) should be extended, in other words, that the territorial limitation contained in the said provisions should be abolished. This proposal did not meet with the Government's approval either. Another similar idea was likewise rejected, namely, that, by the enactment of appropriate legislation, the erection of installations on the high seas without a licence having first been obtained from the authorities should be prohibited. The Minister considered that there were several objections to this proposal: first of all, to place such discretionary powers to grant or refuse licences in the hands of the coastal state would hardly be compatible with the law of nations; secondly, this solution would not create any legal system to govern the installations concerned; and thirdly, it would not provide the state authorities with a legal basis for the effective exercise of jurisdiction over the installation itself.

A final possibility could have been to follow the example of the Belgian and Scandinavian legislatures and prohibit acts of collaboration with broadcasting stations outside national territories, making such acts punishable offences. On this point, the Government made the same objections as in the case of the draft European Agreement for the Prevention of Broadcasts transmitted from Stations outside National Territories. It took the view that it was hardly legitimate to take legal action against accomplices without inflicting the same penalties on the chief culprit. Moreover, such regulations affect only broadcasting, whereas the aim in this case was to create a legal system to govern all installations on the high seas.

The arguments advanced by the Government may not be convincing enough to win everybody over to its point of view. However that may be, the Government decided to give its preference to another solution, which was broader and more far-reaching in its scope. It considered that, even if Radio Noordzee installed on "REM island" provided the *grounds* for enactment of legislation, the *purpose* of such legislation should not be restricted to the broadcasts of REM. Its aim should be to fill the legislative gap not only as far as radio installations at sea were concerned, but also in respect of any kind of installations erected for any purpose whatsoever. Steps must be taken to prevent the springing up a short distance off the coast of installations— except for those intended for the exploration and exploitation of the natural resources of the sea—which would lie outside the scope of any legal system of jurisdiction. Consequently, the Government did not find it necessary to devote attention to the controversial question whether international law does or does not permit the erection of installations affixed to the bed of the sea. It took the view that this question went beyond its immediate concern, which was to bring such installations under its jurisdiction rather than prohibit them.[32]

On the basis of the ideas set forth above, the Government laid before the States General a Bill, an unofficial translation of which is given below:

BILL

... considering that it is desirable to enact legislation to cover installations erected on the bed of the North Sea in that part of the continental shelf over which the Kingdom exercises sovereign rights ...

Article 1   Within the meaning of the present Act, the term "continental shelf" signifies that part of the bed of the North Sea over which the Kingdom exercises sovereign rights, in accordance with the provisions of the Convention on the Continental Shelf, signed in Geneva on 29th April 1958.

Article 2   For the purposes of the application of the legal provisions referred to in the Regulation laid down by the public authorities, installations erected on the continental shelf are regarded as forming part of the territory of the Netherlands.

Article 3   The Regulation laid down by the public authorities, on the basis of Article 2, may exclude or limit the application of the said legal provisions to certain specific installations.

Article 4   With regard to those installations which have been or will be erected on the continental shelf, the Regulation laid down by the public authorities may enact rules governing the interests of navigation, fishing, the conservation of the living resources of the sea and scientific research, or for the purpose of protecting other interests recognized by international law.

The Bill was not accepted without criticism. In two respects, in particular, it gave rise to strong objections on the part of experts in the law of nations and of members of the Chamber of Deputies. The reference to the Convention on the Continental Shelf contained in Article 1 and the legal fiction in Article 2 were ambiguous and might possibly cause confusion. The fiction in Article 2 was too closely related to annexation, which clearly conflicted with the principle of the freedom of the high seas. Furthermore, there appeared to be little justification for the idea of basing the Act on the Convention on the Continental Shelf.

Since the Convention in question was concerned only with the exploration and exploitation of the natural resources of the high seas, any extension of its application to cover other purposes by the unilateral act of one state would have to be regarded as incompatible with the principles of the law of nations.

The Minister soon explained that it was in no way his intention to base the Bill in question on the said Convention. The reference was aimed merely at introducing a criterion of place and the designation of the continental shelf appeared the most appropriate. Without such a reference, the Act would be applicable to any part of the high seas, however distant, and this could not be justified by the aim it was intended to achieve. In this connection, the Government did not consider it a disadvantage that the Convention on the Continental Shelf had not yet been ratified by the Netherlands and that the negotiations with the Federal Republic of Germany on the boundaries of the continental shelf had not yet been concluded. As for the legal fiction contained in Article 2, it has been introduced on the model of the British Continental Shelf Act 1964 and was in no way intended to involve annexation.

In addition to these two objections concerning international law, another serious objection arose, founded on Dutch domestic legislation. It was considered that the delegation of powers to the Crown, as laid down in Article 3 and 4, went too far. The Chamber was reluctant to agree with the proposal that it should be left to the Government to decide, possibly without intervention by Parliament, what legal provisions would or would not be applicable to the installations on the high seas.

The objections listed above and a large number of other criticisms and comments induced the Government to carry out a revision of the Bill. The Consultative Committee on International Law was called upon to give its views, and the comments and suggestions it made served as a basis for the preparation of a revised version of the Bill. When defending the Bill before Parliament, the Minister made a well-documented statement on various aspects of the law of nations and convincingly refuted the arguments advanced by the REM experts (cf. REM publication, note 1, page 151). Finally the following text, of which the translation given here is unofficial, became law.

Act of 3rd December 1964 on
Installations Erected on the Bed of the North Sea

. . . considering that it is desirable, in order to protect legitimate interests, to take steps in respect of installations set up on the bed of that part of the North Sea the boundaries of which are identical to those of that part of the Continental Shelf assigned to the Netherlands, pending the enactment of international regulations on this subject . . .

Article 1 The term "installations at sea", as used in the present Act, means installations erected outside territorial waters on the bed of that part of the North Sea the boundaries of which coincide with those of that part of the continental shelf assigned to the Netherlands.

Article 2   The provisions of Dutch criminal law are applicable to any person committing an infringement on an installation erected at sea.

Article 3   The Regulation laid down by the public authorities will specify the Dutch legal provisions applicable to installations at sea.

Article 4   The Regulation laid down by the public authorities may, with regard to installations at sea, settle the question of the respective jurisdiction *ratione loci* of the authorities, courts of law and officials responsible for implementing the provisions laid down in Article 3, for preparing the case, taking proceedings and passing judgment in connection with breaches of the law or for putting legal decisions into effect.

Article 5   The Regulation laid down by the public authorities may exclude or limit the application of the criminal provisions and of the Dutch legal provisions laid down in Article 3, in respect of certain installations at sea referred to therein.

Article 6   If, within a period of three months from the date of the entry into force of the Regulation laid down by the public authorities on the basis of Article 3 or Article 5, a Bill taking the place of the said Regulation is not laid before the States General, or if the said Bill is withdrawn or thrown out, the Regulation in question shall be withdrawn forthwith.

Article 7   In respect of installations which have been or will be erected on the bed of that part of the North Sea defined in Article 1, the Regulation laid down by the public authorities may provide for special provisions in the interests of navigation, fishing, the conservation of the living resources of the sea, research of a purely scientific nature, the laying and maintenance of submarine cables and pipelines, of preventing the pollution of the sea, or of protecting other interests recognized by the law of nations.

Article 8   Any infringement of the provision enacted on the basis of Article 7 is punishable by the infliction of a fine of up to ten thousand florins. Any infringement of this nature will be treated as an offence.

Article 9   The Act may be referred to as the Act on Installations in the North Sea.

Article 10   This Act shall come into force as from the first day following the date of publication in the *Staatsblad*.

The Act came into force on 5th December 1964. Three Royal decrees were issued on 8th December 1964, being regulations laid down by the public authorities in pursuance of Articles 3 and 4 of the Act. The first decree declares the Code of Criminal Procedure to be applicable. It is worded as follows:

Article 1   The provisions of the Code of Criminal Procedure and the provisions laid down in pursuance of the said Code shall be described as Dutch legal regulations, in accordance with the terms of Article 3 of the Act applicable to and in respect of installations at sea, within the meaning of the Act.

The second decree settles the question of the respective jurisdiction of the criminal judge, the police, the officials carrying out the enquiry, and the government officials, in general, in respect of installations at sea. The third decree declares the Telegraph and Telephone Act and the provisions resulting from this Act to be applicable. All three decrees were issued on 10th December and came into force on 12th December 1964. From then onwards, the broadcasts made by Radio Noordzee constituted a violation of the Act, but the REM nevertheless continued its broadcasts.

On 17th December, the police and post office officials landed on the installation from two helicopters and a Royal Dutch Navy vessel, drew up a report, and put the installation under seal. The public prosecutor opened criminal proceedings, the first step being a preliminary investigation against ten persons, only one of whom was a Dutch national. The new owner of the installation stated, according to reports in the press, that he was considering bringing a legal action against the state.

This is the situation at the time this article was written. It should be noted, in addition, that the Government declared, on the subject of another station, installed on the ship "Veronica," that it was waiting for the European Agreement for the Prevention of Broadcasts transmitted from Stations outside National Territories to be signed. The Government carried out a large-scale enquiry in order to discover where the vessel was registered, but it had meanwhile been sold to be broken up and the station had been transferred to another ship.

The Postmaster General and the Pirates*

The United Kingdom is now surrounded by eight pirate stations established on ships or disused forts and these stations are all engaged in broadcasting programmes of a popular type intended for reception in the United Kingdom. The Postmaster General has repeatedly declared the intention of the Government to suppress the pirate stations, but until recently there has been little sign of any practical steps being taken to implement these declarations. It would seem that the delay has been largely due to the difficulties which the Government has had in deciding what should be put in place of the pirate stations. The Government considers that there is a need for a new service devoted to the provision of a continuous popular music programme, but it may be pointed out that this need would not have arisen if the Government had dealt firmly with the first pirate stations at an early stage in their existence. The Government finally announced in a White Paper of December 1966 that a new popular music programme should be provided by the BBC. At the same time, the Postmaster General reaffirmed the intention of the Government to suppress the pirate stations. These fall in two categories, those operating inside territorial waters and those operating outside.

* By E. C. Robbins, the legal adviser to the British Broadcasting Corporation. Reprinted by permission of the *EBU Review,* and the author.

As regard the pirate stations operating from ships outside territorial waters, the Government has no powers to take action until legislation has been passed in the United Kingdom to give effect to the European Agreement for the prevention of broadcasts transmitted from stations outside national territories, which was signed by the United Kingdom at the Council of Europe in January 1965. A Bill for this purpose, entitled the Marine etc. Broadcasting (Offences) Bill, was presented by the Postmaster General to the House of Commons in July 1966. Apart from the formal first reading of the Bill there has been no further discussion of it in Parliament, but, when the White Paper was issued in December, the Postmaster General announced that the second reading of the Bill would be in the first week of February and that it would become law by July. The text of the Bill as presented may be substantially altered during its passage through both Houses of Parliament and it is, therefore, not proposed to discuss it here.

As regards the pirate stations operating from ships or other installations inside territorial waters, the Postmaster General has existing powers under the Wireless Telegraphy Act 1949. Section 1 of the Act makes it a criminal offence to establish or use any station or apparatus for wireless telegraphy except under the authority of a licence granted by the Postmaster General. Section 6 provides that the Act is to apply to all stations and apparatus in the United Kingdom or the territorial waters adjacent thereto but the meaning of the term "territorial waters" is not defined in the Act. In 1958 the United Kingdom took part in the Law of the Sea Conference at Geneva, and agreement was then reached as to the base lines which should be adopted for the measurement of territorial waters. In September 1964 the Queen in Council approved the Territorial Waters Order to give effect to the agreement reached at the Geneva Conference. So far the Postmaster General has begun proceedings under the Wireless Telegraphy Act against four pirate stations operating inside territorial waters.

In the first case the operators of a station known as Radio 390 were convicted by the magistrates at a Court of Summary Jurisdiction in Kent for infringing Section 1 of the Wireless Telegraphy Act, by using a radio transmitter at Red Sands Tower without the licence of the Postmaster General. Red Sands Tower is a disused fort which formed part of the anti-aircraft defences during the war and it is situated in the Thames Estuary some 4.9 nautical miles from low water mark on the Kent coast, but within three miles of a base line drawn to include a low tide elevation known as Middle Sand. The Postmaster General contended that on these facts the station was being operated in territorial waters as measured under the Territorial Waters Order. The operators of Radio 390 then applied to the Queen's Bench Division of the High Court to set aside the conviction on the grounds that the magistrates had no jurisdiction to try the case. It was also argued on behalf of the operators that the effect of the Wireless Telegraphy Act 1949 was to fix the extent of territorial waters at the limit of three miles then operative, and that it was *ultra vires* for the limit to be subsequently altered by the Crown in Council under the Territorial Waters Order 1964. The application was heard by three judges and was dismissed by a majority decision of two. Lord Chief Justice Parker considered that the magistrates of the area adjacent to the coastline had an implied jurisdiction to deal with the criminal offence created by the Wireless Telegraphy Act. He also considered that the Crown had a prerogative right to define the extent of territorial waters from time to time and that the Crown was not bound by the position as it existed in 1949. Mr. Justice Blain agreed with the judgment of the Lord Chief Justice, but Lord Justice Salmon dissented as he took the view that the term "territorial waters" in the 1949 Act should be considered as meaning the position then existing and that it was not competent for the Crown to alter the position by subsequent prerogative declaration. Following the dismissal of their application the operators of Radio 390 announced that they proposed to discontinue broadcasting from the station and that they did not propose to make a further appeal to the House of Lords. They subsequently declared that they did after all propose to resume broadcasting, as new evidence had come to light which showed that they had in fact been operating outside territorial waters. They alleged that the Crown Survey on which the case for the Postmaster General had been based was out of date and that Middle Sand, the low tide elevation taken into account in measuring the base line, was in fact always covered by water. In his turn the Postmaster General has announced that he is proposing to issue a second summons against the operators of Radio 390.

Another prosecution was started by the Postmaster General against the operators of Radio Essex which was established at Knock John Tower near Foulness Point in the Thames Estuary. The operators were convicted by the magistrates of a Court of Summary Jurisdiction at Rochford in Essex for infringing Section 1 of the Wireless Telegraphy Act. They continued their broadcasts and appealed to the Court of Quarter Sessions at Chelmsford in Essex. This Court dismissed the appeal and held that Knock John Tower was about 1½ miles inside territorial waters and was within the jurisdiction of the Rochford magistrates. The operators of Radio Essex have announced that they propose to continue with their appeal to the High Court, which they will thus reach by a different route from that adopted by Radio 390.

A further prosecution under the Wireless Telegraphy Act has been started by the Postmaster General against Radio Scotland, which has been established on a converted lightship operating off Troon on the Ayrshire coast. This summons will, however, not be heard by the Sheriff Court at Ayr until March.

Since this article was written the magistrates at the Court of Summary Jurisdiction at Rochford have dealt with another summons issued by the Postmaster General against the operator of Radio City, established on the Shivering Sands Fort in the Thames Estuary. The operator was convicted of broadcasting without a licence and it has been announced that there will be no appeal against the conviction and no further broadcasting by Radio City.

NOTES

1. Albert Namurois, "The Prevention of the Activities of 'Pirate' Broadcasting Stations," *EBU Review*, 90B, March 1965, p. 36.
2. *Long Beach Independent*, July 3, 1967, p. B–17.
3. *Ibid.*
4. *EBU Review*, 90B, March 1965, pp. 36–52; 102B, March 1967, pp. 52–53.
5. It will be recalled that the term "telecommunication" includes the following:

> a broadcasting service in which the transmissions are intended for direct reception by the general public: this service may include sound transmissions, television transmissions, or other types of transmissions (facsimile, etc.);
> radiocommunications other than broadcasting, propagated in the ether by means of radio waves with a specific end in view (radiotelegraphy, radiotelephony, etc.).

6. Although making use of this term, I am aware of the fact that the expression "pirate" stations has a clearly defined meaning in international law, which might not be applicable to the stations concerned.
7. Jens Evensen. *Certain Aspects of International Law Concerning the Operation of "Pirate" Stations from Ships or Aircraft.* Oslo, 22nd August 1960. Unpublished. (*Author's note:* Mr. Jens Evensen's legal opinion was sent to the post office authorities in the various countries by the ITU.)
8. These practicable steps fall into two classes. The first is concerned with the quality of the installations, the intention being to ensure that the station concerned in one state does not cause harmful interference to the services or radiocommunications of other states. As Mr. Evensen points out, the prohibitions against harmful interference are couched in general terms comprising "all stations" without restriction. They refer to broadcasting stations as well as to other radio services. They comprise land stations as well as maritime and aeronautical mobile stations, and govern the behaviour of stations inside the territorial limits as well as stations operating outside these limits. The Article further imposes the specific duty on the government concerned to enforce these provisions also against "private operating agencies". This express obligation imposed upon member governments to control the activities of their radio services in order to avoid harmful interference is, in the same way as the various other principles discussed in the foregoing, irreconcilable with acquiescence in the activities of "pirate" stations (*op. cit.*, p. 32).

   The second kind of practicable step is concerned with the range of the broadcasts, which must be viewed from two angles: the useful range, which determines the reception zone, and the harmful range, which determines the distance at which a broadcast may interfere with another broadcast on the same frequency or on a neighbouring frequency.
9. ITU Note on the operation of broadcasting stations on board ships or aircraft outside national territories (1962), Nos. 3.2.1 and 3.2.2.

10. *Op. cit.*, page 41.
11. It might be as well to recall that Number 28 of the same Regulations stipulates that a broadcasting service is a radio-communication service in which the transmissions are intended for direct reception by the general public. This service may include sound transmission, television transmissions, or other types of transmissions (facsimiles, time signals, etc.).
12. ITU Note already referred to, No. 3.2.3. It would appear that no government has as yet issued a licence authorizing the operation of a broadcasting station on board a ship or aircraft, outside the national territory. The ITU points out in this connection that the lack of a licence in no way lessens the responsibility of a government which has entered in its register of shipping a vessel carrying a broadcasting station (Convention on the High Seas, Article 5).
13. Recommendation No. 16 is worded as follows: "The Administrative Radio Conference, Geneva, 1959, *considering*
    a) that the operation of broadcasting stations on board ships or aircraft outside national territories is in conflict with the provisions of Nos. 422 and 962 of the Radio Regulations;
    b) that such operation is contrary to the orderly use of the radio frequency spectrum and may result in chaotic conditions;
    c) that the operation of such broadcasting stations may take place outside the jurisdiction of Member countries, thereby making the direct application of national laws difficult;
    d) that a particularly difficult legal situation arises when such broadcasting stations are operated on board ships or aircraft not duly registered in any country;
    recommends
    1. that administrations ask their Governments to study possible means, direct or indirect, to prevent or suspend such operations, and, where appropriate, take the necessary action,
    2. that administrations inform the Secretary General of the results of these studies and submit any other information which may be of general interest, so that the Secretary General can inform the Members and Associate Members of the Union accordingly."
14. The IFRB is a permanent organ of the ITU, whose essential duties are to effect an orderly recording of frequency assignments made by the different countries so as to establish the date, purpose and technical characteristics of each of these assignments, with a view to ensuring formal international recognition thereof.
15. The text of these provisions was given earlier, under section 7.
16. *"Article 1*
    This Agreement is concerned with broadcasting stations which are installed or maintained on board ships, aircraft or any other floating or airborne objects and which, outside national territories, transmit broadcasts intended for reception or capable of being received, wholly or in part, within the territory of any Contracting Party, or which cause harmful interference to any radiocommunication service operating under the authority of a Contracting Party in accordance with the Radio Regulations."
17. In thus adding to the original text the words "or maintained", the Legal Committee's sole concern was to comply with the request made by the delegation of the Federal Republic of Germany that the text should conform as closely as possible to its national legislation.
18. *"Article 4*

Nothing in this Agreement shall be deemed to prevent a Contracting Party:
(a) ...
(b) from also applying the provisions of this Agreement to broadcasting stations installed or maintained on objects affixed to or supported by the bed of the sea."

19. It should be noted that the International Telecommunication Convention (No. 242) does not state that it is necessary for harmful interference actually to be caused to the radio services of other countries: it is enough that it should be possible. The only criterion by which to determine whether harmful interference exists, is that the station situated in country X is capable of causing such harmful interference, in other words, that by virtue of its purpose, activities and power, etc., it is liable to cause harmful interference to the stations of other member countries of the ITU.

20. "*Article 2*
    1. Each Contracting Party undertakes to take appropriate steps to make punishable as offences, in accordance with its domestic law, the establishment or operation of broadcasting stations referred to in Article 1, as well as acts of collaboration knowingly performed.
    2. The following shall, in relation to broadcasting stations referred to in Article 1, be acts of collaboration:
    (a) the provision, maintenance or repairing of equipment;
    (b) the provision of supplies;
    (c) the provision of transport for, or the transporting of, persons, equipment or supplies;
    (d) the ordering or production of material of any kind, including advertisements to be broadcast;
    (e) the provision of services concerning advertising for the benefit of the stations."

21. "*Article 3*
    Each Contracting Party shall, in accordance with its domestic law, apply the provisions of this Agreement in regard to:
    (a) its nationals who have committed any act referred to in Article 2 on its territory, ships or aircraft, or outside national territories on any ships, aircraft or any other floating or airborne object;
    (b) non-nationals who, on its territory, ships or aircraft, or on board any floating or airborne object under its jurisdiction have committed any act referred to in Article 2."

22. It will be recalled that this term covers the actual territory, territorial waters, ships and aircraft having the nationality of the state in question, as well as the air space over this territory and these waters.

23. Cf. Section 16 (d) above.

24. "*Article 4*
    Nothing in this Agreement shall be deemed to prevent a Contracting Party:
    (a) from also treating as punishable offences acts other than those referred to in Article 2 and also applying the provisions concerned to persons other than those referred to in Article 3;
    (b) ..."

25. Charles De Visscher, *Théories et Réalitiés en Droit International public*, Paris 1960, p. 277.

26. Article 1, § 1, of the Convention on the Territorial Sea: "The sovereignty of a state extends, beyond its land territory and its internal waters, to a belt of sea adjacent to its coast, described as the territorial sea".

27. Article 2, § 1, of the Convention on the High Seas: "The high seas being open to all nations, no state may validly purport to subject any part of them to its sovereignty".

28. Article 1 of the Convention on the Continental Shelf: "For the purpose of these articles, the term "continental shelf" is used as referring (a) to the sea-bed and the subsoil of the submarine areas adjacent to the coast but outside the area of the territorial sea, to a depth of 200 metres or, beyond that limit, to where the depth of the superjacent waters admits of the exploitation of the natural resources of the said areas; (b) to the sea-bed and subsoil of similar submarine areas adjacent to the coasts of islands".

29. Article 2, § 1: "The coastal state exercises over the continental shelf sovereign rights for the purpose of exploring it and exploiting its natural resources".

30. Proclamation by President Truman on 28th September 1945.

31. Prof. A. J. P. Tammes, *EBU Review*, 1964, No. 86B; M. W. Mouton, *International Spectator*, 1963, page 548; Prof. J. P. A. François, *International Spectator*, 1964, page 120; A. M. Verstegen, *Nederlands Juristenblad*, 1964, No. 11; Prof. F. J. F. M. Duynstee, *Nederlands Juristenblad*, 1964, No. 13; Prof. H. F. van Panhuys, *Nederlands Juristenblad*, 1964, No. 22; H. G. M. van der Voort, *Nederlands Juristenblad*, 1964, No. 24; Prof. A. J. P. Tammes, *Nederlands Juristenblad*, 1964, No. 25; Prof. M. Bos, *Nederlands Juristenblad*, 1964, No. 26; A. Bockwinkel, *Nederlands Juristenblad*, 1964, No. 27; A. P. Spaanderman, *Nederlands Juristenblad*, 1964, No. 38; REM publication containing the opinions expressed by foreign experts: Dr. Colombos, Prof. D. Johnson, Prof. C. Rousseau, Sir H. Waldock, Prof. H. Rolin, Prof. F. de Pauw.

32. In its reply to the question raised by Mr. Morman, M.P. on 12th September 1964, the Government expressed the opinion that the fact of constructing an installation at sea did not "in itself" constitute a violation of the law of nations.

APPENDICES

APPENDICES

APPENDIX I

Radio (TV) Programme Regulations Of the Canadian Board Of Broadcast Governors*

Broadcasting Generally

5. (1) No station or network shall broadcast:
   (a) anything contrary to law;
   (b) any abusive comment or abusive pictorial representation on any race, religion or creed;
   (c) any obscene, indecent or profane language or pictorial presentation;
   (d) any false or misleading news;
   (e) any contest or program purporting to be a contest, the results of which are known in advance of, or are known to have been determined in advance of such contest or program;
   (f) any program on the subject of birth control, or venereal disease, unless that program is presented in a manner and at a time approved by a representative of the Board as appropriate to the medium of broadcasting;
   (g) any advertising content in the body of a news broadcast, and for the purpose of this section a summary is deemed to be a part of the body of the broadcast;
   (h) except with the consent in writing of a representative of the Board, any appeal for donations or subscriptions in money or kind on behalf of any person or organization other than

---

* An excerpt from the broadcasting regulations of the Board of Broadcast Governors pursuant to Section 11 of the Broadcasting Act. *CANADA GAZETTE* Part II, XCIII, No. 13 (July 8, 1959), 504. On March 7, 1968, Parliament replaced the Board with the Canadian Radio–Television Commission. At this writing, however, the BBG regulations are still in effect. See Appendix IX for selected provisions of the new law.

     (i) a church or religious body permanently established in Canada and serving the area covered by the station;

    (ii) a recognized charitable institution or organization,

    (iii) a university, or

    (iv) a musical or artistic organization whose principal aim or object is not that of monetary gain; or

   (i) any program involving a lottery, gift enterprise or similar scheme in which the contestant or competitor pays any sum of money in order to be eligible for a prize.

(2) No station shall extend its regular hours of broadcasting into or during the period from six o'clock in the forenoon until twelve o'clock noon, local time, without first submitting to the Board an outline of its proposed programming for the added period and satisfying the Board that it has facilities and resources to program effectively during the added period.

Canadian Content

6. (1) During any period of four weeks, not less than 55% of the broadcast time of any station or network shall be devoted to programs that are basically Canadian in content and character.

(2) For the purposes of subsection (1), the first four week period shall commence on the first Sunday following or including April 1st in any year, and subsequent four week periods shall be measured consecutively from the end of the first such period.

(3) Notwithstanding the provisions of this section, there shall be no specified minimum percentage of broadcast time of stations or networks devoted to programs that are basically Canadian in content and character prior to April 1st, 1961; and from April 1st, 1961 to March 31st, 1962 inclusive, the minimum percentage of broadcast so devoted shall be 45%.

(4) For the purposes of this section, "programs that are basically Canadian in content and character" shall, inter alia, include:

   (a) any program produced by a licensee

    (i) in his studio, or using his remote facilities, and

    (ii) to be broadcast initially by the licensee;

   (b) news broadcasts;

   (c) news commentaries;

   (d) broadcasts of events occurring outside Canada in which Canadians are participating;

   (e) broadcasts of programs featuring special events outside Canada and of general interest to Canadians;

   (f) subject to subsection (5), programs produced outside Canada,

        (i) in Commonwealth countries, or

        (ii) in French language countries, and

    (g) programs of films or other reproductions which have been made in Canada if

        (1) the producing company is incorporated under the laws of Canada or any Province and has a majority of Canadian Directors;

        (2) an application has been submitted to the Board presenting evidence of Canadian and non Canadian content in a form prescribed by the Board; and

        (3) the Board, after consideration of the balance of elements going into the production has approved a Canadian content classification.

(5) For the purposes of this section, in computing the portion of Canadian content of the broadcast time of any station or network, there may be included,

    (a) programs produced outside Canada in Commonwealth countries, to the extent of one-half of the program time of such programs, but the total program time used for this purpose shall not exceed ⅓ of the broadcast time of a station or network;

    (b) programs produced outside Canada in French language countries, to the extent of one-half of the program time of such programs, but the total program time used for this purpose shall not exceed ¼ of the broadcast time of the station or network;

(6) Where, in the opinion of the Board the objects and purposes of the Act would be more fully realized by requiring a licensee to make facilities available at certain hours for programming by other parties, the Board, after hearing representations from the licensee at a public hearing, may require the licensee to enter into program contracts with other parties subject to such fair and equitable conditions as may be prescribed by the Board.

Political Broadcasts

7. (1) Each station shall allocate time for the broadcasting of programs, advertisements or announcements of a partisan political character on an equitable basis to all parties and rival candidates.

    (2) Political programs, advertisements or announcements shall be broadcast by stations in accordance with the directions of the Board issued from time to time respecting:

    (a) the proportion of time which may be devoted to the broadcasting of programs, advertisements or announcements of a partisan political character, and

(b) the assignment of time to all political parties and rival candidates.

Advertising Content

8. (1) No station shall broadcast any program of the length set out in column (1) the advertising content of which exceeds the time set out in column (2).

(1) *Length of Program* (MINUTES)	(2) *Length of Advertising Message* (MINUTES AND SECONDS)
5	1:15
10	2:10
15	3:00
20	3:30
25	4:00
30	4:15
40	5:00
45	5:45
60	7:00

(2) No station shall broadcast paid spot or flash advertisements that exceed five in number of four minutes in total time during any fifteen minute period, except that a station may average the above quotas over any one clock-hour period.

(3) Subsection (2) does not apply to a station during the period of a major emergency within the area served by the station.

Advertising Generally

9. (1) No station shall broadcast any program or any spot or flash announcement sponsored by any person for the purpose of promoting

(a) any act or thing prohibited by the law of Canada or of the Province in which the station is located;

(b) any insurance corporation not authorized by law to carry on business in Canada;

(c) the sale of bonds, shares or other securities, except securities of the Government of Canada or of any Province, Municipality or other public authority; or

(d) the sale of mining, oil or natural gas property or any interest in any mining, oil or natural gas property.

(2) Subsection (1) does not apply to the broadcasting of a sponsored program of general quotations of market prices, presented without comment.

(3) The Board may by notice in writing to any station, require that station to modify the character of any advertisement broadcast by the station, where, in the opinion of a representative of the Board, the advertisement is of an offensive or objectionable nature.

Spirituous Liquors, Beer and Wine

10. (1) Subject to subsection (2) no station shall broadcast any program or spot or flash announcement,

(a) advertising directly or indirectly, any Spirituous Liquor or any Beer, or Wine; or

(b) sponsored by or on behalf of any person or persons whose principal business is the manufacture or sale of Spirituous Liquor, Beer or Wine.

(2) Where in any province, the advertising of Beer and Wine is permitted, a program of not less than ten minutes duration sponsored by a brewery or winery may be broadcast, subject to the following conditions:

(a) the program shall contain no advertising other than sponsorship announcements;

(b) sponsorship announcements may be made only at the beginning and end of the program, but where the program is a program of more than ten minutes duration the name of the sponsor may be introduced at intervals of not less than fifteen minutes in program announcements;

(c) the form of sponsorship announcements shall be in accordance with the following examples.

"This program is presented with the compliments of the ABC Brewery." or

"This program has been presented with the compliments of the ABC Brewery."

(d) no other announcements shall be made or devices used in any such program to advertise directly or indirectly the product of the sponsor; and

(e) the program format, the form of the sponsorship announcements, and the continuity to be used must be approved in advance of the broadcast by a representative of the Board.

Food and Drugs; Proprietary or Patent Medicines

11. (1) No station shall broadcast any advertisement or testimonial for any article to which the Proprietary or Patent Medicine Act or the Food and Drugs Act applies unless the continuity of the advertisement or testimonial has been approved by the Department of National Health and Welfare and by a representative of the Board and bears the registration number assigned by the Board.

(2) No station shall broadcast any recommendation for the prevention, treatment or cure of a disease or ailment unless the continuity thereof has been approved by the Department of National Health and Welfare and by a representative of the Board and bears the registration number assigned by the Board.

(3) Continuities submitted for approval pursuant to this Regulation shall be forwarded to the Board in triplicate at least, two weeks in advance of intended use.

(4) Inspectors of the Food and Drugs Division, Department of National Health and Welfare, are authorized to act as representatives of the Board for the purposes of the enforcement of this section.

Programs of the Corporation

12. (1) Time to be reserved by a private station for broadcast of programs of the Corporation is such as may be agreed on between the station and the Corporation, or, failing agreement, by decision of the Board.

(2) Any time reserved for broadcast of programs of the Corporation shall, except with consent of a representative of the Corporation or, failing agreement, a representative of the Board, be used exclusively for programs of the Corporation.

(3) Stations may be required to broadcast network programs of public interest or significance as determined by the Board.

Rebroadcasting

13. Except with the consent in writing of a representative of the Board, no station shall pick up and rebroadcast any program or portion thereof.

Chain Broadcasting

14. (1) Except with the consent of a representative of the Board or in accordance with the license of the station, no station shall operate as a part of a network inside or outside Canada, but this section shall not be construed so as to preclude a station without reference to the Board from entering into agreements from time to time to carry reproductions of particular programs or series of programs produced by networks or stations operating inside or outside Canada.

(2) Except with the consent of the Board or in accordance with the license of the station, no station or network shall enter into an affiliation with any network or station operating outside or inside Canada but provided a minimum of Canadian content as required by these regulations in its programming is being maintained by a station or network, this subsection shall not be construed so as to preclude a station or network without reference to the Board, from entering into agreements from time to time to carry reproductions of particular programs or series of programs produced by networks or stations outside or inside Canada.

(3) Except with the consent of a representative of the Board, no station shall broadcast a reproduction of a program originating from a network outside of Canada and which has been carried by a network in Canada, during a period of one month after the original broadcast on the Canadian network.

(4) The Board may amend or revoke its approval of a network affiliation of any station given under Section 13 of the Act if, in the opinion of a representative of the Board a broadcasting service which is basically Canadian in content and character is not being maintained.

The British Independent Television Code of Advertising Standards and Practice

1. *Preamble*

The general principle which will govern all television advertising is that it should be legal, clean, honest and truthful. It is recognized that this principle is not peculiar to the television medium, but is one which applies to all reputable advertising in other media in this country. Nevertheless, television, because of its greater intimacy within the home, gives rise to problems which do not necessarily occur in other media and it is essential to maintain a consistently high quality of television advertising.

2. Advertisements must comply in every respect with the law, common or statute. In the case of some Acts, notably the Merchandise Marks Acts, rules applicable to other forms of advertising may not, on a strict interpretation of the Acts, cover television advertising. Advertisements must, however, comply in all respects with the spirit of those Acts.

3. The detailed rules set out below are intended to be applied in the spirit as well as the letter and should be taken as laying down the minimum standards to be observed.

4. The word 'advertisement' has the meaning implicit in the Television Act, i.e. any item of publicity inserted in the programmes broadcast by the Authority in consideration of payment to a programme contractor or to the Authority.

5. *Programme Independence*

No advertisement may include anything that states, suggests or implies, or could reasonably be taken to state, suggest or imply, that any part of any programme broadcast by the Authority has been supplied or suggested by any advertiser—Television Act, 1964, Section 7(6).

6. *Identification of Advertisements*

An advertisement must be clearly distinguishable as such and recognizably separate from the programmes—Television Act, 1964, Schedule 2, paragraph 1(1).

7. *'Subliminal' Advertising*

No advertisement may include any technical device which, by using imagines of very brief duration or by any other means, exploits the possibility of conveying a message to, or otherwise influencing the minds of, members of an audience without their being aware, or fully aware, of what has been done—Television Act, 1964, Section 3(3).

8. *Good Taste*

No advertisement should offend against good taste or decency or be offensive to public feeling—Television Act, 1964, Section 3(1)(a).

9. *Gifts or Prizes*

No advertisement may include an offer of any prize or gift of significant value, being a prize or gift which is available only to television viewers of the advertisement or in relation to which any advantage is given to viewers—Television Act, 1964, Section 3(4).

10. *Stridency*

Audible matter in advertisements must not be excessively noisy or strident—Television Act, 1964, Schedule 2, paragraph 1(4).

11. *Charities*

No advertisement may give publicity to the needs or objects of any association or organization conducted for charitable or benevolent purposes. (This does not preclude the advertising of 'flag days', fêtes or other events organized by charitable organizations or the advertising of publications of general interest.)

12. *Religion and Politics*

No advertisements may be inserted by or on behalf of any body, the objects whereof are wholly or mainly of a religious or political nature, and advertisements must not be directed towards any religious or political end or have any relation to any industrial dispute—Television Act, 1964, Schedule 2, paragraph 8.

13. *Appeals to Fear*

Advertisements must not without justifiable reason play on fear.

14. *Unacceptable Products or Services*

Advertisements for products or services coming within the recognized character of, or specifically concerned with, the following are not acceptable:

(a) money-lenders
(b) matrimonial agencies and correspondence clubs
(c) fortune-tellers and the like
(d) undertakers or others associated with death or burial
(e) unlicensed employment services, registers or bureaux
(f) organizations/companies/persons seeking to advertise for the purpose of giving betting tips
(g) betting (including pools)

(h) cigarettes and cigarette tobacco.

N.B. An advertiser who markets more than one product may not use advertising copy devoted to an acceptable product for purposes of publicizing the brand name or other identification of an unacceptable product.

15. *Reproduction Techniques*

It is accepted that the technical limitations of photography can lead to difficulties in securing a faithful portrayal of a subject, and that the use of special techniques or substitute materials may be necessary to overcome these difficulties. These techniques must not be abused: no advertisement in which they have been used will be acceptable, unless the resultant picture presents a fair and reasonable impression of the product or its effects and is not such as to mislead. Unacceptable devices include, for example, the use of glass or plastic sheeting to simulate the effects of floor or furniture polishes.

16. *Descriptions and Claims*

No advertisement may contain any descriptions, claims or illustrations which directly or by implication mislead about the product or service advertised or about its suitability for the purpose recommended. In particular:

    (a) *Special Claims*—No advertisement shall contain any reference which is likely to lead the public to assume that the product advertised, or an ingredient, has some special property or quality which is incapable of being established.

    (b) *Scientific Terms and Statistics*—Scientific terms, statistics, quotations from technical literature and the like must be used with a proper sense of responsibility to the ordinary viewer. Irrelevant data and scientific jargon must not be used to make claims appear to have a scientific basis they do not possess. Statistics of limited validity should not be presented in such a way as to make it appear that they are universally true.

Advertisers and their agencies must be prepared to produce evidence to substantiate any descriptions, claims or illustrations.

17. *Comparative Advertising and Disparagement*

Substantiated competitive claims inviting fair comparison with a group of products or with other products in the same field may be acceptable. Such claims may not be presented in a way which by distortion or undue emphasis, is likely to mislead. Advertisements may not contain disparaging references to another product or service.

18. *Imitation*

Any imitation likely to mislead viewers, even though it is not of such a kind as to give rise to a legal action for infringement of copyright or for 'passing off', must be avoided.

19. *Price Claims*

Visual and verbal presentations of actual and comparative prices and cost must be accurate and incapable of misleading by undue emphasis or distortion.

20. *Testimonials*

Testimonials must be genuine and must not be used in a manner likely to mislead. Advertisers and their agencies must be prepared to produce evidence in support of any testimonial and any claims therein.

21. *Guarantees*

The word 'guarantee' should be used with caution and sparingly and only in relation to some specific description or quality and the detailed terms of any such guarantee must be available for inspection by the Authority. Where the guarantee is associated with an offer to return the purchase price, it must be made quite clear to what it applies and in what way it protects the purchaser.

22. *Competitions*

Advertisements inviting the public to take part in competitions where allowable under Section 3(4) of the Television Act, 1964, and the Betting, Gaming and Lotteries Act, 1963 (which requires the presence of an element of skill), should state clearly how prospective entrants may obtain the printed conditions including the arrangement for the announcement of results and for the distribution of prizes.

23. *Homework Schemes*

Fullest particulars of any schemes must be supplied and where it is proposed to make a charge for the raw materials or components and where the advertiser offers to buy back the goods made by the home-worker, the advertisement is not acceptable.

24. *Hire-Purchase*

Advertisements relating to the sale of goods on hire-purchase or credit sale must comply with the provisions of the Advertisements (Hire-Purchase) Act, 1957, and from 1st January 1965, Part IV of the Hire-Purchase Act, 1964.

25. *Instructional Courses*

Advertisements offering courses of instruction in trades or subjects leading up to professional or technical examinations must not imply the promise of employment or exaggerate the opportunity of employment or remuneration alleged to be open to those taking such courses; neither should they offer unrecognized 'degrees' or qualifications.

26. *Mail Order Advertising*

Advertisements for the sale of goods by mail order are unacceptable unless adequate stocks of the goods in question are carried and they correspond with the description given in the advertisement. Such advertisements are unacceptable where an accommodation address is given. All advertisements should make it clear that the customer is entitled to return the goods within seven days if not satisfied and to obtain full refund of the purchase price.

27. *Direct Sale Advertising*

Direct sale advertising is that placed by the advertiser with the intention that the articles or services advertised, or some other articles or services, shall be sold or provided at the home of the person responding to the advertisement. Where it is the intention of the advertiser to send a representative to call on persons responding to the advertisement, such fact must be apparent from the advertisement or from the particulars subsequently supplied and the respondent must be given an adequate opportunity of refusing any call.

Direct sale advertisements are not acceptable without adequate assurances from the advertiser and his advertising agency (a) that the articles advertised will be supplied at the price stated in the advertisement within a reasonable time from stocks sufficient to meet potential demand and (b) that sales representatives when calling upon persons responding to the advertisement will demonstrate and make available for sale, the articles advertised.

It will be taken as prima facie evidence of misleading and unacceptable 'bait' advertising for the purpose of 'switch selling' if an advertiser's salesmen seriously disparage or belittle the cheaper article advertised or report unreasonable delays in obtaining delivery or otherwise put difficulties in the way of its purchase.

28. *Financial Advertising*

In view of the importance of giving full information in connection with any offer to the public of debentures, bonds and shares and in view of the difficulty of ensuring that such information is given in the limited time of the normal television advertisement, invitations to invest are limited to the following:

(a) invitations to invest in British Government stocks (including National Savings Certificates), stocks of public boards and nationalized industries in the United Kingdom and Local Government stocks in the United Kingdom.

(b) invitations to place money on deposit or share account with building societies.

(c) invitations to place money on deposit with the Post Office or any Trustee Savings Bank, and, normally, banking companies which are recognized as such for the purposes of the Eighth Schedule to the Companies Act, 1948.

Advertisements by Unit Trusts authorized as such by the Board of Trade may be accepted provided that these are strictly limited to the name and description of the Trust, the address of its manager, and an invitation to viewers to write to the manager for full particulars of the units available. No person may be shown on the screen during the course of the advertisement.

Advertisements announcing the publication in established national and provincial newspapers and journals of prospectuses offering shares or debentures to the public may be accepted provided that these are strictly limited to giving the name of the company whose shares or debentures are being offered, the amount of the offer and the names and dates of publication of the newspapers and journals in which a prospectus may be found. No person may be shown on the screen during the course of advertisement.

No advertisement is acceptable which contains any review of or advice about the stock market or investment prospects, or which offers to advise on investments.

29. *Advertising and Children*

Particular care should be taken over advertising that is likely to be seen by large numbers of children and advertisements in which children are to be employed. More detailed guidance is given in Appendix 1.

30. *Advertising of Medicines and Treatments*

Within the generality of the Independent Television Code the advertising of medicines and treatments is subject to the detailed rules given in Appendix 2.

APPENDIX 1. *Advertising and Children*

1. *The Viewing Child*

No product or service may be advertised and no method of advertising may be used, in association with a programme intended for children or which large numbers of children are likely to see, which might result in harm to them physically, mentally or morally, and no method of advertising may be employed which takes advantage of the natural credulity and sense of loyalty of children.

In particular:

(a) No advertisement which encourages children to enter strange places or to converse with strangers in an effort to collect coupons, wrappers, labels, etc., is allowed. The details of any collecting scheme must be submitted for investigation to ensure that the scheme contains no element of danger to children.

(b) No advertisement for a commercial product or service is allowed if it contains any appeal to children which suggests in any way that unless the children themselves buy or encourage other people to buy the product or service they will be failing in some duty or lacking in loyalty towards some person or organization whether that person or organization is the one making the appeal or not.

(c) No advertisement is allowed which leads children to believe that if they do not own the product advertised they will be inferior in some way to other children or that they are liable to be held in contempt or ridicule for not owning it.

(d) No advertisement dealing with the activities of a club is allowed without the submission of satisfactory evidence that the club is carefully supervised in the matter of the behaviour of the children and the company they keep and that there is no suggestion of the club being a secret society.

(e) While it is recognized the children are not the direct purchasers of many products over which they are naturally allowed to exercise preference, care should be taken that they are not encouraged to make themselves a nuisance to other people in the interests of any particular product or service. In an advertisement for children, the main emphasis of the advertisement must be on the product with which the offer is associated.

(f) If there is to be a reference to a competition for children in an advertisement, the published rules must be submitted for approval before the advertisement can be accepted. The value of prizes and the chances of winning one must not be exaggerated.

(g) To help in the fair portrayal of free gifts for children, an advertisement should, where necessary, make it easy to see the true size of a gift by showing it in relation to some common object against which its scale can be judged.

2. *The Child in Advertisements*

The appearance of children in advertisements is subject to the following conditions:

(a) *Employment*

It should be noted that the conditions under which children are employed in the making of advertisements are governed by certain provisions of the Children and Young Persons Act 1933 (Scotland 1937) and the Act of 1963; the Education Acts 1944 to 1948; and the appropriate by-laws made by Local Authorities in pursuance of these Acts.

(b) *Contributions to Safety*

Any situations in which children are to be seen in television advertisements should be carefully considered from the point of view of safety.

In particular:

(i) children should not appear to be unattended in street scenes unless they are obviously old enough to be responsible for their own safety; should not be shown playing in the road, unless it is clearly shown to be a play-street or other safe area; should not be shown stepping carelessly off the pavement or crossing the road without due care; in busy street scenes should be seen to use zebra crossings in crossing the road; and should be otherwise seen in general, as pedestrians or cyclists, to behave in accordance with the Highway Code.

(ii) children should not be seen leaning dangerously out of windows or over bridges, or climbing dangerous cliffs.

(iii) small children should not be shown climbing up to high shelves or reaching up to take things from a table above their heads.

(iv) medicines, disinfectants, antiseptics and caustic substances must not be shown within reach of children without close parental supervision, nor should children be shown using these products in any way.

(v) children must not be shown using matches or any gas, paraffin, petrol, mechanical or mains-powered appliance which could lead to their suffering burns, electrical shock or other injury.

(vi) children must not be shown driving or riding on agricultural machines (including tractor-drawn carts or implements). Scenes of this kind could encourage contravention of the Agriculture (Safety, Health and Welfare Provisions) Act, 1956.

(vii) an open fire in a domestic scene in an advertisement must always have a fireguard clearly visible if a child is included in the scene.

(c) *Good Manners and Behaviour*

Children seen in advertisements should be reasonably well-mannered and well-behaved.

APPENDIX 2. *The Advertising of Medicines and Treatments*

(a) *Introductory*

1. The rules contained in this Appendix have been adopted by the Independent Television Authority after due consultation under the terms of the Television Act with the Advertising Advisory Committee and the Medical Advisory Panel and with the Postmaster-General in so far as he is concerned with the classes and descriptions of advertisements which must not be broadcast and the methods of advertising which must not be employed.

2. *The British Code of Advertising Practice*

Within the generality of the Independent Television Code of Advertising Standards and Practice and subject to the additional rules below, the Authority's basic requirements in regard to the advertising of medicines and treatments are those laid down in Part II of the British Code of Advertising Practice which is reproduced as part (b) of this Appendix. The preamble to that Code states:

> The harm to the individual that may result from exaggerated, misleading or unwarranted claims justifies the adoption of a very high standard and the inclusion of considerable detail in a Code designed to guide those who are concerned with this form of advertising.

3. *Unacceptable Products or Services*

Advertisements for products or services coming within the recognized character of, or specifically concerned with, the following are not acceptable:

(a) products or treatments for bust development or, except as permitted by the British Code of Advertising Practice, for slimming, weight reduction or limitation, or figure control

(b) contraceptives

(c) smoking cures

(d) products for the treatment of alcoholism

(e) contact or corneal lenses

(f) clinics for the treatment of hair and scalp

(g) products for the treatment of haemorrhoids.

N.B. An advertiser who markets more than one product may not use advertising copy devoted to an acceptable product for the purposes of publicizing the brand name or other identification of an unacceptable product.

4. *Avoidance of Impression of Professional Advice*

In advertisements for medicine, treatments and products which are claimed to promote health or be beneficial in illness, the following are not allowable:

(a) visual presentations of doctors, dentists, pharmaceutical chemists, nurses, midwives, etc., which give the impression of professional advice or recommendation, and

(b) statements giving the impression of professional advice or recommendation made by persons who appear in the advertisements and who are presented, either directly or by implication, as being qualified to give such advice or recommendation.

To avoid misunderstanding about the status of the presenter of a medicine or treatment, it may be necessary to establish positively in the course of an advertisement that the presenter is not a professionally qualified adviser.

5. *Hospital Tests*

No reference may be made to a hospital test unless the Medical Committee of the hospital concerned is prepared to vouch for its validity.

6. *Testimonials*

No advertisement for a medicine or treatment may include a testimonial by a person well known in public life, sport, entertainment, etc.

7. *Tonic*

The use of this expression is not acceptable in advertisement for medicines or treatments or products for which medical or health claims are made.

8. *Vitamins*

No advertisement should state or imply that good health is likely to be endangered solely because people do not supplement their diets with vitamins.

(b) *The British Code of Advertising Practice—Part B*

This part of the Code deals with the Advertising of Medicines and Treatments and it is important that this should be regarded as setting forth the minimum standards to be observed by the parties concerned. The harm to the individual that may result from exaggerated, misleading or unwarranted claims justifies the adoption of a very high standard and the inclusion of considerable detail in a Code designed to guide those who are concerned with this form of advertising. All advertising media are urged not to accept advertisements in respect of any product or treatment from any advertising agency or advertiser who disregards the provisions of this part of the Code in any form of advertising or publicity relating to that product or treatment.

The advance of medical science may influence the view to be taken of the efficacy of medicines, products, appliances or treatments and, therefore, this part of the Code will be subject to periodic review.

The provisions of this part of the Code do not apply to an advertisement published by or under the authority of a Government Ministry or Department, nor to an advertisement published only in so far as is reasonably necessary to bring it to the notice of registered medical or dental practitioners, registered pharmacists or registered nurses.

SECTION I:
GENERAL PRINCIPLES

Advertisements should not contain any of the following:

1. *Cure*

A claim to cure any ailment or symptoms of ill health, nor should an advertisement contain a word or expression used in such a form or context as to mean in the positive sense the extirpation of any ailment, illness or disease.

2. *Illnesses, etc., Properly Requiring Medical Attention*

Any matter which can be regarded as an offer of a medicine or product for, or advice relating to the treatment of, serious diseases, complaints, conditions, indications or symptoms which should rightly receive the attention of a registered medical practitioner.

3. *Misleading or Exaggerated Claims*

Any matter which directly or by implication misleads or departs from the truth as to the composition, character or action of the medicine or treatment advertised or as to its suitability for the purpose for which it is recommended.

4. *Appeals to Fear*

Any statement or illustration calculated to induce fear on the part of the reader that he is suffering, or may without treatment suffer, or suffer more severely, from an ailment, illness or disease.

5. *Competitions*

An offer of any prize competitions or similar schemes. It should be noted that such an advertisement may constitute an offence under Section 47 of the Betting, Gaming and Lotteries Act, 1963.

6. *Diagnosis or Treatment by Correspondence*

An offer to diagnose by correspondence diseases, conditions or any symptoms of ill health in a human being or a request from any person for a statement of his or any other person's symptoms of ill health with a view to advising as to or providing for treatment of such conditions of ill health by correspondence or an offer to treat by correspondence any ailment, illness, disease, or symptoms thereof in a human being.

7. *Disparaging References*

Any direct or implied disparagement of the products, medicines or treatments of another advertiser or manufacturer or registered medical practitioners or the medical profession.

8. *Money-back Offers*

Offers to refund money to dissatisfied users.

9. *College, Clinic, Institute, Laboratory*

The words 'College', 'Clinic', 'Institute', 'Laboratory', or similar terms unless an establishment corresponding to the description used does in fact exist.

10. *Doctors, Hospitals, etc.*

Any reference to doctors, hospitals, or hospital tests, whether British or foreign, unless such reference can be substantiated by independent evidence and can properly be used in the manner proposed; or the name of a product containing the term 'Doctor' or 'Dr' unless the product were so named prior to 1st January, 1944.

11. *Products Offered Particularly to Women*

Offers of products, medicines or treatments for disorders or irregularities peculiar to women, which contain the following or similar expressions which may imply that the product, medicine or treatment advertised can be effective in inducing miscarriage: 'Female Pills', 'Not to be used in cases of pregnancy', 'The stronger the remedy the more effective it is', 'Never known to fail'.

12. *Illustrations*

Any illustration which by itself or in combination with words used in connection therewith is likely to convey a misleading impression, or any reasonable inference which can be drawn infringing the provisions of this Code.

13. *Exaggerated Copy*

Copy which is exaggerated by reason of the improper use of words, phrases or methods of presentation, e.g. the use of the words 'magic', 'magical', 'miracle', 'miraculous'.

14. *'Natural' Remedies*

A claim or suggestion, contrary to the fact, that the article advertised is in the form in which it occurs in nature or that its value lies in its being a 'natural' product.

15. *Special Claims*

Any reference which is calculated to lead the public to assume that the article, product, medicine or treatment advertised, or an ingredient has some special property or quality which is in fact unknown or unrecognized.

16. *Sexual Weakness, Premature Ageing, Loss of Virility*

A claim that the product, medicine or treatment advertised will promote sexual virility or be effective in treating sexual weakness, or habits associated with sexual excess or indulgence, or any ailment, illness or disease associated with those habits.

In particular, such terms as 'premature ageing', 'loss of virility' will be regarded as conditions for which medicines, products, appliances or treatment may not be advertised.

17. *Slimming, Weight Reduction or Limitation, or Figure Control*
An offer of any product or treatment for slimming, weight reduction or limitation or figure control, if the taking or using of the product or following the course of treatment is likely to lead to harmful effects.

18. *Tonic*
The expression 'tonic' if it implies that the product or medicine can be used in the treatment of sexual weakness.

19. *Testimonials*
Any testimonial containing a statement or implication which would not be permitted in the text of the advertisement, or any testimonial other than one limited to the actual views of the writer, or any testimonial given by a doctor other than a registered British medical practitioner unless it is obvious in the advertisement that the writer is not a registered British medical practitioner.

20. *Hypnosis*
Any offer to diagnose or treat complaints or conditions by hypnosis.

21. *Hair and Scalp Products and Treatments*
(a) Any offer of diagnosis by post or telephone or any claim or implication that the product or treatment advertised will do more than arrest loss of hair.
(2) Any particulars of establishments administering treatments for the hair and scalp other than the name, address, telephone number and hours of attendance and the types of treatment available; any reference to specific conditions for which the treatment is intended.

22. *Haemorrhoids*
Any offer of products for the treatment of haemorrhoids unless the following warning notice appears with the directions for use on the container itself or its labels. 'Persons who suffer from haemorrhoids are advised to consult a doctor'.

23. *Products Offered for the Relief of Backache and Rheumatic Pains*
Claims for the relief of backache and rheumatic pains based upon the urinary antiseptic properties of the products advertised.

SECTION II:
RESTRICTIONS IMPOSED BY STATUTE

1. *Cancer*
The Cancer Act, 1939, makes it an offence to take part in the publication of any advertisement which contains an offer to treat any person for cancer, to prescribe any remedy therefor, or to give any advice calculated to lead to its use in the treatment of cancer.

2. *Abortion*
The Pharmacy and Medicines Act, 1941, makes it an offence to take part in

the publication of any advertisement referring to any article in terms which are calculated to lead to the use of the article for procuring the miscarriage of women.

3. *Bright's Disease, Cataract, Diabetes, Epilepsy, Fits, Glaucoma, Locomotor Ataxy, Paralysis, Tuberculosis*

The Pharmacy and Medicines Act, 1941, makes it an offence to take part in the publication of an advertisement referring to any article in terms which are calculated to lead to the use of that article for the purpose of the treatment of these diseases.

(Note: Bright's Disease is sometimes referred to as 'Nephritis', Epilepsy as 'Falling Sickness', and Tuberculosis as 'Phthisis', 'Consumption' or 'Wasting Disease'.)

4. *Venereal Diseases*

The Venereal Diseases Act, 1917, makes it an offence to advertise in any way any preparation or substance of any kind as a medicine for the prevention, cure or relief of venereal diseases.

The above prohibitions do not apply in the case of technical journals which circulate among persons of the classes mentioned in the respective Acts. It is permissible, for example, for advertisements to appear in technical journals intended for circulation mainly among registered medical practitioners, registered pharmacists and nurses (except in the case of (4) above, where no provision is made in the Venereal Diseases Act, for advertising in journals circulating among nurses).

The foregoing is a very broad outline of the effects of the relevant sections of the respective Acts. For further and more detailed information, reference should be made to the Acts.

APPENDIX III

Charter of the BBC

Incorporation

1. The Corporation shall continue to be a body corporate by the name of The British Broadcasting Corporation with perpetual succession and a common seal with power to break, alter and renew the same at discretion: willing and ordaining that the Corporation shall and may sue and be sued in all Courts and be capable in law to take and hold real and personal property and do all matters and things incidental or pertaining to a body corporate, but so that the Corporation shall apply the whole of its income solely in promoting its objects. The Governors of the Corporation shall be the members thereof.

Term of Charter

2. This Charter shall come into operation on the thirtieth day of July One thousand nine hundred and sixty-four and (subject as herein provided) shall continue in force until the thirty-first day of July One thousand nine hundred and seventy-six.

Objects of the Corporation

3. The objects of the Corporation are as follows:
   (a) To provide, as public services, broadcasting services of wireless telegraphy by the method of telephony for general reception in sound, and by the methods of television and telephony in combination for general reception in visual images with sound, in Our United Kingdom of Great Britain and Northern Ireland, the Channel Islands and the Isle of Man and the territorial waters thereof, and on board ships and aircraft (such services being hereafter referred to together as 'the Home Services' and separately as 'the Home Sound Services' and 'the Television Services'), and elsewhere within the British Commonwealth of Nations and in other countries and places overseas (such services being hereinafter referred to as 'the External Services').
   (b) To hold the existing and to construct or acquire and establish and

instal additional stations for wireless telegraphy and apparatus for wireless telegraphy in Our United Kingdom, the Channel Islands and the Isle of Man, and to use the same for the emission and reception of wireless telegraphy by the methods and for the purposes aforesaid, and by any methods for purposes ancillary or related to those purposes.

(c) To hold the existing and to construct or acquire additional equipment and apparatus for line telegraphy in Our United Kingdom, the Channel Islands and the Isle of Man, and to use the same for purposes ancillary or related to the purposes aforesaid.

(d) For all the purposes aforesaid to acquire from time to time from Our Postmaster General a Licence or Licences for such period and subject to such terms, provisions and limitations as he may prescribe, and to exercise the powers herein granted to the Corporation in conformity in all respect therewith and with any agreement or agreements which may from time to time be made by Our Postmaster General with the Corporation, and not in any other manner whatsoever.

(e) To develop, extend and improve the Home Services and the External Services and to those ends to exercise such Licence or Licences in such manner or by such means and methods as may from time to time be agreed by the Corporation and Our Postmaster General, and to concur in any extension, adaptation or modification of the terms, provisions or limitations of any such Licence or Licences as may to Our Postmaster General seem fit.

(f) To hold all other existing property of the Corporation and to acquire additional property, whether such properties be within or without Our United Kingdom, the Channel Islands and the Isle of Man, and to equip and use such properties for carrying out any of the objects of the Corporation.

(g) Subject to the prior consent in writing from time to time of Our Postmaster General and to the acquisition (subject as hereinafter provided) of any requisite licences, concessions, rights or privileges, to construct or acquire and establish, instal, equip and use stations for wireless telegraphy and apparatus for wireless telegraphy in countries or places without Our United Kingdom, the Channel Islands and the Isle of Man, for the purpose of providing, within the scope or ambit of any such consent for the time being in force, and as may be permitted thereby or thereunder, broadcasting services by such method or methods of wireless telegraphy as may in such consent be specified, for reception in such countries or places as may in or under such consent be designated: and for the purpose of receiving wireless telegraphy conveying such matter by such methods for such purposes as may by or under such consent be permitted.

(h) To perform services in any part of the world for and on behalf of any Department of the Government of Our United Kingdom, and in particular to provide, erect, equip and instal, or supervise the provision, erection, equipment and installation of, stations, studios, apparatus, machinery, plant and other equipment for broadcasting and receiving matter by wireless telegraphy by the methods of telephony and television, and to work or manage, or to supervise the working or management of such stations, studios, apparatus, machinery, plant and equipment.

(i) To provide to other bodies by such means and methods as may be convenient matter to be broadcast by the methods of telephony or television, by the wireless telegraphy stations of such bodies, and to receive from other bodies by such means and methods as aforesaid matter to be broadcast by stations of the Corporation.

(j) To compile and prepare, print, publish, issue, circulate and distribute, with or without charge, such papers, magazines, periodicals, books, circulars and other matter as may be conducive to any of the objects of the Corporation.

(k) To organize, provide or subsidize concerts and other entertainments in connection with the broadcasting services of the Corporation or for any purpose incidental thereto.

(l) To collect news and information in any part of the world and in any manner that may be thought fit and to establish and subscribe to news agencies.

(m) For the purposes of the broadcasting services of the Corporation or for any purposes incidental thereto, to produce, manufacture, purchase, acquire, use, sell, rent or dispose of films and records (including tapes and any other devices from which visual images or sounds may be reproduced) and material and apparatus for use in connection with such films and records: Provided that nothing herein contained shall be deemed to authorize the Corporation to display films or play records for the entertainment of the public except as aforesaid.

(n) To apply for and obtain, purchase or otherwise acquire and turn to account in any manner that may be thought fit any Letters Patent or patent rights or any interest in any Letters Patent or patent rights, brevets d'invention, licences, concessions, and the like conferring any right, whether exclusive, non-exclusive or limited, to use any secret or other information as to any invention in relation to any device or machine serving or calculated to serve any useful purpose in connection with any of the objects of the Corporation.

(o) Subject as hereinafter provided, to enter into any arrangement with any Governments or authorities, supreme, municipal, local or otherwise, which may seem conducive to the Corporation's objects or any of them, and to obtain from any such Government or authority any licences, rights, privileges and concessions which the Corporation may think it desirable to obtain, and to carry out, exercise and comply with any such arrangements, licences, rights, privileges and concessions.

(p) To establish and support or aid in the establishment or support of associations, institutions, funds, trusts and amenities calculated to benefit employees or former employees of the Corporation or the dependants or connections of such persons, and to grant pensions and allowances, to make payments toward insurances and to subscribe or guarantee money for charitable or benevolent objects or for any exhibition or for any public, general or useful object.

(q) To purchase, take on lease or in exchange, hire or otherwise acquire any real and personal property and any interests, rights or privileges which the Corporation may think necessary or convenient for the purposes of its business or the furtherance of its objects, and in particular any land, buildings, easements, apparatus, machinery, plant and stock-in-trade.

(r) Subject to the approval of Our Postmaster General, to purchase or otherwise acquire stocks, shares or securities of any company whose objects include any of those hereinbefore mentioned or of any company whose business is capable of being carried on in such a way as to facilitate or advance any of the objects of the Corporation, and to subsidise and assist any such company.

(s) Subject as hereinafter provided, to invest and deal with the moneys of the Corporation not immediately required in such manner as the Corporation may from time to time determine.

(t) Subject as hereinafter provided, to borrow or raise or secure the payment of money in such manner as the Corporation shall think fit, and in particular by mortgage or charge of all or any parts of the property or rights of the Corporation or by the issue of debentures or debenture stock, charged upon all or any of the Corporation's property or rights (both present and future), and to purchase, redeem or pay off any such securities: Provided always that the Corporation shall not borrow or raise or secure the payment of money upon any property, interests or rights now held by the Corporation which Our Postmaster General has decided in consultation with the Corporation that the Corporation is to use exclusively for any purpose of the External Services or upon any property, interests or rights which the Corporation has acquired or may hereafter acquire out of moneys paid to the Corporation out of aids or supplies appropriated by Parliament for any such purpose: Provided also that the aggregate amount of the moneys so borrowed, raised and secured for the purpose of obtaining temporary banking accommodation or facilities and at any one time outstanding shall not exceed £10,000,000 and that the aggregate amount of the moneys so borrowed, raised and secured for the purpose of defraying capital expenditure (including moneys so borrowed or raised for the repayment or replacement of moneys borrowed or raised for that purpose) and at any one time outstanding shall not exceed such sum up to the maximum of £20,000,000 as may from time to time be approved by Our Postmaster General.

(u) To sell, improve, manage, develop, exchange, lease, mortgage, enfranchise, dispose of, turn to account or otherwise deal with all or any part of the property, interests or rights of the Corporation: Provided always that the Corporation shall not, without the prior consent in writing of Our Postmaster General, sell, exchange, lease, mortgage, enfranchise or dispose of any property, interests or rights now held by the Corporation which Our Postmaster General has decided in consultation with the Corporation that the Corporation is to use exclusively for any purpose of the External Services or any property, interests or rights which the Corporation has acquired or may hereafter acquire out of moneys paid to the Corporation out of aids or supplies appropriated by Parliament for any such purpose, and shall not without such prior consent turn to account or deal with any such property, interests or rights otherwise than for the purposes of the External Services.

(v) To enter into, make and perform contracts of guarantee and indemnity of whatsoever kind which may be necessary or convenient for carrying out the objects of the Corporation.

(w) To do all such other things as the Corporation may consider incidental or conducive to the attainment of any of the aforesaid objects or the exercise of any of the aforesaid powers of the Corporation.

Restriction of Oversea Concessions

4. The Corporation shall not acquire any licence, concession, right or privilege from or enter into any arrangement with the Government of any part of the British Commonwealth of Nations or the Government of any other country or place oversea, without having first obtained the consent in writing of Our Postmaster General.

Constitution

5. (1) The Governors of the Corporation shall be such persons as shall from time to time be appointed by Us, Our Heirs or Successors in Council. There shall be nine Governors or such other number as may from time to time be directed by Us, Our Heirs or Successors in Council. The Governors shall be appointed for such respective periods, not exceeding five years, as may be directed by Us, Our Heirs or Successors in Council.

(2) One of such Governors shall be nominated from time to time to be

the Chairman of the Corporation and another of such Governors shall be nominated from time to time to be the Vice-Chairman thereof. Such nomination shall be made at the time when the Governor nominated is appointed to the office of Governor or at any time while he holds that office.

(3) The Governors shall at all times include, in addition to the Chairman and the Vice-Chairman of the Corporation, one person, to be designated as the National Governor for Scotland, a second person, to be designated as the National Governor for Wales, and a third person, to be designated as the National Governor for Northern Ireland. Each person to be designated as a National Governor shall have been selected for appointment as Governor in virtue of his knowledge of the culture, characteristics and affairs of Our People in the country for which he is to be designated as the National Governor and his close touch with opinion in that country. Such designation shall be made by Us, Our Heirs or Successors in Council and may be made at the time when the Governor designated is appointed to the office of Governor or at any time while he holds that office.

6. (1) A retiring Governor shall be eligible for reappointment.

(2) The Governors however appointed, shall (during such time or times as the broadcasting services hereinbefore referred to shall be carried on by the Corporation) receive out of the funds or moneys of the Corporation, by way of remuneration for their services as Chairman, Vice-Chairman, National Governor for Scotland, for Wales or for Northern Ireland, or other Governor (as the case may be) such sums or sum as We, Our Heirs or Successors in Council may at any time or times order.

Each Governor may in addition receive out of the funds or moneys of the Corporation the expenses properly incurred by him in the due performance of his office.

(3) A Governor, however appointed, shall cease to be a Governor of the Corporation (and, if he is such, the Chairman or Vice-Chairman thereof)—

(a) If he shall at any time by notice in writing to Our Postmaster General resign his Governorship;

(b) If his Governorship shall be terminated by Us, Our Heirs or Successors in Council;

(c) If he shall hold any office or place in which his interest may in the opinion of Our Postmaster General conflict with any interest of the Corporation;

(d) If he shall become of unsound mind or bankrupt or shall make an arrangement with his creditors;

(e) If he shall absent himself from the meetings of the Corporation continuously for three months or longer without the consent of the Corporation and the Corporation shall resolve that his office be vacated.

(4) As soon as may be reasonably practicable after a vacancy among

the Governors has arisen or at a convenient time before such a vacancy will arise, the vacancy or approaching vacancy, and, if it involves the Chairmanship or Vice-Chairmanship of the Corporation or the National Governorship for Scotland, for Wales or for Northern Ireland, the fact that it does so, shall be certified to Us, Our Heirs, or Successors by Our Postmaster General under his hand, to the end that We, Our Heirs or Successors in Council may with all convenient speed proceed to the filling of the vacancy or approaching vacancy and, if involved, the nomination of a Chairman or Vice-Chairman of the Corporation or the designation of a National Governor for Scotland, for Wales or for Northern Ireland.

7. (1) The Chairman of the Corporation, or in his absence the Vice-Chairman thereof, shall preside at the meetings thereof.

(2) Subject to any regulations made by the Corporation under the next following paragraph hereof, the Chairman, or an officer authorized by him so to do, shall summon all meetings of the Corporation.

(3) The Corporation shall meet for the transaction of its business and affairs, and shall from time to time make such regulations with respect to the summoning, notice, time, place, management and adjournment of meetings, and generally with respect to the transaction and management of its business and affairs, as the Corporation may think fit, subject to the following conditions—

(a) In addition to meeting in England, the Corporation shall meet in Scotland, in Wales and in Northern Ireland at such intervals as may to the Corporation seem appropriate, regard being had to its representative function;

(b) The quorum for a meeting shall be such number of Governors as Our Postmaster General may from time to time in writing prescribe;

(c) Subject to sub-paragraph (d) of this paragraph, every question shall be decided by a majority of votes of the Governors present at the meeting and voting on that question. In the case of an equality of votes on any question the person presiding at the meeting shall have a second or casting vote;

(d) Any question which cannot by reason of its urgency be decided at a meeting of the Corporation shall be decided by the Chairman, or, if he shall be inaccessible or the office of Chairman shall be vacant, by the Vice-Chairman. The Chairman or the Vice-Chairman, as the case may be, before deciding the question, shall, if and so far as may be reasonably practicable, consult with the other Governors or such of them as may be accessible to him, and as soon as may be after taking his decision shall report the question and his decision thereon to the other Governors.

(4) For the transaction of its business or affairs, the Corporation may from time to time appoint Committees of its members, or Committees of its members and other persons, for such purposes and on such terms and

conditions as the Corporation may think fit. The conclusions of any such Committee shall not be binding on the Corporation unless adopted with or without amendment by the Corporation in meeting assembled.

General Advisory Council and Committees

8. (1) The Corporation shall appoint a General Advisory Council for the purpose of advising the Corporation on all matters which may be of concern to the Corporation or to bodies or persons interested in the broadcasting services of the Corporation.

(2) The said Council shall consist of a Chairman and such other members as may be selected by the Corporation from time to time so as to give the Council a broadly representative character.

(3) The procedure of the said Council, including their quorum, shall be such as they may from time to time determine.

9. The Corporation may from time to time appoint persons or committees for the purpose of advising the Corporation with regard to matters connected with the broadcasting services, business, operations and affairs of the Corporation. Each such person or committee shall be appointed with reference to such matters and on such terms and conditions as the Corporation may decide.

National Broadcasting Councils

10. (1) The Corporation shall appoint for the purposes in this article mentioned two National Broadcasting Councils, to be known respectively as the Broadcasting Council for Scotland and the Broadcasting Council for Wales, and if and when required on behalf of Our Government in Northern Ireland so to do shall establish for the purposes aforesaid a third National Broadcasting Council to be known as the Broadcasting Council for Northern Ireland.

(2) Each National Broadcasting Council shall consist of—

(a) a Chairman, who shall be, in the case of the Broadcasting Council for Scotland, the National Governor for Scotland, in the case of the Broadcasting Council for Wales, the National Governor for Wales, and, in the case of the Broadcasting Council for Northern Ireland if it be established, the National Governor for Northern Ireland; and

(b) not less than eight nor more than twelve members, who shall be persons selected for appointment by the Corporation by a panel of the General Advisory Council nominated for that purpose by the General Advisory Council. In the cases of the Broadcasting Council for Scotland and the Broadcasting Council for Wales, such persons shall be selected after consultation with such representative cultural, religious and other bodies in Scotland or Wales, as the case may be, as the panel of the General Advisory Council think fit. The members of the Broadcasting Council for Northern Ireland, if it be established, shall be selected by the panel of the General Advisory Council from a panel of persons nominated in that behalf by Our Government in Northern Ireland.

(3) (i) The Chairman of each National Broadcasting Council shall cease to be such if he becomes the Chairman or the Vice-Chairman of the Corporation or when he ceases to be a Governor thereof.

(ii) The members, other than the Chairman, of each National Broadcasting Council shall be appointed for such respective periods, not exceeding five years, as the Corporation may think fit. Any such member who is appointed for a period of less than five years shall be eligible for re-appointment for the remainder of the period of five years from the beginning of his appointment, or for any less period. Otherwise any such member shall be eligible for reappointment provided that his reappointment takes effect not less than one year after the expiration of his appointment. Any such member may at any time by notice in writing to the Corporation resign his membership. The membership of any such member may at any time be terminated by notice in writing given to him by the Corporation with the concurrence of the panel of the General Advisory Council.

(4) Each National Broadcasting Council shall be charged with the following functions which shall be exercised with full regard to the distinctive culture, language, interests and tastes of Our People in the country for which the Council is established.

- (a) the function of controlling the policy and content of the programmes in that Service among the Home Sound Services which the Corporation provides primarily for reception in that country;
- (b) the function of controlling the policy and content of those programmes in the Television Services which the Council decides shall be provided primarily for reception in that country in replacement of or in addition to programmes provided by the Corporation for general reception in Our United Kingdom of Great Britain and Northern Ireland;
- (c) such other functions in relation to the said Services as the Corporation may from time to time devolve upon the Council; and
- (d) the function of tendering advice to the Corporation in regard to all matters relating to other broadcasting services of the Corporation which affect the interests of Our People in that country:

Provided that each National Broadcasting Council shall be subject to—
- (a) such reservations and directions as may appear to the Corporation to be necessary from time to time in order to secure the transmission throughout Our United Kingdom of Great Britain and Northern Ireland of Broadcasts by Us, Our Heirs or Successors, of broadcasts by Ministers of Our Government in the United Kingdom of Great Britain and Northern Ireland, of party

political broadcasts and of broadcasts of national importance or interest, and the transmission of broadcasts intended for reception in schools; and

(b) such reservations and directions as may appear to the Corporation to be necessary from time to time for reasons of finance or in the interest of due co-ordination and coherent administration of the operations and affairs of the Corporation.

(5) If and whenever in the opinion of Our Postmaster General an emergency shall have arisen in which it is expedient in the public interests that the functions of the National Broadcasting Councils or any of them under this article shall be suspended, Our Postmaster General may by notices in writing to the National Councils or any of them and to the Corporation give directions accordingly and directions so given shall have effect according to their terms during the currency of the notices. Any such notices may be modified or revoked in writing by Our Postmaster General at such time or times as shall in his opinion be expedient.

(6) In the performance of their functions under this article each National Broadcasting Council shall perform and observe all duties and obligations imposed on and all directions given to the Corporation by or under this Our Charter or any licence or agreement granted or made by Our Postmaster General to or with the Corporation so far as such duties, obligations and directions are capable of being performed and observed by the Council.

(7) (i) Each National Broadcasting Council shall have power to regulate their own procedure and to fix their quorum; Provided that the Chairman may call a meeting of the Council whenever he thinks fit to do so, and shall call a meeting thereof when required so to do by any three members.

(ii) Each National Broadcasting Council shall have power to appoint such advisory committees as they may think fit, and any such committee may include or consist of persons who are not members of the Council.

(8) Each National Broadcasting Council shall make an Annual Report to the Corporation of their proceedings during the preceding financial year or residual part thereof of the Corporation. A National Broadcasting Council may, and if requested so to do by the Corporation shall, make special reports to the Corporation during any year.

(9) Each National Broadcasting Council may select and nominate for employment by the Corporation such officers and servants, to serve wholly on the affairs of the Council (including affairs of any advisory committee) as may appear to the Council to be requisite for the proper exercise and performance of their functions and the Corporation shall employ the officers and servants so nominated and shall not without the concurrence of the Council terminate the employment of any such officer or servant: Provided

that the Corporation may decline to employ or may terminate the employment of any such officer or servant if he is unwilling to accept the rates of remuneration or conditions of employment which the Corporation would offer to him if he were to be employed or were employed otherwise than on the affairs of the Council, or if in the opinion of the Corporation and the Chairman of the General Advisory Council it would be detrimental to the administration of the Corporation to employ or continue to employ him.

(10) The Corporation shall afford to each National Broadcasting Council the use of such accommodation and the services of such staff to be engaged partly on the affairs of the Council (including affairs of any advisory committee) as are requisite for the proper performance of the functions of the Council.

(11) The Corporation shall pay to each member of a National Broadcasting Council or of any advisory committee appointed by a Council such out-of-pocket expenses as such member may reasonably incur in the performance of his functions.

Regional Advisory Councils

11. (1) The Corporation shall appoint in Northern Ireland a council to be known as the Northern Ireland Advisory Council, and in each of its Regions from time to time in being in England (which expression shall in this article and the next following article be deemed to include the Channel Islands and the Isle of Man) a council to be known as the Regional Advisory Council, for the purpose of advising the Corporation on the policy and the content of the programmes which the Corporation provides primarily for reception in Northern Ireland or, as the case may be, in the Region for which the Council are appointed, and on all matters relating to other broadcasting services of the Corporation which affect the interests of persons in Northern Ireland or, as the case may be, in that Region.

(2) The Chairman of the Northern Ireland Advisory Council shall be the National Governor for Northern Ireland. The Chairman of each Regional Advisory Council shall be nominated by the Corporation from among the members thereof.

(3) The members of the Northern Ireland Advisory Council (other than the Chairman thereof) and the members of each Regional Advisory Council (including the Chairman thereof) shall not be less than 15 nor more than 20 in number and shall be persons chosen for the individual qualities who are broadly representative of the general public of Northern Ireland or, as the case may be, the Region for which the Council are appointed.

(4) The members of the Northern Ireland Advisory Council (other than the Chairman thereof) and the members of each Regional Advisory Council (including the Chairman thereof) shall be appointed for such respective periods not exceeding five years as the Corporation may think fit,

and on retirement they shall be eligible for reappointment. Any such member may at any time by notice in writing to the Corporation resign his appointment.

(5) The procedure of each Advisory Council, including their quorum, shall be such as they may determine: Provided that the Chairman may call a meeting of the Council whenever he thinks fit so to do, and shall call a meeting thereof when required so to do by any five members.

(6) The Corporation shall afford to each Advisory Council the use of such accommodation and the services of such staff as are requisite for the proper performance of the functions of the Council.

(7) The Corporation shall pay to each member of an Advisory Council (including the Chairman thereof) such out-of-pocket expenses as such member may reasonably incur in the performance of his functions.

(8) In furtherance of the purposes of this article the Corporation shall ensure that the programmes which the Corporation provides primarily for reception in Northern Ireland or in any one of its Regions in England have full regard to the interests of Our People in Northern Ireland or, as the case may be, in that Region.

(9) In the event of a Broadcasting Council for Northern Ireland being established, the Corporation shall forthwith dissolve the Northern Ireland Advisory Council; and in that event the last preceding paragraph of this article shall cease to apply in respect of Northern Ireland.

Organization

12. (1) The Corporation shall appoint such officers and such staff as it may from time to time consider necessary for the efficient performance of its functions and transactions of its business.

(2) The Corporation shall fix such rates of remuneration and conditions of employment for the officers and the staff so employed as the Corporation shall consider proper. Subject to the provisions of paragraph 9 of article 10 of this Our Charter and to any contract made between the Corporation and any such officer or member of the staff, the Corporation may remove any officer or member of the staff.

13. (1) It shall be the duty of the Corporation, except in so far as the Corporation is satisfied that adequate machinery exists for achieving the purposes of this paragraph, to seek consultation with any organization appearing to the Corporation to be appropriate with a view to the conclusion between the Corporation and that organization of such agreements as appear to the parties to be desirable with respect to the establishment and maintenance of machinery for—

   (a) the settlement by negotiation of terms and conditions of employment of persons employed by the Corporation, with provision for reference to arbitration in default of such settlement in such cases as may be determined by or under the agreements; and

(b) the discussion of matters affecting the safety, health and welfare of persons employed by the Corporation, and of other matters of mutual interest to the Corporation and such persons, including efficiency in the operation of the Corporation's services.

(2) Where the Corporation concludes such an agreement as is mentioned in the preceding paragraph, or any variation is made in such an agreement, the Corporation shall forthwith transmit particulars of the agreement or the variation to Our Postmaster General and Our Minister of Labour.

(3) In relation to any agreement affecting employment in Northern Ireland, the foregoing reference to Our Minister of Labour shall be construed as including a reference to Our Minister of Labour and National Insurance for Northern Ireland.

Provision and Review of Services

14. The Corporation is hereby authorized, empowered and required to provide from time to time all such broadcasting services and facilities and to do all such acts and things as shall from time to time be required by or under any Licence granted by Our Postmaster General to the Corporation or any agreement made by Our Postmaster General with the Corporation.

15. It shall be the duty of the Corporation to devise and make such arrangements as appear to the Corporation to be best adapted to the purpose of bringing the work of the Corporation under constant and effective review from without the Corporation, and to that end the Corporation shall provide suitable and sufficient means for the representation to the Corporation of public opinion on the programmes broadcast in the Home Services and for consideration within the Corporation of criticisms and suggestions so represented.

Financial

16. (1) The Corporation is hereby authorized, empowered and required—

(a) To receive all funds which may be paid by Our Postmaster General out of moneys provided by Parliament in furtherance of the purposes of this Our Charter and to apply and administer such funds in accordance with the terms and conditions which may be attached to the grant thereof;

(b) To receive all other moneys which may be obtained by or given to the Corporation or derived from any source not hereinbefore mentioned and to apply and administer such moneys exclusively in furtherance of the purposes of this Our Charter and in accordance with any terms and conditions upon which such moneys may have been obtained, given or derived: Provided that moneys borrowed or raised in exercise of the power hereinbefore conferred for the purpose of defraying capital expenditure (including the repayment or replacement of moneys borrowed or raised for that purpose) shall be applied to that purpose alone.

(2) Subject to any such terms and conditions as aforesaid and to the proviso to sub-paragraph (b) of paragraph (1) of this article, the Corporation may treat such funds and moneys either as capital or as income at its discretion.

(3) Except as in this Our Charter expressly provided, no funds or moneys of the Corporation derived from any source shall in any event be divided by way of profit or otherwise amongst the Governors of the Corporation.

17. (1) In the event of the Corporation exercising (otherwise than for the purpose of obtaining temporary banking accommodation and facilities) the power hereinbefore contained of borrowing or raising money upon the security of or otherwise charging all or any part of its property or rights to which such power extends, it shall set aside out of its revenue such sums as will be sufficient to provide for the repayment of the amount so borrowed or raised within such period in each instance as the Corporation may with the approval of Our Postmaster General determine.

(2) The Corporation shall make proper provision for meeting depreciation of or for renewing any property of the Corporation: Provided that this paragraph shall not apply in relation to any property, interests or rights now held by the Corporation which Our Postmaster General has decided in consultation with the Corporation that the Corporation is to use exclusively for any purpose of the External Services or to any property, interests or rights which the Corporation has acquired or may hereafter acquire out of moneys paid to the Corporation out of aids or supplies appropriated by Parliament for any such purpose.

(3) The Corporation may set aside as a reserve or carry over out of its revenue such sums as it may deem expedient, and may invest, deal with and apply such sums in such manner as it may think conducive to its objects.

Annual Report and Statement of Accounts

18. (1) The accounts of the Corporation shall be audited annually by an auditor or auditors to be appointed by the Corporation with the approval of Our Postmaster General, and a person shall not be qualified to be so appointed unless he is a member of a body of accountants established in Our United Kingdom and for the time being recognized by the Board of Trade for the purposes of section 161 (1)(a) of the Companies Act 1948.

(2) The Corporation shall, once in every year at least, prepare a General Report of its proceedings during the preceding financial year or residual part thereof of the Corporation, and attach thereto an Account or Accounts of the Income and Expenditure of the Corporation and a Balance Sheet, which Account or Accounts and Balance Sheet shall be duly certified by the auditor or auditors of the Corporation. The Corporation, if required so to do by Our Postmaster General after consultation with the Corporation,

shall include in such Report such information relating to its finance, administration and its work generally as Our Postmaster General may from time to time specify in writing, and shall comply with any directions which may be given in writing by Our Postmaster General, after consultation with the Corporation, as regards the information to be given in such Account or Accounts and Balance Sheet or in appendices thereto.

(3) The Chairman shall, on the completion of every such General Report, Account or Accounts and Balance Sheet, forthwith submit the same, together with the Reports for the same year or residual part thereof made under paragraph (8) of article 10 of this Our Charter by the National Broadcasting Councils, to Our Postmaster General to be considered by him and presented to Parliament.

(4) The Corporation shall at all reasonable times upon demand made give to Our Postmaster General and all other persons nominated by him full liberty to examine the accounts of the Corporation and furnish him and them with all forecasts, estimates, information and documents which he or they may require with regard to the financial transactions and engagements of the Corporation.

General

19. (1) The Corporation may at any time and from time to time apply for and accept a Supplemental Charter, or promote a Bill in Parliament, if it appears to the Corporation that a Supplemental Charter or an Act of Parliament is required for or will be conducive to the carrying into effect of any of the purposes or powers of this Our Charter.

(2) No act or proceeding of the Corporation, or of any Council or Committee appointed under the provisions of this Our Charter, or of any subcommittees appointed by any such Council or Committee, shall be questioned on account of any vacancy or vacancies in the Corporation, or in such Council or Committee, or in such sub-committee.

(3) No defect in the appointment of any person acting as Chairman, Vice-Chairman or Governor of the Corporation or as a member of any Council or Committee appointed by the Corporation, or as a member of any sub-committee appointed by any such Council or Committee shall be deemed to vitiate any proceedings of the Corporation or of such Council or Committee, or of such sub-committee in which he has taken part, in cases where the majority of members parties to such proceedings are duly entitled to act.

(4) Any instrument which, if made by a private person, would be required to be under seal, shall be under the seal of the Corporation and signed by one or more Governors authorized for that purpose by a resolution of the Corporation and countersigned by the proper officer. Any notice, appointment, contract, order, or other document made by or proceeding from the Corporation which is not required to be under seal shall be signed by such Governor or such officer, or by an officer of such class, as the

Corporation may, in relation to any specified document or any document of any specified class, from time to time direct.

(5) The proper officer of the Corporation shall be any officer duly authorized as such by the Corporation.

20. (1) The grant of this Our Charter is made upon the express condition that the Corporation shall strictly and faithfully observe and perform and cause to be observed and performed the provisions prescribed therein or thereunder, and also the provisions prescribed in or under any Licence which Our Postmaster General may from time to time grant to the Corporation or contained in or prescribed under any agreement which Our Postmaster General may from time to time make with the Corporation.

(2) If it is made to appear or appears to Our Postmaster General, either on the representation of any person or body politic or corporate appearing to be interested or in any other manner howsoever, that there is reasonable cause to suppose that any of the provisions prescribed in or under this Our Charter or in or under any such Licence or in or under any such agreement (including any stipulations, directions or instructions of Our Postmaster General) have not been observed, performed, given effect to or complied with by the Corporation, Our Postmaster General may require the Corporation to satisfy him that such provisions have been observed, performed, given effect to or complied with, and if within a time specified by him the Corporation shall fail so to do Our Postmaster General may if he thinks fit certify the same under his hand to Us, Our Heirs or Successors, and upon such certificate being given it shall be lawful for Us, Our Heirs or Successors, if We or They shall be so minded, by Letters made Patent under the Great Seal of the Realm, absolutely to revoke and make void this Our Charter, and everything therein contained: Provided that the power of revocation so hereby reserved shall not have or be construed to have the effect of preventing or barring any proceedings which may be lawfully taken to annul or repeal this Our Charter.

21. And We do further will and declare that on the determination of the said term expiring on the thirty-first day of July One thousand nine hundred and seventy-six the undertaking of the Corporation shall cease, so far as the same may depend upon or be carried on under or by virtue of the powers and provisions herein given and contained, unless We, Our Heirs or Successors, shall by writing under Our or Their Sign Manual declare to the contrary, and shall authorize the continuance of the said undertaking under the provisions of this Our Charter or a further Royal Charter for such further term, and under such provisions and conditions as We, Our Heirs or Successors, shall think fit, and any term for which this Our Charter is so renewed shall be construed to be part of the term of this Our Charter.

Dissolution and Winding-up

22. It shall be lawful for the Corporation to surrender this Our Charter subject to the sanction of Us, Our Heirs or Successors, and upon such terms as

We or They may consider fit, and to wind up or otherwise deal with the affairs of the Corporation in such manner as may be approved by Our Postmaster General.

23. Upon the voluntary or compulsory dissolution of the Corporation the property and assets of the Corporation shall be applied in satisfaction of the debts and liabilities of the Corporation and subject thereto shall be disposed of in accordance with the directions of Our Postmaster General.

General Declaration

24. Lastly We do further will, ordain and declare that these Our Letters or the enrolment or exemplification thereof shall be in and by all things good, firm, valid, sufficient and effectual in law according to the true intent and meaning thereof, and shall be taken, construed and judged in the most favourable and beneficial sense for the best advantage of the Corporation and its successors, as well in all Our Courts of Record as elsewhere by all and singular Judges, Justices, Officers, Ministers and other Our Subjects whatsoever, any non-recital, mis-recital or any other omission, imperfection, defect, matter, cause or thing whatsoever to the contrary thereof in anywise notwithstanding.

IN WITNESS whereof We have caused these Our Letters to be made Patent. Witness Ourself at Westminster the twenty-sixth day of March in the thirteenth year of Our Reign.

BY WARRANT UNDER THE QUEEN'S SIGN MANUAL.

Coldstream

APPENDIX IV

BBC Licence and Agreement

Treasury Minute Dated the 19th December 1963

My Lords have had before them a new Licence and Agreement dated 19th December 1963, granted by the Postmaster General to and concluded by him with the British Broadcasting Corporation.

2. The Licence authorizes the British Broadcasting Corporation to maintain the stations and apparatus for wireless telegraphy established and installed by the Corporation under the terms of Licences granted by the Postmaster General, the last of which expires on 29th July 1964, and to establish and instal other stations and apparatus. Certain provisions are incorporated concerning the working of the stations.

3. The term of the Licence is from 30th July 1964 to 31st July 1976, subject to revocation in the event of non-observance or non-performance by the Corporation of any of its conditions or those of the Royal Charter of the Corporation.

4. Under the new Licence and Agreement the Corporation undertakes, unless prevented by circumstances beyond its control, to send broadcast programmes in the Home Sound Services and the Television Services for reception in the British Islands. The Postmaster General may give directions to the Corporation as to the hours of broadcasting in those services. The Corporation also undertakes to send programmes in the External Services at such times as may be prescribed (after consultation with the Corporation and with the approval of the Postmaster General and My Lords) by the Government Department concerned, for reception in countries and places beyond the seas.

5. For the purposes of the Home Services (Sound and Television) the Postmaster General is to pay to the Corporation (out of moneys provided by Parliament) in respect of the period 30th July 1964 until 31st March 1965 a sum equal to the whole of the net licence revenue (as defined in clause 17(3)) and in respect of the remainder of the term of the Licence a sum or sums equal to the whole of the net licence revenue or to such percentage or percentages thereof as the Treasury may from time to time determine.

6. For the purposes of the External Services and other services performed at the request of any Department of Her Majesty's Government the Postmaster General is to pay to the Corporation (out of moneys provided by Parliament) in each year of the term such sums as My Lords shall authorize. The Corporation is to deliver to the Postmaster General such account of its expenditure on the External Services and other services performed at such request as he may prescribe.

7. The new Licence and Agreement takes account of the recommendations contained in the report of the Committee on Broadcasting (Cmnd 1753) and in particular of the Government's decisions arising out of the report and contained in the two White Papers (Cmnd 1770 and 1893). In addition the requirements of a technical nature have been brought up to date, and in particular the Postmaster General has taken powers to secure co-operation between the Corporation and the Independent Television Authority in the use of broadcasting installations.

8. An Agreement dated 19th February 1954 (Cmnd 9089) relating to the execution of certain defence work is extended until 31st July 1976.

9. My Lords consider the terms of the new Licence and Agreement and the financial provisions made therein to be satisfactory and on those grounds have authorized the Postmaster General to grant and conclude it.

Licence and Agreement

THIS DEED is made the nineteenth day of December one thousand nine hundred and sixty-three BETWEEN THE RIGHT HONOURABLE JOHN REGINALD BEVINS, M.P., Her Majesty's Postmaster General (hereinafter called 'the Postmaster General') on behalf of Her Majesty of the one part and THE BRITISH BROADCASTING CORPORATION whose Chief Office is situated at Broadcasting House Portland Place in the County of London (hereinafter called 'the Corporation') of the other part:

WHEREAS on the 20th December 1926 by Letters made Patent under the Great Seal, a Charter of Incorporation was granted unto the Corporation for the purpose of carrying on a Broadcasting Service within the British Islands:

AND WHEREAS on divers dates by Letters made Patent under the Great Seal a Supplemental Charter and further Charters of Incorporation have been granted and the Postmaster General is applying to Her Majesty for the continuance of the Corporation for a further term beginning on the 30th July 1964 and ending on the 31st July 1976 subject to such provisions and conditions as may to Her Majesty seem fit:

AND WHEREAS the Corporation has applied to the Postmaster General for a further licence authorizing the Corporation to continue to use its existing stations and apparatus for wireless telegraphy and to establish, instal and use additional stations and apparatus and granting unto the Corporation other facilities:

AND WHEREAS the Postmaster General has agreed to grant to the Corporation the further licence hereinafter contained and the Postmaster General and the Corporation have agreed to enter into the arrangements hereinafter expressed:

NOW in consideration of the premises and of the matters hereinafter appearing THIS DEED WITNESSETH and the Postmaster General and the Corporation hereby covenant and agree with one another and declare as follows:—

1. IN these presents, except where the subject or context otherwise requires:

    (a) the following expressions have the meanings hereby respectively assigned to them, that is to say:

        'apparatus' means apparatus for wireless telegraphy;

        'apparatus for wireless telegraphy' has the same meaning as in the Wireless Telegraphy Act 1949;

        'British Islands' means England, Scotland, Wales, Northern Ireland, the Channel Islands and the Isle of Man;

        'broadcast relay station' means a station licensed by the Postmaster General or his predecessors in office to be established and used for the purpose solely or primarily of receiving programmes broadcast by authorized broadcasting stations and relaying them by wire to the premises of subscribers to the licensee's broadcast relay service;

        'injurious affection' in relation to a telegraphic line means any interruption of, interference with or impairment of communication by means of the line;

        'interference' in relation to wireless telegraphy has the same meaning as in the Wireless Telegraphy Act 1949;

        'International Telecommunication Convention' means the Convention signed at Geneva on the 21st December 1959 and the Regulations and Additional Regulations in force thereunder, and includes any Convention and Regulations which may from time to time be in force in substitution therefor or in amendment thereof;

        'messages' include other communications;

        'Postmaster General' includes the Postmaster General's successors in the office of Her Majesty's Postmaster General;

        'sponsored programme' means any matter which is provided at the expense of any sponsor (that is, any person other than the Corporation and the performers) for the purpose of being broadcast and is the subject of a broadcast announcement mentioning the sponsor or his goods or services;

        'station' means station for wireless telegraphy;

        'station for wireless telegraphy' has the same meaning as in the Wireless Telegraphy Act 1949;

'telegraph' has the same meaning as in the Telegraph Act 1869; 'telegraphic line' has the same meaning as in the Telegraph Act 1878;

'wireless telegraphy' has the same meaning as in the Wireless Telegraphy Act 1949.

(b) References to stations or a station or to apparatus are references to stations or a station or to apparatus of the Corporation.

2. Subject to the terms, provisions and limitations hereinafter contained, the Postmaster General, in exercise of all powers him hereunto enabling, hereby grants unto the Corporation, for the term beginning on 30th July 1964 and ending on the 31st July 1976, licence within the territorial extent of the Wireless Telegraphy Act 1949—

(a) to use for the purposes hereinafter stated the existing stations established by the Corporation by virtue of licences granted by predecessors in office of the Postmaster General or by the Postmaster General, and to establish from time to time and use for the said purposes additional stations at such places as the Postmaster General may approve in writing;

(b) to use for the said purposes the existing apparatus installed by the Corporation by virtue of such licences, and to instal from time to time and use for the said purposes additional apparatus at the stations of the Corporation and at such other places and in such vehicles, vessels and aircraft as the Postmaster General may approve in writing;

(c) to use the stations and apparatus aforesaid for emitting, sending, reflecting or receiving:

(1) wireless telegraphy by the method of telephony for the purpose of providing broadcasting services for general reception in sound, and by the methods of television and telephony in combination for the purpose of providing broadcasting services for general reception in visual images with sound, in—

(i) the British Islands and the territorial waters thereof and on board ships and aircraft (such services being hereinafter referred to together as 'the Home Services' and separately as 'the Home Sound Services' and 'the Television Services'); and

(ii) countries and places beyond the seas (such services being hereinafter referred to as 'the External Services'); and

(2) wireless telegraphy for purposes ancillary or related to the broadcasting services aforesaid; and

(d) to connect by existing or additional wires any stations or apparatus of the Corporation with broadcast relay stations, and to send thereby to such broadcast relay stations programmes broadcast in the Home Services.

3. If and whenever, with a view to extending the coverage or to improving the strength or quality either generally or in any area or areas of trans-

missions in the Home Services or any of them, the Postmaster General after consultation with the Corporation shall so require by notice in writing, the Corporation shall establish and use such additional station or stations in such place or places in the British Islands as may be specified in the notice.

4.—(1) At each station, whether now existing or hereafter established, the height of the aerials, the types and frequencies of the waves emitted therefrom, the aerial power and directivity, and the characteristics of the modulating signals shall be such as shall be approved in writing from time to time by the Postmaster General after consultation with the Corporation. The constancy and purity of the waves emitted shall be maintained at as high a standard as may be reasonably practicable.

(2) If and whenever the Postmaster General shall so require by notice in writing given after such consultation as aforesaid, the Corporation shall refrain from adopting or shall cease to use at or in relation to the stations whether now existing or hereafter established or such of them as may be specified in the notice such technical measures or processes as may be so specified.

(3) If and whenever the Postmaster General shall so require by notice in writing given after such consultation as aforesaid, the Corporation shall adopt and use at or in relation to the stations whether now existing or hereafter established or such of them as may be specified in the notice, such technical measures or processes as may be so specified, being measures or processes which in the opinion of the Postmaster General are calculated to increase the coverage or to improve the strength or quality either generally or in any area or areas of the transmissions in the broadcasting services provided by the Corporation or any of them.

5.—(1) The Postmaster General may at any time by notice in writing—

(a) require the Corporation to radiate such of its broadcast transmissions as may be specified in the notice from a mast, tower or other installation belonging to the Independent Television Authority (in this clause referred to as 'the Authority'); or

(b) require the Corporation to permit such of the Authority's broadcast transmissions as may be so specified to be radiated from a mast, tower or other installation belonging to the Corporation; or

(c) require the Corporation to co-operate with the Authority in providing and using an installation and to radiate such of the Corporation's broadcast transmissions as may be so specified from that installation;

and it shall be the duty of the Corporation to comply with any such notice.

(2) Before giving a notice under this clause to the Corporation the Postmaster General shall consult the Corporation and the Authority.

(3) If, after a notice is given under this clause to the Corporation, a dispute between the Corporation and the Authority arising out of the matters to which the notice relates is referred to the Postmaster General by either

body, or it appears to the Postmaster General that there is such a dispute, he may give such directions to the Corporation as he may think expedient for determining the dispute, and it shall be the duty of the Corporation to comply with any such directions.

6.—(1) The stations and apparatus shall be subject to inspection and testing by any officer for the time being nominated for the purpose by the Postmaster General, but such inspection and testing shall be so made and done as not to interfere with the Corporation in the general conduct and operation of any of the stations.

(2) The Corporation shall afford all requisite and proper facilities for such inspection and testing and shall provide or secure for the Postmaster General the right, for the purposes aforesaid or for any other purposes of these presents, of entry from time to time into and on the stations and other premises of the Corporation and any premises which may be in the possession or occupation of any person or persons other than the Corporation.

7. The Corporation shall observe the provisions of the International Telecommunication Convention and of any International Convention or international agreement relating to broadcasting to which Her Majesty or the Postmaster General may be or become a party during the continuance of these presents.

8. In order to prevent interference with the working or use of any station for wireless telegraphy established or any apparatus for wireless telegraphy installed in the British Islands or the territorial waters thereof or on board any ship or aircraft by or for the purposes of the Postmaster General or any Department of Her Majesty's Government in the United Kingdom or the Government of any other part of the British Islands or for commercial purposes, and in particular with the sending and receiving of any ship-and-shore messages or aircraft-and-ground messages, the following provisions shall, without prejudice to the other provisions of these presents, have effect—

    (a) (1) The Corporation shall comply with all reasonable directions which shall be given to the Corporation by the Postmaster General and with all rules and regulations made by the Postmaster General for observance by his licensees with respect to avoiding interference between one station or piece of apparatus for wireless telegraphy and another such station or piece of apparatus.

    (2) The Postmaster General shall give consideration to any objections raised by the Corporation to any directions given by him as aforesaid and to any such rules or regulations as aforesaid, but if the Postmaster General shall after consideration maintain such directions, rules or regulations his decision shall be final and the Corporation shall act in accordance therewith.

    (b) The Corporation shall further, so far as is reasonably practicable having regard to technical considerations, so use the stations and apparatus as not to cause any such interference as aforesaid.

9.—(1) The stations and apparatus for wireless telegraphy and other apparatus and equipment of the Corporation, wherever installed, shall be so established, designed, constructed, installed, maintained and used, and if necessary so altered, that no avoidable injurious affection to any telegraphic line of the Postmaster General (whatever and whenever placed and by whomsoever used) is caused by the use of any station or any such apparatus or equipment.

(2) If any injurious affection (whether avoidable or not) is caused as aforesaid to any such telegraphic line, the Corporation shall pay to the Postmaster General the amount of any expense reasonably incurred by him in providing protection for that line against the injurious affection or in substituting for that line a line of different description in the same place or a line of the same or a different description in another place and providing for the substituted line such protection against the injurious affection as he may consider necessary or expedient.

(3) If on placing any telegraphic line (not being such a substituted line as is referred to in the last foregoing sub-clause) the Postmaster General considers it necessary or expedient to do any or all of the following things for the purpose of preventing any injurious affection from being caused to the line as aforesaid, that is to say—

(a) to provide protection for the line;
(b) to provide a line of a description which he would not otherwise have provided;
(c) to place the line provided in a position in which he would not otherwise have placed it,

the Corporation shall pay to the Postmaster General such of the following amounts as he shall in the particular case have incurred, namely, the amount of the expenses reasonably incurred in providing the protection referred to in paragraph (a) and the estimated amounts of the additional expenses reasonably incurred in providing a line of such a description as is referred to in paragraph (b) and in placing the line provided in such a position as is referred to in paragraph (c).

10. Persons employed by the Corporation in the conduct of the services who are not, or are not deemed to be, British subjects shall be so employed on and subject to such conditions as may from time to time be prescribed in writing by the Postmaster General.

11. No person acting on the Corporation's behalf or by its permission shall or shall be permitted or suffered by the Corporation to divulge to any person (other than a properly authorized official of Her Majesty's Government of the United Kingdom or a competent legal tribunal), or make any use whatever of, any message coming to his knowledge and not intended for reception by means of the stations or any of them or any of the Corporation's apparatus for wireless telegraphy.

12. The stations and apparatus shall not without the previous consent in writing of the Postmaster General be used by the Corporation or by its permission for the sending or emission of any message other than a message authorized by this Licence to be sent or emitted thereby.

13. The Corporation shall not without the consent in writing of the Postmaster General receive money or any valuable consideration from any persons in respect of the sending or emitting, or the refraining from sending or emitting, of any matter whatsoever by means of the stations or any of them, and shall not send or emit by means thereof any sponsored programme.

14.—(1) Unless prevented by circumstances beyond its control, the Corporation shall send efficiently programmes in the Home Sound Services, the Television Services, and the External Services from such stations as after consultation with the Corporation the Postmaster General may from time to time in relation to those Services respectively in writing prescribe.

(2) The Corporation shall broadcast an impartial account day by day prepared by professional reporters of the proceedings in both Houses of the United Kingdom Parliament.

(3) The Corporation shall, whenever so requested by any Minister of Her Majesty's Government in the United Kingdom at the Corporation's own expense, send from all or any of the stations any announcement (with a visual image of any picture or object mentioned in the announcement if it is sent from the television stations or any of them) which such Minister may request the Corporation to broadcast; and shall also, whenever so requested by any such Minister in whose opinion an emergency has arisen or continues, at the like expense send as aforesaid any other matter which such Minister may request the Corporation to broadcast: Provided that the Corporation when sending such an announcement or other matter may at its discretion announce or refrain from announcing that it is sent at the request of a named Minister.

(4) The Postmaster General may from time to time by notice in writing require the Corporation to refrain at any specified time or at all times from sending any matter or matter of any class specified in such notice; and the Postmaster General may at any time or times revoke or vary any such notice. The Corporation may at its discretion announce or refrain from announcing that such a notice has been given or has been varied or revoked.

(5) The Corporation shall send programmes in the External Services to such countries, in such languages and at such times as, after consultation with the Corporation, may from time to time be prescribed, with the approval of the Postmaster General and the Treasury, by such Departments of Her Majesty's Government in the United Kingdom as may from time to time be specified in writing by the Postmaster General; and shall perform such other services by way of monitoring emissions of wireless telegraphy and recording matter intended to be broadcast by wireless telegraphy as

after such consultation as aforesaid may from time to time be prescribed as aforesaid.

The Corporation shall consult and collaborate with the Departments so specified and shall obtain and accept from them such information regarding conditions in, and the policies of Her Majesty's Government aforesaid towards, the countries so prescribed and other countries as will enable the Corporation to plan and prepare its programmes in the External Services in the national interest.

15.—(1) The Postmaster General may from time to time by notice in writing give directions to the Corporation as to the maximum time, the minimum time, or both the maximum and the minimum time, which is to be given in any day, week or other period to broadcasts in the Home Services, and as to the hours of the day in which such broadcasts are or are not to be given.

(2) A direction under paragraph (1) may be framed in any way, and in particular—

(a) may be confined to broadcasts from those stations which transmit, or usually transmit, the same programme, or may be different for different stations, or for different programmes broadcast from the same stations;

(b) may make special provision for annual holidays and other special occasions;

(c) may be confined to a specified day of the week, or may be different for different days of the week;

(d) in imposing a maximum number of hours for any purpose, may allow for programmes or items of specified kinds being left out of account in determining the maximum, whether in all circumstances or depending on the fulfilment of specified conditions as regards programmes or items so specified.

(3) The Postmaster General may, whether or not a direction under paragraph (1) provides for exemptions, exempt the Corporation from any requirement of such a direction on any occasion or in any circumstances.

16. The Corporation shall pay to the Postmaster General on the execution of this Deed an issue fee of £1,000 in respect of the licence hereby granted, and on or before the 30th July in each year from 1965 to 1975 inclusive a renewal fee of £1,000

17.—(1) For the purposes of the Home Services (subject as is and in manner hereinafter provided) the Postmaster General shall pay to the Corporation (out of moneys provided by Parliament) during the period ending on the 31st March 1965 a sum equal to the whole of the net licence revenue (as defined in sub-clause (3)), and thereafter during the continuance of these presents a sum or sums equal to the whole of the net licence revenue or to such percentage or percentages thereof as the Treasury may from time to time determine.

(2) The sums payable by the Postmaster General to the Corporation under the provisions of this clause shall be paid by him in instalments of such amount and at such intervals (not being longer than one month) as the Postmaster General shall think fit and any adjustment between the parties shall be made as soon as conveniently possible.

(3) The expression 'net licence revenue' means the broadcast receiving licence revenue as defined in Section 3 of the Post Office Act 1961 less the expenses incurred by or on behalf of the Postmaster General in the collection of the broadcast receiving licence revenue, in the administration of the licensing system, and in investigating complaints of interference by electro-magnetic energy affecting broadcasting services within the British Islands.

(4) Any account certified by the Comptroller and Accountant General of the Post Office, the Director of Finance and Accounts of the Post Office or a Deputy Director of Finance and Accounts of the Post Office, of any sum payable by the Postmaster General to the Corporation under this clause shall for all purposes be final and conclusive.

18.—(1) For the purposes of the External Services and other services performed pursuant to clause 14 (5) and of any services performed by the Corporation at the request of any Department of Her Majesty's Government in the United Kingdom (other than services performed under clause 14 (3)) the Postmaster General shall pay to the Corporation (out of moneys provided by Parliament) in each year during the continuance of these presents such sums as the Treasury shall authorize.

(2) The Corporation shall deliver to the Postmaster General such accounts of its expenditure on the External Services and on other services referred to in sub-clause (1) covering such periods and at such times as may from time to time be prescribed in writing by the Postmaster General.

19. Sums paid by the Postmaster General to the Corporation under the provisions of clauses 17 and 18 shall be applied and administered by the Corporation in accordance with any terms and conditions which may be attached to the grant thereof by Parliament or by the Treasury.

20.—(1) If and whenever in the opinion of the Postmaster General an emergency shall have arisen in which it is expedient in the public interest that Her Majesty's Government in the United Kingdom shall have control over the transmission of messages or any other matter whatsoever by means of the stations or any of them, it shall be lawful for the Postmaster General to direct and cause the stations or any of them or any part thereof to be taken possession of in the name and on behalf of Her Majesty and to prevent the Corporation from using them, and also to cause the stations or any of them or any part thereof to be used for Her Majesty's service, or to take such other steps as he may think fit to secure control over the stations or any of them, and in that event any person authorized by the Postmaster General may enter upon the stations or any of them and the offices and works of the Corporation or any of them and take possession thereof and use the same as aforesaid.

(2) If and whenever the Postmaster General shall exercise the powers conferred on him by sub-clause (1) he may deduct from the sums payable by him to the Corporation under the provisions of clauses 17 and 18 such amounts as shall be appropriate having regard to the extent and duration of the exercise of such powers, but the Corporation shall be entitled to receive from the Postmaster General—

(a) compensation for any damage done to any property of the Corporation, being damage directly attributable to the exercise of any such powers, and

(b) such sums as are required to defray any expenses which, regard being had to the nature of the emergency, have been properly and necessarily incurred by the Corporation and for meeting which revenue is by reason of the exercise of such powers not otherwise available to the Corporation.

In such case the Postmaster General shall repay or allow to the Corporation such proportionate part of the issue fee or renewal fee payable by the Corporation under the provisions of clause 16 as shall be appropriate, regard being had to the extent and duration of the exercise of such powers.

21. Any contract entered into by the Corporation for the purposes of these presents shall secure the observance and fulfilment by the Corporation's contractor of the obligations upon contractors specified in any resolution of the House of Commons for the time being in force applicable to contracts of Government Departments as if the Corporation were a Department for the purposes of such resolution.

22.—(1) The Corporation shall not:

(a) offer or give or agree to give to any person in Her Majesty's Service any gift or consideration of any kind as an inducement or reward for doing or forbearing to do, or for having done or forborne to do any act in relation to the obtaining or execution of this or any other contract for Her Majesty's Service, or for showing or forbearing to show favour or disfavour to any person in relation to this or any other contract for Her Majesty's service.

(b) enter into this or any other contract with Her Majesty or any Government Department in connection with which commission has been paid or agreed to be paid by the Corporation or on its behalf, or to its knowledge, unless before the contract is made particulars of any such commission and of the terms and conditions of any agreement for the payment thereof have been disclosed in writing to an authorized officer of the Postmaster General.

(2) Any breach of this condition by the Corporation or by anyone employed by the Corporation or acting on its behalf (whether with or

without the knowledge of the Corporation) or the commission of any offence by the Corporation or by anyone employed by the Corporation or acting on its behalf under the Prevention of Corruption Acts 1889 to 1916, in relation to this or any other contract for Her Majesty's Service shall entitle the Postmaster General to determine the contract and recover from the Corporation the amount of any loss resulting from such determination and/or recover from the Corporation the amount or value of any such gift, consideration or commission.

(3) Any dispute, difference or question arising in respect of the interpretation of this condition (except so far as the same may relate to the amount recoverable from the Corporation under sub-clause (2) in respect of any loss resulting from such determination of the contract), the right of the Postmaster General to determine the contract, or the amount or value of any such gift, consideration or commission shall be decided by the Postmaster General whose decision shall be final and conclusive.

23. The Corporation shall not without the consent in writing of the Postmaster General assign, underlet or otherwise dispose of these presents or of the powers or authorities granted by the licence hereinbefore contained or the benefit or advantage or the covenants and provisions herein contained or, except as may be provided in the Royal Charter of the Corporation, assign or charge any sum or sums payable by the Postmaster General to the Corporation hereunder.

24.—(1) In any of the following cases (that is to say):

(a) if at any time during the continuance of these presents the Corporation shall not in the opinion of the Postmaster General have adequately performed the covenant on its part hereinbefore contained to send efficiently programmes in the Home Sound Services, the Television Services and the External Services; or

(b) in case of any breach, non-observance or non-performance by or on the part of the Corporation of any of the provisions or conditions contained in the Royal Charter of the Corporation or in any document made or issued thereunder, or of any of the other covenants or the provisions or conditions contained herein or in any document made or issued hereunder and on the part of the Corporation to be observed and performed, which shall not be remedied, made good or desisted from within a reasonable time of the attention of the Corporation being drawn to the alleged breach, non-observance or non-performance in question; or

(c) in case the Corporation shall pass a resolution for voluntary winding up or in case an Order shall be made by the Court for the winding up of the Corporation compulsorily or under the supervision of the Court, or in case a Receiver or Manager for any debenture holders, mortgagee or other creditor shall be appointed or any debenture holders, mortgagee or other creditor shall enter in possession of any part of the Corporation's property,

then and in any of the said cases the Postmaster General may at any time thereafter by notice in writing to the Corporation revoke and determine these presents and the licences, powers and authorities hereinbefore granted and each and every of them, and thereupon these presents and the said licences, powers and authorities and each and every of them shall (subject and without prejudice to any right of action or remedy for breach of any of the covenants and conditions herein contained which shall then have accrued to either of the parties) absolutely cease, determine and become void.

(2) Nothing in this clause contained shall be deemed to prejudice or affect any statutory power of the Postmaster General.

25. The Corporation shall at all times indemnify the Crown against all actions, claims and demands which may be brought or made against the Crown or any servant or agent of the Crown by any person in respect of any injury arising from any act of the Corporation or of its servants or agents licensed or permitted by these presents.

26.—(1) Any notice, request, consent, approval or other act (whether required to be in writing or not) given or served by the Postmaster General under these presents may be under the hand of the Director General or any other duly authorized officer of the Post Office and may be given or served by being sent by registered post or by the recorded delivery service addressed to the Corporation at its chief office for the time being and any notice given or served by the Corporation under these presents may be given or served by being sent by registered post or by the recorded delivery service addressed to the Director General of the Post Office at the General Post Office, London.

(2) Any notice given by the Postmaster General to the Corporation under the provisions of these presents may be revoked or varied by any subsequent notice in writing given by him.

27. The Agreement dated the 19th February 1954 and made between The Right Honourable Hebrand Edward Dundonald Brassey Earl De La Warr then Her Majesty's Postmaster General on behalf of Her Majesty of the one part and the Corporation of the other part (which relates to the execution of certain defence work) shall continue in force during the continuance of this Deed, and references therein to the Licence therein mentioned shall be deemed to include references to this Deed.

28. It is a condition of this Deed that the contract thereby made shall not be binding until it has been approved of by a resolution of the House of Commons.

APPENDIX V

Members of the European Broadcasting Union

Active Members

Austria	Österreichischer Rundfunk Ges.m.b.H.
Belgium	Radiodiffusion-Télévision Belge — Institut des Services Communs, forming the association of the following organizations:
	Radiodiffusion-Télévision Belge, émissions françaises
	Belgische Radio en Televisie, Nederlandse uitzendingen
Denmark	Danmarks Radio
Finland	Oy. Yleisradio Ab.
France	Office de Radiodiffusion-Télévision Française
Germany (Federal Republic)	Arbeitsgemeinschaft der Öffentlich-Rechtlichen Rundfunkanstalten der Bundesrepublik Deutschland (ARD), comprising:

    Bayerischer Rundfunk
    Hessischer Rundfunk
    Norddeutscher Rundfunk
    Radio Bremen
    Saarländischer Rundfunk
    Sender Freies Berlin
    Süddeutscher Rundfunk
    Südwestfunk
    Westdeutscher Rundfunk
    Deutsche Welle
    Deutschlandfunk
  Zweites Deutsches Fernsehen

Greece	Hellenic National Broadcasting Institute

Iceland	Rikisutvarpid
Ireland	Radio Telefis Éireann
Israel	Israel Broadcasting Authority—Kol Yisrael
Italy	RAI—Radiotelevisione Italiana
Lebanon	Ministère de l'Orientation, de l'Information et du Tourisme
Luxembourg	Compagnie Luxembourgeoise de Télédiffusion (Radio-Télé-Luxembourg)
Monaco	Radio Monte-Carlo
Netherlands	Stichting Nederlandse Radio-Unie, comprising:
	Nederlandse Televisie Stichting
	Algemene Vereniging Radio Omroep
	Katholieke Radio Omroep
	Nederlandse Christelijke Radio Vereniging
	Omroepvereniging VARA
	Vrijzinnig Protestantse Radio Omroep
Norway	Norsk Rikskringkasting
Portugal	Emissora Nacional de Radiodifusão
	RTP—Radiotelevisão Portuguesa S.A.R.L.
Spain	Dirección General de Radiodifusión y Televisión
Sweden	Sveriges Radio
Switzerland	Société Suisse de Radiodiffusion et Télévision
Tunisia	Radiodiffusion-Télévision Tunisienne
Turkey	Türkiye Radyo Televizyon Kurumu Genel Müdürlüğü
United Kingdom	British Broadcasting Corporation
	Independent Television Authority and Independent Television Companies Association Ltd.
Vatican State	Radio Vaticana
Yugoslavia	Jugoslovenska Radiotelevizija

Associate Members

Algiers	Radiodiffusion-Télévision Algérienne
Australia	Australian Broadcasting Commission
	Federation of Australian Commercial Television Stations
Brazil	Associacão Brasileira de Emissoras de Rádio e Televisão
	Diarios Associados Ltda.
	Emissoras Unidas de Radio e Televisão

Canada	Canadian Broadcasting Corporation—La Société Radio-Canada
Ceylon	Ceylon Broadcasting Corporation
Chad	Radiodiffusion Nationale Tchadienne
Congo	Radiodiffusion Nationale Congolaise
Cyprus	Cyprus Broadcasting Corporation
Dahomey	Radiodiffusion du Dahomey
Gabon	Radiodiffusion-Télévision Gabonaise
Ghana	Ghana Broadcasting Corporation
Haiti	Service des Télécommunications
Iran	National Iranian Television
	National Iranian Radio
Ivory Coast	Radiodiffusion Télévision Ivoirienne
Japan	Nippon Hoso Kyokai
	National Association of Commercial Broadcasters in Japan
	Tokyo Broadcasting System, Inc.
	Nippon Educational Television Co., Ltd.
Kenya	The Voice of Kenya
Liberia	Liberian Broadcasting Corporation
Malawi	Malawi Broadcasting Corporation
Malta	Broadcasting Authority—Malta, and Malta Television Service Ltd.
Mexico	Telesistema Mexicano S.A.
Morocco	Radiodiffusion Télévision Marocaine
New Zealand	New Zealand Broadcasting Corporation
Niger	Radio-Niger
Nigeria	Nigerian Broadcasting Corporation
Pakistan	Radio Pakistan
Republic of South Africa	South African Broadcasting Corporation
Rhodesia	Rhodesia Broadcasting Corporation
Tanzania	Tanzania Broadcasting Corporation
United States	American Broadcasting Company
	Broadcasting Foundation of America
	Columbia Broadcasting System, Inc.
	National Association of Educational Broadcasters
	National Broadcasting Company, Inc.
	National Educational Television
	Time-Life Broadcast, Inc.
	U.S. Information Agency
Upper Volta	Radiodiffusion-Télévision Voltaïque

Satellite Communications:

The Challenge and the

Opportunity for

International Cooperation*

ADDRESS BY

John A. Johnson

VICE PRESIDENT—INTERNATIONAL

COMMUNICATIONS SATELLITE CORPORATION

BEFORE THE

Washington World Conference on World Peace Through Law

WORKING SESSION II—SECTION II

SEPTEMBER 14, 1965

Joseph Conrad once wrote, "What all men are really after is some form, or perhaps some formula, of peace." It is fitting that lawyers should seek to provide such a formula through the development of legal principles and institutions which further international cooperation. So today I propose to consider with you a case study which I believe provides tangible evidence of progress in this direction: the international arrangements which have been worked out for the cooperative development of satellite communications on a world-wide basis. Although 46 countries are now parties to these

* Published in the *Federal Communications Bar Journal*, XIX, No. 3 (1964–1965), 88–96. Reprinted by permission of the *Journal* and the author.

arrangements, and the organization which they have established has been functioning effectively for over a year, I doubt that their significance is widely understood among lawyers interested in the development of international organizations.

The inescapable necessity for international cooperation on a world-wide basis is perhaps more self-evident in the organization of satellite communications than in any other area of man's current economic activity. It is in the very nature of international communications that there must be agreement among the parties interested in communicating with one another; but satellite communications presents a challenge and an opportunity for international cooperation on a global basis far beyond anything that has gone before. Both the challenge and the opportunity result from the very nature of the technology involved and from the fact that satellite communications represent man's first effort to exploit for economic benefits the newly opened realm of outer space.

There may be a temptation to oversimplify the challenge and the opportunity by regarding communications satellites as merely another step in the augmentation of earlier means of telecommunications. While communications satellites are indeed already demonstrating this capability, I believe that for the purpose of our discussion this afternoon the differences between satellite communications and older means of telecommunications are perhaps more significant than their similarities.

The special significance of man's activities in outer space was emphasized by Adlai Stevenson in urging passage by the United Nations General Assembly of U. N. Resolution 1721, which was designed to promote exploration and use of outer space through peaceful cooperation. He said:

> In outer space we start with a clean slate—an area yet unmarred by the accumulated conflicts and prejudices of our earthly past. We propose today that the United Nations write on its slate boldly and in an orderly and a creative way to narrow the gap between scientific progress and social invention, to offer to all nations, irrespective of the stage of their economy or scientific development, an opportunity to participate in one of the greatest adventures of man's existence.

In satellite communications we find ourselves, at one and the same time, in two of the most rapidly evolving areas of man's endeavor; communications and outer space. The nexus of these two fields represents the very frontier of man's knowledge and practical achievement.

It was less than eight years ago that outer space was first penetrated by man-made vehicles. The simultaneous development of rocket propulsion and advances in electronic technology opened up a totally new resource for economic exploitation. For the first time man was able to place mechanisms of considerable size far above the earth's atmosphere, to control their positioning and movement with amazing precision, and to utilize them to serve his scientific and economic interests. These technological breakthroughs have made it possible for a satellite such as Early Bird to hover over the earth and provide the means to bridge the gap of miles and oceans in man's dialogue with man. Satellite technology will permit man to reach into the most distant parts of the globe in order to seek out and communicate with other men by means of speech and the projection of visual images —indeed, with no constraints on the type of traffic that can be carried.

In satellite communications, the basic technology itself requires extensive international cooperation. Essentially, the act of communicating through outer space involves the transmission of a signal by an earth station to a satellite which relays it to earth where it is received by another earth station. It is then retransmitted via the terrestrial network that is available in a given geographical area. Ultimately, this results in a message arriving at a telegraph office, in a telephone call being received in an office or home, or in a television program being viewed on receivers after rebroadcast of the audio-video signals by a television broadcasting station. Thus, cooperation is required on the part of a number of people in the retransmission of the signals if intelligible communication is to be addressed to the intended recipient.

The technology also requires another form of cooperation, since satellite communications, which are a form of microwave radio transmission, use one of the most valuable resources available to men—the electromagnetic frequency spectrum. If this limited resource is to be widely used, agreement must be reached among all nations for its allocation among many competing uses, including satellite communications. This was accomplished, in fact, at an Extraordinary Administrative Radio Conference held under the aegis of the International Telecommunication Union in 1963.

There is another fundamental difference between satellites and other means of long distance communication which emphasizes the need for close cooperation on a global basis. Satellites are capable of connecting any point on the earth with all those other points to which the satellite is mutually visible, and without dependence upon linkage through any other country.

Yet, although the technology may make it imperative for international cooperation to take place, men must perceive this necessity and respond to its challenge in a timely manner. In the field of outer space we have seen many effective responses—at the level of the United Nations, in domestic legislation, and in international agreements.

The U. N. General Assembly Resolution previously mentioned, Resolution 1721, which was unanimously adopted on December 20, 1961, declared that "international law, including the Charter of the United Nations, applies to outer space and celestial bodies" and that "outer space and celestial bodies are free for exploration and use by all States in conformity with international law and are not subject to national appropriation." This principle of the freedom of outer space, which is so essential to the use of outer space for commercial purposes, was reaffirmed in the resolution adopted unanimously by the General Assembly of the United Nations on December 13, 1963, entitled "Declaration of Legal Principles Governing the Activities of States in the Exploration of Outer Space." In addition, the United National Declaration stated two principles of particular relevance to the organization and operation of a global communications satellite system. The Declaration states, first, that States bear international responsibility for national activities in outer space, whether carried on by governmental agencies or by non-governmental entities, and, second, that the activities of non-governmental entities in outer space require authorization and continuing supervision by the State concerned.

The United States Government also responded to the challenge in the Communications Satellite Act of 1962, which states the policy and purposes of this country in these words:

> The Congress hereby declares that it is the policy of the United States to establish, in conjunction and in cooperation with other countries, as expeditiously as practicable a commercial communications satellite system, as part of an improved global communications network, which will be responsive to public needs and national objectives, which will serve the communication needs of the United States and other countries, and which will contribute to world peace and understanding.

The 1962 Act created the Communications Satellite Corporation and provided that it should be the United States' participant in the global satellite system. It did not, however, attempt to dictate the form or content of the international arrangements under which the global system would be established. This was left to be worked out in the course of international negotiations.

Let us turn now to the international response of the nations interested in the development of satellite communications as manifested in the international arrangements concluded last year.

Perhaps one of the unique aspects of satellite communications is that political factors have not overwhelmed economic considerations in the creation of an international organization to exploit the technology. I say this is unique because most international organizations, whether they be nominally designated as social, cultural or economic, have had their charters, organizational structure and their *modus operandi* determined primarily by political considerations. This appears to me to be the usual case in the formation and formal structure of international organizations regardless of how the particular organization proceeds to function once it is established. This is demonstrably not so in the case of satellite communications. It is fair to say that among the many factors that had to be considered by those engaged in establishing an international organization in this field, the economic aspects were given at least equal weight with the political factors. It is my belief that this equilibrium contributed greatly to the shaping of an organizational structure which can be responsive to many diverse interests and yet able to move ahead efficiently with its operational responsibilities.

In considering possible international arrangements, it was found useful to conceive of the global system as consisting of a single space segment and a number of earth segments. The space segment includes all of the satellites used in the system and the tracking, control and command facilities required to support the operation of the satellites in orbit. The earth segments comprise the stations located in various countries which are used to send telecommunications traffic to and receive it from the satellites.

Negotiations were undertaken initially with representatives of countries whose potential use of communications satellites was of such a magnitude that their participation in the global system seemed desirable from the outset. We found that these countries, like ourselves, felt that the space segment should be jointly owned and financed by participants from all of the major regions of the world, and that the extent of each participant's financial investment and consequent ownership share should be related to its potential use of the global system. It was also agreed that the various earth segments of the system should be separately owned and financed by telecommunications entities, public or private, authorized by the countries in which they are located or, in certain cases, jointly owned and financed by the telecommunications entities of several countries whose traffic would be handled through a single earth station. This distinction between the form of ownership and financing of the space segment on the one hand and the various earth segments on the other is basic to an understanding of the international arrangements.

The negotiations culminated in the conclusion of two interrelated agreements which were opened for signature on August 20 of last year. These two agreements established an international partnership for the financing, ownership and operation of the space segment of the system. The first agreement, entitled "Agreement Establishing Interim Arrangements for a Global Commercial Communications Satellite System," is an agreement among governments. The second agreement, called the "Special Agreement," is an agreement which may be signed either by the governments themselves or by telecommunications entities, public or private, designated by the governments signing the first agreement.

When these Agreements were first opened for signature, they were signed by the United States and 13 other countries. Today, a total of 46 countries have signed these Agreements and are full-fledged members of this new international joint venture. In the Western Hemisphere, this includes Brazil, Argentina, Chile, Colombia, Canada, and the United States. Seven countries in the African continent, Algeria, Ethiopia, Libya, South Africa, Sudan, Tunisia, and the United Arab Republic are parties to the Agreements; and, in the Far East, Japan, Australia, New Zealand, India, Pakistan, Ceylon, Indonesia and the Republic of China are signatories. The remaining 25 members are from the Middle East and Western Europe. Representing the

Middle East are Iraq, Israel, Jordan, Kuwait, Lebanon, Saudi Arabia, Syria, and Yemen; and, representing Western Europe are Austria, Belgium, Denmark, France, The Federal Republic of Germany, Greece, Ireland, Italy, Monaco, The Netherlands, Norway, Portugal, Spain, Sweden, Switzerland, The United Kingdom and the Vatican City. These 46 countries account for about 90% of the potential world telecommunications traffic that might be served by a global satellite system.*

The first of the two interrelated Agreements, the Interim Agreement, established certain basic political and economic principles and goals to which all of the signatories are committed, as well as the organizational and financial framework of the partnership. I should like to read the Preamble of this Agreement:

> Recalling the principle set forth in Resolution No. 1721 (XVI) of the General Assembly of the United Nations that communications by means of satellites should be available to the nations of the world as soon as practicable on a global and nondiscriminatory basis;
> Desiring to establish a single global commercial communications satellite system as part of an improved global communications network which will provide expanded telecommunications services to all areas of the world and which will contribute to world peace and understanding;
> Determined, to this end, to provide, through the most advanced technology available, for the benefit of all nations of the world, the most efficient and economical service possible consistent with the best and most equitable use of the radio spectrum;
> Believing that satellite communications should be organized in such a way as to permit all States to have access to the global system and those States so wishing to invest in the system with consequent participation in the design, development, construction (including the provision of equipment), establishment, maintenance, operation and ownership of the system;
> Believing that it is desirable to conclude interim arrangements providing for the establishment of a single global commercial communications satellite system at the earliest practicable date, pending the working out of a definitive arrangement for the organization of such a system.

The Interim Agreement, which is open for accession to any State which is a member of the International Telecommunications Union, obligates the partners to cooperate in the establishment of a system which will achieve basic global coverage in the latter part of 1967, with the first phase consisting of one or more satellites in synchronous orbit in 1965. The first of these is the Early Bird satellite now in position over the equator just east of Brazil. Early Bird is at this moment owned by 46 international partners.

On the organizational side, the Interim Agreement established a governing committee, the Interim Communications Satellite Committee, which has

---

* Since Mr. Johnson made this speech in 1965, a sizeable number of additional countries have become members.

overall responsibility for the design, development, construction, establishment, maintenance, and operation of the space segment of the global system. It also provides that the Communications Satellite Corporation shall act as the manager in the design, development, construction, establishment, operation and maintenance of the space segment.

By the terms of the Interim Agreement, the space segment is owned in undivided shares by the signatories to the Special Agreement in proportion to their respective contributions to the costs of the space segment. Arriving at agreement on the investment and ownership quotas to be accorded to each of the participants was, of course, one of the most difficult problems in negotiating the Agreements. The Communications Satellite Corporation, as the United States participant in this joint venture, was initially obligated by the Agreements to contribute 61% of the capital required for the establishment of the space segment during the interim arrangements, estimated to be approximately $200,000,000. The initial investment quotas of all the Western European countries totalled 30.5%, with the remaining 8.5% divided among Canada, Japan and Australia. As additional countries have become parties, the quotas of previous signatories have been reduced pro rata to accommodate the quotas of all parties within the total of 100%. Quotas of new parties are set by the Interim Communications Satellite Committee on their application. A majority of the countries have quotas of less than 1%.

With such a disparity of investment and ownership interests, one of the foremost questions to be solved in the negotiations was the composition of the governing committee and the distribution of voting power among its members. It was decided to limit membership on the Interim Communications Satellite Committee to representatives from each of the partners or groups of partners having an ownership interest and a financial commitment of 1.5% or more. Each member of the Committee has voting power in proportion to the ownership share of the organizations he represents. Although the Communications Satellite Corporation commands more than a majority of the votes by virtue of its investment quota which is presently slightly more than 56%, the Agreements specify a number of important subjects on which decisions require the concurrence of a number of parties in addition to the Communications Satellite Corporation, the necessary accumulation of votes being such that countries located in several major geographic regions of the world must be in agreement.

The Interim Communications Satellite Committee has held eleven meetings at regular periodic intervals since last September. The Committee now has thirteen members each of whom, in accordance with the Agreements, represents a partner with investment and ownership share of 1.5% or more or a group of entities whose combined shares equal at least 1.5%. It seems likely that the membership of the Committee will soon be increased to fifteen, representing a total of 33 signatories.

This, then, is the institutional framework for the development of world-wide satellite communications. It provides an opportunity for all nations to participate in a challenging international venture and to derive practical benefits of incalculable value.

In less than three more years the space segment of a communications satellite system capable of serving the entire world will be in place and ready for operation. In order for a country to be able to utilize this great new resource, it needs only to have an earth station available for its use. With a space segment of global coverage, an earth station will truly provide even the most isolated country with a window upon the whole world. It is estimated that more than 20 earth stations will be tied in with the global system in the next few years, with some of them, as in Western Europe, serving a great many countries. It seems likely that as many as 50 countries may be served during the first year of global coverage.

I wish to emphasize that the Agreements deal only with the space segment portion of the system. Each of the partners must decide for itself whether it wishes to establish an earth station or whether it wishes to make arrangements to use some other earth station, and it must work out for itself the manner in which the station is to be financed.

It is not necessary to be a co-owner of the space segment in order to benefit from the global system. Any country, by using its own earth station or by making suitable arrangements to use a neighboring country's station, may use the satellites on a non-discriminatory basis by paying an appropriate charge for such use to the international consortium which owns the satellites. In order to assure the most efficient utilization of the space segment, the Interim Communications Satellite Committee is charged with approving all earth stations for access to the space segment.

While the first use of communications satellites has been to provide a new means of spanning the oceans, the potential benefits of this new technology are by no means limited to such applications. Satellites can provide top-quality communication over large land masses which could be furnished only with enormous difficulty and high cost by terrestrial means. This is a significant breakthrough for intra-continental communications. One can see, for example, the potential for educational television in countries lacking the means to provide conventional facilities to meet the explosive demand for training in today's skills.

If we look ahead a few years, we can already foresee many other uses of communications satellites of tremendous value to the developing countries. One of the great scientific and engineering educational centers in the United States has proposed that communications satellites be utilized to provide the resources of a master computing center to scientists and engineers working in areas of the world which can not afford to duplicate such a facility. There appears to be no reason why such use of a satellite system should not be feasible.

Perhaps the most revolutionary change promised by communications satellites will come about when direct broadcasting from satellites into the home receiver is realized. The satellites which will be employed in the initial global system will not have this capability, but it is a possible development during the decade of the 1970's. During the early phases of the system, television programs carried by satellite will have to be rebroadcast from stations on the ground to the home receiver. Thus, they pose no radically new problems of national or international control. With the advent of direct broadcasting of television from the satellites, a totally new situation will arise which will test the ingenuity and creativity of the architects of international order.

In conclusion, I think that the following aspects of the Agreements are worthy of special note in the context of this Conference:

First, the concept of an international cooperative enterprise, with very widespread membership, for the purpose of sharing the exploitation of a new resource for the economic benefit of all mankind;

Second, the effort to reduce national rivalries in a new field of economic activity by the concept of a single global system instead of competing national systems;

Third, a form of organization which recognizes the diversity of national economic systems by permitting participation of either public or private entities on behalf of the signatory countries;

Fourth, a form of organization which provides for a wide disparity of investment and ownership reflecting the probable extent of the use of the system by the various participants and which takes this factor into account in the decision-making process; and

Fifth, the careful balance of political and economic factors reflected throughout the Agreements.

It has become a kind of intellectual fashion to view with alarm the alleged inability of the law to keep pace with scientific and technological developments which are changing the outward face of the world. Whatever may be the case in other areas of scientific progress, I believe it is safe to say with respect to satellite communications that the development of legal principles and institutions has not only kept up with technological developments but has, to a considerable extent, anticipated them.

The international arrangements embodied in the two Agreements I have described represent, I believe, the social and legal inventiveness needed to keep abreast of scientific development in what may be termed the race of history. While it would be presumptuous to claim that they furnish the "formula" of peace which Joseph Conrad said all men are seeking, they do provide a significant pattern for the elimination of international rivalries and conflicts.

APPENDIX VII

Annual Report of the President

on Activities and Accomplishments under

the Communications Satellite Act of 1962

January 1 — December 31, 1966

Introduction

I T IS THE POLICY of the United States to continue toward development of a global communications satellite system. This policy was clearly expressed in the Communications Satellite Act of 1962 and reiterated when this country affixed its signature to the Agreement of August 20, 1962, establishing interim arrangements for a global commercial communications satellite system.

This policy affirms the principle that through the combined, purposeful and cooperative efforts of members of the International Telecommunications Satellite Consortium (INTELSAT) mankind can realize the full benefits of communications satellite technology.

In 1964 nineteen nations signed the Agreement establishing INTELSAT. By the end of 1966, the consortium had grown to fifty-five member nations. During 1967, the total is expected to increase by almost one-fifth.

This growth underscores the firmness of the foundation upon which this international partnership has been constructed and encourages the expectation of continued healthy expansion in the years ahead. With each member nation contributing its share toward establishing and operating the global system, and with each nation entitled to its equitable share of earnings, there is also assured a healthy rate of financial growth.

The United States participates in INTELSAT through the Communications Satellite Corporation (COMSAT) which is charged with representing the United States on the Interim Communications Satellite Committee

(ICSC), which is the governing body of INTELSAT. In addition, and by Article VIII of the Agreement of August 20, 1964, COMSAT acts as manager for the design, development, construction, establishment, operation and maintenance of the space segments of the global system. Executive Order 11191, dated January 4, 1965, provided that the Department of State be given principal responsibility for furnishing such guidance to COMSAT as would insure that its activities as United States representative to INTELSAT will present the views and include the assistance of the United States Government.

The steady advance of INTELSAT toward the goal of a global system continued during 1966 and is expected to accelerate during 1967.

The first of three scheduled steps toward attaining the objective of worldwide coverage was completed in 1965 when INTELSAT I (EARLY BIRD) was placed in orbit over the Atlantic. It has continued since then to provide high-quality service between the North American continent and Western Europe. A dramatic measure of the ultimate utility of the system was demonstrated in 1965 when Early Bird carried a live international telecast of the visit of Pope Paul to the United Nations.

The second step was inaugurated in October 1966 when the first of the INTELSAT II satellites was launched into orbit over the Pacific Ocean. Despite the failure to achieve the desired orbital path, it continues to provide effective service during certain hours of each day. Indeed, a historic milestone was reached on November 27, 1966, when, for the first time, millions of people in Japan, Hawaii and the United States viewed live telecasts originating in Hawaii, Japan and the United States and relayed via this satellite.[1]

The INTELSAT II phase will continue during 1967 with the orbiting of a satellite over the Atlantic Ocean.

As INTELSAT's plans for the third step move ahead, mankind may look forward to having at its disposal in 1968 the space segments to which all but a few nations of the world can be linked when the complex of earth stations has been adequately developed.

Realization of the full benefits of this new and expanded means of communication in the interest of all nations and of all peoples now demands equal application of imagination and skill to the solution of the socio-economic and political problems which have already arisen and which will inevitably arise in the future. This demands the painstaking and objective efforts of our people and our agencies to assure the most beneficial use of our capability in telecommunications.

Many suggestions have been advanced on the potentialities of satellite communications for the development of new techniques of education. The specific proposals made by major business organizations and foundations merit careful study and evaluation. Close cooperation between the Congress and the Federal departments and agencies will lead to a resolution of organizational and financial problems and to realizing most effectively the benefits for our own people as well as for the people of other nations.

During 1966, a number of technical proposals and studies have been made to enable us to cope more effectively with the problem of introducing the use of satellites into an already crowded radio spectrum. These appear to warrant the development of new and higher areas of the spectrum not yet in active use. These efforts offer considerable promise for much greater expansion of satellite communication service. They also indicate the need for enlarged and accelerated research and development and the results made available to nations of the world at the earliest possible time.

The solutions to these and other problems are necessary in order to promote the orderly and continuous growth of satellite communications. Industry, science and government of this nation and that of its international partners—working together, recognizing that the fruits of their efforts can benefit all of mankind, and considering the economic, scientific and legal implications of their solutions—are equal to the task.

International Activities

DURING 1966 the Department of State continued directly, and through the Communications Satellite Corporation (COMSAT), to implement the policy of the United States to encourage additional membership in and progress of INTELSAT. During the year, seven nations[2] joined the consortium, bringing international membership to a total of fifty-five.[3]

Five nations[4] have had investment quotas approved by INTELSAT and their formal accession to the Interim Agreement is awaited. Other countries are considering joining the consortium.

Membership on the Interim Communications Satellite Committee (ICSC), which is the governing body of INTELSAT, increased from fourteen to seventeen during 1966. Under the terms of the Agreement, the members of the ICSC represent a total of forty nations of the consortium.[5]

The Supplementary Agreement on Arbitration became effective on November 21, 1966, when all of the signatories of the Special Agreement of August 1964 affixed their signatures to the new Agreement. This provided for the establishment of an arbitral tribunal with the authority to adjudicate disputes arising out of interpretation of the Interim and/or Special Agreements.

Interest continues at a high level in the progressive development of an earth station complex. INTELSAT members, including many developing countries, have evidenced their intent to use the space segment at an early date, either by establishing earth stations within their national boundaries or by linking with a neighboring earth station. By 1969, it is anticipated that there will be in operation approximately forty earth stations, at least half of which may be located in developing nations. Achievements of the latter goal depends upon the availability of adequate funding and the development of necessary technical capabilities for the operation of earth stations. The United States has actively pursued a policy of advising developing countries toward overcoming these and other obstacles.

In conformance with notification and registration procedures adopted by the International Telecommunication Union (ITU) in 1963, and to assure that INTELSAT members are provided the opportunity of satisfying their satellite communication frequency needs, a group of frequency experts, in January 1966, developed a procedure for selecting INTELSAT space segment frequency bands and for filing appropriate information with the ITU. These procedures were submitted to and approved by the nations of the consortium and were placed in effect on September 1, 1966. Each INTELSAT member now has the opportunity to study and comment on proposed uses of the radio spectrum prior to a final decision by the ICSC.

The rapid growth in the use of the radio spectrum, which is accelerated in certain bands by the introduction of communications satellites, is posing problems for the advanced nations which make extensive use of the spectrum. The communications administrations of these countries are coordinating their efforts within the framework of the ITU in order to find ways of making more efficient use of this important national and international resource.

A number of international organizations gave increased attention during 1966 to the growing importance and use of satellite communications technology.

In its role as a contributor to the International Telecommunication Union Technical Assistance Program, the United States sponsored a seminar on earth station technology during the period May 16-27, 1966. Representatives of forty-five nations met at the Department of State and participated in a series of lectures, industrial demonstrations and field trips to technological facilities and to an earth station. This was one of the efforts to acquaint international officials, particularly those of developing countries, with the current state of the art in respect to earth station technology.

During 1966 a number of meetings were held at which United Nations-affiliated international organizations engaged in wide-ranging discussions concerning the expanding promise and importance of satellite communication. Included among these meetings were those of the Plan Committees of the International Telegraph and Telephone Consultative Committee, the XIth Plenary Assembly of the International Radio Consultative Committee, the Communications/Operations Division of the International Civil Aviation Organization and the Aeronautical Extraordinary Administrative Radio Conference.

Through these and other international forums, much is now being done to plan an orderly and effective introduction of satellite technology into the global communications network without creating adverse effects on existing communications services.

National Activities

NATIONAL Aeronautics and Space Administration support of COMSAT includes that of furnishing satellite launch and associated capabilities on a reimbursable basis. The second formal Launch Services Agreement was signed on July 22, 1966, which provides for the required NASA support of the INTELSAT II phase and for replacement of the INTELSAT I (EARLY BIRD) satellite if the requirement arises. The terms of the agreement are essentially similar to those of the agreement covering the Early Bird launch. The approximate cost to INTELSAT of NASA support is $3,570,000 per launch.

As a result of INTELSAT's decisions, COMSAT, in May 1966, contracted for delivery of six operational communication satellites for the INTELSAT III phase; the first of these satellites is scheduled for delivery during the first half of 1968. Decision as to the type of launch vehicle to be used will be made approximately eighteen months prior to launch.

NASA has continued during the past year to engage in a number of technical advisory activities. It provided technical advice and comments to the Federal Communications Commission (FCC) on a number of applications filed by COMSAT with the FCC; and acted as advisor to the Department of State at a Ground Station Seminar held in Washington, D. C., in May 1966, and at the XIth Plenary Assembly of the International Radio Consultative Committee (CCIR), in June 1966 in Oslo. It continues to coordinate with and furnish technical advice and assistance to the Director of Telecommunications Management.

During 1966 NASA continued its broad-based research and development program to advance the state of the art in satellite communications technology. The flight portion of the program is being carried out with a series of Applications Technology Satellites (ATS), the first of which was launched December 6, 1966. These satellites will include experiments using advanced methods of multiple access, passive attitude stabilization, despun antennas, and communication between ground stations and aircraft via satellite relay.

Studies continued during 1966 to develop the technology required for the employment of communications satellites for navigation, traffic control and communications for aircraft and ships; for other services involving simultaneous communication to large numbers of small, transportable earth stations; and for the broadcasting of aural and visual programs. Studies are also continuing on propagation phenomena which influence the feasibility of frequency-sharing between satellite and terrestrial services; and on extending the useful portion of the frequency spectrum.

On July 5, 1966 NASA signed a contract which called for the provision by INTELSAT of six voice-data and two teletypewriter circuits between and among the United States and each of the three earth stations at Carnarvon, Australia; Ascension Island and Grand Canary Island; and each of three instrumentation ships located respectively in the Atlantic, Pacific and Indian Oceans.

The award of this contract had been preceded by a series of negotiations undertaken in conformance with the policy that commercial communications facilities will be used to the maximum feasible extent by all Government agencies.

Discussions of the potential employment of satellite communications within NASA's operational network (NCS/NASCOM) were initiated in June 1965 among representatives of NASA, Department of Defense (DOD), the National Communications System (NCS) and COMSAT. In August, COMSAT submitted a proposal to the Executive Agent of the NCS, and following evaluation and approval by several joint working groups representing NASA, DOD, and NCS, negotiations were begun between NASA and COMSAT and were culminated with the award of a contract.

Concurrent negotiations with communications entities of Australia, United Kingdom and Spain for provision of service between their respective earth stations and the INTELSAT II satellites in the Atlantic and Pacific areas are completed.

The Department of Defense has also arranged for the use of INTELSAT resources both for required expansion of circuits to the Far East and augmentation of DOD's communications capability in Southeast Asia.

On July 26, 1966, a contract was awarded for thirty circuits between Hawaii and Japan, the Philippines and Thailand; and on October 10, 1966, Western Union International, Inc., was requested to provide ten voice-data circuits between the U. S. mainland and Hawaii—both services via INTELSAT II satellite.

As a result of the advent of satellite communication services, the U.S. international common carriers have proposed substantial tariff reductions which will result in significant saving to both private and government users of international services via satellite and cable circuits.

Both the Federal Aviation Agency (FAA) and United States international airline operators are convinced that satellite communications offer the only practical near-term solution to the problem of obtaining the reliability of communications required to assure air safety and traffic control for trans-oceanic flights. Very High Frequency (VHF) services do not have the necessary range and High Frequency (HF) radio is not adequately reliable to provide these essential communications requirements. Moreover, these existing means are incapable of adequate expansion to meet the growing requirements of greatly-increased international air traffic.

To cope with this complex problem, FAA is participating in a coordinated program with the National Aeronautics and Space Administration (NASA). FAA is also conducting an in-house effort to define the magnitude of the problem. Concurrently, the Communications Satellite Corporation (COMSAT), with the close collaboration of the FAA, is applying its resources to a study of the problem.

The FAA is working actively within the framework of the International Civil Aviation Organization (ICAO), first introducing its views on the subject of employing satellite communications for transoceanic air traffic control at a European-Mediterranean Meeting in February 1966. The matter was again discussed in October 1966 at a general meeting in Montreal.

It is considered that the technique of air/ground communications via satellite in the VHF portion of the radio spectrum is well within the present state of the art. Use of satellite technology for this purpose awaits agreement by ICAO members on system standards, funding and operational employment.

For its long-haul point-to-point communications, the FAA will continue to share in and contribute to the National Communications System (NCS) resources. The FAA will consider the use of satellite communications if the price is competitive with the cost of presently-used services. Beyond that, the FAA has no plans for the use of point-to-point communication via satellite.

The Department of Health, Education and Welfare (HEW) has continued to expand its use of telecommunications in support of major social, medical and educational goals. The use of audio-visual techniques has already had a significant impact; the potentialities of other means are being carefully studied. The possibility of employing low-cost, long-distance transmission techniques for home television viewing, for point-to-point interconnection between hospitals, laboratories and educational units, for rapid interrogation of data centers, for more effective coordination of Federal programs, and for the institution of real-time reporting systems— is also being evaluated.

The potential use of satellite technology in the enhancement of these and other goals is drawing increasing attention of HEW and preliminary concepts are being drawn. Plans for an in-depth demonstration of the feasibility of using satellite communications for vast extension of HEW's services to the public are being advanced. Such a demonstration would capitalize on the existence of broad-based activities such as are found in the National Library of Medicine, the Public Health Audio-Visual facility and in the communications structure of the nation's medical institutions. It would contemplate testing two-way transmission of various forms of data, televised instruction, seminars via radio and television, and other innovations in information exchange.

Recognition of the future capability of communication satellites to provide world-wide service is leading HEW to study the feasibility of interconnecting the nation's medical facilities for domestic use and for using this complex as a basis for developing an international service. The value of such a service in the interchange of information resulting from medical research and development can be measured against the fact that more than one-half of ongoing health research which generates knowledge of use to all mankind is initiated by other than American institutions.

NOTES

1. A second INTELSAT II satellite was successfully launched into orbit over the Pacific Ocean on January 11, 1967, and will be capable of providing up to 240 channels of communication. With the approval of INTELSAT, the United States intends to increase satellite service by using a portion of this capability in support of its APOLLO program.

2. Liechtenstein, Malaysia, Mexico, Morocco, Philippines, Singapore and Thailand.

3.

Algeria	Fed. Rep. of	Liechtenstein	South Africa
Argentina	Germany	Malaysia	Spain
Australia	Greece	Mexico	Sudan
Austria	India	Monaco	Sweden
Belgium	Indonesia	Morocco	Switzerland
Brazil	Iraq	Netherlands	Syria
Canada	Ireland	New Zealand	Thailand
Ceylon	Israel	Nigeria	Tunisia
Chile	Italy	Norway	United Arab Republic
Rep. of China	Japan	Pakistan	United Kingdom
Colombia	Jordan	Philippines	United States
Denmark	Kuwait	Portugal	Vatican City
Ethiopia	Lebanon	Saudi Arabia	Venezuela
France	Libya	Singapore	Yemen

4. Ecuador, Korea, Panama, Peru and Tanzania.

5.   *Member of ICSC*   *Other Nations Represented by the ICSC Member*

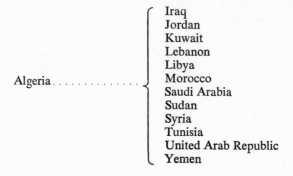

Algeria . . . .
Iraq
Jordan
Kuwait
Lebanon
Libya
Morocco
Saudi Arabia
Sudan
Syria
Tunisia
United Arab Republic
Yemen

Argentina
Australia
Belgium . . . . The Netherlands
Brazil
Canada
Chile . . . . { Colombia
        { Venezuela
France . . . . Monaco
Federal Republic of Germany
Italy . . . . Vatican City
Japan
Mexico
Spain . . . . Portugal
Sweden . . . . { Denmark
        { Norway
Switzerland . . . . { Liechtenstein
        { Austria
United Kingdom . . . . . . Ireland
United States

APPENDIX VIII

The Lexonomics
of Telecommunications:

Legal-Economic Patterns of National
Telecommunications Systems
Throughout the World*

MOST OF US HAVE CLEAR AND RATHER STEREOTYPED IDEAS of the legal and economic patterns prevailing in various countries of the world. The U.S.S.R. stands as the prototype of a socialized industrial economy and the United States represents a highly developed capitalist economy. In general, it is assumed that the states of Western Europe fall into the pattern of capitalist economies whereas those of Eastern Europe, together with some of the African and Asian countries, are socialist. It would appear to be an easy matter to survey the world scene and ascertain how many countries have telecommunications systems fitting one or another of these patterns. In fact, however, such a survey is far more difficult than it appears and any reports based on such a survey are, at best, only approximations.

The Survey

IN an effort to determine the legal-economic patterns governing the telecommunications systems in various parts of the world I have attempted to survey these systems country by country. The first thing that becomes apparent is that there is no single comprehensive and authoritative source

* Written by Lee Loevinger, a former member of the Federal Communications Commission. Reproduced by permission of the *Journal of Broadcasting* and the author.

for such a survey. The best sources I have found are listed and classified in Appendix A. Relying on such sources I have surveyed more than 200 geographical areas. This number is greater than the number of nations which belong to the UN or the ITU as it includes not only sovereign nations but also countries whose political status is in dispute and separate geographical areas that are not independent sovereignties and have political ties to other countries. All of the countries or areas given separate recognition and listing in one of the standard reference sources used have been surveyed and are named in Appendix B.

The identification of countries or geographical areas is relatively easy compared to classification of telecommunications systems. There are government owned and operated telephone and broadcasting systems, systems owned and operated by private commercial enterprises, systems owned by government and operated privately and autonomously, and private systems operated under strict government control. The difficulty is that there is almost every conceivable variation and mixture of these patterns, and each country has its own combination of variants. There are countries with government owned telephone systems and commercial broadcasting systems, like Andorra. There are countries with privately operated and government owned telephone systems and government operated broadcasting systems, like Italy. There are countries with government operated radio systems and commercial television systems, like the Dominican Republic; and there are countries with commercial radio systems and government operated television systems, like Colombia.

For purposes of classification it has been necessary to establish broad categories which are by their nature somewhat arbitrary. The categories that have seemed most appropriate are: First, predominantly government operation; Second, systems involving both government and commercial operation; and Third, predominantly commercial operation. The assignments to categories have been made on the basis of information reported in the reference sources, although in some cases this is equivocal. Further, there is such variation in size, population and other characteristics of countries and areas that more than a mere count of countries is required, though it is difficult to say precisely what additional facts are most important.

The most significant aspect of telecommunications seems to be the scope and efficiency with which it functions, which is indexed by the number of people who are communicated with. This is at least roughly indicated by the numbers of telephones and of radio and television receivers in a country. Here another difficulty arises. It is possible to determine the number of telephones connected to government and commercial systems respectively, but radio and television receivers may be tuned to any station. Nevertheless, some indication of significant patterns may be given by the numbers of receivers in the countries and areas which have predominantly government, commercial, and mixed broadcasting systems. It must be emphasized that set counts for many countries are not altogether reliable, that there are variations in reports among reference sources, that all available reports are more than a year old and that, for these and other reasons, the basic numbers and percentages reported are only approximations. With this reservation, these data do present significant patterns. A tabular summary of the data is attached as Appendix C. The number of countries and areas surveyed is greater than the number of telecommunications systems reported in each category, as some lack certain facilities, such as radio or television stations. Incidentally, this survey has disclosed that there are at least three jurisdictions in which there is a total absence of telephones, radio and television transmitting stations—which some may consider a blessing. These are: Bhutan, a small country in the Himalayas bounded by Sikkim, Tibet and India; Nauru, a trust territory of Australia in the South Pacific; and the Tokelau Islands, also in the South Pacific.

Europe

IN Europe, including the U.S.S.R., the predominant pattern is clearly that of government operation. Twenty-nine countries have telephone systems operated by the government, one country (Norway) has government operation with some private operation, two countries have only commercially operated systems and four countries have predominantly commercial systems with some government operation. Thus, 30 countries have predominantly government operated telephone systems, and six countries have predominantly commercial telephone systems. Eighty-two percent of the telephones are government operated and only 18% are commercially operated.

European radio is government operated in 24 countries, six countries have both government and commercial operation of radio transmitters and three countries have only commercial operation. However, the countries with government operated radio systems have the overwhelming preponderance (88%) of the radio receivers reported for Europe. The countries with government and commercial operation have approximately 15% of the radio receivers and the countries with commercial radio transmitters have less than 1% of the radio receivers in Europe. The commercially operated systems are in the relatively small countries of Andorra, Luxembourg and Monaco, but do reach audiences beyond the borders of these countries.

Twenty-five European countries have government operated television transmitting stations, but at least eight of these accept advertising and rely in part upon advertising revenue for support. The United Kingdom and

Malta have mixed government-commercial operation of television transmitters, and four countries have predominantly commercial operation of television. The countries with government operation have 90% of the television receivers in Europe; the countries with government and commercial operation have approximately 10% of the television receivers in Europe; and the countries with predominantly commercial operation have less than 1% of the television receivers.

Africa

AFRICA presents a picture similar to Europe in this respect. Fifty-one countries in Africa have a government operated telephone system. Three countries have telephones operated both by government and commercial enterprise, and four countries have commercial operation of telephones. However, 99% of the telephones in Africa are connected with government operated systems and only 1% are connected to commercial systems.

In Africa 44 radio broadcast transmitting systems are government operated, of which at least three accept advertising and rely in part on such revenue. Seven African radio broadcasting systems involve both government and commercial operation and only three such systems are predominantly commercial. Seventy per cent of the radio receivers in Africa are in countries with government operated transmitting systems; 30% are in countries with government and commercially operated systems; and approximately 1% are in countries with commercially operated systems.

Nineteen African countries have government operated television systems, and two accept advertising and rely in part on such revenue. Two countries have government operated television together with commercial operation, and one country (Mauritius) is reported to have a commercially operated system. Ninety-three per cent of the television receivers are in countries having government operated transmitting systems; 6% of the receivers are in countries with government and commercially operated systems; and 1% of the receivers are in a country with a commercial system.

Asia

THE pattern in Asia is slightly different, but this is largely due to the predominance in the statistics of the Japanese telecommunications system. Thirty-two countries of Asia have government operated telephone systems, three countries have government and commercially operated systems, and five countries have commercial systems. However, only 33% of the telephones are connected to government operated systems while 67% of the telephones are connected to commercial systems. The overwhelming majority of the latter are in Japan.

Twenty-seven countries of Asia have government operated radio broadcasting systems of which at least two accept advertising. Ten countries (including Japan) have government and commercially operated systems; and the Ryukyu Islands have a commercial system. Forty-three per cent of the radio receivers in Asia are in countries with government operated transmitting systems, and 57% are in countries with government and commercially operated systems. However, more than 70% of the latter are in Japan. Less than 1% of the radio receivers are in the Ryukyu Islands. Eleven Asian countries have government operated television transmitters; seven (including Japan) have government and commercially operated transmitters. The distribution of television receiving sets is quite out of proportion to this distribution of country systems, because nearly 90% of the television receiving sets are in Japan. Thus, 95% of the television receiving sets are in the seven countries (including Japan) that have government and commercially operated transmitters, while only 2% of the receivers are in the 11 countries with government operated transmitters, and 3% of the receivers are in the five countries with commercially operated transmitters.

Oceania

In Australia there is a government operated telephone system, and a mixed government and commercially operated radio and television transmitting system. Australia is by far the largest of the areas that compose Oceania, and, consequently, by far the largest number of telephones as well as radio and television receivers in the Oceanian areas are in countries with government operated telephone systems and with government and commercially operated radio and television systems. However, there are more than 18 other Oceanian islands with government operated telephone systems, as well as 14 with government operated radio systems, and three with government operated television systems. Outside of Australia there is little commercial television.

North America

North America has four countries or geographical areas: Canada, Greenland, St. Pierre & Miquelon, and the United States. The islands have government operated telephone systems as well as radio transmitters. However, the number of telephones and radio and television receivers in Canada and the United States is so great that more than 99% of the telephones in North America are connected to commercial telephone systems, and more than 99% of the radio and television receivers are in those two countries. Canada has a mixed government and commercial broadcasting system. The United States has a predominantly commercial broadcasting system, and has 95% of the radio receivers and 92% of the television receivers in North America. However, as will be noted later, there are a number of broadcasting stations operated by various levels of government in the United States.

Central America and Caribbean

IN Central America and the Caribbean the pattern resembles that of North America, with a commercial rather than government predominance. Twelve countries of this area have government operated telephone systems, four have government and commercially operated systems, and ten have predominantly commercial systems. However 27% of the telephones are connected to government operated systems while 73% are connected to commercial systems. In this area are eight government operated radio broadcast transmitting systems; five countries or areas with government and commercial operation; and 11 countries or areas with predominantly commercial operation. Twenty-three per cent of the receivers are in countries with government operated transmitters; 3% are in areas with government and commercially operated transmitters; and 74% are in countries with predominantly commercial operation. The television systems are even more often commercial. Only two jurisdictions have government operated television transmitters; three have government and commercially operated television transmitters; and 14 have predominantly commercially operated television transmitters. Seventeen per cent of the television receivers are in countries with government operated transmitters; 2% are in countries with government and commercial operation, and 81% are in countries and areas with predominantly commercial TV transmitters.

South America

SOUTH America presents a similar pattern but with a slightly different distribution. Seven countries have government operated telephone systems; two have government and commercially operated systems, and five have predominantly commercial systems. Approximately 50% of the telephones are connected to government operated systems and 50% to commercial systems. Two countries of South America have government operated radio broadcast transmitters; one country (Argentina) has government and commercial transmitters; and eleven countries have predominantly commercial transmitters. The countries with government operated transmitters have less than 1% of the radio receivers. Argentina has approximately 30% of the radio receivers in South America; and approximately 70% are in countries with predominantly commercial transmitters. Two countries of South America have government operated television transmitting systems; Argentina has both government and commercial transmitters; six countries have predominantly commercial systems; and Chile has only educational television transmitters operated by universities. Approximately 5% of the receivers are in countries with government operated transmitters; 30% of the television receivers are in Argentina; approximately 65% of the receivers are in countries with predominantly commercial transmitting stations; and Chile has less than 1% of the television sets.

United States of America

IN order to illustrate the complexity of any classification, and the lack of clear-cut national patterns, it may be worthwhile to add a little more detail about the situation in the United States. As of the first part of 1967, there were in the United States more than 4,000 commercial standard broadcast (AM) radio stations and more than 1,500 commercial FM radio stations on the air. In addition to those, however, there were more than 300 educational FM stations on the air, of which approximately 200 were owned and operated by either city or state governmental agencies. The remainder were owned and operated by non-profit private organizations. There were approximately 615 commercial television stations on the air, plus some 130 educational television stations. Of the latter, about 90 were owned and operated by state or city governmental agencies, and the remainder were owned and operated by private non-profit organizations. Thus, even in the United States, which has a clearly predominant commercial broadcasting system, there are a significant number of government operated broadcasting stations.

Several other elements also deserve attention. There are three major television networks in the United States, and four radio networks. All of these are privately and commercially owned and operated. Furthermore, the stations, as in all the countries of the world, are licensed, and to some degree regulated, by a government agency. The government with the licensing and regulatory authority is the Federal government, whereas it is state and city governments which own and operate the governmental stations. There is some debate as to the precise role which the Federal government should play in attempting to influence program content of commercial stations in the United States, but there is general agreement that the government should not control programming and, in fact, the Federal government exercises little regulatory authority and probably has little influence on programs. It is, therefore, fair to conclude that the broadcasting system of the United States is, in a realistic sense, a privately operated system and that the national government has little participation and only limited regulatory control.

However, a recent statute establishes a federally-chartered public, nonprofit corporation, with a majority of directors appointed by the President, to provide additional broadcast programming, to offer greater diversity and possibly greater cultural depth than commercial network programs. In addition, the Communications Satellite Corporation, commonly known as Comsat, was established by Congress as a private commercial corporation but with three directors appointed by the President and subject to regulation by the FCC in many of its activities. Comsat is also manager of an interim consortium for satellite communications known as Intelsat, which has more than 50 members, most of which are the telecommunications agencies of other countries.

Finally, the United States now has over 100 million telephones, of which well over 90% are owned and operated by two companies and their corporate affiliates. Yet there are nearly 100,000 telephones operated by state or municipal governments in the United States; there are many hundreds of small private commercial telephone companies; and the large companies are subject to government control and regulation as to both service and rates.

Telecommunications Problems

REGARDLESS of the form of legal and economic organization, all telecommunications systems face essentially the same problems. These seem to fall into five major categories. The first major telecommunications problem is obviously that of *establishing technical standards and specifications*. For broadcasting this involves the assignment of frequencies, power, nature of electromagnetic emission and the establishment of many operating characteristics necessary to insure compatibility of transmitters and receivers and to prevent harmful interference among transmitters. In radio transmission AM and FM can be received only on receivers constructed for such types of emission, and the tuning range of the receivers must correspond to the frequencies on which the transmissions take place. In television additional technical characteristics require control in order to insure that transmissions can be received. The number of lines scanned in various systems in use in different parts of the world range from 405 to 819. Channel widths in use range from 5 MHz to 14 MHz with the visual bandwidth ranging from 3 MHz to 10 MHz. Other characteristics involved are the nature of the sound modulation (whether AM or FM), polarity, and the system used for color transmission. This latter is still the subject of international dispute.

Similarly, telephone transmissions must involve instruments at both ends as well as connecting channels or circuits and intermediate switchboards and other equipment, all of which are designed to handle similar electronic messages. The problem of wire transmission is being complicated by increasing demands for the transmission of data generated by computers and similar automatic devices, for the transmission of radio and television programs, and for the transmission of other types of messages requiring varying bandwidths. All these problems necessitate the establishment of common standards within the country, as well as some coordination between countries that desire to communicate with each other, which today includes virtually all countries.

The second problem, or class of problems, is the *availability of instruments*. In telephone systems this means telephone instruments, and in radio and television it means receivers and transmitters. This problem has been dealt with in a variety of ways. In the United States, which has almost completely a commercial telephone system, the manufacture of telephone instruments is largely monopolized by companies affiliated with the various telephone operating companies. On the other hand, in most European and Asian countries which have government operated telephone systems, the telephone instruments and equipment are manufactured and provided by competition of private enterprises which are not owned or controlled by the operating system. The superiority of telephone communications in the United States to that in many other countries is due, in large part, to the availability of instruments and equipment. This, in turn, results from the fact that the operating company is commercial and is able to devote its revenue to equipment, service and profits. In government operated systems of many countries revenue from telephone service is used to subsidize other, less profitable, services, such as the post office. As a result, these countries are unable to provide as much equipment as there is demand for and service lags.

So far as radio and television are concerned, the availability of receivers and the ability and willingness of the public to purchase and use receivers is an important element in establishing the broadcasting system. For example, in the United States the profitability of FM radio and television broadcasting in the UHF band depends very largely on availability of receivers in the community in which the station is located.

This suggests the third great class of problems faced by all telecommunications systems, which is *financial support*. Again, it is interesting to note that essentially the same problems are faced by both private and government operated systems. The three principal sources of funds for the support of broadcasting are dedicated funds (such as license fees), government grants from general revenue, and advertising revenue. In broadcasting systems operated by government the most common source of funds seems to be that of revenue derived from annual license fees on receiving sets. However, these are increasingly coming to be inadequate and are being supplemented both by government grants from general revenue and by advertising revenue. A number of observers report that the tendency in Europe is increasingly toward advertising support for broadcasting. Separate commercial television services are now in operation in Britain, Holland and Finland. Advertising is accepted on government operated television systems in Austria, West Germany, Ireland, Italy, and Switzerland. Commercial television is in operation in Portugal where the system is also financed in part by license fees on receiving sets. The systems of Monaco and Luxembourg rely entirely upon commercial revenue. The broadcasting system of Luxembourg is an outstanding example of a popular and successful commercial operation. It reaches a very substantial part of the European market, is one of the most popular and successful broadcasting operations in the world, shares profits with the government and thus provides the second largest source of revenue for the state of Luxembourg.

In the United States the great majority of broadcasting stations rely upon and are supported by revenue from commercial advertising. However, a substantial number of educational stations are supported by government grants from state, local and Federal governments, and it is now being urged that dedicated government funds be used to support the Corporation for Public Broadcasting. Correspondingly, in a number of European systems operated by government, financial support is secured from dedicated funds and government grant and is supplemented by advertising revenue. Even in Yugoslavia, a socialist country with a nationalized broadcasting system, what is called "economic publicity" or advertising provides a substantial amount of programming time and support to the system. Thus, the problems of financial support tend to be met by recourse to the same methods and sources regardless of the legal-economic structure of the system.

The problems that are probably most important for the broadcasting media have to do with *programming*. Regardless of whether a broadcasting system is operated by the government, a commercial enterprise, or a private non-profit organization, it can have no effect or influence unless it has an audience, and it cannot attract an audience unless it presents programs that people desire to hear or see. Thus, the first problem of any broadcasting system is that of ascertaining the desires and needs of the public. Broadcasting systems, whether operated by government or commercial interests, approach this problem in similar ways and arrive at roughly similar results. Music and news tend to be the dominant program elements of radio presentation in most of the broadcasting systems of the world. Although reliable figures are hard to come by, the percentage of news seems generally to vary from 5% to 20% of broadcast time. A substantial amount of time on both radio and television in all countries is devoted to sports, and the dominant programming element in television in almost all countries is entertainment.

In a communication to me from the U.S.S.R., it was said that Radio Moscow broadcasts "various features to suit the tastes and interests of all ages and professions. . . . In general, broadcasts are as varied as possible, about the same as all over the world. Some things are altogether missing from Soviet radio and television programs. We do not stand for sex, violence, and murder." These comments are in general agreement with those from other sources, including American observers. The most noticeable national differences in broadcast programming appear to be in the treatment of such things as sex, violence and religion, and in the amount of propaganda, or government bias, in news and public affairs programs. Reports of observers who have attempted to make a comparison indicate that American programs tend to show more scenes of violence than European programs while the latter are less restrained in showing scenes relating to sex. Government broadcasting systems frequently are subject to government influence in presenting news and public affairs and are always subject to that suspicion.

The general public demand in all countries is for entertaining broadcast programs. There are "pirate," or unauthorized broadcasting stations operating in or near several European countries and providing programming that meets public demand for popular entertainment which is apparently not satisfied by government operated or authorized stations. A number of these pirate stations have been remarkably successful in attracting audience. Britain has recently put stringent laws into effect to close its offshore pirate radio stations, but at the same time BBC radio has taken over much of the pirate radio programming, which has been mainly popular music.

Probably the greatest problem in television programming is that of securing an adequate amount of program material worth broadcasting. Television is the most voracious consumer of audio-visual material that the world has ever seen. Furthermore, television programming is expensive to prepare, to record and to present. As a result, the availability of television programming is limited in all countries by the amount of money the system can afford to spend for this purpose.

In most countries television broadcasting stations operate for a limited period, typically an hour or two at mid-day and four to six hours during the evening, with some additional time on Saturday or Sunday afternoons. In the United States, the typical pattern for commercial broadcasting stations is to operate from early morning until late evening, with most commercial stations operating from 5,000 to 6,500 hours a year. With three national networks, a substantial number of independent television stations, and a large number of educational television stations, this creates a tremendous demand for television program material. As a result, many American television programs are not as high quality as some people would like, and American television is subject to a good deal of disparagement and derision by professional critics. European television, which is subject to more government control, tends to reach a slightly higher cultural level and come closer to meeting the standards of critics. However, it is noteworthy that the programs produced by American commercial networks are popular and in demand throughout the world. Considering the more limited broadcasting time of television stations in Europe and the rest of the world as compared with American stations, it appears that the difference in program quality is not great, and the similarity of programming is far more striking than the differences, insofar as can be judged by reports and sporadic observation.

The methods of determining program popularity and audience response, by and large, are the same regardless of the structure and nature of the system. These methods are essentially those of survey research, and the limitations are principally those imposed by amounts of money available for the purpose. Some government operated broadcasting systems of Europe, such as BBC, engage in proportionately more audience survey research than American commercial broadcasters.

Some countries have situations that present special problems of broadcasting. For example, Canada has both French and English speaking people and thus there is demand for programs in both languages. Similar problems exist in Belgium and Switzerland, which require three languages each, and in many other countries. In the Netherlands there is a traditionally strong interest in religion. While the government has established a broadcasting system, the programming is presented largely by religious and cultural organizations, and thus Dutch broadcasting has a stronger religious element than is common in other countries.

An interesting variant of broadcasting communication is the transmission of broadcast programming by wire or cable. In Russia about two-thirds of radio reception is by wired connection, the situation is similar in Communist China, and in Hong Kong television is distributed primarily by cable. The apparent reason for adoption of this technique is a shortage of sufficient equipment, both transmitting and receiving, to meet public demand by wireless broadcasting. However, it is also interesting to note that cable systems of television program distribution are developing rapidly in the United States. Because of cost, the limitations of program source material, the philosophy of the basic television frequency allocation plan, and other reasons, television broadcasting stations in the United States are largely limited to metropolitan areas. There are less than 250 of these areas. However, there are many other communities that seek television reception, and what have been called community antenna television systems (or

CATV) have developed to bring television programming by cable to the people in these communities. About 1700 communities are now served by such systems and the number is increasing. Some metropolitan areas receive additional service through CATV. These systems are almost entirely privately owned and operated. Thus, while there are significant differences between Russia and China, on the one hand, and the United States on the other, it is interesting to note that the socialized telecommunications systems of two of the world's largest countries have utilized substantially the same technique as the private enterprise system of the largest capitalist country.

A final group of problems is that which involves the kind and degree of *government control*. Superficially it would appear that the degree of government control is directly related to the ownership and mode of operation. It is certainly true that the probability of government control is greater where the government owns and operates the telecommunications system than where it is operated by private enterprise. However, the correlation is by no means simple and direct. Rather, it appears that the kind and degree of control exercised by government depends upon traditions and attitudes of the society more than upon the form of organization of the telecommunications enterprises. Thus, Britain has had a long and strong tradition of free speech and dissent. Although BBC is a government-controlled corporation, it is reported to operate with substantial autonomy and a good deal of freedom in programming; but the government recently has shown its power by appointing the former head of ITA (British commercial television) as head of BBC. On the other hand, in countries which have historically had authoritarian governments and where commercial systems are permitted to operate, it is reported that freedom to express unorthodox or dissenting views is considerably less than in Britain.

Lexonomic Analysis

IN observing and discussing telecommunications systems of the world, as well as many other aspects of social and economic activity, it is usual to note and remark upon differences between national systems. This is commonly done by contrasting the theory of national systems, regarding one as socialist and another as capitalist. While there is tremendous variety in the telecommunications systems of the world, as had been suggested, there is another viewpoint that may be even more significant. Just as there are differences among the systems of the various countries so are there striking similarities. To some extent differences that we note are the result of conceptual schemes that we use in observation, or intellectual models that exist in the ideology of each of the countries. There is no country in which actual institutions correspond completely to the intellectual models of its ideology.

Rather, the intellectual models reflect our efforts at analysis and represent abstractions of ideas that we somehow extract from observation. But there is a very involved circular relationship between theory and observation. We cannot observe without having some idea as to what we are looking at, which implies that we have some intellectual models to begin with. On the other hand, we cannot construct models of reality without having some data derived from observation. As a child learns the simple facts about his physical environment by looking and testing, so social scientists and philosophers learn about more complex and abstract phenomena of social, legal, economic, and technical activities by observing, abstracting, theorizing, and again observing and testing.

One observation that seems to me basic in this field is that there is a fundamental and inescapable relationship between legal and economic institutions. The most simple economic elements we can think of, things such as property, contract and money, are creations of law. Certainly, complex organizations like corporations and government agencies are wholly created by law. Most laws that deal with things other than personal relations have some economic significance. On the other hand, virtually all economic institutions in organized society depend upon a legal framework. Therefore I propose that we recognize law and economics as essentially different ways of looking at similar aspects of organized society. I propose the name "lexonomy" as an appropriate term for this social structure. Certainly in examining and analyzing the telecommunications systems of the world we are dealing with the lexonomy of each nation and area under observation. I urge the use of this term partly as a matter of convenience but more importantly because the use of such term will emphasize the integral relationship between the legal and political system and the economic institutions of each country.

On the basis of this summary survey of telecommunications systems and their lexonomic aspects, I suggest that the traditional dichotomy of lexonomies into capitalist and socialist is no longer adequate as a means of either observing or describing the relevant phenomena of national activity. A more realistic conceptual scheme for observing and describing lexonomic institutions would recognize that there are four basic elements involved, any combination of which may be present in any given situation.

The first basic element of lexonomic analysis is *legislation*. Although this term can be, and frequently is, used more broadly, I suggest its use in a restricted sense to mean government promulgation of rules or principles of general applicability subject to specific interpretation and application by non-legislative tribunals on the basis of facts in particular cases. Thus statutes regulating conduct generally are examples of legislation. In the telecommunications field, laws prohibiting the transmission of obscenity over broadcasting stations or telephones are examples of legislation. Laws establishing the enforceability of contract, codes for business corporations, and rules for the acquisition and transfer of property are examples of legislation.

The second element of lexonomic analysis is *intervention*. Government "intervention" is influence exerted in economic affairs by government participation in a market economy as one enterprise among several, without coercing other participants. An example of government intervention in lexonomic affairs is the sale of stockpiled commodities in order to influence prices. The government here acts as a seller seeking to influence the market, rather than as sovereign establishing prices by virtue of coercive power. There are many examples of government action by intervention in the telecommunications field. The government establishment and operation of broadcasting stations or systems in countries with independent commercial enterprises is an example of intervention. Other examples are the establishment of a Corporation for Public Broadcasting and the making of financial grants to broadcasting enterprises.

The third element of lexonomic analysis is *regulation*. "Regulation" is government control of activity by means of orders to named enterprises or individuals requiring or permitting specified activities. Regulation is common, indeed almost universal, in the field of telecommunications. In virtually every country the government regulates radio transmission by licensing named enterprises or individuals, and by specifying and requiring transmission on particular frequencies with specified power, modes of emission, and other technical characteristics. Examples of government regulation are legion through the lexonomies of the world.

The fourth element of lexonomic analysis is *operation*. Government "operation" is precisely what the term implies, control by government of the major enterprise in an economic field by ownership. Government operation is usually and essentially government monopoly of a field; although there may be situations where there is major government operation with private competition permitted.

The Lexonomics of Telecommunications

IF we apply this mode of analysis to telecommunications it will be readily apparent that there are substantial aspects of each element in the telecommunications lexonomy of most countries. The typical telecommunications system in Europe, Africa and Asia involves a "PTT," which is a government agency operating the post office, the telephone, the telegraph and the broadcasting system. In general, telephone and telegraph equipment is purchased competitively from private enterprise, and in almost all cases all broadcasting equipment is so procured. Telecommunications systems are commonly financed by charges to users of telephones and telegraphs and by license fees or taxes upon radio and television receivers. Increasingly even government operated systems are accepting commercial advertising as a source of revenue. Furthermore, private communications systems involving radio communication for private companies, for safety uses such as air lines and ships at sea, and for business enterprises and individuals, are generally permitted subject to regulation by the appropriate government agency. Thus under these systems there is legislation establishing the general framework, government intervention in the field of advertising and marketing, government regulation with respect to the assignment of frequencies and licenses to operate, and government operation of major elements of the telecommunication system.

As has been noted, all four elements of lexonomic analysis may also be observed in the United States. In America we have a government owned and operated postal system, which is not, however, directly related to our telephone and telegraph system. We have privately owned telephone and telegraph companies, which are essentially monopolistic in their operation, but which are subject to regulation by government as to almost all aspects of operation. The American broadcasting system is predominantly a private commercial system which operates pursuant to legislation and subject to limited regulation. In general, the regulatory authority is forbidden to control or censor programming. There are also a number of broadcasting stations owned and operated by city and state governments in the United States. Further, it is now being proposed that government increase its intervention in the broadcasting field through the Corporation for Public Broadcasting and by increasing government grants to educational and cultural broadcasting stations.

Thus, surveying the world scene we observe that there are the same elements in the telecommunications system of every country, and that each country deals with essentially the same problems. It is also clear that each country has developed its own mix of the four lexonomic elements to provide its own means of dealing with the problems confronting it, and it seems probable that the variety of conditions confronting the countries of the world requires variety in combining these elements to provide tolerably satisfactory solutions to the problems.

However, another striking fact is that even the variety of combinations of lexonomic elements in the telecommunications systems of the world has not produced as much difference in results as might be expected. The American telephone system connects with more than 95% of the telephones of the world, and most of these telephones can be connected with each other. Internationally we have established systems for satellite communication which represent a complete mixture of lexonomic elements, and we are establishing facilities which will permit the transmission of both private communications and broadcast messages over wider areas with greater efficiency and economy than ever before. Even with respect to broadcast programming, which reflects national cultures more than any other element of telecommunications, there is a striking similarity. Observers of television in the countries of Europe, including the U.S.S.R., as well as in the Americas and Asia report that programs are essentially similar except for language differences, the observance of somewhat differing taboos, and slightly different mixtures of program categories.

One can emphasize either differences or similarities in a survey such as this. Realism suggests that we try to give equal attention to both. Certainly there is infinite variety in detail among telecommunications systems. Yet it seems to me that taking the broadest view, the most striking and significant fact is that of technical compatibility and basic similarity in operation of the telecommunications systems of the world.

The lexonomies of the world's countries, as well as the telecommunications systems, are like the inhabitants of those countries. The inhabitants of the numerous countries of the world differ in many respects. They speak different languages, wear different clothes, belong to different churches, eat different foods, and have almost infinite cultural diversity, although culture patterns are clearly converging. On the other hand, the inhabitants of all countries of the world are human beings who walk upright on two legs, have two arms, one head with a brain, two eyes and a mouth. They can converse with others, they require essentially the same elements for preserving and enjoying life, and they seek, the overwhelming majority of them, the same things: sustenance, security, family, dignity, and a peaceful and prosperous world. As we examine the lexonomic framework of the world's telecommunications systems it seems to me that likewise the similarities are more profound and more significant than the differences.

APPENDIX VIII–A

Sources and Bibliography

MANY STATEMENTS in the text and tabulations of the underlying analysis are based on several sources, and a number of sources listed relate to many statements in the text. In some respects, the sources were not wholly consistent, and some data presented involve reconciliation or weighing of several sources. Thus, it has not been practical to relate specific statements or conclusions to particular sources by conventional footnotes. However, the published sources listed contain data supporting all factual statements and conclusions of the text.

Personal Interviews and Correspondence:
Personal interviews with telecommunications officials of: Belgium, Canada, China (Taiwan), Finland, France, Ireland, Italy, Netherlands, Sweden, Switzerland, United Kingdom, United States, and other countries, and correspondence with U.S.S.R.

Directories and Standard Reference Guides:
World Radio TV Handbook, 1967—21st Edition (World Radio-Television Handbook Co., Ltd., Hellerup, Denmark)
The World's Telephones 1966 (American Telephone & Telegraph Co., 195 Broadway, New York, N.Y. 10007)
World Communications—press, radio, television, film (UNESCO 1964).
Broadcasting (1967 Yearbook Issue), p. A–167, et seq.
Television Factbook, 1967 ed., p. 932–b, et seq.

Books and Monographs:
BBC Handbook—1967
Emery, Walter B., *Five European Broadcasting Systems* (Belgium; Netherlands; Portugal; Hungary, Yugoslavia), Journalism Monographs, No. 1, August 1966 (Assn. for Education in Journalism, University of Texas, Austin, Texas).
Firestone, O. J., *Broadcast Advertising in Canada* (Ottawa: U. of Ottawa Press, 1966).
Inkeles, Alex, "Domestic Broadcasting In the U.S.S.R.," in *Communications Research, 1948–1949,* ed. by Paul F. Lazarsfeld and Frank N. Stanton (New York: Harper & Bros., 1949), pp. 223–293.
ITV 1966 (A Guide to Independent Television, published by ITA, London, 1966).
Kominski, John J., "Political Broadcasting in Other Democracies," 113 *Cong. Rec.* S 12019 (daily ed.) 90th Cong., 1st Sess.
Paulu, Burton, *British Broadcasting* (Minneapolis: U. of Minnesota Press, 1956), and *British Broadcasting in Transition* (Minneapolis: U. of Minnesota Press, 1961).
Weir, E. Austin, *The Struggle for National Broadcasting in Canada* (Toronto: McClelland and Stewart, 1965).

Articles in Scholarly Journals:
Ranjan Borra, "TV in India," *Television Quarterly,* 5:4:51 (1966).
James C. Ching, "Mass Communications in the Republic of the Congo (Leopoldville)," *Journalism Quarterly,* 41:237 (1964).
Wilson P. Dizard, "The Political Impact of Television Abroad," *Journal of Broadcasting,* 9:195 (Summer, 1965).
Walter B. Emery, "Broadcasting in Mexico," *Journal of Broadcasting,* 8:257 (Summer, 1964).
Walter B. Emery, "Radio Luxembourg: 'The Station of the Stars,'" *Journal of Broadcasting,* 10:31 (1966).

Richard R. Fagen, "Mass Media Growth: A Comparison of Communist and Other Countries," *Journalism Quarterly,* 41:563 (1964).

Richard R. Fagen, "Relation of Communication Growth to National Political Systems in the Less Developed Countries," *Journalism Quarterly,* 41:87 (1964).

Vincent Farace and Lewis Donohew, "Mass Communication in National Social Systems: A Study of 43 Variables in 115 Countries," *Journalism Quarterly,* 42:253 (1965).

Leonard J. Fein and Victoria E. Bonnell, "Press and Radio in Rumania: Some Recent Developments," *Journalism Quarterly,* 42:443 (1965).

Richard Hauser, "Small Screens and Serving Girls—TV in France," *Television Quarterly,* 5:4:43 (1966).

Mark W. Hopkins, "Lenin, Stalin, Khrushchev: Three Concepts of the Press," *Journalism Quarterly,* 42:523 (1965).

Frank Iezzi, "The Politics of Piracy," *Television Quarterly,* 5:4:25 (1966).

Jay Jensen and Richard Bayley, "Highlights of the Development of Russian Journalism, 1553–1917," *Journalism Quarterly,* 41:403 (1964).

Richard Kahlenberg and David Attenborough, "BBC–2: An Experiment in Diversity," *Television Quarterly,* 5:4:9 (1966).

Alan Ping-lin Liu, "Growth and Modernizing Function of Rural Radio in Communist China," *Journalism Quarterly,* 41:573 (1964).

Elmer W. Lower, "Television, Soviet Style—1967," *Television Quarterly,* 6:3:29 (1967).

John D. Mitchell, "Thailand's Unexamined Media: Nondaily Newspapers and Radio-TV," *Journalism Quarterly,* 42:87 (1965).

Doreen Stephens, "Children's TV in Britain," *Television Quarterly,* 5:4:61 (1966).

"Television in Eastern Europe," *Television Quarterly,* 6:3:34 (1967).

Richard Tuber, "A Survey of Programming on the Central Studios of Television, Moscow, U.S.S.R.," *Journal of Broadcasting,* 3:315 (Fall, 1960).

Frederick Williams, "The Soviet Philosophy of Broadcasting," *Journal of Broadcasting,* 6:3 (Winter, 1961–62).

Reports in Newspapers and News Magazines, Etc.:
Broadcasting: Aug. 7, 1967 (p. 69); April 24, 1967 (p. 75); etc.

Christian Science Monitor: July 31, 1967 (p. 2); June 14, 1967 (p. 12); etc.

EBU Review: No. 97B (May 1966) Special Religious Broadcasting Number.

London Times: July 30, 1967 (p. 1); July 27, 1967 (p. 1); May 31, 1964 (p. 1); Oct. 30, 1963 (p. 9); Mar. 9, 1961 (p. 11).

(London) *Daily Express, The Observer, The Daily Telegraph:* July 30, 1967; July 27, 1967.

National Observer: July 17, 1967 (p. 6).

Newsweek: March 6, 1961 (p. 98); etc.

New York Herald-Tribune: Jan. 10, 1966 (p. 21).

New York Herald-Tribune, International Edition: Jan. 24, 1964 (p. 10).

New York Times: Oct. 2, 1967 (p. 94); Aug. 15, 1967 (p. 17); Aug. 10, 1967 (p. 8); June 16, 1967 (p. 75); June 15, 1967 (p. 83); June 12, 1967 (p. 77); June 6, 1967 (p. 78); April 6, 1967 (p. 17); March 22, 1966 (p. 2); Aug. 20, 1965 (p. 59); Nov. 10, 1964 (p. 1); Nov. 9, 1964 (p. 11); April 23, 1964 (p. 15); etc.

New York Times International Edition: Feb. 17, 1964; Feb. 24, 1964 (p. 6); May 27, 1964 (p. 5).

New York World-Telegram: Feb. 25, 1965 (p. 33).

Saturday Review: Aug. 12, 1967 (p. 60); July 8, 1967 (p. 47); June 9, 1962 (p. 23); etc.

Sponsor: March 23, 1964 (p. 41).

Time: Sept. 15, 1967 (p. 70); March 10, 1967 (p. 50).

TV Guide: May 13, 1967 (p. 14); April 29, 1967 (p. 14); etc.

Variety: Sept. 13, 1967; Aug. 30, 1967 (p. 44); Aug. 23, 1967 (p. 38); Feb. 5, 1964 (p. 24).

The Viewer: Oct. 12, 1961.

Washington Post: Aug. 10, 1967; May 19, 1967 (p. D 4); etc.

Washington Star: Aug. 27, 1967 (p. C 4); etc.

APPENDIX VIII – B

List of Countries and Geographical Areas Surveyed

This list is compiled from the sources indicated in Appendix A. No opinion or conclusion is suggested or implied by this listing or by the names used to identify countries and geographical areas, as these are taken from the sources. In general, data reported are as of 1966.

Europe

Albania
Andorra
Austria
Azores (Portugal)
Belgium
Bulgaria
Channel Islands
   (U.K.)
Czechoslovakia
Denmark
Finland
France
Germany—East
   (German Demo-
   cratic Republic)

Germany—West
   (Federal Republic
   of Germany)
Gibralter
Greece
Hungary
Iceland
Ireland
Italy
Liechtenstein
Luxembourg
Malta
Monaco
Netherlands
Norway

Poland
Portugal
Rumania
San Marino
Spain
Sweden
Switzerland
Turkey
Union of Soviet
   Socialist Republics
United Kingdom
Yugoslavia

Africa

Algeria
Angola
Ascension Island
Botswana
Burundi
Cameroon
Cape Verde Islands
Central African
   Republic
Chad
Comoro Islands
Congo (Brazzaville)
Congo, Democratic
   Republic of
Dahomey
Ethiopia
Gabon
Gambia
Ghana
Guinea, Republic of
Ifni (Spanish)
Ivory Coast

Kenya
Lesotho
Liberia
Libya
Malagasy Republic
   (Madagascar)
Malawi
Mali
Mauritania
Mauritius
Morocco
Mozambique
Niger
Nigeria
Portuguese Guinea
Reunion
Rhodesia
Rwanda
Sahara, Spanish
St. Helena
Sao Tome
   & Principe

Senegal
Seychelles
Sierra Leone
Somalia
Somaliland (French)
South Africa
South West Africa
Spanish Equatorial
   Africa
Spanish North Africa
   (Centa & Melilla)
Sudan
Swaziland
Tanzania
Togo
Tunisia
Uganda
United Arab Republic
Upper Volta
Zambia

Asia

Aden (U.K.)
Afghanistan
Bahrein
Bhutan
Brunei
Burma
Cambodia
Ceylon
China—Mainland
(People's Republic
of China)
China—Taiwan
(Republic of
China)
Cyprus
Hong Kong (U.K.)
India
Indonesia
Iran

Iraq
Israel
Japan
Jordan
Korea—North
(People's Demo-
cratic Republic of)
Korea—South
(Republic of
Korea)
Kuwait
Laos
Lebanon
Macao
Malaysia
Maldive Islands
Mongolia
Muscat & Oman
Nepal

Pakistan
Philippine Republic
Portuguese Timor
Ryukyu Islands
Saudi Arabia
Sikkim
Singapore
Syria
Thailand
Trucial Oman
Vietnam—North
(Democratic Re-
public of Vietnam)
Vietnam—South
(Republic of Viet-
nam)
West Irian
Yemen

Oceania

Australia
British Solomon
Islands
Caroline Islands
Christmas Island
Cook Islands
Fiji Islands
Gilbert & Ellice
Islands

Guam
Marshall Islands
Midway Island
Nauru
New Caledonia
New Hebrides
New Zealand
Nieue
Norfolk Island

Papua & New Guinea
Polynesia, French
Samoa, American
Samoa, Western
Tokelau Islands
Tonga
Wake Island

North America

Canada
Greenland

St. Pierre
& Miquelon

United States of
America

Central America and Caribbean

Bahama Islands	El Salvadore	Netherlands Antilles
Barbados	Guadeloupe	Nicaragua
Bermuda	Guatemala	Panama
British Honduras	Haiti	Puerto Rico
Canal Zone	Honduras, Republic of	Trinidad & Tobago
Cayman Islands	Jamaica	Turks & Caicos
Costa Rica	Leeward Islands	Islands
Cuba	Martinique	Virgin Islands
Dominican Republic	Mexico	Windward Islands

South America

Argentina	Ecuador	Peru
Bolivia	Falkland Islands	Surinam (Dutch
Brazil	French Guiana	Guiana)
Chile	Guyana	Uruguay
Colombia	Paraguay	Venezuela

APPENDIX VIII–C

Lexonomic Patterns of Telecommunications Systems

Region and System	Government Operation		Government and Commercial Operation		Commercial Operation	
	NUMBER OF SYSTEMS	APPROX. % OF INSTRUMENTS IN SYSTEMS OR RECEIVERS IN COUNTRIES	NUMBER OF SYSTEMS	APPROX. % OF INSTRUMENTS IN SYSTEMS OR RECEIVERS IN COUNTRIES	NUMBER OF SYSTEMS	APPROX. % OF INSTRUMENTS IN SYSTEMS OR RECEIVERS IN COUNTRIES
EUROPE						
Telephone	29	82%	1	*	6	18%
Radio	24	85%	6	15%	3	<1%
Television	25	90%	2	10%	4	<1%
AFRICA						
Telephone	51	99%	3	*	4	1%
Radio	44	70%	7	30%	3	1%
Television	19	93%	2	6%	1	1%
ASIA						
Telephone	32	33%	3	*	5	67%
Radio	27	43%	10	57%	1	<1%
Television	11	2%	7	95%	5	3%

OCEANIA						
Telephone	19	92%	—	—	I	8%
Radio	14	25%	I	73%	I	2%
Television	3	17%	I	82%	I	1%
NORTH AMERICA						
Telephone	2	1%	—	—	2	99%
Radio	2	1%	I	5%	I	95%
Television	—	—	I	8%	I	92%
CENTRAL AMERICA & CARIBBEAN						
Telephone	12	27%	4	*	10	73%
Radio	8	23%	5	3%	11	74%
Television	2	17%	3	2%	14	81%
SOUTH AMERICA						
Telephone	7	50%	2	*	5	50%
Radio	2	<1%	I	30%	11	70%
Television	2	5%	I	30%	6	65%

*Although some countries have telephone systems with both government and commercial operations, it is possible to ascertain the system to which a telephone is connected, and this Appendix shows the percentages of telephones connected to "government operated" and "commercially operated" telephone systems, rather than the proportion of telephones in countries with mixed (government and commercial) systems. Appendix B lists the countries and geographical areas surveyed to compile the data in Appendix C. Not all of the countries or areas listed in Appendix B have radio and television broadcasting systems, so the numbers of systems reported in Appendix C does not necessarily total the same as the number of countries listed in Appendix B.

Appendix A lists the sources of data. Most data relating to numbers of telephones and receiving sets and organizations of systems are as of the first part of 1966. Some data are more recent. It should be noted that the reference sources report data that are not altogether consistent. These data were reconciled for purposes of summary in Appendix C, but the results must be regarded as approximations.

APPENDIX IX

The Canadian Broadcasting Act

of 1968

CHAPTER IV contains an account of activities leading up to the passage of the Broadcasting Act of 1968. At the time the chapter was written, the Canadian Parliament had not yet enacted the law but, as pointed out, a House Standing Committee had already made recommendations and new legislation was imminent.

On March 7, 1968, Parliament passed the Broadcasting Act (16017 Elizabeth II, Chapter 25, pp. 203–237). The changes which it made in the Broadcasting Act of 1958 (7 Elizabeth II, Chapter 22, pp. 137–151) should be noted.

Basic Broadcasting Services

PART I of the new Act recites the broad policies which shall govern broadcasting in Canada, namely, (1) that broadcasting undertakings (including stations, networks and cable systems) use radio frequencies that are public property and that all such undertakings constitute one single system comprising public and private elements; (2) that the Canadian broadcasting system should be effectively controlled by Canadians in the national interest; (3) that broadcast licensees have public responsibilities, but freedom of expression, within the framework of law and regulations, is unquestioned; (4) that programming should be of high quality, be balanced and serve the multiple and varied interest of listeners and viewers in all areas of the country; (5) that opportunities should be provided for the expression of differing views on subjects of public importance; and (6) that broadcasting in English and French should be provided as public funds become available.

Furthermore, the law states, emphasis should be placed upon the development of national unity and the need "for a continuing expression of Canadian identity," and "where any conflict arises between the national broadcasting and the interest of the private element," it must be resolved in the national and public interest.

A special provision requires that facilities be provided for educational broadcasting, and that regulation of all broadcasting, both commercial and noncommercial, be flexible and "readily adaptable to scientific and technical advances."

To achieve these objectives most effectively, the law declares that there should be one single, independent agency vested with authority to supervise and regulate the total broadcasting system in the country.

Establishment of Commission and Executive Committee

ACCORDINGLY, the Canadian Radio–Television Commission (CRTC) was created, replacing the Board of Broadcast Governors. The Commission, with broader regulatory powers than those vested in the BBG, consists of five full-time and ten part-time members, all appointed by the Governor in Council. Section 8, Par. I of the Act provides that the Governor in Council shall designate one full-time member as Chairman.

An Executive Committee, consisting of the Chairman, Vice-Chairman and the other three full-time members, has been vested with major regulatory authority and responsibilities. In fact, what powers the Commission exercises stem largely from recommendations of this Committee. Based upon these recommendations, the Commission may do the following things:

(a) prescribe classes of broadcasting licenses;
(b) make regulations applicable to all broadcast stations with reference to program standards; character of advertising and amount of time that may be devoted to it; assignment of time for political broadcasting; the conditions for operation of broadcasting stations as part of a network and the conditions for the broadcasting of network programs, and the amount of fees to be paid by licensees; and the kind of reports regarding management and operation of stations that must be filed with the Commission.

The Executive Committee, after consultation with part-time members in attendance at a meeting, may issue broadcasting licenses for terms not exceeding five years and prescribe the conditions for operation, issue renewals not exceeding five years, suspend licenses other than those held by the Canadian Broadcasting Corporation, and review and consider any technical matter relating to broadcasting referred to the Commission by the Minister of Transport and make recommendations to him relating thereto. The full Commission, subject to prescribed hearing procedures set forth in the Act, is empowered to revoke any broadcasting license, excluding those which are held by the Corporation.

Canadian Broadcasting Corporation

THE new law provides for the continuation of the CBC but increases the number of directors from eleven to fifteen and makes it more subject to the regulatory policies of the Commission than it was to the Board of Broadcast Governors. Section 39 of the Act states that the Corporation is established for the purpose of providing the national broadcasting service, in accordance "with the conditions of any licence or licences issued to it by the Commission and subject to any applicable regulations of the Commission." To carry out this purpose the Corporation is authorized, among other things, to perform the following functions:

(a) establish, equip, maintain and operate broadcasting undertakings;

(b) make operating agreements with licensees for the broadcasting of programs;

(c) originate programs, and secure programs from within or outside Canada by purchase, exchange or otherwise, and make arrangements necessary for their transmission;

(d) make contracts with any person, within or outside Canada, in connection with the production or presentation of programs originated or secured by the Corporation;

(e) make contracts with any person, within or outside Canada, for performances in connection with the programs of the Corporation;

(f) with the approval of the Minister, act as agent for or on behalf of any person in providing broadcasting service to any part of Canada not served by any other licensee;

(g) publish, distribute and preserve, whether for a consideration or otherwise, such audio-visual material, papers, periodicals and other literary matter as may seem conducive to the purposes of the Corporation;

(h) collect news relating to current events in any part of the world and establish and subscribe to news agencies;

(i) acquire copyrights and trade marks;

(j) acquire and use any patent, or patent rights, licences or concessions that the Corporation considers useful for its purposes;

(k) make arrangements or agreements with any organization for the use of any rights, privileges or concessions that the Corporation considers useful for its purposes;

(l) acquire broadcasting undertakings either by lease or by purchase;

(m) subject to the approval of the Governor in Council, acquire, hold and dispose of shares of the capital stock of any company or corporation authorized to carry on any business that is incidental or conducive to the attainment of the objects of the Corporation; and

(n) do all such things as the Corporation deems incidental or conducive to the attainment of the purposes of the Corporation.

The Act also provides that the Corporation may, "within the conditions of any licence or licences issued to it by the Commission and subject to any applicable regulations of the Commission, act as agent for or on behalf of any Minister of the Crown or as an agent of Her Majesty in right of Canada or of any province, in respect of any broadcasting operations that it may be directed by the Governor in Council to carry out, including the provision of an international service."

Both the Commission and Corporation are required to submit annual reports to the Secretary of State regarding their operations. The Secretary in turn is required to transmit these reports to Parliament within fifteen days after receiving them.

Minister of Transport

SECTION 48(2c) of the law provides that the Minister of Transport may prescribe classes of radio licenses, and may grant technical construction and operating certificates. He regulates and controls all technical matters relating to the planning, construction and operation of broadcasting facilities; determines the power, radio frequency and call letters used by broadcasting undertakings; and prescribes technical requirements regarding equipment, etc.

Section 51 states that the Minister "shall take such action as may be necessary to secure, by international regulation or otherwise, the rights of Her Majesty in right of Canada in telecommunications matters and shall consult the Canadian Radio–Television Commission with respect to all such matters that, in his opinion, affect or concern broadcasting." Moreover, he is under statutory mandate to "undertake, sponsor, promote or assist in research relating to radiocommunication including the technical aspects of broadcasting," and "encourage the development and more efficient operation of radiocommunication services and increasing their usefulness and availability in the public interest."

Licenses

SECTION 22 states that no broadcasting licence will be issued, amended or renewed in contravention of any direction to the Commission issued by the Governor in Council under the authority of the Broadcast Act respecting the maximum number of channels or frequencies for the use of which licenses may be issued within a geographical area designated by the directive. The same prohibition applies to the reservation of channels or frequencies for the use of the Corporation or for any special purpose designated in a directive by the Governor in Council. Nor will any license be granted, amended or renewed "unless the Minister of Transport certifies to the Commission that the applicant has satisfied the requirements of the *Radio Act** and regulations thereunder and has been or will be issued a technical construction and operating certificate under that Act with respect to the radio apparatus that the applicant would be entitled to operate under the broadcasting licence applied for or sought to be amended or renewed." Furthermore, "no broadcasting licence is of any force or effect during any period while the technical construction and operating certificate issued under the *Radio Act* with respect to the radio apparatus that the holder of the broadcasting licence is entitled to operate thereunder is suspended or revoked."

Revocation and Suspension of Licenses

As previously pointed out, the Executive Committee may suspend the licenses of broadcasting stations but only the full Commission may revoke them. In both cases, however, licensees may be officially notified as to the reasons for the proposed action and must be afforded opportunity for a public hearing. In the case of the Canadian Broadcasting Corporation, if, after affording it an opportunity to be heard, the Commission concludes that the Corporation has violated or failed to comply with any condition of a broadcasting license or any regulation, the Commission is required to submit a report to the Secretary of State setting forth its findings of fact together with recommendations for action. A copy of this report must be presented by the Secretary, within fifteen days, to the Parliament. If Parliament is not in session at the time, the report must be presented within fifteen days after the Parliament reconvenes.

The law provides for appeal from the decisions and orders of the Commission to the Supreme Court of Canada upon questions of law or jurisdiction, upon leave being obtained from the Court, or within such further time as the Court or a judge thereof under special circumstances may allow.

Penalties for Infractions of the Law

SEVERE penalties are prescribed for the transmission via radio of false or fraudulent messages. The same applies to the interception of radiocommuni-

---

* A statute separate from the Broadcasting Act, which includes requirements of a technical nature pertaining to all radio stations regardless of class or type.

cations (other than broadcasting) and the divulgence thereof. Likewise, there are criminal sanctions against the establishment of any kind of radio station without governmental authority.

BBG Regulations Continued until
Repealed or Altered by the Commission

SECTION 62, Part V of the new law provides that the regulations made by the Board of Broadcast Governors under the former Act continue in effect until modified or repealed by the Canadian Radio–Television Commission. As of this writing, the BBG regulations (see Appendix I) were still applicable to all broadcasting stations in Canada.

Harry Boyle, Vice-Chairman of the Commission, has indicated that the CRTC will aim at "encouraging rather than discouraging" broadcasters, both public and private, "to get the best possible form of broadcasting." The "Canadian content" regulations [6(1) to 6(6)], which varied from forty-five to fifty-five percent of programming time under the old law, were described by Mr. Boyle as a "negating" approach. Under the new Act, the Commission is empowered to set programming standards for each station on an individual basis. Mr. Boyle has stated that "the first priority is to assure full coverage by the second network," that is, the establishment of private television stations in those areas now served only by the Corporation. Beyond that, no revolutionary changes are expected in the present broadcasting structure or in the program regulations. (See *Ottawa Star*, April 20, 1968, p. 4.)

APPENDIX X

The Yugoslav Broadcasting
Law of 1965*

General Provisions

Art. 1

RADIOBROADCASTING institutions within the meaning of this law are organizations broadcasting their own public programs through their radio transmitting stations and/or television stations.

Art. 2

Radiobroadcasting institutions inform the public on the events and development concerning all spheres of life in Yugoslavia and abroad, initiate discussions on matters of public interest and broadcast opinions of citizens, organizations and public organs on such matters, make and broadcast cultural, artistic, educational, entertainment and other programs with the view to satisfying cultural requirements and other interests of citizens.

Radiobroadcasting institutions shall care for building, development and maintenance of the radio transmitting network and for securing material means required for advancement of radiobroadcasting and for development and advancement of radiobroadcasting programs.

Art. 3

The affairs of radiobroadcasting institutions concerning the drawing up and transmission of programs and those connected with building, development and maintenance of the radiotransmitting network are affairs of special social concern.

In managing the affairs of special social concern of radiobroadcasting

* The Basic Law on Radiobroadcasting Institutions was promulgated April 1, 1965. Translation published in the *1966 Yugoslav Radio and Television Yearbook*, pp. 274–282.

institutions representatives of the social community shall also take part, in accordance with this law and the statute of the radiobroadcasting institution.

Art. 4

The social community shall care for development of radiobroadcasting and for that purpose shall create favourable conditions for establishment and operation of radiobroadcasting institutions and for building and development of the radio transmitting network.

Art. 5

Radiobroadcasting institutions shall autonomously draw up and broadcast their programs.

No notification or permission are required for transmission of programs of radiobroadcasting institutions.

Programs of radiobroadcasting institutions are not subject to censorship.

Art. 6

Radiobroadcasting institutions are bound to comply with the regulations concerning radio communications and with international conventions on radio communications in force in Yugoslavia.

Art. 7

The affairs connected with building, development and maintenance of the radio transmitting network and ensuring reception of radiobroadcasting programs on the territory of a Republic are discharged by one or more radiobroadcasting institutions provided by republican regulations.

Art. 8

Each radiobroadcasting institution shall have a statute.

The statute of the radio broadcasting institution shall be sent for consideration to the municipal assembly on the territory of which the radiobroadcasting institution is located, and the statute of the radiobroadcasting institution under article 7 of this law—to the republican and/or provincial assembly.

Art. 9

The provisions of the Law on the Press and Other Media of Information shall apply accordingly to the matters concerning broadcasting and diffusion of information in transmissions of radiobroadcasting institutions, freedom of exchange of information with other countries, accessibility to the sources of information, duties and responsibilities of the persons engaged in drawing up and broadcasting the programs of the radiobroadcasting institutions, right to reply to the information communicated in the transmissions of the radiobroadcasting institution and prohibition to transmit programs of radiobroadcasting institutions, as well as qualifications for discharging the functions of responsible editor and his liability.

Art. 10

Except where otherwise provided by this law, the provisions of the Basic Law on Institutions shall apply to the radiobroadcasting institutions.

Establishment

Art. 11

Radiobroadcasting institutions may be established by the socio-political community and the working and other self-governing organization under the conditions provided by law.

Art. 12

Before bringing the act of establishment the founder shall obtain permission for erection of a radio station and/or television station under the general regulations of radio communications.

Art. 13

The act of establishment of a radiobroadcasting institution shall contain, besides the particulars required by the general regulations on institutions, also the particulars concerning the character of the program of the radiobroadcasting institution (information, entertainment, educational, advertising program etc.) and the language in which the program shall be transmitted.

Art. 14

The radiobroadcasting institution shall within eight days after receiving the decision on registration send the republican organ of administration competent for affairs of information the following particulars:

1) the name of the radiobroadcasting institution and its location;
2) the date of registration of the radiobroadcasting institution;
3) the name of the founder;
4) the character of the program of the radiobroadcasting institution;
5) the language in which the program is to be transmitted;
6) the time of transmission of the program;
7) personal name and residence of the responsible editor;
8) address of editorial offices of the radiobroadcasting institution and of the offices of its transmitting station.

Together with the particulars under paragraph 1 of this article the radio-broadcasting institution shall submit the necessary proofs that no disabilities under article 30 of the Law on the Press and Other Media of Information attach to the editor-in-chief.

Art. 15

All changes in the particulars under article 14 of this law must be notified by the radiobroadcasting institution to the republican organ of administration competent for affairs of information within eight days upon their occurrence.

Activities

Art. 16

Activities of the radiobroadcasting institutions comprise the affairs connected with drawing up and transmission of programs and maintenance and development of the radio transmitting network.

For the purpose of creating favourable conditions for discharge of their tasks radiobroadcasting institutions may engage in supplementary business of production and sale of special technical articles required for operation of radio stations and television stations, production and sale of television films, phonographic and videographic articles, organization and arrangement of public cultural performances, issuing of publications concerning radiobroadcasting, transmission of economic advertisements and utilization of the ground surrounding radio transmitters.

Art. 17

Radiobroadcasting institutions may, besides their own programs, transmit also the programs of other radiobroadcasting institutions.

Two or more radiobroadcasting institutions may prepare and transmit a common program, in part or in whole.

When a radiobroadcasting institution transmits the program of another radiobroadcasting institution or radiobroadcasting institutions prepare and transmit a common program, their mutual relations shall be regulated by contract.

In the case under paragraph 3 of this article obligations against third persons fall on the mother broadcasting institution.

Art. 18

Radiobroadcasting institutions shall transmit specified programs designed for foreign countries and programs in the languages of the peoples of Yugoslavia when so required by the federal and/or republican organ of administration competent for affairs of information.

For transmission of programs under paragraph 1 of this article the radiobroadcasting institution shall be entitled to compensation of actual costs.

Art. 19

Radiobroadcasting institutions shall without delay and free of charge transmit communications concerning emergencies or other events of special concern for the public, if their urgent transmission is required by the organ of administration of the socio-political community competent for affairs of information.

Art. 20

The radiobroadcasting institution under article 7 of this law shall keep the record of users of radio receivers and charge a fee for the use of such receivers.

In a republic where there are several radiobroadcasting institutions under article 7 of this law, republican regulations shall designate the radiobroadcasting institution to keep the record of users of radio receivers and charge fees for the use of such receivers, as well as the manner of distribution of the fees among such institutions.

A radio receiver within the meaning of this law is deemed to be any apparatus or other device designed for reception of radio programs.

Art. 21

For the purpose of ensuring technical conditions for transmission and improvement of reception of radio programs, radiobroadcasting institutions may lay down the necessary technical installations on the grounds and other objects in social civil property in conformity with the regulations on expropriation.

Together with the request for expropriation the radiobroadcasting institution shall submit a certificate of the republican organ of administration competent for affairs of radio communications showing that the erection of installation under paragraph 1 of this article is necessary.

Art. 22

Radiobroadcasting institutions may request orders for transmission of economic and other advertisements on the whole territory of Yugoslavia and abroad.

Such orders may be received for the radiobroadcasting institutions by authorised persons in its employment, business agents engaged for that purpose with agreed remuneration, as well as by the working organizations licenced therefore.

Art. 23

It is the duty of the radiobroadcasting institutions to make their activities accessible to the public. For that purpose the radiobroadcasting institutions shall publish in the newspapers not less than once annually their plans of development, plans of radio programs, annual reports of operation and such general acts as may be of interest for the public.

Management

Art. 24

The organs of management of radiobroadcasting institutions are: the council, the board of management and the director.

Other organs of management of radiobroadcasting institutions may be created by their statutes.

Art. 25

In a radiobroadcasting institution having less than 30 workers the functions of the council shall be exercised by the working community, and in a radiobroadcasting institution having less than 15 workers the working community shall also immediately exercise the functions of the board of management.

Art. 26

Representatives of the social community in a radiobroadcasting institution of the statute of the radiobroadcasting institution, except the provisions relating to the organization of work and distribution of personal revenue, as well as in determination of the plan and program of development of the radiobroadcasting institution, issuing of directives for development and improvement of the program of the radiobroadcasting institution, cooperation with other radiobroadcasting institutions in the matters of program, distribution of the income into a portion for personal revenue and common needs of workers and a portion for enlargement of the material basis of work of the radiobroadcasting institution, offering opinion on appointment and removal of the director and in other affairs specified by law or by the statute of the radiobroadcasting institution in accordance with the Constitution.

Art. 27

Representatives of the social community in a radiobroadcasting institution established by the socio-political community shall be appointed and recalled by the organ designated in the act of establishment of such radio-broadcasting institution, and in a radiobroadcasting institution established by a working or other self-governing organization—by the municipal assembly in the territory of which the radiobroadcasting institution is located.

The number of representatives of the social community may not exceed one third of membership of the council elected by the working community and/or one third of membership of the working community of the radiobroadcasting institution not electing the council.

Representatives of the social community in the radiobroadcasting institution are appointed for the term of two years, but they may be removed even before the expiration of this period.

Art. 28

Representatives of the social community participate in deciding upon the matters under article 26 of this law as members of the council of the radiobroadcasting institution.

In a radiobroadcasting institution not electing its council, representatives of the social community shall participate in deciding upon the matters under article 26 of this law at the meetings of the working community.

Art. 29

Decision upon the matters under article 26 of this law may be brought if the majority of the council membership elected by the working community and majority of representatives of the social community are present at the meeting of the council of the radiobroadcasting institution.

Decision of the council of the radiobroadcasting institution are brought by majority vote of the members present.

Art. 30

Representatives of the social community shall vote separately from the council members elected by the working community of the radiobroadcasting institution if this is required by not less than half the membership of the social community present at the meeting of the council.

Where representatives of the social community are voting separately from the council members elected by the working community of the radiobroadcasting institution, decision shall be considered taken if voted by the majority of representatives and majority of the council members elected by the working community.

Art. 31

Where in deciding on a matter no agreement is reached between the representatives of the social community and the council members elected by the working community of the radiobroadcasting institution, a joint commission shall be formed to consider such matter and propose a solution. Representatives of the social community and the council members elected by the working community of the radiobroadcasting institutions shall appoint members to such commission by equal numbers.

If the commission under paragraph 1 of this article fails to reach agreement, or the council meeting fail to approve its proposal, a new commission shall be formed to which representatives of the social community and the council members elected by the working community shall be appointed by equal numbers, while the chairman of the commission shall be appointed by the organ appointing representatives of the social community to the radiobroadcasting institution (article 27, paragraph 1).

The commission decision under paragraph 2 of this article shall be taken by majority vote and shall be final.

Art. 32

The provisions of articles 29–31 of this law shall apply according in the case where the functions of the council or a radiobroadcasting institution are exercised by the working community.

Art. 33

The director of the radiobroadcasting institution established by the socio-political community shall be appointed and removed by the organ designated by the act of establishment of the radiobroadcasting institution, and the director of the radiobroadcasting institution established by a working or other self-governing organization—by the municipal assembly on the territory of which such radiobroadcasting institution is located.

The director shall be appointed and/or removed upon previous opinion of the council of the radiobroadcasting institution.

Fees for Use of Radio Receivers

Art. 34

The user of a radio receiver shall notify the purchase thereof and give a notice in case of destruction, durable unusability, alienation or other disposition of his receiving set.

Notification and notices shall be given to the radiobroadcasting institution under article 7 of this law within 30 days after the obligation of notification and/or notice was created.

Art. 35

The user of a radio receiver shall pay the radiobroadcasting institution under article 7 of this law a fixed monthly fee for the use of the receiving set.

The user of the radio receiver shall pay the fee for the use of the receiving set all until he shall have given the notice thereof.

In the case of alienation or other disposition of a radio receiver the former user shall pay the fee for its use all until he shall have given the notice and/or until the new user shall have notified it.

Art. 36

The amount of the fee for the use of the radio receiver shall be fixed by the radiobroadcasting institution under article 7 of this law.

Art. 37

The user of a radio receiver desiring to discontinue the use thereof may notify discontinuation to the radiobroadcasting institution under article 7 of this law and require the institution to seal the receiver.

The expenses connected with the sealing of a radio receiver shall be borne by the user of such receiver.

Art. 38

The radiobroadcasting institution under article 7 of this law may have the fees for use of radio receivers collected by another working organization, by authorized persons in its employment or by business agents engaged for that purpose with agreed remuneration.

Art. 39

The working organization selling radio receivers shall notify the sale of every receiver to the radiobroadcasting institution under article 7 of this law and state the type, model and factory number of the receiver, as well as the name and residence of the buyer.

Customs officers shall also send to the radiobroadcasting institution under article 7 of this law the particulars under paragraph 1 of this law for any radio receiver imported by individual persons.

If the importer of radio receivers is a working organization selling receivers the customs officer shall send to the radiobroadcasting institution under article 7 of this law only the name of the working organization and the number of the receivers imported.

Art. 40

The user of a radio receiver is entitled to place an antenna on the roof of the neighbouring dwelling building if it is indispensable for reception of radio programs and if it does not interfere with reception of radio programs by the dwellers of the neighbouring building.

Art. 41

Detailed provisions on the mode of notification and notices of radio receivers and the system of recording radio receivers and their users, as well as the manner of collection and payment of fees for the use of radio receivers shall be made by republican regulations.

Financial Provisions

Art. 42

Radiobroadcasting institutions shall create their financial means from the fees charged for the services rendered, the revenue derived from their supplementary business and from other sources.

Art. 43

The socio-political community and the working or other self-governing organization, founder of the radiobroadcasting institution may provide for the radiobroadcasting institution to render, within the framework of its basic activities, specified services at a fixed charge to all or a determined class of beneficiaries of such services, provided that the founder shall compensate the difference between the fixed charges and actual costs of such services.

Art. 44

Radiobroadcasting institutions carrying on economic activities as a supplementary business shall in discharge of such business calculate and pay their dues to the social community according to the regulations governing the enterprises carrying on the respective economic activity.

Art. 45

Radiobroadcasting institutions shall calculate and pay the amortization for their basic means and/or use the amortization means according to the regulations governing economic organizations.

Exceptionally, the Federal Executive Council may fix the rates of amortization of radiobroadcasting installations and other radio materials at a higher level than the one applied to such installations and materials in economic organizations.

Winding Up

Art. 46

A radiobroadcasting institution shall be wound up:

1) if there is no need for its basic activity;

2) if the technical and other conditions required for operation of the radiobroadcasting institution cease to exist;

3) if it becomes merged with another radiobroadcasting institution, or associated with another radiobroadcasting institution, or divided into two or more radiobroadcasting institutions;

4) if it is no longer capable of discharging its obligations and the founder is not willing to consolidate it.

Art. 47

The act of winding up of a radiobroadcasting institution in the case under article 46, item 1 of this law shall be brought by the assembly of the socio-political community which has established the radiobroadcasting institution.

Where the radiobroadcasting institution was established by the working or other self-governing organization, the act of winding up in the case under article 46, item 1 of this law shall be brought by the municipal assembly in the territory of which the radiobroadcasting institution is located, upon previous opinion of the founder of such radiobroadcasting institution.

In the case under article 46, item 2 of this law the act of winding up shall be brought by the municipal assembly in the territory of which the radiobroadcasting institution is located.

Where a radiobroadcasting institution established by the socio-political community is wound up for reasons provided under article 46, item 3 of this law, the acts of the organs of management of the radiobroadcasting institution deciding upon its merger, association or division shall be subject to approval by the assembly of the respective socio-political community; and where a radiobroadcasting institution established by the working or other self-governing organization is wound up for the same reasons the acts of the organs of management of the radiobroadcasting institution deciding on its merger, association or division shall be subject to approval by the municipal assembly in the territory of which the radiobroadcasting institution is located.

Art. 48

In the case of winding up of a radiobroadcasting institution the country economic court where it was registered shall send the notice that it has been scratched out of the register to the republican organ of administration competent for affairs of information.

Penal Clauses

Art. 49

The radiobroadcasting institution shall be punished for transgression by a fine not exceeding 200.000 dinars:

1) if it fails to send to the competent organ within the period prescribed any of the particulars provided in article 14, paragraph 1 of this law, or to submit the proofs concerning the responsible editor provided in article 14, paragraph 2 of this law;

2) if it fails to notify the competent organ within the period prescribed any changes in the particulars provided in article 14 of this law (article 15);

3) if it fails to transmit the communication required by the competent organ under article 19 of this law.

The responsible person of the radiobroadcasting institution shall be punished for the offence under item 1 or 2, paragraph 1 of this article by a fine not exceeding 50.000 dinars, and for the offence under item 3, paragraph 1 of this article by a fine not exceeding 50.000 dinars or detention for a period not exceeding 30 days.

Art. 50

Any person failing to notify the purchase of a radio receiver under article 34 of this law shall be punished for transgression by a fine not exceeding 30.000 dinars.

Any working or other self-governing organization and any civil-legal person shall be punished for the offence under paragraph 1 of this article by a fine not exceeding 50.000 dinars, and the responsible person of such corporate bodies—by a fine not exceeding 15.000 dinars.

The responsible person of a state organ shall be punished for transgression by a fine not exceeding 15.000 dinars if he fails to notify the purchase of a radio receiver for requirements of the respective organ under article 34 of this law.

Art. 51

Any user of the radio receiver breaking the seal or otherwise using the receiver sealed by the radiobroadcasting institution (article 37) for reception of radio programs during the time for which he has not paid the user's fee shall be punished for transgression by a fine not exceeding 50.000 dinars.

Any working or other self-governing organization and any civil-legal person shall be punished for the offence under paragraph 1 of this article by a fine not exceeding 100.000 dinars, and the responsible person of such corporate bodies—by a fine not exceeding 30.000 dinars.

The responsible person of the state organ using a radio receiver shall be punished for the offence under paragraph 1 of this article by a fine not exceeding 30.000 dinars.

Art. 52

Any working or other self-governing organization selling radio receivers shall be punished for transgression by a fine not exceeding 300.000 dinars if it fails to notify the sale of a radio receiver to the competent radio broadcasting institution as provided in article 39 of this law.

The responsible person of such organization shall be punished for the offence under paragraph 1 of this article by a fine not exceeding 50.000 dinars.

Transitional and Final Provisions

Art. 53

The existing radiobroadcasting institutions shall conform their organization and operation with the provisions of this law within six months after the coming in force of this law.

The existing radiobroadcasting institutions shall apply for registration to the competent court within the period fixed in paragraph 1 of this article.

If an existing radiobroadcasting institution fails to apply for registration within the time provided under paragraph 2 of this article, the municipal assembly in the territory of which such radiobroadcasting institution is located shall bring the act of winding up.

Art. 54

Radiobroadcasting institutions are exempt from payment of the contribution from the income and the interest on the operational fund.

The contribution from the income and the interest on the operational fund shall be calculated and paid into the operational fund of the radiobroadcasting institution.

Art. 55

On the day of coming in force of this law there shall be repealed:

1) The Law on Radio Transmission Stations (Official Gazette of the FPRY, No. 52/55 and Official Gazette of the SFRY, No. 11/65).

2) The Decision determining the percentage of the licence fee in the territory of the People's Republic of Serbia payable as revenue of the radio station "Radio Beograd I" (Official Gazette of the FPRY, No. 20/49).

Art. 56

The Rules on payment of radio licence fees (Official Gazette of the FPRY, No. 57/51) shall cease to apply in the territory of the respective republic as from the date of coming in force of the republican regulation under article 41 of this law, but not later than six months after the date of coming in force of this law.

Art. 57

This law shall come in force the day after its publication in the Official Gazette of the SFRY.

SELECTED PROVISIONS OF THE LAW ON THE
PRESS AND OTHER MEDIA OF INFORMATION*

Art. 1

In order to ensure the democratic rights of citizens, to strengthen the role of public opinion in social life and to provide the fullest possible information for the benefit on events and developments in all domains of life in the country and abroad, the freedom of the press and other media of information is guaranteed.

Art. 2

The citizens of Yugoslavia, irrespective of differences in nationality, race, language or religion, have the right to express their opinions and make them known through media of information. They have the right to make use of such media for personal information. They have the right to disseminate information, to publish papers and other publications, to issue instructions and set up organizations for disseminating information, and to take part in managing the means of public information under the condition laid down by this Law.

The rights provided for by the previous paragraph of this article shall

* Excerpts from Chapters I and III of the Law of the Press and Other Media of Information, as amended and supplemented in the *Official Journal* of the Socialist Federal Republic of Yugoslavia, No. 15, 1965. Translation published in the *1966 Yugoslav Radio and Television Yearbook*, pp. 298–300.

not be misused for the purpose of undermining the foundations of the socialist democratic government established by the Constitution, for the purpose of jeopardizing peace or the international cooperation and independence of the state, for the purpose of stirring national, racial or religious hatred or intolerance, or for the purpose of initiating criminal actions; nor shall they be misused to the detriment of public morals.

Art. 3

No special application or approval is necessary for the dissemination of information.

There is no censorship of the press or other media of information, except in the case of war, or when the immediate danger of war is confirmed by the act of the competent organ.

Art. 4

The social community shall aid in setting up institutions and organizations engaged in the dissemination of information for the benefit of the public, put some material resources at the former's disposal, provide them with material and other facilities for the performance of their tasks, and assist in the training and specialization of expert personnel.

Art. 5

Institutions and organizations engaged in the dissemination of information shall enjoy full independence in the performance of their tasks.

These institutions and organizations are managed according to the principles of social self-management.

The state organs have only those rights and duties towards institutions and organizations engaged in the dissemination of information as provided for by this Law.

Art. 6

Exchange of information between Yugoslavia and other countries is free.

This exchange can only be restricted in cases provided for by this Law to protect the country's independence, security and free development, and to ensure the full respect of human rights and freedoms, of public and law order, and of international cooperation in the spirit of the United Nations Charter.

According to the principles of reciprocity, international agreements and other forms of cooperation with other states ensure special conditions for the exchange of information between Yugoslavia and such states to facilitate mutual understanding.

Art. 7

The publication of information that damages the honour, reputation or rights of citizens, or the interests of the social community, constitutes an abuse of freedom of information, and incurs responsibility as provided for by the law.

The dissemination of information can be restricted only to prevent abuse of the freedom of information, and in cases specifically provided for by this Law.

Art. 8

Sources of information are accessible under equal conditions to all organs, institutions, organizations and individuals engaged in the dissemination of information. The manner in which information concerning each respective field of activity is provided is defined in the regulations on the organization of the state organ or in the rules of the respective institution or organization.

Art. 9

All citizens, working organizations, and other civilian legal persons are guaranteed the right to request a public reply to any published information under conditions provided for by this Law.

Art. 10

Journalists and other persons engaged in the dissemination of information are bound to perform their work in keeping with the principles of professional ethics and social responsibility, upholding truth, human rights and peaceful cooperation among nations.

Assistance will be extended and facilities provided for the most successful possible activity of journalists' associations and other similar professional associations and institutions, engaged in the dissemination of information and in the professional training of journalists and others, in keeping with their statutes and respecting the professional ethics and social responsibility to be borne by such individuals.

Art. 11

In order to further international relations and all-around cooperation with other countries in the field of information this Law lays down the rights and duties of foreign press offices, correspondents and information services, and the conditions in which they may engage in the dissemination of information in Yugoslavia.

In exercising the rights provided for in this Law, foreign institutions and correspondents engaged in the dissemination of information in Yugoslavia are bound to adhere in every respect to Yugoslav regulations.

Art. 12

The State Secretariat for Information and the republican administrative bodies competent for the dissemination of information on their territories are bound to offer institutions and organizations similarly engaged the necessary facilities for obtaining official and other information and for performing their tasks in accordance with the principles of international cooperation in the field of information.

Art. 13

In accordance with this Law, information includes news, data, opinions and other informative items published in the press or through other public information media.

In accordance with this Law, other informative items include information received through sound and television broadcasts, films and other channels provided for by this Law.

Art. 14

Special regulations have been laid down for the establishment, organization and work of the press and film enterprises and institutions, sound broadcasting and sound and television broadcasting stations.

Art. 80

In accordance with this Law sound and television information media include all broadcasts transmitted by sound and sound and television stations disseminating information.

Art. 81

Every sound and sound and television broadcasting station transmitting programmes for the public must have a responsible editor.

Sound and sound and television broadcasting stations may have several responsible editors. Such editors are directly in charge of editing the various broadcasts of the respective sound and television broadcasting station. The provisions of this Law laying down conditions for the performance of work on the part of the responsible editor of a newspaper and covering the scope of his responsibility regulate conditions for the performance of the work of the responsible editor of a sound or sound television broadcasting station and the scope of his responsibility (Art. 29 and 30).

Art. 82

The publication of a reply to any information may also be requested in the case of information published through a broadcast transmitted by a sound or sound and television broadcasting station.

In exercising the right to request a reply, and in initiating the procedure for exercising this right in the case of a sound or sound and television broadcasting station, the provisions of the Law are applied as in the case of newspapers and periodicals (Art. 34 to 49).

Art. 83

If there is no reason to refuse to publish a reply, it may be published within two days after the request has been received by the sound or sound and television station. This is usually done at the same scheduled time and in a similar broadcast as that during which the original information was transmitted.

In the case of television, the reply is broadcast only by sound.

Art. 84

It is not permissible to broadcast programmes by sound or sound and television broadcasting stations if they contain matter as listed in Art. 52 of this Law.

In the banning of such broadcasts and the procedure for deciding on the ban, the provisions of this Law referring to the prohibition of press distribution and on procedure for issuing this decision are applicable (Art. 52 to 66).

BIBLIOGRAPHY

BIBLIOGRAPHY

National Systems of Broadcasting

Books

Atkinson, William C. *A History of Spain and Portugal.* Baltimore: Penguin Books, 1961.

Awasthy, G. C. *Broadcasting in India.* Bombay: Allied Publishers Private Limited, 1965.

Barghoorn, Frederick. *The Soviet Cultural Offensive.* Princeton, N.J.: Princeton University Press, 1960.

Barnouw, Eric. *A Tower in Babel: A History of Broadcasting in the United States, Vol. I—to 1933.* New York: Oxford University Press, 1966.

Briggs, Asa. *The Birth of Broadcasting—The History of Broadcasting in the United Kingdom,* Vol. I London: Oxford University Press, 1961.

Briggs, Charles F., and Maverick, Augustus. *The Story of Telegraph and History of the Great Atlantic Cable.* New York: Rudd and Carlton, 1958.

British Broadcasting Corporation. *Annual Reports and Accounts of the British Broadcasting Corporation.* London: Her Majesty's Stationery Office, 1928 to date.

British Broadcasting Corporation. *1967 Handbook.* London, 1967.

Brounthal, Julius. *The Tragedy of Austria.* London: Victor Gollancz, Ltd., 1948.

Buzek, Antony. *How The Communist Press Works.* New York: Frederick A. Praeger, 1964.

Canadian Broadcasting Corporation. *Broadcasting in Canada: History and Development of the National System.* Ottawa: Canadian Broadcasting Corporation, 1960.

Canadian Institute on Public Affairs. *The Price of Being Canadian, 7th Winter Conference.* D. L. B. Hamlin (ed.). Toronto: Toronto University Press, 1961.

Cantril, Hadley. *Soviet Leaders and Mastery over Man.* New Brunswick, N.J.: Rutgers University Press, 1960.

Center for the Study of Democratic Institutions. *Broadcasting in a Free Society: An Occasional Paper on the Role of the Mass Media in a Free Society.* 1959.

Coase, R. H. *British Broadcasting: A Study in Monopoly.* Cambridge, Mass.: Harvard University Press, 1950.

Collison, Robert L. *Broadcasting in Britain: A Bibliography.* Cambridge, England: The University Press, 1961.

Coons, John E. (ed.). *Freedom & Responsibility in Broadcasting.* Evanston, Ill.: Northwestern University Press, 1961.

Dumazedier, Joffre. *Television and Rural Adult Education: The Tele-Clubs in France.* Paris: UNESCO, 1956.

Durham, F. Gayle. *News Broadcasting on Soviet Radio and Television.* Cambridge, Mass.: Center for International Studies, Massachusetts Institute for Technology, 1965.

Emery, Walter B. *Broadcasting and Government: Responsibilities and Regulations.* East Lansing: Michigan State University Press, 1961.

————. *Five European Broadcasting Systems. Journalism Monographs,* 1. August 1966.

Fahie, J. J. *A History of Electric Telegraphy to the Year 1837.* London: E. and F. N. Spon, 1844.

Fernandez, Jose Luis. *Derecho de la Radiodifusion.* Mexico City: Impreso en los telleres linotipograficos de la "Editorial Olimpo," Imprenta 205, 1960.

Gordon, Lincoln. *The Public Corporation in Great Britain.* New York: Oxford University Press, 1938.

Gorham, Maurice. *Sound and Fury: Twenty-One Years in the B.B.C.* London: Percival Marshall, 1948.

Hand, Learned. *The Spirit of Liberty: Papers and Addresses of Learned Hand.* New York: Alfred A. Knopf, 1952.

Harris, Robert D. G. *A Report from Spain—The Press in an Authoritarian State.* Los Angeles: University of California Press, 1964.

Hearder, H., and Waley, D. P. *A Short History of Italy.* London: Cambridge University Press, 1963.

Independent Television Authority. *ITV 1967: A Guide to Independent Television.* London, 1967.

India, Ministry of Information and Broadcasting. *Aspects of Broadcasting in India.* New Delhi: Ministry of Information, 1959.

Inglis, Brian. *The Story of Ireland.* London: Faber and Faber, 1960.

Instituto de la Opinion Publica. *Estudio sobre los Medios de Comunicacion de Masas en Espana.* Second Part. 1964.

King, Vincent S. *A General Study of the Channels of Communication between Communist China and the Western World.* Cambridge: Center for International Studies, Massachusetts Institute of Technology, 1964.

Kumar, Narendra. *School Broadcasting in India.* Jaipur, India: Nai Shiksha Prakashan, 1958.

Kumata, H., and Schramm, W. *Four Working Papers in Propaganda Theory.* Washington, D.C.: USIA, 1955.

Landry, Robert John. *This Fascinating Radio Business.* New York: The Bobbs-Merrill Co., 1946.

Lippmann, Walter. *Essays in Public Philosophy.* Boston: Little, Brown and Company, 1955.

Liu, Alan P. L. *Radio Broadcasting in Communist China.* Cambridge: Center for International Studies, Massachusetts Institute of Technology, 1964.

Louis, Roger, and Rovan, Joseph. *Television and Tele-Clubs in Rural Communities: An Experiment in France.* New York: UNESCO, 1955.

Mackay, Ian K. *Broadcasting in Australia.* Melbourne: Melbourne University Press, 1957.

Malone, William. *Broadcast Regulation in Canada: A Legislative History.* Distributed by the Canadian Association of Broadcasters. 1962.

Marconi, Degna. *My Father Marconi.* New York: McGraw Hill Book Company, Inc., 1962.

Mehlen, Raymon. *Les Cahiers, Luxembourgeois, Radio-Tele Luxembourg, Imprimeria Bourg.* Luxembourg: Bourger, 1961.

Milton, John A. *Aereopagitica for the Liberty of Unlicensed Printing.* London: Oxford at the Clarendon Press, 1886.

Namurois, Albert. *The Organization of Broadcasting: Problems of Structure and Organization of Broadcasting in the Framework of Radiocommunications,* Legal Monograph 2. Geneva: European Broadcasting Union, 1964.

National Association of Broadcasters. *NAB Handbook.* Japan: National Association of Broadcasters, Annual Publication.

Neurath, Paul M. *Radio Farm Forum in India.* New Delhi: Government of India Press, 1960.

NHK. *The History of Broadcasting in Japan.* Tokyo: NHK Press, 1967.

————. Radio and Television Culture Research Institute. *Studies in Broadcasting.* 1967.

Nicol, John; Shea, Albert A.; and Simmins, G. J. P. *Canada's Farm Radio Forum.* Paris: UNESCO, 1954.

Nils, Andren. *Government and Politics in the Norden Countries.* Stockholm: Almquist and Wiksell, 1964.

O'Brien, Terence H. *British Experiments in Public Ownership and Control.* London: George Allen and Unwin, Ltd., 1937.

Osterreichischer Rundfunk. *Forty Years of Broadcasting in Austria (40 Jahre Rundfunk in Osterreich), Chronik 1924–1938.* Vienna, 1964.

Paulu, Burton. *British Broadcasting.* Minneapolis: University of Minnesota Press, 1958.

————. *British Broadcasting in Transition.* Minneapolis: University of Minnesota Press, 1961.

————. *British Broadcasting: Radio and Television in the United Kingdom.* Minneapolis: University of Minnesota Press, 1956.

Pingaud, Bernard. *Holland: A Land Afloat.* New York: Viking Press, 1962.

Pirenne, Henry. *Early Democracies in the Low Countries.* New York: Harper and Row, 1963.

Radio Luxembourg, Inc. *Radio Luxembourg: The Station of the Stars.* London: Gordon Ross Company, undated.

RAI, Radiotelevisione Italiana. *Proceedings of the International Conference of Broadcasting Organizations on Sound and Television School Broadcasting.* Rome, 1961.

Rappard, William E. *The Government of Switzerland.* New York: D. Van Nostrand Company, Inc., 1936.

Ruiz, Anibal Arias. *La Radiodifusión Española.* Madrid: Publicaciones Españolas, No. 453, 1964.

Schramm, Wilbur. *Mass Media and National Development.* Stanford, Calif.: Stanford University Press and Paris: UNESCO, 1964.

————. *Responsibility in Mass Communication.* New York: Harper, 1957.

Schurmann, Franz. *Ideology and Organization in Communist China.* Berkeley and Los Angeles: University of California Press, 1966.

Shea, Albert A. *Broadcasting: The Canadian Way.* Montreal: Harvest House, 1963.

Skornia, Harry J. *Television and Society.* New York: McGraw-Hill Book Company, 1965.

Summers, Robert E. and Summers, Harrison B. *Broadcasting and the Public.* Belmont, Calif.: Wadsworth Publishing Co., 1966.

Taplin, Walter. *The Origin of Television Advertising in the United Kingdom.* London: Pitman, 1961.

UNESCO. *Developing Mass Media in Asia.* New York: UNESCO Publications Center, 1960.

————. *Mass Media in the Developing Countries.* Paris: UNESCO, 1961.

————. *Social Education through Television: An All India–Radio UNESCO Pilot Project.* New York: UNESCO Publications Center, 1963.

Van der Essen, Leon. *A Short History of Belgium.* Chicago: University of Chicago Press, 1915.

Wilson, H. H. *Pressure Group: The Campaign for Commercial Television in England.* New Brunswick, N.J.: Rutgers University Press, 1961.

Yu, Frederick T. C. *Mass Persuasion in Communist China.* New York and London: Frederick A. Praeger, 1964.

Zeman, Z. A. B. *Nazi Propaganda.* London: Oxford University Press, 1964.

Periodicals

Alisky, Marvin. "Broadcasting in Peru," *Journal of Broadcasting,* III (Spring 1959), 118–127.

————. "The End of Nicaragua's Radio Freedom," *Journal of Broadcasting,* V (Fall 1961), 311–314.

————. "The Mass Media in Central America," *Journalism Quarterly,* XXXII (1955), 479–486.

————. "Radio's Role in Mexico: A First Hand Survey," *Journalism Quarterly,* XXXI (1954), 66–72.

————. "Spain's Press and Broadcasting: Conformity and Censorship," *Journalism Quarterly,* XXXIX (Winter 1962), 63–70.

Australian Royal Commission on Television. "Control of Political Broadcasting in English-Speaking Countries," *Journal of Broadcasting,* II (Spring 1958), 123–136.

Birkrem, Hans J. "Development and Future Plans of Television for Schools in Norway," *EBU Review,* 90B (March 1965), 32–33.

"Broadcasting in the Ivory Coast," *EBU Review,* 81B (September 1963), 15–18.

"Broadcasting in the Netherlands," *NAEB Journal,* XIX (July–August 1960), 9–15.

Browne, Don R. "Radio Guinea: A Voice of Independent Africa," *Journal of Broadcasting,* VII (Spring 1963), 113–122.

————. "Radio in Africa: Problems and Prospects," *NAEB Journal,* XXII (November–December 1963), 32–35.

Butt, Asghar. "Radio Pakistan Today," *EBU Review,* 81B (September 1963), 28–31.

Carr, John. "Television and the Welsh," *Contrast,* II (Spring 1963), 210–215.

Ching, James C. "Mass Communications in the Republic of the Congo (Leopoldville)," *Journalism Quarterly,* XLI (Spring 1964), 237–244.

Cobin, Martin. "An Introduction to Japanese Broadcasting," *Speech Monographs,* XXXII (March 1965), 13–24.

Cohen, Nathan. "The Broadcasting Authority in Israel," *EBU Review,* 94B (November 1965), 73–74.

Crawford, Robert P. "Comparative Aspects of British and American Commercial Television," *Journal of Broadcasting,* X (Spring 1966), 103–110.

Curran, C. J. "The BBC's Advisory Bodies," *EBU Review,* 95B (January 1966), 10–15.

DaPiedade, H. "Radio-Dahomey: The First Ten Years," *EBU Review,* 78B (March 1963), 6–7.

Deutschmann, Paul J. "The Mass Media in an Underdeveloped Village," *Journalism Quarterly,* XL (Winter 1963), 27–35.

———; McNelly, John; and Ellingsworth, Huber. "Mass Media Use by Sub-Elites in 11 Latin American Countries," *Journalism Quarterly,* XXXVI (Autumn 1961), 460–472.

"Development of Television in the Chinese People's Republic," *Radio and Television (OIRT),* III (September 1962), 49–52.

Diamond, Leslie A. W. "Bringing Radio and Television to Northern Nigeria," *EBU Review,* 93B (September 1965), 27–29.

Eisler, Gerhart. "Twenty Years of the German Democratic Radio," *Radio and Television (OIRT),* VI (March 1965), 6–10.

Ellingsworth, Huber. "Broadcast Use by a Latin American Professional and Technical Group," *Journal of Broadcasting,* VII (Spring 1963), 173–182.

Emery, Walter B. "Broadcasting in Mexico," *Journal of Broadcasting,* VIII (Summer 1964), 257–274.

———. "A Comparative Study of Broadcasting Law and Regulations in Mexico and the United States," *Journal of Broadcasting,* VIII (Spring 1964), 185–202.

Emmett, B. P. "A Brief History of Broadcasting Research in the United Kingdom, 1936–1965," *Studies of Broadcasting,* 4 (March 1966), 77–100.

Fagen, Richard R. "Mass Media Growth: A Comparison of Communist and Other Countries," *Journalism Quarterly,* XLI (Autumn 1964), 563–567.

Fein, Leonard J., and Bonnell, Victoria E. "Press and Radio in Rumania: Some Recent Developments," *Journalism Quarterly,* XLII (Summer 1965), 443–449.

"Finnish Radio and Television," *Radio and Television (OIRT),* III (January 1962), 14–20.

Gardner, Leroy W. "A Content Analysis of Japanese and American Television," *Journal of Broadcasting,* VI (Winter 1961), 45–52.

Gilson, Paul. "The Present State of Sound Broadcasting in France," *EBU Review*, 78B (March 1963), 21–24.

Givton, Hanoch. "Introducing Television into Israel," *EBU Review*, 93B (September 1965), 10–12.

Göğüs, Ali Ihsan. "Turkish Broadcasting Faces the Future," *EBU Review*, 89B (January 1965), 16–17.

Graham, Archie. "Advertising on Independent Television in Britain," *EBU Review*, 87B (September 1964), 11–14.

Grant, Douglas. "Television in Liberia—A Sturdy Newcomer," *EBU Review*, 90B (March 1965), 20–22.

Gutierrez, Lazaro Barajas. "Television in Latin America," *Telecommunication Journal*, XXVIII (November 1961), 711–715.

Hahr, Henrik. "The Code of Broadcasting Practice in Sweden," *EBU Review*, 76B (November 1962), 41–43.

Harris, Bill. "Kenya Broadcasting Corporation," *EBU Review*, 81B (September 1963), 24–27.

Hartner, A. "Forty Years of Broadcasting in Austria," *EBU Review*, 87B (September 1964), 6–10.

Head, Sydney. "NAEB Goes to Sudan," *NAEB Journal*, XXI (March–April 1962), 48.

———. "NAEB Goes to Tanganyika," *NAEB Journal*, XXI (May–June 1962), 25–27.

Headland, Frederick H. "The Malawi Broadcasting Corporation," *EBU Review*, 89B (January 1965), 24–26.

Hood, Stuart. "American Programs and British Audiences," *Television Quarterly*, II (Winter 1963), 20–24.

Hurlbert, Raymond D. "Japan Uses ETV," *NAEB Journal*, XXI (September–October 1962), 3–5.

Iezzi, Frank. "Italy: Its Television Revisited," *NAEB Journal*, XIX (July–August 1960), 62–70.

Kadlecova, Zdenka. "The Czechoslovak Radio and its Listeners," *Radio and Television (OIRT)*, III (January 1962), 21–23.

Kaser, Tom. "Classroom TV Comes to Samoa," *Saturday Review*, XLVIII (June 19, 1965), 58–59.

Koumantos, George A. "Broadcasting in Greece: Structure, Organization and Operation," *EBU Review*, 95B (January 1966), 53–57.

Lamb, Kenneth. "Freedom and Responsibility in Religious Broadcasting," *EBU Review*, 97B (May 1966), 45–48.

Lewis, J. David. "Revolution by Radio," *NAEB Journal*, XIX (November–December 1960), 47–55.

Lightfoot, Donald A. "The Zambia Broadcasting Corporation," *EBU Review*, 89B (January 1965), 27–29.

Lindblad, Ingemar. "The Future of Swedish Broadcasting," *EBU Review*, 92B (July 1965), 15–18.

Liu, Alan Ping-lin. "Growth and Modernizing Function of Rural Radio in Communist China," *Journalism Quarterly*, XLI (Autumn 1964), 573–577.

Maclin, Rev. H. T. "Religious Broadcasting in Africa," *EBU Review*, 97B (May 1966), 53–58.

Maletzke, Gerhard. "The Development of Broadcasting Research in Germany," *Studies of Broadcasting*, 2 (March 1963), 23–40.

Mathur, J. C. "Television in India," *EBU Review*, 60B (March 1960), 13–14.

Moreira, Maria da Silva. "The Legal Position of Broadcasting in Portugal," *EBU Review*, 82B (November 1963), 53–61.

Namurois, Albert. "The New Charter for Broadcasting in Belgium," *EBU Review*, 63B (September 1960), 2–10.

Nettheim, Garth. "Public Broadcasting and Government," *Australian Quarterly*, XXXV (March 1963), 36–42.

Newman, John F. "Radio Newscasting in Latin America," *Journal of Broadcasting*, X (Winter 1965–66), 25–32.

Norgaard, P. "Radio and Television in Denmark," *EBU Review*, 67B (1961), 2.

Numminen, Inari. "Television in the Land of the Thousand Lakes," *EBU Review*, 98B (July 1966), 14–15.

Nuttall, C. G. F. "TV Commercial Audiences in the United Kingdom," *Journal of Advertising Research*, II (September 1962), 19–28.

Okabe, Keizo. "Broadcasting Research in Post-War Japan," *Studies of Broadcasting*, 1 (March 1963), 7–48.

O'Reilly, Michael. "Network TV in Ireland," *Broadcasting* (April 22, 1963), 86–88.

"The Organization of Broadcasting in Holland," *EBU Bulletin*, III (1952), 270.

Patrick, P. E. "Broadcasting in the Republic of South Africa," *EBU Review*, 73B (May 1962), 13–16.

Paz, Magdeleine. "Educational Radio in France," *NAEB Journal*, XIX (July–August 1960), 28–30.

Perez, Itial. "Television in Cuba," *Radio and Television (OIRT)*, II (April 1961), 51–54.

Petry, Thomas. "West German TV—The Way Ahead," *Television Quarterly*, II (Summer 1963), 58–67.

"The Principality of Monaco and Radio Monte Carlo," *EBU Bulletin*, IV (1953), 635.

Puglisi, Maria G. "Television and the Fight Against Illiteracy," *EBU Review*, 82B (November 1963), 6–11.

Punter, Otto. "Advertising on Swiss Television," *EBU Review*, 90B (March 1965), 33–34.

Ragsdale, Wilmot. "A Program for Developing the Media of Southeast Asia," *Journalism Quarterly*, XXXVII (Spring 1960), 275–279.

Ragueneau, Philippe. "The Second French Television Programme," *EBU Review*, 86B (July 1964), 9–12.

Rainsberry, F. B. "Educational TV in Canada," *NAEB Journal*, XIX (July–August 1960), 92–104.

Razzi, Giulio. "Sound Broadcasting in Italy Today," *EBU Review*, 78B (March 1963), 30–31.

Reich, Donald R. "Accident and Design: The Reshaping of German Broad-

casting under Military Government," *Journal of Broadcasting*, VII
(Summer 1963), 191–208.

Richter, Erich. "The History of the German Democratic Radio," *Radio and
Television (OIRT)*, VI (September 1965), 23–25.

Rigopoulou, Popy. "A Brief Survey of Greek Religious Broadcasting," *EBU
Review*, 97B (May 1966), 24–25.

Robbins, E. C. "The New Royal Charter and Licence of the British Broadcasting Corporation," *EBU Review*, 86B (July 1964), 36–38.

Rydbeck, Olof. "Broadcasting in Sweden," *EBU Review*, 80B (July 1963), 6–10.

Sakai, Saburo. "A History of the National Association of Commercial Broadcasters in Japan," *EBU Review*, 74B (July 1962), 9–12.

Sakiyama, Seiki. "The International Broadcasting of Japan," *Studies of Broadcasting*, 3 (1965), 5–32.

Sakontikov, N. "The Experience of the Central Television of the USSR in the
Field of Political Broadcasts," *Radio and Television (OIRT)*, III (November 1962), 3–6.

Salu, Adekunle. "Educational Broadcasting in Modern Nigeria," *EBU Review*,
95B (January 1966), 25–27.

Sandor, Gyorgy. "The Experience of the Hungarian Television," *Radio and
Television (OIRT)*, V (July 1964), 6–9.

Scheller, Fred. "Spain Changes Broadcasting Regulations," *NAEB Journal*,
XXV (March–April 1966), 54–56.

Schwass, Rodger. "Radio in Canadian Adult Education," *International Journal
of Adult and Youth Education*, XVI (1964), 5–10.

Shang-Simpson, K. "The Ghana Broadcasting Corporation," *EBU Review*, 78B
(March 1963), 8–14.

Shaw, Colin. "The Regional Structure of the BBC," *EBU Review*, 90B (March
1965), 13–17.

Sington, Derrick. "Broadcasting in East Africa," *The Listener*, LXVI (August 3,
1961), 167–169.

Sizov, N. "Main Theme of Our Broadcasting: Some Questions of Communist
Propaganda on the Soviet Radio," *Radio and Television (OIRT)*, III
(May 1962), 3–6.

Snare, Austin. "The Development and Problems of Australian Broadcast Services," *Journal of Broadcasting*, VII (Winter 1962), 23–34.

Sokorski, Wlodzimierz. "Radio and Television Work in Poland," *Radio and
Television (OIRT)*, I (October 1960), 189–192.

Sorensen, Robert C. and Meyer, Leszek L. "Local Uses of Wired Radio in Com-
munist-Ruled Poland," *Journalism Quarterly*, XXXII (Summer 1955),
343–348.

Sroga, Alojzy. "Economic and Agricultural Broadcasts of the Polish Radio,"
Radio and Television (OIRT), V (March 1964), 17–20.

Stephen, D. A. "This is Radio Rhodesia," *EBU Review*, 93B (September 1965),
23–26.

Stringer, Gilbert H. "The New Zealand Broadcasting Corporation," *EBU Review* (January 1964), 18–21.

Takayanagi, Kenjiro. "Television in Asia," *Telecommunication Journal (ITU)*
(December 1961), 775–777.

Takkenberg, Bernard F. "The Structure of Religious Broadcasting on Nether-lands Radio and Television," *EBU Review*, 97B (May 1966), 29–31.

Tavares, Renato. "What is the ABERT?" (Broadcasting in Brazil), *EBU Review*, 92B (July 1965), 29–31.

Tedros, Gabriel. "Television in Africa," *Telecommunication Journal*, XXVIII (September 1961), 595–596.

Todorov, Davin. "Press and Broadcasting in Present-Day Bulgaria," *Journalism Quarterly*, XXXIX (Spring 1962), 212–215.

Tolga, Sedat. "Legislation Setting up the Radio–Television Association of Turkey (TRT)," *EBU Review*, 88B (November 1964), 48–52.

Tschannen, Lance. "Swiss Radio System Reflects Regional, Lingual Diversities," *Journalism Quarterly*, XXVII (Spring 1950), 193–197.

Tuber, Richard. "A Survey of Programming on the Central Studies of Television, Moscow, U.S.S.R., January–June, 1960," *Journal of Broadcasting*, IV (Fall 1960), 315–325.

Uchikawa, Yoshimi. "Process of Establishment of the New System of Broad-casting in Post-War Japan," *Studies of Broadcasting*, 2 (March 1964), 51–80.

Walker, Dean. "Canadian TV—The Wasteland and the Pasture," *Television Quarterly*, I (August 1962), 23–38.

Williams, Paul B. "Panamanian Television," *NAEB Journal*, XXI (May–June 1962), 79–83.

Williams, Richard. "The Soviet Philosophy of Broadcasting," *Journal of Broadcasting*, VI (Winter 1961), 3–10.

Willis, Edgar E. "Sound Broadcasting in Great Britain," *Journal of Broadcasting*, VIII (Fall 1964), 331–340.

Wisniewska, Maria. "School Television Programmes in Poland," *Radio and Television (OIRT)*, VI (January 1965), 10–12.

Wolff, Hermann H. "West German Television and Television in the Soviet Zone," *Gazette*, II (1956), 235–242.

Wood, R. " 'Radio Australia'—The Australian Broadcasting Commission's Overseas Service," *EBU Bulletin*, III (1952), 129.

Woolston, Howard. "Propaganda in Soviet Russia," *American Journal of Sociology*, XXXVIII (July 1932), 32–40.

Xenofontov, V. "Broadcasts for Children in the Soviet Television," *Radio and Television (OIRT)*, V (November 1964), 7–12.

Yamamoto, Toru. "The Growth of Television in Japan," *Studies of Broadcasting*, 2 (March 1964), 81–126.

Zentai, Janos, and Bozo, Laszlo. "The Place of the Hungarian Radio in the System of the Arts and Education," *Radio and Television (OIRT)*, VI (May 1965), 3–13.

International Broadcasting

Books

Barghoorn, Frederick C. *Soviet Foreign Propaganda*. Princeton, N.J.: Princeton University Press, 1964.

Barrett, Edward W. *Truth Is Our Weapon*. New York: Funk and Wagnalls Company, 1953.

Bramstead, Earnest K. *Goebbels and National Socialist Propaganda, 1925–1945*. East Lansing: Michigan State University Press, 1965.

Childs, Harwood, and Whitton, John B. *Propaganda by Short Waves*. Princeton, N.J.: Princeton University Press, 1942.

Clews, John C. *Communist Propaganda Techniques*. New York: Frederick A. Praeger, 1964.

Codding, George A., Jr. *Broadcasting Without Barriers*. Paris: UNESCO, 1959.

——. *The International Telecommunication Union*. Leiden: E. J. Brill, 1952.

Cohen, Maxwell (ed.). *Law and Politics in Space*. Montreal: McGill University Press, 1964.

Daugherty, William, and Janowitz, Morris. *A Psychological Warfare Case Book*. Baltimore: John Hopkins Press, 1958.

Davison, W. Phillips. *International Political Communication*. New York: Frederick Praeger, 1965.

Dizard, Wilson P. *The Strategy of Truth: The Story of the U.S. Information Service*. Washington, D.C.: Public Affairs Press, 1961.

——. *Television: A World View*, Syracuse, N.Y.: Syracuse University Press, 1966.

Dumazedier, Joffre. *Television and Rural Adult Education*. Paris: UNESCO, 1956.

Frenkel, Herbert M., and Frenkel, Richard E. *World Peace via Satellite Communications*. New York: Telecommunications Research Associates, 1965.

Gatland, Kenneth W. *Telecommunications Satellites*. Englewood Cliffs, N.J.: Prentice-Hall, 1964.

Gorham, Maurice. *Broadcasting and Television Since 1900*. London: Andrew Dakers, Ltd., 1952.

Haley, Andrew G. *Space Law and Government*. New York: Appleton-Century-Crofts, 1963.

Harlow, Alvin F. *Old Wires and New Waves*. New York: D. Appleton-Century-Company, 1936.

Hodapp, William; Gordon, George; and Falk, Irving. *The Idea Invaders*. New York: Hastings House, 1963.

Holt, Robert T. *Radio Free Europe*. Minneapolis: University of Minnesota Press, 1958.

International Broadcasting Union. *The Problems of Broadcasting*. Geneva: International Broadcasting Union, 1935.

International Telecommunications Union. *From Semaphore to Satellite*. Geneva: International Telecommunications Union, 1965.

Jaffe, Leonard. *Communications in Space*. New York: Holt, Rinehart and Winston, 1964.

Johansen, O. Lund. *World Radio Handbook*. Copenhagen, 1958 to date.

Kinane, K. *Educational Television in Developing Countries*. Tokyo: Nippon Hoso Kyokai, 1965.

Kirkpatrick, Evron M. *Target: The World, Communist Propaganda Activities in 1955*. New York: The Macmillan Co., 1956.

Kris, Ernst, and Speier, Hans. *German Radio Propaganda*. New York: Oxford University Press, 1944.

McLuhan, Marshall. *Understanding Media: The Extensions of Man*. New York: McGraw-Hill Book Company, 1964.

Markham, James W. *Voices of the Red Giants*. Ames: Iowa State University Press, 1967.

Michie, Allen A. *Voices Through the Iron Curtain: The Radio Free Europe Story*. New York: Dodd, Mead and Company, 1963.

National Association of Broadcasters. *International Broadcasting*. Washington, D.C.: National Association of Broadcasters, 1962.

Paulu, Burton. *Radio and TV Broadcasting on the European Continent*. Minneapolis: University of Minnesota Press, 1967.

Pons, Eugene. *License Fees for Radio and Television Sets*. Geneva: European Broadcasting Union, 1964.

Pye, Lucian W. (ed.). *Communications and Political Development*. Princeton, N.J.: Princeton University Press, 1963.

Qualter, Terrence H. *Propaganda and Psychological Warfare*. New York: Random House, 1962.

Sargent, William. *Battle for the Mind*. New York: Doubleday and Company, 1957.

Schramm, Wilbur. *Mass Media and National Development*. Stanford, Calif.: Stanford University Press, 1964.

Siebert, Frederick S.; Peterson, T.; and Schramm, W. *Four Theories of the Press*. Urbana: University of Illinois Press, 1956.

Siepmann, Charles. *Radio, Television and Society*. New York: Oxford University Press, 1950.

Skolnik, Roger. *A Bibliography of Selected Publications on Foreign and International Broadcasting*. East Lansing: Michigan State University, 1966.

Smith, Bruce L., and Smith, Chitra M. *International Communication and Political Opinion—A Guide to the Literature*. Princeton, N.J.: Princeton University Press, 1956.

Summers, Robert E. *Wartime Censorship of Press and Radio*. New York: W. H. Wilson Co., 1942.

Terrou, Fernand. *Legislation for Press, Film and Radio*. Paris: UNESCO, 1951.

Thomason, F. S., and Wolcott, P. A. *Breaking the Illiteracy Barrier Through Radio.* Washington, D.C.: U.S. Government Printing Office, 1960.

Tomlinson, John D. *The International Control of Radio Communications.* Ann Arbor, Mich.: Edward Brothers, 1945.

UNESCO. *Broadcasting to Schools.* Paris: UNESCO, 1949.

————. *Radio Broadcasting Serves Rural Development.* New York: UNESCO Publications Center, 1965.

————. *Social Education Through Television.* Paris: UNESCO, 1963.

————. *Space Communication and the Mass Media.* New York: UNESCO Publications Center, 1964.

————. *World Communications: Press, Radio, Television, Film.* New York: UNESCO Publications Center, 1964.

Urban, George R. (ed.). *Scaling the Wall: Talking to Eastern Europe.* Detroit: Wayne State University Press, 1964.

Vasari, Bruno. *Financial Aspects of Broadcasting.* Geneva: European Broadcasting Union, 1965.

White, Llewellyn, and Leigh, Robert D. *Peoples Speaking to Peoples: A Report on International Mass Communication from the Commission on Freedom of the Press.* Chicago: University of Chicago Press, 1946.

Williams, J. Grenfell. *Radio in Fundamental Education in Underdeveloped Areas.* Paris: UNESCO, 1950.

World Radio TV Handbook 1967. Hellerup, Denmark: World Radio–Television Handbook Company, Ltd., 1968.

Wright, Charles R. *Mass Communication, a Sociological Perspective.* New York: Random House, 1959.

Zeman, Z.A.B. *Nazi Propaganda.* London: Oxford University Press, 1964.

Periodicals

Bermel, Albert. "The Split Personality of USIA," *Harpers,* CCXXXI (November 1965), 116–124.

Bezencon, Marcel. "Eurovision and its Objectives," *EBU Review,* 74B (September 1962), 4–5.

Brown, Thomas H. "RFE . . . Its Audience and Its Policies," *NAEB Journal,* XIX (July–August 1960), 82–88.

Browne, Don R. "The Limits of the Limitless Medium—International Broadcasting," *Journalism Quarterly,* XLII (Winter 1965), 82–86.

Burns, Lloyd. "Past and Future of Overseas TV Syndication," *Broadcasting,* LXV (September 9, 1963), 102.

Caldwell, William S. "Soviet Specialty: Political Warfare," *Communist Affairs,* I (September 1963), 3–7.

Cassirer, Henry. "Television in Developing Countries," *Telecommunication Journal,* XXX (December 1963), 374–377.

Dieuzeide, Henri. "The Present Position of School Television in Europe," *EBU Review,* 61B (May 1960), 2–10.

Dizard, Wilson P. "Europe's TV Networks," *Television Quarterly,* IV (Winter 1965), 7–18.

————. "The Political Impact of Television Abroad," *Journal of Broadcasting*, IX (Summer 1965), 195–214.

————. "Television's Foreign Markets," *Television Quarterly*, III (Summer 1964), 57–73.

Dreyfus, Lee S., and Gumpert, Gary. "Students Visit via Satellite," *NAEB Journal*, XXV (May–June 1966), 6–13.

Eyde, Kay. "Satellites and International Television," *NAEB Journal*, XXIV (March–April 1965), 51–60.

Fagen, Richard. "Relations of Communication Growth to National Political Systems in Less Developed Countries," *Journalism Quarterly*, XLI (Winter 1964), 87–94.

Harwood, Kenneth. "The International Radio and Television Organization," *Journal of Broadcasting*, V (Winter 1960), 61–72.

————. *Radio and Television Works Added to the Library of the British Museum, 1881–1950: A Bibliography*. University Park: The University of Southern California, 1965 (mimeo).

————. "A World Bibliography of Selected Periodicals on Broadcasting," *Journal of Broadcasting*, V (Summer 1961), 251–278.

Hillig, Hans-Peter. "The New Copyright Law in the Federal Republic of Germany from the Broadcasting Viewpoint," *EBU Review*, 95B (January 1966), 39–52.

Howell, William S. "The North American Service of Radio Moscow," *Quarterly Journal of Speech*, XLVI (October 1960), 262–269.

Iezzi, Frank. "TV Piracy on the High Seas," *Television Quarterly*, IV (Winter 1965), 23–28.

"Intervision," *Radio and Television (OIRT)*, III (March 1962), 3–16.

Janowitz, Morris. "Mass Persuasion and International Relations," *Public Opinion Quarterly* (Winter 1962), 560–570.

Kaul, Professor. "Copyright Regulations in the German Democratic Radio and the Television of the German Democratic Republic," *Radio and Television (OIRT)*, VI (January 1965), 19–20.

Kragem, Björg. "The Norwegian Copyright Bill," *EBU Review*, 63B (September 1960), 30–33.

Kroeger, Albert R. "International Television," *Television Magazine*, XX (July 1963), 44–49, 74–84.

Lerch, John. "Diverse Techniques in International Broadcasting," *Journal of Broadcasting*, II (Summer 1958), 213–224.

Lindsay, Robert. "What Will the Satellites Communicate?" *NAEB Journal*, XXIII (July–August 1964), 37–44.

Loevinger, Lee. "The Lexonomics of Telecommunications," *Journal of Broadcasting*, XI (Fall 1967), 285–311.

MacNeill, Rev. Don. "Near East Radio Broadcasting," *The East and West Review* (July 1964).

Maddison, John. "TV and International Understanding," *Television Quarterly*, I (November 1962), 55–60.

Marks, Leonard H. "Communications Satellites: New Horizons for Broadcasters," *Journal of Broadcasting*, IX (Spring 1965), 97–101.

———. "Early Bird—A New Horizon for Broadcasters," *EBU Review*, 93B (September 1965), 41–44.

———. "The Role of Broadcasters in Space Communications," *EBU Review*, 84B (March 1964), 46–50.

Marosi, Jenö. "Questions of Copyright in the Practice of the Hungarian Radio and Television," *Radio and Television (OIRT)*, V (September 1964), 1014.

Masouye, Claude. "Copyright in Africa," *EBU Review*, 92B (July 1965), 41–45.

Moreira, Mario da Silva. "The International Law on Radio Interference, Parts I and II," *EBU Review*, 73B and 74B (May and July 1962).

Namurois, Albert. "The International Convention for the Protection of Performers, Producers of Phonograms and Broadcasting Organizations," EBU Review, 72B and 73B (March and May 1962).

———. "The Prevention of the Activities of 'Pirate' Broadcasting Stations: A European Agreement," *EBU Review*, 90B (March 1965), 36–46.

Paglin, Max D. "Some Regulatory and International Problems Facing Establishment of Communication Satellite Systems," *Journal of Broadcasting*, VI (Fall 1962), 285–294.

Persin, Jean. "Will Space Be Open to Piracy?" *Telecommunication Journal*, XXX (April 1963), 112–115.

Ploman, Edward W. "Some Observations on Space Communications," *EBU Review*, 96B (March 1966), 33–36.

Pollock, Donald K., and Woods, David L. "A Study in International Communication—Eurovision," *Journal of Broadcasting*, III (Spring 1959), 101–117.

Pulling, Martin. "International Television," *EBU Review*, 79B (May 1963), 11–15.

Remes, Karel. "Prevention of Broadcasts Transmitted from Artificial Islands: Dutch Legislation," *EBU Review*, 90B (March 1965), 47–52.

Robbins, E.C. "The Postmaster General and the Pirates," *EBU Review*, 102B (March 1967), 52–53.

Rutkowski, G. "Television in the OIRT Countries," *Telecommunication Journal*, XXVIII (August 1961), 521–526.

Rydbeck, Olof. "How the EBU is Fostering the Development of Television," *Broadcasting* (October 29, 1962), 74–75.

Scupham, John. "New Trends in School Broadcasting: Some Reflections on the Tokyo Conference," *EBU Review*, 88B (November 1964), 9–15.

Semmler, C. "Glimpses of World Television," *Australian Quarterly*, XXXV (March 1963), 58–67.

Skatchko, Nikolai. "Five Years of Intervision," *Radio and Television (OIRT)*, VI (March 1965), 3–5.

———. "Intervision—Years of Development," *Radio and Television (OIRT)*, VII (March 1966), 3–6.

Smith, Don. "Is there a U.S. Audience for International Broadcasts?" *Journalism Quarterly*, XXXIX (Winter 1962), 86–87.

———. "Radio Moscow's North American Broadcasts: An Exploratory Study," *Journalism Quarterly*, XLII (Autumn 1965), 643–645.

Smythe, Dallas W. "Space-Satellite Broadcasting: Threat or Promise?" *Journal of Broadcasting,* IV (Summer 1960), 191–198.

Spelman, Franz. "What the Hungarians Say About Western Propaganda," *Harpers,* CCXIV (April 1957), 70–74.

Tchistiakov, Nikolai. "Popov and the Birth of Radio," *Telecommunication Journal,* XXX (June 1963), 172–174.

Tebbel, John. "How Europe Fights Commercial TV," *Saturday Review* (August 10, 1963), 46–47.

"Vatican Radio," *EBU Review,* 97B (May 1966), 12–15.

"The War We're Losing—The Communications Crisis: What Persuaders Can Do," *Printers' Ink,* CCLXXX (September 14, 1962), 27–73.

Wilhoit, Grover C. "USIA's Television Service," *NAEB Journal,* XXI (September–October 1962), 62–72.

Ziebarth, E. W. "The Mass Media in International Communication," *Journal of Communication,* II (1952), 24–28.

Zini Lamberti, Carlo. "The Rome Convention for the Protection of Performer, Producers of Phonograms and Broadcasting Organizations, Parts I and II," *EBU Review,* 75B and 76B (September and November 1962).

Government Publications

Australian Broadcasting Commission. *33rd Annual Report, 1964–65.* Canberra, 1965.

Canada. *Report of the Committee on Broadcasting.* Ottawa: Queen's Printer, 1965.

———. *Report of Royal Commission on Broadcasting.* Ottawa: Queen's Printer and Controller of Stationery, March 15, 1957.

———. *Report of Royal Commission on National Development in the Arts, Letters and Science.* Ottawa: Edmond Cloutier, Printer to the King's Most Excellent Majesty, 1951.

———. *Report of the Royal Commission on Radio Broadcasting.* Ottawa: F. A. Aclaud, Printer to the King's Most Excellent Majesty, 1929.

———. *White Paper on Broadcasting.* Ottawa: La Marsh, Judy, Secretary of State, 1966.

Canada Year Book 1965. Ottawa: Queen's Printer, 1965.

Commonwealth of Australia. *Annual Reports.* Canberra: Australian Broadcasting Commission.

———. *Eleventh Annual Report of the Australian Control Board for the Year 1959–60.* Canberra, 1960.

———. *The History and Development of the A.B.C.* Canberra: Australian Broadcasting Commission, undated.

————. *Report of the Advisory Committee on Educational Television Services to the Australian Broadcasting Control Board*. Tasmania: Government Printer, 1964.

Denmark. *Official Handbook*. Copenhagen: Royal Danish Ministry of Foreign Affairs, 1964.

Federal Communications Commission. *Public Service Responsibility of Broadcast Licensees*. Washington, D.C., 1946.

Fourth National Radio Conference. *Proceedings and Recommendations for Regulation*. Washington, D.C., 1925.

Government of India. *India 1952—A Reference Annual*. New Delhi: Ministry of Information and Broadcasting, 1965.

————. *A Reference Annual*. New Delhi, 1956–62.

————. *Second Five Year Plan*. New Delhi: Planning Commission, 1956.

————. *Third Five Year Plan*. New Delhi: Planning Commission, 1961.

Ireland. *Report of the Television Commission, 1959*. Dublin: Stationery Office, 1960.

United Kingdom. *Report of the Broadcasting Committee 1949*. London: Cmnd. 8116, 1949.

————. *Report of Committee on Broadcasting 1960*. London: Cmnd. 1753, 1962.

————. *Report of Crawford Committee 1925*. London: Cmnd. 2599, 1926.

United States Information Agency. *Annual Reports*. Washington, D.C., 1954–1967.

————. *Facts About the USIA*. Washington, D.C., 1964.

————. *Greece: A Communications Fact Book*. Washington, D.C., 1962.

U.S. Senate, Committee on Commerce. *Communications Satellite Legislation*. Washington, D.C.: U.S. Government Printing Office, 1962.

U.S. Senate, Subcommittee on Monopoly of the Select Committee on Small Business. *Public Policy Questions on the Ownership and Control of a Space Satellite Communication System*. Washington, D.C.: U.S. Government Printing Office, 1961.

Yugoslavia. *Statistical Pocket-Book of Yugoslavia 1965*. Belgrade: Federal Institute for Statistics, 1965.

INDEX

ABU, *see* Asian Broadcasting Union

Adamov, Joe, 389, 390

Adult education: in Australia, 502, 504; Austria, 316, 318; Belgium, 129, 130, 135, 136; Cameroun, 444; Canada, 59, 63; China, 472, 476, 477; Denmark, 179, 180; East Germany, 307; Finland, 223; France, 239, 244, 245, 248, 249, 255; Greece, 287, 288, 289; Hungary, 398, 399; Iceland, 183, 184; India, 455, 456, 458, 459; Italy, 272, 273, 274, 275, 276; Japan, 487; Luxembourg, 163; Mexico, 35; Netherlands, 149; Niger, 444; Norway, 188, 189, 195; Portugal, 372, 375, 376, 378; Soviet Union (Russia), 390, 392; Sweden, 198, 202, 216; Switzerland, 330, 334, 335; Yugoslavia, 405, 406, 411; Zambia, 443, 444

Advertising: current trends, xxx; nature of and requirements relating to, in Australia, 495, 505; Austria, 319; Belgium, 129, 137, 138; Canada, 602, 604; England, 609–617; Germany, 304; Greece, 286, 287; Hungary, 400; Iceland, 182; Ireland, 114, 119; Japan, 484, 485; Luxembourg, 158, 160, 162, 168; Mexico, 18, 25, 33, 42, 43; Portugal, 377; Spain, 360, 364; Switzerland, 335, 336; Turkey, 427; United Kingdom, 96, 100, 102, 103, 106; Yugoslavia, 417

Africa: advantages of mass communication in, 438, 439, 440; broadcast financing, problems of, 448; colonial exploitation, 437; creating national spirit, 441, 442; improving educational system, 442, 443, 444; modernizing economic system, 444, 445, 446; problems of communication, 437; programs (broadcasting), 441, 442

Agreement (international): for global, commercial communications satellite system, 656–658; North American Regional, 53; for prevention of "pirate" stations, 568–578; Stockholm, 564

Aird Commission: appointment of, 47; recommendations by, 48, 49

Akar, John, 447

Alcohol: restrictions on broadcast advertising of, in Canada, 603; Finland, 231; Mexico, 25

Algemeene Vereenig Radio Omroep, 141

All India Radio: establishment of, 452; experiments (TV) by, 458, 459; objectives of, 455; organization and operation of, 460; programs, 455, 456; transmitters, 452, 453; *see also* India

Amateur operators: role of, in Austria, 309, 310; Belgium, 124; Denmark, 174; Finland, 222; France, 238; Germany, 295, 296; Netherlands, 141; Portugal, 368;

Soviet Union, 381; Switzerland, 324; Yugoslavia, 403

American Committee for Liberation: organization of, 545, 546

American Forces Network (Europe), 551–556

Andora: broadcasting pattern in, 672

Andreyev, I., 383, 384

Angola: Portuguese broadcasting in, 373

Arase, Yutaka, 491

Arbeitsgemeinschaft der Offentlich-rechtlichen Rundfunkanstalten der Bundesrepublik Deutschland (ARD), 300; *see also* Germany

Argentina: pattern of broadcasting in, 676

Artificial islands: broadcasts from, *see* "Pirate" stations

Asian Broadcasting Union, 523–525

Audience (radio and TV): in Australia, 505, 506; Luxembourg, 165, 167; United Kingdom, 100; of "pirate" stations, 560; U.S. Armed Services Radio, 553, 554; Voice of America, 405, 406, 540

Australia: early broadcast history, 492; establishment of Australian Broadcasting Commission (ABC), 493; ABC's powers and limitations, 493; regulatory problems, 494; major objectives, 494; broadcast expansion, 495; new broadcasting law enacted, 495, 496; Australian Broadcasting Control Board created, 496; passage of Broadcasting and Television Act of 1956, 497; amendments thereto, 497, 498; ABC membership, 497, 498; Commission stations not permitted to broadcast commercials, 498; granting, renewal, transfer and revocation of licenses, 498, 499; political broadcasting, 500; indecent programming prohibited, 500; broadcasting growth since World War II, 500, 501, 502; recent patterns of programming, 502; Radio Australia, 503; ABC television, 503, 504, 505; commercial television, 505, 506

Australian Broadcasting Act, *see* Australia

Australian Broadcasting Commission, *see* Australia

Australian Broadcasting Control Board, *see* Australia

Austria: financial collapse after World War I, 309; establishment of democratic republic, 309; creation of first broadcasting station, 309, 310; establishment of joint stock company (broadcast), 310; broadcast facilities expanded, 310, 311; German control during World War II, 311, 312; postwar control decentralized by Allies, 312; new broadcasting law, 313, 314; Austrian Radio Company (Oste-